EUSEBIUS

I

EUSEBIUS
THE ECCLESIASTICAL HISTORY

WITH AN ENGLISH TRANSLATION BY

KIRSOPP LAKE, D.D., D.Litt.

WINN PROFESSOR OF ECCLESIASTICAL HISTORY
IN THE UNIVERSITY OF HARVARD

IN TWO VOLUMES

I

CAMBRIDGE, MASSACHUSETTS
HARVARD UNIVERSITY PRESS
LONDON
WILLIAM HEINEMANN LTD
MCMLXXX

American
ISBN 0-674-99169-9

British
ISBN 0 434 99153 8

First printed 1926
Reprinted 1949, 1953, 1959, 1965, 1975, 1980

Printed in Great Britain

CONTENTS OF VOLUME I

	PAGE
PREFACE	vii
EDITORIAL NOTE	viii
INTRODUCTION	ix
BOOK I	2
BOOK II	98
BOOK III	190
BOOK IV	300
BOOK V	400

PREFACE

THE text of the *Historia Ecclesiastica* of Eusebius in the following pages is that of E. Schwartz in volumes i. and ii. of Part II. of the edition of Eusebius in *Die griechischen christlichen Schriftsteller der erstern drei Jahrhunderte*, published by the Berlin Academy. Changes have only been introduced in a few very small points, such as the accentuation of the proper names in the genealogy of Christ.

I am most grateful to the Academy for its kindness in allowing me the use of this magnificent example of how a text ought to be edited.

In preparing the English I have in difficult passages frequently consulted the translation of A. C. M'Giffert and have derived much benefit from his notes. I am also greatly indebted to my friends Mrs. Frederick Winslow, Professor Robert P. Blake, who read proof-sheets and suggested many improvements, and Miss Edith Coe, who helped at every stage, and undertook the laborious work of verifying and inserting the references which were taken from Schwartz.

Editorial Note (1974): Occasion to reprint affords an opportunity of noticing that the last fifty years have added much to the scholarly literature which Kirsopp Lake surveyed in his introduction; a convenient guide to this material will be furnished by the bibliographies in the *Oxford Dictionary of the Christian Church*, 2nd ed. rev. F. L. Cross and E. A. Livingstone, 1974.

With reference to page xxxvii, note 1 and page xl respectively, the works of Josephus (9 vols., 1926–1965) and Philo (12 vols., 1929–1953) are now fully available in the Loeb Classical Library; and the fourth volume of Stählin's Clement (*cf.* page xlvi, line 3) appeared in 1936.

G. P. G.

INTRODUCTION

No contemporary biography of Eusebius is now extant, for though one was published by Acacius, his successor as bishop of Caesarea, it has been lost, and we are dependent on a few vague statements in later writers and on the evidence of his extant writings.

He was probably born about the year 260. This date is fixed by (1) the fact that he speaks of Dionysius of Alexandria as having been alive in his time : Dionysius was bishop of Alexandria from about 247 to 265. (2) He speaks of Paul of Samosata as a contemporary : Paul was deposed in 270. (3) He speaks of Manes as belonging " to yesterday and our times " : Manes lived during the episcopate of Felix at Rome in 270–274. (4) After speaking of Dionysius of Alexandria, who became bishop in 247, and before speaking of Dionysius of Rome (A.D. 259), he seems to draw a chronological line, stating that he now proposes to relate the history of his own generation.[1]

His parentage and the place of his birth are unknown. It is true that Arius in writing to Eusebius of Nicomedia spoke of him as the brother of the latter, but it is probable that this meant no more than " brother bishop." He was sometimes referred to

[1] *H.E.* iii. 28, v. 28, vii. 26, vii. 31 ; *Theoph.* iv. 30.

as " the Palestinian," but this again was probably merely to distinguish him from the other Eusebius, and alluded to his Palestinian bishopric. His most usual designation was "Eusebius of Pamphilus." This doubtless means some close relationship, and has been interpreted as son, nephew, friend, or slave of Pamphilus. All these are possible, but none certain, and in the absence of evidence a decision between them cannot be made.[1] Pamphilus was a native of Phoenicia who had studied in Alexandria and settled in Caesarea. He here collected a large library, including some of the works of Origen and the original of the Hexapla.[2] This library and the similar one made by Bishop Alexander at Jerusalem were the main sources from which Eusebius derived the material for his books.

It is unknown at what time he was ordained deacon or priest, and it has been doubted whether he was in clerical orders at all until his election to the see of Caesarea. He was imprisoned during the persecution at Caesarea under the governor Firmilianus in the year 309 but was neither tortured nor executed. Many years afterwards, at the Council of Tyre (A.D. 335), he was accused by Potammon, the bishop of Heraclea, of having betrayed the faith during the persecution and having thus escaped. But no evidence appears to have been produced that this was so, and in the controversies of that time neither side was unduly reluctant to blacken the character of their opponents; had there been any evidence it would surely have been adduced.

After the end of the persecution in 313 Eusebius

---

[1] Theodoret, *H.E.* i. 1 ; Nicephorus Callistus, *H.E.* vi. 37.
[2] Eus. *H.E.* vi. 32.

was made bishop of Caesarea, but the exact date is doubtful ; it must, however, have been before 315, when as bishop of Caesarea he attended the consecration of the church in Tyre. In 325 he was present at the Council of Nicaea, where he held a very prominent place on the right hand of the Emperor Constantine. It has sometimes been stated that he was actually the president of the Council, but this cannot be proved and is even improbable. Both before and after this time he appears to have been the chief theological adviser of Constantine. His general attitude during and after the Council was that of the moderate man. He was not in agreement with the party of Alexander,[1] and appears to have done his best to induce the Council to adopt a less drastic creed. On the whole he probably was more in agreement with Arius and with his namesake, Eusebius of Nicomedia, than with the opposite party, but his policy and that of the Emperor was to seek a formula of comprehension, while Alexander on the one hand and Arius on the other desired formulae which would exclude their opponents. In the end he was obliged to yield to the pressure of numbers and appears to have voted with the majority in the final decision ; but he was never really convinced, and for the rest of his life was an opponent of the Athanasian party, and a firm supporter of all attempts to evict its leaders and to modify the creed so as to leave room for more difference of opinion on metaphysical questions.

Six years after the Council of Nicaea he was present at the Council of Antioch (A.D. 331), which

[1] The Bishop of Alexandria, whose quarrel with Arius was the immediate cause of the Arian controversy and of the Council of Nicaea.

deposed Eustathius, one of the leaders of the anti-Arian party. On this occasion he was offered the bishopric of Antioch, but refused it, nominally at least, because he was unwilling to transgress the ecclesiastical rule that a bishop must not leave one see for another. Three years later (A.D. 334) a proposal was made to depose Athanasius. An attempt was apparently made to hold a council for this purpose at Caesarea, but it was unsuccessful, and the Synod was not actually held till a year later at Tyre (A.D. 335). At this meeting, which Eusebius attended, Athanasius was condemned on evidence which though apparently convincing was, to say the least of it, mostly fraudulent. Athanasius was accused of having cut off the hand of a certain bishop. The hand was actually produced as evidence, but not the bishop, whom Athanasius afterwards discovered and convicted of possessing both hands.

In the same year Eusebius was the leading figure at the Synod of Jerusalem during which was held the consecration of the new church. This Synod was distinctly Arian in tendency as, indeed, were most of the councils of the eastern clergy. It was decided to re-admit Arius, and action was begun against Marcellus of Ancyra.[1] In pursuance of this policy a little later during the same year Eusebius attended a Synod at Constantinople. Arius died on the eve of his restoration, but Marcellus was condemned, and during the proceedings Eusebius was the chosen

---

[1] Marcellus, bishop of Ancyra, was one of the leaders of the extreme anti-Arian party. He was accused of Sabellianism,—the heresy which regarded the Logos or Son as merely a name for God when acting in a certain way, and not as a separate " existence " or—to use the later word—hypostasis. See especially Th. Zahn, *Marcellus von Ancyra.*

orator at the famous " tricennalia," the celebration
of the thirtieth year of Constantine's reign.

In 337 Constantine died and Eusebius did not long
survive him. The day of his death is known with
tolerable certainty, but not the year, for the Syriac
martyrology of the fourth century, which probably
represents the old calendar of Nicomedia, merely
says that Eusebius died on May the 30th. Since
Socrates, *H.E.* ii. 4, mentions his death in connexion
with events which took place in 339 and 340, and
since in 341, at the Synod of Antioch, Acacius, the
successor of Eusebius, was present as bishop of
Caesarea, the death of Eusebius must have taken
place on May the 30th in 339 or 340. A definite
choice between these years is impossible, but, as
Lightfoot points out, the general impression made by
the statements in Socrates and Sozomen is that the
death of Eusebius took place before that of the
younger Constantine and the second exile of Athanasius. These events were probably earlier in 340 than
May the 30th, so that probability slightly favours
339 rather than 340 as the year of his death.[1]

Important though his ecclesiastical and political
career undoubtedly was, his literary achievements
are his chief claim to fame. Once more, there is
not extant any complete list of his writings. Jerome,
Nicephorus Callistus, and Ebed Jesu, the Syriac
writer, have given partial lists, and scattered through
the writings of Photius are references to other works.
These are some help, but Eusebius himself is our
chief source of information.

He began to write in the last years of the third
century or at the beginning of the fourth. To the

---

[1] Socrates, *H.E.* ii. 4 f. ; Sozomen, *H.E.* iii. 2.

INTRODUCTION

earliest period probably belong two books of controversy with heathen writers. One, *Adversus Hieroclem*, was an answer to the *Philalethes* of Hierocles, who had compared Christ and Apollonius of Tyana. The work of Hierocles is unfortunately lost, but Eusebius's book is extant. It is written in a style rather markedly different from his later works, and he never quotes it. There is, however, scarcely sufficient reason for doubting its authenticity. It was probably a work of his youth. The other book of the same kind was an answer to Porphyry, a heathen controversialist living in Caesarea, who had attacked Origen and other Christians. The text of this book is wholly lost, but a fragment which may belong to it has been published by E. von der Goltz in *Texte und Untersuchungen*, xvii. 4. pp. 41 ff. It is also probable that to the same early period should be ascribed a collection of the lives of the early martyrs. This collection, which would be of inestimable value, has unfortunately been lost, but it was used by the Old Syriac martyrology and other traces of it have been found in later collections of the lives of saints. Finally, it is generally thought that a lost work of his, Περὶ τῆς τῶν παλαιῶν ἀνδρῶν πολυπαιδίας, quoted by Basil the Great, *De Spiritu Sancto*, cap. 29, and mentioned in Eusebius, *Praeparatio*, vii. 8. 29 and *Demonstratio*, i. 9. 20, may belong to this period.

The next period of his life is the ten years of the Diocletian persecution, 303–313. During this time, and possibly even before it, Eusebius was busy with a great project of connected works dealing with the history and philosophy of Christianity. Though they have not all been preserved the greater part of these books remain and are the most valuable extant

monument of Christianity as it was immediately before the Council of Nicaea. Part of his great claim to distinction is that when writing philosophy he never neglects history, or philosophy when writing history.

The position of Eusebius is that the Logos existed from the beginning with God the Father. As might be expected from one who wrote earlier than the Council of Nicaea and was afterwards suspected of a tendency to Arianism, he expresses himself with some ambiguity as to whether the Son, or Logos, was created by the Father. The Father was the creator of the universe and all creation within it the work of the Logos. Man, however, was made by the Father, though the Logos shared in the plan of his creation. After the creation it was the Logos who appeared to the righteous ; and Eusebius thus explains the visions of Abraham, Moses, Jacob, and Joshua, as well as all references to Wisdom in the sapiential books. He explains that this doctrine of the Logos would have been promulgated long ago, had not men been too wicked to understand it, and that it was actually, though obscurely, contained in the Old Testament, as is shown by passages in the Old Testament which should be regarded as foretelling even the names of Jesus and of Christ. Jesus, according to him, was the incarnate Logos, who came to announce himself and to point out to men the duty of reverencing and worshipping him. Finally, he maintains that the teaching of Christianity was neither new nor strange. What was new was the Church, the race of Christians. Their corporate existence, their general piety, and their increasing influence were indeed new, but their teaching was

not. It had been followed centuries before them by Abraham and Moses and the later prophets ; and the religion of the patriarchs was identical with that of the Christians. All history was a contest between God, acting through Patriarchs, Prophets, and the Church, on the one hand, and the Devil, instigating Jews, Persecutors, and Heretics, on the other. It is a contest in which the Devil always gets the worst of it in the long run, but the righteous suffer considerably in the process ; and part of the plan of Eusebius is to reveal the machinations of the Evil One and his followers, and to show the catastrophes which befell Persecutors, Jews, and Heretics.

The student of church history will have little difficulty in recognizing that this teaching is in the direct line of Justin Martyr, Aristides, Clement of Alexandria, and Origen. In some ways he was the last and the greatest of the Apologists, for after his time, when the Church was accepted within the Empire, there was no reason for anyone to write quite the same argumentative justification of Christian religion as was incumbent upon him. It would be interesting if we could know how far his works, incomparably more logical than those of his predecessors, converted the educated classes in the Empire. Origen, no doubt, and Clement of Alexandria were his superiors as philosophers, but neither of them had the same grasp of history and of historical presentation.

To attempt to arrange in chronological order the books which he wrote during this period is misleading. He was doubtless constantly working on the material used in them all, and although it is possible to make a few statements about their relative chronology,

this applies only to the dates at which they were begun or at which they were finally put into writing.

At the head of the series must be placed the *Chronicon*. Eusebius perceived that the foundation of history is accurate chronology and for this purpose, using no doubt as the basis of his work the earlier efforts of Julius Africanus and others, and partly at least controverting their position, he produced a work which is now extant in the form of elaborate tables arranged in parallel columns illustrating the whole history of the world year by year. These form the Χρονικοὶ κανόνες, which have been preserved in an Armenian translation and in the Latin version of Jerome. Whether this was the original form of Eusebius's own work is open to question. Possibly it is a later, more precise but less trustworthy recension.[1] To these tables was prefixed a Χρονογραφία, or explanation and introduction, which has unfortunately been lost. From references in *Eclogae* i. 1 and i. 8, it would appear that this work was produced before 303, but according to Jerome Eusebius afterwards re-edited it, carrying it down to 325.

During the years of persecution which followed he began two great connected works entitled the *Praeparatio Evangelica* and the *Demonstratio Evangelica*, dedicated to Theodotus, bishop of Laodicaea. The beginning of these books can be dated as after 303 and before 313, for both *Praeparatio*, xii. 10. 7 and *Demonstratio*, iii. 5. 7 refer to the persecution as

[1] See Schwartz's Prolegomena to the *Hist. Eccl.* pp. ccxv ff.

still raging. Nevertheless, the *Demonstratio* was not finished until after the peace, to which a reference is made in *Demonstratio*, v. 3. 11.

The *Praeparatio* is fully extant, but of the *Demonstratio*, which originally contained twenty books, only the first ten are preserved. Taken together they constitute a statement of the positive and negative cases for Christianity as Eusebius conceived them. The *Praeparatio* is especially concerned with the treatment of heathenism which it describes and refutes. The *Demonstratio* shows how the prophets foretold Christianity, and how the religion of the Christians was not new but was identical with that which had been followed by the patriarchs and saints of Old Testament days even before the time of Moses. It is thus incidentally an answer to Jewish controverversalists.

Closely connected with these two books is a third called Ἡ καθόλου στοιχειώδης εἰσαγωγή, or *General Elementary Introduction*, in ten books, of which four are extant in the form of the Προφητικαὶ ἐκλογαί, commonly quoted as the *Eclogae*, or *Prophetic Extracts*. It is not quite clear what was the relation of this book to the Εἰσαγωγή, but apparently it was an extract from the larger work. It must have been begun before 313, as it contains a reference to the persecution as still continuing (*Ecl.* i. 8). It presents another version of the same argument from prophecy as is contained in the *Demonstratio*, and lists of passages are given from the Old Testament, which are held to refer to the person and work of Christ. The first book of the *Eclogae* is devoted to the historical books of the Old Testament, the second to the Psalms, the third to the remaining poetical books

and the other prophets, the fourth to Isaiah. The other books of the Εἰσαγωγή are lost.

If Photius can be trusted, Eusebius also wrote, possibly at this time, two other books of a similar nature, the *Praeparatio Ecclesiastica*, and the *Demonstratio Ecclesiastica*. Both of these have entirely perished, but it is supposed that they dealt with the church in the same way as the *Praeparatio Evangelica* and *Demonstratio Evangelica* dealt with the coming of Christ. Lightfoot thinks that there is an allusion to the *Demonstratio Ecclesiastica* in the *Praeparatio Evangelica*, i. 3. 11, where Eusebius says that he had gathered together in a special work the sayings of Christ relative to the foundation of his church and had compared them with the events. Lightfoot also thinks that it is possible that Book IV. of the *Theophania* may have been adapted from the *Demonstratio Ecclesiastica*, just as other parts of the *Theophania* (for instance Book V.) are adapted from the *Demonstratio Evangelica*.

Before Eusebius had finished writing the *Demonstratio Evangelica* the persecution was ended (or at least seemed to be ended) by the Edict of Toleration in 311, and Eusebius seems to have broken off from his dogmatic writings to write a history of the church on the basis of the facts which he had already collected and in part published in the *Chronicon*.

This *Church History*, translated in the present volumes, passed during the life of Eusebius himself through several stages which may not unfairly be called editions.

1. The first edition consisted of Books I.-VIII. It was planned in 311, for in the preface to the first

book Eusebius says that he will describe " the martyrdoms of our own time and the gracious and favouring help of our Saviour in them all," and in Book viii. 16. 1 he says that the Edict of Tolerance in 311 was " the gracious and favouring interposition of God." The similarity of phrase suggests that the same event—the Edict of Tolerance—is intended in both passages. This conclusion may be supported by small differences of plan which show that the ninth book was not part of the original scheme, and that the original text of the eighth book has been somewhat modified in the later editions, to which all the extant MSS. belong. The details can best be found in Schwartz's introduction, page lvi.

2. The second edition added Book IX., which was necessary because the persecution, which seemed to have ceased in 311, was revived by Maximin, and the defeat of Maximin by Licinius appeared the really decisive moment. This second edition was probably produced in 315

3. The third edition added the tenth book in order to close the story with the dedication of the basilica at Tyre. Eusebius says that he did this at the request of Paulinus, bishop of Tyre, " adding at this time the tenth book to those that were already completed of the *Ecclesiastical History*" (*H.E.* x. 1. 2). Schwartz thinks that he also moved a collection of documents from their original position in Book IX. to the end of Book X., and added a paragraph to the eighth book on the death of the four emperors. This edition would belong to the year 317.

4. The fourth edition came after the fall of Licinius in 323, and consisted in the main of the removal of

passages inconsistent with the *Damnatio Memoriae* of Licinius. The evidence for this last edition is in the main textual. The group of manuscripts ATER contain a number of passages omitted in BDM, and a large proportion of them seem to be connected with Licinius. It is thought that though all the existing manuscripts represent the fourth edition, from which these passages had been omitted in accordance with the *Damnatio Memoriae* of Licinius, the group ATER had been corrected from a copy of the third edition, which, of course, contained these passages.

This theory of four editions of the *Ecclesiastical History* is taken from E. Schwartz's Prolegomena, pp. xlvii ff. which should be carefully studied, as they supersede all earlier investigations. It should be noted that the evidence for the 3rd and 4th editions is textual, for the 2nd and 3rd internal and logical.

A rival theory has been propounded by H. J. Lawlor in his *Eusebiana*, pp. 243 ff. He thinks that Eusebius had begun to write his Church History somewhat earlier than the date assigned by Schwartz, and in this agrees with the view stated by Harnack in his *Chronologie*, ii. pp. 111 ff. The theory has the advantage that it gives Eusebius rather more time for completing so large a book ; and it necessitates the view, by no means improbable in itself, that he wrote the Introduction in Book I. after he had finished the narrative properly so called. He had, according to Lawlor, nearly completed the Seventh Book of the *History*, which brought the story down to his own time, when suddenly the Edict of Toleration was issued by Galerius and his colleagues. This event, which appeared to have ushered in a period of

peace to the church after a most cruel persecution, was seized upon by him as the natural end of his story. He therefore wrote a sketch of the history of the persecution as the eighth and last book of his work, and published the whole. A little later he added an abridged form of his *Palestinian Martyrs*, which he had written in the interval as a supplement to the eighth book, and this addition, according to Lawlor, may be regarded as a second edition of the *Church History*. But the persecution was resumed, and when the Edict of Milan once more re-established toleration, Eusebius produced a third edition of the *Historia Ecclesiastica*, revising Book VIII., making a few changes in Book VII. and in the *Palestinian Martyrs*, and adding Book IX., thus bringing the whole to an end with the text of the letter of Licinius dated June the 13th, 313. The date of this edition would therefore be soon after the end of 313. A fourth edition was produced eleven years later, adding the tenth Book, and the whole work in its present form was finished in 324 or a little later.

The weakest spot in this theory seems to be that it attaches too little weight to the statement of Eusebius that he added the tenth book in order to please the bishop of Tyre, which certainly suggests an earlier date than 323, inasmuch as the church at Tyre was dedicated in 317. But Lawlor's suggestion that there was never more than one edition of Book X. is important for textual reasons. It would on the whole tend to give greater value to the ATER group and rather less to the BDM group, which Schwartz on the whole prefers. The opinion of the present editor inclines somewhat to Schwartz's interpretation of the phenomena, but the suggestion that the first

edition of the *Historia Ecclesiastica* was begun rather earlier than Schwartz suggests has many advantages.

It is probable that the *Chronicon,* the *Historia Ecclesiastica,* the *Praeparatio Evangelica,* the *Demonstratio Evangelica,* the *Eclogae Propheticae,* and possibly the *Demonstratio* and *Praeparatio Ecclesiastica,* comprise the whole of the original plan of Eusebius. But the exigencies of events which forced him somewhat to change the plan of the *Historia Ecclesiastica* also led to his writing some subsidiary books during this period.

The most important of these is the *Palestinian Martyrs,* which has, like the *Historia Ecclesiastica,* a complicated textual history. It is known in two forms, the longer found only in Syriac, though undoubtedly based on a lost Greek original, and the shorter preserved in the group ATER of the manuscripts of the *Historia Ecclesiastica,* and inserted immediately after Book VIII. The relation of these two forms to each other and to the *Historia Ecclesiastica* affords a problem which will probably never be solved. Lightfoot and Lawlor believe that the longer form is the earlier ; Schwartz thinks that the shorter is Eusebius's original draft, but that he lengthened it himself. All agree that it is extremely probable that both forms are due to Eusebius himself. The relation of the shorter form to the *Historia Ecclesiastica* depends somewhat on the view taken of the textual history of the *Historia.* On Schwartz's view of the manuscript evidence it seems almost certain that the *Palestinian Martyrs* was omitted from the last edition of the *Historia Ecclesiastica,* but that it probably belonged to the third which influenced the group of manuscripts ATER. Yet it is scarcely

probable that it was not inserted before the third
edition. Its position between the eighth and the
ninth books suggests that it was added by Eusebius to
the first edition which ended with Book VIII., and
this addition constitutes Lawlor's " second edition."
But there can be, from the nature of the case, no
certainty on this point. All that is clear is that the
book has every claim of internal evidence to be
regarded as a true work of Eusebius, and that when
the recension ATER was made the scribe had access
to another manuscript, not that which he was actually
copying, which contained its text after the end of
Book VIII. What that manuscript was must remain
uncertain, as there is no evidence whatever on the
subject. Similarly, it is not likely that complete
certainty will ever be attained as to the relation
between the two forms of the text ; the evidence
is too conflicting.

With regard to the whole complicated series of
problems afforded by the composition and text of
the *Historia Ecclesiastica* and the *Palestinian Martyrs*,
it may be said that the wisest method for a student
to pursue is to begin by reading the essay of Lightfoot in the *Dictionary of Christian Biography*, supple-
menting it by Harnack's treatment in his *Altchristliche Literatur* and in his *Chronologie*, and then, and
not till then, to go on to the more detailed, more
thorough, but far more difficult books of Schwartz and
Lawlor, both of which are quite indispensable to a
proper knowledge of the subject.

During the last years of the persecution, Eusebius
collaborated with Pamphilus in writing a *Defence of
Origen*. When Pamphilus was martyred he finished

the work by himself, and also wrote the *Life of Pamphilus*. Both books are unfortunately lost. He also wrote, in two volumes, a work called by Jerome the *De evangeliorum diaphonia*, but in the Greek entitled the Ζητήματα καὶ λύσεις εἰς τὴν γενεαλογίαν τοῦ Σωτῆρος ἡμῶν πρὸς Στέφανον and the Ζητήματα καὶ λύσεις εἰς τὴν ἀνάστασιν τοῦ Σωτῆρος πρὸς Μαρῖνον. These are only extant in the form of an epitome, but large fragments of the original have been found. It is possible, but quite uncertain, that there may be some connexion between this book and the system of " Canons " which Eusebius invented to facilitate the comparative study of the Gospels. These canons divide the paragraphs of the Gospels, quoted by the numbers given by Ammonius,[1] into ten groups, according as the material in them is found in all four Gospels, in only one, or in any of the possible combinations of two or three Gospels. Eusebius published this apparatus with an explanation in a " letter to Carpianus," of whom nothing is known. The earliest manuscript of the New Testament which contains this system is the Codex Sinaiticus which may have been written in Caesarea during the life of Eusebius, but more probably is a little later and came from Alexandria.

After Nicaea Eusebius scarcely produced so many books as he did in the time of the persecution and the days immediately succeeding it. This, no doubt, was due to his elevation to the bishopric of Caesarea. He seems to have busied himself with exegetical writing, and there are large fragments

---

[1] A scholar of Alexandria who divided the gospels into chapters in order to facilitate their use. These chapters are commonly found in Greek mss. and are known as the " Ammonian sections."

extant of a commentary on the Psalms, another on
Luke, another on Isaiah, and perhaps another on
1 Corinthians, which probably belong to this period,
but none are fully extant and their further recovery
depends in the main on the study of catenae.[1]

He also produced four connected works dealing
with the geography of the Bible. These comprise a
translation into Greek of foreign words found in the
Bible; a description of ancient Judaea, a plan of
Jerusalem and the temple, and a treatise on the
names of the places mentioned in the Bible. The
first three have been lost, but the last was translated
by Jerome and is still extant. According to him it
was written after the *Church History,* and from
internal evidence it appears to have been published
before the death of Paulinus of Tyre in 328. It is
usually quoted as the Τοπικά or sometimes as the
Onomasticon.

Of doubtful authenticity, but sometimes ascribed
to Eusebius and to this period, is a little book on the
nomenclature of the book of the Prophets containing
a short account of the several prophets and their
works.

In the last years of his life Eusebius was busy with
two main achievements. He regarded Marcellus of
Ancyra with somewhat the same feelings as Athanasius regarded Arius, that is to say as the real leader
of the attempts to disturb the peace and unity of the
church by essentially one-sided and erroneous teaching. He therefore wrote two treatises against
Marcellus, one generally known as the *Contra
Marcellum,* the other as the *De ecclesiastica theo-*

---

[1] That is, commentaries made up of selections from early
interpreters linked together into a " chain " of comment.

logia. Both of these were published after 335. He also wrote and published a book on the life of Constantine, which was not so much a full biography as a panegyric, important to us because it contains much information about the Council of Nicaea and the further ecclesiastical activities of the Emperor. With this, or closely connected with it, came also the publication of the speech known as the *De laudibus Constantini,* which Eusebius delivered in honour of Constantine on his thirtieth anniversary, and an edition of the speech which Constantine himself made to the Synod. Finally, it is probable that during his last years he was engaged in writing the volume known as the *Theophania,* which is in the main a repetition of the same arguments as those found in the *Demonstratio,* and in the opening chapters of the *Historia Ecclesiastica* with regard to the appearance of the Logos in the world. It was probably his last work; it is extant only in Syriac, and apparently was never finished, but there is still controversy among critics as to its date and relation to the *Demonstratio.*

II. The Manuscripts of the *Historia Ecclesiastica*

The primary mss. of the *Historia Ecclesiastica* fall into two main groups :

1. The group BDMΣL.

> B, Codex Parisinus, 1431 (vellum, s. xi-xii), formerly Colbert. 621 and Reg. 2280, called E by Burton. In the Bibliothèque Nationale.

D, Codex Parisinus 1433 (vellum, s. xi-xii), called F by Heikel. In the Bibliothèque Nationale.

M, Codex Marcianus 338 (vellum, s. xii), called H by Burton. In St. Mark's Library at Venice.

Σ, an ancient Syriac version, probably made early in the fifth century.

L, the translation of Rufinus made in 402.

In this group M most frequently differs from B and D. Generally this seems due to error in M, but sometimes BD have an error in common against M owing to their having been influenced by a later "learned" recension which did not affect M (see p. xxix). The combination MD is usually inferior, so that B is on the whole the best ms. of the group. The decision between B and M can often be made by comparison with the second group of mss. The Syriac version is far better than Rufinus, who frequently paraphrases and seems to have found Eusebius very difficult to render literally, as, indeed, he is.

2. The group ATER :

A, Codex Parisinus 1430 (vellum, s. xi), formerly in the possession of Cardinal Mazarin. Called C by Burton. In the Bibliothèque Nationale.

T, Codex Laurentianus 70, 7 (vellum, s. x-xi), called I by Burton. In the Laurentian library in Florence.

E, Codex Laurentianus 70, 20 (vellum, s. x), called K by Burton. In the Laurentian library in Florence.

R, Codex Mosquensis 50 (vellum, s. xii), called J by Heikel. In Moscow.

INTRODUCTION

In this group A is, generally speaking, the best, though it has many individual errors. TER seem to have a common element, and probably represent a later recension.

Schwartz thinks that BDMΣL represent the text of the 4th edition of Eusebius, with mistakes but no deliberate emendations. ATER represent the same text often corrected by a copy of the third edition. It is, however, often free from the individual errors of BDMΣL, which it serves to correct.

It can also be shown that there was a later " learned " recension which has affected mss. of both groups, and is now found in ERBD and in some corrections in T, quoted as Tᶜ.

From these primary mss. are derived the secondary mss. of the *Historia Ecclesiastica*. Schwartz has investigated the text of all of them, and his results can be shown most clearly in the following scheme.

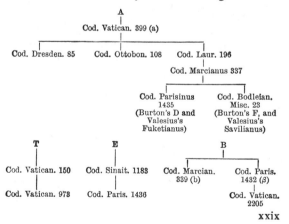

Besides these codices which are unmixed descendants of primary MSS. there are three others in which the text of one of the primary MSS. has been "crossed" with readings found in the others. These are :

(1) Codex Parisinus, 1437 (paper, s. xiv), a descendant of B, crossed with some readings derived from the A-family, probably from Cod. Dresden. 85 (or some similar MS.), rather than A or a. It was the basis of the *editio princeps* of Stephanus (1544), and is quoted by Valesius as Regius, by Burton as A, and by Schwegler as a and q. This double use by Schwegler is due to a curious accident : Burton (following Stroth and Heinichen) referred to this MS. by error as Paris. 1436, but he also possessed a collation of it with the right number, and his posthumous editor, not realizing that this collation referred to Burton's A, published it in an appendix. Schwegler was misled by this, and thus manufactured two MSS. out of two collations of one MS.

(2) Codex Parisinus, 1434 (paper, s. xvi), a descendant of A crossed with B or a descendant of B. It was occasionally used by Stephanus, and is quoted by Valesius as Medicaeus, and by Burton as B.

(3) Codex Arundelianus, 539, in the British Museum (paper, s. xv), a carelessly written descendant of A (not of a) crossed with the B group. Quoted by Burton as G.

III. THE PRINTED TEXT OF THE *HISTORIA ECCLESIASTICA*

The following independent editions of the Greek text of the *Historia Ecclesiastica* have been published.

(1) Stephanus : Paris, 1544. Reprinted several

times ; the best of the later editions being at Geneva in 1612. It was based on codd. Paris. 1437 and 1434.

(2) Valesius : Paris, 1659. This was based on four MSS., the two used by Stephanus which Valesius (Henri de Valois) called Regius (cod. Paris. 1437) and Medicaeus (cod. Paris. 1434) and two others at Paris, cod. Paris. 1430 (A), which was then in the possession of Cardinal Mazarin, and cod. Paris. 1435, which he called Fuketianus. To the text he added many valuable notes which still are indispensable.

The edition of Valesius was reprinted at least three times in the seventeenth century, at Mainz in 1672, at Paris in 1677, and at Amsterdam in 1695. An excellent reprint, containing some more notes of Valesius collected from scattered sources, was issued in 1720 by Reading in Cambridge ; this was reprinted in Turin in 1746, and in Migne's *Patrologia Graeca* in Paris in 1857.

(3) Stroth : Halle, 1779. This edition was never completed, nor has it now any value ; but it deserves to be mentioned if only for the pious memory of a man whose aims and vision were greater than his means. F. A. Stroth collected much new information as to MSS., but was unable to afford the expense of obtaining collations, so that his real apparatus remained that of Valesius.

(4) Zimmermann : Frankfort, 1822. E. Zimmerman's edition was in the main little more than a reprint of the text of Valesius and added nothing of importance to the material for reconstructing the text.

(5) Heinichen, ed. 1 : Leipzig, 1827. Heinichen's edition of Eusebius is a good example of the waste of labour incurred by those who edit texts on the basis of inaccurate collations. His first edition was

published in 1827. It did not go much beyond the
work of Zimmerman, or, in other words, of Valesius.
In 1840 he published a *Supplementa notarum ad
Eusebii Historiam Ecclesiasticum*, which contained a
statement of the variants found in Burton and of
cod. Dresden. 185. Finally in 1868 he published a
second edition in which he collected all the information which was to be found in previous editions of
Eusebius. Some of the collations for this edition he
made himself, or had made for him, but they prove
to have been in almost every instance far from
satisfactory Nor did he seem to understand
perfectly the collations found in other editions. The
result is that his book cannot be trusted and was
never likely to lead to true results.

(6) Burton: Oxford, 1838. This edition, by Edward
Burton, building on and adding to the work of Stroth,
was unfortunately also based on imperfect collations.
But it contained for the first time the readings of
ATEBM and of cod. Arundelianus. It was published,
after his death, at Oxford in 1838 and reissued in 1845,
and again in 1856 ; it also served as the text of a
partial edition by W. Bright, issued in 1872 and 1881.

(7) Schwegler: Tübingen, 1852. This edition
was in method a great improvement on its predecessors; but its material was really that of Burton,
and Schwegler's results are nullified by the inaccuracy
of the collations.

(8) Laemmer: Schaffhausen, 1859-62. This was a
thoroughly bad text, being in the main Schwegler's,
changed in many places to agree with cod. Marcianus
338 (M), which Laemmer thought was the best MS.

(9) Dindorf: Leipzig, 1871. This is perhaps the
best known of all editions of Eusebius, as it was

issued in the convenient "Teubner texts," but it
is merely an inaccurate reprint of Schwegler.

(10) Schwartz : Leipzig, 1903. This edition has
rendered obsolete all except that of Valesius. It is
based on new and probably accurate collations of all the
known MSS. Its text is followed in the present volumes.
It is possible that some future editor may conceivably
reopen the question of the merits of the two groups of
primary MSS., but he will have to build on Schwartz's
work. It is not a commentary, but much of the
material on which a commentary could be based is
to be found in the references given in its apparatus.

The fullest statement of the printed editions of
Eusebius and the manuscripts upon which they are
based is to be found in an article by A. C. Headlam in
the *Journal of Theological Studies* for October 1902,
pp. 93 ff. It is stated at the beginning of this
article that it is a draft of prolegomena for a projected
edition, but nothing more has yet appeared of this
great undertaking.

One other book remains to be mentioned although
it is not an edition of the text. The translation
of the *Historia Ecclesiastica* by A. C. M'Giffert in
the Nicene and Post-Nicene Fathers, Second Series,
vol. i., 1904, is provided with historical notes which
furnish the only valuable continuous supplement to
Valesius : no student of Eusebius can afford to neglect
them.

IV. THE PLAN OF EUSEBIUS IN THE *HISTORIA ECCLESIASTICA* AND THE SOURCES WHICH HE USED

The general plan of the *Historia Ecclesiastica* is
clear and lucid. The chronology adopted is that of

INTRODUCTION

the Roman Emperors, and the events are arranged reign by reign. But there is little or no attempt to give any closer dating than this, and the relation between events during the same reign is not indicated. To this there is one exception. The bishops of Rome, Alexandria, Antioch, and Jerusalem are given, and in the case of Rome and Alexandria the exact dates are given. Where did Eusebius obtain this information? The researches of Lipsius, Lightfoot, and Harnack have shown that he used the chronological material collected by Hippolytus and Africanus, and Lightfoot thought that there was a still earlier list compiled by Hegesippus, but to discuss at due length the problems involved would demand more space than is at present available; since Harnack's *Chronologie* the main contributions have been in reviews and periodicals, the chief English writers being H. J. Lawlor, C. H. Turner, and J. K. Fotheringham.

One further observation is necessary. The object of the whole book was to present the Christian " Succession," which did not merely mean, though it certainly included, the apostolic succession of the bishops of the four great " thrones," but rather the whole intellectual, spiritual, and institutional life of the Church. It cannot be too strongly emphasised that Eusebius, like all early church historians, can be understood only if it be recognized that whereas modern writers try to trace the development, growth, and change of doctrines and institutions, their predecessors were trying to prove that nothing of the kind ever happened. According to them the Church had had one and only one teaching from the beginning; it had been preserved by the " Succes-

sion " and heresy was the attempt of the Devil to change it.

In tracing " the succession " Eusebius quotes and refers to many writers. To give any complete description of them would be to write a handbook to early Christian literature ; but it seems desirable to give a short account of the chief writings referred to in the books translated in this volume, book by book, and to indicate the points of interest and difficulty which they present.

BOOK I.—The chief sources drawn on by Eusebius, apart from the New Testament, are Josephus, Africanus, and the Archives of Edessa.

Josephus.—Josephus, the son of Matthias, who took the name of Flavius in honour of the emperors of the Flavian house, was born in A.D. 37 or 38. He belonged to the highest Jewish aristocracy, being descended on his mother's side from Jonathan the Maccabee. After studying all the sects of the Jews he became a Pharisee. He went to Rome when he was twenty-six years old on a political mission, and hereafter he appears to have been quite sincere in his desire, though somewhat shifty in his tactics, to bring about better relations between the Jews and the Romans. During the Jewish war which began in 66 he belonged to the moderate party, and was entrusted with the command of Galilee. His career here was much hindered by the opposition of John of Gischala. He was besieged in Jotatata, and at last was forced to surrender. As he had preferred surrender to death the Jews regarded him as a renegade, and attributed the worst motives to his persistent efforts to secure peace before the inevitable catastrophe which he foresaw. He became friendly

with Vespasian and Titus, and when the war ended obtained a grant of lands in Palestine, the privilege of Roman citizenship, and other distinctions. He appears to have lived until after the year 100, as his autobiography was written after the death of Agrippa II., who died in that year.

After the fall of Jerusalem in A.D. 70 he wrote the history of the Jewish war (*Bellum Iudaicum*) in seven books. In this the first two books give an introductory history from the reign of Antiochus Epiphanes to the beginning of the war ; Books III.-VI. describe the war down to the capture of Jerusalem ; and Book VII. describes the last scenes. This work is said to have been accepted and even revised by Vespasian and Titus. Its main object no doubt was to make the Jews and the Romans understand each other better, but a desire that they should appreciate Josephus's own service to both sides can be clearly seen.

Some years later Josephus supplemented this work by a larger one giving the history of the Jewish people up to the beginning of the war. This was arranged in twenty books and was called the Ἀρχαιολογία Ἰουδαϊκή. This was translated into Latin as the *Antiquitates Iudaeorum*, and it is therefore usually quoted in English as the *Antiquities*. It was probably completed about A.D. 93.

Almost immediately after this Josephus also wrote a work in two books in answer to Apion. This Apion was a famous controversialist who lived in the middle of the first century and wrote a history of Egypt and a book against the Jews. He figures largely in the Clementine homilies. None of his works are extant, but the fragments which remain are collected in

Müller, *Fragmenta Hist. Graec.* (See also the article by Lightfoot in the *Dictionary of Christian Biography*.)

Finally in old age he wrote his autobiography, usually quoted as the *Vita*.

Eusebius makes many quotations from Josephus, which are usually accurate. Only in the account of the death of Agrippa the First is there any serious divergence, and this is probably accidental (see pp. 130 f.).

The best text of Josephus is that of Niese, Berlin, 1887. Niese also published in 1888 a smaller edition omitting the apparatus criticus.

The first translation[1] in English was that of Whiston, which has been often reprinted, and was superficially revised by Shilleto in 1889–90. It is not free from inaccuracies, but Josephus is very difficult to render, as his Greek is bad and his style obscure. Explanation as well as a new translation is desirable, and there are few books more needed by scholars at the present time than an historical commentary on the second half of the *Antiquities* and on the *Jewish War*. At present there is on neither any commentary.

Julius Africanus. — Julius Africanus, sometimes, but probably wrongly, called Sextus or Sextus Julius, is stated by Suidas to have been a Libyan who served in the army of Severus in 195, and afterwards settled in Emmaus (Nicopolis) though he probably also spent some time in Alexandria. When his home was ruined he went, in 221 or a little later, on an embassy to the Emperor, either Elagabalus or Alexander Severus, and was made the head of a reparation commission which rebuilt the city under the name of Nicopolis. The exact time of his death

[1] Vol. I. of a new translation by H. St. J. Thackeray has appeared in the Loeb Classical Library, and Vol. II. is in the Press.

is unknown, but he was still alive in 240 when he corresponded with Origen. Besides the information given in the *Historia Ecclesiastica* of Eusebius and in Eusebius, *Chron.* ann. 221, some details are found in Sozomen, *Hist. Eccl.* v. 1 ; in Jerome, *De viris illustribus*, 63 ; in George Syncellus, who may have used the lost introduction to the *Chronicon* of Eusebius ; in Cedrenus, *Hist. Comp.* 207, and in Moses of Chorene, ii. 27.

He was one of the most learned of the writers in the third century. His chief work was a treatise on chronology in five books on which the *Chronicon* of Eusebius was largely based. This began with the creation and went down at least to the year 221. It appears to have consisted, like most chronological books of the period, of two parts, a " Chronology " and a " Canon." The " Chronology " was an essay, or a series of essays, on critical questions ; the " Canon " [1] was a series of tables in which a summary of events was arranged in parallel columns showing how the numbers of years in one system, such as the Greek Olympiads, corresponded to another, such as the years after Christ. He appears to have written in order to prove the " chiliastic " view of history rather than in the interests of pure chronology, and on this point Eusebius was controverting rather than copying him. Apart from this, however, his work was doubtless the source of much of the framework of the *Historia Ecclesiastica* (see especially Schwartz, *Prolegomena*, pp. ccxv ff.).

Besides this great book Africanus wrote a letter to Aristides, whose identity is unknown, on the dis-

---

[1] It should be noted that the word "Chronicon" is properly used of the canon, not of the chronology.

crepancies between the genealogies in Matthew and Luke. This is quoted in part by Eusebius, *H.E.* i. 7. And he also wrote a letter to Origen on the authenticity of the book of Susanna. This is referred to by Eusebius, *H.E.* vi. 31, and is preserved in several manuscripts of Origen.

The authenticity of these writings is undoubted. There is also ascribed to him a work called Κεστοί, which means *Girdles*. It apparently consisted of a collection of essays varying in character from Agriculture to the Art of War. A few extracts from this book remain, but not sufficient to prove or disprove its ascription to Africanus.

The most convenient collection of the fragments of Africanus is still that of Routh, *Rel. Sacr.* vol. ii. The most important work on his writing has been done by H. Gelzer, *Sextus Julius Africanus*, 1880 and 1885, but except for detailed study of the points raised by Gelzer, a sufficient account is provided by the article on Africanus in the *Dictionary of Christian Biography*, and by Harnack, *Chronologie*, ii. pp. 89 ff.

The Archives of Edessa.—According to *H.E.* i. 12. 3 ff. Eusebius made use of material in the Archives of Edessa. These appear to have consisted of two divisions. There was an ancient royal archive at Edessa and a later ecclesiastical one which was probably not instituted until the beginning of the fourth century. According to Moses of Chorene Julius Africanus made use of all this material, which was also known to the editor of the *Chronicon Edessenum*. It is not certain whether Eusebius had himself seen this archive or made use of it only at second-hand through the writings of Julius Africanus, but in any case there is no reason to doubt the statement

that the apocryphal story of Abgar Uchama was found in the archives at Edessa, which is also the probable source—direct or indirect—for most of the information contained in Eusebius as to the history of Christianity outside the Roman Empire in the region of Mesopotamia and such details as the story of Mani. The rather complicated questions concerning the story of this archive can be studied best in Hallier, *Untersuchungen über die edess. Chronik* (*Texte u. Unters.* ix. 1, 1892).

Book II.—In the second book Josephus is again used, and extracts are made from Philo, Clement of Alexandria and Hegesippus.

Philo.—Philo was probably born about the year 30 B.C., and lived on until the beginning of the second half of the first century A.D. He belonged to a wealthy and distinguished family in Alexandria. His brother, Alexander, was the Alabarch [1] of the city and had close relations with the imperial family in Rome. Philo was essentially a philosopher, and spent his life endeavouring to reconcile the Jewish Law with the Platonic Faith. He was also a voluminous writer and his books were treasured by Origen, and so passed into the library at Caesarea and thence into the general tradition of Christian writings.

The statements about Philo's writings in Book II. of the *Historia Ecclesiastica* are so confused that it is desirable to give the facts about them in somewhat clearer form.

[1] The name of a high local official in Alexandria. From Josephus, *Antiq.* xviii. 8. 1 it appears to be the name of the head of the Jewish colony in Alexandria, but Cicero, *Att.* ii. 17 applies the word to Pompey, apparently with the meaning " tax-collector."

xl

INTRODUCTION

Philo wrote three great books on the Pentateuch :

(1) The *Quaestiones et solutiones* (Ζητήματα καὶ λύσεις). How far Philo carried this book, which dealt with the problems of the Pentateuch, is not known, but Eusebius, like ourselves, was unacquainted with any work going beyond Exodus.

(2) The *Legum allegoriae*. This was divided into a number of books of which three are known as *Legum allegoriarum libri* i., ii., and iii., but the others which follow, each with separate titles, were apparently without numbers. The list of these books is *De cherubim et flammeo gladio* (Gen. iii. 24), *De sacrificiis Abelis et Caini* (Gen. iv. 2-4), *Quod deterius potiori insidiari soleat* (Gen. iv. 8-15), *De posteritate Caini sibi visi sapientis et quo pacto sedem mutat* (Gen. iv. 16-25), *De gigantibus* (Gen. vi. 1-4), *De agricultura* (Gen. ix. 20), *De ebrietate* (Gen. ix. 21), *De sobrietate* (Gen. ix. 24-27), *De confusione linguarum* (Gen. xi. 1-9), *De migratione Abrahami* (Gen. xii. 1-6), *Quis rerum divinarum haeres sit* (Gen. xv. 2-8), *De congressu quaerendae eruditionis causa* (Gen. xvi. 1-6), *De profugis* (Gen. xvi. 6-14), *De mutatione nominum* (Gen. xvii. 1-22), *De somniis* liber i. (Gen. xxviii. 12 ff.).

(3) *A Systematic Description of the Mosaic Legislation.* It is divided into three parts : The first deals with the creation of the world ; this is known as the *De mundi opificio*. In the manuscripts and editions of Philo this work has been placed at the beginning of Philo's works, before the first book of the *Legum allegoriae*, but it probably ought to be put back into the position here claimed for it. The second part deals with the biographies of the virtuous men of the Old Testament, and is known as the Νόμοι ἄγραφοι. Of it are extant the *De Abrahamo*, and the *De Iosepho*,

also known as *The Statesman* (ὁ Πολιτικός), because Joseph was treated by Philo as illustrating the virtues of civic life. The third part of the *Systematic Description* went on to deal with the consideration of the Mosaic legislation properly so-called, and was divided into two subdivisions, (*a*) the *De Decalogo* and (*b*) the *De specialibus legibus* or the " consideration of the special laws which follow the Ten Commandments and are connected with them." This was contained in four books. To these were added two appendices, one on three virtues, *De fortitudine*, *De caritate*, *De poenitentia*, with the possible addition of a fourth, *De nobilitate*, and one on the treatment of the good and evil under the title of *De praemiis et poenis* and *De execrationibus*.

Besides these three great books on the Pentateuch Philo also wrote various single works: (1) the *Vita Mosis*. (2) *Quod omnis probus liber*, with which went another book now lost, *Quod omnis improbus servus*. (3) A great work which was apparently intended to do something similar to that which Lactantius did afterwards for the Christians in his book *De mortibus persecutorum*, and to show that no one persecuted the Jews without suffering from the punishment of God at the end of his life, while the Jews received the rewards of their virtues. Probably he dealt in this way with the careers of Sejanus, Flaccus, Caligula, and Pilate, but it is only the story of Flaccus which is at all fully preserved in the *Adversus Flaccum* and the *Legatio ad Caium*. It would appear that there were originally five books in this work of which only the two mentioned have been preserved.

Another work published separately is the *De providentia*, only found now in Armenian, which is

also the case with the *De Alexandro et quod propriam
rationem muta animalia habeant*.

Finally two books, now only partially preserved,
appear to have been entitled the Ὑποθετικά and the
Defence of the Jews. Whether these were two or one
seems doubtful. To these most critics add a long
book, still extant, *De vita contemplativa*, giving an
account of the Therapeutae in Egypt, but there are
still a few who think that this is not a genuine work
of Philo.

It will be seen by comparing this list of the writings
of Philo with the references made in Eusebius ii. 18
that Eusebius has referred to the greater number of
writings of Philo which are still extant, but he has
confused the order of the books so that if we did not
possess other information it would be quite impossible
for us to reconstruct the relation of the sub-titles
which Eusebius quotes to the great divisions into
which Philo's works really fall. The most probable
suggestion is that of Dr. Lawlor, who thinks that
Eusebius knew Philo only through volumes of tracts
which were preserved in the library at Caesarea, and
that he copied out the titles without always recognizing the relation of one tract to another, being
misled by the accidents of binding (see Lawlor,
Eusebiana, pp. 138–145).

The fullest and best sources of information on
Philo's writings are E. Schürer, *Geschichte des jüdisches
Volkes*, ed. 4, vol. iii. pp. 633–716 ; the prolegomena of
Cohn and Wendland's edition, and the article in
the *Dictionary of Christian Biography*. The two
fullest editions are Mangey, London, 1742, and Cohn
and Wendland, Berlin, 1896–1915, which includes
everything except the fragments, for which Mangey

must still be consulted, and the Armenian texts published by Aucher, *Paralipomena Armena*, 1826. There is also a valuable edition of the *De vita contemplativa* by F. C. Conybeare.

Clement of Alexandria. — Clement of Alexandria was probably born in the middle of the second century. According to Julius Africanus, quoted by Cedrenus, he came into fame in the reign of Commodus (A.D. 180–193) and the *Chronicon* of Eusebius apparently assigns the date 193 to his ordination as presbyter. According to Eusebius, *Praeparatio evangelica*, ii. 2. 64, he was converted to Christianity from heathenism and was not born in the church, and according to Epiphanius his birthplace was claimed by Athens as well as by Alexandria. He travelled much in the east, and towards the end of the second century became head of the catechetical school at Alexandria. He appears to have retired from public life in Alexandria during the persecution under Severus, A.D. 202 ff. According to the letter of Alexander,[1] who was bishop of Jerusalem in 212, and, wrote about 211 from prison to the church at Antioch, Clement had been living in the Cappadocian Caesarea and must have been still alive when he wrote, as he was going to carry Alexander's letter. According to a later letter of the same Alexander to Origen Clement died soon after this, for this second letter, which can hardly be later than 217 and may have been earlier, implies that he was dead.

The list of Clement's writings is given by Eusebius, *H.E.* vi. 13. Of those to which he refers the Προτρεπτικός or *Exhortation to the Greeks*,[2] is completely

---

[1] Quoted in Eusebius vi. 2. 6.

[2] This and the *Quis dives salvetur* are translated by G. W. Butterworth in the Loeb Classical Library.

INTRODUCTION

preserved as is also the Παιδαγωγός, or *Instructor*, which is in three books. These two works seem to have been intended as the first two parts of a connected series. The first, the Προτρεπτικός, deals with the Logos in relation to the conversion of the heathen ; the Παιδαγωγός also deals with the Logos but in relation to morality ; and the third book was intended to deal with the Logos as the teacher who initiated man into true knowledge. It is possible, but far from certain, that the Στρωματεῖς [1] mentioned by Eusebius and still partially preserved represent this third volume.

Of the other works mentioned by Eusebius only fragments are found except the small treatise known as *Quis dives salvetur*. The loss of the *Hypotyposes* [2] is greatly to be regretted, but in addition to the quotations preserved in Eusebius three other fragments have been thought to have originally belonged to them. These are the *Excerpta Theodoti*,[3] the *Eclogae propheticae*, and the *Adumbrationes in epistolas canonicas*. It has, however, been suggested that the *Excerpta Theodoti* really belong to the eighth book of the Στρωματεῖς. In any case they are very valuable information as to the teaching of Theodotus, for they seem to represent the notes which Clement had made rather than a finished literary production.

The best edition of Clement is that of Stählin, in *Die griechischen christlichen Schriftsteller der ersten drei*

---

[1] Sometimes called *Stromata*; the word means literally " patchwork " and hence " miscellanies."

[2] This appears to have been a commentary on selected parts of the Bible.

[3] Theodotus was a Gnostic of the Valentinian School, from whose writings Clement made a series of extracts with the intention of refuting them.

Jahrhunderte, issued by the Berlin Academy. The three volumes containing the text and introduction of this edition are published ; the fourth volume, which has not yet appeared, will contain the index and some additional dissertations, but even as it stands Stählin's edition takes the place of all others. For the study of Clement special reference should be made to the writings of de Faye, especially his *Clément d'Alexandrie*, 1898 (see also the article on Clement of Alexandria in Harnack's *Chronologie* vol. ii. pp. 1 ff.).

Hegesippus. — Hegesippus appears to have been of Hebrew birth (Eusebius, *H.E.* iv. 22), but there is no evidence whether he was born a Christian or converted from Judaism. He certainly visited, and perhaps lived in Rome. If Eusebius means in the passage referred to that he lived until the time of Eleutherus his death must have been between 175 and 189. The book from which Eusebius derived much of his information as to the early church was entitled Πέντε ὑπομνήματα ἐκκλησιαστικῶν πραξέων, *Five Treatises on the Acts of the Church.* Whether this was an ordered history or a collection of miscellaneous observations cannot be proved, but the latter view is more usually held, and the most probable theory is that of Lawlor, who thinks that the ὑπομνήματα were an apologetic work which only contained a few scattered references to history. Some confusion periodically arises from the fact that in a recension of Josephus, of which a Latin version appeared in the fifth century, the name " Josephus " was spelt " Hegesippus."

The extant fragments of the genuine Hegesippus can be found in Routh, *Rel. Sacr.* vol. i. pp. 207-219,

but more fully and with more complete reference to the authorities in Lawlor's *Eusebiana*, pp. 98-107, and the problems connected with him may be studied best in that work and in the articles in Smith's *Dictionary of Christian Biography* and in Herzog's *Real-Encyklopädie*.

BOOK III.—In this book Josephus remains the chief source of information about the Jews, while Hegesippus and Clement are drawn on for the history of the Church; but besides them Papias, Caius, Clement of Rome, and Ignatius are quoted or referred to.

Papias.—Papias according to Eusebius (iii. 36) was bishop of Hierapolis, but we do not know the exact chronology of his life. Irenaeus (*Adv. haer.* v. 33. 4) says that he was a companion of Polycarp, and he is quoted by Eusebius (iii. 39. 9) as claiming to have seen the daughters of Philip the Evangelist, so that he can scarcely have been born later than the end of the first century. In one of the fragments of his work preserved by Philip Sidetes (edited by De Boor in *Texte und Untersuchungen*, v. 2) he refers to the belief that those whom Christ raised from the dead lived " until the time of Hadrian," so that he can hardly have written earlier than 140.[1] On the other hand, as Irenaeus regarded him as belonging to a past generation, he can scarcely have written later than 160. Thus the middle of the second century is probably the period at which he wrote. His work, from which Eusebius quotes, was entitled Λογίων κυριακῶν ἐξήγησις. Unfortunately the book is lost, and no one knows what the title means. Λόγια generally means " oracles," and is frequently used of the Old Testament, but it might be used of

[1] Hadrian reigned from 117 to 137.

the teaching of Jesus. The quotation given by Eusebius iii. 39, which may come from the preface of Papias, suggests, but does not prove, that the title should be translated *Oracles of the Lord* rather than *Oracles about the Lord*. Thus it is uncertain whether it was a work on the interpretation of the Old Testament or on the Gospels or on traditions behind the Gospels. There is an enormous literature on the subject, but most of it is in the interests of some theory of the origin of the Synoptic Gospels and is almost worthless. The clearest and best statement of the facts is in Harnack's *Chronologie*, i. pp. 356 ff., and on the interpretation of the quotation in Eusebius, *H.E.* iii. 39, Dom Chapman's *John the Presbyter* (Oxford, 1910), is peculiarly lucid and thorough.

Clement of Rome and Ignatius.—Both these writers have left extant works which are published in the Loeb Classical Library, *The Apostolic Fathers*, vol. i.

Caius.—Nothing is known of him except what Eusebius tells us, but his writings and his relation to the Alogi, who rejected the Gospel of John, have been the subject of an extensive literature, to which the latest and most thorough contribution is made by C. Schmidt in an elaborate appendix to his edition of the "Epistola Apostolorum" published in 1919 as *Gespräche Jesu* in *Texte und Untersuchungen* xliii.

BOOK IV.—In the fourth book Eusebius deals with the last rebellion of the Jews, referring to Aristo of Pella, with the Apologists of the time of Hadrian, with the Gnostics of the second century, with Justin Martyr, with Polycarp and other martyrs, and with Tatian. In the 21st chapter he gives a list of the chief Christian writers of the time of Marcus Aurelius.

Aristo of Pella.—In *Hist. Eccl.* iv 6 Eusebius

xlviii

describes the last war of the Jews against the Romans in A.D. 132. He refers to the account given by Aristo of Pella. The natural interpretation is that Aristo had written a history of this time. But nothing is known of him except that in the seventh century Maximus the Confessor says that Aristo wrote the Dialogue of Jason and Papiscus, which was mentioned by Clement of Alexandria, who seems to have attributed it to Luke the Evangelist, though the text of this statement may be corrupt. It is therefore possible that Eusebius is merely referring to some reference introduced into this lost Dialogue (see Harnack, *Altchristliche Literatur*, i. pp. 92 ff.).

Quadratus and Aristides.—Eusebius mentions two apologists of the reign of Hadrian—Quadratus and Aristides. The work of Quadratus is lost, but the apology of Aristides has been recently discovered, though in an imperfect condition. A Syriac translation was found by J. Rendel Harris in 1889 on Mount Sinai, and it was then recognized by J. Armitage Robinson as extant in Greek in the speech put into the mouth of the Christian Nachor in the story of Barlaam and Josaphat. The Syriac and the Greek differ widely, and it is disputed which of the two is nearer the original. Both forms are given in Rendel Harris's " The Apology of Aristides " in *Texts and Studies* i. 1. The Syriac, which alone has the title of Apology, suggests that it was addressed to Antoninus Pius rather than to Hadrian, but the text is in any case corrupt and the point is not certain. Harnack's *Altchristliche Literatur* i. pp. 96 ff. and ii. 2. pp. 271 ff. gives the best statement of the facts and references to other books, but to these should be added Geffcken's *Zwei griechische Apologien.*

INTRODUCTION

The Gnostic Writers.—In *Hist. Eccl.* iv. 7 and 11
Eusebius mentions the chief Gnostic writers known
to him. His information was apparently derived in
main from Irenaeus with probably some use of
Clement of Alexandria, Hippolytus, and a lost work
(the Syntagma) of Justin Martyr. The best modern
books introductory to the subject of Gnosticism are
those of Lipsius (especially his *Quellen der ältesten
Ketzergeschichten* and his articles in the *Dictionary of
Christian Biography*), Harnack's *Quellenkritik der Geschichte des Gnosticismus*, and De Faye's *Gnostiques et
Gnosticisme*, but it is probably quicker and certainly
better to begin by reading Irenaeus, Hippolytus, and
—quite especially—the *Excerpta Theodoti* of Clement
of Alexandria.

Justin Martyr.—Justin according to his own
account (at the beginning of his dialogue with
Trypho) was born in Samaria and became in his youth
a zealous but unsuccessful student of philosophy.
He was converted to Christianity before A.D. 135 (the
time to which the Dialogue refers) and died as a
martyr under Junius Rusticus, who was praetor under
Marcus Aurelius between 163 and 167. The *Chronicon
Paschale* fixes the year of his martyrdom as 165, and
there is no reason why this should not be correct.

According to Eusebius he wrote at least ten books,
of which he gives the list in *Hist. Eccl.* iv. 18. 2-9. Of
these two are extant (1) *The Apology to Antoninus
Pius*, and (2) *The Dialogue with Trypho* ; but there
is a curious literary puzzle in connexion with the
Apology. The printed texts of Justin (which represent the Paris manuscript, Paris. 450 of the year 1364,
of which all other manuscripts are copies) give two
apologies of Justin, and Eusebius also states that he

1

wrote two apologies. It would therefore be natural to conclude that we possess the two which Eusebius had. But except in *Hist. Eccl.* iv. 16. 1 ff. which is ambiguous, Eusebius quotes as the first Apology passages from both the printed books. The point has not been completely cleared up, but it seems probable that the printed texts make up the Eusebian first apology and that the second one known to Eusebius has been lost.

Three other works of Justin mentioned by Eusebius purport to be given in the printed texts—the *Oratio contra Graecos*, the *Cohortatio ad Graecos*, and the *De monarchia*—but it is generally held that these texts are spurious, and it is unlikely that they are those to which Eusebius refers.

The best edition of Justin is that of Otto, 3rd edition, 1876. The best statements of the manuscripts and the ecclesiastical tradition are by Harnack in his *Altchristliche literatur* i. pp. 99 ff., and ii. 1 ff., 274 ff., and in the *Texte und Untersuchungen* I. i. 2. The most complete discussion of Justin's teaching is by Goodenough, *Justin Martyr*, 1923, which also contains a very full bibliography.

The Acts of the Martyrs.—Though Eusebius was active in collecting evidence as to the martyrdoms of the earliest Christians, and made a collection of documents describing them (see p. xiv) he has surprisingly little to tell in his history. In the first five books he relates the martyrdom of James and Simeon, the Lord's brothers, but his information is from Hegesippus; he also mentions the martyrdom of Telesphorus, Bishop of Rome, Publius, Bishop of Athens, Ignatius of Antioch, Justin, Ptolemaeus, Lucius, and Sagaris; but he gives no details and

seems to have had no documents about them, though the *Acta* of Justin are extant in a probably genuine form. He had the *Acta* of Polycarp, of Pionius, of Carpus, Papylus and Agathonice, and of Apollonius, all of which are still extant, and the account of the martyrs of Lyons and Vienne, which has disappeared except for his extensive quotations at the beginning of the fifth book.

Tatian.—The only work of Tatian which is extant in its original form is the *Oratio ad Graecos*, which was once preserved in the famous Arethas manuscript Paris. 451 of the year A.D. 914. The pages containing Tatian's work are missing, but several later MSS. are direct or indirect copies.

The Diatessaron of Tatian is not wholly lost. There is an Arabic version, in which, however, the text has been accommodated to the later Syrian text of the Gospels; there is some connexion between it and the Harmony found and edited by Victor of Capua about the year 545; and it is possible that some mediaeval Dutch and German harmonies indicate the existence of an Old Latin harmony based on Tatian's works.[1] Besides these, and in many ways more important than these, are a series of quotations in early Syriac writers and the commentary of Ephraim on the Diatessaron, partially preserved in Armenian.

The best edition of the *Oratio ad Graecos* is that of E. Schwartz, and of the Diatessaron that given in the *Ante-Nicene Church Fathers*. See also especially Zahn's *Forschungen* i. and the treatment of Tatian in his *Geschichte des N.T. Kanon*.

---

[1] See D. Plooij, *A Primitive Text of the Diatessaron*, Leiden, 1923.

INTRODUCTION

Writers in the time of Marcus Aurelius.—In *Hist. Eccl.* iv. 20 f. Eusebius gives a list of the writers of the end of the second century: Theophilus of Antioch, Hegesippus, Dionysius of Corinth, Pinytus of Crete, Philip of Gortyna, Apollinarius of Hierapolis, Melito, Musanus, Modestus, and Irenaeus. In the following chapters he gives a short summary of the writings of each of them with the exception of Irenaeus whom he reserves for the next book. None of these writings are extant except a few fragments of Melito in Syriac, and the three books of Theophilus *Ad Autolycum*, published in Otto's *Corpus Apologeticum* and in other collections. The first printed edition was issued at Zürich in 1546. The facts relating to Hegesippus have been dealt with above on p. xlvi.

Book V.—In this book Eusebius deals first with the persecution of the Christians in the time of Marcus Aurelius, illustrating it by long quotations from the letter of the churches of Lyons and Vienne referred to above (p. lii). He then describes the works of Irenaeus, and Rhodo, and then turns to Montanism, the Paschal controversy, and the heresy of Artemon and the two Theodoti.

Irenaeus.—Irenaeus was probably a native of the province of Asia and in his youth saw Florinus and Polycarp, presumably at Smyrna. Polycarp was put to death in 155, so that Irenaeus can hardly have been born much later than 140. Florinus became a Gnostic about 190; he was probably a little older than Irenaeus, who says that as a boy he had admired his splendid position in the Emperor's court. Therefore, unless Florinus was converted when quite old, Irenaeus cannot have been born much earlier than

140—ten years seems the extreme of possibility, and every year earlier than 140 becomes less and less likely.

It is unknown how or when he left Asia, but it is certain that in 177, the year of the persecution at Lyons and Vienne, he went to Rome with the report of the churches on the martyrdom of some of their members, and he is described as being at that time a presbyter. Shortly after this he became Bishop of Lyons, and supported the Asiatic side in the Paschal controversy with Victor of Rome in 190. Nothing certain is known of his death. Jerome (but no earlier writer) speaks of him as a martyr, and it has been thought that he was put to death in the persecution of Septimius Severus in 202, but this is merely a guess.

Of his many writings mentioned by Eusebius (see especially *Hist. Eccl.* iv. 11, 20, 26) only two are fully extant and neither in the original language. The Πρὸς Αἱρέσεις or Ἔλεγχος καὶ ἀνατροπὴ τῆς ψευδωνύμου γνώσεως,[1] quoted as the *Adversus Haereses*, is found in Latin; the best edition is that of Harvey (Cambridge, 1857). The Ἀπόδειξις τοῦ ἀποστολικοῦ κηρύγματος[2] or *Apostolic Preaching*, a treatise sent by Irenaeus to his friend Marcianus, is found in Armenian and was published in 1907 in the *Texte und Untersuchungen*, xxxi. 1.

Probably the best description of the theology of Irenaeus is not in any book devoted to him, but in W. Bousset's *Kyrios Christos*.

The anti-Montanist Writers.—In the fifth book, after long extracts from the letter of the Churches of Lyons and Vienne about their martyrs, and some extracts

[1] " Refutation and overthrow of 'knowledge falsely so called.'"
[2] " Demonstration of the Apostolic Preaching."

from Irenaeus, Eusebius goes on to describe the work of Clement of Alexandria (see above, pp. xliv-xlv) and of Rhodo, of whom nothing more is known, and then turns to a discussion of Montanism, or the Phrygian heresy. For this he makes use of five sources, of which unfortunately nothing more is known beyond what he tells us himself. These are Apollinarius of Hierapolis, Apollonius, Serapion, an anonymous writer who addressed a letter to Abercius, and either Miltiades or Alcibiades. The Abercius addressed by the anonymous writer is the centre of one of the romances of epigraphy. In the *Acta Sanctorum* for October 22 is given a life of Abercius, which has all the marks of lateness, but it contains an epitaph which Lightfoot and others regarded as genuine. Other scholars doubted this, but in 1883 W. M. Ramsay [1] discovered the epitaph in Hieropolis (not Hierapolis). The fifth document to which he refers presents a curious puzzle as to its authorship, for it is impossible to be sure what was the name of the writer, as in the existing manuscripts Eusebius clearly speaks of Miltiades, but the source which he quotes equally clearly speaks of Alcibiades. One name or the other must be wrong, but there is no sufficient evidence for a choice between them (see *Hist. Eccl.* v. 17). For a discussion of these documents and of other evidence relating to Montanism the best modern book is N. Bonwetsch's *Montanisme*.

The Paschal Controversy.—In *Hist. Eccl.* v. 27 Eusebius gives a short list of writers of the beginning of the third century, but none of them have left extant works. He then goes on to discuss the Paschal controversy. This dispute divided the East

[1] See his *Cities and Bishoprics of Phrygia*, pp. 424 ff.

from the West. The East held that the fast before Easter should end on the 14th of Nisan (hence the name " Quartodecimans ") with the feast of the resurrection following at once independently of the day of the week, while the West followed the present custom of observing the feast of the Resurrection on a Sunday independently of the day of the month, and arranged the end of the fast accordingly. Eusebius quotes Polycrates of Ephesus, whose writings are not now extant, and Irenaeus, and mentions various synods whose decrees were known to him but have since been lost. For a discussion of the action of Victor of Rome, and of the whole question see Hefele's *History of the Councils*, preferably in the French translation which has many valuable additional notes.

The Heresy of Artemon.—The last part of the fifth book is largely taken up with an anonymous quotation from a work against the Adoptionist teaching of Artemon and the two Theodoti, whose teaching that Jesus was a man who by the power of God became divine is sometimes described by modern writers as " Dynamic Monarchianism." Theodoret, who also used this writing, says that it was called the " Little Labyrinth," obviously in allusion to the work of Hippolytus against heresy, which is sometimes called " The Labyrinth." Modern scholars generally think that the " Little Labyrinth " was itself the work of Hippolytus but this is by no means certain.

For further information as to these or any other writers mentioned by Eusebius, the best and clearest guides are Harnack's *Geschichte der altchristlichen Litteratur*, Bardenhewer's *Geschichte der altkirchlichen Literatur*, and the *Dictionary of Christian Biography*.

THE ECCLESIASTICAL
HISTORY OF EUSEBIUS

Ᾱ

Τάδε ἡ πρώτη περιέχει βίβλος τῆς·
Ἐκκλησιαστικῆς ἱστορίας

Ᾱ Τίς ἡ τῆς ἐπαγγελίας ὑπόθεσις.

Β̄ Ἐπιτομὴ κεφαλαιώδης περὶ τῆς κατὰ τὸν
σωτῆρα καὶ κύριον ἡμῶν τὸν Χριστὸν τοῦ
θεοῦ προυπάρξεώς τε καὶ θεολογίας.

Γ̄ Ὡς καὶ τὸ Ἰησοῦ ὄνομα καὶ αὐτὸ δὴ τὸ τοῦ
Χριστοῦ ἔγνωστό τε ἀνέκαθεν καὶ τετίμητο
παρὰ τοῖς θεσπεσίοις προφήταις.

Δ̄ Ὡς οὐ νεώτερος οὐδὲ ξενίζων ἦν ὁ τρόπος
τῆς πρὸς αὐτοῦ καταγγελθείσης πᾶσι τοῖς
ἔθνεσιν εὐσεβείας.

Ε̄ Περὶ τῶν χρόνων τῆς ἐπιφανείας αὐτοῦ τῆς
εἰς ἀνθρώπους.

Ϛ̄ Ὡς κατὰ τοὺς χρόνους αὐτοῦ ἀκολούθως ταῖς
προφητείαις ἐξέλιπον ἄρχοντες οἱ τὸ πρὶν
ἐκ προγόνων διαδοχῆς τοῦ Ἰουδαίων ἔθνους
ἡγούμενοι πρῶτός τε ἀλλόφυλος βασιλεύει
αὐτῶν Ἡρῴδης.

Ζ̄ Περὶ τῆς ἐν τοῖς εὐαγγελίοις νομιζομένης
διαφωνίας τῆς περὶ τοῦ Χριστοῦ γενεαλογίας.

Η̄ Περὶ τῆς Ἡρῴδου κατὰ τῶν παίδων ἐπι-

CONTENTS OF BOOK I

*The first book of the Ecclesiastical History
contains the following :*

I. What are the presuppositions of the Promise.

II. A summary account of the pre-existence of, and attribution of divinity to, our Saviour and Lord, the Christ of God.

III. How both the name of Jesus and even that of Christ itself were known from the first and honoured by the inspired prophets.

IV. How there was nothing revolutionary or strange in the character of the religion announced by him to all the nations.

V. Concerning the time of his appearance to men.

VI. How in his time in agreement with prophecy the previous line of ancestral rulers of the Jewish nation died out, and Herod, the first foreigner, was their king.

VII. Concerning the supposed discrepancy in the Gospels on the genealogy as to Christ.

VIII. Concerning the plot of Herod against the

βουλῆς καὶ οἷα μετῆλθεν αὐτὸν καταστροφὴ
βίου.

Θ̄ Περὶ τῶν κατὰ Πιλᾶτον χρόνων.

Ῑ Περὶ τῶν παρὰ Ἰουδαίοις ἀρχιερέων καθ᾽
οὓς ὁ Χριστὸς τὴν διδασκαλίαν ἐποιήσατο.

ῙΑ Τὰ περὶ Ἰωάννου τοῦ βαπτιστοῦ καὶ τοῦ
Χριστοῦ μεμαρτυρημένα.

ῙΒ Περὶ τῶν μαθητῶν τοῦ σωτῆρος ἡμῶν.

ῙΓ Ἱστορία περὶ τοῦ τῶν Ἐδεσσηνῶν δυνάστου.[1]

---

[1] At the end E adds :—ὅρα ὁ ἀναγινώσκων μὴ συναρπαγῇς
τῇ αἱρετικῇ ὑπολήψει τοῦ συγγραφέως· εἰ γὰρ καὶ τὰ μάλιστά
ἐστιν ὠφελιμωτάτη κατὰ τὴν ἱστορίαν ἡ παροῦσα βίβλος, ἀλλ᾽
ὅμως ὅπου μὲν ἀπολύτως περὶ θεοῦ φαίνεται θεολογῶν, οὐ δοκεῖ
τισὶ κακοδοξεῖν, ὅπου δὲ περὶ τοῦ πατρὸς καὶ τοῦ υἱοῦ καὶ τοῦ
ἁγίου πνεύματος λέγει τι, πανταχοῦ ὑποβεβηκότα καὶ δεύτερον καὶ
ὑπουργὸν τοῦ πατρὸς ἐμφαίνει τὸν υἱόν, Ἀρειανὸς ὢν καὶ τὴν ἑαυτοῦ
δόξαν ἐπικεκρυμμένως ἐπιδεικνύων.

children and the catastrophe which overtook him in his life.

IX. Concerning the times of Pilate.

X. Concerning the high priests among the Jews
in whose time the Christ gave his teaching.

XI. The evidence relating to John the Baptist and
the Christ.

XII. Concerning the disciples of our Saviour.

XIII. A narrative concerning the ruler of the
Edessenes.[1]

[1] One manuscript adds, " Beware, reader, of being caught by the heretical tendency of the writer, for though his present book is peculiarly valuable as history, nevertheless though in some places he speaks unconditionally concerning God and attributes divinity to him, and here to some his opinions seem sound, yet in others he speaks of the Father and the Son and the Holy Spirit and everywhere represents the Son as subordinate and secondary and the servant of the Father, for he was an Arian and guardedly manifests his opinion."

ΕΥΣΗΒΙΟΥ

ΕΚΚΛΗΣΙΑΣΤΙΚΗΣ ΙΣΤΟΡΙΑΣ

Α

I. Τὰς τῶν ἱερῶν ἀποστόλων διαδοχὰς σὺν καὶ 1
τοῖς ἀπὸ τοῦ σωτῆρος ἡμῶν καὶ εἰς ἡμᾶς διηνυ-
σμένοις χρόνοις, ὅσα τε καὶ πηλίκα πραγματευθῆναι
κατὰ τὴν ἐκκλησιαστικὴν ἱστορίαν λέγεται, καὶ
ὅσοι ταύτης διαπρεπῶς ἐν ταῖς μάλιστα ἐπιση-
μοτάταις παροικίαις ἡγήσαντό τε καὶ προέστησαν,
ὅσοι τε κατὰ γενεὰν ἑκάστην ἀγράφως ἢ καὶ διὰ
συγγραμμάτων τὸν θεῖον ἐπρέσβευσαν λόγον,
τίνες τε καὶ ὅσοι καὶ ὁπηνίκα νεωτεροποιίας
I Tim. 6, 20 ἱμέρῳ πλάνης εἰς ἔσχατον ἐλάσαντες, ψευδωνύμου
γνώσεως εἰσηγητὰς ἑαυτοὺς ἀνακεκηρύχασιν,
Acts 20, 29 ἀφειδῶς οἷα λύκοι βαρεῖς τὴν Χριστοῦ ποίμνην
ἐπεντρίβοντες, πρὸς ἐπὶ τούτοις καὶ τὰ παραυτίκα 2
τῆς κατὰ τοῦ σωτῆρος ἡμῶν ἐπιβουλῆς τὸ πᾶν
Ἰουδαίων ἔθνος περιελθόντα, ὅσα τε αὖ καὶ ὁποῖα
καθ᾽ οἵους τε χρόνους πρὸς τῶν ἐθνῶν ὁ θεῖος
πεπολέμηται λόγος, καὶ πηλίκοι κατὰ καιροὺς
τὸν δι᾽ αἵματος καὶ βασάνων ὑπὲρ αὐτοῦ διεξῆλθον ἀγῶνα, τά τ᾽ ἐπὶ τούτοις καὶ καθ᾽ ἡμᾶς

6

THE ECCLESIASTICAL HISTORY OF EUSEBIUS

BOOK I

I. I HAVE purposed to record in writing the successions of the sacred apostles, covering the period stretching from our Saviour to ourselves; the number and character of the transactions recorded in the history of the Church; the number of those who were distinguished in her government and leadership in the provinces of greatest fame; the number of those who in each generation were the ambassadors of the word of God either by speech or pen; the names, the number and the age of those who, driven by the desire of innovation to an extremity of error, have heralded themselves as the introducers of Knowledge, falsely so-called, ravaging the flock of Christ unsparingly, like grim wolves. To this I will add the fate which has beset the whole nation of the Jews from the moment of their plot against our Saviour; moreover, the number and nature and times of the wars waged by the heathen against the divine word [1] and the character of those who, for its sake, passed from time to time through the contest of blood and torture; furthermore the

---

[1] Or possibly " the Divine Logos."

αὐτοὺς μαρτύρια καὶ τὴν ἐπὶ πᾶσιν ἵλεω καὶ
εὐμενῆ τοῦ σωτῆρος ἡμῶν ἀντίληψιν γραφῇ παραδοῦναι προῃρημένος, οὐδ' ἄλλοθεν ἢ ἀπὸ πρώτης
ἄρξομαι τῆς κατὰ τὸν σωτῆρα καὶ κύριον ἡμῶν
Ἰησοῦν τὸν Χριστὸν τοῦ θεοῦ οἰκονομίας. ἀλλά 3
μοι συγγνώμην εὐγνωμόνων ἐντεῦθεν ὁ λόγος
αἰτεῖ, μείζονα ἢ καθ' ἡμετέραν δύναμιν ὁμολογῶν
εἶναι τὴν ἐπαγγελίαν ἐντελῆ καὶ ἀπαράλειπτον
ὑποσχεῖν, ἐπεὶ καὶ πρῶτοι νῦν τῆς ὑποθέσεως
ἐπιβάντες οἷά τινα ἐρήμην καὶ ἀτριβῆ ἰέναι ὁδὸν
ἐγχειροῦμεν, θεὸν μὲν ὁδηγὸν καὶ τὴν τοῦ κυρίου
συνεργὸν σχήσειν εὐχόμενοι δύναμιν, ἀνθρώπων
γε μὴν οὐδαμῶς εὑρεῖν οἷοί τε ὄντες ἴχνη γυμνὰ
τὴν αὐτὴν ἡμῖν προωδευκότων, μὴ ὅτι σμικρὰς
αὐτὸ μόνον προφάσεις, δι' ὧν ἄλλος ἄλλως ὧν
διηνύκασι χρόνων μερικὰς ἡμῖν καταλελοίπασι
διηγήσεις, πόρρωθεν ὥσπερ εἰ πυρσοὺς τὰς ἑαυτῶν
προανατείνοντες φωνὰς καὶ ἄνωθέν ποθεν ὡς ἐξ
ἀπόπτου καὶ ἀπὸ σκοπῆς βοῶντες καὶ διακελευό-
μενοι, ᾗ χρὴ βαδίζειν καὶ τὴν τοῦ λόγου πορείαν
ἀπλανῶς καὶ ἀκινδύνως εὐθύνειν. ὅσα τοίνυν 4
εἰς τὴν προκειμένην ὑπόθεσιν λυσιτελεῖν ἡγούμεθα
τῶν αὐτοῖς ἐκείνοις σποράδην μνημονευθέντων,
ἀναλεξάμενοι καὶ ὡς ἂν ἐκ λογικῶν λειμώνων
τὰς ἐπιτηδείους αὐτῶν τῶν πάλαι συγγραφέων
ἀπανθισάμενοι φωνάς, δι' ὑφηγήσεως ἱστορικῆς
πειρασόμεθα σωματοποιῆσαι, ἀγαπῶντες, εἰ καὶ
μὴ ἁπάντων, τῶν δ' οὖν μάλιστα διαφανεστάτων
τοῦ σωτῆρος ἡμῶν ἀποστόλων τὰς διαδοχὰς
κατὰ τὰς διαπρεπούσας ἔτι καὶ νῦν μνημονευο-
μένας ἐκκλησίας ἀνασωσαίμεθα. ἀναγκαιότατα δέ 5
μοι πονεῖσθαι τὴν ὑπόθεσιν ἡγοῦμαι, ὅτι μηδένα

martyrdoms of our own time, and the gracious and favouring help of our Saviour in them all. My starting-point is therefore no other than the first dispensation of God touching our Saviour and Lord, Jesus the Christ. Even at that point the project at once demands the lenience of the kindly, for confessedly it is beyond our power to fulfil the promise, complete and perfect, since we are the first to enter on the undertaking, as travellers on some desolate and untrodden way. We pray God to give us his guidance, and that we may have the help of the power of the Lord, for nowhere can we find even the bare footsteps of men who have preceded us in the same path, unless it be those slight indications by which in divers ways they have left to us partial accounts of the times through which they have passed, raising their voices as a man holds up a torch from afar, calling to us from on high as from a distant watch-tower, and telling us how we must walk, and how to guide the course of our work without error or danger. We have therefore collected from their scattered memoirs all that we think will be useful for the present subject, and have brought together the utterances of the ancient writers themselves that are appropriate to it, culling, as it were, the flowers of intellectual fields. We shall endeavour to give them unity by historical treatment, rejoicing to rescue the successions, if not of all, at least of the most distinguished of the apostles of our Saviour throughout those churches of which the fame is still remembered. To work at this subject I consider especially necessary, because I am not aware

EUSEBIUS

πω εἰς δεῦρο τῶν ἐκκλησιαστικῶν συγγραφέων
διέγνων περὶ τοῦτο τῆς γραφῆς σπουδὴν πεποιη-
μένον τὸ μέρος· ἐλπίζω δ' ὅτι καὶ ὠφελιμωτάτη
τοῖς φιλοτίμως περὶ τὸ χρηστομαθὲς τῆς ἱστορίας
ἔχουσιν ἀναφανήσεται. ἤδη μὲν οὖν τούτων καὶ 6
πρότερον ἐν οἷς διετυπωσάμην χρονικοῖς κανόσιν
ἐπιτομὴν κατεστησάμην, πληρεστάτην δ' οὖν ὅμως
αὐτῶν ἐπὶ τοῦ παρόντος ὡρμήθην τὴν ἀφήγησιν
ποιήσασθαι.

Καὶ ἄρξεταί γέ μοι ὁ λόγος, ὡς ἔφην, ἀπὸ τῆς 7
κατὰ τὸν Χριστὸν ἐπινοουμένης ὑψηλοτέρας καὶ
κρείττονος ἢ κατὰ ἄνθρωπον οἰκονομίας τε καὶ
θεολογίας. καὶ γὰρ τὸν γραφῇ μέλλοντα τῆς 8
ἐκκλησιαστικῆς ὑφηγήσεως παραδώσειν τὴν ἱστορίαν, ἄνωθεν ἐκ πρώτης τῆς κατ' αὐτὸν τὸν
Χριστόν, ὅτιπερ ἐξ αὐτοῦ καὶ τῆς προσωνυμίας
ἠξιώθημεν, θειοτέρας ἢ κατὰ τὸ δοκοῦν τοῖς
πολλοῖς οἰκονομίας ἀναγκαῖον ἂν εἴη κατάρξασθαι.

II. Διττοῦ δὲ ὄντος τοῦ κατ' αὐτὸν τρόπου, καὶ τοῦ 1
μὲν σώματος ἐοικότος κεφαλῇ, ᾗ θεὸς ἐπινοεῖται,
τοῦ δὲ ποσὶ παραβαλλομένου, ᾗ τὸν ἡμῖν ἄνθρωπον
ὁμοιοπαθῆ τῆς ἡμῶν αὐτῶν ἕνεκεν ὑπέδυ σωτηρίας,
γένοιτ' ἂν ἡμῖν ἐντεῦθεν ἐντελὴς ἡ τῶν ἀκολούθων
διήγησις, εἰ τῆς κατ' αὐτὸν ἱστορίας ἁπάσης ἀπὸ
τῶν κεφαλαιωδεστάτων καὶ κυριωτάτων τοῦ λόγου
τὴν ὑφήγησιν ποιησαίμεθα· ταύτῃ δὲ καὶ τῆς
Χριστιανῶν ἀρχαιότητος τὸ παλαιὸν ὁμοῦ καὶ
θεοπρεπὲς τοῖς νέαν αὐτὴν καὶ ἐκτετοπισμένην,
χθὲς καὶ οὐ πρότερον φανεῖσαν, ὑπολαμβάνουσιν
ἀναδειχθήσεται.

I Cor. 11, 8

---

[1] Literally, " ecclesiastical "; but the antithesis to the
word used is either " heathen " (as here) or " heretical."

that any Christian [1] writer has until now paid attention to this kind of writing; and I hope that its high value will be evident to those who are convinced of the importance of a knowledge of the history. I have already summarized the material in the chronological tables which I have drawn up, but nevertheless in the present work I have undertaken to give the narrative in full detail.

I will begin with what, apprehended in relation to Christ, is beyond man in its height and greatness, —the dispensation of God, and the ascription of divinity.[2] For he who plans to hand on in writing the history of Christian origins is forced to begin from the first dispensation concerning the Christ himself, which is more divine than it seems to most, seeing that from him we claim to derive our very name.

II. Now his nature was twofold; on the one hand like the head of the body, in that he is recognized as God, on the other comparable to the feet, in that he put on for the sake of our own salvation, man of like passions with us. Therefore to make our description of what follows complete we should start the whole narrative concerning him by the most capital and dominant points of the discussion. By this means, moreover, the real antiquity and divine character of Christianity will be equally demonstrated to those who suppose that it is recent and foreign, appearing no earlier than yesterday.

[2] οἰκονομία and θεολογία are semi-technical terms. The οἰκονομία or " dispensation " with regard to Christ was the incarnation of the divine Logos; the θεολογία was the ascription of divinity to him. Hence this passage might almost be rendered freely as " the divine and human natures of Christ, which pass man's understanding."

Γένους μὲν οὖν καὶ ἀξίας αὐτῆς τε οὐσίας τοῦ 2
Χριστοῦ καὶ φύσεως οὔτις ἂν εἰς ἔκφρασιν αὐτάρκης
γένοιτο λόγος, ᾗ καὶ τὸ πνεῦμα τὸ θεῖον ἐν προφητείαις "τὴν γενεὰν αὐτοῦ" φησὶν "τίς διηγή-
σεται;" ὅτι δὴ οὔτε τὸν πατέρα τις ἔγνω, εἰ μὴ
ὁ υἱός, οὔτ' αὖ τὸν υἱόν τις ἔγνω ποτὲ κατ' ἀξίαν,
εἰ μὴ μόνος ὁ γεννήσας αὐτὸν πατήρ, τό τε φῶς 3
τὸ προκόσμιον καὶ τὴν πρὸ αἰώνων νοερὰν καὶ
οὐσιώδη σοφίαν τόν τε ζῶντα καὶ ἐν ἀρχῇ παρὰ
τῷ πατρὶ τυγχάνοντα θεὸν λόγον τίς ἂν πλὴν τοῦ
πατρὸς καθαρῶς ἐννοήσειεν, πρὸ πάσης κτίσεως καὶ
δημιουργίας ὁρωμένης τε καὶ ἀοράτου τὸ πρῶτον
καὶ μόνον τοῦ θεοῦ γέννημα, τὸν τῆς κατ' οὐρανὸν
λογικῆς καὶ ἀθανάτου στρατιᾶς ἀρχιστράτηγον,
τὸν τῆς μεγάλης βουλῆς ἄγγελον, τὸν τῆς ἀρρήτου
γνώμης τοῦ πατρὸς ὑπουργόν, τὸν τῶν ἁπάντων
σὺν τῷ πατρὶ δημιουργόν, τὸν δεύτερον μετὰ τὸν
πατέρα τῶν ὅλων αἴτιον, τὸν τοῦ θεοῦ παῖδα
γνήσιον καὶ μονογενῆ, τὸν τῶν γενητῶν ἁπάντων
κύριον καὶ θεὸν καὶ βασιλέα τὸ κῦρος ὁμοῦ καὶ
τὸ κράτος αὐτῇ θεότητι καὶ δυνάμει καὶ τιμῇ
παρὰ τοῦ πατρὸς ὑποδεδεγμένον, ὅτι δὴ κατὰ τὰς
περὶ αὐτοῦ μυστικὰς τῶν γραφῶν θεολογίας "ἐν
ἀρχῇ ἦν ὁ λόγος, καὶ ὁ λόγος ἦν πρὸς τὸν θεόν,
καὶ θεὸς ἦν ὁ λόγος· πάντα δι' αὐτοῦ ἐγένετο, καὶ
χωρὶς αὐτοῦ ἐγένετο οὐδὲ ἕν." τοῦτό τοι καὶ 4
ὁ μέγας Μωυσῆς, ὡς ἂν προφητῶν ἁπάντων
παλαιότατος, θείῳ πνεύματι τὴν τοῦ παντὸς
οὐσίωσίν τε καὶ διακόσμησιν ὑπογράφων, τὸν
κοσμοποιὸν καὶ δημιουργὸν τῶν ὅλων αὐτῷ δὴ
τῷ Χριστῷ καὶ οὐδὲ ἄλλῳ ἢ τῷ θείῳ δηλαδὴ καὶ

Is. 53, 8
Matt. 11, 27
John 1, 9. 10
Prov. 8, 23
John 1, 4. 2
Col. 1, 15. 16
Jos. 5, 14
Is. 9, 6
John 1, 1. 3

No treatise, indeed, could be sufficient for a statement of the origin and dignity, the very being and nature of the Christ: as indeed the divine spirit says in prophecies, " Who will declare his generation ? " seeing that neither does any know the Father save the Son, neither did any ever know the Son properly, save only the Father who begat him. And who except the Father would ever clearly conceive the ante-mundane light, and that wisdom which was intellectual and real [1] before the ages, the living Logos who was, in the beginning, God by the side of the Father, the first and only offspring of God, before all creation and fabrication,[2] both visible and invisible, the captain of the spiritual and immortal host of heaven, the angel of great counsel, the minister of the ineffable plan of the Father, the fabricator of all things along with the Father, the true and only begotten child of God, the Lord and God and King of all begotten, who has received lordship and might, together with deity itself, and power and honour from the Father, according to the mysterious ascription of divinity to him in the Scriptures, " In the beginning was the Logos and the Logos was with God and the Logos was God, all things were through him, and without him was no single thing " ? This, indeed, is also the teaching of the great Moses, as the most ancient of all prophets, when by divine inspiration he described the coming into being, and the ordering of the universe, that the creator and fabricator of all things gave up to the Christ himself, and to no other than his

[1] Or " substantial "—but not in the sense of " material."
[2] " Creation " and " fabrication " are almost but not quite synonyms. " Creation " means making out of nothing, and " fabrication " making out of existent matter.

13

πρωτογόνῳ ἑαυτοῦ λόγῳ τὴν τῶν ὑποβεβηκότων
ποίησιν παραχωροῦντα διδάσκει αὐτῷ τε κοινο-

Gen. 1, 26 λογούμενον ἐπὶ τῆς ἀνθρωπογονίας· '' εἶπεν γὰρ ''
φησὶν '' ὁ θεός· ' ποιήσωμεν ἄνθρωπον κατ'
εἰκόνα ἡμετέραν καὶ καθ' ὁμοίωσιν.' '' ταύτην 5
δὲ ἐγγυᾶται τὴν φωνὴν προφητῶν ἄλλος, ὧδέ πως

Ps. 32, 9;
148, 5 ἐν ὕμνοις θεολογῶν '' αὐτὸς εἶπεν, καὶ ἐγενήθησαν·
αὐτὸς ἐνετείλατο, καὶ ἐκτίσθησαν,'' τὸν μὲν πατέρα
καὶ ποιητὴν εἰσάγων ὡς ἂν πανηγεμόνα βασιλικῷ
νεύματι προστάττοντα, τὸν δὲ τούτῳ δευτερεύοντα
θεῖον λόγον, οὐχ ἕτερον τοῦ πρὸς ἡμῶν κηρυτ-
τομένου, ταῖς πατρικαῖς ἐπιτάξεσιν ὑπουργοῦντα.
τοῦτον καὶ ἀπὸ πρώτης ἀνθρωπογονίας πάντες 6
ὅσοι δὴ δικαιοσύνῃ καὶ θεοσεβείας ἀρετῇ διαπρέψαι λέγονται, ἀμφί τε τὸν μέγαν θεράποντα
Μωυσέα καὶ πρό γε αὐτοῦ πρῶτος Ἀβραὰμ
τούτου τε οἱ παῖδες καὶ ὅσοι μετέπειτα δίκαιοι
πεφήνασιν καὶ προφῆται, καθαροῖς διανοίας ὄμμασι
φαντασθέντες ἔγνωσάν τε καὶ οἷα θεοῦ παιδὶ τὸ
προσῆκον ἀπένειμαν σέβας, αὐτός τε, οὐδαμῶς 7
ἀπορραθυμῶν τῆς τοῦ πατρὸς εὐσεβείας, διδάσκαλος
τοῖς πᾶσι τῆς πατρικῆς καθίστατο γνώσεως.

Gen. 18, 1-3 ὦφθαι γοῦν κύριος ὁ θεὸς ἀνείρηται οἷά τις κοινὸς
ἄνθρωπος τῷ Ἀβραὰμ καθημένῳ παρὰ τὴν δρῦν
τὴν Μαμβρῆ· ὁ δ' ὑποπεσὼν αὐτίκα, καίτοι γε
ἄνθρωπον ὀφθαλμοῖς ὁρῶν, προσκυνεῖ μὲν ὡς
θεόν, ἱκετεύει δὲ ὡς κύριον, ὁμολογεῖ τε μὴ

Gen. 18, 25 ἀγνοεῖν ὅστις εἴη, ῥήμασιν αὐτοῖς λέγων '' κύριε

---

[1] The point of this quotation is obscured by its shortness.
Eusebius is really influenced by Ps. xxxii. 6, " By the word
of the Lord were the heavens established." He takes

divine and first-born Logos, the making of subordinate things and communed with him concerning the creation of man. " For," he says, " God said, let us make man in our own image and likeness." Another of the prophets confirms this saying, ascribing divinity to him in one place in hymns, " He spake and they were begotten, he commanded and they were created."[1] On the one hand he introduces the Father and Maker as a universal sovereign, commanding by his royal nod, and on the other the divine Logos—no other than him who is proclaimed by us—as secondary to him, and ministering to his Father's commands. Him even from the creation of mankind did all who are said to have been pre-eminent in righteousness and virtuous piety recognize by the contemplation of the pure eyes of the mind, and pay him the reverence due to a child of God; thus did Moses, the great servant, and his fellows, and even before him Abraham, the first, and his children, and all the righteous and prophets who have since appeared; and he himself, never wearying of piety toward the Father, has been a teacher to all men of knowledge of the Father. Thus the Lord God is said to have appeared as an ordinary man to Abraham, while he was seated by the oak of Mamre. But he fell down immediately, even though he saw him as a man with his eyes, worshipped him as God, besought him as Lord, and confessed that he was not ignorant who he was, saying in his own words,

" word " as meaning Logos, and thus connects the " he " of the verse which he actually quotes with the Logos, not the Father. This was a traditional Christian interpretation and was probably so familiar to Eusebius that he overlooked his omission of the connecting link in the argument.

ὁ κρίνων πᾶσαν τὴν γῆν, οὐ ποιήσεις κρίσιν;" εἰ 8
γὰρ μηδεὶς ἐπιτρέποι λόγος τὴν ἀγένητον καὶ
ἄτρεπτον οὐσίαν θεοῦ τοῦ παντοκράτορος εἰς
ἀνδρὸς εἶδος μεταβάλλειν μηδ' αὖ γενητοῦ μηθενὸς
φαντασίᾳ τὰς τῶν ὁρώντων ὄψεις ἐξαπατᾶν μηδὲ
μὴν ψευδῶς τὰ τοιαῦτα πλάττεσθαι τὴν γραφήν,
θεὸς καὶ κύριος ὁ κρίνων πᾶσαν τὴν γῆν καὶ ποιῶν
κρίσιν, ἐν ἀνθρώπου ὁρώμενος σχήματι, τίς ἂν
ἕτερος ἀναγορεύοιτο, εἰ μὴ φάναι θέμις τὸ πρῶτον
τῶν ὅλων αἴτιον, ἢ μόνος ὁ προὼν αὐτοῦ λόγος;

Ps. 106, 20 περὶ οὗ καὶ ἐν ψαλμοῖς ἀνείρηται " ἀπέστειλεν
τὸν λόγον αὐτοῦ, καὶ ἰάσατο αὐτούς, καὶ ἐρρύσατο
αὐτοὺς ἐκ τῶν διαφθορῶν αὐτῶν." τοῦτον δεύ- 9
τερον μετὰ τὸν πατέρα κύριον σαφέστατα Μωυσῆς

Gen. 19, 24 ἀναγορεύει λέγων " ἔβρεξε κύριος ἐπὶ Σόδομα
καὶ Γόμορρα θεῖον καὶ πῦρ παρὰ κυρίου·" τοῦτον
καὶ τῷ Ἰακὼβ αὖθις ἐν ἀνδρὸς φανέντα σχήματι,
θεὸν ἡ θεία προσαγορεύει γραφή, φάσκοντα τῷ

Gen. 32, 28 Ἰακὼβ " οὐκέτι κληθήσεται τὸ ὄνομά σου Ἰακώβ,
ἀλλ' Ἰσραὴλ ἔσται τὸ ὄνομά σου, ὅτι ἐνίσχυσας

Gen. 32, 30 μετὰ θεοῦ," ὅτε καὶ " ἐκάλεσεν Ἰακὼβ τὸ ὄνομα
τοῦ τόπου ἐκείνου Εἶδος θεοῦ," λέγων " εἶδον
γὰρ θεὸν πρόσωπον πρὸς πρόσωπον, καὶ ἐσώθη
μου ἡ ψυχή." καὶ μὴν οὐδ' ὑποβεβηκότων ἀγγέλων 10
καὶ λειτουργῶν θεοῦ τὰς ἀναγραφείσας θεοφανείας
ὑπονοεῖν θέμις, ἐπειδὴ καὶ τούτων ὅτε τις ἀνθρώποις
παραφαίνεται, οὐκ ἐπικρύπτεται ἡ γραφή, ὀνομαστὶ
οὐ θεὸν οὐδὲ μὴν κύριον, ἀλλ' ἀγγέλους χρηματίσαι
λέγουσα, ὡς διὰ μυρίων μαρτυριῶν πιστώσασθαι
ῥᾴδιον. τοῦτον καὶ ὁ Μωυσέως διάδοχος Ἰησοῦς, 11

" O Lord, that judgest all the earth, wilt thou not
do judgement ? " For inasmuch as no reason would
allow that the uncreated and unchangeable substance of the Almighty was converted into the form
of man, or deceived the eyes of the beholders by
the phantasm of anything created, or that the Scripture has falsely invented such a story, who other
could be described as God, and as the Lord who
judges all the earth and does judgement, appearing
in the form of man (seeing that it is improper to
call him the first cause of the universe), than his
pre-existent Logos alone ? And concerning him it
was said in the Psalms, " He sent forth his Logos
and healed them, and he rescued them from their
corruptions." Of him, too, Moses clearly speaks
as a second Lord, after the Father, when he says,
" The Lord rained on Sodom and Gomorrah brim-
stone and fire from the Lord." Him the divine
Scripture also calls God when he appears in human
form to Jacob, saying to Jacob, " Thy name shall
no more be called Jacob, but Israel shall be thy
name because thou hadst power with God." Then,
too, " Jacob called the name of the place ' the Vision
of God,' saying, ' For I saw God face to face and
my life was saved.' " [1] And it cannot be right to
suppose that the Theophanies described were the
appearances of subordinate angels and ministers of
God, for whenever one of these appears to men the
Scripture does not conceal it, but says definitely
that they are called angels, not God or Lord, as
it is easy to prove from countless passages. Him,
too, Joshua, the successor of Moses, calls the chief
captain of the host of the Lord, as if he were the

[1] The allusion is to the Septuagint text of Gen. xxxii. 30.

17

ὡς ἂν τῶν οὐρανίων ἀγγέλων καὶ ἀρχαγγέλων τῶν
τε ὑπερκοσμίων δυνάμεων ἡγούμενον καὶ ὡς ἂν
εἰ τοῦ πατρὸς ὑπάρχοντα δύναμιν καὶ σοφίαν καὶ
τὰ δευτερεῖα τῆς κατὰ πάντων βασιλείας τε καὶ
ἀρχῆς ἐμπεπιστευμένον, ἀρχιστράτηγον δυνάμεως
κυρίου ὀνομάζει, οὐκ ἄλλως αὐτὸν ἢ αὖθις ἐν
ἀνθρώπου μορφῇ καὶ σχήματι θεωρήσας. γέγραπται γοῦν '' καὶ ἐγενήθη, ὡς ἦν Ἰησοῦς ἐν
Ἰεριχώ, καὶ ἀναβλέψας ὁρᾷ ἄνθρωπον ἑστηκότα
κατέναντι αὐτοῦ, καὶ ἡ ῥομφαία ἐσπασμένη ἐν
τῇ χειρὶ αὐτοῦ, καὶ προσελθὼν Ἰησοῦς εἶπεν,
'ἡμέτερος εἶ ἢ τῶν ὑπεναντίων;' καὶ εἶπεν αὐτῷ,
'ἐγὼ ἀρχιστράτηγος δυνάμεως κυρίου· νυνὶ παρα-
γέγονα.' καὶ Ἰησοῦς ἔπεσεν ἐπὶ πρόσωπον ἐπὶ
τὴν γῆν καὶ εἶπεν αὐτῷ, 'δέσποτα, τί προστάσσεις
τῷ σῷ οἰκέτῃ;' καὶ εἶπεν ὁ ἀρχιστράτηγος κυρίου
πρὸς Ἰησοῦν, 'λῦσαι τὸ ὑπόδημα ἐκ τῶν ποδῶν
σου· ὁ γὰρ τόπος, ἐν ᾧ σὺ ἕστηκας, τόπος ἅγιός
ἐστιν.''' ἔνθα καὶ ἐπιστήσεις ἀπὸ τῶν αὐτῶν
ῥημάτων ὅτι μὴ ἕτερος οὗτος εἴη τοῦ καὶ Μωυσεῖ
κεχρηματικότος, ὅτι δὴ αὐτοῖς ῥήμασι καὶ ἐπὶ
τῷδέ φησιν ἡ γραφή '' ὡς δὲ εἶδεν κύριος ὅτι
προσάγει ἰδεῖν, ἐκάλεσεν αὐτὸν κύριος ἐκ τοῦ
βάτου λέγων, 'Μωυσῆ Μωυσῆ'· ὁ δὲ εἶπεν,
'τί ἐστιν;' καὶ εἶπεν, 'μὴ ἐγγίσῃς ὧδε· λῦσαι
τὸ ὑπόδημα ἐκ τῶν ποδῶν σου· ὁ γὰρ τόπος, ἐν
ᾧ σὺ ἕστηκας ἐπ' αὐτοῦ, γῆ ἁγία ἐστίν.' καὶ
εἶπεν αὐτῷ, 'ἐγώ εἰμι ὁ θεὸς τοῦ πατρός σου,
θεὸς Ἀβραὰμ καὶ θεὸς Ἰσαὰκ καὶ θεὸς Ἰακώβ.'''
καὶ ὅτι γέ ἐστιν οὐσία τις προκόσμιος ζῶσα καὶ
ὑφεστῶσα, ἡ τῷ πατρὶ καὶ θεῷ τῶν ὅλων εἰς τὴν
τῶν γενητῶν ἁπάντων δημιουργίαν ὑπηρετησαμένη,

18

1 Cor. 1, 24

Jos. 5, 13-15

Exod. 3, 4-6

leader of the heavenly angels and archangels, and
the supernal powers, and as if he were of the
power and wisdom of the Father, entrusted with
the second rank in his universal kingdom and rule,
though Joshua, too, saw him in none but human
form and shape. It is written at least, " And it
came to pass, while Joshua was in Jericho that he
looked up and saw a man standing over against
him, and his sword was drawn in his hand, and
Joshua went to him and said, Art thou for us or
for our adversaries ? And he said to him, As chief
captain of the host of the Lord am I now come.
And Joshua fell on his face on the earth, and said
to him, Lord, what dost thou command thy servant ?
And the chief captain of the Lord said to Joshua,
Loose thy shoe from off thy feet, for the place
whereon thou standest is a holy place." Here, too,
you will perceive from the words themselves that
this is none other than he who spoke also to Moses,
for of him also the Scripture uses the same words,
" And when the Lord saw that he drew nigh to see,
the Lord called him out of the bush saying, Moses,
Moses. And he said, What is it ? And he said,
Do not draw near here. Loose thy shoe from off
thy feet, for the place whereon thou standest is
holy ground. And he said to him, I am the God
of thy Father, the God of Abraham, and God of
Isaac and God of Jacob." And that there really is
a certain being living and existent before the world,
who ministered to the Father and God of the universe for the fabrication of all created things, called

19

λόγος θεοῦ καὶ σοφία χρηματίζουσα, πρὸς ταῖς
τεθειμέναις ἀποδείξεσιν ἔτι καὶ αὐτῆς ἐξ ἰδίου
προσώπου τῆς σοφίας ἐπακοῦσαι πάρεστιν, διὰ
Σολομῶνος λευκότατα ὧδέ πως τὰ περὶ αὐτῆς

Prov. 8, 12.
15. 16 μυσταγωγούσης " ἐγὼ ἡ σοφία κατεσκήνωσα
βουλήν, καὶ γνῶσιν καὶ ἔννοιαν ἐγὼ ἐπεκαλεσάμην.
δι' ἐμοῦ βασιλεῖς βασιλεύουσιν, καὶ οἱ δονάσται
γράφουσι δικαιοσύνην· δι' ἐμοῦ μεγιστᾶνες μεγα-
λύνονται, καὶ τύραννοι δι' ἐμοῦ κρατοῦσι γῆς·"

Prov. 8. 22–
25. 27. 28.
30. 31 οἷς ἐπιλέγει " κύριος ἔκτισέν με ἀρχὴν ὁδῶν αὐ- 15
τοῦ εἰς ἔργα αὐτοῦ, πρὸ τοῦ αἰῶνος ἐθεμελίωσέν
με· ἐν ἀρχῇ πρὸ τοῦ τὴν γῆν ποιῆσαι, πρὸ τοῦ
προελθεῖν τὰς πηγὰς τῶν ὑδάτων, πρὸ τοῦ ὄρη
ἑδρασθῆναι, πρὸ δὲ πάντων βουνῶν γεννᾷ με.
ἡνίκα ἡτοίμαζεν τὸν οὐρανόν, συμπαρήμην αὐτῷ,
καὶ ὡς ἀσφαλεῖς ἐτίθει πηγὰς τῆς ὑπ' οὐρανόν,
ἤμην σὺν αὐτῷ ἁρμόζουσα. ἐγὼ ἤμην ᾗ προσ-
έχαιρεν καθ' ἡμέραν, εὐφραινόμην δὲ ἐνώπιον
αὐτοῦ ἐν παντὶ καιρῷ, ὅτε εὐφραίνετο τὴν οἰκουμένην συντελέσας." ὅτι μὲν οὖν προῆν καὶ τισίν, 16
εἰ καὶ μὴ τοῖς πᾶσιν, ὁ θεῖος λόγος ἐπεφαίνετο,
ταῦθ' ἡμῖν ὡς ἐν βραχέσιν εἰρήσθω.

Τί δὴ οὖν οὐχὶ καθάπερ τὰ νῦν, καὶ πάλαι 17
πρότερον εἰς πάντας ἀνθρώπους καὶ πᾶσιν ἔθνεσιν
ἐκηρύττετο, ὧδε ἂν γένοιτο πρόδηλον. οὐκ ἦν
πω χωρεῖν οἷός τε τὴν τοῦ Χριστοῦ πάνσοφον
καὶ πανάρετον διδασκαλίαν ὁ πάλαι τῶν ἀνθρώπων
βίος. εὐθὺς μέν γε ἐν ἀρχῇ μετὰ τὴν πρώτην ἐν 18
μακαρίοις ζωὴν ὁ πρῶτος ἄνθρωπος ἧττον τῆς
θείας ἐντολῆς φροντίσας, εἰς τουτονὶ τὸν θνητὸν
καὶ ἐπίκηρον βίον καταπέπτωκεν καὶ τὴν ἐπάρατον
ταυτηνὶ γῆν τῆς πάλαι ἐνθέου τρυφῆς ἀντικατηλλά-

the Logos and Wisdom of God, can be learned from the actual person of Wisdom herself, in addition to the preceding proofs, for in one place she tells her own secret very clearly through Solomon, " I, Wisdom, made Counsel my habitation and I invoked Knowledge and Thought ; through me kings reign, and the mighty inscribe justice ; by me great men are magnified, and sovereigns rule the earth through me." And to this she adds, " The Lord created me as the beginning of his ways for his works ; he established me before the world ; in the beginning, before the making of the earth, before the springs of water came forth, before the mountains were founded, and before all hills, he begat me. When he prepared the heaven, I was present with him, and when he made safe the springs which are under heaven, I was with him giving them order. I was she in whom he rejoiced daily and I exulted before him at all times, when he exulted that he had completed the world." Thus let this be our short proof that the divine Logos pre-existed, and appeared to some, if not to all, men.

It must now be demonstrated why this announcement was not formerly made, long ago, to all men and all nations, as it is now. The life of men in the past was not capable of receiving the complete wisdom and virtue of the teaching of Christ. For at the beginning, after the first life in blessedness. the first man, despising the command of God, fell at once to this mortal and perishable life, and exchanged the former divine delights for this earth

ξατο, οἵ τε ἀπὸ τούτου τὴν καθ᾽ ἡμᾶς σύμπασαν
πληρώσαντες πολὺ χείρους ἀναφανέντες ἐκτὸς
ἑνός που καὶ δευτέρου, θηριώδη τινὰ τρόπον καὶ
βίον ἀβίωτον ἐπανῄρηντο· ἀλλὰ καὶ οὔτε πόλιν 19
οὔτε πολιτείαν, οὐ τέχνας, οὐκ ἐπιστήμας ἐπὶ νοῦν
ἐβάλλοντο, νόμων τε καὶ δικαιωμάτων καὶ προσέτι
ἀρετῆς καὶ φιλοσοφίας οὐδὲ ὀνόματος μετεῖχον,
νομάδες δὲ ἐπ᾽ ἐρημίας οἷά τινες ἄγριοι καὶ
ἀπηνεῖς διῆγον, τοὺς μὲν ἐκ φύσεως προσήκοντας
λογισμοὺς τά τε λογικὰ καὶ ἥμερα τῆς ἀνθρώπων
ψυχῆς σπέρματα αὐτοπροαιρέτου κακίας ὑπερβολῇ
διαφθείροντες, ἀνοσιουργίαις δὲ πάσαις ὅλους
σφᾶς ἐκδεδωκότες, ὡς τοτὲ μὲν ἀλληλοφθορεῖν,
τοτὲ δὲ ἀλληλοκτονεῖν, ἄλλοτε δὲ ἀνθρωποβορεῖν,
θεομαχίας τε καὶ τὰς παρὰ τοῖς πᾶσιν βοωμένας
γιγαντομαχίας ἐπιτολμᾶν, καὶ γῆν μὲν ἐπιτειχίζειν
οὐρανῷ διανοεῖσθαι, μανίᾳ δὲ φρονήματος ἐκτόπου
αὐτὸν τὸν ἐπὶ πᾶσιν πολεμεῖν παρασκευάζεσθαι·
ἐφ᾽ οἷς τοῦτον ἑαυτοῖς εἰσάγουσι τὸν τρόπον 20
κατακλυσμοῖς αὐτοὺς καὶ πυρπολήσεσιν ὥσπερ
ἀγρίαν ὕλην κατὰ πάσης τῆς γῆς κεχυμένην
θεὸς ὁ πάντων ἔφορος μετῄει, λιμοῖς τε συνεχέσι
καὶ λοιμοῖς πολέμοις τε αὖ καὶ κεραυνῶν βολαῖς
ἄνωθεν αὐτοὺς ὑπετέμνετο, ὥσπερ τινὰ δεινὴν
καὶ χαλεπωτάτην νόσον ψυχῶν πικροτέροις ἀνέχων
τοῖς κολαστηρίοις. τότε μὲν οὖν, ὅτε δὴ καὶ 21
πολὺς ἦν ἐπικεχυμένος ὀλίγου δεῖν κατὰ πάντων
ὁ τῆς κακίας κάρος, οἷα μέθης δεινῆς, τὰς ἁπάντων σχεδὸν ἀνθρώπων ἐπισκιαζούσης καὶ ἐπισκο-
τούσης ψυχάς, ἡ πρωτόγονος καὶ πρωτόκτιστος
τοῦ θεοῦ σοφία καὶ αὐτὸς ὁ προὼν λόγος φιλανθρωπίας ὑπερβολῇ τοτὲ μὲν δι᾽ ὀπτασίας ἀγγέλων

with its curse ; and after him those who filled all
our world were manifestly much worse, with the
exception of one or two, and chose some brutal
habit of life, unworthy of the name. They gave no
thought to city or state, to art or knowledge, they
had not even the name of laws and decrees or virtue
and philosophy, but they lived as nomads in the
wildernesses like savage and unbridled beings ; they
destroyed by their excess of self-chosen wickedness
the natural reasonings, and the germs of thought
and gentleness in the human soul ; they gave themselves up completely to all iniquity so that at one
time they corrupted one another, at another they
murdered one another, at another they were can-
nibals ; they ventured on conflicts with God and on
the battles of the giants famous among all men ;
they thought to wall up the earth to heaven, and
in the madness of a perverted mind prepared for
war against the supreme God himself. While they
were leading this life, God, the guardian of all,
pursued them with floods and conflagrations, as
though they had been a wild forest scattered throughout the whole earth ; he cut them off with perpetual
famines and plagues, by wars and by thunderbolts
from on high, as if he were restraining by bitter
chastisement some terrible and grievous disease of
their souls. Then, indeed, when the great flood
of evil had come nigh overwhelming all men, like a
terrible intoxication overshadowing and darkening
the souls of almost all, the first-begotten and first-
created Wisdom of God, the pre-existent Logos
himself, in his exceeding kindness appeared to his
subjects, at one time by a vision of angels, at another

I Cor. 1, 24

τοῖς ὑποβεβηκόσι, τοτὲ δὲ καὶ δι' ἑαυτοῦ οἷα θεοῦ
δύναμις σωτήριος ἑνί που κ̣αὶ δευτέρῳ τῶν πάλαι
θεοφιλῶν ἀνδρῶν οὐκ ἄλλως ἢ δι' ἀνθρώπου μορφῆς,
ὅτι μηδ' ἑτέρως ἦν δυνατὸν αὐτοῖς, ὑπεφαίνετο.

Ὡς δ' ἤδη διὰ τούτων τὰ θεοσεβείας σπέρ- 22
ματα εἰς πλῆθος ἀνδρῶν καταβέβλητο ὅλον τε
ἔθνος ἐπὶ γῆς θεοσεβείᾳ προσανέχον ἐκ τῶν
ἀνέκαθεν Ἑβραίων ὑπέστη, τούτοις μέν, ὡς ἂν
εἰ πλήθεσιν ἔτι ταῖς παλαιαῖς ἀγωγαῖς ἐκδεδιῃτη-
μένοις, διὰ τοῦ προφήτου Μωυσέως εἰκόνας καὶ
σύμβολα σαββάτου τινὸς μυστικοῦ καὶ περιτομῆς
ἑτέρων τε νοητῶν θεωρημάτων εἰσαγωγάς, ἀλλ'
οὐκ αὐτὰς ἐναργεῖς παρεδίδου μυσταγωγίας· ὡς 23
δὲ τῆς παρὰ τούτοις νομοθεσίας βοωμένης καὶ
πνοῆς δίκην εὐώδους εἰς ἅπαντας ἀνθρώπους
διαδιδομένης, ἤδη τότε ἐξ αὐτῶν καὶ τοῖς πλείοσιν
τῶν ἐθνῶν διὰ τῶν πανταχόσε νομοθετῶν τε καὶ
φιλοσόφων ἡμέρωτο τὰ φρονήματα, τῆς ἀγρίας
καὶ ἀπηνοῦς θηριωδίας ἐπὶ τὸ πρᾷον μεταβεβλη-
μένης, ὡς καὶ εἰρήνην βαθεῖαν φιλίας τε καὶ
ἐπιμιξίας πρὸς ἀλλήλους ἔχειν, τηνικαῦτα πᾶσι
δὴ λοιπὸν ἀνθρώποις καὶ τοῖς ἀνὰ τὴν οἰκουμένην
ἔθνεσιν ὡς ἂν προωφελημένοις καὶ ἤδη τυγχάνουσιν ἐπιτηδείοις πρὸς παραδοχὴν τῆς τοῦ
πατρὸς γνώσεως, ὁ αὐτὸς δὴ πάλιν ἐκεῖνος ὁ τῶν
ἀρετῶν διδάσκαλος, ὁ ἐν πᾶσιν ἀγαθοῖς τοῦ
πατρὸς ὑπουργός, ὁ θεῖος καὶ οὐράνιος τοῦ θεοῦ
λόγος, δι' ἀνθρώπου κατὰ μηδὲν σώματος οὐσίᾳ
τὴν ἡμετέραν φύσιν διαλλάττοντος ἀρχομένης τῆς
Ῥωμαίων βασιλείας ἐπιφανείς, τοιαῦτα ἔδρασέν
τε καὶ πέπονθεν, οἷα ταῖς προφητείαις ἀκόλουθα
ἦν, ἄνθρωπον ὁμοῦ καὶ θεὸν ἐπιδημήσειν τῷ βίῳ

24

personally to one or two of the God-fearing men of old, as a saving power of God, yet in no other form than human, for they could not receive him otherwise.

But when the seeds of true religion had been strewn by them among a multitude of men, and a whole nation, sprung from the Hebrews, existed on earth, cleaving to true religion, he handed on to them, through the prophet Moses, images and symbols of a certain mysterious sabbath and of circumcision and instruction in other spiritual principles, but not unveiled initiation itself, for many of them had still been brought up in the old practices. Their Law became famous and spread among all men like a fragrant breeze. Beginning with them the minds of most of the heathen were softened by the lawgivers and philosophers who arose everywhere. Savage and unbridled brutality was changed to mildness, so that deep peace, friendship, and mutual intercourse obtained. Then, at last, when all men, even the heathen throughout the world, were now fitted for the benefits prepared for them beforehand, for the reception of knowledge of the Father, then again that same divine and heavenly Logos of God, the teacher of virtues, the minister of the Father in all good things, appeared at the beginning of the Roman Empire through man. In nothing did he change our nature as touching bodily substance ; his acts and sufferings were such as were consistent with the prophecies which foretell that man and God shall live together to do marvellous

25

παραδόξων ἔργων ποιητὴν καὶ τοῖς πᾶσιν ἔθνεσιν
διδάσκαλον τῆς τοῦ πατρὸς εὐσεβείας ἀναδειχ-
θήσεσθαι τό τε παράδοξον αὐτοῦ τῆς γενέσεως
καὶ τὴν καινὴν διδασκαλίαν καὶ τῶν ἔργων τὰ
θαύματα ἐπί τε τούτοις τοῦ θανάτου τὸν τρόπον
τήν τε ἐκ νεκρῶν ἀνάστασιν καὶ ἐπὶ πᾶσιν τὴν εἰς
οὐρανοὺς ἔνθεον ἀποκατάστασιν αὐτοῦ προκηρυτ-
τούσαις. τὴν γοῦν ἐπὶ τέλει βασιλείαν αὐτοῦ 24
Δανιὴλ ὁ προφήτης θείῳ πνεύματι συνορῶν, ὧδέ
πη ἐθεοφορεῖτο, ἀνθρωπινώτερον τὴν θεοπτίαν
Dan. 7, 9. 10 ὑπογράφων· "ἐθεώρουν γὰρ" φησίν "ἕως οὗ
θρόνοι ἐτέθησαν, καὶ παλαιὸς ἡμερῶν ἐκάθητο.
καὶ τὸ ἔνδυμα αὐτοῦ ὡς εἰ χιὼν λευκόν, καὶ ἡ
θρὶξ τῆς κεφαλῆς αὐτοῦ ὡς εἰ ἔριον καθαρόν· ὁ
θρόνος αὐτοῦ φλὸξ πυρός, οἱ τροχοὶ αὐτοῦ πῦρ
φλέγον· ποταμὸς πυρὸς εἷλκεν ἔμπροσθεν αὐτοῦ.
χίλιαι χιλιάδες ἐλειτούργουν αὐτῷ, καὶ μύριαι
μυριάδες παρειστήκεισαν ἔμπροσθεν αὐτοῦ. κριτή-
ριον ἐκάθισεν, καὶ βίβλοι ἠνεῴχθησαν." καὶ ἑξῆς 25
Dan. 7, 13. 14 "ἐθεώρουν," φησίν "καὶ ἰδοὺ μετὰ τῶν νεφελῶν
τοῦ οὐρανοῦ ὡς εἰ υἱὸς ἀνθρώπου ἐρχόμενος, καὶ
ἕως τοῦ παλαιοῦ τῶν ἡμερῶν ἔφθασεν, καὶ ἐνώπιον
αὐτοῦ προσηνέχθη· καὶ αὐτῷ ἐδόθη ἡ ἀρχὴ καὶ
ἡ τιμὴ καὶ ἡ βασιλεία, καὶ πάντες οἱ λαοὶ φυλαὶ
γλῶσσαι αὐτῷ δουλεύσουσιν. ἡ ἐξουσία αὐτοῦ
ἐξουσία αἰώνιος, ἥτις οὐ παρελεύσεται· καὶ ἡ
βασιλεία αὐτοῦ οὐ διαφθαρήσεται." ταῦτα δὲ 26
σαφῶς οὐδ' ἐφ' ἕτερον, ἀλλ' ἐπὶ τὸν ἡμέτερον
John 1, 1 σωτῆρα, τὸν ἐν ἀρχῇ πρὸς τὸν θεὸν θεὸν λόγον,
ἀναφέροιτο ἄν, υἱὸν ἀνθρώπου διὰ τὴν ὑστάτην
ἐνανθρώπησιν αὐτοῦ χρηματίζοντα. ἀλλὰ γὰρ ἐν 27
οἰκείοις ὑπομνήμασιν τὰς περὶ τοῦ σωτῆρος

26

deeds, and to teach to all Gentiles the worship of the Father, and that the marvel of his birth and his new teaching and the wonder of his deeds will be made manifest together with the manner of his death and resurrection from the dead, and, above all, his divine restoration to Heaven. Daniel the prophet, in a moment of inspiration, saw by the divine spirit his final sovereignty, and describes the vision of God in human wise : " For I beheld," he said, " until thrones were set and an Ancient of Days did sit. And his garment was white like snow and the hair of his head was like pure wool ; his throne was a flame of fire, his wheels were flaming fire, a river of fire ran before him, thousand thousands ministered unto him and ten thousand times ten thousand stood before him, the judgement sat, and books were opened." And he goes on to say, " I beheld, and lo, one like to a son of man coming with the clouds of Heaven, and he came to the Ancient of Days and was brought before him. And to him was given the sovereignty and honour and kingdom, and all the people, tribes, and tongues shall serve him. His power is an everlasting power, which shall not pass away, and his kingdom shall not be destroyed." Clearly this would apply to none but our Saviour, the God-Logos who was in the beginning with God, called " son of man " because of his ultimate incarnation. However, since we have collected in special treatises the

27

ἡμῶν Ἰησοῦ Χριστοῦ προφητικὰς ἐκλογὰς συν-
αγαγόντες ἀποδεικτικώτερόν τε τὰ περὶ αὐτοῦ
δηλούμενα ἐν ἑτέροις συστήσαντες, τοῖς εἰρημένοις
ἐπὶ τοῦ παρόντος ἀρκεσθησόμεθα.

III. Ὅτι δὲ καὶ αὐτὸ τοὔνομα τοῦ τε Ἰησοῦ καὶ δὴ 1
καὶ τοῦ Χριστοῦ παρ' αὐτοῖς τοῖς πάλαι θεοφιλέσιν
προφήταις τετίμητο, ἤδη καιρὸς ἀποδεικνύναι.
σεπτὸν ὡς ἔνι μάλιστα καὶ ἔνδοξον τὸ Χριστοῦ 2
ὄνομα πρῶτος αὐτὸς γνωρίσας Μωυσῆς τύπους
οὐρανίων καὶ σύμβολα μυστηριώδεις τε εἰκόνας

Heb. 8, 5
(Exod. 25,
40)

ἀκολούθως χρησμῷ φήσαντι αὐτῷ '' ὅρα, ποιήσεις
πάντα κατὰ τὸν τύπον τὸν δειχθέντα σοι ἐν τῷ
ὄρει '' παραδούς, ἀρχιερέα θεοῦ, ὡς ἐνῆν μάλιστα

Lev. 4, 5. 16;
6, 22

δυνατὸν ἄνθρωπον, ἐπιφημίσας, τοῦτον Χριστὸν
ἀναγορεύει, καὶ ταύτῃ γε τῇ κατὰ τὴν ἀρχιερωσύνην ἀξίᾳ, πᾶσαν ὑπερβαλλούσῃ παρ' αὐτῷ τὴν
ἐν ἀνθρώποις προεδρίαν, ἐπὶ τιμῇ καὶ δόξῃ τὸ
τοῦ Χριστοῦ περιτίθησιν ὄνομα· οὕτως ἄρα τὸν
Χριστὸν θεῖόν τι χρῆμα ἠπίστατο. ὁ δ' αὐτὸς 3
καὶ τὴν τοῦ Ἰησοῦ προσηγορίαν εὖ μάλα πνεύματι θείῳ προϊδὼν πάλιν τινὸς ἐξαιρέτου προ-
νομίας καὶ ταύτην ἀξιοῖ. οὔποτε γοῦν πρότερον
ἐκφωνηθὲν εἰς ἀνθρώπους, πρὶν ἢ Μωυσεῖ γνω-

Num. 13, 17

σθῆναι, τὸ τοῦ Ἰησοῦ πρόσρημα τούτῳ Μωυσῆς
πρώτῳ καὶ μόνῳ περιτίθησιν, ὃν κατὰ τύπον αὖθις
καὶ σύμβολον ἔγνω μετὰ τὴν αὐτοῦ τελευτὴν
διαδεξόμενον τὴν κατὰ πάντων ἀρχήν. οὐ πρό- 4
τερον γοῦν τὸν αὐτοῦ διάδοχον, τῇ τοῦ Ἰησοῦ
κεχρημένον προσηγορίᾳ, ὀνόματι δὲ ἑτέρῳ τῷ
Αὐσῇ, ὅπερ οἱ γεννήσαντες αὐτῷ τέθεινται, καλούμενον, Ἰησοῦν αὐτὸς ἀναγορεύει, γέρας ὥσπερ
τίμιον, παντὸς πολὺ μεῖζον βασιλικοῦ διαδήματος,

prophetic utterances concerning our Saviour Jesus Christ, and in others have given a fuller demonstration of our statements concerning him, we will rest content in the present work with what has now been said.

III. It is now time to demonstrate that the very names " Jesus," and especially " Christ," were held in honour by the ancient God-loving prophets themselves. Moses was himself the first to recognize how peculiarly august and glorious is the name of Christ, when he delivered the tradition of the types and symbols of heavenly things, and the mysterious images, in accordance with the oracle which said to him, " See thou shalt make all things according to the type which was shown thee in the mount " ; for in describing the High Priest of God as a man of supreme power, he calls him Christ, and, as a mark of honour and glory, surrounds with the name of Christ this rank of the High Priesthood, which with him surpassed all pre-eminence among men. Thus then he knew the divine character of " Christ." He himself also was inspired very clearly to foresee the title " Jesus," and it again he endued with special privilege. Though before it was made known to Moses it had never been previously pronounced to men, Moses gave the title, Jesus, to him first, and to him alone, who, once more typically and symbolically, he knew would receive the rule over all after his death. His successor, at any rate, had not previously used the title " Jesus," but was called by another name, " Auses," which his parents had given him, and Moses calls him Jesus, as a precious privilege greater than any royal crown, giving to

τοὔνομα αὐτῷ δωρούμενος, ὅτι δὴ καὶ αὐτὸς ὁ
τοῦ Ναυῆ Ἰησοῦς τοῦ σωτῆρος ἡμῶν τὴν εἰκόνα
ἔφερεν, τοῦ μόνου μετὰ Μωυσέα καὶ τὸ συμπέρασμα
τῆς δι᾽ ἐκείνου παραδοθείσης συμβολικῆς λατρείας,
τῆς ἀληθοῦς καὶ καθαρωτάτης εὐσεβείας τὴν
ἀρχὴν διαδεξαμένου. καὶ Μωυσῆς μὲν ταύτῃ πῃ 5
δυσὶ τοῖς κατ᾽ αὐτὸν ἀρετῇ καὶ δόξῃ παρὰ πάντα
τὸν λαὸν προφέρουσιν ἀνθρώποις, τῷ μὲν ἀρχιερεῖ,
τῷ δὲ μετ᾽ αὐτὸν ἡγησομένῳ, τὴν τοῦ σωτῆρος
ἡμῶν Ἰησοῦ Χριστοῦ προσηγορίαν ἐπὶ τιμῇ τῇ
μεγίστῃ περιτέθειται· σαφῶς δὲ καὶ οἱ μετὰ 6
ταῦτα προφῆται ὀνομαστὶ τὸν Χριστὸν προανε-
φώνουν, ὁμοῦ τὴν μέλλουσαν ἔσεσθαι κατ᾽ αὐτοῦ
συσκευὴν τοῦ Ἰουδαίων λαοῦ, ὁμοῦ δὲ καὶ τὴν
τῶν ἐθνῶν δι᾽ αὐτοῦ κλῆσιν προμαρτυρόμενοι,

Lam. 4, 20 τοτὲ μὲν ὧδέ πως Ἱερεμίας λέγων " πνεῦμα
προσώπου ἡμῶν Χριστὸς κύριος συνελήφθη ἐν
ταῖς διαφθοραῖς αὐτῶν, οὗ εἴπομεν ' ἐν τῇ σκιᾷ
αὐτοῦ ζησόμεθα ἐν τοῖς ἔθνεσιν,' " τοτὲ δὲ ἀμηχανῶν

Ps. 2, 1. 2 Δαυὶδ διὰ τούτων " ἵνα τί ἐφρύαξαν ἔθνη καὶ λαοὶ
ἐμελέτησαν κενά; παρέστησαν οἱ βασιλεῖς τῆς
γῆς, καὶ οἱ ἄρχοντες συνήχθησαν ἐπὶ τὸ αὐτό,
κατὰ τοῦ κυρίου καὶ κατὰ τοῦ Χριστοῦ αὐτοῦ ".
οἷς ἑξῆς ἐπιλέγει ἐξ αὐτοῦ δὴ προσώπου τοῦ

Ps. 2, 7. 8 Χριστοῦ " κύριος εἶπεν πρός με ' υἱός μου εἶ σύ,
ἐγὼ σήμερον γεγέννηκά σε. αἴτησαι παρ᾽ ἐμοῦ,
καὶ δώσω σοι ἔθνη τὴν κληρονομίαν σου, καὶ τὴν
κατάσχεσίν σου τὰ πέρατα τῆς γῆς.' " οὐ μόνους 7
δὲ ἄρα τοὺς ἀρχιερωσύνῃ τετιμημένους, ἐλαίῳ
σκευαστῷ τοῦ συμβόλου χριομένους ἕνεκα, τὸ τοῦ
Χριστοῦ κατεκόσμει παρ᾽ Ἑβραίοις ὄνομα, ἀλλὰ

---

[1] In the LXX. of Numb. xiii. 17 (which relates the chang-

him the name because Jesus the son of Nave [1]
himself bore the image of our Saviour who alone,
after Moses and the completion of the symbolic
worship [2] delivered by Moses, did receive the rule of
the true and pure religion. In this way Moses as a
mark of the greatest honour surrounds with the name
of our Saviour Jesus Christ the two men who in
his day excelled all the people in virtue and glory
—the High Priest and him who should rule after
him. Clearly, too, did the later prophets foretell
the Christ by name, giving their testimony beforehand alike to the future intrigue of the people of
the Jews against him, and to the calling of the
Gentiles through him. At one time Jeremiah says,
" The spirit of our face, Christ the Lord was taken
in their corruptions, and we said we will live in his
shadow among the Gentiles." At another time
David in perplexity says as follows, " Wherefore
did the heathen rage, and the peoples imagine vain
things ? The kings of the earth stood up, and the
rulers were gathered together, against the Lord and
against his Christ." In the following verses he
goes on to speak in the person of Christ himself,
" The Lord said to me, Thou art my son, to-day have
I begotten thee. Ask of me and I will give thee
the heathen for thine inheritance and the uttermost
parts of the earth for thy possession." However it
was not only those that were honoured with the
High Priesthood, and anointed for the sake of the
symbol with prepared oil, that were decorated
among the Hebrews with the name " Christ " ; but

ing of the name of Hoshea, son of Nun, to Joshua) the name
Hoshea is spelt Auses, Joshua is spelt Jesus, and Nun is
spelt Nave.

  [2] *i.e.* the Jewish worship symbolized the future Christianity.

31

καὶ τοὺς βασιλέας, οὓς καὶ αὐτοὺς νεύματι θείῳ
προφῆται χρίοντες εἰκονικούς τινας Χριστοὺς
ἀπειργάζοντο, ὅτι δὴ καὶ αὐτοὶ τῆς τοῦ μόνου καὶ
ἀληθοῦς Χριστοῦ, τοῦ κατὰ πάντων βασιλεύοντος
θείου λόγου, βασιλικῆς καὶ ἀρχικῆς ἐξουσίας
τοὺς τύπους δι’ ἑαυτῶν ἔφερον. ἤδη δὲ 8
καὶ αὐτῶν τῶν προφητῶν τινὰς διὰ χρίσματος
Χριστοὺς ἐν τύπῳ γεγονέναι παρειλήφαμεν, ὡς
τούτους ἅπαντας τὴν ἐπὶ τὸν ἀληθῆ Χριστόν, τὸν
ἔνθεον καὶ οὐράνιον λόγον, ἀναφορὰν ἔχειν, μόνον
ἀρχιέρεα τῶν ὅλων καὶ μόνον ἁπάσης κτίσεως
βασιλέα καὶ μόνον προφητῶν ἀρχιπροφήτην τοῦ
πατρὸς τυγχάνοντα. τούτου δ’ ἀπόδειξις τὸ μηδένα 9
πω τῶν πάλαι διὰ τοῦ συμβόλου κεχρισμένων,
μήτε ἱερέων μήτε βασιλέων μήτε μὴν προφητῶν,
τοσαύτην ἀρετῆς ἐνθέου δύναμιν κτήσασθαι, ὅσην
ὁ σωτὴρ καὶ κύριος ἡμῶν Ἰησοῦς ὁ μόνος καὶ
ἀληθινὸς Χριστὸς ἐπιδέδεικται. οὐδεὶς γέ τοι 10
ἐκείνων, καίπερ ἀξιώματι καὶ τιμῇ ἐπὶ πλείσταις
ὅσαις γενεαῖς παρὰ τοῖς οἰκείοις διαλαμψάντων,
τοὺς ὑπηκόους πώποτε ἐκ τῆς περὶ αὐτοὺς εἰκο-
νικῆς τοῦ Χριστοῦ προσρήσεως Χριστιανοὺς ἐπ-
εφήμισεν· ἀλλ’ οὐδὲ σεβάσμιός τινι τούτων πρὸς
τῶν ὑπηκόων ὑπῆρξε τιμή· ἀλλ’ οὐδὲ μετὰ τὴν
τελευτὴν τοσαύτη διάθεσις, ὡς καὶ ὑπεραπο-
θνήσκειν ἑτοίμως ἔχειν τοῦ τιμωμένου· ἀλλ’ οὐδὲ
πάντων τῶν ἀνὰ τὴν οἰκουμένην ἐθνῶν περί τινα
τῶν τότε τοσαύτη γέγονε κίνησις, ἐπεὶ μηδὲ
τοσοῦτον ἐν ἐκείνοις ἡ τοῦ συμβόλου δύναμις οἷα
τε ἦν ἐνεργεῖν, ὅσον ἡ τῆς ἀληθείας παράστασις
διὰ τοῦ σωτῆρος ἡμῶν ἐνδεικνυμένη· ὃς οὔτε 11
σύμβολα καὶ τύπους ἀρχιερωσύνης παρά του λαβών,

32

also the kings, for they also, at the bidding of God, were made Christs in a certain symbolism by the prophets who anointed them, inasmuch as they also bore in themselves the types of the royal and sovereign power of the only true Christ, the divine Logos who reigns over all. We have also received the tradition that some of the prophets themselves had by anointing already become Christs in type, seeing that they all refer to the true Christ, the divine and heavenly Logos, of the world the only High Priest, of all creation the only king, of the prophets the only archprophet of the Father. The proof of this is that no one of those symbolically anointed of old, whether priests or kings or prophets, obtained such power of divine virtue as our Saviour and Lord, Jesus, the only real Christ, has exhibited. None indeed of them, though renowned in rank and honour for so many generations among their own people, ever gave the name of Christian to their subjects from the symbolical application to themselves of the name of Christ. The honour of worship was not paid to any of them by their subjects, nor did they hold them in such affection after their death as to be ready to die for him whom they honoured. For none of the men of those days was there such disturbance of all the nations throughout all the world, since the power of the symbol was incapable of producing such an effect among them as the presence of the reality manifested by our Saviour ; for he received from none the symbol and types of the High Priesthood, nor did he trace his

ἀλλ' οὐδὲ γένος τὸ περὶ σῶμα ἐξ ἱερωμένων
κατάγων, οὐδ' ἀνδρῶν δορυφορίαις ἐπὶ βασιλείαν
προαχθεὶς οὐδὲ μὴν προφήτης ὁμοίως τοῖς πάλαι
γενόμενος, οὐδ' ἀξίας ὅλως ἤ τινος παρὰ Ἰουδαίοις
τυχὼν προεδρίας, ὅμως τοῖς πᾶσιν, εἰ καὶ μὴ
τοῖς συμβόλοις, ἀλλ' αὐτῇ γε τῇ ἀληθείᾳ παρὰ
τοῦ πατρὸς κεκόσμητο, οὐχ ὁμοίων δ' οὖν οἷς 12
προειρήκαμεν, τυχών, πάντων ἐκείνων καὶ Χριστὸς
μᾶλλον ἀνηγόρευται, καὶ ὡς ἂν μόνος καὶ ἀληθὴς
αὐτὸς ὢν ὁ Χριστὸς τοῦ θεοῦ, Χριστιανῶν τὸν
πάντα κόσμον, τῆς ὄντως σεμνῆς καὶ ἱερᾶς αὐτοῦ
προσηγορίας, κατέπλησεν, οὐκέτι τύπους οὐδὲ
εἰκόνας, ἀλλ' αὐτὰς γυμνὰς ἀρετὰς καὶ βίον
οὐράνιον αὐτοῖς ἀληθείας δόγμασιν τοῖς θιασώταις
παραδούς, τό τε χρῖσμα, οὐ τὸ διὰ σωμάτων 13
σκευαστόν, ἀλλ' αὐτὸ δὴ πνεύματι θείῳ τὸ θεο-
πρεπές, μετοχῇ τῆς ἀγεννήτου καὶ πατρικῆς θεότητος
ἀπειλήφει· ὃ καὶ αὐτὸ πάλιν Ἡσαΐας διδάσκει,
ὡς ἂν ἐξ αὐτοῦ ὧδέ πως ἀναβοῶν τοῦ Χριστοῦ

Luke 4, 18. "πνεῦμα κυρίου ἐπ' ἐμέ, οὗ εἵνεκεν ἔχρισέν με·
19 Is. (61, 1) εὐαγγελίσασθαι πτωχοῖς ἀπέσταλκέν με, κηρῦξαι
αἰχμαλώτοις ἄφεσιν καὶ τυφλοῖς ἀνάβλεψιν." καὶ
οὐ μόνος γε Ἡσαΐας, ἀλλὰ καὶ Δαυὶδ εἰς τὸ αὐτοῦ
Ps. 44, 7. 8 πρόσωπον ἀναφωνεῖ λέγων "ὁ θρόνος σου, ὁ θεός,
εἰς τὸν αἰῶνα τοῦ αἰῶνος· ῥάβδος εὐθύτητος ἡ
ῥάβδος τῆς βασιλείας σου. ἠγάπησας δικαιοσύνην
καὶ ἐμίσησας ἀνομίαν· διὰ τοῦτο ἔχρισέν σε ὁ
θεός, ὁ θεός σου ἔλαιον ἀγαλλιάσεως παρὰ τοὺς
μετόχους σου"· ἐν οἷς ὁ λόγος ἐν μὲν τῷ πρώτῳ
στίχῳ θεὸν αὐτὸν ἐπιφημίζει, ἐν δὲ τῷ δευτέρῳ
σκήπτρῳ βασιλικῷ τιμᾷ, εἶθ' ἑξῆς ὑποβὰς μετὰ

34

physical descent from the race of priests, nor was
he promoted to a kingdom by the armed force of
men, nor did he become a prophet in the same way
as those of old, nor did he hold any rank at all or
precedence among the Jews, yet with all these he
had been adorned, not in symbols, but in actual
reality by the Father. Though he did not obtain
the honours of which we have spoken before, he is
called Christ more than any of them, and inasmuch
as he is himself the only true Christ of God, he filled
the whole world with Christians—his truly reverend
and sacred name. He no longer gave to his initiates
types or images but the uncovered virtues themselves and the heavenly life, in the actual doctrines
of truth, and he has received the chrism, not that
which is prepared materially [1] but the divine anointing
itself with the spirit of God, by sharing in the unbegotten divinity of the Father. Again, Isaiah teaches
this very point, for in one place he exclaims as if
from Christ himself, " The spirit of the Lord was
upon me, wherefore he anointed me : he sent me
to preach the gospel to the poor, to announce release
to prisoners, and sight to the blind." [2] And not
only Isaiah but also David speaks with reference to
him and says, " Thy throne, O God, is for ever
and ever, a rod of uprightness is the rod of thy
kingdom. Thou didst love righteousness and didst
hate iniquity. For this cause God, even thy God,
anointed thee with the oil of gladness above thy
fellows." In this the text calls him God in the
first verse, and in the second honours him with the
royal sceptre, and then goes on, after royal and

[1] Or, if ἀρωμάτων be read, " with spices."
[2] The punctuation of this passage is based on Eusebius's
Ecl. Proph. 229. 13.

τὴν ἔνθεον καὶ βασιλικὴν δύναμιν τρίτῃ τάξει
Χριστὸν αὐτὸν γεγονότα, ἐλαίῳ οὐ τῷ ἐξ ὕλης
σωμάτων, ἀλλὰ τῷ ἐνθέῳ τῆς ἀγαλλιάσεως
ἠλειμμένον, παρίστησιν· παρ᾽ ὃ καὶ τὸ ἐξαίρετον
αὐτοῦ καὶ πολὺ κρεῖττον καὶ διάφορον τῶν πάλαι
διὰ τῶν εἰκόνων σωματικώτερον κεχρισμένων
ὑποσημαίνει. καὶ ἀλλαχοῦ δὲ ὁ αὐτὸς ὧδέ πως 16
Ps. 109, 1 τὰ περὶ αὐτοῦ δηλοῖ λέγων " εἶπεν ὁ κύριος τῷ
κυρίῳ μου· ' κάθου ἐκ δεξιῶν μου, ἕως ἂν θῶ τοὺς
Ps. 109, 3. 4
Heb. 7, 11–
25 ἐχθρούς σου ὑποπόδιον τῶν ποδῶν σου,' " καὶ " ἐκ
γαστρὸς πρὸ ἑωσφόρου ἐγέννησά σε. ὤμοσεν κύριος
καὶ οὐ μεταμεληθήσεται· σὺ εἶ ἱερεὺς εἰς τὸν αἰῶνα
κατὰ τὴν τάξιν Μελχισεδέκ." οὗτος δὲ εἰσ- 17
άγεται ἐν τοῖς ἱεροῖς λόγοις ὁ Μελχισεδὲκ ἱερεὺς
τοῦ θεοῦ τοῦ ὑψίστου, οὐκ ἐν σκευαστῷ τινι
χρίσματι ἀναδεδειγμένος, ἀλλ᾽ οὐδὲ διαδοχῇ γένους
προσήκων τῇ καθ᾽ Ἑβραίους ἱερωσύνῃ· δι᾽ ὃ
κατὰ τὴν αὐτοῦ τάξιν, ἀλλ᾽ οὐ κατὰ τὴν τῶν ἄλλων
σύμβολα καὶ τύπους ἀνειληφότων Χριστὸς καὶ
ἱερεὺς μεθ᾽ ὅρκου παραλήψεως ὁ σωτὴρ ἡμῶν
ἀνηγόρευται· ὅθεν οὐδὲ σωματικῶς παρὰ Ἰου- 18
δαίοις χρισθέντα αὐτὸν ἡ ἱστορία παραδίδωσιν,
ἀλλ᾽ οὐδ᾽ ἐκ φυλῆς τῶν ἱερωμένων γενόμενον,
ἐξ αὐτοῦ δὲ θεοῦ πρὸ ἑωσφόρου μέν, τοῦτ᾽ ἐστὶν
πρὸ τῆς τοῦ κόσμου συστάσεως, οὐσιωμένον,
ἀθάνατον δὲ καὶ ἀγήρω τὴν ἱερωσύνην εἰς τὸν
ἄπειρον αἰῶνα διακατέχοντα. τῆς δ᾽ εἰς αὐτὸν 19
γενομένης ἀσωμάτου καὶ ἐνθέου χρίσεως μέγα
καὶ ἐναργὲς τεκμήριον τὸ μόνον αὐτὸν ἐξ ἁπάντων
τῶν πώποτε εἰς ἔτι καὶ νῦν παρὰ πᾶσιν ἀνθρώποις

---

[1] Eusebius means that this is the significance of " above
thy fellows."

divine power, to present him in the third place
as having become Christ, anointed not with oil
made of material substances but with the divine
" oil of gladness." And in addition to this he
indicates his peculiar distinction and superiority
to those who in the past had been more materially
anointed as types.[1] And in another place too the
same David explains his position as follows : " The
Lord said to my Lord, Sit thou on my right hand,
until I make thine enemies the footstool of thy
feet." And, " Before the day-star I begat thee
from the womb. The Lord sware and will not repent,
Thou art a priest for ever after the order of Melchisedek." Now this Melchisedek is introduced in
the sacred books as priest of the most high God,
without having been so marked out by any material
unction, or even as belonging by racial descent to
the priesthood of the Hebrews. For this reason our
Saviour has been called Christ and priest, on the
authority of an oath, according to his order and not
according to that of the others who received symbols
and types. For this reason, too, the narrative does
not relate that he was anointed physically by the
Jews or even that he was of the tribe of those who
hold the priesthood, but that he received his being
from God himself before the day-star, that is to
say, before the construction of the world, and holds
his priesthood to boundless eternity, ageless and
immortal. A weighty and clear proof of the
immaterial [2] and divine anointing effected on him
is that he alone, out of all who have ever yet been

---

[2] Gk. ἀσώματος. The use of this word as a technical
term meaning "immaterial" has a long history, but it was
popularized in Christian metaphysics, especially by Origen.

EUSEBIUS

καθ' ὅλου τοῦ κόσμου Χριστὸν ἐπιφημίζεσθαι
ὁμολογεῖσθαί τε καὶ μαρτυρεῖσθαι πρὸς ἁπάντων
ἐπὶ τῇ προσηγορίᾳ παρά τε Ἕλλησι καὶ βαρβάροις μνημονεύεσθαι, καὶ εἰς ἔτι νῦν παρὰ τοῖς
ἀνὰ τὴν οἰκουμένην αὐτοῦ θιασώταις τιμᾶσθαι
μὲν ὡς βασιλέα, θαυμάζεσθαι δὲ ὑπὲρ προφήτην,
δοξάζεσθαί τε ὡς ἀληθῆ καὶ μόνον θεοῦ ἀρχιερέα,
καὶ ἐπὶ πᾶσι τούτοις, οἷα θεοῦ λόγον προόντα καὶ
πρὸ αἰώνων ἁπάντων οὐσιωμένον τήν τε σεβάσμιον
τιμὴν παρὰ τοῦ πατρὸς ὑπειληφότα, καὶ προσκυ-
νεῖσθαι ὡς θεόν· τό γε μὴν πάντων παραδοξότατον, 20
ὅτι μὴ φωναῖς αὐτὸ μόνον καὶ ῥημάτων ψόφοις
αὐτὸν γεραίρομεν οἱ καθωσιωμένοι αὐτῷ, ἀλλὰ καὶ
πάσῃ διαθέσει ψυχῆς, ὡς καὶ αὐτῆς προτιμᾶν τῆς
ἑαυτῶν ζωῆς τὴν εἰς αὐτὸν μαρτυρίαν.

IV. Ταῦτα μὲν οὖν ἀναγκαίως πρὸ τῆς ἱστορίας 1
ἐνταῦθά μοι κείσθω, ὡς ἂν μὴ νεώτερόν τις εἶναι
νομίσειεν τὸν σωτῆρα καὶ κύριον ἡμῶν Ἰησοῦν τὸν
Χριστὸν διὰ τοὺς τῆς ἐνσάρκου πολιτείας αὐτοῦ
χρόνους. ἵνα δὲ μηδὲ τὴν διδασκαλίαν αὐτοῦ νέαν
εἶναι καὶ ξένην, ὡς ἂν ὑπὸ νέου καὶ μηδὲν τοὺς λοιποὺς
διαφέροντος ἀνθρώπους συστᾶσαν, ὑπονοήσειέν τις,
φέρε, βραχέα καὶ περὶ τούτου διαλάβωμεν. τῆς 2
μὲν γὰρ τοῦ σωτῆρος ἡμῶν Ἰησοῦ Χριστοῦ
παρουσίας νεωστὶ πᾶσιν ἀνθρώποις ἐπιλαμψάσης,
νέον ὁμολογουμένως ἔθνος, οὐ μικρὸν οὐδ' ἀσθενὲς
οὐδ' ἐπὶ γωνίας ποι γῆς ἱδρυμένον, ἀλλὰ καὶ
πάντων τῶν ἐθνῶν πολυανθρωπότατόν τε καὶ
θεοσεβέστατον ταύτῃ τε ἀνώλεθρον καὶ ἀήττητον, ᾗ
καὶ εἰς ἀεὶ τῆς παρὰ θεοῦ βοηθείας τυγχάνει,
χρόνων προθεσμίαις ἀρρήτοις ἀθρόως οὕτως ἀνα-
πέφηνεν, τὸ παρὰ τοῖς πᾶσι τῇ τοῦ Χριστοῦ

38

until now, is called Christ among all men throughout the whole world ; that under this title he is confessed and borne witness to by all, and is mentioned thus by Jews, Greeks, and barbarians ; that until this present day he is honoured by his worshippers throughout the world as king, wondered at more than a prophet, and glorified as the true and only High Priest of God, and, above all, as the Logos of God, pre-existent, having his being before all ages, and having received the right of reverence from the Father, and that he is worshipped as God. Strangest of all, we, who have been consecrated to him, honour him not only with our voices and with the sound of words, but with the whole disposition of our soul, so as to value testimony to him more than our very life itself.

IV. Let these observations suffice me, as needed before beginning the history, that no one might think of our Saviour and Lord, Jesus Christ, as a novelty because of the date of his ministry in the flesh. But that no one may suppose that his teaching either was new and strange, inasmuch as it was put together by a youth no better than the rest of men, come, let us discuss this point briefly. For when the advent of our Saviour, Jesus Christ, recently shone forth on all men, it was confessedly a new race which has thus appeared in such numbers, in accordance with the ineffable prophecies of the date, and is honoured by all by the name of Christ, but it is not little nor weak, nor founded in some obscure corner of the earth, but the most populous of all nations, and most pious towards God, alike innocent and invincible in that it ever finds help from God.

προσηγορίᾳ τετιμημένον. τοῦτο καὶ προφητῶν 3
κατεπλάγη τις, θείου πνεύματος ὀφθαλμῷ τὸ
μέλλον ἔσεσθαι προθεωρήσας, ὡς καὶ τάδε ἀνα-
φθέγξασθαι " τίς ἤκουσεν τοιαῦτα, καὶ τις ἐλάλησεν
οὕτως; εἰ ὤδινεν γῆ ἐν μιᾷ ἡμέρᾳ, καὶ εἰ ἐτέχθη
ἔθνος εἰς ἅπαξ." ὑποσημαίνει δέ πως καὶ τὴν
μέλλουσαν ὁ αὐτὸς προσηγορίαν, λέγων " τοῖς
δὲ δουλεύουσίν μοι κληθήσεται ὄνομα καινόν, ὃ
εὐλογηθήσεται ἐπὶ τῆς γῆς." ἀλλ' εἰ καὶ νέοι 4
σαφῶς ἡμεῖς καὶ τοῦτο καινὸν ὄντως ὄνομα τὸ
Χριστιανῶν ἀρτίως παρὰ πᾶσιν ἔθνεσιν γνωρίζεται,
ὁ βίος δ' οὖν ὅμως καὶ τῆς ἀγωγῆς ὁ τρόπος
αὐτοῖς εὐσεβείας δόγμασιν ὅτι μὴ ἔναγχος ὑφ'
ἡμῶν ἐπιπέπλασται, ἐκ πρώτης δ' ὡς εἰπεῖν ἀνθρωπογονίας φυσικαῖς ἐννοίαις τῶν πάλαι θεοφιλῶν ἀνδρῶν κατωρθοῦτο, ὧδέ πως ἐπιδείξομεν.
οὐ νέον, ἀλλὰ καὶ παρὰ πᾶσιν ἀνθρώποις ἀρχαιότητι 5
τετιμημένον ἔθνος, τοῖς πᾶσι καὶ αὐτὸ γνώριμον,
τὸ Ἑβραίων τυγχάνει. λόγοι δὴ παρὰ τούτῳ
καὶ γράμματα παλαιοὺς ἄνδρας περιέχουσιν,
σπανίους μὲν καὶ ἀριθμῷ βραχεῖς, ἀλλ' ὅμως
εὐσεβείᾳ καὶ δικαιοσύνῃ καὶ πάσῃ τῇ λοιπῇ
διενεγκόντας ἀρετῇ, πρὸ μέν γε τοῦ κατακλυσμοῦ
διαφόρους, μετὰ δὲ καὶ τοῦτον ἑτέρους, τῶν τε
τοῦ Νῶε παίδων καὶ ἀπογόνων ἀτὰρ καὶ τὸν
Ἀβραάμ, ὃν ἀρχηγὸν καὶ προπάτορα σφῶν αὐτῶν
παῖδες Ἑβραίων αὐχοῦσι. πάντας δὴ ἐκείνους
ἐπὶ δικαιοσύνῃ μεμαρτυρημένους, ἐξ αὐτοῦ Ἀβραὰμ
ἐπὶ τὸν πρῶτον ἀνιοῦσιν ἄνθρωπον, ἔργῳ Χρι-

Is. 66, 8

Is. 65, 15. 16

It was at this that one of the prophets was amazed when, by the eye of the divine spirit, he foresaw the future which was to be, so that he exclaimed, " Who heard these things and who spoke thus ? Did the earth travail in one day, and was a nation born at once ? " And the same writer also indicates in one place its future title, saying, " And a new name shall be called on those who serve me, which shall be blessed on the earth." But even if we are clearly new, and this really fresh name of Christians is recently known among all nations, nevertheless our life and method of conduct, in accordance with the precepts of religion, has not been recently invented by us, but from the first creation of man, so to speak, has been upheld by the natural concepts of the men of old who were the friends of God, as we will here demonstrate. The race of the Hebrews is not new but is honoured among all men for its antiquity and is itself well known to all. Now, stories and documents belonging to it concern ancient men, few and scarce in number, yet remarkable for piety and righteousness and for all other virtues. Divers of them, indeed, were before the flood, and after it were others, and, (to say nothing of the children and descendants of Noah), especially Abraham, whom the children of the Hebrews boast as their own originator and ancestor. If the line be traced back from Abraham to the first man, anyone who should describe those who have obtained a good testimony for righteousness, as Christians in fact,

στιανούς, εἰ καὶ μὴ ὀνόματι, προσειπών τις οὐκ
ἂν ἐκτὸς βάλοι τῆς ἀληθείας. ὃ γάρ τοι δηλοῦν 7
ἐθέλοι τοὔνομα, τὸν Χριστιανὸν ἄνδρα διὰ τῆς τοῦ
Χριστοῦ γνώσεως καὶ διδασκαλίας σωφροσύνῃ
καὶ δικαιοσύνῃ καρτερίᾳ τε βίου καὶ ἀρετῆς
ἀνδρείᾳ εὐσεβείας τε ὁμολογίᾳ ἑνὸς καὶ μόνου
τοῦ ἐπὶ πάντων θεοῦ διαπρέπειν, τοῦτο πᾶν ἐκείνοις
οὐ χεῖρον ἡμῶν ἐσπουδάζετο. οὔτ' οὖν σώματος 8
αὐτοῖς περιτομῆς ἔμελεν, ὅτι μηδὲ ἡμῖν, οὐ
σαββάτων ἐπιτηρήσεως, ὅτι μηδὲ ἡμῖν, ἀλλ' οὐδὲ
τῶν τοιῶνδε τροφῶν παραφυλακῆς οὐδὲ τῶν
ἄλλων διαστολῆς, ὅσα τοῖς μετέπειτα πρῶτος
ἁπάντων Μωυσῆς ἀρξάμενος ἐν συμβόλοις τελεῖσθαι
παραδέδωκεν, ὅτι μηδὲ νῦν Χριστιανῶν τὰ τοιαῦτα·
ἀλλὰ καὶ σαφῶς αὐτὸν ᾔδεσαν τὸν Χριστὸν τοῦ
Gen. 18, 1.
26, 2. 35, 1 θεοῦ, εἴ γε ὦφθαι μὲν τῷ Ἀβραάμ, χρηματίσαι
δὲ τῷ Ἰσαάκ, λελαληκέναι δὲ τῷ Ἰσραήλ, Μωυσεῖ
τε καὶ τοῖς μετὰ ταῦτα προφήταις ὡμιληκέναι
προδέδεικται· ἔνθεν αὐτοὺς δὴ τοὺς θεοφιλεῖς 9
ἐκείνους εὕροις ἂν καὶ τῆς τοῦ Χριστοῦ κατ-
ηξιωμένους ἐπωνυμίας, κατὰ τὴν φάσκουσαν περὶ
Ps. 104, 15 αὐτῶν φωνήν " μὴ ἅψησθε τῶν Χριστῶν μου,
καὶ ἐν τοῖς προφήταις μου μὴ πονηρεύεσθε"·
ὥστε σαφῶς πρώτην ἡγεῖσθαι δεῖν καὶ πάντων 10
παλαιοτάτην τε καὶ ἀρχαιοτάτην θεοσεβείας εὕρεσιν
αὐτῶν ἐκείνων τῶν ἀμφὶ τὸν Ἀβραὰμ θεοφιλῶν
ἀνδρῶν τὴν ἀρτίως διὰ τῆς τοῦ Χριστοῦ διδασκαλίας πᾶσιν ἔθνεσιν κατηγγελμένην. εἰ δὲ δὴ 11
μακρῷ ποθ' ὕστερον περιτομῆς φασι τὸν Ἀβραὰμ
ἐντολὴν εἰληφέναι, ἀλλὰ πρό γε ταύτης δικαιοσύνην
διὰ πίστεως μαρτυρηθεὶς ἀνείρηται, ὧδέ πως τοῦ
Gen. 15, 6 θείου φάσκοντος λόγου " ἐπίστευσεν δὲ Ἀβραὰμ

if not in name, would not shoot wide of the truth. For the name signifies that through the knowledge of Christ and his teaching the Christian man excels in sobriety and righteousness, in control of life and courageous virtue, and in the confession that God over all is but one ; and for zeal in all this they were not inferior to us. They had no care for bodily circumcision any more than we, nor for the keeping of Sabbaths any more than we, nor for abstinence [1] from certain foods nor the distinction between others (such as Moses afterwards first began to hand down to their successors) nor for symbolic ceremony any more than Christians care for such things now, but they clearly knew him as the Christ of God, seeing that it has already been demonstrated that he appeared to Abraham, addressed Isaac, spoke to Israel, and conversed with Moses and the later prophets. Whence you would find that those God-loving men obtained even the name of Christ according to the word spoken concerning them, " Touch not my Christs and act not wickedly among my prophets." So that it must clearly be held that the announcement to all the Gentiles, recently made through the teaching of Christ, is the very first and most ancient and antique discovery of true religion by Abraham and those lovers of God who followed him. And even if they say that Abraham received the command of circumcision long afterwards, it has been related that, before this command, he received a good testimony for righteousness through faith, as the divine word says, " And Abraham be-

---

[1] Literally " observation," *i.e.* in order to avoid.

τῷ θεῷ, καὶ ἐλογίσθη αὐτῷ εἰς δικαιοσύνην." καὶ 12
δὴ τοιούτῳ πρὸ τῆς περιτομῆς γεγονότι χρησμὸς
ὑπὸ τοῦ φήναντος ἑαυτὸν αὐτῷ θεοῦ (οὗτος δ'
ἦν αὐτὸς ὁ Χριστός, ὁ τοῦ θεοῦ λόγος) περὶ τῶν
ἐν τοῖς μετέπειτα χρόνοις τὸν ὅμοιον αὐτῷ δι-
καιοῦσθαι τρόπον μελλόντων ῥήμασιν αὐτοῖς προ-
επήγγελται λέγων " καὶ ἐνευλογηθήσονται ἐν σοὶ
πᾶσαι αἱ φυλαὶ τῆς γῆς," καὶ ὡς ὅτι " ἔσται εἰς
ἔθνος μέγα καὶ πολύ, καὶ ἐνευλογηθήσονται ἐν
αὐτῷ πάντα τὰ ἔθνη τῆς γῆς." τούτῳ δὲ καὶ 13
ἐπιστῆσαι εἰς ἡμᾶς ἐκπεπληρωμένῳ πάρεστιν.
πίστει μὲν γὰρ ἐκεῖνος τῇ εἰς τὸν ὀφθέντα αὐτῷ
τοῦ θεοῦ λόγον τὸν Χριστὸν δεδικαίωτο, πατρῴας
μὲν ἀποστὰς δεισιδαιμονίας καὶ πλάνης βίου
προτέρας, ἕνα δὲ τὸν ἐπὶ πάντων ὁμολογήσας θεὸν
καὶ τοῦτον ἔργοις ἀρετῆς οὐχὶ δὲ θρησκείᾳ νόμου
τοῦ μετὰ ταῦτα Μωυσέως θεραπεύσας, τοιούτῳ τε
ὄντι εἴρητο ὅτι δὴ πᾶσαι αἱ φυλαὶ τῆς γῆς καὶ
πάντα τὰ ἔθνη ἐν αὐτῷ εὐλογηθήσεται· ἔργοις 14
δὲ λόγων ἐναργεστέροις ἐπὶ τοῦ παρόντος παρὰ
μόνοις Χριστιανοῖς καθ' ὅλης τῆς οἰκουμένης ἀσκούμενος αὐτὸς ἐκεῖνος ὁ τῆς θεοσεβείας τοῦ Ἀβραὰμ
ἀναπέφηνε τρόπος. τί δὴ οὖν λοιπὸν ἐμποδὼν 15
ἂν εἴη, μὴ οὐχὶ ἕνα καὶ τὸν αὐτὸν βίον τε καὶ
τρόπον εὐσεβείας ἡμῖν τε τοῖς ἀπὸ Χριστοῦ καὶ
τοῖς πρόπαλαι θεοφιλέσιν ὁμολογεῖν; ὥστε μὴ νέαν
καὶ ξένην, ἀλλ' εἰ δεῖ φάναι ἀληθεύοντα, πρώτην
ὑπάρχειν καὶ μόνην καὶ ἀληθῆ κατόρθωσιν εὐσεβείας
τὴν διὰ τῆς τοῦ Χριστοῦ διδασκαλίας παραδοθεῖσαν
ἡμῖν ἀποδείκνυσθαι. καὶ ταῦτα μὲν ὧδε ἐχέτω.

Rom. 4, 3

Gen. 12, 3
Gen. 18, 18

Gen. 12, 1

---

[1] As usual, it is impossible to represent in English the
fact that in Christian Greek the same word means " nations "

lieved God and it was reckoned to him for righteousness." And to him, just as he was, before circumcision, was the oracle given by the God who showed himself to him (and this was the Christ himself, the word of God), concerning those who in time to come would be justified in the same manner as himself, in the following promise, " And in thee shall all the tribes of the earth be blessed," and, " It shall be a great and numerous nation, and all the nations of the earth shall be blessed in it." Now this is obviously intelligible as fulfilled in us ; for it was by faith towards the Logos of God, the Christ who had appeared to him, that he was justified, and gave up the superstition of his fathers, and his former erroneous life, and confessed the God who is over all to be one ; and him he served by virtuous deeds, not by the worship of the law of Moses, who came later. To him, just as he was then, was it said that all the tribes of the earth and all the nations [1] will be blessed in him ; and more clearly than any words do facts show that at the present moment it is only among Christians throughout the whole world that the manner of religion which was Abraham's can actually be found in practice. What objection then can there be to admitting that the life and pious conduct of us, who belong to Christ, and of the God-loving men of old is one and the same? Thus we have demonstrated that the practice of piety handed down by the teaching of Christ is not new or strange, but, if one must speak truthfully, is primitive, unique, and true. And let this suffice.

---

or " heathen." The Church took over from Hellenistic Judaism the usage of calling itself " the people " (ὁ λαός) as distinguished from " the nations " (τὰ ἔθνη).

V. Φέρε δὲ ἤδη, μετὰ τὴν δέουσαν προκατασκευὴν 1
τῆς προτεθείσης ἡμῖν ἐκκλησιαστικῆς ἱστορίας ἤδη
λοιπὸν ἀπὸ τῆς ἐνσάρκου τοῦ σωτῆρος ἡμῶν
ἐπιφανείας οἷά τινος ὁδοιπορίας ἐφαψώμεθα, τὸν
τοῦ λόγου πατέρα θεὸν καὶ τὸν δηλούμενον αὐτὸν
Ἰησοῦν Χριστὸν τὸν σωτῆρα καὶ κύριον ἡμῶν, τὸν
οὐράνιον τοῦ θεοῦ λόγον, βοηθὸν ἡμῖν καὶ συνεργὸν
τῆς κατὰ τὴν διήγησιν ἀληθείας ἐπικαλεσάμενοι.
ἦν δὴ οὖν τοῦτο δεύτερον καὶ τεσσαρακοστὸν ἔτος 2
τῆς Αὐγούστου βασιλείας, Αἰγύπτου δ’ ὑποταγῆς
καὶ τελευτῆς Ἀντωνίου καὶ Κλεοπάτρας, εἰς ἣν
ὑστάτην ἡ κατ’ Αἴγυπτον τῶν Πτολεμαίων κατέ-
ληξε δυναστεία, ὄγδοον ἔτος καὶ εἰκοστόν, ὁπηνίκα

Luke 2, 2 ὁ σωτὴρ καὶ κύριος ἡμῶν Ἰησοῦς ὁ Χριστὸς ἐπὶ
τῆς τότε πρώτης ἀπογραφῆς, ἡγεμονεύοντος
Κυρινίου τῆς Συρίας, ἀκολούθως ταῖς περὶ αὐτοῦ
Mich. 5, 2 προφητείαις ἐν Βηθλεὲμ γεννᾶται τῆς Ἰουδαίας.
ταύτης δὲ τῆς κατὰ Κυρίνιον ἀπογραφῆς καὶ ὁ 3
τῶν παρ’ Ἑβραίοις ἐπισημότατος ἱστορικῶν Φλα-
ύιος Ἰώσηπος μνημονεύει, καὶ ἄλλην ἐπισυνάπτων
ἱστορίαν περὶ τῆς τῶν Γαλιλαίων κατὰ τοὺς
αὐτοὺς ἐπιφυείσης χρόνους αἱρέσεως, ἧς καὶ παρ’
ἡμῖν ὁ Λουκᾶς ἐν ταῖς Πράξεσιν μνήμην ὧδέ πως
Acts 5, 37 λέγων πεποίηται “ μετὰ τοῦτον ἀνέστη Ἰούδας

---

[1] That is, 1 B.C., the next year being the *annus Domini*.
The same date is given by Clement of Alexandria, *Strom.* 1,
but Irenaeus and Tertullian place the nativity one year earlier.
Neither date can be reconciled with the statement of Matthew
ii. 1 that Jesus was born in the reign of Herod the Great,
who died in 4 B.C.

[2] Eusebius assumes that the census mentioned by
Josephus, which led to a revolt, is the same as that referred
to in Luke and in Acts. If he be right Luke and Matthew

V. So then, after the necessary preliminaries to the history of the Church proposed by us, let us begin, as if starting a journey, with the appearance of our Saviour in the flesh, after invoking God, the Father of the Logos, and Jesus Christ himself, our Saviour and Lord, the heavenly Logos of God, to give us help and assistance to truth in the narrative. It was, then, the forty-second year of the reign of Augustus,[1] and the twenty-eighth year after the submission of Egypt and the death of Antony and Cleopatra (and with her the Egyptian dynasty of the Ptolemies came to an end), when our Saviour and Lord Jesus Christ, in accordance with the prophecies concerning him, was born in Bethlehem of Judaea at the time of the census which then first took place, while Quirinius was Governor of Syria. This census in the time of Quirinius,[2] Flavius Josephus, the most famous of the historians among the Hebrews, also mentions, and joins to the narrative another concerning the sect of the Galileans which arose at the same time. Our own Luke has also mentioned this in one place in the Acts, saying " After this man arose Judas the Galilean, in the

---

cannot be reconciled, for the census of Quirinius referred to by Josephus and also in Acts v. 37 was in A.D. 6. Sir W. M. Ramsay thinks that there may have been an earlier census in the reign of Herod during a former governorship of Quirinius in Syria, which did not then include the domain of Herod. There is good evidence for the former governorship of Quirinius, but none for a census in Judaea during his governorship by (or for) Herod. See Eusebius, *Ecl. proph.* 158 ff.

ὁ Γαλιλαῖος ἐν ταῖς ἡμέραις τῆς ἀπογραφῆς, καὶ
ἀπέστησε λαὸν ὀπίσω αὐτοῦ· κἀκεῖνος ἀπώλετο,
καὶ πάντες ὅσοι ἐπείσθησαν αὐτῷ, διεσκορπί-
σθησαν." τούτοις δ' οὖν καὶ ὁ δεδηλωμένος ἐν 4
ὀκτωκαιδεκάτῳ τῆς Ἀρχαιολογίας συνᾴδων ταῦτα
παρατίθεται κατὰ λέξιν· " Κυρίνιος δὲ τῶν εἰς τὴν
βουλὴν συναγομένων, ἀνὴρ τάς τε ἄλλας ἀρχὰς
ἐπιτετελεκὼς καὶ διὰ πασῶν ὁδεύσας ὕπατος
γενέσθαι τά τε ἄλλα ἀξιώματι μέγας, σὺν ὀλίγοις
ἐπὶ Συρίας παρῆν, ὑπὸ Καίσαρος δικαιοδότης
τοῦ ἔθνους ἀπεσταλμένος καὶ τιμητὴς τῶν οὐσιῶν
γενησόμενος." καὶ μετὰ βραχέα φησίν· " Ἰούδας 5
δέ, Γαυλανίτης ἀνὴρ ἐκ πόλεως ὄνομα Γαμαλά,
Σάδδοκον Φαρισαῖον προσλαβόμενος, ἠπείγετο ἐπὶ
ἀποστάσει, τήν τε ἀποτίμησιν οὐδὲν ἄλλο ἢ ἄντικρυς
δουλείαν ἐπιφέρειν λέγοντες καὶ τῆς ἐλευθερίας ἐπ'
ἀντιλήψει παρακαλοῦντες τὸ ἔθνος." καὶ ἐν τῇ 6
δευτέρᾳ δὲ τῶν ἱστοριῶν τοῦ Ἰουδαϊκοῦ πολέμου
περὶ τοῦ αὐτοῦ ταῦτα γράφει· " ἐπὶ τούτου τις
ἀνὴρ Γαλιλαῖος Ἰούδας ὄνομα εἰς ἀποστασίαν
ἐνῆγε τοὺς ἐπιχωρίους, κακίζων εἰ φόρον τε
Ῥωμαίοις τελεῖν ὑπομενοῦσιν καὶ μετὰ τὸν θεὸν
οἴσουσι θνητοὺς δεσπότας." ταῦτα ὁ Ἰώσηπος.

VI. Τηνικαῦτα δὲ καὶ τοῦ Ἰουδαίων ἔθνους Ἡρώ- 1
δου πρώτου τὸ γένος ἀλλοφύλου διειληφότος τὴν
βασιλείαν ἡ διὰ Μωυσέως περιγραφὴν ἐλάμβανεν
προφητεία " οὐκ ἐκλείψειν ἄρχοντα ἐξ Ἰούδα οὐδὲ
ἡγούμενον ἐκ τῶν μηρῶν αὐτοῦ" φήσασα, " ἕως
ἂν ἔλθῃ ᾧ ἀπόκειται," ὃν καὶ ἀποφαίνει προσ- 2
δοκίαν ἔσεσθαι ἐθνῶν. ἀτελῆ γέ τοι τὰ τῆς προρ-

days of the census, and led away the people after him and he perished and all who obeyed him were scattered." In agreement with this, in the eighteenth book of the *Antiquities* the writer referred to also gives the following details: " And Quirinius, one of those called to the Senate, who had filled the other offices and passed through all of them to become Consul, and was otherwise of high rank, reached Syria with a small staff, having been sent by Caesar to administer the people and to make a valuation of their property." And a little later he says, " And Judas, the Gaulonite, of the city called Gamala, took with him Zadok, a Pharisee, and instigated a revolt, for they said that the valuation led to nothing but plain slavery, and they called on the people to rally for liberty." And in the second book of the *History of the Jewish War* he writes concerning the same man, " At this time a Galilean called Judas incited the inhabitants to revolt, calling them cowards to suffer the payment of tribute to the Romans, and after serving God to endure mortal masters." So far Josephus.

VI. Now at this time, when Herod was the first foreigner to hold the sovereignty of the Jewish nation, the prophecy made through Moses that " A ruler shall not fail from Judah nor a leader from his loins until he come for whom it is reserved "[1] began to be fulfilled. Moses also shows that this one will be the " expectation of the Gentiles." Obviously the terms of the prediction were unfulfilled so long

---

[1] The Hebrew text of this passage is, accurately rendered, " until Shiloh come," but has no discoverable meaning. The text of the LXX. varies between " until there come him for whom it is reserved " and " until there come the things reserved for him."

49

ρήσεως ἦν καθ᾽ ὃν ὑπὸ τοῖς οἰκείοις τοῦ ἔθνους
ἄρχουσι διάγειν αὐτοῖς ἐξῆν χρόνον, ἄνωθεν ἐξ
αὐτοῦ Μωυσέως καταρξαμένοις καὶ εἰς τὴν Αὐγούστου βασιλείαν διαρκέσασιν, καθ᾽ ὃν πρῶτος
ἀλλόφυλος Ἡρώδης τὴν κατὰ Ἰουδαίων ἐπι-
τρέπεται ὑπὸ Ῥωμαίων ἀρχήν, ὡς μὲν Ἰώσηπος
παραδίδωσιν, Ἰδουμαῖος ὢν κατὰ πατέρα τὸ γένος
Ἀράβιος δὲ κατὰ μητέρα, ὡς δ᾽ Ἀφρικανός (οὐχ
ὁ τυχὼν δὲ καὶ οὗτος γέγονε συγγραφεύς), φασὶν
οἱ τὰ κατ᾽ αὐτὸν ἀκριβοῦντες Ἀντίπατρον (τοῦτον
δ᾽ εἶναι αὐτῷ πατέρα) Ἡρώδου τινὸς Ἀσκαλω-
νίτου τῶν περὶ τὸν νεὼ τοῦ Ἀπόλλωνος ἱερο-
δούλων καλουμένων γεγονέναι· ὃς Ἀντίπατρος ὑπὸ 3
Ἰδουμαίων λῃστῶν παιδίον αἰχμαλωτισθεὶς σὺν
ἐκείνοις ἦν, διὰ τὸ μὴ δύνασθαι τὸν πατέρα πτωχὸν
ὄντα καταθέσθαι ὑπὲρ αὐτοῦ, ἐντραφεὶς δὲ τοῖς
ἐκείνων ἔθεσιν ὕστερον Ὑρκανῷ τῷ Ἰουδαίων
ἀρχιερεῖ φιλοῦται. τούτου γίνεται ὁ ἐπὶ τοῦ
σωτῆρος ἡμῶν Ἡρώδης. εἰς δὴ οὖν τὸν τοιοῦτον 4
τῆς Ἰουδαίων περιελθούσης βασιλείας, ἐπὶ θύραις
ἤδη καὶ ἡ τῶν ἐθνῶν ἀκολούθως τῇ προφητείᾳ
προσδοκία παρῆν, ἅτε διαλελοιπότων ἐξ ἐκείνου
τῶν παρ᾽ αὐτοῖς ἐξ αὐτοῦ Μωυσέως κατὰ διαδοχὴν
ἀρξάντων τε καὶ ἡγησαμένων. πρὸ μέν γε τῆς 5
αἰχμαλωσίας αὐτῶν καὶ τῆς εἰς Βαβυλῶνα μετανα-
στάσεως ἐβασιλεύοντο, ἀπὸ Σαοὺλ πρώτου καὶ
Δαυὶδ ἀρξάμενοι· πρὸ δὲ τῶν βασιλέων ἄρχοντες
αὐτοὺς διεῖπον, οἱ προσαγορευόμενοι κριταί, ἄρξαν-
τες καὶ αὐτοὶ μετὰ Μωυσέα καὶ τὸν τούτου διάδοχον
Ἰησοῦν· μετὰ δὲ τὴν ἀπὸ Βαβυλῶνος ἐπάνοδον 6
οὐ διέλιπον πολιτείᾳ χρώμενοι ἀριστοκρατικῇ μετὰ
ὀλιγαρχίας (οἱ γὰρ ἱερεῖς προεστήκεσαν τῶν

Joseph, A.I.
14, 8. 121.
B.I. 1, 123.
181

Joseph. A.I.
11, 112. 111

as it was possible for the Jews to live under the native rulers of the nation, beginning with Moses himself and lasting down to the reign of Augustus ; but in his time the first foreigner, Herod, was entrusted by the Romans with the government of the Jews. He was, as Josephus relates, an Idumaean on his father's side and an Arab on his mother's, but according to Africanus (nor was he any ordinary historian) those who give accurate information concerning Herod say that Antipater (he was his father) was the son of a certain Herod of Ascalon, and one of those called *hierodouloi* [1] in the temple of Apollo. This Antipater was captured as a child by Idumaean brigands, and stayed with them because his father was unable on account of poverty to pay ransom for him. He was brought up in their customs and later on was befriended by Hyrcanus the high priest of the Jews. His child was the Herod of our Saviour's time. When therefore the kingdom of the Jews came to such a man as this the expectation of the Gentiles, in accordance with the prophecy, was already at the door, inasmuch as the succession from Moses of rulers and governors ceased with him. Before their captivity and removal to Babylon, kings had ruled them, beginning with Saul, the first king, and David ; and before the kings, rulers called judges administered them and these began after Moses and his successor, Joshua. After the return from Babylon a constitution of oligarchic aristocracy was continuous (for the

[1] That is " temple servants " : their functions were various.

πραγμάτων), ἄχρι οὗ Πομπήιος Ῥωμαίων στρατηγὸς ἐπιστὰς τὴν μὲν Ἱερουσαλὴμ πολιορκεῖ
κατὰ κράτος μιαίνει τε τὰ ἅγια μέχρι τῶν ἀδύτων
τοῦ ἱεροῦ προελθών, τὸν δ᾽ ἐκ προγόνων διαδοχῆς
εἰς ἐκεῖνο τοῦ καιροῦ διαρκέσαντα βασιλέα τε
ὁμοῦ καὶ ἀρχιερέα, Ἀριστόβουλος ὄνομα ἦν αὐτῷ,
δέσμιον ἐπὶ Ῥώμης ἅμα τέκνοις ἐκπέμψας,
Ὑρκανῷ μὲν τῷ τούτου ἀδελφῷ τὴν ἀρχιερωσύνην
παραδίδωσιν, τὸ δὲ πᾶν Ἰουδαίων ἔθνος ἐξ ἐκείνου
Ῥωμαίοις ὑπόφορον κατεστήσατο. αὐτίκα γοῦν καὶ 7
Ὑρκανοῦ, εἰς ὃν ὕστατον τὰ τῆς τῶν ἀρχιερέων
περιέστη διαδοχῆς, ὑπὸ Πάρθων αἰχμαλώτου
ληφθέντος, πρῶτος, ὡς γοῦν ἔφην, ἀλλόφυλος
Ἡρῴδης ὑπὸ τῆς συγκλήτου Ῥωμαίων Αὐγούστου
τε βασιλέως τὸ Ἰουδαίων ἔθνος ἐγχειρίζεται, καθ᾽ 8
ὃν ἐναργῶς τῆς τοῦ Χριστοῦ παρουσίας ἐνστάσης,
καὶ τῶν ἐθνῶν ἡ προσδοκωμένη σωτηρία τε καὶ
κλῆσις ἀκολούθως τῇ προφητείᾳ παρηκολούθησεν·
ἐξ οὗ δὴ χρόνου τῶν ἀπὸ Ἰούδα ἀρχόντων τε καὶ
ἡγουμένων, λέγω δὲ τῶν ἐκ τοῦ Ἰουδαίων ἔθνους,
διαλελοιπότων, εἰκότως αὐτοῖς καὶ τὰ τῆς ἐκ
προγόνων εὐσταθῶς ἐπὶ τοὺς ἔγγιστα διαδόχους
κατὰ γενεὰν προϊούσης ἀρχιερωσύνης παραχρῆμα
συγχεῖται. ἔχεις καὶ τούτων ἀξιόχρεων τὸν 9

Joseph. A.I.
20, 247. 249 Ἰώσηπον μάρτυρα, δηλοῦντα ὡς τὴν βασιλείαν
παρὰ Ῥωμαίων ἐπιτραπεὶς Ἡρῴδης οὐκέτι τοὺς
ἐξ ἀρχαίου γένους καθίστησιν ἀρχιερεῖς, ἀλλά
τισιν ἀσήμοις τὴν τιμὴν ἀπένεμεν· τὰ ὅμοια δὲ
πρᾶξαι τῷ Ἡρῴδῃ περὶ τῆς καταστάσεως τῶν
ἱερέων Ἀρχέλαόν τε τὸν παῖδα αὐτοῦ καὶ μετὰ
τοῦτον Ῥωμαίους, τὴν ἀρχὴν τῶν Ἰουδαίων
παρειληφότας. ὁ δ᾽ αὐτὸς δηλοῖ ὡς ἄρα καὶ τὴν 10

priests were at the head of affairs), until Pompey, a Roman general, attacked Jerusalem, besieged it in force, and defiled the holy places by intruding into the secret parts of the temple. He sent to Rome as a prisoner with his children the king and high priest, Aristobulus by name, who had continued the succession of his ancestors until then. To Hyrcanus, the brother of Aristobulus, he handed over the high-priesthood, but made the whole nation of the Jews from that time tributary to the Romans. As soon as Hyrcanus, the last to whom belonged the high-priestly succession, was taken prisoner by the Parthians, Herod, the first foreigner, as I just said, was entrusted with the nation of the Jews by the Senate of the Romans and the Emperor Augustus. The advent of the Christ clearly came in his time, and thus the expected salvation and calling of the Gentiles followed consistently with the prophecy ; moreover, from the time when the rulers and governors from Judah, that is to say those of the Jewish race, had ceased, immediate confusion naturally ensued in the affairs of the priesthood which passed steadily to the nearest heirs from generation to generation from the ancestors. Of this, too, you have Josephus as a valuable witness, for he explains how Herod, when he was entrusted with the kingdom by the Romans, no longer appointed high priests of the ancient race but assigned the honour to certain obscure persons ; and that Herod's policy with regard to the appointment of the priests was followed by his son Archelaus, and after him by the Romans, when they took over the government of the Jews. The same writer explains how Herod

ἱερὰν στολὴν τοῦ ἀρχιερέως πρῶτος Ἡρώδης
ἀποκλείσας ὑπὸ ἰδίαν σφραγῖδα πεποίηται, μηκέτ'
αὐτὴν τοῖς ἀρχιερεῦσιν ἔχειν ὑφ' ἑαυτοὺς ἐπιτρέψας·
ταὐτὸν δὲ καὶ τὸν μετ' αὐτὸν Ἀρχέλαον καὶ μετὰ
τοῦτον Ῥωμαίους διαπράξασθαι. καὶ ταῦτα δ' 11
ἡμῖν εἰρήσθω εἰς ἑτέρας ἀπόδειξιν προφητείας
κατὰ τὴν ἐπιφάνειαν τοῦ σωτῆρος ἡμῶν Ἰησοῦ
Χριστοῦ πεπερασμένης. σαφέστατα γοῦν ἐν τῷ

Dan. 9, 24-
27

Δανιὴλ ἑβδομάδων τινῶν ἀριθμὸν ὀνομαστὶ ἕως
Χριστοῦ ἡγουμένου περιλαβὼν ὁ λόγος, περὶ ὧν
ἐν ἑτέροις διειλήφαμεν, μετὰ τὸ τούτων συμπέρασμα
ἐξολοθρευθήσεσθαι τὸ παρὰ Ἰουδαίοις χρῖσμα
προφητεύει· καὶ τοῦτο δὲ σαφῶς κατὰ τὸν καιρὸν
τῆς τοῦ σωτῆρος ἡμῶν Ἰησοῦ Χριστοῦ γενέσεως
ἀποδείκνυται συμπεπληρωμένον. ταῦτα δ' ἡμῖν
ἀναγκαίως εἰς παράστασιν τῆς τῶν χρόνων ἀληθείας προτετηρήσθω.

VII. Ἐπειδὴ δὲ τὴν περὶ τοῦ Χριστοῦ γενεαλογίαν 1
διαφόρως ἡμῖν ὅ τε Ματθαῖος καὶ ὁ Λουκᾶς
εὐαγγελιζόμενοι παραδεδώκασι διαφωνεῖν τε νομί-
ζονται τοῖς πολλοῖς τῶν τε πιστῶν ἕκαστος
ἀγνοίᾳ τἀληθοῦς εὑρεσιλογεῖν εἰς τοὺς τόπους
πεφιλοτίμηται, φέρε, καὶ τὴν περὶ τούτων κατ-
ελθοῦσαν εἰς ἡμᾶς ἱστορίαν παραθώμεθα, ἣν δι'
ἐπιστολῆς Ἀριστείδῃ γράφων περὶ συμφωνίας
τῆς ἐν τοῖς εὐαγγελίοις γενεαλογίας ὁ μικρῷ
πρόσθεν ἡμῖν δηλωθεὶς Ἀφρικανὸς ἐμνημόνευσεν,
τὰς μὲν δὴ τῶν λοιπῶν δόξας ὡς ἂν βιαίους καὶ
διεψευσμένας ἀπελέγξας, ἣν δ' αὐτὸς παρείληφεν
ἱστορίαν τούτοις αὐτοῖς ἐκτιθέμενος τοῖς ῥήμασιν·

" Ἐπειδὴ γὰρ τὰ ὀνόματα τῶν γενῶν ἐν Ἰσραὴλ 2
ἠριθμεῖτο ἢ φύσει ἢ νόμῳ, φύσει μέν, γνησίου

was the first to lock up and keep under his own seal
the sacred robe of the high priest, for he no longer
allowed the high priests to keep it in their own
charge, and his successor, Archelaus, and after him
the Romans, pursued the same policy. These facts
may also serve us as proof of the fulfilment of
another prophecy on the manifestation of our Saviour
Jesus Christ. It is quite obvious that in Daniel
the text defines the number of certain weeks, which
I have treated of elsewhere, in so many words as
" until Christ the ruler," and prophesies that after
the accomplishment of these weeks the anointing
among the Jews shall be destroyed. The fulfilment
of this at the time of the birth of our Saviour
Jesus Christ is clearly demonstrated. These points
must suffice as preliminary observations necessary
to establish the truth of the date.

VII. Since Matthew and Luke, having given us
different traditions in their gospels concerning the
genealogy of Christ, are considered by many to
disagree ; and since each of the faithful in ignorance
of the truth has been zealous in making guesses
on these passages, come, let us set out the
story that has reached us concerning them, which
the Africanus mentioned by us a short time ago
narrated in a letter which he wrote to Aristides on
the harmony of the genealogies in the Gospels,
confuting the opinions of others as forced and
fictitious and setting out his own traditions in the
following words : " Since the names of the families
in Israel were numbered either by nature or by law ;

σπέρματος διαδοχῇ, νόμῳ δέ, ἑτέρου παιδοποιου-
μένου εἰς ὄνομα τελευτήσαντος ἀδελφοῦ ἀτέκνου
(ὅτι γὰρ οὐδέπω δέδοτο ἐλπὶς ἀναστάσεως σαφής,
τὴν μέλλουσαν ἐπαγγελίαν ἀναστάσει ἐμιμοῦντο
θνητῇ, ἵνα ἀνέκλειπτον τὸ ὄνομα μείνῃ τοῦ μετ-
ηλλαχότος)· ἐπεὶ οὖν οἱ τῇ γενεαλογίᾳ ταύτῃ 3
ἐμφερόμενοι, οἱ μὲν διεδέξαντο παῖς πατέρα
γνησίως, οἱ δὲ ἑτέροις μὲν ἐγεννήθησαν, ἑτέροις
δὲ προσετέθησαν κλήσει, ἀμφοτέρων γέγονεν ἡ
μνήμη, καὶ τῶν γεγεννηκότων καὶ τῶν ὡς γεγεννηκότων. οὕτως οὐδέτερον τῶν εὐαγγελίων
ψεύδεται, καὶ φύσιν ἀριθμοῦν καὶ νόμον. ἐπεπλάκη 4
γὰρ ἀλλήλοις τὰ γένη, τό τε ἀπὸ τοῦ Σολομῶνος
καὶ τὸ ἀπὸ τοῦ Ναθάν, ἀναστάσεσιν ἀτέκνων καὶ
δευτερογαμίαις καὶ ἀναστάσει σπερμάτων, ὡς
δικαίως τοὺς αὐτοὺς ἄλλοτε ἄλλων νομίζεσθαι,
τῶν μὲν δοκούντων πατέρων, τῶν δὲ ὑπαρχόντων·
ὡς ἀμφοτέρας τὰς διηγήσεις κυρίως ἀληθεῖς
οὔσας ἐπὶ τὸν Ἰωσὴφ πολυπλόκως μέν, ἀλλ᾽
ἀκριβῶς κατελθεῖν. ἵνα δὲ σαφὲς ᾖ τὸ λεγό- 5
μενον, τὴν ἐναλλαγὴν τῶν γενῶν διηγήσομαι.
ἀπὸ τοῦ Δαυὶδ διὰ Σολομῶνος τὰς γενεὰς καταρι-

---

[1] This is the only possible translation of the Greek; but
it appears to be a mistake in copying on the part of Eusebius,
and according to cod. *q* of the *Quaestiones ad Stephanum*
(Mai, *Nova patrum bibl.* iv. 231 f.) Africanus wrote " the
deaths of the childless."

[2] The point of this obscure argument is that among the
Jews if a man died childless his brother was charged with
the duty of begetting children by the widow, who was still
reckoned as the wife of the deceased. Such children were
legally regarded as the sons of the dead brother, though
known to be actually the children of the living one. This

by nature, in the succession of legitimate birth; by law, when a man begat children in the name of a brother who had died childless; for because no certain hope of resurrection had as yet been given they portrayed the future promise by a mortal resurrection, in order that the name of him who had passed away might not fail to remain. Since then by following this kind of genealogy some succeeded in the legitimate order of father and son, but others were reckoned in name to one father though the children of another, the memory of both was retained, both of the actual and of the fictitious parents. Thus neither of the Gospels misstates, reckoning both nature and law. For the two families, the one descended from Solomon and the other from Nathan, were connected with each other by the ' resurrections ' [1] of the childless and second marriages and the raising up of seed, so that the same persons could be correctly regarded as the children of different persons at different times, either of their fictitious or of their real fathers. Thus both accounts are strictly true in coming down to Joseph in a manner complicated but accurate. In order that what has been said may be clear I will explain the relation of the families.[2] Reckoning the generations from David through Solomon the third from

happened in the case of Joseph. He was legally the son of Eli, physically of Jacob. A further complication was that Eli and Jacob were only half brothers. They were the sons of the same mother, Estha, but Eli was the son of her second husband, Melchi, descended from Nathan the son of David, and Jacob was the son of her first husband Matthan, descended from Solomon the son of David. Thus Matthew giving the physical descent of Jesus traces it through Jacob to Solomon, but Luke (who avoids the word " begat ") giving the legal descent traces it through Eli to Nathan.

57

Matt. 1, 15. 16 θμουμένοις τρίτος ἀπὸ τέλους εὑρίσκεται Ματθάν,
ὃς ἐγέννησε τὸν Ἰακώβ, τοῦ Ἰωσὴφ τὸν πατέρα·
Luke 3, 23. 24 ἀπὸ δὲ Ναθὰν τοῦ Δαυὶδ κατὰ Λουκᾶν ὁμοίως
τρίτος ἀπὸ τέλους Μελχί· Ἰωσὴφ γὰρ υἱὸς Ἡλὶ
τοῦ Μελχί. σκοποῦ τοίνυν ἡμῖν κειμένου τοῦ 6
Ἰωσήφ, ἀποδεικτέον πῶς ἑκάτερος αὐτοῦ πατὴρ
ἱστορεῖται, ὅ τε Ἰακὼβ ὁ ἀπὸ Σολομῶνος καὶ Ἡλὶ
ὁ ἀπὸ τοῦ Ναθὰν ἑκάτερος κατάγοντες γένος,
ὅπως τε πρότερον οὗτοι δή, ὅ τε Ἰακὼβ καὶ ὁ
Ἡλί, δύο ἀδελφοί, καὶ πρό γε, πῶς οἱ τούτων
πατέρες, Ματθὰν καὶ Μελχί, διαφόρων ὄντες γενῶν,
τοῦ Ἰωσὴφ ἀναφαίνονται πάπποι. καὶ δὴ οὖν 7
ὅ τε Ματθὰν καὶ ὁ Μελχί, ἐν μέρει τὴν αὐτὴν
ἀγαγόμενοι γυναῖκα, ὁμομητρίους ἀδελφοὺς ἐπαιδοποιήσαντο, τοῦ νόμου μὴ κωλύοντος χηρεύουσαν,
ἤτοι ἀπολελυμένην ἢ καὶ τελευτήσαντος τοῦ
ἀνδρός, ἄλλῳ γαμεῖσθαι· ἐκ δὴ τῆς Ἐσθὰ (τοῦτο 8
γὰρ καλεῖσθαι τὴν γυναῖκα παραδέδοται) πρῶτος
Ματθάν, ὁ ἀπὸ τοῦ Σολομῶνος τὸ γένος κατάγων,
τὸν Ἰακὼβ γεννᾷ, καὶ τελευτήσαντος τοῦ Ματθὰν
Μελχί, ὁ ἐπὶ τὸν Ναθὰν κατὰ γένος ἀναφερόμενος,
χηρεύουσαν, ἐκ μὲν τῆς αὐτῆς φυλῆς, ἐξ ἄλλου
δὲ γένους ὤν, ὡς προεῖπον, ἀγαγόμενος αὐτήν,
ἔσχεν υἱὸν τὸν Ἡλί. οὕτω δὴ διαφόρων δύο 9
γενῶν εὑρήσομεν τόν τε Ἰακὼβ καὶ τὸν Ἡλὶ
ὁμομητρίους ἀδελφούς, ὧν ὁ ἕτερος, Ἰακώβ,
ἀτέκνου τοῦ ἀδελφοῦ τελευτήσαντος Ἡλί, τὴν
γυναῖκα παραλαβών, ἐγέννησεν ἐξ αὐτῆς τρίτον
τὸν Ἰωσήφ, κατὰ φύσιν μὲν ἑαυτῷ (καὶ κατὰ
Matt. 1, 16 λόγον, δι' ὃ γέγραπται ' Ἰακὼβ δὲ ἐγέννησεν
τὸν Ἰωσήφ '), κατὰ νόμον δὲ τοῦ Ἡλὶ υἱὸς ἦν·
ἐκείνῳ γὰρ ὁ Ἰακώβ, ἀδελφὸς ὤν, ἀνέστησεν

58

the end is found to be Matthan who begat Jacob
the father of Joseph ; but from Nathan, the son of
David, according to Luke, the corresponding third
from the end is Melchi ; for Joseph was a son of
Eli the son of Melchi. So then fixing our attention
on Joseph, it must be demonstrated how each is
called his father, Jacob tracing his family from
Solomon and Eli from Nathan, and how first they,
that is Jacob and Eli, were two brothers, and, still
earlier, how their fathers, Matthan and Melchi,
belonging to different families, are represented as
the grandfathers of Joseph. Now Matthan and
Melchi, inasmuch as they took the same wife, were
the fathers of step-brothers, for the law does not
prevent a woman who has lost her husband either by
her own divorce or by his death from being married
to another. Now from Estha, for this is the traditional name of the woman, first Matthan, who
reckoned his descent from Solomon, begat Jacob
and when Matthan was dead, Melchi, who traced
himself by family to Nathan, took his widow, for he
was of the same tribe though of another family,
as I said before, and had a son, Eli. Thus we shall
find that though the two families were different
Jacob and Eli were step-brothers of the same mother,
and the first of them, Jacob, when his brother Eli
died without children, took his wife, and begat of
her the third,[1] Joseph, according to nature, for
himself (and so also according to reason, for which
cause it is written, ' And Jacob begat Joseph '),
but according to law he was the son of Eli, for
to him Jacob, being his brother, raised up

---

[1] That is, the third from Estha.

EUSEBIUS

σπέρμα. δι' ὅπερ οὐκ ἀκυρωθήσεται καὶ ἡ κατ'
αὐτὸν γενεαλογία· ἦν Ματθαῖος μὲν ὁ εὐαγγελιστὴς 10
ἐξαριθμούμενος ' Ἰακὼβ δέ' φησίν ' ἐγέννησεν
τὸν Ἰωσήφ,' ὁ δὲ Λουκᾶς ἀνάπαλιν ' ὃς ἦν, ὡς
ἐνομίζετο (καὶ γὰρ καὶ τοῦτο προστίθησιν) τοῦ
Ἰωσὴφ τοῦ Ἡλὶ τοῦ Μελχί.' τὴν γὰρ κατὰ νόμον
γένεσιν ἐπισημότερον οὐκ ἦν ἐξειπεῖν, καὶ τὸ
' ἐγέννησεν' ἐπὶ τῆς τοιᾶσδε παιδοποιίας ἄχρι
τέλους ἐσιώπησεν, τὴν ἀναφορὰν ποιησάμενος
ἕως ' τοῦ Ἀδὰμ τοῦ θεοῦ' κατ' ἀνάλυσιν. οὐδὲ 11
μὴν ἀναπόδεικτον ἢ ἐσχεδιασμένον ἐστὶν τοῦτο.
τοῦ γοῦν σωτῆρος οἱ κατὰ σάρκα συγγενεῖς, εἴτ'
οὖν φανητιῶντες εἴθ' ἁπλῶς ἐκδιδάσκοντες, πάντως
δὲ ἀληθεύοντες, παρέδοσαν καὶ ταῦτα· ὡς Ἰδου-
μαῖοι λῃσταὶ Ἀσκάλωνι πόλει τῆς Παλαιστίνης
ἐπελθόντες, ἐξ εἰδωλείου Ἀπόλλωνος, ὃ πρὸς
τοῖς τείχεσιν ἵδρυτο, Ἀντίπατρον Ἡρώδου τινὸς
ἱεροδούλου παῖδα πρὸς τοῖς ἄλλοις σύλοις αἰχμά-
λωτον ἀπῆγον, τῷ δὲ λύτρα ὑπὲρ τοῦ υἱοῦ καταθέσθαι μὴ δύνασθαι τὸν ἱερέα ὁ Ἀντίπατρος τοῖς
τῶν Ἰδουμαίων ἔθεσιν ἐντραφείς, ὕστερον Ὑρκανῷ
φιλοῦται τῷ τῆς Ἰουδαίας ἀρχιερεῖ· πρεσβεύσας 12
δὲ πρὸς Πομπήιον ὑπὲρ τοῦ Ὑρκανοῦ καὶ τὴν
βασιλείαν ἐλευθερώσας αὐτῷ ὑπὸ Ἀριστοβούλου
τοῦ ἀδελφοῦ περικοπτομένην, αὐτὸς ηὐτύχησεν,
ἐπιμελητὴς τῆς Παλαιστίνης χρηματίσας· διαδέχεται δὲ τὸν Ἀντίπατρον, φθόνῳ τῆς πολλῆς
εὐτυχίας δολοφονηθέντα, υἱὸς Ἡρῴδης, ὃς ὕστερον
ὑπ' Ἀντωνίου καὶ τοῦ σεβαστοῦ συγκλήτου
δόγματι τῶν Ἰουδαίων ἐκρίθη βασιλεύειν· οὗ
παῖδες Ἡρῴδης οἵ τ' ἄλλοι τετράρχαι. ταῦτα

---
[1] i.e. Herod the Great.

seed. Wherefore the genealogy concerning him will not be inaccurate. Matthew, the evangelist, reckoned it in this way, saying, ' And Jacob begat Joseph,' but Luke, on the other hand, said, ' Who was, as it was supposed ' (for he adds this also), ' the son of Joseph, the son of Eli, the son of Melchi,' for it was impossible to express legal descent more pointedly, and up to the end he suppressed the word ' begat ' concerning such raising of children, for he traces the list back to its source with ' Adam the son of God.' This is neither devoid of proof, nor is it conjecture, for the human relatives of the Saviour have handed on this tradition, either from family pride, or merely to give information, but in any case speaking the truth. When Idumaean brigands attacked the city of Ascalon in Palestine among their other spoils they took away captive from the temple of Apollo, which was built on the walls, Antipater the child of a certain Herod, a *hierodoulos*, and since the priest was unable to pay ransom for his son, Antipater was brought up in the customs of the Idumaeans and later was befriended by Hyrcanus the high priest of Judaea. When sent on a mission to Pompey on behalf of Hyrcanus he won for him the freedom of the kingdom which had been taken away by his brother Aristobulus, and so was himself fortunate enough to gain the title of overseer of Palestine. Antipater was assassinated from envy of his great good fortune, and succeeded by a son Herod,[1] who later was appointed by Antony and by decree of the august Senate to be king of the Jews. His children were Herod[2] and the other tetrarchs. So much is shared

---

[2] *i.e.* Herod Antipas and his brothers.

μὲν δὴ κοινὰ καὶ ταῖς Ἑλλήνων ἱστορίαις· ἀνα- 13
γράπτων δὲ εἰς τότε ἐν τοῖς ἀρχείοις ὄντων τῶν
Ἑβραϊκῶν γενῶν καὶ τῶν ἄχρι προσηλύτων
ἀναφερομένων, ὡς Ἀχιὼρ τοῦ Ἀμμανίτου καὶ
Ῥοὺθ τῆς Μωαβίτιδος, τῶν τε ἀπ' Αἰγύπτου
συνεκπεσόντων ἐπιμίκτων, ὁ Ἡρῴδης, οὐδέν τι
συμβαλλομένου τοῦ τῶν Ἰσραηλιτῶν γένους αὐτῷ
καὶ τῷ συνειδότι τῆς δυσγενείας κρουόμενος,
ἐνέπρησεν αὐτῶν τὰς ἀναγραφὰς τῶν γενῶν,
οἰόμενος εὐγενὴς ἀναφανεῖσθαι τῷ μηδ' ἄλλον
ἔχειν ἐκ δημοσίου συγγραφῆς τὸ γένος ἀνάγειν
ἐπὶ τοὺς πατριάρχας ἢ προσηλύτους τούς τε
καλουμένους γειώρας, τοὺς ἐπιμίκτους. ὀλίγοι δὴ 14
τῶν ἐπιμελῶν, ἰδιωτικὰς ἑαυτοῖς ἀπογραφὰς ἢ
μνημονεύσαντες τῶν ὀνομάτων ἢ ἄλλως ἔχοντες
ἐξ ἀντιγράφων, ἐναβρύνονται σῳζομένῃ τῇ μνήμῃ
τῆς εὐγενείας· ὧν ἐτύγχανον οἱ προειρημένοι,
δεσπόσυνοι καλούμενοι διὰ τὴν πρὸς τὸ σωτήριον
γένος συνάφειαν ἀπό τε Ναζάρων καὶ Κωχάβα
κωμῶν Ἰουδαϊκῶν τῇ λοιπῇ γῇ ἐπιφοιτήσαντες
καὶ τὴν προκειμένην γενεαλογίαν ἔκ τε τῆς Βίβλου
τῶν ἡμερῶν, ἐς ὅσον ἐξικνοῦντο, ἐξηγησάμενοι.
εἴτ' οὖν οὕτως εἴτ' ἄλλως ἔχοι, σαφεστέραν
ἐξήγησιν οὐκ ἂν ἔχοι τις ἄλλος ἐξευρεῖν, ὡς
ἔγωγε νομίζω πᾶς τε ὃς εὐγνώμων τυγχάνει, καὶ
ἡμῖν αὕτη μελέτω, εἰ καὶ ἀμάρτυρός ἐστιν,
τῷ μὴ κρείττονα ἢ ἀληθεστέραν ἔχειν εἰπεῖν·
τό γέ τοι εὐαγγέλιον πάντως ἀληθεύει.'' καὶ
ἐπὶ τέλει δὲ τῆς αὐτῆς ἐπιστολῆς προστίθησι
ταῦτα· '' Ματθὰν ὁ ἀπὸ Σολομῶνος ἐγέννησε τὸν

Judith 14, 10
Exod. 12, 38
Deut. 23, 8

with the histories of the Greeks also. But since the
Hebrew families and those traceable to proselytes,
such as Achior the Ammonite, and Ruth the Moabi-
tess, and the mixed families which had come out of
Egypt, had until then been enrolled in the archives,
Herod, because the family of the Israelites contri-
buted nothing to him, and because he was goaded
by his own consciousness of his base birth, burned
the records of their families, thinking to appear
noble if no one else was able by public documents
to trace his family to the patriarchs or proselytes,
or to the so-called *gers* [1] of mixed descent. Now
a few who were careful, having private records for
themselves, either remembering the names or
otherwise deriving them from copies, gloried in
the preservation of the memory of their good birth ;
among these were those mentioned above, called
desposyni, because of their relation to the family
of the Saviour,[2] and from the Jewish villages of
Nazareth and Cochaba they traversed the rest of
the land and expounded the preceding genealogy
of their descent, and from the book of Chronicles
so far as they went.[3] Whether this be so or
not no one could give a clearer account, in my
opinion and in that of all well-disposed persons, and
it may suffice us even though it is not corroborated,
since we have nothing better or truer to say : in
any case the gospel speaks the truth." And at
the end of the same letter Africanus adds this :
" Matthan of the line of Solomon begat Jacob.[4] On

---

[1] A Hellenized form of the Hebrew word translated
" stranger " in the phrase the " stranger within the gates."
[2] Because he is the Lord or " Despot."
[3] Literally " the book of days "—from the Hebrew.
[4] *Cf.* Eusebius, *Quaest. ad Steph.* pp. 232 and 224.

Ἰακώβ. Ματθὰν ἀποθανόντος, Μελχὶ ὁ ἀπὸ Ναθὰν ἐκ τῆς αὐτῆς γυναικὸς ἐγέννησε τὸν Ἡλί. ὁμομήτριοι ἄρα ἀδελφοὶ Ἡλὶ καὶ Ἰακώβ. Ἡλὶ ἀτέκνου ἀποθανόντος ὁ Ἰακὼβ ἀνέστησεν αὐτῷ σπέρμα, γεννήσας τὸν Ἰωσήφ, κατὰ φύσιν μὲν ἑαυτῷ, κατὰ νόμον δὲ τῷ Ἡλί. οὕτως ἀμφοτέρων ἦν υἱὸς ὁ Ἰωσήφ."

Τοσαῦτα ὁ Ἀφρικανός. καὶ δὴ τοῦ Ἰωσὴφ 17 ὧδέ πως γενεαλογουμένου, δυνάμει καὶ ἡ Μαρία σὺν αὐτῷ πέφηνεν ἐκ τῆς αὐτῆς οὖσα φυλῆς, εἴ γε κατὰ τὸν Μωυσέως νόμον οὐκ ἐξῆν ἑτέραις Num. 36, 8. 9 ἐπιμίγνυσθαι φυλαῖς· ἑνὶ γὰρ τῶν ἐκ τοῦ αὐτοῦ δήμου καὶ πατριᾶς τῆς αὐτῆς ζεύγνυσθαι πρὸς γάμον παρακελεύεται, ὡς ἂν μὴ περιστρέφοιτο τοῦ γένους ὁ κλῆρος ἀπὸ φυλῆς ἐπὶ φυλήν. ὡδὶ μὲν οὖν καὶ ταῦτα ἐχέτω.

VIII. Ἀλλὰ γὰρ τοῦ Χριστοῦ γεννηθέντος ταῖς 1 προφητείαις ἀκολούθως ἐν Βηθλεὲμ τῆς Ἰουδαίας κατὰ τοὺς δεδηλωμένους χρόνους, Ἡρώδης ἐπὶ τῇ τῶν ἐξ ἀνατολῆς μάγων ἀνερωτήσει ὅπη εἴη διαπυνθανομένων ὁ τεχθεὶς βασιλεὺς τῶν Ἰουδαίων, ἑορακέναι γὰρ αὐτοῦ τὸν ἀστέρα καὶ τῆς τοσῆσδε πορείας τοῦτ᾽ αἴτιον αὐτοῖς γεγονέναι, οἷα θεῷ προσκυνῆσαι τῷ τεχθέντι διὰ σπουδῆς πεποιημένοις, οὐ σμικρῶς ἐπὶ τῷ πράγματι, ἅτε κινδυνευούσης, ὥς γε δὴ ᾤετο, αὐτῷ τῆς ἀρχῆς, διακινηθείς, πυθόμενος τῶν παρὰ τῷ ἔθνει νομοδιδασκάλων ποῦ τὸν Χριστὸν γεννηθήσεσθαι προσ- Mich. 5, 2 δοκῶεν, ὡς ἔγνω τὴν Μιχαίου προφητείαν ἐν Βηθλεὲμ προαναφωνοῦσαν, ἑνὶ προστάγματι τοὺς ὑπομαζίους ἔν τε τῇ Βηθλεὲμ καὶ πᾶσι τοῖς ὁρίοις αὐτῆς ἀπὸ διετοῦς καὶ κατωτέρω παῖδας, κατὰ

the death of Matthan, Melchi of the line of Nathan begat Eli from the same woman. Thus Eli and Jacob were step-brothers with the same mother. When Eli died without children, Jacob raised up seed for him, begetting Joseph as his own natural son but the legal son of Eli. Thus Joseph was son of both." Thus far Africanus. Now since this was the nature of the genealogy of Joseph, it is potential proof that Mary belonged to the same tribe as he, seeing that according to the law of Moses, it was not lawful for the different tribes to mix, for the command is given to join in marriage with one of the same people and same family, in order that the inheritance of the race might not be changed from tribe to tribe. Thus let this suffice on this point.

VIII. Now when Christ was born, in accordance with the prophecy, at Bethlehem of Judaea at the time mentioned, Herod was asked by the Magi from the East where might he be who was born king of the Jews, for they had seen his star, and this had been the cause of their long journey in their zeal to worship the infant as God. The request caused him to be not a little disturbed at the situation for, as he thought, his sovereignty was in danger. He therefore inquired from the teachers of the Law among the people where they expected the Christ to be born, and when he learnt the prophecy of Micah, foretelling that it should be in Bethlehem, he gave a comprehensive order to put to death all the infants which were being nursed in Bethlehem and the whole neighbourhood, of two years old and less, according to the time indicated

τὸν ἀπηκριβωμένον αὐτῷ χρόνον παρὰ τῶν μάγων,
ἀναιρεθῆναι προστάττει, πάντως που καὶ τὸν
Ἰησοῦν, ὥς γε ἦν εἰκός, τῆς αὐτῆς τοῖς ὁμήλιξι
συναπολαῦσαι συμφορᾶς οἰόμενος. φθάνει γε μὴν 2
τὴν ἐπιβουλὴν εἰς Αἴγυπτον διακομισθεὶς ὁ παῖς,
δι' ἐπιφανείας ἀγγέλου τὸ μέλλον προμεμαθηκότων

Matt. 2, 1–7
ff. αὐτοῦ τῶν γονέων. ταῦτα μὲν οὖν καὶ ἡ ἱερὰ
τοῦ εὐαγγελίου διδάσκει γραφή· ἄξιον δ' ἐπὶ 3
τούτοις συνιδεῖν τἀπίχειρα τῆς Ἡρῴδου κατὰ
τοῦ Χριστοῦ καὶ τῶν ὁμηλίκων αὐτῷ τόλμης, ὡς
παραυτίκα, μηδὲ σμικρᾶς ἀναβολῆς γεγενημένης, ἡ
θεία δίκη περιόντα ἔτ' αὐτὸν τῷ βίῳ μετελήλυθεν,
τὰ τῶν μετὰ τὴν ἐνθένδε ἀπαλλαγὴν διαδεξομένων
αὐτὸν ἐπιδεικνῦσα προοίμια. ὡς μὲν οὖν τὰς 4
κατὰ τὴν βασιλείαν αὐτῷ νομισθείσας εὐπραγίας
ταῖς κατὰ τὸν οἶκον ἐπαλλήλοις ἠμαύρωσεν
συμφοραῖς, γυναικὸς καὶ τέκνων καὶ τῶν λοιπῶν
τῶν μάλιστα πρὸς γένους ἀναγκαιοτάτων τε καὶ
φιλτάτων μιαιφονίαις, οὐδὲ οἷόν τε νῦν καταλέγειν,
τραγικὴν ἅπασαν δραματουργίαν ἐπισκιαζούσης
τῆς περὶ τούτων ὑποθέσεως, ἣν εἰς πλάτος ἐν ταῖς
κατ' αὐτὸν ἱστορίαις ὁ Ἰώσηπος διελήλυθεν· ὡς 5
δ' ἅμα τῇ κατὰ τοῦ σωτῆρος ἡμῶν καὶ τῶν ἄλλων
νηπίων ἐπιβουλῇ θεήλατος αὐτὸν καταλαβοῦσα
μάστιξ εἰς θάνατον συνήλασεν, οὐ χεῖρον καὶ τῶν
φωνῶν τοῦ συγγραφέως ἐπακοῦσαι, κατὰ λέξιν
ἐν ἑπτακαιδεκάτῳ τῆς Ἰουδαϊκῆς Ἀρχαιολογίας τὴν
καταστροφὴν τοῦ κατ' αὐτὸν βίου τοῦτον γράφοντος

Joseph. A.I.
17,168–170 τὸν τρόπον· '' Ἡρῴδῃ δὲ μειζόνως ἡ νόσος ἐνεπι-
κραίνετο, δίκην ὧν παρηνόμησεν ἐκπρασσομένου τοῦ
θεοῦ. πῦρ μὲν γὰρ μαλακὸν ἦν, οὐχ ὧδε πολλὴν
ἀποσημαῖνον τοῖς ἐπαφωμένοις τὴν φλόγωσιν, ὅσην

to him by the Magi, supposing, as was natural, that Jesus also would enjoy the same fate as the children of his age. However the child forestalled the plot by being taken to Egypt, as by the manifestation of an angel his parents had learned beforehand what was to happen. This is also taught by the sacred scripture of the Gospel, but it is worth noticing in this connexion the result of the crime of Herod against the Christ and the children of his age ; for immediately, without even a short delay, the justice of God overtook him while he was still in life, showing the prelude of what awaited him when he had passed hence. It is not now possible even to give a summary list of the ways by which he darkened what were reckoned the glories of his reign, by the successive misfortunes of his house, by the foul murder of wife and children and of the rest who were closest to him in family and in affection ; for the shadows in their story, which Josephus has narrated at length in the history of Herod, are darker than any in tragic drama. But it is well to hear from the words of that writer how, from the moment of the plot against our Saviour and the other innocents, a scourge sent from God seized him and drove him to death. In the seventeenth book of the *Jewish Antiquities* he writes of the catastrophe of Herod's life in this way : " But in Herod disease kept growing ever more cruel as God exacted punishment for his crimes. For there was a slow fire which did not give much indication to those who touched him of the

τοῖς ἐντὸς προσετίθει τὴν κάκωσιν, ἐπιθυμία δὲ
δεινὴ τοῦ δέξασθαί τι, οὐδὲ ἦν μὴ οὐχ ὑπουργεῖν,
καὶ ἕλκωσις τῶν τε ἐντέρων καὶ μάλιστα τοῦ
κόλου δειναὶ ἀλγηδόνες καὶ φλέγμα ὑγρὸν περὶ
τοὺς πόδας καὶ διαυγές· παραπλησία δὲ καὶ περὶ 7
τὸ ἦτρον κάκωσις ἦν, ναὶ μὴν καὶ τοῦ αἰδοίου σῆψις,
σκώληκας ἐμποιοῦσα, πνεύματός τε ὀρθία ἔντασις,
καὶ αὐτὴ λίαν ἀηδὴς ἀχθηδόνι τε τῆς ἀποφορᾶς
καὶ τῷ πυκνῷ τοῦ ἄσθματος, ἐσπασμένος τε περὶ
πᾶν ἦν μέρος, ἰσχὺν οὐχ ὑπομενητὴν προστιθέμενος.
ἐλέγετο γοῦν ὑπὸ τῶν θειαζόντων καὶ οἷς ταῦτα 8
προαποφθέγγεσθαι σοφία πρόκειται, ποινὴν τοῦ
πολλοῦ καὶ δυσσεβοῦς ταύτην ὁ θεὸς εἰσπράττεσθαι
παρὰ τοῦ βασιλέως."

Ταῦτα μὲν ἐν τῇ δηλωθείσῃ γραφῇ παρα-
σημαίνεται ὁ προειρημένος· καὶ ἐν τῇ δευτέρᾳ 9
δὲ τῶν Ἱστοριῶν τὰ παραπλήσια περὶ τοῦ αὐτοῦ
παραδίδωσιν, ὧδέ πως γράφων·

B.I. 1, 656–
660 "Ἔνθεν αὐτοῦ τὸ σῶμα πᾶν ἡ νόσος διαλαβοῦσα
ποικίλοις πάθεσιν ἐμέριζεν. πυρετὸς μὲν γὰρ ἦν
χλιαρός, κνησμὸς δ' ἀφόρητος τῆς ἐπιφανείας
ὅλης καὶ κόλου συνεχεῖς ἀλγηδόνες περί τε τοὺς
πόδας ὡς ὑδρωπιῶντος οἰδήματα τοῦ τε ἤτρου
φλεγμονὴ καὶ δι' αἰδοίου σηπεδὼν σκώληκα
γεννῶσα, πρὸς τούτοις ὀρθόπνοια καὶ δύσπνοια
καὶ σπασμοὶ πάντων τῶν μελῶν, ὥστε τοὺς
ἐπιθειάζοντας ποινὴν εἶναι τὰ νοσήματα λέγειν.
ὁ δὲ παλαίων τοσούτοις πάθεσιν ὅμως τοῦ ζῆν 10
ἀντείχετο, σωτηρίαν τε ἤλπιζεν, καὶ θεραπείας
ἐπενόει. διαβὰς γοῦν τὸν Ἰορδάνην τοῖς κατὰ
Καλλιρόην θερμοῖς ἐχρῆτο· ταῦτα δὲ ἔξεισιν
μὲν εἰς τὴν Ἀσφαλτῖτιν λίμνην, ὑπὸ γλυκύτητος

burning which within was increasing his evil plight, and an awful desire for nourishment, which could not be ministered to, and ulceration of the intestines, and especially awful pain in the colon, and a moist and transparent dropsy in his feet ; similar too was an inflammation of the bladder, and even mortification of the genitals breeding worms. There was also a shrill acceleration of his breathing, and this was very offensive from the nature of the discharge and rapidity of his breath. He was convulsed in every part with intolerable severity.[1] Thus it was said by those who looked on, and had the wisdom to pronounce on these things, that God was exacting this penalty from the king for his many impieties."

The writer mentioned above gives this account in the treatise quoted, and in the second book of the *Jewish Wars* he gives a similar tradition, writing as follows :

" Then the disease spread through his whole body, and attacked each part with divers sufferings. The fever rose, there was intolerable itching of the whole surface, incessant pain in the colon, his feet were swollen as though with dropsy, there was inflammation of the bladder, and gangrene of the genitals, breeding worms. In addition to this, his breathing was difficult and impossible if he lay down, and there were spasms in every limb, so that the divines said that his illness was a punishment. Yet though he was struggling with such great suffering he still clung to life, hoping for health and thinking of cure. So he crossed the Jordan and took the warm baths at Callirhoë which flow out into the Dead

---

[1] The Greek of Eusebius seems impossible, but the text of Josephus is plainer, " Convulsion was in every limb, adding intolerable severity."

δέ ἐστι καὶ πότιμα. δόξαν ἐνταῦθα τοῖς ἰατροῖς 11
ἐλαίῳ θερμῷ πᾶν ἀναθάλψαι τὸ σῶμα χαλασθὲν
εἰς ἐλαίου πλήρη πύελον, ἐκλύει καὶ τοὺς ὀφθαλμοὺς
ὡς ἐκλυθεὶς ἀνέστρεψεν. θορύβου δὲ τῶν θερα-
πόντων γενομένου, πρὸς μὲν τὴν πληγὴν ἀνήνεγκεν,
εἰς δὲ τὸ λοιπὸν ἀπογνοὺς τὴν σωτηρίαν, τοῖς τε
στρατιώταις ἀνὰ δραχμὰς πεντήκοντα ἐκέλευσεν
διανεῖμαι καὶ πολλὰ χρήματα τοῖς ἡγεμόσι καὶ
τοῖς φίλοις. αὐτὸς δ' ὑποστρέφων εἰς Ἱεριχοῦντα 12
παραγίνεται, μελαγχολῶν ἤδη καὶ μόνον οὐκ
ἀπειλῶν αὐτῷ τι τῷ θανάτῳ· προέκοψεν δ' εἰς
ἐπιβουλὴν ἀθεμίτου πράξεως. τοὺς γὰρ ἀφ'
ἑκάστης κώμης ἐπισήμους ἄνδρας ἐξ ὅλης Ἰουδαίας
συναγαγὼν εἰς τὸν καλούμενον ἱππόδρομον ἐκέλευσεν συγκλεῖσαι, προσκαλεσάμενος δὲ Σαλώμην 13
τὴν ἀδελφὴν καὶ τὸν ἄνδρα ταύτης Ἀλεξᾶν
'οἶδα' ἔφη 'Ἰουδαίους τὸν ἐμὸν ἑορτάσοντας
θάνατον, δύναμαι δὲ πενθεῖσθαι δι' ἑτέρων καὶ
λαμπρὸν ἐπιτάφιον σχεῖν, ἂν ὑμεῖς θελήσητε
ταῖς ἐμαῖς ἐντολαῖς ὑπουργῆσαι. τούσδε τοὺς
φρουρουμένους ἄνδρας, ἐπειδὰν ἐκπνεύσω, τάχιστα
κτείνατε περιστήσαντες τοὺς στρατιώτας, ἵνα
πᾶσα Ἰουδαία καὶ πᾶς οἶκος καὶ ἄκων ἐπ' ἐμοὶ
Joseph. B.I.
1, 662 δακρύσῃ.'" καὶ μετὰ βραχέα φησίν "αὖθις 14
δέ, καὶ γὰρ ἐνδείᾳ τροφῆς καὶ βηχὶ σπα-
σμώδει διετείνετο, τῶν ἀλγηδόνων ἡσθεὶς φθά-
σαι τὴν εἱμαρμένην ἐπεβάλλετο· λαβὼν δὲ μῆλον,
ᾔτησε καὶ μαχαίριον· εἰώθει γὰρ ἀποτέμνων
ἐσθίειν· ἔπειτα περιαθρήσας μή τις ὁ κωλύσων
αὐτὸν εἴη, ἐπῆρεν τὴν δεξιὰν ὡς πλήξων ἑαυτόν."
Joseph. A.I.
17, 187. 191 ἐπὶ δὲ τούτοις ὁ αὐτὸς ἱστορεῖ συγγραφεὺς
ἕτερον αὐτοῦ γνήσιον παῖδα πρὸ τῆς ἐσχάτης

Sea but are sweet and drinkable. There it was decided by his physicians to warm up his whole body with hot oil by letting it down into a tub full of oil, but he collapsed and turned up his eyes as though dying. Disturbance arose among the attendants and he came back to his sufferings, but for the future gave up hope of cure and ordered fifty drachmas each to be distributed to the soldiers and much money to the governors and his friends. He then returned and reached Jericho, full of melancholy and scarcely refraining from the threat of suicide. But he gained strength enough to plan one more execrable crime ; for he brought together the notables from every village from all Judaea and commanded them to be shut up in the so-called Hippodrome. He then summoned Salome, his sister, and her husband, Alexas, and said, ' I know that the Jews will celebrate my death with festivity, but I can be mourned by others and have a splendid funeral if you are willing to administer my commands. Station soldiers around these men who are shut up, and as soon as I expire kill them with all speed, that all Judaea and every house may weep over me even against its will.' " After a little Josephus says : " Later on, racked by lack of food and a convulsive cough, the pains he felt urged him to anticipate fate. He took an apple and asked for a knife, for it was his custom to peel it and eat it. Then, having turned round, lest there should be any to prevent him, he raised his right hand as if he were going to stab himself." Moreover, the same historian relates that he ordered the murder of another legitimate son before the end of his life,

71

B.I. 1, 664.
665

Matt. 2, 19.
20

Matt. 2, 22

Luke 3, 1

Joseph. *A.I.*
18, 32. 33. 35.
89

τοῦ βίου τελευτῆς, τρίτον ἐπὶ δυσὶν ἤδη προανῃρημένοις, δι' ἐπιτάξεως ἀνελόντα, παραχρῆμα τὴν ζωὴν οὐ μετὰ σμικρῶν ἀλγηδόνων ἀπορρῆξαι. καὶ τοιοῦτο μὲν τὸ πέρας τῆς Ἡρώδου γέγονεν τελευτῆς, ποινὴν δικαίαν ἐκτίσαντος ὧν ἀμφὶ τὴν Βηθλεὲμ ἀνεῖλεν παίδων τῆς τοῦ σωτῆρος ἡμῶν ἐπιβουλῆς ἕνεκα· μεθ' ἣν ἄγγελος ὄναρ ἐπιστὰς ἐν Αἰγύπτῳ διατρίβοντι τῷ Ἰωσὴφ ἀπᾶραι ἅμα τῷ παιδὶ καὶ τῇ τούτου μητρὶ ἐπὶ τὴν Ἰουδαίαν παρακελεύεται, τεθνηκέναι δηλῶν τοὺς ἀναζητοῦντας τὴν ψυχὴν τοῦ παιδίου. τούτοις δ' ὁ εὐαγγελιστὴς ἐπιφέρει λέγων " ἀκούσας δὲ ὅτι Ἀρχέλαος βασιλεύει ἀντὶ Ἡρώδου τοῦ πατρὸς αὐτοῦ ἐφοβήθη ἐκεῖ ἀπελθεῖν· χρηματισθεὶς δὲ κατ' ὄναρ ἀνεχώρησεν εἰς τὰ μέρη τῆς Γαλιλαίας."

IX. Τῇ δ' ἐπὶ τὴν ἀρχὴν μετὰ τὸν Ἡρώδην τοῦ Ἀρχελάου καταστάσει συνᾴδει καὶ ὁ προειρημένος ἱστορικός, τόν τε τρόπον ἀναγράφων, καθ' ὃν ἐκ διαθηκῶν Ἡρώδου τοῦ πατρὸς ἐπικρίσεώς τε Καίσαρος Αὐγούστου τὴν κατὰ Ἰουδαίων βασιλείαν διεδέξατο, καὶ ὡς τῆς ἀρχῆς μετὰ δεκαέτη χρόνον ἀποπεσόντος οἱ ἀδελφοὶ Φίλιππός τε καὶ ὁ νέος Ἡρώδης ἅμα Λυσανίᾳ τὰς ἑαυτῶν διεῖπον τετραρχίας.

Ὁ δ' αὐτὸς ἐν ὀκτωκαιδεκάτῳ τῆς Ἀρχαιολογίας κατὰ τὸ δωδέκατον ἔτος τῆς Τιβερίου βασιλείας (τοῦτον γὰρ τὴν καθ' ὅλων ἀρχὴν διαδέξασθαι ἑπτὰ ἐπὶ πεντήκοντα ἔτεσιν τὴν ἡγεμονίαν ἐπικρατήσαντος Αὐγούστου) Πόντιον Πιλᾶτον τὴν Ἰουδαίαν ἐπιτραπῆναι δηλοῖ, ἐνταῦθα δὲ ἐφ' ὅλοις ἔτεσιν δέκα σχεδὸν εἰς αὐτὴν παραμεῖναι τὴν Τιβερίου τελευτήν. οὐκοῦν σαφῶς

72

making the third in addition to the two others already put to death, and immediately gave up his life, torn by great agony. Such was the end of Herod : he paid a just penalty for the children that he murdered at Bethlehem for the sake of his plot against our Saviour. After this an angel appeared in a dream to Joseph, who was staying in Egypt, and commanded him to return to Judaea with the child and his mother, and announced that those who sought the life of the little child were dead. The evangelist continues by saying, " Now when he heard that Archelaus was king in the room of Herod his father, he was afraid to depart there, and, being warned in a dream, retired to the districts of Galilee."

IX. The historian already mentioned corroborates the accession to power of Archelaus after Herod, describing both the way in which he succeeded to the kingdom of the Jews by the testaments of Herod his father and the decision of Caesar Augustus, and how, when he fell from power after ten years, his brothers Philip and the younger Herod, together with Lysanias, administered their own tetrarchies.

In the eighteenth book of the *Antiquities* the same Josephus explains how Pontius Pilate was given the administration of Judaea in the twelfth year of Tiberius (for he had succeeded to universal sove-reignty after Augustus had held the government for fifty-seven years), and for ten whole years he remained in office, almost until the death of Tiberius.

ἀπελήλεγκται τὸ πλάσμα τῶν κατὰ τοῦ σωτῆρος
ἡμῶν ὑπομνήματα χθὲς καὶ πρῴην διαδεδωκότων,
ἐν οἷς πρῶτος αὐτὸς ὁ τῆς παρασημειώσεως
χρόνος τῶν πεπλακότων ἀπελέγχει τὸ ψεῦδος.
ἐπὶ τῆς τετάρτης δ' οὖν ὑπατείας Τιβερίου, ἣ 4
γέγονεν ἔτους ἑβδόμου τῆς βασιλείας αὐτοῦ, τὰ
περὶ τὸ σωτήριον πάθος αὐτοῖς τολμηθέντα περιέχει, καθ' ὃν δείκνυται χρόνον μηδ' ἐπιστάς πω τῇ
Ἰουδαίᾳ Πιλᾶτος, εἴ γε τῷ Ἰωσήπῳ μάρτυρι
χρήσασθαι δέον, σαφῶς οὕτως σημαίνοντι κατὰ
τὴν δηλωθεῖσαν αὐτοῦ γραφὴν ὅτι δὴ δωδεκάτῳ
ἐνιαυτῷ τῆς Τιβερίου βασιλείας ἐπίτροπος τῆς
Ἰουδαίας ὑπὸ Τιβερίου καθίσταται Πιλᾶτος.

Luke 3, 1
X. Ἐπὶ τούτων δὴ οὖν, κατὰ τὸν εὐαγγελιστὴν 1
ἔτος πεντεκαιδέκατον Τιβερίου Καίσαρος ἄγοντος
τέταρτον δὲ τῆς ἡγεμονίας Ποντίου Πιλάτου, τῆς
τε λοιπῆς Ἰουδαίας τετραρχούντων Ἡρώδου καὶ
Λυσανίου καὶ Φιλίππου, ὁ σωτὴρ καὶ κύριος
Luke 3, 23 ἡμῶν Ἰησοῦς ὁ Χριστὸς τοῦ θεοῦ, ἀρχόμενος
ὡς εἰ ἐτῶν τριάκοντα, ἐπὶ τὸ Ἰωάννου βάπτισμα
παραγίνεται, καταρχήν τε ποιεῖται τηνικαῦτα τοῦ
κατὰ τὸ εὐαγγέλιον κηρύγματος.

Luke, 3, 2
Φησὶν δὲ αὐτὸν ἡ θεία γραφὴ τὸν πάντα τῆς 2
διδασκαλίας διατελέσαι χρόνον ἐπὶ ἀρχιερέως
Ἄννα καὶ Καϊάφα, δηλοῦσα ὅτι δὴ ἐν τοῖς μεταξὺ

---

[1] The word translated " reports " is used of official
documents, such as the *Acta Pilati* claimed to be ; the
Latin is *commentarii*—well known from its use by Caesar.
The *Acta Pilati* now extant are Christian forgeries of uncertain date. Those to which Eusebius refers were heathen
forgeries introduced in the time of the great persecution
under Maximin.

[2] Eusebius reckons the baptism of Christ as taking place

So that there is clear proof of the forgery of those who recently or formerly have issued a series of Pilate's Reports[1] about our Saviour; for in them the dates mentioned convict the forgers of untruth. They relate that the crime of the Saviour's death fell in the fourth consulship of Tiberius, which was the seventh year of his reign, but at that time it has been shown that Pilate was not yet in charge of Judaea, if Josephus may be used as a witness, for he clearly shows, in the writing quoted from him above, that it was actually in the twelfth year of the reign of Tiberius that Pilate was appointed procurator of Judaea by Tiberius.

X. In the time of these rulers then, according to the evangelist, when Tiberius Caesar was in the fifteenth year of his reign and Pontius Pilate the fourth of his governorship, and Herod, Lysanias, and Philip were tetrarchs of the rest of Judaea, our Saviour and Lord, Jesus the Christ of God, " beginning to be about thirty years old," came to the baptism of John and there began the proclamation of the gospel.[2]

The divine Scripture says that he completed the whole time of his teaching while Annas and Caiaphas were high priest,[3] showing that the

in the fifteenth year of Tiberius, dating his accession from the death of Augustus. As he was then in his thirtieth year he was born in the forty-second year of Augustus, fourteen years before his death. This is the reckoning of time known as the Christian era (see p. 46).

[3] The singular " high priest " is somewhat harsher in English than in Greek, but represents the fact that according to Jewish custom there was never more than one high priest at the same time. Luke's statement seems to contradict this fact, and Eusebius tries to explain it by interpreting the difficult phrase as meaning the period between the high priesthoods of Annas and Caiaphas.

τῆς τούτων ἔτεσιν λειτουργίας ὁ πᾶς τῆς διδασκαλίας αὐτῷ συνεπεράνθη χρόνος. ἀρξαμένου
μὲν οὖν κατὰ τὴν τοῦ Ἄννα ἀρχιερωσύνην,
μέχρι δὲ τῆς ἀρχῆς τοῦ Καϊάφα παραμείναντος
οὐδ' ὅλος ὁ μεταξὺ τετραέτης παρίσταται χρόνος.
τῶν γάρ τοι κατὰ τὸν νομον ἤδη πως καθαιρου- 3
μένων ἐξ ἐκείνου θεσμῶν, λέλυτο μὲν ᾧ διὰ βίου
καὶ ἐκ προγόνων διαδοχῆς τὰ τῆς τοῦ θεοῦ θεραπείας προσήκοντα ἦν, ὑπὸ δὲ τῶν Ῥωμαϊκῶν
ἡγεμόνων ἄλλοτε ἄλλοι τὴν ἀρχιερωσύνην ἐπι-
τρεπόμενοι, οὐ πλεῖον ἔτους ἑνὸς ἐπὶ ταύτης 4
διετέλουν. ἱστορεῖ δ' οὖν ὁ Ἰώσηπος τέσσαρας
κατὰ διαδοχὴν ἐπὶ Καϊάφαν ἀρχιερεῖς μετὰ τὸν
Ἄνναν διαγενέσθαι, κατὰ τὴν αὐτὴν τῆς Ἀρχαιο-
Joseph. A.I.
18, 34. 35 λογίας γραφὴν ὧδέ πως λέγων '' Οὐαλέριος
Γρᾶτος, παύσας ἱερᾶσθαι Ἄνανον, Ἰσμάηλον
ἀρχιερέα ἀποφαίνει τὸν τοῦ Φαβι, καὶ τοῦτον
δὲ μετ' οὐ πολὺ μεταστήσας, Ἐλεάζαρον τὸν
Ἀνάνου τοῦ ἀρχιερέως υἱὸν ἀποδείκνυσιν ἀρχιερέα. ἐνιαυτοῦ δὲ διαγενομένου καὶ τόνδε
παύσας, Σίμωνι τῷ Καμίθου τὴν ἀρχιερωσύνην 5
παραδίδωσιν. οὐ πλέον δὲ καὶ τῷδε ἐνιαυτοῦ
τὴν τιμὴν ἔχοντι διεγένετο χρόνος, καὶ Ἰώσηπος,
ὁ καὶ Καϊάφας, διάδοχος ἦν αὐτῷ.'' οὐκοῦν 6
ὁ σύμπας οὐδ' ὅλος τετραέτης ἀποδείκνυται
τῆς τοῦ σωτῆρος ἡμῶν διδασκαλίας χρόνος,
τεσσάρων ἐπὶ τέσσαρσιν ἔτεσιν ἀρχιερέων ἀπὸ
τοῦ Ἄννα καὶ ἐπὶ τὴν τοῦ Καϊάφα κατά-
στασιν ἐνιαύσιον λειτουργίαν ἐκτετελεκότων. τόν
Matt. 26, 3.
51
John 11, 49
John 18, 13.
24. 28 γέ τοι Καϊάφαν ἀρχιερέα εἰκότως τοῦ ἐνιαυτοῦ,
καθ' ὃν τὰ τοῦ σωτηρίου πάθους ἐπετελεῖτο, ἡ
τοῦ εὐαγγελίου παρεσημήνατο γραφή, ἐξ ἧς καὶ

whole time of his teaching was bounded by the
years which cover their administration. Since,
then, he began in the high priesthood of Annas
and continued to the reign of Caiaphas the intervening time does not extend to a full four years.
For since the regulations of the law were at that
time already in process of destruction the rule had
been relaxed by which the duties of the service of
God were held for life and by inherited succession,
and the Roman governors entrusted the high priesthood at different times to different men, who did not
hold this office for more than one year. Moreover
Josephus relates that four high priests intervened in
succession between Annas and Caiaphas, and speaks
as follows in the text of the *Antiquities* :

" Valerius Gratus, having deprived Ananus of the
priesthood, appoints as high priest Ishmael the
son of Phabi. Him, too, he removes shortly and
nominates as high priest Eliezer the son of Ananus
the high priest. But when a year was past he
removes him also and hands over the high priesthood to Simon the son of Kamithus. But neither
did his tenure of office last for more than a year,
and Josephus, who is also called Caiaphas, was his
successor." Thus the whole time of the teaching of
our Saviour is shown to be not even a full four years ;
since from Annas to the appointment of Caiaphas
in four years four high priests held the yearly office.
Naturally, then, the scripture of the gospel has indicated Caiaphas as high priest of the year in which the
Saviour's passion was completed, and from this also
the time of the teaching of Christ is shown to be not

77

αὐτῆς οὐκ ἀπάδων τῆς προκειμένης ἐπιτηρήσεως
ὁ τῆς τοῦ Χριστοῦ διδασκαλίας ἀποδείκνυται
χρόνος. ἀλλὰ γὰρ ὁ σωτὴρ καὶ κύριος ἡμῶν 7
οὐ μετὰ πλεῖστον τῆς καταρχῆς τοῦ κηρύγματος
τοὺς δώδεκα ἀποστόλους ἀνακαλεῖται, οὓς καὶ
μόνους τῶν λοιπῶν αὐτοῦ μαθητῶν κατά τι γέρας
ἐξαίρετον ἀποστόλους ὠνόμασεν, καὶ αὖθις ἀνα-
δείκνυσιν ἑτέρους ἑβδομήκοντα, οὓς καὶ αὐτοὺς
ἀπέστειλεν ἀνὰ δύο δύο πρὸ προσώπου αὐτοῦ εἰς
πάντα τόπον καὶ πόλιν οὗ ἤμελλεν αὐτὸς ἔρχεσθαι.

XI. Οὐκ εἰς μακρὸν δὲ τοῦ βαπτιστοῦ Ἰωάννου 1
ὑπὸ τοῦ νέου Ἡρῴδου τὴν κεφαλὴν ἀποτμηθέντος
μνημονεύει μὲν καὶ ἡ θεία τῶν εὐαγγελίων γραφή,
συνιστορεῖ γε μὴν καὶ ὁ Ἰώσηπος, ὀνομαστὶ τῆς
τε Ἡρῳδιάδος μνήμην πεποιημένος καὶ ὡς ἀδελφοῦ
γυναῖκα οὖσαν αὐτὴν ἠγάγετο πρὸς γάμον Ἡρῴδης,
ἀθετήσας μὲν τὴν προτέραν αὐτῷ κατὰ νόμους
γεγαμημένην (Ἀρέτα δὲ ἦν αὕτη τοῦ Πετραίων
βασιλέως θυγάτηρ), τὴν δὲ Ἡρῳδιάδα ζῶντος
διαστήσας τοῦ ἀνδρός· δι' ἣν καὶ τὸν Ἰωάννην
ἀνελὼν πόλεμον αἴρεται πρὸς τὸν Ἀρέταν, ὡς
ἂν ἠτιμασμένης αὐτῷ τῆς θυγατρός, ἐν ᾧ πολέμῳ 2
μάχης γενομένης πάντα φησὶν τὸν Ἡρῴδου
στρατὸν διαφθαρῆναι καὶ ταῦτα πεπονθέναι τῆς
ἐπιβουλῆς ἕνεκεν τῆς κατὰ τοῦ Ἰωάννου γεγενημένης. ὁ δ' αὐτὸς Ἰώσηπος ἐν τοῖς μάλιστα 3
δικαιότατον καὶ βαπτιστὴν ὁμολογῶν γεγονέναι
τὸν Ἰωάννην, τοῖς περὶ αὐτοῦ κατὰ τὴν τῶν
εὐαγγελίων γραφὴν ἀναγεγραμμένοις συμμαρτυρεῖ,
ἱστορεῖ δὲ καὶ τὸν Ἡρῴδην τῆς βασιλείας ἀπο-
πεπτωκέναι διὰ τὴν αὐτὴν Ἡρῳδιάδα, μεθ' ἧς
αὐτὸν καὶ εἰς τὴν ὑπερορίαν ἀπεληλάσθαι, Βίενναν

Matt. 10, 1 ff.
Mark 3, 14 ff.
Luke 6, 13.
9, 1 ff.

Luke 10, 1

Matt. 14, 1-12
Mark 6, 14-29
Luke 3, 19.
20. 9, 7-9
Joseph. A.I.
18, 109-114

Joseph. A.I.
18, 117. 18, 240-255

discordant with the preceding observation. However, our Lord and Saviour called the twelve apostles not long after the beginning of his preaching, and to them alone of all his disciples did he give the name of apostles as a special privilege. Afterwards he appointed seventy others, and them also he sent[1] out in advance of him, two by two, to every place and city where he was to come himself.

XI. The divine scripture of the gospels relates that not long afterwards John the Baptist was beheaded by Herod the younger, and Josephus confirms the narrative, mentioning Herodias by name, and telling how, though she was his brother's wife, Herod took her in marriage, by putting aside her who had formerly been legally married to him (and she was the daughter of Aretas the king of the Petraeans) and separating Herodias from her husband who was alive. For her sake, too, after killing John, he waged war with Aretas for the dishonour done his daughter ; and Josephus says that in a battle in this war the whole army of Herod was destroyed, and that he suffered this because of the plot against John. The same Josephus admits that John was peculiarly righteous, and a baptist, confirming the testimony recorded in the text of the gospels concerning him. He also relates that Herod was deprived of his kingdom for the sake of the same Herodias, and was exiled with

---

[1] It is impossible in English to bring out the fact that the word " sent " is the same as that implied by the word " apostle."

τῆς Γαλλίας πόλιν οἰκεῖν καταδικασθέντα. καὶ 4
ταῦτά γε αὐτῷ ἐν ὀκτωκαιδεκάτῳ τῆς Ἀρχαιολογίας δεδήλωται, ἔνθα συλλαβαῖς αὐταῖς περὶ
τοῦ Ἰωάννου ταῦτα γράφει

Joseph. A.I.
18, 116-119

"Τισὶ δὲ τῶν Ἰουδαίων ἐδόκει ὀλωλέναι τὸν
Ἡρῴδου στρατὸν ὑπὸ τοῦ θεοῦ, καὶ μάλα δικαίως
τιννυμένου κατὰ ποινὴν Ἰωάννου τοῦ καλου-
μένου βαπτιστοῦ. κτείνει γὰρ τοῦτον Ἡρῴδης, 5
ἀγαθὸν ἄνδρα καὶ τοῖς Ἰουδαίοις κελεύοντα ἀρετὴν
ἐπασκοῦσιν καὶ τὰ πρὸς ἀλλήλους δικαιοσύνῃ καὶ
πρὸς τὸν θεὸν εὐσεβείᾳ χρωμένους βαπτισμῷ
συνιέναι· οὕτω γὰρ δὴ καὶ τὴν βάπτισιν ἀποδεκτὴν
αὐτῷ φανεῖσθαι, μὴ ἐπί τινων ἁμαρτάδων παραι-
τήσει χρωμένων, ἀλλ' ἐφ' ἁγνείᾳ τοῦ σώματος,
ἅτε δὴ καὶ τῆς ψυχῆς δικαιοσύνῃ προεκκεκαθ-
αρμένης. καὶ τῶν ἄλλων συστρεφομένων (καὶ γὰρ 6
ἤρθησαν ἐπὶ πλεῖστον τῇ ἀκροάσει τῶν λόγων),
δείσας Ἡρῴδης τὸ ἐπὶ τοσόνδε πιθανὸν αὐτοῦ τοῖς
ἀνθρώποις, μὴ ἐπὶ ἀποστάσει τινὶ φέροι (πάντα
γὰρ ἐοίκεσαν συμβουλῇ τῇ ἐκείνου πράξοντες),
πολὺ κρεῖττον ἡγεῖται, πρίν τι νεώτερον ὑπ'
αὐτοῦ γενέσθαι, προλαβὼν ἀναιρεῖν, ἢ μεταβολῆς
γενομένης εἰς πράγματα ἐμπεσὼν μετανοεῖν. καὶ
ὁ μὲν ὑποψίᾳ τῇ Ἡρῴδου δέσμιος εἰς τὸν Μαχαι-
ροῦντα πεμφθείς, τὸ προειρημένον φρούριον, ταύτῃ
κτίννυται."

Ταῦτα περὶ τοῦ Ἰωάννου διελθών, καὶ τοῦ 7

---

[1] Eusebius has slightly altered the text of Josephus.
This ran : " For Herod killed him, a good man and one who
commanded the Jews training themselves in virtue and practising righteousness towards one another and piety towards
God to come together for baptism." It would seem to
mean that John was preaching to ascetics and suggested

her, being condemned to live in Vienne, a city of Gaul. The account of these things is given in the eighteenth book of the *Antiquities*, where he writes concerning John exactly as follows :

" Now to some of the Jews it seemed that the army of Herod had been destroyed by God and that he was paying a very just penalty for John who was called the Baptist. For Herod killed him, a good man and one who commanded the Jews, training themselves in virtue, to practise righteousness towards one another and piety towards God, and to come together for baptism. For he said that baptism would prove acceptable to him only in those who used it not to escape from any sins but for bodily purity, on condition that the soul also had been previously cleansed thoroughly by righteousness. And when the rest collected, for they were greatly excited at hearing his words, Herod feared his great persuasiveness with men lest it should lead to some rising, for they appeared ready to do everything under his advice. He therefore considered it much better, before a revolt should spring from John, to put him to death in anticipation, rather than be involved in difficulties through the actual revolution and then regret it. And John, through Herod's suspicion, was sent a prisoner to Macherus, the prison mentioned already, and was there put to death." [1]

After narrating these things about John in the

baptism as a final act of perfection. This explains the reference to " when the rest collected." So long as John preached to ascetics Herod did not mind but was disturbed when the rest of the public manifested interest. Whiston's translation of Josephus and an unnecessary emendation in the text of Niese's edition of Josephus have conspired to obscure these facts.

σωτῆρος ἡμῶν κατὰ τὴν αὐτὴν τοῦ συγγράμματος
ἱστορίαν ὧδέ πως μέμνηται

Joseph. A.I.
18, 63. 64 " Γίνεται δὲ κατὰ τοῦτον τὸν χρόνον Ἰησοῦς,
σοφὸς ἀνήρ, εἴ γε ἄνδρα αὐτὸν λέγειν χρή. ἦν
γὰρ παραδόξων ἔργων ποιητής, διδάσκαλος ἀνθρώπων τῶν ἡδονῇ τἀληθῆ δεχομένων, καὶ πολλοὺς
μὲν τῶν Ἰουδαίων, πολλοὺς δὲ καὶ ἀπὸ τοῦ
Ἑλληνικοῦ ἐπηγάγετο. ὁ Χριστὸς οὗτος ἦν, καὶ 8
αὐτὸν ἐνδείξει τῶν πρώτων ἀνδρῶν παρ' ἡμῖν
σταυρῷ ἐπιτετιμηκότος Πιλάτου, οὐκ ἐπαύσαντο
οἱ τὸ πρῶτον ἀγαπήσαντες· ἐφάνη γὰρ αὐτοῖς
τρίτην ἔχων ἡμέραν πάλιν ζῶν, τῶν θείων προφητῶν ταῦτά τε καὶ ἄλλα μυρία περὶ αὐτοῦ θαυμάσια εἰρηκότων. εἰς ἔτι τε νῦν τῶν Χριστιανῶν
ἀπὸ τοῦδε ὠνομασμένων οὐκ ἐπέλιπε τὸ φῦλον."

Ταῦτα τοῦ ἐξ αὐτῶν Ἑβραίων συγγραφέως 9
ἀνέκαθεν τῇ ἑαυτοῦ γραφῇ περί τε τοῦ βαπτιστοῦ
Ἰωάννου καὶ τοῦ σωτῆρος ἡμῶν παραδεδωκότος,
τίς ἂν ἔτι λείποιτο ἀποφυγὴ τοῦ μὴ ἀναισχύντους
ἀπελέγχεσθαι τοὺς τὰ κατ' αὐτῶν πλασαμένους
ὑπομνήματα; ἀλλὰ ταῦτα μὲν ἐχέτω ταύτῃ.

XII. Τῶν γε μὴν τοῦ σωτῆρος ἀποστόλων παντὶ
τῳ σαφὴς ἐκ τῶν εὐαγγελίων ἡ πρόσρησις· τῶν δὲ
ἑβδομήκοντα μαθητῶν κατάλογος μὲν οὐδεὶς οὐδαμῇ
φέρεται, λέγεταί γε μὴν εἷς αὐτῶν Βαρναβᾶς
γεγονέναι, οὗ διαφόρως μὲν καὶ αἱ Πράξεις τῶν
ἀποστόλων ἐμνημόνευσαν, οὐχ ἥκιστα δὲ καὶ
Gal. 2, 1. 9.
13
1 Cor. 1, 1 Παῦλος Γαλάταις γράφων. τούτων δ' εἶναί φασι
καὶ Σωσθένην τὸν ἅμα Παύλῳ Κορινθίοις ἐπιστεί-
λαντα· ἡ δ' ἱστορία παρὰ Κλήμεντι κατὰ τὴν
πέμπτην τῶν Ὑποτυπώσεων· ἐν ᾗ καὶ Κηφᾶν,
Gal. 2, 11 περὶ οὗ φησιν ὁ Παῦλος " ὅτε δὲ ἦλθεν Κηφᾶς

same historical work he speaks as follows concerning our Saviour :

" At this time arose Jesus, a wise man, if indeed he must be called a man, for he was a doer of marvellous deeds, a teacher of men who received the truth with pleasure, and he led after him many of the Jews and many also of the Gentile population. This was the Christ ; and when Pilate had condemned him to the cross at the instigation of the leading men among us, those who had first loved him did not cease to do so, for he appeared to them when three days dead restored to life, and the divine prophets had told these and ten thousand other wonders concerning him. And up till now the tribe of Christians which are named after him has not died out."

When a writer sprung from the Hebrews themselves handed on in his own writing these details concerning John the Baptist and our Saviour, what alternative is there but to convict of shamelessness those who have concocted the Reports about them ?[1] But let this suffice.

XII. Now the names of the apostles of our Saviour are plain to everyone from the gospels, but no list of the Seventy is anywhere extant. It is said, however, that one of them was Barnabas, and of him the Acts of the Apostles has also made special mention, and so also has Paul when writing to the Galatians. And they say that Sosthenes too, who wrote with Paul to the Corinthians, was one of them. And there is the story in Clement, in the fifth book of the *Hypotyposes*, in which he says that Cephas, concerning whom Paul says " and when Cephas

---

[1] The reference is again to the heathen Acts of Pilate.

εἰς Ἀντιόχειαν, κατὰ πρόσωπον αὐτῷ ἀντέστην,"
ἕνα φησὶ γεγονέναι τῶν ἑβδομήκοντα μαθητῶν,
ὁμώνυμον Πέτρῳ τυγχάνοντα τῷ ἀποστόλῳ. καὶ

Acts 1, 23–26 Ματθίαν δὲ τὸν ἀντὶ Ἰούδα τοῖς ἀποστόλοις
συγκαταλεγέντα τόν τε σὺν αὐτῷ τῇ ὁμοίᾳ ψήφῳ
τιμηθέντα τῆς αὐτῆς τῶν ἑβδομήκοντα κλήσεως
ἠξιῶσθαι κατέχει λόγος. καὶ Θαδδαῖον δὲ ἕνα
τῶν αὐτῶν εἶναί φασι, περὶ οὗ καὶ ἱστορίαν ἐλθοῦσαν εἰς ἡμᾶς αὐτίκα μάλα ἐκθήσομαι. καὶ
τῶν ἑβδομήκοντα δὲ πλείους τοῦ σωτῆρος πεφη-
νέναι μαθητὰς εὕροις ἂν ἐπιτηρήσας, μάρτυρι

1 Cor. 15, 5–7 χρώμενος τῷ Παύλῳ, μετὰ τὴν ἐκ νεκρῶν ἔγερσιν
ὦφθαι αὐτὸν φήσαντι πρῶτον μὲν Κηφᾷ, ἔπειτα
τοῖς δώδεκα, καὶ μετὰ τούτους ἐπάνω πεντα-
κοσίοις ἀδελφοῖς ἐφάπαξ, ὧν τινὰς μὲν ἔφασκεν
κεκοιμῆσθαι, τοὺς πλείους δ' ἔτι τῷ βίῳ, καθ'
ὃν καιρὸν αὐτῷ ταῦτα συνετάττετο, περιμένειν·
ἔπειτα δ' ὦφθαι αὐτὸν Ἰακώβῳ φησίν· εἷς δὲ
καὶ οὗτος τῶν φερομένων τοῦ σωτῆρος ἀδελφῶν
ἦν· εἶθ' ὡς παρὰ τούτους κατὰ μίμησιν τῶν
δώδεκα πλείστων ὅσων ὑπαρξάντων ἀποστόλων,
οἷος καὶ αὐτὸς ὁ Παῦλος ἦν, προστίθησι λέγων
" ἔπειτα ὤφθη τοῖς ἀποστόλοις πᾶσιν." ταῦτα
μὲν οὖν περὶ τῶνδε.

XIII. Τῆς δὲ περὶ τὸν Θαδδαῖον ἱστορίας τοιοῦτος γέγονεν ὁ τρόπος. ἡ τοῦ κυρίου καὶ σωτῆρος
ἡμῶν Ἰησοῦ Χριστοῦ θειότης, εἰς πάντας ἀνθρώπους τῆς παραδοξοποιοῦ δυνάμεως ἕνεκεν βοωμένη,
μυρίους ὅσους καὶ τῶν ἐπ' ἀλλοδαπῆς πορρωτάτω
ὄντων τῆς Ἰουδαίας νόσων καὶ παντοίων παθῶν
ἐλπίδι θεραπείας ἐπήγετο. ταύτῃ τοι βασιλεὺς
Ἄβγαρος, τῶν ὑπὲρ Εὐφράτην ἐθνῶν ἐπιση-

came to Antioch I withstood him to the face," was one of the seventy disciples, who had the same name as the apostle Peter. Tradition also relates that Matthias, who was reckoned with the apostles in the place of Judas, and he who was honoured with him at the same casting of lots had been called among the Seventy. They also say that Thaddaeus was one of them, and I will shortly recount a narrative which has reached us concerning him. And consideration would show you that there were more disciples of the Saviour than the Seventy, if you used Paul as a witness, for he says that after the resurrection from the dead Jesus was seen first by Cephas, afterwards by the twelve, and after these by above five hundred brethren at once ; of whom he says that some had fallen asleep, but the majority remained alive at the time that he composed this account. He says that he was then seen by James, who was one of the alleged brethren of the Saviour, and then, as though in addition to these there had been numberless apostles, on the model of the twelve, like Paul himself, he goes on to say " then he was seen by all the apostles." This then suffices for them.

XIII. The manner of the narrative concerning Thaddaeus is as follows. The divinity of our Lord and Saviour Jesus Christ became famous among all men because of his wonder-working power, and led to him myriads even of those who in foreign lands were far remote from Judaea, in the hope of healing from diseases and from all kinds of sufferings. In this way King Abgar, the celebrated monarch of the

μότατα δυναστεύων, πάθει τὸ σῶμα δεινῷ καὶ
οὐ θεραπευτῷ ὅσον ἐπ' ἀνθρωπείᾳ δυνάμει κατα-
φθειρόμενος, ὡς καὶ τοὔνομα τοῦ Ἰησοῦ πολὺ καὶ
τὰς δυνάμεις συμφώνως πρὸς ἁπάντων μαρτυ-
ρουμένας ἐπύθετο, ἱκέτης αὐτοῦ πέμψας δι' ἐπι-
στοληφόρου γίνεται, τῆς νόσου τυχεῖν ἀπαλλαγῆς
ἀξιῶν. ὁ δὲ μὴ τότε καλοῦντι ὑπακούσας, ἐπι- 3
στολῆς γοῦν αὐτὸν ἰδίας καταξιοῖ, ἕνα τῶν αὐτοῦ
μαθητῶν ἀποστέλλειν ἐπὶ θεραπείᾳ τῆς νόσου
ὁμοῦ τε αὐτοῦ σωτηρίᾳ καὶ τῶν προσηκόντων
ἁπάντων ὑπισχνούμενος. οὐκ εἰς μακρὸν δὲ ἄρα 4
αὐτῷ ἐπληροῦτο τὰ τῆς ἐπαγγελίας. μετὰ γοῦν
τὴν ἐκ νεκρῶν ἀνάστασιν αὐτοῦ καὶ τὴν εἰς οὐρανοὺς
ἄνοδον Θωμᾶς, τῶν ἀποστόλων εἷς τῶν δώδεκα,
Θαδδαῖον, ἐν ἀριθμῷ καὶ αὐτὸν τῶν ἑβδομήκοντα
τοῦ Χριστοῦ μαθητῶν κατειλεγμένον, κινήσει
θειοτέρᾳ ἐπὶ τὰ Ἔδεσσα κήρυκα καὶ εὐαγγελιστὴν
τῆς περὶ τοῦ Χριστοῦ διδασκαλίας ἐκπέμπει,
πάντα τε δι' αὐτοῦ τὰ τῆς τοῦ σωτῆρος ἡμῶν
τέλος ἐλάμβανεν ἐπαγγελίας. ἔχεις καὶ τούτων
ἀνάγραπτον τὴν μαρτυρίαν, ἐκ τῶν κατὰ Ἔδεσσαν
τὸ τηνικάδε βασιλευομένην πόλιν γραμματο-
φυλακείων ληφθεῖσαν· ἐν γοῦν τοῖς αὐτόθι δη-
μοσίοις χάρταις, τοῖς τὰ παλαιὰ καὶ τὰ ἀμφὶ
τὸν Ἄβγαρον πραχθέντα περιέχουσι, καὶ ταῦτα
εἰς ἔτι νῦν ἐξ ἐκείνου πεφυλαγμένα εὕρηται,
οὐδὲν δὲ οἷον καὶ αὐτῶν ἐπακοῦσαι τῶν ἐπιστολῶν,
ἀπὸ τῶν ἀρχείων ἡμῖν ἀναληφθεισῶν καὶ τόνδε
αὐτοῖς ῥήμασιν ἐκ τῆς Σύρων φωνῆς μεταβληθεισῶν
τὸν τρόπον·

nations beyond the Euphrates, perishing from terrible suffering in his body, beyond human power to heal, when he heard much of the name of Jesus and of the miracles attested unanimously by all men, became his suppliant and sent to him by the bearer of a letter, asking to find relief from his disease. Jesus did not give heed to his request at the time, yet vouchsafed him a letter of his own, promising to send one of his disciples for the cure of his disease, and for the salvation alike of himself and of all his relations. Nor were the terms of his promise long in being fulfilled. After his resurrection from the dead and return into heaven, Thomas, one of the twelve apostles, was divinely moved to send to Edessa Thaddaeus, who was himself reckoned among the number of the Seventy disciples, as herald and evangelist of the teaching about Christ, and through him all the terms of our Saviour's promise received fulfilment. There is also documentary evidence of these things taken from the archives at Edessa which was at that time a capital city. At least, in the public documents there, which contain the things done in antiquity and at the time of Abgar, these things too are found preserved from that time to this ; but there is nothing equal to hearing the letters themselves, which we have extracted from the archives, and when translated from the Syriac they are verbally as follows :

EUSEBIUS

ΑΝΤΙΓΡΑΦΟΝ ΕΠΙΣΤΟΛΗΣ ΓΡΑΦΕΙΣΗΣ ΥΠΟ ΑΒΓΑΡΟΥ
ΤΟΠΑΡΧΟΥ ΤΩΙ ΙΗΣΟΥ ΚΑΙ ΠΕΜΦΘΕΙΣΗΣ ΑΥΤΩΙ
ΔΙ᾽ ΑΝΑΝΙΟΥ ΤΑΧΥΔΡΟΜΟΥ ΕΙΣ ΙΕΡΟΣΟΛΥΜΑ

" "Αβγαρος Οὐχαμα τοπάρχης Ἰησοῦ σωτῆρι 6
ἀγαθῷ ἀναφανέντι ἐν τόπῳ Ἱεροσολύμων χαίρειν.
ἤκουσταί μοι τὰ περὶ σοῦ καὶ τῶν σῶν ἰαμάτων,
ὡς ἄνευ φαρμάκων καὶ βοτανῶν ὑπὸ σοῦ γινομένων. ὡς γὰρ λόγος, τυφλοὺς ἀναβλέπειν ποιεῖς,
χωλοὺς περιπατεῖν, καὶ λεπροὺς καθαρίζεις, καὶ
ἀκάθαρτα πνεύματα καὶ δαίμονας ἐκβάλλεις, καὶ
τοὺς ἐν μακρονοσίᾳ βασανιζομένους θεραπεύεις,
καὶ νεκροὺς ἐγείρεις. καὶ ταῦτα πάντα ἀκούσας 7
περὶ σοῦ, κατὰ νοῦν ἐθέμην τὸ ἕτερον τῶν δύο,
ἢ ὅτι σὺ εἶ ὁ θεὸς καὶ καταβὰς ἀπὸ τοῦ οὐρανοῦ
ποιεῖς ταῦτα, ἢ υἱὸς εἶ τοῦ θεοῦ ποιῶν ταῦτα.
διὰ τοῦτο τοίνυν γράψας ἐδεήθην σου σκυλῆναι 8
πρός με καὶ τὸ πάθος, ὃ ἔχω, θεραπεῦσαι. καὶ
γὰρ ἤκουσα ὅτι καὶ Ἰουδαῖοι καταγογγύζουσί σου
καὶ βούλονται κακῶσαί σε. πόλις δὲ μικροτάτη 9
μοί ἐστι καὶ σεμνή, ἥτις ἐξαρκεῖ ἀμφοτέροις.¹ ''

ΤΑ ΑΝΤΙΓΡΑΦΕΝΤΑ ΥΠΟ ΙΗΣΟΥ ΔΙΑ ΑΝΑΝΙΟΥ ΤΑΧΥ-
ΔΡΟΜΟΥ ΤΟΠΑΡΧΗΙ ΑΒΓΑΡΩΙ

" Μακάριος εἶ πιστεύσας ἐν ἐμοί, μὴ ἑορακώς 1
με. γέγραπται γὰρ περὶ ἐμοῦ τοὺς ἑορακότας
με μὴ πιστεύσειν ἐν ἐμοί, καὶ ἵνα οἱ μὴ ἑορακότες
με αὐτοὶ πιστεύσωσι καὶ ζήσονται. περὶ δὲ οὗ

Side notes:
Matt. 11, 5
Luke 7, 22
Eccl. 9, 14
John 20, 29
Is. 6, 9 ff.
Matt.13,14ff.
John 12,39 ff.

¹ ἀμφοτέροισ ΑΤΜΣΛ : ἀμφοτέροισ· καὶ ταῦτα μὲν οὗτοσ [οὕτωσ
Β] ἔγραφεν [ἔγραψε R] τῆσ θείασ αὐτὸν τέωσ μικρὸν αὐγασάσησ
ἐλλάμψεωσ· ἄξιον δὲ καὶ τῆσ πρὸσ τοῦ ῑυ αὐτῷ διὰ τοῦ αὐτοῦ
γραμματοκομιστοῦ ἀποσταλείσησ ἐπακοῦσαι ὀλιγοστίχου μὲν πολυ-
δυνάμου δὲ ἐπιστολῆσ τοῦτον ἐχούσησ καὶ αὐτῆσ τὸν τρόπον
ERBD.

88

A copy of a letter written by Abgar the Toparch to Jesus and sent to him to Jerusalem by the courier Ananias.

" Abgar Uchama, the Toparch, to Jesus the good Saviour who has appeared in the district of Jerusalem, greeting. I have heard concerning you and your cures, how they are accomplished by you without drugs and herbs. For, as the story goes, you make the blind recover their sight, the lame walk, and you cleanse lepers, and cast out unclean spirits and demons, and you cure those who are tortured by long disease and you raise dead men. And when I heard all these things concerning you I decided that it is one of the two, either that you are God, and came down from heaven to do these things, or are a Son of God for doing these things. For this reason I write to beg you to hasten to me and to heal the suffering which I have. Moreover I heard that the Jews are mocking you, and wish to ill-treat you. Now I have a city very small and venerable which is enough for both." [1]

The reply from Jesus to Abgar, the Toparch, by the courier Ananias.

" Blessed art thou who didst believe in me not having seen me, for it is written concerning me that those who have seen me will not believe on me, and that those who have not seen me will believe and live. Now concerning what you wrote to me,

[1] In some manuscripts the following is added : " 9. And he wrote thus when the divine illumination had but a little shined on him. But it is also worth while to hear the letter sent to him by Jesus by the same bearer of the letter ; it has only a few lines but great power, and runs as follows."

89

ἔγραψάς μοι ἐλθεῖν πρὸς σέ, δέον ἐστὶ πάντα δι'
ἃ ἀπεστάλην ἐνταῦθα, πληρῶσαι καὶ μετὰ τὸ
πληρῶσαι οὕτως ἀναληφθῆναι πρὸς τὸν ἀποστείλαντά με. καὶ ἐπειδὰν ἀναληφθῶ, ἀποστελῶ
σοί τινα τῶν μαθητῶν μου, ἵνα ἰάσηταί σου τὸ
πάθος καὶ ζωήν σοι καὶ τοῖς σὺν σοὶ παράσχηται.''

Ταύταις δὲ ταῖς ἐπιστολαῖς ἔτι καὶ ταῦτα 11
συνῆπτο τῇ Σύρων φωνῇ·

''Μετὰ δὲ τὸ ἀναληφθῆναι τὸν Ἰησοῦν ἀπέστειλεν αὐτῷ Ἰούδας, ὁ καὶ Θωμᾶς, Θαδδαῖον
ἀπόστολον, ἕνα τῶν ἑβδομήκοντα· ὃς ἐλθὼν
κατέμενεν πρὸς Τωβίαν τὸν τοῦ Τωβία. ὡς δὲ
ἠκούσθη περὶ αὐτοῦ,[1] ἐμηνύθη τῷ Ἀβγάρῳ ὅτι
ἐλήλυθεν ἀπόστολος ἐνταῦθα τοῦ Ἰησοῦ, καθὰ

Matt. 4, 23. ἐπέστειλέν σοι. ἤρξατο οὖν ὁ Θαδδαῖος ἐν δυνάμει 12
9, 35. 10, 1 θεοῦ θεραπεύειν πᾶσαν νόσον καὶ μαλακίαν, ὥστε
πάντας θαυμάζειν· ὡς δὲ ἤκουσεν ὁ Ἄβγαρος τὰ
μεγαλεῖα καὶ τὰ θαυμάσια ἃ ἐποίει, καὶ ὡς ἐθερά-
πευεν, ἐν ὑπονοίᾳ γέγονεν ὡς ὅτι αὐτός ἐστιν περὶ
οὗ ὁ Ἰησοῦς ἐπέστειλεν λέγων ' ἐπειδὰν ἀναληφθῶ,
ἀποστελῶ σοί τινα τῶν μαθητῶν μου, ὃς τὸ πάθος
σου ἰάσεται.' μετακαλεσάμενος οὖν τὸν Τωβίαν, 13
παρ' ᾧ κατέμενεν, εἶπεν ' ἤκουσα ὅτι ἀνήρ τις
δυνάστης ἐλθὼν κατέμεινεν ἐν τῇ σῇ οἰκίᾳ· ἀνάγαγε αὐτὸν πρός με.'[2] ἐλθὼν δὲ ὁ Τωβίας παρὰ
Θαδδαίῳ, εἶπεν αὐτῷ ' ὁ τοπάρχης Ἄβγαρος
μετακαλεσάμενός με εἶπεν ἀναγαγεῖν σε παρ'
αὐτῷ, ἵνα θεραπεύσῃς αὐτόν.' καὶ ὁ Θαδδαῖος,

---

[1] αὐτοῦ ΑΤ¹ΜΣΛ : αὐτοῦ καὶ δῆλοσ γέγονε [γέγονεν D] διὰ τῶν
ἐπιτελουμένων παρ' αὐτοῦ θαυμασίων TcERBD.

[2] ἀνάγαγε αὐτὸν πρόσ με ΑΤΜΣΛ : καὶ πολλὰσ ἰάσεισ ἐπ' ὀνόματι
ῑυ ἐργάζεται· ὁ δὲ εἶπεν [εἶπε R] ναὶ κε ξένοσ τισ ἐλθὼν ἐνώκησεν

to come to you, I must first complete here all for which I was sent, and after thus completing it be taken up to him who sent me, and when I have been taken up, I will send to you one of my disciples to heal your suffering, and give life to you and those with you."

To these letters the following is further appended in the Syriac :

" Now after the ascension of Jesus, Judas, who is also Thomas, sent Thaddaeus to him as an apostle, being one of the Seventy, and he came and stayed with Tobias, the son of Tobias. Now when news of him was heard,[1] it was reported to Abgar that an Apostle of Jesus has come here, as he wrote to you. So Thaddaeus began in the power of God to heal every disease and weakness so that all marvelled And when Abgar heard the great and wonderful deeds which he was doing, and how he was working cures, he began to suspect that this was he of whom Jesus had written saying, ' When I have been taken up, I will send you one of my disciples who will heal your suffering.' So he summoned Tobias, with whom Thaddaeus was staying, and said, ' I hear that a certain man of power has come and is staying in your house. Bring him to me.'[2] And Tobias came to Thaddaeus and said to him, ' The Toparch, Abgar, summoned me and bade me bring you to him in order to heal him.' And Thad-

---

[1] Some manuscripts add : " And he had become manifest by the wonders wrought by him."

[2] Some manuscripts continue : " ' And he is working many cures in the name of Jesus.' And he said, ' Yes, Lord. A certain stranger came and is living with me, and is working many wonders.' And Abgar said, ' Bring him to me.' "

[ἐνώκησε R, ἐνοίκησεν ED] παρ' ἐμοὶ καὶ πολλὰ θαύματα ἐπιτελεῖ· ὁ δὲ ἀνάγαγε αὐτὸν ἔφη πρόσ με ERBD.

'ἀναβαίνω,' ἔφη, 'ἐπειδήπερ δυνάμει παρ' αὐτῷ
ἀπέσταλμαι.' ὀρθρίσας οὖν ὁ Τωβίας τῇ ἑξῆς καὶ 14
παραλαβὼν τὸν Θαδδαῖον ἦλθεν πρὸς τὸν Ἄβγαρον.
ὡς δὲ ἀνέβη, παρόντων καὶ ἑστώτων τῶν μεγι-
στάνων αὐτοῦ, παραχρῆμα ἐν τῷ εἰσιέναι αὐτὸν
ὅραμα μέγα ἐφάνη τῷ Ἀβγάρῳ ἐν τῷ προσώπῳ
τοῦ ἀποστόλου Θαδδαίου· ὅπερ ἰδὼν Ἄβγαρος
προσεκύνησεν τῷ Θαδδαίῳ, θαῦμά τε ἔσχεν
πάντας τοὺς περιεστῶτας· αὐτοὶ γὰρ οὐχ ἑοράκασι
τὸ ὅραμα, ὃ μόνῳ τῷ Ἀβγάρῳ ἐφάνη· ὃς καὶ 15
τὸν Θαδδαῖον ἤρετο εἰ 'ἐπ' ἀληθείας μαθητὴς
εἶ Ἰησοῦ τοῦ υἱοῦ τοῦ θεοῦ, ὃς εἰρήκει πρός με
" ἀποστελῶ σοί τινα τῶν μαθητῶν μου, ὅστις
ἰάσεταί σε καὶ ζωήν σοι παρέξει."' καὶ ὁ Θαδδαῖος ἔφη 'ἐπεὶ μεγάλως πεπίστευκας εἰς τὸν
ἀποστείλαντά με, διὰ τοῦτο ἀπεστάλην πρὸς σέ.
καὶ πάλιν, ἐὰν πιστεύσῃς ἐν αὐτῷ, ὡς ἂν πιστεύσῃς ἔσται σοι τὰ αἰτήματα τῆς καρδίας σου.'
καὶ ὁ Ἄβγαρος πρὸς αὐτόν 'οὕτως ἐπίστευσα,' 16
φησίν, 'ἐν αὐτῷ, ὡς καὶ τοὺς Ἰουδαίους τοὺς
σταυρώσαντας αὐτὸν βουληθῆναι δύναμιν παραλαβὼν κατακόψαι, εἰ μὴ διὰ τὴν βασιλείαν τὴν
Ῥωμαίων ἀνεκόπην τούτου.' καὶ ὁ Θαδδαῖος
εἶπεν 'ὁ κύριος ἡμῶν τὸ θέλημα τοῦ πατρὸς
αὐτοῦ πεπλήρωκεν καὶ πληρώσας ἀνελήφθη πρὸς
τὸν πατέρα.' λέγει αὐτῷ Ἄβγαρος 'κἀγὼ πε- 17
πίστευκα εἰς αὐτὸν καὶ εἰς τὸν πατέρα αὐτοῦ.'
καὶ ὁ Θαδδαῖος 'διὰ τοῦτο,' φησίν, 'τίθημι τὴν
χεῖρά μου ἐπὶ σὲ ἐν ὀνόματι αὐτοῦ.' καὶ τοῦτο
πράξαντος, παραχρῆμα ἐθεραπεύθη τῆς νόσου καὶ
τοῦ πάθους οὗ εἶχεν. ἐθαύμασέν τε ὁ Ἄβγαρος 18
ὅτι καθὼς ἤκουσται αὐτῷ περὶ τοῦ Ἰησοῦ, οὕτως

daeus said, ' I will go up since I have been miraculously sent to him.' So Tobias rose up early the next day and taking Thaddaeus came to Abgar. Now as he went up, while the king's magnates were standing present, as soon as he entered a great vision appeared to Abgar on the face of the Apostle Thaddaeus. And when Abgar saw this, he did reverence to Thaddaeus, and wonder held all who were standing by, for they had not seen the vision, which appeared only to Abgar. And he asked Thaddaeus, ' Are you of a truth a disciple of Jesus, the Son of God, who said to me, " I will send you one of my disciples who will heal you and give you life " ? ' And Thaddaeus said, ' Since you have had great faith in him who sent me, I was sent to you for this reason. And again, if you believe in him, the request of your heart shall be to you as you believe.' And Abgar said to him, ' I have such belief in him as to have wished to take force and destroy the Jews who crucified him, had I not been prevented from this by the Roman Empire.' And Thaddaeus said, ' Our Lord has fulfilled the will of his Father, and after fulfilling it has been taken up to the Father.' And Abgar said to him, ' I too have believed on him and on his Father.' And Thaddaeus said, ' For this cause I put my hand on you in his name.' And when he did this immediately he was healed from the disease and the sufferings he had. And Abgar wondered that just as he had heard concerning Jesus

93

τοῖς ἔργοις παρέλαβεν διὰ τοῦ μαθητοῦ αὐτοῦ
Θαδδαίου, ὃς αὐτὸν ἄνευ φαρμακείας καὶ βοτανῶν
ἐθεράπευσεν, καὶ οὐ μόνον, ἀλλὰ καὶ ῎Αβδον τὸν
τοῦ ῎Αβδου, ποδάγραν ἔχοντα· ὃς καὶ αὐτὸς
προσελθὼν ὑπὸ τοὺς πόδας αὐτοῦ ἔπεσεν, εὐχάς
τε διὰ χειρὸς λαβὼν ἐθεραπεύθη, πολλούς τε
ἄλλους συμπολίτας αὐτῶν ὁ αὐτὸς ἰάσατο, θαυ-
μαστὰ καὶ μεγάλα ποιῶν καὶ κηρύσσων τὸν λόγον
τοῦ θεοῦ. μετὰ δὲ ταῦτα ὁ ῎Αβγαρος ‘ σὺ Θαδ- 19
δαῖε,’ ἔφη, ‘ σὺν δυνάμει τοῦ θεοῦ ταῦτα ποιεῖς
καὶ ἡμεῖς αὐτοὶ ἐθαυμάσαμεν· ἀλλ’ ἐπὶ τούτοις
δέομαί σου, διήγησαί μοι περὶ τῆς ἐλεύσεως τοῦ
᾿Ιησοῦ πῶς ἐγένετο, καὶ περὶ τῆς δυνάμεως αὐτοῦ,
καὶ ἐν ποίᾳ δυνάμει ταῦτα ἐποίει ἅτινα ἤκουσταί
μοι.’ καὶ ὁ Θαδδαῖος ‘ νῦν μὲν σιωπήσομαι,’ 20
ἔφη, ‘ ἐπεὶ δὲ κηρῦξαι τὸν λόγον ἀπεστάλην,
αὔριον ἐκκλησίασόν μοι τοὺς πολίτας σου πάντας,
καὶ ἐπ’ αὐτῶν κηρύξω καὶ σπερῶ ἐν αὐτοῖς τὸν
λόγον τῆς ζωῆς, περί τε τῆς ἐλεύσεως τοῦ ᾿Ιησοῦ
καθὼς ἐγένετο, καὶ περὶ τῆς ἀποστολῆς αὐτοῦ,
καὶ ἕνεκα τίνος ἀπεστάλη ὑπὸ τοῦ πατρός, καὶ
περὶ τῆς δυνάμεως καὶ τῶν ἔργων αὐτοῦ καὶ
μυστηρίων ὧν ἐλάλησεν ἐν κόσμῳ, καὶ ποίᾳ
δυνάμει ταῦτα ἐποίει, καὶ περὶ τῆς καινῆς αὐτοῦ
κηρύξεως, καὶ περὶ τῆς μικρότητος καὶ περὶ τῆς
Phil. 2, 8 ταπεινώσεως, καὶ πῶς ἐταπείνωσεν ἑαυτὸν καὶ
ἀπέθετο καὶ ἐσμίκρυνεν αὐτοῦ τὴν θεότητα, καὶ
ἐσταυρώθη, καὶ κατέβη εἰς τὸν ῞Αιδην, καὶ διέσχισε
φραγμὸν τὸν ἐξ αἰῶνος μὴ σχισθέντα, καὶ ἀν-
ήγειρεν νεκροὺς καὶ κατέβη μόνος, ἀνέβη δὲ μετὰ
πολλοῦ ὄχλου πρὸς τὸν πατέρα αὐτοῦ.¹’ ἐκέλευσεν 21

so he had in fact received through his disciple Thaddaeus, who cured him without drugs and herbs, and not only him but also Abdus the son of Abdus who had the gout; for he too came and fell at his feet, and received his prayer at his hands, and was healed. And the same Thaddaeus healed many others of their fellow-citizens, performing many wonderful deeds and preaching the word of God. And after this Abgar said, 'O Thaddaeus, it is by the power of God that you do these things, and we ourselves have wondered. But in addition to this I beg you, explain to me concerning the coming of Jesus, how it happened, and concerning his power, and by what power he did these things of which I have heard.' And Thaddaeus said, 'I will now be silent, but since I was sent to preach the word, summon for me to-morrow an assembly of all your citizens, and I will preach before them, and sow in them the word of life, both concerning the coming of Jesus, how it happened, and concerning his mission, and for what reason he was sent by the Father, and concerning his power, and his deeds, and the mysteries which he spoke in the world, and by what power he did these things, and concerning his new preaching, and concerning his lowliness and humiliation, and how he humbled himself, and put aside and made little his divinity, and was crucified, and descended into Hades, and rent the partition which had not been rent from the beginning of the world, and raised the dead, and he went down alone, but with a great multitude did he go up to his

---

[1] *αὐτοῦ* ATMΣΛ: *αὐτοῦ καὶ πῶσ κάθηται ἐν δεξιᾷ τοῦ θυ καὶ πρσ μετὰ δόξησ ἐν τοῖσ οὐνοισ καὶ πῶσ ἐλεύσεσθαι μέλλει πάλιν μετὰ δυνάμεωσ κρῖναι ζῶντασ καὶ νεκρούσ* ERBD.

οὖν ὁ Ἄβγαρος τῇ ἕωθεν συνάξαι τοὺς πολίτας αὐτοῦ καὶ ἀκοῦσαι τὴν κήρυξιν Θαδδαίου, καὶ μετὰ ταῦτα προσέταξεν δοθῆναι αὐτῷ χρυσὸν καὶ ἄσημον. ὁ δὲ οὐκ ἐδέξατο, εἰπών ' εἰ τὰ ἡμέτερα καταλελοίπαμεν, πῶς τὰ ἀλλότρια ληψόμεθα;' ἐπράχθη ταῦτα τεσσαρακοστῷ καὶ τριακο- 22 σιοστῷ ἔτει."

῝Α καὶ οὐκ εἰς ἄχρηστον πρὸς λέξιν ἐκ τῆς Σύρων μεταβληθέντα φωνῆς ἐνταῦθά μοι κατὰ καιρὸν κείσθω.

---

[1] Some manuscripts add : " And how he is seated on the right hand of God and the Father with glory in the Heavens, and how he will come again with power to judge the living and the dead."

Father.' [1] So Abgar commanded his citizens to assemble in the morning and to hear the preaching of Thaddaeus, and after this he ordered him to be given gold and plate, but he did not receive it, saying, ' If we have left our own things, how shall we take those of others ? ' These things were done in the 340th year." [2]

Let this valuable and literal translation from the Syriac suffice me for the present.

[2] The three hundredth and fortieth year of the Edessene era, which began 310 B.C., would be A.D. 30, which agrees with the date of the crucifixion given by Tertullian but is one year earlier than the date given in Jerome's version of the Chronicle of Eusebius and two years earlier than that given in the Armenian version of the same book.

B̄

Τάδε καὶ ἡ β̄ περιέχει βίβλος τῆς
Ἐκκλησιαστικῆς ἱστορίας

Ā Περὶ τῆς μετὰ τὴν ἀνάληψιν τοῦ Χριστοῦ
διαγωγῆς τῶν ἀποστόλων.

B̄ Ὅπως Τιβέριος ὑπὸ Πιλάτου τὰ περὶ τοῦ
Χριστοῦ διδαχθεὶς ἐκινήθη.

Γ̄ Ὅπως εἰς πάντα τὸν κόσμον ἐν βραχεῖ
χρόνῳ διέδραμεν ὁ περὶ τοῦ Χριστοῦ λόγος.

Δ̄ Ὡς μετὰ Τιβέριον Γάϊος Ἰουδαίων βασιλέα
καθίστησιν Ἀγρίππαν, τὸν Ἡρώδην ἀϊδίῳ
ζημιώσας φυγῇ.

Ē Ὡς Φίλων ὑπὲρ Ἰουδαίων πρεσβείαν ἐστεί-
λατο πρὸς Γάϊον.

Ϛ̄ Ὅσα Ἰουδαίοις συνερρύη κακὰ μετὰ τὴν
κατὰ τοῦ Χριστοῦ τόλμαν.

Ζ̄ Ὡς καὶ Πιλάτος ἑαυτὸν διεχρήσατο.

 Η̄ Περὶ τοῦ κατὰ Κλαύδιον λιμοῦ.

Θ̄ Μαρτύριον Ἰακώβου τοῦ ἀποστόλου.

Ī Ὡς Ἀγρίππας ὁ καὶ Ἡρώδης τοὺς ἀποστόλους διώξας τῆς θείας παραυτίκα δίκης
ᾔσθετο.

ĪĀ Περὶ Θευδᾶ τοῦ γόητος.

ĪB̄ Περὶ Ἑλένης τῆς τῶν Ἀδιαβηνῶν βασιλίδος.

ĪΓ̄ Περὶ Σίμωνος τοῦ μάγου.

98

CONTENTS OF BOOK II

The contents of the second book of the History of the Church is as follows :

   I. On the life of the Apostles after the Ascension of Christ.
  II. On the emotion of Tiberius at learning from Pilate the story of Christ.
 III. How in a short time the message concerning Christ ran through the whole world.
  IV. How after Tiberius Caius appointed Agrippa as King of the Jews and punished Herod with perpetual banishment.
   V. How Philo was sent on an embassy to Caius on behalf of the Jews.
  VI. All the evils which accumulated on the Jews after their crime against Christ.
 VII. How Pilate, too, committed suicide.
VIII. Concerning the famine in the time of Claudius.
  IX. The martyrdom of James the Apostle.
   X. How Agrippa, who was also called Herod, persecuted the Apostles and at once felt the punishment of God.
  XI. On Theudas the magician.
 XII. On Helena the Queen of the Adiabeni.
XIII. On Simon Magus.

ΙΔ Περὶ τοῦ κατὰ Ῥώμην κηρύγματος Πέτρου
    τοῦ ἀποστόλου.

ΙΕ Περὶ τοῦ κατὰ Μάρκον εὐαγγελίου.

ΙϚ Ὡς πρῶτος Μάρκος τοῖς κατ' Αἴγυπτον
    τὴν εἰς τὸν Χριστὸν γνῶσιν ἐκήρυξεν.

ΙΖ Οἷα περὶ τῶν κατ' Αἴγυπτον ἀσκητῶν ὁ
    Φίλων ἱστορεῖ.

ΙΗ Ὅσα τοῦ Φίλωνος εἰς ἡμᾶς περιῆλθεν συγ-
    γράμματα.

ΙΘ Οἷα τοὺς ἐν Ἱεροσολύμοις Ἰουδαίους συμ-
    φορὰ μετῆλθεν ἐν τῇ τοῦ πάσχα ἡμέρᾳ.

Κ Οἷα καὶ κατὰ Νέρωνα ἐν τοῖς Ἱεροσολύμοις
    ἐπράχθη.

ΚΑ Περὶ τοῦ Αἰγυπτίου, οὗ καὶ τῶν ἀποστόλων
    αἱ Πράξεις ἐμνημόνευσαν.

ΚΒ Ὡς ἐκ τῆς Ἰουδαίας εἰς τὴν Ῥώμην δέσμιος
    ἀναπεμφθεὶς Παῦλος ἀπολογησάμενος πά-
    σης ἀπελύθη αἰτίας.

ΚΓ Ὡς ἐμαρτύρησεν Ἰάκωβος ὁ τοῦ κυρίου
    χρηματίσας ἀδελφός.

ΚΔ Ὡς μετὰ Μάρκον πρῶτος ἐπίσκοπος τῆς
    Ἀλεξανδρέων ἐκκλησίας Ἀννιανὸς κατέστη.

ΚΕ Περὶ τοῦ κατὰ Νέρωνα διωγμοῦ, καθ' ὃν
    ἐπὶ Ῥώμης Παῦλος καὶ Πέτρος τοῖς ὑπὲρ
    εὐσεβείας μαρτυρίοις κατεκοσμήθησαν.

ΚϚ Ὡς μυρίοις κακοῖς περιηλάθησαν Ἰουδαῖοι,
    καὶ ὡς τὸν ὕστατον πρὸς Ῥωμαίους ἤραντο
    πόλεμον.

Συνῆκται ἡμῖν ἡ βίβλος ἀπὸ τῶν Κλήμεντος
Τερτυλλιανοῦ Ἰωσήπου Φίλωνος.

XIV. On the preaching of Peter the Apostle at Rome.

XV. On the Gospel according to Mark.

XVI. How Mark was the first to preach the knowledge of Christ to those in Egypt.

XVII. The narrative of Philo on the Ascetics in Egypt.

XVIII. The treatises of Philo which have come down to us.

XIX. The misfortunes which overtook the Jews in Jerusalem on the day of the Passover.

XX. What was done at Jerusalem under Nero.

XXI. On the Egyptian whom the Acts of the Apostles also mentioned.

XXII. How Paul was sent a prisoner to Rome from Judaea and after defending himself was acquitted of all guilt.

XXIII. How James who was called the brother of the Lord suffered martyrdom.

XXIV. How after Mark Annianus was the first to be appointed bishop of the church of the Alexandrians.

XXV. On the persecution under Nero in which Paul and Peter at Rome were adorned with martyrdom for religion's sake.

XXVI. How the Jews were pursued by countless evils and how they began the final war against the Romans.

Our book was compiled from those of Clement, Tertullian, Josephus, and Philo.

II

Ὅσα μὲν τῆς ἐκκλησιαστικῆς ἱστορίας ἐχρῆν 1
ὡς ἐν προοιμίῳ διαστείλασθαι τῆς τε θεολογίας
πέρι τοῦ σωτηρίου λόγου καὶ τῆς ἀρχαιολογίας
τῶν τῆς ἡμετέρας διδασκαλίας δογμάτων ἀρ-
χαιότητός τε τῆς κατὰ Χριστιανοὺς εὐαγγελικῆς
πολιτείας, οὐ μὴν ἀλλὰ καὶ ὅσα περὶ τῆς γενομένης ἔναγχος ἐπιφανείας αὐτοῦ, τά τε πρὸ τοῦ
πάθους καὶ τὰ περὶ τῆς τῶν ἀποστόλων ἐκλογῆς,
ἐν τῷ πρὸ τούτου, συντεμόντες τὰς ἀποδείξεις,
διειλήφαμεν· φέρε δ᾽, ἐπὶ τοῦ παρόντος ἤδη καὶ 2
τὰ μετὰ τὴν ἀνάληψιν αὐτοῦ διασκεψώμεθα, τὰ
μὲν ἐκ τῶν θείων παρασημαινόμενοι γραμμάτων,
τὰ δ᾽ ἔξωθεν προσιστοροῦντες ἐξ ὧν κατὰ καιρὸν
μνημονεύσομεν ὑπομνημάτων.

I. Πρῶτος τοιγαροῦν εἰς τὴν ἀποστολὴν ἀντὶ 1
τοῦ προδότου Ἰούδα κληροῦται Ματθίας, εἷς καὶ
αὐτός, ὡς δεδήλωται, τῶν τοῦ κυρίου γενόμενος
μαθητῶν. καθίστανται δὲ δι᾽ εὐχῆς καὶ χειρῶν
Acts 6, 1-6 ἐπιθέσεως τῶν ἀποστόλων εἰς διακονίαν ὑπηρεσίας
ἕνεκα τοῦ κοινοῦ ἄνδρες δεδοκιμασμένοι, τὸν
ἀριθμὸν ἑπτά, οἱ ἀμφὶ τὸν Στέφανον. ὃς καὶ
Acts 7, 58. 59 πρῶτος μετὰ τὸν κύριον ἅμα τῇ χειροτονίᾳ,
ὥσπερ εἰς αὐτὸ τοῦτο προαχθείς, λίθοις εἰς θάνατον
πρὸς τῶν κυριοκτόνων βάλλεται, καὶ ταύτῃ πρῶ-
102

BOOK II

ALL that needed stating by way of preface in the history of the Church—the proof of the divinity of the saving Logos, the ancient history of our teaching, and the antiquity of the dogmas of the Christian life according to the Gospel, particularly all the points concerning his recently fulfilled advent, the events before his Passion, and the story of the choice of the Apostles—all this we traced in the preceding book, summarizing the demonstration. Let us now consider in the present book what followed his Ascension, noting some things from the divine writings, and adding what is taken from other sources from treatises which we will quote from time to time.

I. Matthias was the first to be chosen to the Apostolate instead of the traitor Judas. As has been shown, he had himself been one of the Lord's disciples, For the administration of the common fund tried men, seven in number, led by Stephen, were appointed to the ministry by prayer and the laying on of the Apostles' hands. And Stephen was first after his Lord not only in ordination, but, as though he had been put forward for this very purpose, also in that he was stoned to death by the Lord's murderers, and so was the first to carry off the crown,

103

τος τὸν αὐτῷ φερώνυμον τῶν ἀξιονίκων τοῦ Χριστοῦ μαρτύρων ἀποφέρεται στέφανον.

Τότε δῆτα καὶ Ἰάκωβον, τὸν τοῦ κυρίου λεγό- 2 μενον ἀδελφόν, ὅτι δὴ καὶ οὗτος τοῦ Ἰωσὴφ ὠνό- μαστο παῖς, τοῦ δὲ Χριστοῦ πατὴρ ὁ Ἰωσήφ, ᾧ μνηστευθεῖσα ἡ παρθένος, πρὶν ἢ συνελθεῖν

Matt. 1, 18 αὐτούς, εὑρέθη ἐν γαστρὶ ἔχουσα ἐκ πνεύματος ἁγίου, ὡς ἡ ἱερὰ τῶν εὐαγγελίων διδάσκει γραφή· τοῦτον δὴ οὖν αὐτὸν Ἰάκωβον, ὃν καὶ δίκαιον ἐπίκλην οἱ πάλαι δι᾿ ἀρετῆς ἐκάλουν προτερήματα, πρῶτον ἱστοροῦσιν τῆς ἐν Ἱεροσολύμοις ἐκκλη- σίας τὸν τῆς ἐπισκοπῆς ἐγχειρισθῆναι θρόνον· Κλήμης ἐν ἕκτῳ τῶν Ὑποτυπώσεων γράφων 3 ὧδε παρίστησιν " Πέτρον γάρ φησι καὶ Ἰάκωβον καὶ Ἰωάννην μετὰ τὴν ἀνάληψιν τοῦ σωτῆρος, ὡς ἂν καὶ ὑπὸ τοῦ σωτῆρος προτετιμημένους, μὴ ἐπιδικάζεσθαι δόξης, ἀλλὰ Ἰάκωβον τὸν δίκαιον ἐπίσκοπον τῶν Ἱεροσολύμων ἑλέσθαι." ὁ δ᾿ αὐτὸς 4 ἐν ἑβδόμῳ τῆς αὐτῆς ὑποθέσεως ἔτι καὶ ταῦτα περὶ αὐτοῦ φησιν " Ἰακώβῳ τῷ δικαίῳ καὶ Ἰωάννῃ καὶ Πέτρῳ μετὰ τὴν ἀνάστασιν παρ- έδωκεν τὴν γνῶσιν ὁ κύριος, οὗτοι τοῖς λοιποῖς ἀποστόλοις παρέδωκαν, οἱ δὲ λοιποὶ ἀπόστολοι τοῖς ἑβδομήκοντα· ὧν εἷς ἦν καὶ Βαρναβᾶς. δύο 5 δὲ γεγόνασιν Ἰάκωβοι, εἷς ὁ δίκαιος, ὁ κατὰ τοῦ πτερυγίου βληθεὶς καὶ ὑπὸ γναφέως ξύλῳ πληγεὶς εἰς θάνατον, ἕτερος δὲ ὁ καρατομηθείς."

Αὐτοῦ δὴ τοῦ δικαίου καὶ ὁ Παῦλος μνημονεύει Gal. 1, 19 γράφων " ἕτερον δὲ τῶν ἀποστόλων οὐκ εἶδον, εἰ μὴ Ἰάκωβον τὸν ἀδελφὸν τοῦ κυρίου."

Ἐν τούτοις καὶ τὰ τῆς τοῦ σωτῆρος ἡμῶν πρὸς 6 τὸν τῶν Ὀσροηνῶν βασιλέα τέλος ἐλάμβανεν

implied by his name,[1] which was gained by the martyrs of Christ found worthy of victory.

At that same time also James, who was called the brother of the Lord, inasmuch as the latter too was styled the child of Joseph, and Joseph was called the father of Christ, for the Virgin was betrothed to him when, before they came together, she was discovered to have conceived by the Holy Spirit, as the sacred writing of the Gospels teaches—this same James, to whom the men of old had also given the surname of Just for his excellence of virtue, is narrated to have been the first elected to the throne of the bishopric of the Church in Jerusalem. Clement in the sixth book of the *Hypotyposes* adduces the following : " For," he says, " Peter and James and John after the Ascension of the Saviour did not struggle for glory, because they had previously been given honour by the Saviour, but chose James the Just as bishop of Jerusalem." The same writer in the seventh book of the same work says in addition this about him, " After the Resurrection the Lord gave the tradition of knowledge to James the Just and John and Peter, these gave it to the other Apostles and the other Apostles to the seventy, of whom Barnabas also was one. Now there were two Jameses, one James the Just, who was thrown down from the pinnacle of the temple and beaten to death with a fuller's club, and the other he who was beheaded." Paul also mentions the same James the Just when he writes, " And I saw none other of the Apostles save James the brother of the Lord."

At this time too the terms of our Saviour's promise [2] to the king of the Osrhoenes were receiving fulfil-

---

[1] Stephen in Greek means *crown.*   [2] See pp. 84 ff.

ὑποσχέσεως. ὁ γοῦν Θωμᾶς τὸν Θαδδαῖον κινήσει
θειοτέρᾳ ἐπὶ τὰ Ἔδεσσα κήρυκα καὶ εὐαγγελιστὴν
τῆς περὶ τοῦ Χριστοῦ διδασκαλίας ἐκπέμπει,
ὡς ἀπὸ τῆς εὑρεθείσης αὐτόθι γραφῆς μικρῷ
πρόσθεν ἐδηλώσαμεν· ὁ δὲ τοῖς τόποις ἐπιστάς, 7
τόν τε Ἄβγαρον ἰᾶται τῷ Χριστοῦ λόγῳ καὶ
τοὺς αὐτόθι πάντας τοῖς τῶν θαυμάτων παραδόξοις
ἐκπλήττει, ἱκανῶς τε αὐτοὺς τοῖς ἔργοις διαθεὶς
καὶ ἐπὶ σέβας ἀγαγὼν τῆς τοῦ Χριστοῦ δυνάμεως,
μαθητὰς τῆς σωτηρίου διδασκαλίας κατεστήσατο,
εἰς ἔτι τε νῦν ἐξ ἐκείνου ἡ πᾶσα τῶν Ἐδεσσηνῶν
πόλις τῇ Χριστοῦ προσανάκειται προσηγορίᾳ,
οὐ τὸ τυχὸν ἐπιφερομένη δεῖγμα τῆς τοῦ σωτῆρος
ἡμῶν καὶ εἰς αὐτοὺς εὐεργεσίας. καὶ ταῦτα δ' 8
ὡς ἐξ ἀρχαίων ἱστορίας εἰρήσθω· μετίωμεν δ'
αὖθις ἐπὶ τὴν θείαν γραφήν.

Acts 8, 1 Γενομένου ῥῆτα ἐπὶ τῇ τοῦ Στεφάνου μαρτυρίᾳ
πρώτου καὶ μεγίστου πρὸς αὐτῶν Ἰουδαίων
κατὰ τῆς ἐν Ἱεροσολύμοις ἐκκλησίας διωγμοῦ
πάντων τε τῶν μαθητῶν πλὴν ὅτι μόνων τῶν
δώδεκα ἀνὰ τὴν Ἰουδαίαν τε καὶ Σαμάρειαν
Acts 11, 19 διασπαρέντων, τινές, ᾗ φησιν ἡ θεία γραφή,
διελθόντες ἕως Φοινίκης καὶ Κύπρου καὶ Ἀντιοχείας
οὔπω μὲν ἔθνεσιν οἷοί τε ἦσαν τοῦ τῆς πίστεως
μεταδιδόναι λόγου τολμᾶν, μόνοις δὲ τοῦτον
Acts 8, 3 Ἰουδαίοις κατήγγελλον. τηνικαῦτα καὶ Παῦλος 9
ἐλυμαίνετο εἰς ἔτι τότε τὴν ἐκκλησίαν, κατ'
οἴκους τῶν πιστῶν εἰσπορευόμενος σύρων τε
ἄνδρας καὶ γυναῖκας καὶ εἰς φυλακὴν παραδιδούς.
Acts 6, 5 ἀλλὰ καὶ Φίλιππος, εἷς τῶν ἅμα Στεφάνῳ προ- 10
Acts 8, 5-13 χειρισθέντων εἰς τὴν διακονίαν, ἐν τοῖς διασπα-
ρεῖσιν γενόμενος, κάτεισιν εἰς τὴν Σαμάρειαν,

ment. Thomas was divinely moved to send Thaddaeus to Edessa as herald and evangelist of the teaching concerning Christ, as we have shown just previously from the writing preserved there. When he reached the place Thaddaeus healed Abgar by the word of Christ, and amazed all the inhabitants by his strange miracles. By the mighty influence of his deeds he brought them to reverence the power of Christ, and made them disciples of the saving teaching. From that day to this the whole city of the Edessenes has been dedicated[1] to the name of Christ, thus displaying no common proof of the beneficence of our Saviour to them. Let this suffice from the history of the ancients and let us pass again to the divine Scripture.

On the martyrdom of Stephen there arose the first and greatest persecution of the Church in Jerusalem by the Jews. All the disciples, with the single exception of the Twelve, were scattered throughout Judaea and Samaria; some, as the divine Scripture says, traversed as far as Phoenice, Cyprus and Antioch, but they were not yet in a position to venture to transmit the word of faith to Gentiles, and announced it only to Jews. At that time Paul also was still ravaging the Church, entering into the houses of the faithful, dragging out men and women, and handing them over to prison. Philip, however, one of those who with Stephen had been already ordained to the diaconate, was among those who were scattered abroad, and went down to Samaria, where, filled with divine

---

[1] This seems merely to mean "became converted to Christianity."

EUSEBIUS

θείας τε ἔμπλεως δυνάμεως κηρύττει πρῶτος
τοῖς αὐτόθι τὸν λόγον, τοσαύτη δ' αὐτῷ θεία
συνήργει χάρις, ὡς καὶ Σίμωνα τὸν μάγον μετὰ
πλείστων ὅσων τοῖς αὐτοῦ λόγοις ἐλχθῆναι. ἐπὶ 11
τοσοῦτον δ' ὁ Σίμων βεβοημένος κατ' ἐκεῖνο
καιροῦ τῶν ἠπατημένων ἐκράτει γοητείᾳ, ὡς
τὴν μεγάλην αὐτὸν ἡγεῖσθαι εἶναι δύναμιν τοῦ
θεοῦ. τότε δ' οὖν καὶ οὗτος τὰς ὑπὸ τοῦ Φιλίππου δυνάμει θείᾳ τελουμένας καταπλαγεὶς παραδοξοποιίας, ὑποδύεται καὶ μέχρι λουτροῦ τὴν
εἰς Χριστὸν πίστιν καθυποκρίνεται· ὃ καὶ θαυμά- 12
ζειν ἄξιον εἰς δεῦρο γινόμενον πρὸς τῶν ἔτι καὶ
νῦν τὴν ἀπ' ἐκείνου μιαρωτάτην μετιόντων αἵρεσιν,
οἳ τῇ τοῦ σφῶν προπάτορος μεθόδῳ τὴν ἐκκλησίαν λοιμώδους καὶ ψωραλέας νόσου δίκην ὑπο-
δυόμενοι, τὰ μέγιστα λυμαίνονται τοὺς οἷς ἐν-
απομάξασθαι οἷοί τε ἂν εἶεν τὸν ἐν αὐτοῖς ἀπο-
κεκρυμμένον δυσαλθῆ καὶ χαλεπὸν ἰόν. ἤδη γέ
τοι πλείους τούτων ἀπεώσθησαν, ὁποῖοί τινες
εἶεν τὴν μοχθηρίαν ἁλόντες, ὥσπερ οὖν καὶ ὁ
Acts 8, 18-23 Σίμων αὐτὸς πρὸς τοῦ Πέτρου καταφωραθεὶς
ὃς ἦν, τὴν προσήκουσαν ἔτισεν τιμωρίαν. ἀλλὰ 13
γὰρ εἰς αὔξην ὁσημέραι προϊόντος τοῦ σωτηρίου
Acts 8, 26-38 κηρύγματος, οἰκονομία τις ἦγεν ἀπὸ τῆς Αἰθιόπων
γῆς τῆς αὐτόθι βασιλίδος, κατά τι πάτριον ἔθος
ὑπὸ γυναικὸς τοῦ ἔθνους εἰς ἔτι νῦν βασιλευο-
μένου, δυνάστην· ὃν πρῶτον ἐξ ἐθνῶν πρὸς τοῦ
Φιλίππου δι' ἐπιφανείας τὰ τοῦ θείου λόγου ὄργια
μετασχόντα τῶν τε ἀνὰ τὴν οἰκουμένην πιστῶν
ἀπαρχὴν γενόμενον, πρῶτον κατέχει λόγος ἐπὶ
τὴν πάτριον παλινοστήσαντα γῆν εὐαγγελίσασθαι
τὴν τοῦ τῶν ὅλων θεοῦ γνῶσιν καὶ τὴν ζωοποιὸν

power, he was the first to preach the word to those there. So great was the grace of God, which worked with him, that even Simon Magus, with countless others, was captivated by his words. At that time Simon had obtained such fame by his magical power over his victims that he was held to be the Great Power of God ; but even he was then so overwhelmed by the marvels wrought by Philip by divine power, that he submitted, and feigned faith in Christ even to the point of baptism. It is worthy of wonder that this is still done by those who continue his most unclean heresy to the present day, for following the method of their progenitor they attach themselves to the Church like a pestilential and scurfy disease, and ravage to the utmost all whom they are able to inoculate with the deadly and terrible poison hidden in them. Most of these, however, have already been driven out, as many as have been detected in their wickedness, just as Simon himself, when his real nature was detected by Peter, paid the proper punishment. While the saving preaching was daily progressing and growing, some providence brought from the land of the Ethiopians an officer of the queen of that land, for the nation, following ancestral customs, is still ruled by a woman. Tradition says that he, who was the first of the Gentiles to receive from Philip by revelation the mysteries of the divine word, and was the first-fruits of the faithful throughout the world, was also the first to return to his native land and preach the Gospel of the knowledge of the God of the universe and the sojourn of our

EUSEBIUS

εἰς ἀνθρώπους τοῦ σωτῆρος ἡμῶν ἐπιδημίαν,
ἔργῳ πληρωθείσης δι' αὐτοῦ τῆς "Αἰθιοπία
προφθάσει χεῖρα αὐτῆς τῷ θεῷ" περιεχούσης
προφητείας. ἐπὶ τούτοις Παῦλος, τὸ τῆς ἐκλογῆς 14
σκεῦος, οὐκ ἐξ ἀνθρώπων οὐδὲ δι' ἀνθρώπων,
δι' ἀποκαλύψεως δ' αὐτοῦ Ἰησοῦ Χριστοῦ καὶ
θεοῦ πατρὸς τοῦ ἐγείραντος αὐτὸν ἐκ νεκρῶν,
ἀπόστολος ἀναδείκνυται, δι' ὀπτασίας καὶ τῆς
κατὰ τὴν ἀποκάλυψιν οὐρανίου φωνῆς ἀξιωθεὶς
τῆς κλήσεως.

II. Καὶ δὴ τῆς παραδόξου τοῦ σωτῆρος ἡμῶν 1
ἀναστάσεώς τε καὶ εἰς οὐρανοὺς ἀναλήψεως τοῖς
πλείστοις ἤδη περιβοήτου καθεστώσης, παλαιοῦ
κεκρατηκότος ἔθους τοῖς τῶν ἐθνῶν ἄρχουσι τὰ
παρὰ σφίσιν καινοτομούμενα τῷ τὴν βασίλειον
ἀρχὴν ἐπικρατοῦντι σημαίνειν, ὡς ἂν μηδὲν αὐτὸν
διαδιδράσκοι τῶν γινομένων, τὰ περὶ τῆς ἐκ
νεκρῶν ἀναστάσεως τοῦ σωτῆρος ἡμῶν Ἰησοῦ
εἰς πάντας ἤδη καθ' ὅλης Παλαιστίνης βεβοη-
μένα Πιλᾶτος Τιβερίῳ βασιλεῖ κοινοῦται, τάς 2
τε ἄλλας αὐτοῦ πυθόμενος τεραστίας καὶ ὡς ὅτι
μετὰ θάνατον ἐκ νεκρῶν ἀναστὰς ἤδη θεὸς εἶναι
παρὰ τοῖς πολλοῖς πεπίστευτο. τὸν δὲ Τιβέριον
ἀνενεγκεῖν ἐπὶ τὴν σύγκλητον ἐκείνην τ' ἀπώσα-
σθαί φασι τὸν λόγον, τῷ μὲν δοκεῖν, ὅτι μὴ πρότερον αὐτὴ τοῦτο δοκιμάσασα ἦν, παλαιοῦ νόμου
κεκρατηκότος μὴ ἄλλως τινὰ παρὰ Ῥωμαίοις
θεοποιεῖσθαι μὴ οὐχὶ ψήφῳ καὶ δόγματι συγκλήτου, τῇ δ' ἀληθείᾳ, ὅτι μηδὲ τῆς ἐξ ἀνθρώπων
ἐπικρίσεώς τε καὶ συστάσεως ἡ σωτήριος τοῦ
θείου κηρύγματος ἐδεῖτο διδασκαλία· ταύτῃ δ' 3
οὖν ἀπωσαμένης τὸν προσαγγελθέντα περὶ τοῦ

Psalm 67, 32
Acts 9, 15
Gal. 1, 1
Acts 9, 3-6
Tert. Apol.
21

Saviour which gives life to men, so that by him was actually fulfilled the prophecy which says, " Ethiopia shall stretch out her hand to God." In addition to these Paul, the chosen vessel neither of men nor through men but through revelation of Jesus Christ himself and God the Father who raised him from the dead, was appointed an Apostle, being vouchsafed this calling by a vision and the heavenly voice of revelation.

II. The wonderful resurrection and ascension into heaven of our Saviour was now already generally famous, and in accordance with an ancient custom that those who were ruling over the nations should report to him who held the imperial office any new movement among them, in order that no event might escape his notice, Pilate communicated to the Emperor Tiberius the story of the resurrection from the dead of our Saviour Jesus as already famous among all throughout all Palestine, together with the information he had gained of his other wonders and how he was already believed by many to be a God, in that after death he had risen from the dead.[1] They say that Tiberius referred the report to the Senate, which rejected it ostensibly because it had not previously tested the matter, for an ancient law prevailed that no one should be held as a God by the Romans except by a vote and decree of the Senate, but in truth because the saving teaching of the divine message needed no ratification and commendation from men. In this way the council of

[1] Several versions of Pilate's report are extant, all obviously fictitious. See Tischendorf, *Evangelia apocrypha*, and the article of Lipsius on Apocryphal Gospels in the *Dictionary of Christian Biography*, vol. ii. pp. 707 ff.

σωτῆρος ἡμῶν λόγον τῆς Ῥωμαίων βουλῆς, τὸν Τιβέριον ἦν καὶ πρότερον εἶχεν γνώμην τηρήσαντα, μηδὲν ἄτοπον κατὰ τῆς τοῦ Χριστοῦ διδασκαλίας ἐπινοῆσαι.

Ταῦτα Τερτυλλιανὸς τοὺς Ῥωμαίων νόμους ἠκρι- 4 βωκώς, ἀνὴρ τά τε ἄλλα ἔνδοξος καὶ τῶν μάλιστα ἐπὶ Ῥώμης λαμπρῶν, ἐν τῇ γραφείσῃ μὲν αὐτῷ Ῥωμαίων φωνῇ, μεταβληθείσῃ δ᾽ ἐπὶ τὴν Ἑλλάδα γλῶτταν ὑπὲρ Χριστιανῶν ἀπολογίᾳ τίθησιν, κατὰ λέξιν τοῦτον ἱστορῶν τὸν τρόπον

Tert. Apol. 5 '' ἵνα δὲ καὶ ἐκ τῆς γενέσεως διαλεχθῶμεν τῶν 5 τοιούτων νόμων, παλαιὸν ἦν δόγμα μηδένα θεὸν ὑπὸ βασιλέως καθιεροῦσθαι, πρὶν ὑπὸ τῆς συγκλήτου δοκιμασθῆναι. Μάρκος Αἰμίλιος οὕτως περί τινος εἰδώλου πεποίηκεν Ἀλβούρνου. καὶ τοῦτο ὑπὲρ τοῦ ἡμῶν λόγου πεποίηται, ὅτι παρ᾽ ὑμῖν ἀνθρωπείᾳ δοκιμῇ ἡ θεότης δίδοται. ἐὰν μὴ ἀνθρώπῳ θεὸς ἀρέσῃ, θεὸς οὐ γίνεται· οὕτως κατά γε τοῦτο ἄνθρωπον θεῷ ἵλεω εἶναι προσῆκεν. Τιβέριος οὖν, ἐφ᾽ οὗ τὸ τῶν Χριστιανῶν 6 ὄνομα εἰς τὸν κόσμον εἰσελήλυθεν, ἀγγελθέντος αὐτῷ ἐκ Παλαιστίνης τοῦ δόγματος τούτου, ἔνθα πρῶτον ἤρξατο, τῇ συγκλήτῳ ἀνεκοινώσατο, δῆλος ὢν ἐκείνοις ὡς τῷ δόγματι ἀρέσκεται. ἡ δὲ σύγκλητος, ἐπεὶ οὐκ αὐτὴ δεδοκιμάκει, ἀπώσατο· ὁ δὲ ἐν τῇ αὐτοῦ ἀποφάσει ἔμεινεν, ἀπειλήσας θάνατον τοῖς τῶν Χριστιανῶν κατηγόροις.''

Τῆς οὐρανίου προνοίας κατ᾽ οἰκονομίαν τοῦτ᾽ αὐτῷ πρὸς νοῦν βαλλομένης, ὡς ἂν ἀπαραποδίστως ἀρχὰς ἔχων ὁ τοῦ εὐαγγελίου λόγος πανταχόσε γῆς διαδράμοι.

III. Οὕτω δῆτα οὐρανίῳ δυνάμει καὶ συνεργίᾳ 1

the Romans rejected the report sent to it concerning our Saviour, but Tiberius kept the opinion which he had formerly held and made no wicked plans against the teaching of Christ.

Tertullian, who had an accurate knowledge of Roman law, a man especially famous among those most distinguished in Rome, has noted this in the Apology for the Christians which was written by him in Latin but translated into the Greek language ; he tells the story as follows : " But, in order that we may discuss such laws from their origin, there was an ancient decree that none should be consecrated as a god by an Emperor before being approved by the Senate. Marcus Aemilius has acted thus concerning a certain idol Alburnus. And this supports our argument that among you godship has been given by human approval. If a god does not please man, he does not become god, so that, according to this, man must be gracious to God. Tiberius, therefore, in whose time the name of Christian came into the world, when this doctrine was reported to him from Palestine, where it first began, communicated it to the Senate, and made it plain to them that he favoured the doctrine, but the Senate, because it had not itself tested it, rejected it ; but he continued in his own opinion and threatened death to the accusers of the Christians." [1] For heavenly providence had designed putting this in his mind in order that the word of the Gospel might have an unimpeded beginning, and traverse the earth in all directions.

III. Thus by the power and assistance of Heaven

[1] Eusebius seems to imply that the following sentence is part of Tertullian. This is not so in the Latin manuscripts.

ἀθρόως οἷά τις ἡλίου βολὴ τὴν σύμπασαν οἰκουμένην ὁ σωτήριος κατηύγαζε λόγος. αὐτίκα ταῖς θείαις ἑπομένως γραφαῖς ἐπὶ "πᾶσαν" προῄει

Psalm 18, 5 "τὴν γῆν ὁ φθόγγος" τῶν θεσπεσίων εὐαγγελιστῶν αὐτοῦ καὶ ἀποστόλων, "καὶ εἰς τὰ πέρατα τῆς οἰκουμένης τὰ ῥήματα αὐτῶν." καὶ δῆτα 2 ἀνὰ πάσας πόλεις τε καὶ κώμας, πληθυούσης

Matt. 3, 12 ἅλωνος δίκην, μυρίανδροι καὶ παμπληθεῖς ἀθρόως

Luke 3, 17 ἐκκλησίαι συνεστήκεσαν, οἵ τε ἐκ προγόνων διαδοχῆς καὶ τῆς ἀνέκαθεν πλάνης παλαιᾷ νόσῳ δεισιδαιμονίας εἰδώλων τὰς ψυχὰς πεπεδημένοι, πρὸς τῆς τοῦ Χριστοῦ δυνάμεως διὰ τῆς τῶν φοιτητῶν αὐτοῦ διδασκαλίας τε ὁμοῦ καὶ παραδοξοποιίας ὥσπερ δεινῶν δεσποτῶν ἀπηλλαγμένοι εἱργμῶν τε χαλεπωτάτων λύσιν εὑράμενοι, πάσης μὲν δαιμονικῆς κατέπτυον πολυθεΐας, ἕνα δὲ μόνον εἶναι θεὸν ὡμολόγουν, τὸν τῶν συμπάντων δημιουργόν, τοῦτόν τε αὐτὸν θεσμοῖς ἀληθοῦς εὐσεβείας δι᾽ ἐνθέου καὶ σώφρονος θρησκείας τῆς ὑπὸ τοῦ σωτῆρος ἡμῶν τῷ τῶν ἀνθρώπων βίῳ κατασπαρείσης ἐγέραιρον. ἀλλὰ γὰρ τῆς 3 χάριτος ἤδη τῆς θείας καὶ ἐπὶ τὰ λοιπὰ χεομένης ἔθνη καὶ πρώτου μὲν κατὰ τὴν Παλαιστίνων

Acts 10 Καισάρειαν Κορνηλίου σὺν ὅλῳ τῷ οἴκῳ δι᾽ ἐπιφανείας θειοτέρας ὑπουργίας τε Πέτρου τὴν εἰς Χριστὸν πίστιν καταδεξαμένου πλείστων τε

Acts 11, 20-30 καὶ ἄλλων ἐπ᾽ Ἀντιοχείας Ἑλλήνων, οἷς οἱ κατὰ τὸν Στεφάνου διωγμὸν διασπαρέντες ἐκήρυξαν, ἀνθούσης ἄρτι καὶ πληθυούσης τῆς κατὰ Ἀντιόχειαν ἐκκλησίας ἐν ταὐτῷ τε ἐπιπαρόντων πλείστων ὅσων τῶν τε ἀπὸ Ἱεροσολύμων προφητῶν καὶ σὺν αὐτοῖς Βαρναβᾶ καὶ Παύλου ἑτέρου τε

114

the saving word began to flood the whole world with light like the rays of the sun. At once, in accordance with the divine Scriptures, the voice of its inspired evangelists and Apostles " went forth to the whole earth and their words to the end of the world." In every city and village arose churches crowded with thousands of men, like a teeming threshing-floor. Those who by hereditary succession and original error had their souls bound by the ancient disease of the superstition of idols were set free as if from fierce masters and found release from fearful bondage by the power of Christ through the teaching of his followers and their wonderful deeds. They rejected all the polytheism of the demons, and confessed that there is only one God, the Creator of the universe. Him they honoured with the rites of true piety by the divine and rational worship which was implanted by our Saviour in the life of men. But indeed it was when the grace of God was already being poured out even on the other nations—when faith in Christ had been received, first by Cornelius with all his house in Palestinian Caesarea through divine manifestation and the ministration of Peter, and also by many other Greeks in Antioch, to whom those preached who had been scattered in the persecution about Stephen, and the Church in Antioch was already flourishing and multiplying—it was at that moment and in that place, when so many of the prophets from Jerusalem were also present, and with them Barnabas and Paul, and a number of the other

πλήθους ἐπὶ τούτοις ἀδελφῶν, ἡ Χριστιανῶν προσηγορία τότε πρῶτον αὐτόθι ὥσπερ ἀπ' εὐθαλοῦς καὶ γονίμου πηγῆς ἀναδίδοται. καὶ Ἄγα- 4 βος μέν, εἷς τῶν συνόντων αὐτοῖς προφητῶν, περὶ τοῦ μέλλειν ἔσεσθαι λιμὸν προθεσπίζει, Παῦλος δὲ καὶ Βαρναβᾶς ἐξυπηρετησόμενοι τῇ τῶν ἀδελφῶν παραπέμπονται διακονίᾳ.

Joseph. A.I.
18, 224 ; B.I.
2, 180

IV. Τιβέριος μὲν οὖν ἀμφὶ τὰ δύο καὶ εἴκοσι βα- 1 σιλεύσας ἔτη τελευτᾷ, μετὰ δὲ τοῦτον Γάϊος τὴν ἡγεμονίαν παραλαβών, αὐτίκα τῆς Ἰουδαίων ἀρχῆς Ἀγρίππᾳ τὸ διάδημα περιτίθησιν, βασιλέα καταστήσας αὐτὸν τῆς τε Φιλίππου καὶ τῆς Λυσανίου τετραρχίας, πρὸς αἷς μετ' οὐ πολὺν αὐτῷ χρόνον καὶ τὴν Ἡρῴδου τετραρχίαν παραδίδωσιν, ἀϊδίῳ φυγῇ τὸν Ἡρῴδην (οὗτος δ' ἦν ὁ κατὰ τὸ πάθος τοῦ σωτῆρος) σὺν καὶ τῇ γυναικὶ Ἡρῳδιάδι

Joseph. A.I
18, 237. 252.
255

πλείστων ἕνεκα ζημιώσας αἰτιῶν. μάρτυς Ἰώσηπος καὶ τούτων.

Κατὰ δὴ τοῦτον Φίλων ἐγνωρίζετο πλείστοις, ἀνὴρ οὐ μόνον τῶν ἡμετέρων, ἀλλὰ καὶ τῶν ἀπὸ τῆς ἔξωθεν ὁρμωμένων παιδείας ἐπισημότατος. τὸ μὲν οὖν γένος ἀνέκαθεν Ἑβραῖος ἦν, τῶν δ' ἐπ' Ἀλεξανδρείας ἐν τέλει διαφανῶν οὐδενὸς χείρων, περὶ δὲ τὰ θεῖα καὶ πάτρια μαθήματα ὅσον τε καὶ ὁπηλίκον εἰσενήνεκται πόνον, ἔργῳ πᾶσι δῆλος, καὶ περὶ τὰ φιλόσοφα δὲ καὶ ἐλευθέρια τῆς ἔξωθεν παιδείας οἷός τις ἦν, οὐδὲν δεῖ λέγειν, ὅτε μάλιστα τὴν κατὰ Πλάτωνα καὶ Πυθαγόραν ἐζηλωκὼς ἀγωγήν, διενεγκεῖν ἅπαντας τοὺς καθ' ἑαυτὸν ἱστορεῖται. V. καὶ δὴ τὰ κατὰ Γάϊον οὗτος Ἰουδαίοις συμβάντα πέντε βιβλίοις παραδίδωσιν, ὁμοῦ τὴν Γαΐου διεξιὼν

116

brethren besides them, that the name of Christian was first given, as from a fresh and life-giving fountain. Agabus also, one of the prophets with them, made predictions that there was to be a famine, and Paul and Barnabas were sent to give assistance to the ministry of the brethren.

IV. Tiberius died after reigning about twenty-two years.[1] After him Caius received the sovereignty and at once gave to Agrippa[2] the crown of the rule of the Jews. He made him king of the tetrarchies of Philip and Lysanias, and after a short time added to them the tetrarchy of Herod, sentencing Herod (he was the Herod of the Passion of the Saviour) for many offences to perpetual banishment, together with his wife Herodias. Of this too Josephus is witness.

In his reign Philo became generally known as a man of the greatest distinction, not only among our own people but also among those of heathen education. He was a Hebrew by racial descent but inferior to none of the magnates in authority in Alexandria. The extent and quality of the labour he bestowed on the theological learning of his race is in fact patent to all, and it is not necessary to say anything of his position in philosophy and the liberal studies of the heathen world since he is related to have surpassed all his contemporaries, especially in his zeal for the study of Plato and Pythagoras. V. Now this writer has narrated in five books what happened to the Jews in the time of Caius; he has in this work combined the stories of the insanity of Caius,

[1] He died March 16, A.D. 37.
[2] See Introduction for the family of the Herod. This is Agrippa I., son of Aristobulus and grandson of Herod the Great. The Herod mentioned in the next sentence is Herod Antipas, Agrippa's uncle.

φρενοβλάβειαν, ὡς θεὸν ἑαυτὸν ἀναγορεύσαντος
καὶ μυρία περὶ τὴν ἀρχὴν ἐνυβρικότος, τάς τε
κατ' αὐτὸν Ἰουδαίων ταλαιπωρίας καὶ ἣν αὐτὸς
στειλάμενος ἐπὶ τῆς Ῥωμαίων πόλεως ὑπὲρ τῶν
κατὰ τὴν Ἀλεξάνδρειαν ὁμοεθνῶν ἐποιήσατο πρεσβείαν, ὅπως τε ἐπὶ τοῦ Γαΐου καταστὰς ὑπὲρ
τῶν πατρίων νόμων, οὐδέν τι πλέον γέλωτος καὶ
διασυρμῶν ἀπηνέγκατο, μικροῦ δεῖν καὶ τὸν
περὶ τῆς ζωῆς ἀνατλὰς κίνδυνον.

Μέμνηται καὶ τούτων ὁ Ἰώσηπος, ἐν ὀκτω- 2
καιδεκάτῳ τῆς Ἀρχαιολογίας κατὰ λέξιν ταῦτα
Joseph. A.I.
18, 257-260 γράφων " καὶ δὴ στάσεως ἐν Ἀλεξανδρείᾳ γενομένης Ἰουδαίων τε οἳ ἐνοικοῦσι, καὶ Ἑλλήνων, τρεῖς
ἀφ' ἑκατέρας τῆς στάσεως πρεσβευταὶ αἱρεθέντες
παρῆσαν πρὸς τὸν Γάιον. καὶ ἦν γὰρ τῶν Ἀλε- 3
ξανδρέων πρέσβεων εἷς Ἀπίων, ὃς πολλὰ εἰς
τοὺς Ἰουδαίους ἐβλασφήμησεν, ἄλλα τε λέγων
καὶ ὡς τῶν Καίσαρος τιμῶν περιορῶεν· πάντων
γοῦν, ὅσοι τῇ Ῥωμαίων ἀρχῇ ὑποτελεῖς εἶεν,
βωμοὺς τῷ Γαΐῳ καὶ ναοὺς ἱδρυμένων τά τε
ἄλλα ἐν πᾶσιν αὐτὸν ὥσπερ τοὺς θεοὺς δεχομένων, μόνους τούσδε ἄδοξον ἡγεῖσθαι ἀνδριάσι
τιμᾶν καὶ ὅρκιον αὐτοῦ τὸ ὄνομα ποιεῖσθαι·
πολλὰ δὲ καὶ χαλεπὰ Ἀπίωνος εἰρηκότος, ὑφ' 4
ὧν ἀρθῆναι ἤλπιζεν τὸν Γάιον καὶ εἰκὸς ἦν, Φίλων
ὁ προεστὼς τῶν Ἰουδαίων τῆς πρεσβείας, ἀνὴρ
τὰ πάντα ἔνδοξος Ἀλεξάνδρου τε τοῦ ἀλαβάρχου
ἀδελφὸς ὢν καὶ φιλοσοφίας οὐκ ἄπειρος, οἷός
τε ἦν ἐπ' ἀπολογίᾳ χωρεῖν τῶν κατηγορημένων,
διακλείει δ' αὐτὸν Γάιος, κελεύσας ἐκποδὼν ἀπελθεῖν, περιοργής τε ὢν φανερὸς ἦν ἐργασόμε-
νός τι δεινὸν αὐτούς. ὁ δὲ Φίλων ἔξεισι περι-

how he announced himself as a god and perpetrated innumerable acts of insolence during his reign, of the misery of the Jews in his time, of the mission which he was himself entrusted to make to the city of the Romans on behalf of those of his own race in Alexandria, and of how, when he appeared before Caius on behalf of his ancestral laws, he received nothing but laughter and ridicule, and narrowly escaped risking his life.

Josephus also relates these facts and writes as follows in the eighteenth book of the *Antiquities* : " Now when a disturbance took place in Alexandria between the Jews who lived there and the Greeks, three of each side were chosen to go as representatives to Caius. One of the Alexandrian representatives was Apion, who uttered many calumnies against the Jews, saying especially that they neglected to give honour to Caesar, and that while all who are subject to the rule of the Romans build altars and temples to Caius, and in all other respects receive him as they do the gods, these men alone think it improper to honour him with statues or to swear by his name. Now though Apion had made many serious charges by which he naturally hoped that Caius would be roused, Philo, the chief of the embassy of the Jews, a man of high reputation in every respect, for he was the brother of Alexander the Alabarch and a philosopher of no little skill, was able in his reply to deal with the accusations, but Caius cut him short, bade him get out of the way, and was so enraged that he clearly was on the point of serious measures against them. So Philo went

ὑβρισμένος, καί φησιν πρὸς τοὺς Ἰουδαίους
οἳ περὶ αὐτὸν ἦσαν, ὡς χρὴ θαρρεῖν, Γαΐου μὲν
αὐτοῖς ὠργισμένου, ἔργῳ δὲ ἤδη τὸν θεὸν ἀντι-
παρεξάγοντος."

Philo, Leg.
ad Gai. 24. 38
Ταῦτα ὁ Ἰώσηπος. καὶ αὐτὸς δὲ ὁ Φίλων 6
ἐν ᾗ συνέγραψεν Πρεσβείᾳ τὰ κατὰ μέρος ἀκριβῶς
τῶν τότε πραχθέντων αὐτῷ δηλοῖ, ὧν τὰ πλεῖστα
παρείς, ἐκεῖνα μόνα παραθήσομαι, δι' ὧν τοῖς
ἐντυγχάνουσι προφανὴς γενήσεται δήλωσις τῶν
ἅμα τε καὶ οὐκ εἰς μακρὸν τῶν κατὰ τοῦ Χριστοῦ
τετολμημένων ἕνεκεν Ἰουδαίοις συμβεβηκότων.
πρῶτον δὴ οὖν κατὰ Τιβέριον ἐπὶ μὲν τῆς Ῥω- 7
μαίων πόλεως ἱστορεῖ Σηιανόν, τῶν τότε παρὰ
βασιλεῖ πολλὰ δυνάμενον, ἄρδην τὸ πᾶν ἔθνος
ἀπολέσθαι σπουδὴν εἰσαγηοχέναι, ἐπὶ δὲ τῆς
Ἰουδαίας Πιλᾶτον, καθ' ὃν τὰ περὶ τὸν σωτῆρα
τετόλμητο, περὶ τὸ ἐν Ἱεροσολύμοις ἔτι τότε
συνεστὸς ἱερὸν ἐπιχειρήσαντά τι παρὰ τὸ Ἰουδαίοις ἐξόν, τὰ μέγιστα αὐτοὺς ἀναταράξαι,
VI. μετὰ δὲ τὴν Τιβερίου τελευτὴν Γάιον τὴν ἀρχὴν 1
παρειληφότα, πολλὰ μὲν εἰς πολλοὺς καὶ ἄλλα
ἐνυβρίσαι, πάντων δὲ μάλιστα τὸ πᾶν Ἰουδαίων
ἔθνος οὐ σμικρὰ καταβλάψαι· ἃ καὶ ἐν βραχεῖ
πάρεστιν διὰ τῶν αὐτοῦ καταμαθεῖν φωνῶν, ἐν
αἷς κατὰ λέξιν ταῦτα γράφει

Philo, Leg.
ad Gai. 43
''Τοσαύτη μὲν οὖν τις ἡ τοῦ Γαΐου περὶ τὸ 2
ἦθος ἦν ἀνωμαλία πρὸς ἅπαντας, διαφερόντως
δὲ πρὸς τὸ Ἰουδαίων γένος, ᾧ χαλεπῶς ἀπ-
εχθανόμενος τὰς μὲν ἐν ταῖς ἄλλαις πόλεσιν
προσευχάς, ἀπὸ τῶν κατ' Ἀλεξάνδρειαν ἀρξάμενος,
σφετερίζεται, καταπλήσας εἰκόνων καὶ ἀνδριάντων
τῆς ἰδίας μορφῆς (ὁ γὰρ ἑτέρων ἀνατιθέντων

out, deeply insulted, and told the Jews who were with him that they must keep up their courage, for though Caius was enraged against them he was in fact already fighting against God."

So far Josephus. Philo himself in the *Embassy* which he wrote gives an accurate and detailed account of what he did at the time. I shall pass over the greater part and cite only those points which plainly demonstrate to students the misfortunes which came upon the Jews, all at once and after a short time, in consequence of their crimes against Christ. In the first place he relates that, in the time of Tiberius, in the city of the Romans, Sejanus, the most influential of the Emperor's court at the time, took measures completely to destroy the whole race, and in Judaea Pilate, under whom the crime against the Saviour was perpetrated, made an attempt on the temple, still standing in Jerusalem, contrary to the privileges granted to the Jews, and harassed them to the utmost, (VI.) while after the death of Tiberius Caius received the sovereignty and inflicted many injuries on many, but more than all did the greatest harm to the whole nation of the Jews. This may be learned shortly from his own words, in which he writes exactly as follows: "Now the character of Caius was extremely capricious towards all, but particularly towards the race of Jews. He hated them bitterly; in other cities, beginning with Alexandria, he seized the synagogues and filled them with images and statues of his own form (for by giving permission to

ἐφιείς, αὐτὸς ἱδρύετο δυνάμει), τὸν δ' ἐν τῇ ἱερο-
πόλει νεών, ὃς λοιπὸς ἦν ἄψαυστος, ἀσυλίας
ἠξιωμένος τῆς πάσης, μεθηρμόζετο καὶ μετε-
σχημάτιζεν εἰς οἰκεῖον ἱερόν, ἵνα Διὸς Ἐπιφα-
νοῦς Νέου χρηματίζῃ Γαΐου.''

Μυρία μὲν οὖν ἄλλα δεινὰ καὶ πέρα πάσης 3
διηγήσεως ὁ αὐτὸς κατὰ τὴν Ἀλεξάνδρειαν
συμβεβηκότα Ἰουδαίοις ἐπὶ τοῦ δηλουμένου ἐν
δευτέρῳ συγγράμματι ᾧ[1] ἐπέγραψεν '' Περὶ
ἀρετῶν'' ἱστορεῖ· συνᾴδει δ' αὐτῷ καὶ ὁ Ἰώσηπος, ὁμοίως ἀπὸ τῶν Πιλάτου χρόνων καὶ
τῶν κατὰ τοῦ σωτῆρος τετολμημένων τὰς κατὰ
παντὸς τοῦ ἔθνους ἐνάρξασθαι σημαίνων συμ-
φοράς. ἄκουε δ' οὖν οἷα καὶ οὗτος ἐν δευτέρῳ 4
τοῦ Ἰουδαϊκοῦ πολέμου αὐταῖς συλλαβαῖς δηλοῖ
λέγων

Joseph. B.J.
2, 169. 170
'' Πεμφθεὶς δὲ εἰς Ἰουδαίαν ἐπίτροπος ὑπὸ
Τιβερίου Πιλᾶτος νύκτωρ κεκαλυμμένας εἰς Ἱεροσόλυμα παρεισκομίζει τὰς Καίσαρος εἰκόνας· ση-
μαίαι καλοῦνται. τοῦτο μεθ' ἡμέραν μεγίστην
ταραχὴν ἤγειρεν τοῖς Ἰουδαίοις. οἵ τε γὰρ
ἐγγὺς πρὸς τὴν ὄψιν ἐξεπλάγησαν, ὡς πεπατη-
μένων αὐτοῖς τῶν νόμων· οὐδὲν γὰρ ἀξιοῦσιν
ἐν τῇ πόλει δείκηλον τίθεσθαι.''

Ταῦτα δὲ συγκρίνας τῇ τῶν εὐαγγελίων γραφῇ, 5
εἴσῃ ὡς οὐκ εἰς μακρὸν αὐτοὺς μετῆλθεν ἣν
ἔρρηξαν ἐπ' αὐτοῦ Πιλάτου φωνήν, δι' ἧς οὐκ
John 19, 15 ἄλλον ἢ μόνον ἔχειν ἐπεβόων Καίσαρα βασιλέα.

---

[1] Schwartz prefers the reading of BD, ὧν ἐπέγραψεν, but to
make sense this would require the article τῷ before δευτέρῳ.
It is possible that the τῷ slipped out by a primitive error, in
which case ὧν would be the better reading.

others to install them he did in fact put them there),
and in Jerusalem the temple, which had hitherto
been untouched and held worthy of preservation
from all violation, he tried to change and transform
to a shrine of his own to be called that of 'Caius
the new Zeus manifest.'"

The same writer narrates in a second treatise
entitled *On the Virtues*[1] innumerable other atro-
cities, beyond all description, perpetrated on Jews
in Alexandria in the same reign, and Josephus
confirms him, showing in the same way that the
universal misfortunes of the nation began with the
time of Pilate and the crimes against the Saviour.
Listen then to the actual words of his statement in
the second book of the *Jewish War*. "Now Pilate,
sent as procurator to Judaea by Tiberius, brought
into Jerusalem at night and covered up the images
of Caesar which are called ensigns. When day
came this roused the greatest commotion among
the Jews, for they were horrified at what they
saw close by since their laws had been trampled
on, for they do not permit any image to be set up
in the city."

Now comparing this with the writing of the Gospels
you will see that it was not long before they were over-
taken by the cry which they uttered in the presence of
Pilate himself, with which they shouted out that they
had no other king than Caesar only. The same writer

---

[1] This is the only possible translation of the Greek as it
stands. Yet there is little doubt but that *On the Virtues* is an
alternative title of the *Embassy*. Either Eusebius made a
slip, or there is a primitive error in the text, which should be
emended and translated in agreement with the rendering of
Rufinus, "In the second of the books which he entitled
On the Virtues."

Joseph. B.I.
2, 175-177

εἶτα δὲ καὶ ἄλλην ἑξῆς ὁ αὐτὸς συγγραφεὺς 6
ἱστορεῖ μετελθεῖν αὐτοὺς συμφορὰν ἐν τούτοις
'' μετὰ δὲ ταῦτα ταραχὴν ἑτέραν ἐκίνει, τὸν
ἱερὸν θησαυρόν, καλεῖται δὲ κορβανᾶς, εἰς κατα-
γωγὴν ὑδάτων ἐξαναλίσκων· κατῄει δὲ ἀπὸ
τριακοσίων σταδίων. πρὸς τοῦτο τοῦ πλήθους
ἀγανάκτησις ἦν, καὶ τοῦ Πιλάτου παρόντος εἰς
Ἱεροσόλυμα, περιστάντες ἅμα κατεβόων. ὁ δὲ 7
προῄδει γὰρ αὐτῶν τὴν ταραχὴν καὶ τῷ πλήθει
τοὺς στρατιώτας ἐνόπλους, ἐσθήσεσιν ἰδιωτικαῖς
κεκαλυμμένους, ἐγκαταμίξας καὶ ξίφει μὲν χρήσασθαι κωλύσας, ξύλοις δὲ παίειν τοὺς κεκρα-
γότας ἐγκελευσάμενος, σύνθημα δίδωσιν ἀπὸ τοῦ
βήματος. τυπτόμενοι δὲ οἱ Ἰουδαῖοι πολλοὶ μὲν
ὑπὸ τῶν πληγῶν, πολλοὶ δὲ ὑπὸ σφῶν αὐτῶν
ἐν τῇ φυγῇ καταπατηθέντες ἀπώλοντο, πρὸς
δὲ τὴν συμφορὰν τῶν ἀνῃρημένων καταπλαγὲν
τὸ πλῆθος ἐσιώπησεν.''

Ἐπὶ τούτοις μυρίας ἄλλας ἐν αὐτοῖς Ἱεροσο- 8
λύμοις κεκινῆσθαι νεωτεροποιίας ὁ αὐτὸς ἐμφαίνει,
παριστὰς ὡς οὐδαμῶς ἐξ ἐκείνου διέλιπον τήν τε
πόλιν καὶ τὴν Ἰουδαίαν ἅπασαν στάσεις καὶ
πόλεμοι καὶ κακῶν ἐπάλληλοι μηχαναί, εἰς ὅτε
τὸ πανύστατον ἡ κατὰ Οὐεσπασιανὸν αὐτοὺς
μετῆλθεν πολιορκία. Ἰουδαίους μὲν οὖν ὧν κατὰ
τοῦ Χριστοῦ τετολμήκασιν, ταύτῃ πῃ τὰ ἐκ τῆς
θείας μετῄει δίκης.

VII. Οὐκ ἀγνοεῖν δὲ ἄξιον ὡς καὶ αὐτὸν ἐκεῖνον 1
τὸν ἐπὶ τοῦ σωτῆρος Πιλᾶτον κατὰ Γάϊον, οὗ τοὺς
χρόνους διέξιμεν, τοσαύταις περιπεσεῖν κατέχει λόγος
συμφοραῖς, ὡς ἐξ ἀνάγκης αὐτοφονευτὴν ἑαυτοῦ
καὶ τιμωρὸν αὐτόχειρα γενέσθαι, τῆς θείας, ὡς

then goes on to relate another misfortune which overtook them, as follows : " And after this he roused another commotion by expending the sacred treasure, called Corban, for an aqueduct which he brought from a distance of three hundred stadia. Popular indignation was aroused at this, and when Pilate came to Jerusalem the people stood round with howls of execration ; but he had foreseen their disturbance and had mixed with the crowd armed soldiers disguised in civilian clothes, with orders not to use their swords but to club those who had shouted. He gave the signal for this from his judgement-seat ; and as the Jews were smitten many perished from the blows, many from being trampled upon by their fellows in their flight, and the mob, overcome at the calamity of those who perished, was silent."

The same writer shows that besides this innumerable other revolts were started in Jerusalem itself, affirming that from that time risings and war and the mutual contrivance of evil never ceased in the city and throughout Judaea, until the time when the siege under Vespasian came upon them as the last scene of all. Thus the penalty of God pursued the Jews for their crimes against Christ.

VII. It is also worthy of notice that tradition relates that that same Pilate, he of the Saviour's time, in the days of Caius, whose period we have described, fell into such great calamity that he was forced to become his own slayer and to punish himself with his own hand, for the penalty of God, as it seems,

125

ἔοικεν, δίκης οὐκ εἰς μακρὸν αὐτὸν μετελθούσης.
ἱστοροῦσιν Ἑλλήνων οἱ τὰς Ὀλυμπιάδας ἅμα
τοῖς κατὰ χρόνους πεπραγμένοις ἀναγράψαντες.

Joseph. A.I. 19, 201 ; B.I. 2, 204

VIII. Ἀλλὰ γὰρ Γάϊον οὐδ' ὅλοις τέτταρσιν ἔτε- 1
σιν τὴν ἀρχὴν κατασχόντα Κλαύδιος αὐτοκράτωρ

Acts 11, 28 διαδέχεται· καθ' ὃν λιμοῦ τὴν οἰκουμένην πιέσαντος (τοῦτο δὲ καὶ οἱ πόρρω τοῦ καθ' ἡμᾶς
λόγου συγγραφεῖς ταῖς αὐτῶν ἱστορίαις παρέδοσαν), ἡ κατὰ τὰς Πράξεις τῶν ἀποστόλων
Ἀγάβου προφήτου περὶ τοῦ μέλλειν ἔσεσθαι
λιμὸν ἐφ' ὅλην τὴν οἰκουμένην πέρας ἐλάμβανεν
πρόρρησις. τὸν δὲ κατὰ Κλαύδιον λιμὸν ἐπι- 2
σημηνάμενος ἐν ταῖς Πράξεσιν ὁ Λουκᾶς ἱστο-

Acts 11, 29. 30 ρήσας τε ὡς ἄρα διὰ Παύλου καὶ Βαρναβᾶ οἱ
κατὰ Ἀντιόχειαν ἀδελφοὶ τοῖς κατὰ τὴν Ἰουδαίαν ἐξ ὧν ἕκαστος ηὐπόρει διαπεμψάμενοι

Acts 12, 1. 2 εἶησαν, ἐπιφέρει λέγων· (IX.) "κατ' ἐκεῖνον δὲ τὸν 1
καιρόν, δῆλον δ' ὅτι τὸν ἐπὶ Κλαυδίου, ἐπέβαλεν
Ἡρῴδης ὁ βασιλεὺς τὰς χεῖρας κακῶσαί τινας
τῶν ἀπὸ τῆς ἐκκλησίας, ἀνεῖλεν δὲ Ἰάκωβον
τὸν ἀδελφὸν Ἰωάννου μαχαίρᾳ." περὶ τούτου 2
δ' ὁ Κλήμης τοῦ Ἰακώβου καὶ ἱστορίαν μνήμης
ἀξίαν ἐν τῇ τῶν Ὑποτυπώσεων ἑβδόμῃ παρατίθεται ὡς ἂν ἐκ παραδόσεως τῶν πρὸ αὐτοῦ
φάσκων ὅτι δὴ ὁ εἰσαγαγὼν αὐτὸν εἰς δικαστήριον,
μαρτυρήσαντα αὐτὸν ἰδὼν κινηθείς, ὡμολόγησεν
εἶναι καὶ αὐτὸς ἑαυτὸν Χριστιανόν. "συναπήχθησαν 3
οὖν ἄμφω," φησίν, "καὶ κατὰ τὴν ὁδὸν ἠξίωσεν
ἀφεθῆναι αὐτῷ ὑπὸ τοῦ Ἰακώβου· ὁ δὲ ὀλίγον σκε-
ψάμενος, 'εἰρήνη σοι' εἶπεν καὶ κατεφίλησεν αὐτόν.
καὶ οὕτως ἀμφότεροι ὁμοῦ ἐκαρατομήθησαν." [1]

[1] Cf. George Syncellus 633, 11-18.

126

followed hard after him. Those who record the
Olympiads of the Greeks with the annals of events
relate this.[1]

VIII. Caius had not completed four years of
sovereignty when Claudius succeeded him as
Emperor.[2] In his time famine seized the world
(and this also writers[3] with a purpose quite other
than ours have recorded in their histories), and so
what the prophet Agabus had foretold, according
to the Acts of the Apostles, that a famine would
be over the whole world, received fulfilment. Luke
in the Acts describes the famine in the time
of Claudius and narrates how the Christians at
Antioch sent to those in Judaea, each according
to his ability, by Paul and Barnabas, and he goes
on to say, (IX.) " Now at that time,"—obviously
that of Claudius,—" Herod the king put forth his
hand to vex certain of the church and killed James
the brother of John with the sword." Concerning
this James, Clement adds in the seventh book of the
Hypotyposes a story worth mentioning, apparently
from the tradition of his predecessors, to the effect
that he who brought him to the court was so moved
at seeing him testify as to confess that he also was
himself a Christian. " So they were both led away
together," he says, " and on the way he asked for
forgiveness for himself from James. And James
looked at him for a moment and said, ' Peace be to
you,' and kissed him. So both were beheaded at the
same time."

[1] No extant records confirm this statement.
[2] Jan. 24, A.D. 41.
[3] *Cf.* Tacitus, *Ann.* xii. 13, and Dio Cassius lx. 11. But
Eusebius, influenced by Acts xi. 28, exaggerates the
universal character of the famine.

Acts 12, 3-17 Τότε δῆτα, ὥς φησιν ἡ θεία γραφή, ἰδὼν Ἡρώδης 4
ἐπὶ τῇ τοῦ Ἰακώβου ἀναιρέσει πρὸς ἡδονῆς
γεγονὸς τὸ πραχθὲν τοῖς Ἰουδαίοις, ἐπιτίθεται
καὶ Πέτρῳ, δεσμοῖς τε αὐτὸν παραδούς, ὅσον
οὔπω καὶ τὸν κατ' αὐτοῦ φόνον ἐνήργησεν ἄν,
εἰ μὴ διὰ θείας ἐπιφανείας, ἐπιστάντος αὐτῷ
νύκτωρ ἀγγέλου, παραδόξως τῶν εἰργμῶν ἀπαλ-
λαγείς, ἐπὶ τὴν τοῦ κηρύγματος ἀφεῖται διακονίαν.
καὶ τὰ μὲν κατὰ Πέτρον οὕτως εἶχεν οἰκονομίας.

X. Τὰ δέ γε τῆς κατὰ τῶν ἀποστόλων ἐγχειρή- 1
σεως τοῦ βασιλέως οὐκέτ' ἀναβολῆς εἴχετο, ἅμα γέ
τοι αὐτὸν ὁ τῆς θείας δίκης τιμωρὸς διάκονος
μετῄει, παραυτίκα μετὰ τὴν τῶν ἀποστόλων
Acts 12, 19.
21-23 ἐπιβουλήν, ὡς ἡ τῶν Πράξεων ἱστορεῖ γραφή,
ὁρμήσαντα μὲν ἐπὶ τὴν Καισάρειαν, ἐν ἐπισήμῳ
δ' ἐνταῦθα ἑορτῆς ἡμέρᾳ λαμπρᾷ καὶ βασιλικῇ
κοσμησάμενον ἐσθῆτι ὑψηλόν τε πρὸ βήματος
δημηγορήσαντα· τοῦ γάρ τοι δήμου παντὸς ἐπ-
ευφημήσαντος ἐπὶ τῇ δημηγορίᾳ ὡς ἐπὶ θεοῦ
φωνῇ καὶ οὐκ ἀνθρώπου, παραχρῆμα τὸ λόγιον
πατάξαι αὐτὸν ἄγγελον κυρίου ἱστορεῖ, γενό-
μενόν τε σκωληκόβρωτον ἐκψῦξαι. θαυμάσαι δ' 2
ἄξιον τῆς περὶ τὴν θείαν γραφὴν καὶ ἐν τῷδε τῷ
παραδόξῳ συμφωνίας τὴν τοῦ Ἰωσήπου ἱστορίαν,
καθ' ἣν ἐπιμαρτυρῶν τῇ ἀληθείᾳ δῆλός ἐστιν,
ἐν τόμῳ τῆς Ἀρχαιολογίας ἐννεακαιδεκάτῳ, ἔνθα
αὐτοῖς γράμμασιν ὧδέ πως τὸ θαῦμα διηγεῖται.

Joseph. A.I.
19, 343-351 "Τρίτον δ' ἔτος αὐτῷ βασιλεύοντι τῆς ὅλης 3
Ἰουδαίας πεπλήρωτο, καὶ παρῆν εἰς πόλιν Καισάρειαν, ἣ τὸ πρότερον Στράτωνος πύργος ἐκα-

---

[1] The feast was probably that *Pro salute Caesaris* which
was celebrated every four years (see E. Schwartz, "Zur

At that time, as the divine Scripture says, Herod, seeing that his action in the murder of James had given pleasure to the Jews, turned to Peter also, put him in prison, and would have perpetrated his murder also had it not been for Divine intervention at the last moment, for an angel appeared to him by night and he was miraculously released from his bonds and set free for the ministry of preaching. Such was the dispensation of heaven for Peter.

X. As to the king's attempt on the Apostles there was no more delay, but the avenging minister of the sentence of God overtook him at once, immediately after his plot against the Apostles, as the Scripture relates in the Acts. He had gone to Caesarea, and there on the set day of the feast,[1] adorned with splendid and royal robes, he addressed the people, standing on high before his judgement-seat. The whole people applauded his address, as though at the voice of a god and not of a man, and the story[2] relates that an angel of the Lord smote him at once, and he was eaten of worms and expired. It is worthy of wonder how in this marvel also the narrative of Josephus agrees with the divine Scripture. He clearly testifies to the truth in the nineteenth book of the *Antiquities*, where the wonder is related in the following words : " Now the third year of his reign over all Judaea had been finished when he came to the city of Caesarea, which was formerly called the

Chronologie des Paulus," *Gött. Nachr.* 1907), and was due in A.D. 44 when Herod probably died.

[2] Note that Eusebius uses the word λόγιον of the Acts; in view of the fact that the word, literally " oracle," is generally used of the Old Testament it might almost be rendered by " Scripture

λεῖτο. συνετέλει δ' ἐνταῦθα θεωρίας εἰς τὴν
Καίσαρος τιμήν, ὑπὲρ τῆς ἐκείνου σωτηρίας
ἑορτήν τινα ταύτην ἐπιστάμενος, καὶ παρ' αὐτὴν
ἤθροιστο τῶν κατὰ τὴν ἐπαρχίαν ἐν τέλει καὶ
προβεβηκότων εἰς ἀξίαν πλῆθος. δευτέρα δὲ τῶν 4
θεωριῶν ἡμέρᾳ στολὴν ἐνδυσάμενος ἐξ ἀργύρου
πεποιημένην πᾶσαν, ὡς θαυμάσιον ὑφὴν εἶναι,
παρῆλθεν εἰς τὸ θέατρον ἀρχομένης ἡμέρας.
ἔνθα ταῖς πρώταις τῶν ἡλιακῶν ἀκτίνων ἐπιβολαῖς
ὁ ἄργυρος καταυγασθείς, θαυμασίως ἀπέστιλβεν,
μαρμαίρων τι φοβερὸν καὶ τοῖς εἰς αὐτὸν ἀτενί-
ζουσι φρικῶδες. εὐθὺς δὲ οἱ κόλακες τὰς οὐδὲν 5
ἐκείνῳ πρὸς ἀγαθοῦ ἄλλος ἄλλοθεν φωνὰς ἀνεβόων,
θεὸν προσαγορεύοντες ' εὐμενής ' τε ' εἴης ' ἐπι-
λέγοντες, ' εἰ καὶ μέχρι νῦν ὡς ἄνθρωπον ἐφο-
βήθημεν, ἀλλὰ τοὐντεῦθεν κρείττονά σε θνητῆς
φύσεως ὁμολογοῦμεν.' οὐκ ἐπέπληξεν τούτοις
ὁ βασιλεὺς οὐδὲ τὴν κολακείαν ἀσεβοῦσαν ἀπε- 6
τρίψατο. ἀνακύψας δὲ μετ' ὀλίγον, τῆς ἑαυτοῦ
κεφαλῆς ὑπερκαθεζόμενον εἶδεν ἄγγελον. τοῦτον
Joseph. A.J.
18, 195 εὐθὺς ἐνόησεν κακῶν εἶναι αἴτιον, τὸν καί ποτε
τῶν ἀγαθῶν γενόμενον, καὶ διακάρδιον ἔσχεν
ὀδύνην, ἄθρουν δ' αὐτῷ τῆς κοιλίας προσέφυσεν
ἄλγημα, μετὰ σφοδρότητος ἀρξάμενον. ἀναθεω- 7
ρῶν οὖν πρὸς τοὺς φίλους, ' ὁ θεὸς ὑμῖν ἐγώ,'
φησίν, ' ἤδη καταστρέφειν ἐπιτάττομαι τὸν βίον,
παραχρῆμα τῆς εἱμαρμένης τὰς ἄρτι μου κατ-
εψευσμένας φωνὰς ἐλεγχούσης. ὁ κληθεὶς ἀθά-
νατος ὑφ' ὑμῶν, ἤδη θανεῖν ἀπάγομαι. δεκτέον
δὲ τὴν πεπρωμένην, ᾗ θεὸς βεβούληται. καὶ

---

[1] Eusebius is usually very accurate in his quotations, but
here he varies from the text of Josephus, who says " he saw

tower of Strato. There he was celebrating games
in honour of Caesar, because he knew that this was
a kind of feast for his safety, and at it was assembled
a multitude of those in office and of high rank in
the province. On the second day of the games he
put on a robe made entirely of silver, so that it was
a wonderful fabric, and proceeded to the theatre at
the beginning of the day. Then when the silver was
refulgent with the first glint of the rays of the sun
it gleamed marvellously with a peculiar sheen, fearful
and terrifying to those who gazed at it. At once
the flatterers raised their voices from various quarters
—but no good did it do him—and addressed him as
a god, saying, ' Be thou propitious ! even if until
now we feared thee as man, yet from henceforth
we confess thee as of more than mortal nature.' The
king was not dismayed at these words, nor did he
reject the impious flattery.

But after a little looking up he saw an angel
seated above his head.[1] This he at once perceived to
be the harbinger of evil, as it had formerly been of
good ;[1] he had pain in his heart, and agony rapidly
beginning spread increasingly through his stomach.
So he looked up to his friends and said, ' I, who am
your god, am now commanded to give up my life,
for fate has immediately reproved the lying words
just uttered about me. I, whom you called immortal, am now being taken off to die. Fate
must be accepted as God has willed, yet I have

an owl sitting on a certain rope over his head, and at once
understood that it was a messenger (ἄγγελος) of evil, as it had
formerly been of good." The allusion is to the story that
when Agrippa, at the lowest ebb of his misfortunes, was in
prison in Rome he saw an owl and regarded it as a harbinger
of better days, which did indeed soon come (Josephus, *Ant.*
xviii. 6. 7).

131

γὰρ βεβιώκαμεν οὐδαμῇ φαύλως, ἀλλ᾽ ἐπὶ τῆς
μακαριζομένης μακρότητος.' ταῦτα δὲ λέγων ἐπι-
τάσει τῆς ὀδύνης κατεπονεῖτο· μετὰ σπουδῆς
οὖν εἰς τὸ βασίλειον ἐκομίσθη, καὶ διῆξε λόγος
εἰς πάντας ὡς ἔχοι τοῦ τεθνάναι παντάπασι μετ᾽
ὀλίγον. ἡ πληθὺς δ᾽ αὐτίκα σὺν γυναιξὶ καὶ
παισὶν ἐπὶ σάκκον καθεσθεῖσα τῷ πατρίῳ νόμῳ
τὸν θεὸν ἱκέτευον ὑπὲρ τοῦ βασιλέως, οἰμωγῆς
τε πάντ᾽ ἦν ἀνάπλεα καὶ θρήνων. ἐν ὑψηλῷ δ᾽
ὁ βασιλεὺς δωματίῳ κατακείμενος καὶ κάτω
βλέπων αὐτοὺς πρηνεῖς προπίπτοντας, ἄδακρυς
οὐδ᾽ αὐτὸς ἔμενεν. συνεχεῖς δ᾽ ἐφ᾽ ἡμέρας πέντε
τῷ τῆς γαστρὸς ἀλγήματι διεργασθείς, τὸν βίον
κατέστρεψεν, ἀπὸ γενέσεως ἄγων πεντηκοστὸν
ἔτος καὶ τέταρτον, τῆς δὲ βασιλείας ἕβδομον.
τέσσαρας μὲν οὖν ἐπὶ Γαΐου Καίσαρος ἐβασί-
λευσεν ἐνιαυτούς, τῆς Φιλίππου μὲν τετραρχίας
εἰς τριετίαν ἄρξας, τῷ τετάρτῳ δὲ καὶ τὴν Ἡρώδου
προσειληφώς, τρεῖς δ᾽ ἐπιλαβὼν τῆς Κλαυδίου
Καίσαρος αὐτοκρατορίας.'' ταῦτα τὸν Ἰώσηπον
μετὰ τῶν ἄλλων ταῖς θείαις συναληθεύοντα γραφαῖς
ἀποθαυμάζω· εἰ δὲ περὶ τὴν τοῦ βασιλέως προσηγορίαν δόξειέν τισιν διαφωνεῖν, ἀλλ᾽ ὅ γε χρόνος
καὶ ἡ πρᾶξις τὸν αὐτὸν ὄντα δείκνυσιν, ἤτοι κατά
τι σφάλμα γραφικὸν ἐνηλλαγμένου τοῦ ὀνόματος
ἢ καὶ διωνυμίας περὶ τὸν αὐτόν, οἷα καὶ περὶ
πολλούς, γεγενημένης.

Acts 5, 34–36 XI. Ἐπεὶ δὲ πάλιν ὁ Λουκᾶς ἐν ταῖς Πράξεσιν
εἰσάγει τὸν Γαμαλιὴλ ἐν τῇ περὶ τῶν ἀποστόλων
σκέψει λέγοντα ὡς ἄρα κατὰ τὸν δηλούμενον
χρόνον ἀνέστη Θευδᾶς λέγων ἑαυτὸν εἶναί τινα,
ὃς κατελύθη, καὶ πάντες ὅσοι ἐπείσθησαν αὐτῷ,

lived no mean life, but in the spaciousness which men deem-happy.' While he was saying this, he began to be overwhelmed by the intensity of his pain ; he was therefore carried hastily into the palace, and the report was spread among all that he would certainly die shortly. But the multitude seated on sackcloth with their wives and children, according to the law of their fathers, at once began to beseech God for the king and the whole place was filled with wailing and lamentations. The king lying in a room on high, and looking down on them as they fell prostrate, did not remain without tears himself. After being racked by pain in the stomach for five successive days he passed from life in the fifty-fourth year of his age and the seventh of his reign.[1] He had reigned four years in the time of Caius Caesar. For three years he possessed the tetrarchy of Philip, but in the fourth received also that of Herod, and he continued for three more years in the reign of Claudius Caesar." I am surprised how in this and other points Josephus confirms the truth of the divine Scriptures. Even if he seem to some to differ as to the name of the king, nevertheless the date and the events show that he is the same, and either that the name has been changed by some clerical error or that there were two names for the same man, as has happened with many

XI. Since Luke in the Acts introduces Gamaliel as saying at the inquiry about the Apostles that at the time indicated Theudas arose, saying that he was somebody, and that he was destroyed and all who

---

[1] This would be A.D. 44, which fits in well with all the other data, except the fact that there are coins of Agrippa referring to his eighth and ninth years: they are usually thought to be spurious, but the point is obscure.

διελύθησαν· φέρε, καὶ τὴν περὶ τούτου παραθώμεθα τοῦ Ἰωσήπου γραφήν. ἱστορεῖ τοίνυν αὖθις
κατὰ τὸν ἀρτίως δεδηλωμένον αὐτοῦ λόγον αὐτὰ

Joseph. A.I.
20, 97. 98

δὴ ταῦτα κατὰ λέξιν, '' Φάδου δὲ τῆς Ἰουδαίας 2
ἐπιτροπεύοντος, γόης τις ἀνήρ, Θευδᾶς ὀνόματι,
πείθει τὸν πλεῖστον ὄχλον ἀναλαβόντα τὰς κτήσεις
ἕπεσθαι πρὸς τὸν Ἰορδάνην ποταμὸν αὐτῷ· προφήτης γὰρ ἔλεγεν εἶναι, καὶ προστάγματι τὸν
ποταμὸν σχίσας δίοδον ἔφη παρέξειν αὐτοῖς ῥᾳ-
δίαν, καὶ ταῦτα λέγων πολλοὺς ἠπάτησεν. οὐ 3
μὴν εἴασεν αὐτοὺς τῆς ἀφροσύνης ὀνάσθαι Φάδος,
ἀλλ' ἐξέπεμψεν ἴλην ἱππέων ἐπ' αὐτούς, ἥτις
ἐπιπεσοῦσα ἀπροσδοκήτως αὐτοῖς, πολλοὺς μὲν
ἀνεῖλεν, πολλοὺς δὲ ζῶντας ἔλαβεν, αὐτόν τε τὸν
Θευδᾶν ζωγρήσαντες ἀποτέμνουσιν τὴν κεφαλὴν
καὶ κομίζουσιν εἰς Ἱεροσόλυμα.''

Τούτοις ἑξῆς καὶ τοῦ κατὰ Κλαύδιον γενομένου

Joseph. A.I.
20, 101

λιμοῦ μνημονεύει ὧδέ πως· XII. '' ἐπὶ τούτοις [1]
γε καὶ τὸν μέγαν λιμὸν κατὰ τὴν Ἰουδαίαν συνέβη
γενέσθαι, καθ' ὃν καὶ ἡ βασίλισσα Ἑλένη πολλῶν
χρημάτων ὠνησαμένη σῖτον ἀπὸ τῆς Αἰγύπτου,
διένειμεν τοῖς ἀπορουμένοις.'' σύμφωνα δ' ἂν

Acts 11, 29.
30

εὕροις καὶ ταῦτα τῇ τῶν Πράξεων τῶν ἀποστόλων γραφῇ, περιεχούσῃ ὡς ἄρα τῶν κατ'
Ἀντιόχειαν μαθητῶν καθὼς ηὐπορεῖτό τις,
ὥρισαν ἕκαστος εἰς διακονίαν ἀποστεῖλαι τοῖς
κατοικοῦσιν ἐν τῇ Ἰουδαίᾳ· ὃ καὶ ἐποίησαν,
ἀποστείλαντες πρὸς τοὺς πρεσβυτέρους διὰ χειρὸς
Βαρναβᾶ καὶ Παύλου. τῆς γέ τοι Ἑλένης, ἧς δὴ
καὶ ὁ συγγραφεὺς ἐποιήσατο μνήμην, εἰς ἔτι νῦν

---

[1] It is remarkable that Eusebius did not notice that this

obeyed him were scattered ; come, let us compare the writing of Josephus with regard to him.[1] In his work lately mentioned he gives the following narrative. " Now when Fadus was procurator of Judaea a certain impostor named Theudas persuaded a great multitude to take their possessions and follow him to the river Jordan, for he said that he was a prophet and undertook to divide the river by his commands and provide an easy crossing for them. By saying this he deceived many ; Fadus, however, did not allow them to enjoy their delusion, but sent a squadron of cavalry against them which attacked them unexpectedly, killed many and took many alive, captured Theudas himself, cut off his head, and brought it to Jerusalem."

After this he also mentions as follows the famine which took place in the time of Claudius : XII. " At the same time it happened that the great famine took place in Judaea, in which Queen Helena bought corn from Egypt at great expense and distributed it to those who were in need." You would find that this too agrees with the writing of the Acts of the Apostles, which records how the disciples in Antioch, each according to his several ability, determined to send to the relief of the dwellers in Judaea, which they did, sending it to the elders by the hand of Barnabas and Paul. Splendid monuments of the Helena whom the historian has commemorated are

Theudas cannot really have been referred to by Gamaliel, who was speaking many years before the time of Fadus. Most modern writers on Acts think that nevertheless the Theudas of Acts is the Theudas of Josephus and explain the speech as literary fiction. Some think that " Luke " was misled by Josephus, who happens to mention Theudas in the same context as Judas of Galilee.

στῆλαι διαφανεῖς ἐν προαστείοις δείκνυνται τῆς νῦν Αἰλίας· τοῦ δὲ Ἀδιαβηνῶν ἔθνους αὕτη βασιλεῦσαι ἐλέγετο.

XIII. Ἀλλὰ γὰρ τῆς εἰς τὸν σωτῆρα καὶ κύριον ἡμῶν Ἰησοῦν Χριστὸν εἰς πάντας ἀνθρώπους ἤδη διαδιδομένης πίστεως, ὁ τῆς ἀνθρώπων πολέμιος σωτηρίας τὴν βασιλεύουσαν προαρπάσασθαι πόλιν μηχανώμενος, ἐνταῦθα Σίμωνα τὸν πρόσθεν δεδηλωμένον ἄγει, καὶ δὴ ταῖς ἐντέχνοις τἀνδρὸς συναιρόμενος γοητείαις πλείους τῶν τὴν Ῥώμην οἰκούντων ἐπὶ τὴν πλάνην σφετερίζεται. δηλοῖ δὲ τοῦθ᾽ ὁ μετ᾽ οὐ πολὺ τῶν ἀποστόλων ἐν τῷ καθ᾽ ἡμᾶς διαπρέψας λόγῳ Ἰουστῖνος, περὶ οὗ τὰ προσήκοντα κατὰ καιρὸν παραθήσομαι· ὃς δὴ ἐν τῇ προτέρᾳ πρὸς Ἀντωνῖνον ὑπὲρ τοῦ καθ᾽ ἡμᾶς δόγματος ἀπολογίᾳ γράφων ὧδέ φησιν·

Justin, *Apol.* 1 26

"Καὶ μετὰ τὴν ἀνάληψιν τοῦ κυρίου εἰς οὐρανὸν προεβάλλοντο οἱ δαίμονες ἀνθρώπους τινὰς λέγοντας ἑαυτοὺς εἶναι θεούς, οἳ οὐ μόνον οὐκ ἐδιώχθησαν ὑφ᾽ ὑμῶν, ἀλλὰ καὶ τιμῶν ἠξιώθησαν· Σίμωνα μέν τινα Σαμαρέα, τὸν ἀπὸ κώμης λεγομένης Γίτθων, ὃς ἐπὶ Κλαυδίου Καίσαρος διὰ τῆς τῶν ἐνεργούντων δαιμόνων τέχνης δυνάμεις μαγικὰς ποιήσας ἐν τῇ πόλει ὑμῶν τῇ βασιλίδι Ῥώμῃ θεὸς ἐνομίσθη καὶ ἀνδριάντι παρ᾽ ὑμῶν ὡς θεὸς τετίμηται ἐν τῷ Τίβερι ποταμῷ μεταξὺ τῶν δύο γεφυρῶν, ἔχων ἐπιγραφὴν Ῥωμαϊκὴν ταύτην· SIMONI DEO SANCTO," ὅπερ ἐστὶν Σίμωνι θεῷ ἁγίῳ.[1] "καὶ σχεδὸν μὲν πάντες Σαμαρεῖς, ὀλίγοι δὲ καὶ ἐν ἄλλοις ἔθνεσιν ὡς τὸν πρῶτον θεὸν ἐκεῖνον

---

[1] *Cf.* George Syncellus 630, 15–631, 8 and Zonaras 11. 11, 36, 27–37, ed. Dindorf.

still shown in the suburbs of the present Aelia[1];
she was said to be queen of the nation of
Adiabene.

XIII. Seeing that the faith in our Saviour and
Lord Jesus Christ was already being given to all men,
the enemy of men's salvation planned to capture the
capital in advance, and sent there Simon, who was
mentioned above, and by aiding the fellow's tricky
sorcery won over to error many of the inhabitants
of Rome. This is told by Justin, who was an
ornament of our faith not long after the Apostles,
and I will set out the necessary information about
him in due course. In his first *Apology* to Antoninus
for our opinions he writes as follows : " And after
the ascension of the Lord into heaven the demons
put forward men who said that they were gods,
and they not only escaped persecution by you
but were even vouchsafed honours. There was a
certain Simon, a Samaritan, from a village called
Gittho, who in the time of Claudius Caesar worked
miracles by magic through the art of the demons
possessing him ; he was reckoned as a god in Rome,
your capital city, and honoured as a god among you
by a statue on the river Tiber between the two
bridges, with this inscription in Latin—simoni deo
sancto,[2] " that is, to Simon a holy god, " and almost
all Samaritans and a few in other nations as well,
recognize him as the chief god and worship him, and

---

[1] The name given to Jerusalem by Hadrian.
[2] In 1574 a statue was found on the island of St. Sebastian
to which Justin probably referred. Unfortunately for him
it bears the inscription semoni sanco deo, that is to say, to
the god semo sancus, thus explaining but not confirming
Justin's improbable story. Semo Sancus was an old Sabine
deity, not a Samaritan sorcerer.

EUSEBIUS

ὁμολογοῦντες προσκυνοῦσιν. καὶ Ἑλένην τινά, τὴν
συμπερινοστήσασαν αὐτῷ κατ' ἐκεῖνο τοῦ καιροῦ,
πρότερον ἐπὶ τέγους σταθεῖσαν '' ἐν Τύρῳ τῆς
Iren. 1, 23, 2 Φοινίκης, '' τὴν ἀπ' αὐτοῦ πρώτην ἔννοιαν λέγουσιν.''

Ταῦτα μὲν οὗτος· συνᾴδει δ' αὐτῷ καὶ Εἰρη-
Iren. 1, 23, ναῖος, ἐν πρώτῳ τῶν πρὸς τὰς αἱρέσεις ὁμοῦ τὰ 5
1-4 περὶ τὸν ἄνδρα καὶ τὴν ἀνοσίαν καὶ μιαρὰν αὐτοῦ
διδασκαλίαν ὑπογράφων, ἣν ἐπὶ τοῦ παρόντος
περιττὸν ἂν εἴη καταλέγειν, παρὸν τοῖς βουλομένοις καὶ τῶν μετ' αὐτὸν κατὰ μέρος αἱρεσιαρχῶν
τὰς ἀρχὰς καὶ τοὺς βίους καὶ τῶν ψευδῶν δογμάτων τὰς ὑποθέσεις τά τε πᾶσιν αὐτοῖς ἐπι-
τετηδευμένα διαγνῶναι, οὐ κατὰ πάρεργον τῇ
δεδηλωμένῃ τοῦ Εἰρηναίου παραδεδομένα βίβλῳ.
πάσης μὲν οὖν ἀρχηγὸν αἱρέσεως πρῶτον γενέσθαι
τὸν Σίμωνα παρειλήφαμεν· ἐξ οὗ καὶ εἰς δεῦρο
οἱ τὴν κατ' αὐτὸν μετιόντες αἵρεσιν τὴν σώφρονα
καὶ διὰ καθαρότητα βίου παρὰ τοῖς πᾶσιν βεβοη-
μένην Χριστιανῶν φιλοσοφίαν ὑποκρινόμενοι, ἧς
μὲν ἔδοξαν ἀπαλλάττεσθαι περὶ τὰ εἴδωλα δεισιδαιμονίας οὐδὲν ἧττον αὖθις ἐπιλαμβάνονται,
καταπίπτοντες ἐπὶ γραφὰς καὶ εἰκόνας αὐτοῦ τε
τοῦ Σίμωνος καὶ τῆς σὺν αὐτῷ δηλωθείσης Ἑλένης
θυμιάμασίν τε καὶ θυσίαις καὶ σπονδαῖς τούτους
θρησκεύειν ἐγχειροῦντες, τὰ δὲ τούτων αὐτοῖς
ἀπορρητότερα, ὧν φασι τὸν πρῶτον ἐπακούσαντα
ἐκπλαγήσεσθαι καὶ κατά τι παρ' αὐτοῖς λόγιον
ἔγγραφον θαμβωθήσεσθαι, θάμβους ὡς ἀληθῶς
καὶ φρενῶν ἐκστάσεως καὶ μανίας ἔμπλεα τυγχάνει, τοιαῦτα ὄντα, ὡς μὴ μόνον μὴ δυνατὰ εἶναι

---

[1] In the curious mixture of philosophical language with
138

they say that a certain Helena, who travelled about with him at that time but had formerly lived in a house of ill-fame " in Tyre of Phoenicia, " was the first Idea[1] from him."

This is what Justin says, and Irenaeus agrees with him in the first book against heresies where he collects the stories about Simon and his unholy and foul teaching. It would be superfluous to relate this in the present work since those who desire it can study in detail the origin and life and the false doctrinal principles of the heresiarchs who followed him and the customs introduced by them all, for they are carefully preserved in the above-mentioned book of Irenaeus. Thus we have received the tradition that Simon was the first author of all heresy. From him, and down to the present time, those who have followed, feigning the Christian philosophy, with its sobriety and universal fame for purity of life, have in no way improved on the idolatrous superstition from which they thought to be set free, for they prostrate themselves before pictures and images of Simon himself and of Helena, who was mentioned with him, and undertake to worship them with incense and sacrifices and libations. Their more secret rites, at which they say that he who first hears them will be astonished, and according to a scripture current among them will be " thrown into marvel," truly are full of marvel and frenzy and madness; for they are of such a kind that they not merely

mythological concepts which characterized the theology of the Graeco-Roman world of the first four centuries after Christ, the word here translated " idea " was one of those used of the various beings proceeding from the original godhead, and bridging as it were the gap between God and Creation.

139

παραδοθῆναι γραφῇ, ἀλλ' οὐδὲ χείλεσιν αὐτὸ μόνον δι' ὑπερβολὴν αἰσχρουργίας τε καὶ ἀρρητοποιίας ἀνδράσι σώφροσι λαληθῆναι. ὅ τι ποτὲ 8 γὰρ ἂν ἐπινοηθείη παντὸς αἰσχροῦ μιαρώτερον, τοῦτο πᾶν ὑπερηκόντισεν ἡ τῶνδε μυσαρωτάτη αἵρεσις, ταῖς ἀθλίαις καὶ παντοίων ὡς ἀληθῶς 2 Tim. 3, 6 κακῶν σεσωρευμέναις γυναιξὶν ἐγκαταπαιζόντων. XIV. τοιούτων κακῶν πατέρα καὶ δημιουργὸν τὸν 1 Σίμωνα κατ' ἐκεῖνο καιροῦ ὥσπερ εἰ μέγαν καὶ μεγάλων ἀντίπαλον τῶν θεσπεσίων τοῦ σωτῆρος ἡμῶν ἀποστόλων ἡ μισόκαλος καὶ τῆς ἀνθρώπων ἐπίβουλος σωτηρίας πονηρὰ δύναμις προυστήσατο. ὅμως δ' οὖν ἡ θεία καὶ ὑπερουράνιος χάρις τοῖς 2 αὑτῆς συναιρομένη διακόνοις, δι' ἐπιφανείας αὐτῶν καὶ παρουσίας ἀναπτομένην τοῦ πονηροῦ τὴν 2 Cor. 10, 5 φλόγα ᾗ τάχος ἐσβέννυ, ταπεινοῦσα δι' αὐτῶν καὶ καθαιροῦσα πᾶν ὕψωμα ἐπαιρόμενον κατὰ τῆς γνώσεως τοῦ θεοῦ. διὸ δὴ οὔτε Σίμωνος οὔτ' 3 ἄλλου του τῶν τότε φυέντων συγκρότημά τι κατ' αὐτοὺς ἐκείνους τοὺς ἀποστολικοὺς ὑπέστη χρόνους. ὑπερενίκα γάρ τοι καὶ ὑπερίσχυεν ἅπαντα τὸ τῆς ἀληθείας φέγγος ὅ τε λόγος αὐτὸς ὁ θεῖος ἄρτι θεόθεν ἀνθρώποις ἐπιλάμψας ἐπὶ γῆς τε ἀκμάζων καὶ τοῖς ἰδίοις ἀποστόλοις ἐμπολιτευόμενος. αὐ- 4 Acts 8, 18-23 τίκα ὁ δηλωθεὶς γόης ὥσπερ ὑπὸ θείας καὶ παραδόξου μαρμαρυγῆς τὰ τῆς διανοίας πληγεὶς ὄμματα ὅτε πρότερον ἐπὶ τῆς Ἰουδαίας ἐφ' οἷς ἐπονηρεύσατο πρὸς τοῦ ἀποστόλου Πέτρου κατεφωράθη, μεγίστην καὶ ὑπερπόντιον ἀπάρας πορείαν τὴν ἀπ' ἀνατολῶν ἐπὶ δυσμὰς ᾤχετο φεύγων, μόνως ταύτῃ βιωτὸν αὐτῷ κατὰ γνώμην εἶναι οἰόμενος· ἐπιβὰς δὲ τῆς Ῥωμαίων πόλεως, συν- 5

cannot be related in writing, but are so full of baseness and unspeakable conduct that they cannot even be mentioned by the lips of decent men. For whatever foulness might be conceived beyond all that is base, it is surpassed by the utter foulness of the heresy of these men, who make a mocking sport of wretched women, " weighed down," as is truly said, by every kind of evil. XIV. Of such evil was Simon the father and fabricator, and the Evil Power, which hates that which is good and plots against the salvation of men, raised him up at that time as a great antagonist for the great and inspired Apostles of our Saviour. Nevertheless the grace of God which is from heaven helped its ministers and quickly extinguished the flames of the Evil One by their advent and presence, and through them humbled and cast down " every high thing that exalteth itself against the knowledge of God." Wherefore no conspiracy, either of Simon, or of any other of those who arose at that time, succeeded in those Apostolic days ; for the light of the truth and the divine Logos himself, which had shone from God upon men by growing up on the earth and dwelling among his own Apostles, was overcoming all things in the might of victory. The aforesaid sorcerer, as though the eyes of his mind had been smitten by the marvellous effulgence of God when he had formerly been detected in his crimes in Judaea by the Apostle Peter, at once undertook a great journey across the sea, and went off in flight from east to west, thinking that only in this way could he live as he wished. He came to the city of the Romans,

αἰρομένης αὐτῷ τὰ μεγάλα τῆς ἐφεδρευούσης
ἐνταῦθα δυνάμεως, ἐν ὀλίγῳ τοσοῦτον τὰ τῆς
ἐπιχειρήσεως ἤνυστο, ὡς καὶ ἀνδριάντος ἀναθέσει
πρὸς τῶν τῇδε οἷα θεὸν τιμηθῆναι. οὐ μὴν εἰς
μακρὸν αὐτῷ ταῦτα προυχώρει. παρὰ πόδας 6
γοῦν ἐπὶ τῆς αὐτῆς Κλαυδίου βασιλείας ἡ παν-
άγαθος καὶ φιλανθρωποτάτη τῶν ὅλων πρόνοια τὸν
καρτερὸν καὶ μέγαν τῶν ἀποστόλων, τὸν ἀρετῆς
ἕνεκα τῶν λοιπῶν ἁπάντων προήγορον, Πέτρον,
ἐπὶ τὴν Ῥώμην ὡς ἐπὶ τηλικοῦτον λυμεῶνα βίου
Eph. 6, 14-17
1 Thess. 5, 8 χειραγωγεῖ· ὃς οἷά τις γενναῖος θεοῦ στρατηγὸς
τοῖς θείοις ὅπλοις φραξάμενος, τὴν πολυτίμητον
ἐμπορίαν τοῦ νοητοῦ φωτὸς ἐξ ἀνατολῶν τοῖς
John 1, 9 κατὰ δύσιν ἐκόμιζεν, φῶς αὐτὸ καὶ λόγον ψυχῶν
σωτήριον, τὸ κήρυγμα τῆς τῶν οὐρανῶν βασιλείας, εὐαγγελιζόμενος. XV. οὕτω δὴ οὖν ἐπιδημή- 1
σαντος αὐτοῖς τοῦ θείου λόγου, ἡ μὲν τοῦ Σίμωνος
ἀπέσβη καὶ παραχρῆμα σὺν καὶ τῷ ἀνδρὶ κατα-
λέλυτο δύναμις.

Τοσοῦτον δ᾽ ἐπέλαμψεν ταῖς τῶν ἀκροατῶν τοῦ
Πέτρου διανοίαις εὐσεβείας φέγγος, ὡς μὴ τῇ εἰς
ἅπαξ ἱκανῶς ἔχειν ἀρκεῖσθαι ἀκοῇ μηδὲ τῇ ἀγράφῳ
τοῦ θείου κηρύγματος διδασκαλίᾳ, παρακλήσεσιν
δὲ παντοίαις Μάρκον, οὗ τὸ εὐαγγέλιον φέρεται,
ἀκόλουθον ὄντα Πέτρου, λιπαρῆσαι ὡς ἂν καὶ διὰ
γραφῆς ὑπόμνημα τῆς διὰ λόγου παραδοθείσης
αὐτοῖς καταλείψοι διδασκαλίας, μὴ πρότερόν τε
ἀνεῖναι ἢ κατεργάσασθαι τὸν ἄνδρα, καὶ ταύτῃ
αἰτίους γενέσθαι τῆς τοῦ λεγομένου κατὰ Μάρκον
εὐαγγελίου γραφῆς. γνόντα δὲ τὸ πραχθέν φασι 2
τὸν ἀπόστολον ἀποκαλύψαντος αὐτῷ τοῦ πνεύματος, ἡσθῆναι τῇ τῶν ἀνδρῶν προθυμίᾳ κυρῶσαί
142

where the power which obsessed him wrought with him greatly, so that in a short time he achieved such success that he was honoured as a god by the erection of a statue by those who were there. But he did not prosper long. Close after him in the same reign of Claudius the Providence of the universe in its great goodness and love towards men guided to Rome, as against a gigantic pest on life, the great and mighty Peter, who for his virtues was the leader of all the other Apostles. Like a noble captain of God, clad in divine armour, he brought the costly merchandise of the spiritual light from the east to the dwellers in the west, preaching the Gospel of the light itself and the word which saves souls, the proclamation of the Kingdom of Heaven. XV. Thus when the divine word made its home among them the power of Simon was extinguished and perished immediately, together with the fellow himself.

But a great light of religion shone on the minds of the hearers of Peter, so that they were not satisfied with a single hearing or with the unwritten teaching of the divine proclamation, but with every kind of exhortation besought Mark, whose Gospel is extant, seeing that he was Peter's follower, to leave them a written statement of the teaching given them verbally, nor did they cease until they had persuaded him, and so became the cause of the Scripture called the Gospel according to Mark. And they say that the Apostle, knowing by the revelation of the spirit to him what had been done, was pleased at their

143

τε τὴν γραφὴν εἰς ἔντευξιν ταῖς ἐκκλησίαις.
Κλήμης ἐν ἕκτῳ τῶν Ὑποτυπώσεων παρατέθειται τὴν ἱστορίαν, συνεπιμαρτυρεῖ δὲ αὐτῷ
καὶ ὁ Ἱεραπολίτης ἐπίσκοπος ὀνόματι Παπίας,
τοῦ δὲ Μάρκου μνημονεύειν τὸν Πέτρον ἐν τῇ
προτέρᾳ ἐπιστολῇ· ἣν καὶ συντάξαι φασὶν ἐπ'
αὐτῆς Ῥώμης, σημαίνειν τε τοῦτ' αὐτόν, τὴν
πόλιν τροπικώτερον Βαβυλῶνα προσειπόντα διὰ
1 Peter 5, 13 τούτων " ἀσπάζεται ὑμᾶς ἡ ἐν Βαβυλῶνι συνεκ-
λεκτὴ καὶ Μάρκος ὁ υἱός μου."

XVI. Τοῦτον δὲ [Μάρκον] πρῶτόν φασιν ἐπὶ τῆς
Αἰγύπτου στειλάμενον, τὸ εὐαγγέλιον, ὃ δὴ καὶ
συνεγράψατο, κηρῦξαι, ἐκκλησίας τε πρῶτον ἐπ'
αὐτῆς Ἀλεξανδρείας συστήσασθαι. τοσαύτη δ'
ἄρα τῶν αὐτόθι πεπιστευκότων πληθὺς ἀνδρῶν
τε καὶ γυναικῶν ἐκ πρώτης ἐπιβολῆς συνέστη δι'
ἀσκήσεως φιλοσοφωτάτης τε καὶ σφοδροτάτης,
ὡς καὶ γραφῆς αὐτῶν ἀξιῶσαι τὰς διατριβὰς καὶ
τὰς συνηλύσεις τά τε συμπόσια καὶ πᾶσαν τὴν ἄλλην
τοῦ βίου ἀγωγὴν τὸν Φίλωνα· XVII. ὃν καὶ λόγος
ἔχει κατὰ Κλαύδιον ἐπὶ τῆς Ῥώμης εἰς ὁμιλίαν
ἐλθεῖν Πέτρῳ, τοῖς ἐκεῖσε τότε κηρύττοντι. καὶ
οὐκ ἀπεικὸς ἂν εἴη τοῦτό γε, ἐπεὶ καὶ ὃ φαμεν
αὐτὸ σύγγραμμα, εἰς ὕστερον καὶ μετὰ χρόνους
αὐτῷ πεπονημένον, σαφῶς τοὺς εἰς ἔτι νῦν καὶ
εἰς ἡμᾶς πεφυλαγμένους τῆς ἐκκλησίας περιέχει
κανόνας· ἀλλὰ καὶ τὸν βίον τῶν παρ' ἡμῖν ἀσκητῶν
ὡς ἔνι μάλιστα ἀκριβέστατα ἱστορῶν, γένοιτ' ἂν
ἔκδηλος οὐκ εἰδὼς μόνον, ἀλλὰ καὶ ἀποδεχόμενος
ἐκθειάζων τε καὶ σεμνύνων τοὺς κατ' αὐτὸν
ἀποστολικοὺς ἄνδρας, ἐξ Ἑβραίων, ὡς ἔοικε,
γεγονότας ταύτῃ τε ἰουδαϊκώτερον τῶν παλαιῶν

144

zeal, and ratified the scripture for study in the churches. Clement quotes the story in the sixth book of the *Hypotyposes*, and the bishop of Hierapolis, named Papias, confirms him. He also says that Peter mentions Mark in his first Epistle, and that he composed this in Rome itself, which they say that he himself indicates, referring to the city metaphorically as Babylon, in the words, " the elect one in Babylon greets you, and Marcus my son."

XVI. They say that this Mark was the first to be sent to preach in Egypt the Gospel which he had also put into writing, and was the first to establish churches in Alexandria itself. The number of men and women who were there converted at the first attempt was so great, and their asceticism was so extraordinarily philosophic, that Philo thought it right to describe their conduct and assemblies and meals and all the rest of their manner of life. XVII. Tradition says that he came to Rome in the time of Claudius to speak to Peter, who was at that time preaching to those there. This would, indeed, be not improbable since the treatise to which we refer, composed by him many years later, obviously contains the rules of the Church which are still observed in our own time. Moreover, from his very accurate description of the life of our ascetics it will be plain that he not only knew but welcomed, reverenced, and recognized the divine mission of the apostolic men of his day, who were, it appears, of Hebrew origin, and thus still preserved most of the ancient

145

ἔτι τὰ πλεῖστα διατηροῦντας ἐθῶν. πρῶτόν γέ 3
τοι τὸ μηθὲν πέρα τῆς ἀληθείας οἴκοθεν καὶ ἐξ
ἑαυτοῦ προσθήσειν οἷς ἱστορήσειν ἔμελλεν, ἀπ-
ισχυρισάμενος ἐν ᾧ ἐπέγραψεν λόγῳ Περὶ βίου
θεωρητικοῦ ἢ ἱκετῶν, θεραπευτὰς αὐτοὺς καὶ τὰς
σὺν αὐτοῖς γυναῖκας θεραπευτρίδας ἀποκαλεῖσθαί
φησιν, τὰς αἰτίας ἐπειπὼν τῆς τοιᾶσδε προσρήσεως, ἤτοι παρὰ τὸ τὰς ψυχὰς τῶν προσιόντων
αὐτοῖς τῶν ἀπὸ κακίας παθῶν ἰατρῶν δίκην
ἀπαλλάττοντας ἀκεῖσθαι καὶ θεραπεύειν, ἢ τῆς
περὶ τὸ θεῖον καθαρᾶς καὶ εἰλικρινοῦς θεραπείας
τε καὶ θρησκείας ἕνεκα. εἴτ᾽ οὖν ἐξ ἑαυτοῦ 4
ταύτην αὐτοῖς ἐπιτέθειται τὴν προσηγορίαν, οἰκείως ἐπιγράψας τῷ τρόπῳ τῶν ἀνδρῶν τοὔνομα,
εἴτε καὶ ὄντως τοῦτ᾽ αὐτοὺς ἐκάλουν κατ᾽ ἀρχὰς
οἱ πρῶτοι, μηδαμῶς τῆς Χριστιανῶν πω προσρήσεως ἀνὰ πάντα τόπον ἐπιπεφημισμένης, οὔ
τί πω διατείνεσθαι ἀναγκαῖον· ὅμως δ᾽ οὖν ἐν 5
πρώτοις τὴν ἀπόταξιν αὐτοῖς τῆς οὐσίας μαρτυρεῖ,
φάσκων ἀρχομένους φιλοσοφεῖν ἐξίστασθαι τοῖς
προσήκουσι τῶν ὑπαρχόντων, ἔπειτα πάσαις ἀπο-
ταξαμένους ταῖς τοῦ βίου φροντίσιν, ἔξω τειχῶν
προελθόντας, ἐν μοναγρίοις καὶ κήποις τὰς διατριβὰς ποιεῖσθαι, τὰς ἐκ τῶν ἀνομοίων ἐπιμιξίας
ἀλυσιτελεῖς καὶ βλαβερὰς εὖ εἰδότας, τῶν κατ᾽
ἐκεῖνο καιροῦ τοῦθ᾽, ὡς εἰκός, ἐπιτελούντων,
ἐκθύμῳ καὶ θερμοτάτῃ πίστει τὸν προφητικὸν
ζηλοῦν ἀσκούντων βίον. καὶ γὰρ οὖν κἂν ταῖς 6
ὁμολογουμέναις τῶν ἀποστόλων Πράξεσιν ἐμ-
φέρεται ὅτι δὴ πάντες οἱ τῶν ἀποστόλων γνώριμοι

Philo, p. 471, 6. 7
Philo, p. 471, 15-472, 3
Philo, p. 473, 18-22
Philo, p. 474, 17-34
Acts 2, 45

---

[1] The ambiguity is due to the fact that the Greek
word may mean " service " or " healing."
146

customs in a strictly Jewish manner. In the first place he promises not to go beyond the truth in any detail or to add anything of his own invention to what he was going to relate in the treatise which he entitled *On the Contemplative Life or Suppliants*. He then says that they and the women with them were called Therapeutae and Therapeutrides, and enters upon the reason for such a name. It was given either because, like physicians, they relieve from the passions of evil the souls of those who come to them and so cure and heal them, or because of their pure and sincere service[1] and worship of the Divine. Thus it is not necessary to discuss at length whether he gave them this description of himself, naturally adapting the name to their manner of life, or whether the first ones really called themselves this from the beginning, since the title of Christian had not yet become well known everywhere. At any rate he bears witness especially to their abandonment of property, and states that when they begin to follow philosophy they give up their possessions to their relations, and then, having bade farewell to all the cares of life, go outside the walls to make their dwellings in deserts and oases,[2] for they are well aware that intercourse with those of another way is unprofitable and harmful, and it was the practice at that time, so it seems, of those who were thus initiated to emulate the life of the prophets in zealous and warm faith. For even in the canonical Acts of the Apostles it is related that all the acquaintances of the Apostles

[2] Literally " gardens."

τὰ κτήματα καὶ τὰς ὑπάρξεις διαπιπράσκοντες
ἐμέριζον ἅπασιν καθ' ὃ ἄν τις χρείαν εἶχεν, ὡς
μηδὲ εἶναί τινα ἐνδεῆ παρ' αὐτοῖς· ὅσοι γοῦν
κτήτορες χωρίων ἢ οἰκιῶν ὑπῆρχον, ὡς ὁ λόγος
φησίν, πωλοῦντες ἔφερον τὰς τιμὰς τῶν πιπρα-
σκομένων, ἐτίθεσάν τε παρὰ τοὺς πόδας τῶν
ἀποστόλων, ὥστε διαδίδοσθαι ἑκάστῳ καθ' ὅτι ἄν
τις χρείαν εἶχεν.

Τὰ παραπλήσια δὲ τούτοις μαρτυρήσας τοῖς 7
δηλουμένοις ὁ Φίλων συλλαβαῖς αὐταῖς ἐπιφέρει
λέγων· "πολλαχοῦ μὲν οὖν τῆς οἰκουμένης ἐστὶν
τὸ γένος· ἔδει γὰρ ἀγαθοῦ τελείου μετασχεῖν καὶ
τὴν Ἑλλάδα καὶ τὴν βάρβαρον· πλεονάζει δ' ἐν
Αἰγύπτῳ καθ' ἕκαστον τῶν ἐπικαλουμένων
νομῶν καὶ μάλιστα περὶ τὴν Ἀλεξάνδρειαν. οἱ δὲ 8
πανταχόθεν ἄριστοι, καθάπερ εἰς πατρίδα θερα-
πευτῶν, ἀποικίαν στέλλονται πρός τι χωρίον
ἐπιτηδειότατον, ὅπερ ἐστὶν ὑπὲρ λίμνης Μαρείας
κείμενον ἐπὶ γεωλόφου χθαμαλωτέρου, σφόδρα
εὐκαίρως ἀσφαλείας τε ἕνεκα καὶ ἀέρος εὐκρασίας."
εἶθ' ἑξῆς τὰς οἰκήσεις αὐτῶν ὁποῖαί τινες ἦσαν 9
διαγράψας, περὶ τῶν κατὰ χώραν ἐκκλησιῶν ταῦτά
φησιν· "ἐν ἑκάστῃ δὲ οἰκίᾳ ἐστὶν οἴκημα ἱερὸν
ὃ καλεῖται σεμνεῖον καὶ μοναστήριον, ἐν ᾧ μο-
νούμενοι τὰ τοῦ σεμνοῦ βίου μυστήρια τελοῦνται,
μηδὲν εἰσκομίζοντες, μὴ ποτόν, μὴ σιτίον, μηδέ
τι τῶν ἄλλων ὅσα πρὸς τὰς τοῦ σώματος χρείας
ἀναγκαῖα, ἀλλὰ νόμους καὶ λόγια θεσπισθέντα διὰ
προφητῶν καὶ ὕμνους καὶ τἄλλα οἷς ἐπιστήμη καὶ
εὐσέβεια συναύξονται καὶ τελειοῦνται."

Καὶ μεθ' ἕτερά φησιν·

"Τὸ δ' ἐξ ἑωθινοῦ μέχρις ἑσπέρας διάστημα 1

Acts 4, 34–35

Philo, p. 474, 35–44

Philo, p. 475, 14–22

Philo, p. 475, 34–476, 2

sold their goods and possessions and divided them to all according as anyone had need so that none was in want among them ; and as many as were possessors of lands or houses, so the story says, sold them and brought the price of what had been sold and laid it at the feet of the Apostles, so that it might be divided to each according as any had need.

To practices like those which have been related Philo bears witness and continues in the following words : " The race is found in many places in the world, for it was right that both Greece and barbarism should share in perfect good, but it abounds in Egypt in each of the so-called nomes and especially around Alexandria. The noblest from every region send a colony to a district well suited for their purpose, as though it were the land of the Therapeutae. This district is situated above Lake Mareia [1] on a low hill, very convenient for its safety and the temperateness of the climate." He then goes on to describe the nature of their dwellings, and says this about the churches in various districts : " In each house there is a sacred dwelling which is called ' a sanctuary and monastery,' in which they celebrate in seclusion the mysteries of the sacred life, and bring nothing into it, either drink or food or any of the other things necessary for bodily needs, but law and inspired oracles given by the prophets and hymns and other things by which knowledge and religion are increased and perfected." And further on he says : " The whole period from dawn

[1] More often known as Lake Mareotis, a little south of Alexandria.

σύμπαν αὐτοῖς ἐστιν ἄσκησις. ἐντυγχάνοντες γὰρ
τοῖς ἱεροῖς γράμμασιν φιλοσοφοῦσιν τὴν πάτριον
φιλοσοφίαν ἀλληγοροῦντες, ἐπειδὴ σύμβολα τὰ
τῆς ῥητῆς ἑρμηνείας νομίζουσιν ἀποκεκρυμμένης
φύσεως, ἐν ὑπονοίαις δηλουμένης. ἔστι δ' αὐτοῖς 11
καὶ συγγράμματα παλαιῶν ἀνδρῶν, οἳ τῆς αἱρέσεως αὐτῶν ἀρχηγέται γενόμενοι, πολλὰ μνημεῖα
τῆς ἐν τοῖς ἀλληγορουμένοις ἰδέας ἀπέλιπον, οἷς
καθάπερ τισὶν ἀρχετύποις χρώμενοι μιμοῦνται τῆς
προαιρέσεως τὸν τρόπον.''

Ταῦτα μὲν οὖν ἔοικεν εἰρῆσθαι τῷ ἀνδρὶ τὰς 12
ἱερὰς ἐξηγουμένων αὐτῶν ἐπακροασαμένῳ γραφάς,
τάχα δ' εἰκός, ἃ φησιν ἀρχαίων παρ' αὐτοῖς εἶναι
συγγράμματα, εὐαγγέλια καὶ τὰς τῶν ἀποστόλων
γραφὰς διηγήσεις τέ τινας κατὰ τὸ εἰκὸς τῶν
πάλαι προφητῶν ἑρμηνευτικάς, ὁποίας ἥ τε πρὸς
Ἑβραίους καὶ ἄλλαι πλείους τοῦ Παύλου περιέχουσιν ἐπιστολαί, ταῦτ' εἶναι. εἶτα πάλιν ἑξῆς 13
περὶ τοῦ νέους αὐτοὺς ποιεῖσθαι ψαλμοὺς οὕτως
Philo, p. 476,
2–5 γράφει· ''ὥστ' οὐ θεωροῦσι μόνον, ἀλλὰ καὶ
ποιοῦσιν ᾄσματα καὶ ὕμνους εἰς τὸν θεὸν διὰ
παντοίων μέτρων καὶ μελῶν ἀριθμοῖς σεμνοτέροις
ἀναγκαίως χαράσσοντες.''

Πολλὰ μὲν οὖν καὶ ἄλλα περὶ ὧν ὁ λόγος, ἐν 14
ταὐτῷ διέξεισιν, ἐκεῖνα δ' ἀναγκαῖον ἐφάνη δεῖν
ἀναλέξασθαι, δι' ὧν τὰ χαρακτηριστικὰ τῆς
ἐκκλησιαστικῆς ἀγωγῆς ὑποτίθεται. εἰ δέ τῳ 15
μὴ δοκεῖ τὰ εἰρημένα ἴδια εἶναι τῆς κατὰ τὸ
εὐαγγέλιον πολιτείας, δύνασθαι δὲ καὶ ἄλλοις
παρὰ τοὺς δεδηλωμένους ἁρμόττειν, πειθέσθω κἂν
ἀπὸ τῶν ἑξῆς αὐτοῦ φωνῶν, ἐν αἷς ἀναμφ-
ήριστον, εἰ εὐγνωμονοίη, κομίσεται τὴν περὶ τοῦδε

to eve is for them a religious exercise ; they study the sacred scriptures and expound their national philosophy by allegory, for they regard the literal interpretation as symbolic of a concealed reality indicated in what is beneath the surface. They have also some writings of men of old, who were the founders of their sect, who left many memorials of the meaning allegorically expounded, which they use as models and copy their method of treatment.

This seems to have been said by a man who had listened to their expositions of the sacred scriptures, and it is perhaps probable that the writings of men of old, which he says were found among them, were the Gospels, the writings of the Apostles, and some expositions of prophets after the manner of the ancients, such as are in the Epistle to the Hebrews and many other of the epistles of Paul. He then goes on to write thus about their composition of new psalms : " So that they not only contemplate but make songs and hymns to God in all kinds of metres and melodies, though they perforce arrange them in the more sacred measures."

He discusses many other points as well in the same book, but it seemed necessary to enumerate those by which the characteristics of the life of the Church are exhibited ; but if anyone doubt that what has been said is peculiar to life according to the Gospel, and think that it can be applied to others besides those indicated, let him be persuaded by the following words of Philo in which he will find, if he be fair, indisputable testimony on this point. He

151

Philo, p. 476,
36-39 μαρτυρίαν. γράφει γὰρ ὧδε· "ἐγκράτειαν δ' 16
ὥσπερ τινὰ θεμέλιον προκαταβαλλόμενοι τῇ
ψυχῇ, τὰς ἄλλας ἐποικοδομοῦσιν ἀρετάς. σιτίον
ἢ ποτὸν οὐδεὶς ἂν αὐτῶν προσενέγκαιτο πρὸ
ἡλίου δύσεως, ἐπεὶ τὸ μὲν φιλοσοφεῖν ἄξιον
φωτὸς κρίνουσιν εἶναι, σκότους δὲ τὰς τοῦ
σώματος ἀνάγκας· ὅθεν τῷ μὲν ἡμέραν, ταῖς δὲ
νυκτὸς βραχύ τι μέρος ἔνειμαν. ἔνιοι δὲ καὶ διὰ 17
τριῶν ἡμερῶν ὑπομιμνήσκονται τροφῆς, οἷς πλείων
ὁ πόθος ἐπιστήμης ἐνίδρυται, τινὲς δὲ οὕτως
ἐνευφραίνονται καὶ τρυφῶσιν ὑπὸ σοφίας ἑστιώ-
μενοι πλουσίως καὶ ἀφθόνως τὰ δόγματα χορη-
γούσης, ὡς καὶ πρὸς διπλασίονα χρόνον ἀντέχειν
καὶ μόγις δι' ἓξ ἡμερῶν ἀπογεύεσθαι τροφῆς
ἀναγκαίας, ἐθισθέντες."

Ταύτας τοῦ Φίλωνος σαφεῖς καὶ ἀναντιρρήτους 18
περὶ τῶν καθ' ἡμᾶς ὑπάρχειν ἡγούμεθα λέξεις.
εἰ δ' ἐπὶ τούτοις ἀντιλέγων τις ἔτι σκληρύνοιτο,
καὶ οὗτος ἀπαλλαττέσθω τῆς δυσπιστίας, ἐναργε-
στέραις πειθαρχῶν ἀποδείξεσιν, ἃς οὐ παρά τισιν
ἢ μόνῃ τῇ Χριστιανῶν εὑρεῖν ἔνεστιν κατὰ τὸ
Philo, p. 482,
8-11 εὐαγγέλιον θρησκείᾳ. φησὶν γὰρ τοῖς περὶ ὧν ὁ 19
λόγος καὶ γυναῖκας συνεῖναι, ὧν αἱ πλεῖσται γηρα-
λέαι παρθένοι τυγχάνουσιν, τὴν ἁγνείαν οὐκ
ἀνάγκῃ, καθάπερ ἔνιαι τῶν παρ' Ἕλλησιν ἱερειῶν,
φυλάξασαι μᾶλλον ἢ καθ' ἑκούσιον γνώμην, διὰ
ζῆλον καὶ πόθον σοφίας, ᾗ συμβιοῦν σπουδά-
σασαι τῶν περὶ τὸ σῶμα ἡδονῶν ἠλόγησαν, οὐ
θνητῶν ἐκγόνων, ἀλλ' ἀθανάτων ὀρεχθεῖσαι, ἃ
μόνη τίκτειν ἀφ' ἑαυτῆς οἷά τέ ἐστιν ἡ θεοφιλὴς
ψυχή. εἶθ' ὑποκαταβάς, ἐμφαντικώτερον ἐκτίθε- 20
Philo, p. 483,
42-484, 1 ται ταῦτα· "αἱ δ' ἐξηγήσεις τῶν ἱερῶν γραμμάτων

writes thus : " Having laid down for the soul continence as a foundation they build the other virtues
on it. None of them would take food or drink
before sunset, for they think that philosophy deserves the daylight and the necessities of the body
darkness ; for this reason they allot the day to the
one, and a small part of the night to the others.
Some of them neglect food for three days for the
great love of knowledge dwelling in them, and some
so delight and luxuriate in the banquet of doctrine,
so richly and ungrudgingly presided over by wisdom,
that they abstain for twice that time, and are
accustomed scarcely to taste necessary food every
six days."

We think that these words of Philo are clear and
indisputably refer to our communion. But if after
this anyone obstinately deny it let him be converted from his scepticism and be persuaded by
clearer indications which cannot be found among
any, save only in the worship of Christians according
to the Gospel. For Philo says that women belong
also to those under discussion and that most of them
are aged virgins who kept their chastity from no
compulsion, like some of the priestesses among the
Greeks, but rather from voluntary opinion, from zeal
and yearning for wisdom, with which they desired
to live, and paid no attention to bodily pleasures,
longing not for mortal but for immortal children,
which only the soul that loves God is capable of
bearing of itself. He then proceeds to expound
this more clearly. " But the interpretations of the

γίνονται αὐτοῖς δι᾽ ὑπονοιῶν ἐν ἀλληγορίαις. ἅπα-
σα γὰρ ἡ νομοθεσία δοκεῖ τοῖς ἀνδράσι τούτοις
ἐοικέναι ζῴῳ καὶ σῶμα μὲν ἔχειν τὰς ῥητὰς δια-
τάξεις, ψυχὴν δὲ τὸν ἐναποκείμενον ταῖς λέξεσιν
ἀόρατον νοῦν, ὃν ἤρξατο διαφερόντως ἡ οἰκία
αὕτη θεωρεῖν, ὡς διὰ κατόπτρου τῶν ὀνομάτων ἐξαίσια κάλλη νοημάτων ἐμφαινόμενα κατ-
ιδοῦσα.''

Philo, p. 476, 23–34
Τί δεῖ τούτοις ἐπιλέγειν τὰς ἐπὶ ταὐτὸν συν- 2
όδους καὶ τὰς ἰδίᾳ μὲν ἀνδρῶν, ἰδίᾳ δὲ γυναικῶν
ἐν ταὐτῷ διατριβὰς καὶ τὰς ἐξ ἔθους ἔτι καὶ
Philo, p. 481 22–24
νῦν πρὸς ἡμῶν ἐπιτελουμένας ἀσκήσεις, ἃς διαφερόντως κατὰ τὴν τοῦ σωτηρίου πάθους ἑορτὴν
ἐν ἀσιτίαις καὶ διανυκτερεύσεσιν προσοχαῖς τε
τῶν θείων λόγων ἐκτελεῖν εἰώθαμεν, ἅπερ ἐπ᾽ 2
ἀκριβέστερον αὐτὸν ὃν καὶ εἰς δεῦρο τετήρηται
Philo, p. 484, 33–34
παρὰ μόνοις ἡμῖν τρόπον ἐπισημηνάμενος ὁ
δηλωθεὶς ἀνὴρ τῇ ἰδίᾳ παρέδωκεν γραφῇ, τὰς
τῆς μεγάλης ἑορτῆς παννυχίδας καὶ τὰς ἐν ταύ-
Philo, p. 484, 10–21
ταις ἀσκήσεις τούς τε λέγεσθαι εἰωθότας πρὸς
ἡμῶν ὕμνους ἱστορῶν, καὶ ὡς ἑνὸς μετὰ ῥυθμοῦ
κοσμίως ἐπιψάλλοντος οἱ λοιποὶ καθ᾽ ἡσυχίαν
ἀκροώμενοι τῶν ὕμνων τὰ ἀκροτελεύτια συνεξ-
Philo, p. 482, 18–21; p.483, 4–10
ηχοῦσιν, ὅπως τε κατὰ τὰς δεδηλωμένας ἡμέρας
ἐπὶ στιβάδων χαμευνοῦντες οἴνου μὲν τὸ παρά-
παν, ὡς αὐτοῖς ῥήμασιν ἀνέγραψεν, οὐδ᾽ ἀπο-
γεύονται, ἀλλ᾽ οὐδὲ τῶν ἐναίμων τινός, ὕδωρ δὲ
μόνον αὐτοῖς ἐστι ποτόν, καὶ προσόψημα μετ᾽
Philo, p. 481, 32–34. 42; p. 482, 3. 24. 25; p.483, 17; p. 484, 6
ἄρτου ἅλες καὶ ὕσσωπον. πρὸς τούτοις γράφει 2
τὸν τῆς προστασίας τρόπον τῶν τὰς ἐκκλησια-
στικὰς λειτουργίας ἐγκεχειρισμένων διακονίας τε
καὶ τὰς ἐπὶ πᾶσιν ἀνωτάτω τῆς ἐπισκοπῆς προ-

sacred scriptures are given them figuratively in allegories, for the whole law seems to these men to be like a living being ; for a body it has the spoken precepts, but for a soul the invisible mind underlying the words ; and it is this which this sect has begun especially to contemplate, so that in the mirror of the words it sees manifested surpassing beauty of thought."

What need is there to add to this a description of their meetings, and of how the men live separately and the women separately in the same place, and of the customary exercises which are still celebrated among us, particularly those which we are accustomed to celebrate at the feast of the Passion of the Saviour by abstinence from food and vigils and attention to the word of God ? The writer referred to has given in his own writing a description of this, which exactly agrees with the manner which is still observed by us and by us alone ; he relates the vigils for the entire night of the great feast, and the exercises during them, and the hymns which we are accustomed to recite, and how while one sings regularly with cadence, the rest listen in silence and join in singing only the refrain of the hymns, and how on stated days they sleep on the ground on straw, how they completely refrain from wine, as he expressly states, and from all kinds of flesh, drinking only water and using salt and hyssop to season their bread. In addition to this he writes of the order of precedence of those who have been appointed to the service of the Church, both to the diaconate and to the supremacy of the episcopate

ἐδρίας. τούτων δ' ὅτῳ πόθος ἔνεστι τῆς ἀκριβοῦς ἐπιστάσεως, μάθοι ἂν ἐκ τῆς δηλωθείσης τοῦ ἀνδρὸς ἱστορίας· ὅτι δὲ τοὺς πρώτους κήρυκας 24 τῆς κατὰ τὸ εὐαγγέλιον διδασκαλίας τά τε ἀρχῆθεν πρὸς τῶν ἀποστόλων ἔθη παραδεδομένα καταλαβὼν ὁ Φίλων ταῦτ' ἔγραφεν, παντί τῳ δῆλον.

XVIII. Πολύς γε μὴν τῷ λόγῳ καὶ πλατὺς ταῖς 1 διανοίαις, ὑψηλός τε ὢν καὶ μετέωρος ἐν ταῖς εἰς τὰς θείας γραφὰς θεωρίαις γεγενημένος, ποικίλην καὶ πολύτροπον τῶν ἱερῶν λόγων πεποίηται τὴν ὑφήγησιν, τοῦτο μὲν εἱρμῷ καὶ ἀκολουθίᾳ τὴν τῶν εἰς τὴν Γένεσιν διεξελθὼν πραγματείαν ἐν οἷς ἐπέγραψεν Νόμων ἱερῶν ἀλληγορίας, τοῦτο δὲ κατὰ μέρος διαστολὰς κεφαλαίων τῶν ἐν ταῖς γραφαῖς ζητουμένων ἐπιστάσεις τε καὶ διαλύσεις πεποιημένος ἐν οἷς καὶ αὐτοῖς καταλλήλως Τῶν ἐν Γενέσει καὶ τῶν ἐν Ἐξαγωγῇ ζητημάτων καὶ λύσεων τέθειται τὴν ἐπιγραφήν. ἔστι δ' αὐτῷ 2 παρὰ ταῦτα προβλημάτων τινῶν ἰδίως πεπονημένα σπουδάσματα, οἷά ἐστι τὰ Περὶ γεωργίας δύο, καὶ τὰ Περὶ μέθης τοσαῦτα, καὶ ἄλλα ἄττα διαφόρου καὶ οἰκείας ἐπιγραφῆς ἠξιωμένα, οἷος ὁ Περὶ ὧν νήψας ὁ νοῦς εὔχεται καὶ καταρᾶται καὶ Περὶ συγχύσεως τῶν διαλέκτων, καὶ ὁ Περὶ φυγῆς καὶ εὑρέσεως, καὶ ὁ Περὶ τῆς πρὸς τὰ παιδεύματα συνόδου, Περί τε τοῦ τίς ὁ τῶν θείων ἐστὶ κληρονόμος ἢ Περὶ τῆς εἰς τὰ ἴσα καὶ ἐναντία τομῆς, καὶ ἔτι τὸ Περὶ τῶν τριῶν ἀρετῶν ἃς σὺν ἄλλαις ἀνέγραψεν Μωυσῆς, πρὸς τούτοις ὁ Περὶ 3 τῶν μετονομαζομένων καὶ ὧν ἕνεκα μετονομάζονται, ἐν ᾧ φησι συντεταχέναι καὶ Περὶ διαθηκῶν α' β'· ἔστιν δ' αὐτοῦ καὶ Περὶ ἀποικίας 4

at the head over all. Anyone who has a love of accurate knowledge of these things can learn from the narrative of the author quoted already, and it is plain to everyone that Philo perceived and described the first heralds of teaching according to the Gospel and the customs handed down from the beginning by the Apostles.

XVIII. Philo was rich in language and broad in thought, sublime and elevated in his views of the divine writings, and had made various and diverse his exposition of the sacred words. He first went through the subject of the events in Genesis in connected sequence, in the books which he entitled " The Allegories of the Sacred Laws." He then made detailed arrangement into chapters of the difficulties in the Scriptures and gave their statement and solution in the books to which he gave the suitable title of " The Problems and Solutions in Genesis and in Exodus." There are, besides this, some specially elaborated treatises of his on certain problems, such as the two books " On Agriculture," and as many " On Drunkenness," and others with various appropriate titles, such as " The Things which the Sober Mind desires and execrates," " On the Confusion of Tongues," " On Flight and Discovery," " On Assembly for Instruction," and " On the Question who is Heir of the Divine Things," or " On the Distinction between Odd and Even," and further " On the three Virtues which Moses describes with others," in addition to this, " On those whose names have been changed and why they were," in which he says that he has also composed Books I. and II. " On the Covenants." There is also a book of his " On Migration and the wise life of the Man

καὶ βίου σοφοῦ τοῦ κατὰ δικαιοσύνην τελειωθέντος ἢ νόμων ἀγράφων, καὶ ἔτι Περὶ γιγάντων
ἢ περὶ τοῦ μὴ τρέπεσθαι τὸ θεῖον, Περί τε τοῦ
κατὰ Μωυσέα θεοπέμπτους εἶναι τοὺς ὀνείρους
αʹ βʹ γʹ δʹ εʹ. καὶ ταῦτα μὲν τὰ εἰς ἡμᾶς ἐλθόντα
τῶν εἰς τὴν Γένεσιν, εἰς δὲ τὴν Ἔξοδον ἔγνωμεν 5
αὐτοῦ Ζητημάτων καὶ λύσεων αʹ βʹ γʹ δʹ εʹ, καὶ
τὸ Περὶ τῆς σκηνῆς, τό τε Περὶ τῶν δέκα λογίων,
καὶ τὰ Περὶ τῶν ἀναφερομένων ἐν εἴδει νόμων
εἰς τὰ συντείνοντα κεφάλαια τῶν δέκα λόγων αʹ
βʹ γʹ δʹ, καὶ τὸ Περὶ τῶν εἰς τὰς ἱερουργίας ζώων
καὶ τίνα τὰ τῶν θυσιῶν εἴδη, καὶ τὸ Περὶ τῶν
προκειμένων ἐν τῷ νόμῳ τοῖς μὲν ἀγαθοῖς ἄθλων,
τοῖς δὲ πονηροῖς ἐπιτιμίων καὶ ἀρῶν. πρὸς 6
τούτοις ἅπασιν καὶ μονόβιβλα αὐτοῦ φέρεται
ὡς τὸ Περὶ προνοίας, καὶ ὁ Περὶ Ἰουδαίων αὐτῷ
συνταχθεὶς λόγος, καὶ ὁ Πολιτικός, ἔτι τε ὁ Ἀλέξανδρος ἢ περὶ τοῦ λόγον ἔχειν τὰ ἄλογα ζῷα,
ἐπὶ τούτοις ὁ Περὶ τοῦ δοῦλον εἶναι πάντα φαῦλον,
ᾧ ἑξῆς ἐστιν ὁ Περὶ τοῦ πάντα σπουδαῖον ἐλεύθερον εἶναι· μεθ' οὓς συντέτακται αὐτῷ ὁ Περὶ 7
βίου θεωρητικοῦ ἢ ἱκετῶν, ἐξ οὗ τὰ περὶ τοῦ βίου
τῶν ἀποστολικῶν ἀνδρῶν διεληλύθαμεν, καὶ τῶν
ἐν νόμῳ δὲ καὶ προφήταις Ἑβραϊκῶν ὀνομάτων
αἱ ἑρμηνεῖαι τοῦ αὐτοῦ σπουδὴ εἶναι λέγονται.
οὗτος μὲν οὖν κατὰ Γάιον ἐπὶ τῆς Ῥώμης ἀφ- 8
ικόμενος, τὰ περὶ τῆς Γαΐου θεοστυγίας αὐτῷ
γραφέντα, ἃ μετὰ ἤθους καὶ εἰρωνείας Περὶ
ἀρετῶν ἐπέγραψεν, ἐπὶ πάσης λέγεται τῆς Ῥωμαίων συγκλήτου κατὰ Κλαύδιον διελθεῖν, ὡς
καὶ τῆς ἐν βιβλιοθήκαις ἀναθέσεως θαυμασθέντας
αὐτοῦ καταξιωθῆναι τοὺς λόγους.

initiated into Righteousness, or Unwritten Laws," and
also " On Giants or the Immutability of God," and
Books I., II., III., IV., V., " On the Divine Origin of
Dreams according to Moses." These are the books
which have come down to us dealing with Genesis.
On Exodus we know Books I., II., III., IV., V. of
his " Problems and Solutions," the book " On the
Tabernacle," and that "On the Ten Commandments,"
and Books I., II., III., IV., " On the Laws specially
referring to the principal divisions of the Ten Commandments," and the book " On Animals for Sacrifice
and the Varieties of Sacrifice," and " On the Rewards
fixed in the Law for the Good and the Penalties and
Curses for the Wicked." In addition to all this there
are also some single volumes of his, such as the book
" On Providence," and the treatise composed by him
" On the Jews," and " The Statesman," moreover
" Alexander, or that irrational animals have reason."
In addition to this the " That every wicked man is a
slave," to which is appended the " That every good
man is free." After these he composed the book
" On the Contemplative Life, or Suppliants," from
which we have quoted the passages dealing with the
life of the men of the Apostolic age, and the interpretations of the Hebrew names in the Law and the
Prophets are said to be his work. He came to Rome
in the time of Caius, and in the reign of Claudius is
said to have read before the whole Senate of the
Romans his description of the impiety of Caius, which
he entitled, with fitting irony, " Concerning Virtues,"
and his words were so much admired as to be granted
a place in libraries.

Rom. 15, 19   Κατὰ δὲ τούσδε τοὺς χρόνους Παύλου τὴν ἀπὸ 9
Ἱερουσαλὴμ καὶ κύκλῳ πορείαν μέχρι τοῦ Ἰλλυ-
Acts 18, 2. ρικοῦ διανύοντος, Ἰουδαίους Ῥώμης ἀπελαύνει
18. 19. 23   Κλαύδιος, ὅ τε Ἀκύλας καὶ Πρίσκιλλα μετὰ
τῶν ἄλλων Ἰουδαίων τῆς Ῥώμης ἀπαλλαγέντες
ἐπὶ τὴν Ἀσίαν καταίρουσιν, ἐνταῦθά τε Παύλῳ
τῷ ἀποστόλῳ συνδιατρίβουσιν, τοὺς αὐτόθι τῶν
ἐκκλησιῶν ἄρτι πρὸς αὐτοῦ καταβληθέντας θεμελίους ἐπιστηρίζοντι. διδάσκαλος καὶ τούτων ἡ
ἱερὰ τῶν Πράξεων γραφή.

Joseph. B.I.   XIX. Ἔτι δὲ Κλαυδίου τὰ τῆς βασιλείας διέπον- 1
2 227   τος, κατὰ τὴν τοῦ πάσχα ἑορτὴν τοσαύτην ἐπὶ τῶν
Ἱεροσολύμων στάσιν καὶ ταραχὴν ἐγγενέσθαι
συνέβη, ὡς μόνων τῶν περὶ τὰς ἐξόδους τοῦ
ἱεροῦ βίᾳ συνωθουμένων τρεῖς μυριάδας Ἰουδαίων
ἀποθανεῖν πρὸς ἀλλήλων καταπατηθέντων, γενέσθαι
τε τὴν ἑορτὴν πένθος μὲν ὅλῳ τῷ ἔθνει, θρῆνον
δὲ καθ᾽ ἑκάστην οἰκίαν. καὶ ταῦτα δὲ κατὰ
Joseph. B.I.   λέξιν ὁ Ἰώσηπος. Κλαύδιος δὲ Ἀγρίππαν, Ἀγρίπ- 2
2, 247. 248   που παῖδα, Ἰουδαίων καθίστησι βασιλέα, Φήλικα
τῆς χώρας ἁπάσης Σαμαρείας τε καὶ Γαλιλαίας
καὶ προσέτι τῆς ἐπικαλουμένης Περαίας ἐπίτροπον ἐκπέμψας, διοικήσας δὲ αὐτὸς τὴν ἡγεμονίαν
ἔτεσιν τρισὶν καὶ δέκα πρὸς μησὶν ὀκτώ, Νέρωνα
τῆς ἀρχῆς διάδοχον καταλιπών, τελευτᾷ.

XX. Κατὰ δὲ Νέρωνα, Φήλικος τῆς Ἰουδαίας 1
ἐπιτροπεύοντος, αὐτοῖς ῥήμασιν αὖθις ὁ Ἰώσηπος
τὴν εἰς ἀλλήλους τῶν ἱερέων στάσιν ὧδέ πως
ἐν εἰκοστῷ τῆς Ἀρχαιολογίας γράφει·
Joseph. A.I.   " Ἐξάπτεται δὲ καὶ τοῖς ἀρχιερεῦσι στάσις 2
20, 180. 181   πρὸς τοὺς ἱερεῖς καὶ τοὺς πρώτους τοῦ πλήθους
τῶν Ἱεροσολύμων, ἕκαστός τε αὐτῶν στῖφος

At this time, while Paul was finishing his journey from Jerusalem and round about unto Illyricum, Claudius banished the Jews from Rome, and Aquila and Priscilla, with the other Jews, left Rome and came into Asia, and lived there with Paul the Apostle, while he was strengthening the foundations of the churches there which had recently been laid by him. The sacred Scripture of the Acts teaches this also.

XIX. Now while Claudius was still administering the Empire there was a riot and confusion in Jerusalem at the feast of the Passover so great that, merely among those who were violently crowded together at the ways leading out of the temple, thirty thousand Jews perished by trampling on each other, and the feast was turned into mourning for the whole nation and into lamentation in each house. This too Josephus relates in so many words. Claudius appointed Agrippa, the child of Agrippa, as king of the Jews, and sent out Felix as Procurator of the whole district of Samaria and Galilee, together with that called Peraea. He had administered the government for thirteen years and eight months when he died and left Nero his successor in the sovereignty.

XX. In the time of Nero, while Felix was Procurator of Judaea, Josephus again relates the quarrel of the priests with one another in the following words in a passage in the twentieth book of the *Antiquities* : " Now a quarrel arose between the High Priests and the priests and leaders of the people of Jerusalem.

ἀνθρώπων τῶν θρασυτάτων καὶ νεωτεριστῶν ἑαυτῷ ποιήσας, ἡγεμὼν ἦν, καὶ συρράσσοντες ἐκακο-
λόγουν τε ἀλλήλους καὶ λίθοις ἔβαλλον· ὁ δ'
ἐπιπλήξων ἦν οὐδὲ εἷς, ἀλλ' ὡς ἐν ἀπροστατήτῳ
πόλει ταῦτ' ἐπράσσετο μετ' ἐξουσίας. τοσαύτη 3
δὲ τοὺς ἀρχιερεῖς κατέλαβεν ἀναίδεια καὶ τόλμα,
ὥστε ἐκπέμπειν δούλους ἐτόλμων ἐπὶ τὰς ἅλωνας
τοὺς ληψομένους τὰς τοῖς ἱερεῦσιν ὀφειλομένας
δεκάτας. καὶ συνέβαινε τοὺς ἀπορουμένους τῶν
ἱερέων ὑπ' ἐνδείας ἀπολλυμένους θεωρεῖν· οὕτως
ἐκράτει τοῦ δικαίου παντὸς ἡ τῶν στασιαζόντων
βία.''

Joseph. B.I.
2, 254–256 Πάλιν δὲ ὁ αὐτὸς συγγραφεὺς κατὰ τοὺς αὐτοὺς 4
χρόνους ἐν Ἱεροσολύμοις ὑποφυῆναι λῃστῶν τι
εἶδος ἱστορεῖ, οἳ μεθ' ἡμέραν, ὥς φησιν, καὶ
ἐν μέσῃ τῇ πόλει ἐφόνευον τοὺς συναντῶντας.
μάλιστα γὰρ ἐν ταῖς ἑορταῖς μιγνυμένους τῷ 5
πλήθει καὶ ταῖς ἐσθήσεσιν ὑποκρύπτοντας μικρὰ
ξιφίδια, τούτοις νύττειν τοὺς διαφόρους· ἔπειτα
πεσόντων, μέρος γίνεσθαι τῶν ἐπαγανακτούντων
αὐτοὺς τοὺς πεφονευκότας· διὸ καὶ παντάπασιν
ὑπ' ἀξιοπιστίας ἀνευρέτους γενέσθαι. πρῶτον μὲν 6
οὖν ὑπ' αὐτῶν Ἰωνάθην τὸν ἀρχιερέα κατα-
σφαγῆναι, μετὰ δ' αὐτὸν καθ' ἡμέραν ἀναιρεῖσθαι
πολλούς, καὶ τῶν συμφορῶν τὸν φόβον εἶναι
χαλεπώτερον, ἑκάστου καθάπερ ἐν πολέμῳ καθ'
ὥραν τὸν θάνατον προσδεχομένου.

XXI. Ἑξῆς δὲ τούτοις ἐπιφέρει μεθ' ἕτερα λέγων· 1
Joseph. B.I.
2, 261–263 ''μείζονι δὲ τούτων πληγῇ Ἰουδαίους ἐκάκωσεν
ὁ Αἰγύπτιος ψευδοπροφήτης. παραγενόμενος γὰρ
εἰς τὴν χώραν ἄνθρωπος γόης καὶ προφήτου
πίστιν ἐπιθεὶς ἑαυτῷ, περὶ τρισμυρίους μὲν ἀθροίζει

162

Each of them made for himself a band of the
boldest revolutionaries, of which he was the leader,
and when they met they used to abuse each other
and throw stones. There was not a single one
to rebuke this, but it was done with licence as though
in a city without government. Such shamelessness
and audacity seized the High Priests that they
ventured to send slaves to the threshing-floors to
take the tithes owed to the priests, and it was a
common occurrence to see destitute priests perishing
of want. Thus the violence of the factions conquered
all justice."

The same writer again relates that at the same
time a certain kind of bandits arose in Jerusalem,
who, as he says, murdered daily those whom they
met, even in the midst of the city. In particular at
the feasts they used to mingle with the crowd and
concealing short daggers in their clothes used to
stab distinguished people with them ; then, when
they had fallen, the murderers themselves shared
in the indignation. In this way they evaded discovery through the confidence generally placed in
them. Jonathan the High Priest was the first to be
slain by them, but after him many were murdered
daily, and fear was worse than the disasters, for as if
in war every man was hourly expecting death.

XXI. He continues his narrative after other details
as follows : " The Egyptian false prophet afflicted the
Jews with a worse scourge than this, for this man
appeared in the country as a sorcerer and secured
for himself the faith due to a prophet. He assembled
about thirty thousand who had been deceived and

τῶν ἠπατημένων, περιαγαγὼν δ' αὐτοὺς ἐκ τῆς
ἐρημίας εἰς τὸ Ἐλαιῶν καλούμενον ὄρος, ἐκεῖθεν
οἷός τε ἦν εἰς Ἱεροσόλυμα παρελθεῖν βιάζεσθαι
καὶ κρατήσας τῆς τε Ῥωμαϊκῆς φρουρᾶς καὶ
τοῦ δήμου τυραννικῶς χρώμενος τοῖς συνεισ-
πεσοῦσιν δορυφόροις. φθάνει δ' αὐτοῦ τὴν ὁρμὴν 2
Φῆλιξ, ὑπαντιάσας μετὰ τῶν Ῥωμαϊκῶν ὁπλιτῶν, καὶ πᾶς ὁ δῆμος συνεφήψατο τῆς ἀμύνης,
ὥστε συμβολῆς γενομένης τὸν μὲν Αἰγύπτιον
φυγεῖν μετ' ὀλίγων, διαφθαρῆναι δὲ καὶ ζωγρηθῆ-
ναι πλείστους τῶν σὺν αὐτῷ."

Ταῦτα ἐν τῇ δευτέρᾳ τῶν Ἱστοριῶν ὁ Ἰώσηπος· 3
ἐπιστῆσαι δὲ ἄξιον τοῖς ἐνταῦθα κατὰ τὸν Αἰγύπτιον δεδηλωμένοις καὶ τοῖς ἐν ταῖς Πράξεσι
τῶν ἀποστόλων, ἔνθα κατὰ Φήλικα πρὸς τοῦ ἐν
Ἱεροσολύμοις χιλιάρχου εἴρηται τῷ Παύλῳ, ὁπηνίκα κατεστασίαζεν αὐτοῦ τὸ τῶν Ἰουδαίων
Acts 21, 38 πλῆθος· "οὐκ ἄρα σὺ εἶ ὁ Αἰγύπτιος ὁ πρὸ
τούτων τῶν ἡμερῶν ἀναστατώσας καὶ ἐξαγαγὼν
ἐν τῇ ἐρήμῳ τοὺς τετρακισχιλίους ἄνδρας τῶν
σικαρίων;" ἀλλὰ τὰ μὲν κατὰ Φήλικα τοιαῦτα.

Acts 25, 8-12; 27. 1 XXII. Τούτου δὲ Φῆστος ὑπὸ Νέρωνος διάδοχος 1
πέμπεται, καθ' ὃν δικαιολογησάμενος ὁ Παῦλος
δέσμιος ἐπὶ Ῥώμης ἄγεται· Ἀρίσταρχος αὐτῷ
Col. 4, 10 συνῆν, ὃν καὶ εἰκότως συναιχμάλωτόν που τῶν
ἐπιστολῶν ἀποκαλεῖ. καὶ Λουκᾶς, ὁ καὶ τὰς
Acts 28, 30. 31 πράξεις τῶν ἀποστόλων γραφῇ παραδούς, ἐν
τούτοις κατέλυσε τὴν ἱστορίαν, διετίαν ὅλην ἐπὶ
τῆς Ῥώμης τὸν Παῦλον ἄνετον διατρῖψαι καὶ
τὸν τοῦ θεοῦ λόγον ἀκωλύτως κηρῦξαι ἐπισημηνάμενος τότε μὲν οὖν ἀπολογησάμενον, αὖθις 2
ἐπὶ τὴν τοῦ κηρύγματος διακονίαν λόγος ἔχει
164

led them round from the wilderness to the mount
called Olivet, where he was in a position to force
an entry into Jerusalem and overpower the Roman
garrison and the people by a despotic use of the
soldiers who had joined him. But Felix, anticipating
his attack, met him with the Roman forces, and all
the people agreed in the defence, so that when
battle was joined the Egyptian fled with a few
men and the greater part of those with him were
destroyed or captured."

Josephus relates this in the second book of the
Wars, but it is worth noting what is said about the
Egyptian there and in the Acts of the Apostles,
where, in the time of Felix, the centurion at Jerusalem said to Paul, when the mob of the Jews was
rioting against him, " Art thou not that Egyptian
who before these days made an uproar and led out
in the wilderness four thousand men of the Sicarii [1] ? "
Such was the course of events under Felix.

XXII. Festus was sent as his successor by Nero, and
Paul was tried before him and taken as a prisoner to
Rome ; Aristarchus was with him, and he naturally
called him his fellow-prisoner in a passage in the
Epistles. Luke also, who committed the Acts of
the Apostles to writing, finished his narrative at this
point by the statement that Paul spent two whole
years in Rome in freedom, and preached the word
of God without hindrance. Tradition has it that
after defending himself the Apostle was again sent

[1] The Sicarii were the special group of revolutionaries in
Jerusalem who practised the assassination of their opponents
by means of a short dagger or *sica* which could be
conveniently concealed in the sleeve, see p. 163.

στείλασθαι τὸν ἀπόστολον, δεύτερον δ' ἐπιβάντα
τῇ αὐτῇ πόλει τῷ κατ' αὐτὸν τελειωθῆναι μαρ-
τυρίῳ· ἐν ᾧ δεσμοῖς ἐχόμενος, τὴν πρὸς Τιμόθεον δευτέραν ἐπιστολὴν συντάττει, ὁμοῦ σημαίνων τήν τε προτέραν αὐτῷ γενομένην ἀπολογίαν
καὶ τὴν παρὰ πόδας τελείωσιν. δέχου δὴ καὶ 3
τούτων τὰς αὐτοῦ μαρτυρίας· " ἐν τῇ πρώτῃ μου,"
φησίν, " ἀπολογίᾳ οὐδείς μοι παρεγένετο, ἀλλὰ
πάντες με ἐγκατέλιπον (μὴ αὐτοῖς λογισθείη), ὁ
δὲ κύριός μοι παρέστη καὶ ἐνεδυνάμωσέν με,
ἵνα δι' ἐμοῦ τὸ κήρυγμα πληροφορηθῇ καὶ ἀκού-
σωσι πάντα τὰ ἔθνη, καὶ ἐρρύσθην ἐκ στόματος
λέοντος." σαφῶς δὴ παρίστησιν διὰ τούτων 4
ὅτι δὴ τὸ πρότερον, ὡς ἂν τὸ κήρυγμα τὸ δι'
αὐτοῦ πληρωθείη, ἐρρύσθη ἐκ στόματος λέοντος, τὸν Νέρωνα ταύτῃ, ὡς ἔοικεν, διὰ τὸ ὠμό-
θυμον προσειπών. οὔκουν ἑξῆς προστέθεικεν
παραπλήσιόν τι τῷ " ῥύσεταί με ἐκ στόματος
λέοντος·" ἑώρα γὰρ τῷ πνεύματι τὴν ὅσον
οὔπω μέλλουσαν αὐτοῦ τελευτήν, δι' ὃ φησιν ἐπι- 5
λέγων τῷ " καὶ ἐρρύσθην ἐκ στόματος λέοντος" τὸ
" ῥύσεταί με ὁ κύριος ἀπὸ παντὸς ἔργου πονηροῦ
καὶ σώσει εἰς τὴν βασιλείαν αὐτοῦ τὴν ἐπουρά-
νιον," σημαίνων τὸ παραυτίκα μαρτύριον. ὁ
καὶ σαφέστερον ἐν τῇ αὐτῇ προλέγει γραφῇ,
φάσκων " ἐγὼ γὰρ ἤδη σπένδομαι, καὶ ὁ καιρὸς
τῆς ἐμῆς ἀναλύσεως ἐφέστηκεν."[1] νῦν μὲν οὖν
ἐπὶ τῆς δευτέρας ἐπιστολῆς τῶν πρὸς Τιμόθεον
τὸν Λουκᾶν μόνον γράφοντι αὐτῷ συνεῖναι δηλοῖ,
κατὰ δὲ τὴν προτέραν ἀπολογίαν οὐδὲ τοῦτον·
ὅθεν εἰκότως τὰς τῶν ἀποστόλων Πράξεις ἐπ'

[1] Cf. George Syncellus 634, 13-635, 21.

166

on the ministry of preaching, and coming a second time to the same city suffered martyrdom under Nero. During this imprisonment he wrote the second Epistle to Timothy, indicating at the same time that his first defence had taken place and that his martyrdom was at hand. Notice his testimony on this point : " At my first defence," he says, " no man was with me, but all deserted me (may it not be laid to their charge), but the Lord stood by me and strengthened me that the preaching might be fulfilled by me and all the Gentiles might hear, and I was delivered from the lion's mouth." He clearly proves by this that on the first occasion, in order that the preaching which took place through him might be fulfilled, he was delivered from the lion's mouth, apparently referring to Nero thus for his ferocity. He does not go on to add any such words as " he will deliver me from the lion's mouth," for he saw in the spirit that his death was all but at hand, wherefore after the words " And I was delivered from the lion's mouth," he goes on to say, " The Lord will deliver me from all evil and save me for his heavenly kingdom," indicating his impending martyrdom. And this he foretells even more clearly in the same writing, saying, " For I am already offered up and the time of my release is at hand." Now in the second Epistle of those to Timothy, he states that only Luke was with him as he wrote, and at his first defence not even he ; wherefore Luke probably wrote the Acts of the Apostles at that time, carrying

ἐκεῖνον ὁ Λουκᾶς περιέγραψε τὸν χρόνον, τὴν
μέχρις ὅτε τῷ Παύλῳ συνῆν ἱστορίαν ὑφηγησά-
μενος. ταῦτα δ᾽ ἡμῖν εἴρηται παρισταμένοις ὅτι 7
μὴ καθ᾽ ἣν ὁ Λουκᾶς ἀνέγραψεν ἐπὶ τῆς Ῥώμης
ἐπιδημίαν τοῦ Παύλου τὸ μαρτύριον αὐτῷ συν-
επεράνθη· εἰκός γέ τοι κατὰ μὲν ἀρχὰς ἠπιώτερον 8
τοῦ Νέρωνος διακειμένου, ῥᾷον τὴν ὑπὲρ τοῦ
δόγματος τοῦ Παύλου καταδεχθῆναι ἀπολογίαν,
προελθόντος δ᾽ εἰς ἀθεμίτους τόλμας, μετὰ τῶν
ἄλλων καὶ τὰ κατὰ τῶν ἀποστόλων ἐγχειρηθῆναι.

Acts 25, 11.
12; 27, 1

XXIII. Ἰουδαῖοί γε μὴν τοῦ Παύλου Καίσαρα 1
ἐπικαλεσαμένου ἐπί τε τὴν Ῥωμαίων πόλιν ὑπὸ

Acts 23, 13-
15; 25, 3

Φήστου παραπεμφθέντος, τῆς ἐλπίδος καθ᾽ ἣν ἐξήρ-
τυον αὐτῷ τὴν ἐπιβουλήν, ἀποπεσόντες, ἐπὶ Ἰάκωβον τὸν τοῦ κυρίου τρέπονται ἀδελφόν, ᾧ πρὸς τῶν
ἀποστόλων ὁ τῆς ἐπισκοπῆς τῆς ἐν Ἱεροσολύμοις
ἐγκεχείριστο θρόνος. τοιαῦτα δὲ αὐτοῖς καὶ τὰ
κατὰ τούτου τολμᾶται. εἰς μέσον αὐτὸν ἀγα- 2
γόντες ἄρνησιν τῆς εἰς τὸν Χριστὸν πίστεως ἐπὶ
παντὸς ἐξήτουν τοῦ λαοῦ· τοῦ δὲ παρὰ τὴν ἁπάντων γνώμην ἐλευθέρᾳ φωνῇ καὶ μᾶλλον ἢ προσ-
εδόκησαν ἐπὶ τῆς πληθύος ἁπάσης παρρησια-
σαμένου καὶ ὁμολογήσαντος υἱὸν εἶναι θεοῦ τὸν
σωτῆρα καὶ κύριον ἡμῶν Ἰησοῦν, μηκέθ᾽ οἷοί
τε τὴν τοῦ ἀνδρὸς μαρτυρίαν φέρειν τῷ καὶ δικαιότατον αὐτὸν παρὰ τοῖς πᾶσιν δι᾽ ἀκρότητα
ἧς μετῄει κατὰ τὸν βίον φιλοσοφίας τε καὶ θεοσεβείας πιστεύεσθαι, κτείνουσι, καιρὸν εἰς ἐξου-
σίαν λαβόντες τὴν ἀναρχίαν, ὅτι δὴ τοῦ Φήστου
κατ᾽ αὐτὸ τοῦ καιροῦ ἐπὶ τῆς Ἰουδαίας τελευτήσαντος, ἄναρχα καὶ ἀνεπίτροπευτα τὰ τῆς αὐτόθι
διοικήσεως καθειστήκει. τὸν δὲ τῆς τοῦ Ἰακώ- 3

down his narrative until the time when he was with Paul. We have said this to show that Paul's martyrdom was not accomplished during the sojourn in Rome which Luke describes. Probably at the beginning Nero's disposition was gentler and it was easier for Paul's defence on behalf of his views to be received, but as he advanced towards reckless crime the Apostles were attacked along with the rest.

XXIII. When Paul appealed to Caesar and was sent over to Rome by Festus the Jews were disappointed of the hope in which they had laid their plot against him and turned against James, the brother of the Lord, to whom the throne of the bishopric in Jerusalem had been allotted by the Apostles. The crime which they committed was as follows. They brought him into the midst and demanded a denial of the faith in Christ before all the people, but when he, contrary to the expectation of all of them, with a loud voice and with more courage than they had expected, confessed before all the people that our Lord and Saviour Jesus Christ is the son of God, they could no longer endure his testimony, since he was by all men believed to be most righteous because of the height which he had reached in a life of philosophy and religion, and killed him, using anarchy as an opportunity for power since at that moment Festus had died in Judaea, leaving the district without government or procurator. The manner of

βου τελευτῆς τρόπον ἤδη μὲν πρότερον αἱ παρα-
τεθεῖσαι τοῦ Κλήμεντος φωναὶ δεδηλώκασιν, ἀπὸ
τοῦ πτερυγίου βεβλῆσθαι ξύλῳ τε τὴν πρὸς θάνατον
πεπλῆχθαι αὐτὸν ἱστορηκότος· ἀκριβέστατά γε μὴν
τὰ κατ᾽ αὐτὸν ὁ Ἡγήσιππος, ἐπὶ τῆς πρώτης τῶν
ἀποστόλων γενόμενος διαδοχῆς, ἐν τῷ πέμπτῳ
αὐτοῦ ὑπομνήματι τοῦτον λέγων ἱστορεῖ τὸν τρόπον·

" Διαδέχεται τὴν ἐκκλησίαν μετὰ τῶν ἀποστόλων 4
ὁ ἀδελφὸς τοῦ κυρίου Ἰάκωβος, ὁ ὀνομασθεὶς
ὑπὸ πάντων δίκαιος ἀπὸ τῶν τοῦ κυρίου χρόνων
μέχρι καὶ ἡμῶν, ἐπεὶ πολλοὶ Ἰάκωβοι ἐκαλοῦντο,
οὗτος δὲ ἐκ κοιλίας μητρὸς αὐτοῦ ἅγιος ἦν, οἶνον 5
καὶ σίκερα οὐκ ἔπιεν οὐδὲ ἔμψυχον ἔφαγεν, ξυρὸν
ἐπὶ τὴν κεφαλὴν αὐτοῦ οὐκ ἀνέβη, ἔλαιον οὐκ
ἠλείψατο, καὶ βαλανείῳ οὐκ ἐχρήσατο. τούτῳ 6
μόνῳ ἐξῆν εἰς τὰ ἅγια εἰσιέναι· οὐδὲ γὰρ ἐρεοῦν
ἐφόρει, ἀλλὰ σινδόνας. καὶ μόνος εἰσήρχετο εἰς
τὸν ναὸν ηὑρίσκετό τε κείμενος ἐπὶ τοῖς γόνασιν
καὶ αἰτούμενος ὑπὲρ τοῦ λαοῦ ἄφεσιν, ὡς ἀπ-
εσκληκέναι τὰ γόνατα αὐτοῦ δίκην καμήλου, διὰ
τὸ ἀεὶ κάμπτειν ἐπὶ γόνυ προσκυνοῦντα τῷ θεῷ
καὶ αἰτεῖσθαι ἄφεσιν τῷ λαῷ. διά γέ τοι τὴν 7
ὑπερβολὴν τῆς δικαιοσύνης αὐτοῦ ἐκαλεῖτο ὁ
δίκαιος καὶ ὠβλίας, ὅ ἐστιν Ἑλληνιστὶ περιοχὴ
τοῦ λαοῦ, καὶ δικαιοσύνη, ὡς οἱ προφῆται δηλοῦσιν
περὶ αὐτοῦ. τινὲς οὖν τῶν ἑπτὰ αἱρέσεων τῶν 8
ἐν τῷ λαῷ, τῶν προγεγραμμένων μοι (ἐν τοῖς
Ὑπομνήμασιν), ἐπυνθάνοντο αὐτοῦ τίς ἡ θύρα
τοῦ Ἰησοῦ, καὶ ἔλεγεν τοῦτον εἶναι τὸν σωτῆρα·
ἐξ ὧν τινες ἐπίστευσαν ὅτι Ἰησοῦς ἐστιν ὁ Χρι- 9
στός. αἱ δὲ αἱρέσεις αἱ προειρημέναι οὐκ ἐπίστευον οὔτε ἀνάστασιν οὔτε ἐρχόμενον ἀποδοῦναι

Lev. 10, 9
Num. 6, 3
Luke 1, 15

Num. 6, 5

Is. 3, 10?

Cf. Eus. iv.
22. 7
John 10, 9

James's death has been shown by the words of Clement already quoted, narrating that he was thrown from the battlement and beaten to death with a club, but Hegesippus, who belongs to the generation after the Apostles, gives the most accurate account of him speaking as follows in his fifth book : " The charge of the Church passed to James the brother of the Lord, together with the Apostles. He was called the ' Just ' by all men from the Lord's time to ours, since many are called James, but he was holy from his mother's womb. He drank no wine or strong drink, nor did he eat flesh ; no razor went upon his head ; he did not anoint himself with oil, and he did not go to the baths. He alone was allowed to enter into the sanctuary, for he did not wear wool but linen, and he used to enter alone into the temple and be found kneeling and praying for forgiveness for the people, so that his knees grew hard like a camel's because of his constant worship of God, kneeling and asking forgiveness for the people. So from his excessive righteousness he was called the Just and Oblias, that is in Greek, ' Rampart of the people and righteousness,' as the prophets declare concerning him. Thus some of the seven sects among the people, who were described before by me (in the Commentaries), inquired of him what was the ' gate of Jesus,' and he said that he was the Saviour. Owing to this some believed that Jesus was the Christ. The sects mentioned above did not believe either in resurrection or in one who shall

ἑκάστῳ κατὰ τὰ ἔργα αὐτοῦ· ὅσοι δὲ καὶ
ἐπίστευσαν, διὰ Ἰάκωβον. πολλῶν οὖν καὶ τῶν 10
ἀρχόντων πιστευόντων, ἦν θόρυβος τῶν Ἰουδαίων
καὶ γραμματέων καὶ Φαρισαίων λεγόντων ὅτι
κινδυνεύει πᾶς ὁ λαὸς Ἰησοῦν τὸν Χριστὸν προσ-
δοκᾶν. ἔλεγον οὖν συνελθόντες τῷ Ἰακώβῳ·
'παρακαλοῦμέν σε, ἐπίσχες τὸν λαόν, ἐπεὶ ἐπλανήθη εἰς Ἰησοῦν, ὡς αὐτοῦ ὄντος τοῦ Χριστοῦ.
παρακαλοῦμέν σε πεῖσαι πάντας τοὺς ἐλθόντας
εἰς τὴν ἡμέραν τοῦ πάσχα περὶ Ἰησοῦ· σοὶ γὰρ
πάντες πειθόμεθα. ἡμεῖς γὰρ μαρτυροῦμέν σοι

Luke 20, 21 καὶ πᾶς ὁ λαὸς ὅτι δίκαιος εἶ καὶ ὅτι πρόσωπον
οὐ λαμβάνεις. πεῖσον οὖν σὺ τὸν ὄχλον περὶ 11
Ἰησοῦ μὴ πλανᾶσθαι· καὶ γὰρ πᾶς ὁ λαὸς καὶ
πάντες πειθόμεθά σοι. στῆθι οὖν ἐπὶ τὸ πτερύγιον τοῦ ἱεροῦ, ἵνα ἄνωθεν ᾖς ἐπιφανὴς καὶ ᾖ
εὐάκουστά σου τὰ ῥήματα παντὶ τῷ λαῷ. διὰ
γὰρ τὸ πάσχα συνεληλύθασι πᾶσαι αἱ φυλαὶ
μετὰ καὶ τῶν ἐθνῶν.' ἔστησαν οὖν οἱ προ- 12
ειρημένοι γραμματεῖς καὶ Φαρισαῖοι τὸν Ἰάκωβον
ἐπὶ τὸ πτερύγιον τοῦ ναοῦ, καὶ ἔκραξαν αὐτῷ καὶ
εἶπαν ' δίκαιε, ᾧ πάντες πείθεσθαι ὀφείλομεν,
ἐπεὶ ὁ λαὸς πλανᾶται ὀπίσω Ἰησοῦ τοῦ σταυρωθέντος, ἀπάγγειλον ἡμῖν τίς ἡ θύρα τοῦ Ἰησοῦ.'

Matt. 26, 64 καὶ ἀπεκρίνατο φωνῇ μεγάλῃ ' τί με ἐπερωτᾶτε 13
Mark 14, 62 περὶ τοῦ υἱοῦ τοῦ ἀνθρώπου, καὶ αὐτὸς κάθηται
ἐν τῷ οὐρανῷ ἐκ δεξιῶν τῆς μεγάλης δυνάμεως,
καὶ μέλλει ἔρχεσθαι ἐπὶ τῶν νεφελῶν τοῦ οὐρανοῦ;' καὶ πολλῶν πληροφορηθέντων καὶ δο- 14
ξαζόντων ἐπὶ τῇ μαρτυρίᾳ τοῦ Ἰακώβου καὶ

---

[1] The tradition is obviously confused. Oblias may be an

come to reward each according to his deeds, but as many as believed did so because of James. Now, since many even of the rulers believed, there was a tumult of the Jews and the Scribes and Pharisees saying that the whole people was in danger of looking for Jesus as the Christ. So they assembled and said to James, 'We beseech you to restrain the people since they are straying after Jesus as though he were the Messiah. We beseech you to persuade concerning Jesus all who come for the day of the Passover, for all obey you. For we and the whole people testify to you that you are righteous and do not respect persons. So do you persuade the crowd not to err concerning Jesus, for the whole people and we all obey you. Therefore stand on the battlement of the temple that you may be clearly visible on high, and that your words may be audible to all the people, for because of the Passover all the tribes, with the Gentiles also, have come together.' So the Scribes and Pharisees mentioned before made James stand on the battlement of the temple, and they cried out to him and said, 'Oh, just one, to whom we all owe obedience, since the people are straying after Jesus who was crucified, tell us what is the gate of Jesus ?[1]' And he answered with a loud voice, 'Why do you ask me concerning the Son of Man ? He is sitting in heaven on the right hand of the great power, and he will come on the clouds of heaven.' And many were convinced and confessed[2] at the testimony of

---

inaccurate transliteration of the Hebrew for " Rampart of the People," but the reference to the prophets defies explanation. The " Gate " of Jesus is also a puzzle, but it may be connected with the early Christians' name for themselves of " the Way."

[2] Literally " glorified." *Cf.* Jo. ix. 24.

λεγόντων ‘ὡσαννὰ τῷ υἱῷ Δαυίδ,’ τότε πάλιν
οἱ αὐτοὶ γραμματεῖς καὶ Φαρισαῖοι πρὸς ἀλλήλους ἔλεγον ‘κακῶς ἐποιήσαμεν τοιαύτην μαρτυρίαν παρασχόντες τῷ ᾿Ιησοῦ· ἀλλὰ ἀναβάντες
καταβάλωμεν αὐτόν, ἵνα φοβηθέντες μὴ πιστεύ-
σωσιν αὐτῷ.’ καὶ ἔκραξαν λέγοντες ‘ὢ ὤ, 15
καὶ ὁ δίκαιος ἐπλανήθη,’ καὶ ἐπλήρωσαν τὴν
γραφὴν τὴν ἐν τῷ ᾿Ησαΐᾳ γεγραμμένην ‘ἄρωμεν
τὸν δίκαιον, ὅτι δύσχρηστος ἡμῖν ἐστιν· τοίνυν
τὰ γενήματα τῶν ἔργων αὐτῶν φάγονται.’ ἀνα- 16
βάντες οὖν κατέβαλον τὸν δίκαιον. καὶ ἔλεγον
ἀλλήλοις ‘λιθάσωμεν ᾿Ιάκωβον τὸν δίκαιον,’
καὶ ἤρξαντο λιθάζειν αὐτόν, ἐπεὶ καταβληθεὶς
οὐκ ἀπέθανεν· ἀλλὰ στραφεὶς ἔθηκε τὰ γόνατα
λέγων ‘παρακαλῶ, κύριε θεὲ πάτερ, ἄφες αὐτοῖς·
οὐ γὰρ οἴδασιν τί ποιοῦσιν.’ οὕτως δὲ κατα- 17
λιθοβολούντων αὐτόν, εἷς τῶν ἱερέων τῶν υἱῶν
῾Ρηχὰβ υἱοῦ ῾Ραχαβείμ, τῶν μαρτυρουμένων ὑπὸ
᾿Ιερεμίου τοῦ προφήτου, ἔκραζεν λέγων ‘παύ-
σασθε· τί ποιεῖτε; εὔχεται ὑπὲρ ὑμῶν ὁ δίκαιος.’
καὶ λαβών τις ἀπ’ αὐτῶν, εἷς τῶν γναφέων, τὸ 18
ξύλον, ἐν ᾧ ἀποπιέζει τὰ ἱμάτια, ἤνεγκεν κατὰ
τῆς κεφαλῆς τοῦ δικαίου, καὶ οὕτως ἐμαρτύρησεν. καὶ ἔθαψαν αὐτὸν ἐπὶ τῷ τόπῳ παρὰ τῷ
ναῷ, καὶ ἔτι αὐτοῦ ἡ στήλη μένει παρὰ τῷ ναῷ.
μάρτυς οὗτος ἀληθὴς ᾿Ιουδαίοις τε καὶ ῞Ελλησιν
γεγένηται ὅτι ᾿Ιησοῦς ὁ Χριστός ἐστιν. καὶ
εὐθὺς Οὐεσπασιανὸς πολιορκεῖ αὐτούς.’’ [1]

Is. 3, 10

Luke 23, 34

Jer. 42

[1] *Cf.* George Syncellus 638, 3–641, 2.

[1] The first part of the quotation is from the Wisdom of
Solomon, not Isaiah.

[2] This story is confused and improbable. The text of

174

James and said, ' Hosanna to the Son of David.'
Then again the same Scribes and Pharisees said to
one another, ' We did wrong to provide Jesus with
such testimony, but let us go up and throw him
down that they may be afraid and not believe him.'
And they cried out saying, ' Oh, oh, even the just
one erred.' And they fulfilled the Scripture written
in Isaiah,[1] ' Let us take the just man for he is
unprofitable to us. Yet they shall eat the fruit of
their works.' So they went up and threw down the
Just, and they said to one another, ' Let us stone
James the Just,' and they began to stone him since
the fall had not killed him, but he turned and knelt
saying, ' I beseech thee, O Lord, God and Father,
forgive them, for they know not what they do.'
And while they were thus stoning him one of the
priests of the sons of Rechab, the son of Rechabim,[2]
to whom Jeremiah the prophet bore witness, cried
out saying, ' Stop ! what are you doing ? The Just
is praying for you.' And a certain man among them,
one of the laundrymen, took the club with which
he used to beat out the clothes, and hit the Just on
the head, and so he suffered martyrdom. And they
buried him on the spot by the temple, and his grave-
stone still remains by the temple. He became a true
witness both to Jews and to Greeks that Jesus is the
Christ, and at once Vespasian began to besiege them.''

Hegesippus must be corrupt, for Rechabim is only the
Hebrew plural and merely repeats the previous phrase.
Moreover the Rechabites were a tribe of Kenites who were
adopted into Israel (cf. 1 Chron. ii. 55 and Jer. xxxv. 19).
There is no evidence that a Rechabite was ever counted as a
Levite, or that the name was that of a sect to which a priest
or Levite could have belonged. Epiphanius (Haer. lxxviii.
14) replaces this mysterious Rechabite by Simeon the son
of Clopas.

Ταῦτα διὰ πλάτους, συνῳδά γέ τοι τῷ Κλή- 19
μεντι καὶ ὁ Ἡγήσιππος. οὕτω δὲ ἄρα θαυμάσιός
τις ἦν καὶ παρὰ τοῖς ἄλλοις ἅπασιν ἐπὶ δικαιοσύνῃ βεβόητο ὁ Ἰάκωβος, ὡς καὶ τοὺς Ἰουδαίων
ἔμφρονας δοξάζειν ταύτην εἶναι τὴν αἰτίαν τῆς
παραχρῆμα μετὰ τὸ μαρτύριον αὐτοῦ πολιορκίας
τῆς Ἱερουσαλήμ, ἣν δι᾽ οὐδὲν ἕτερον αὐτοῖς
συμβῆναι ἢ διὰ τὸ κατ᾽ αὐτοῦ τολμηθὲν ἄγος.

Ἀμέλει γέ τοι ὁ Ἰώσηπος οὐκ ἀπώκνησεν καὶ 20
τοῦτ᾽ ἐγγράφως ἐπιμαρτύρασθαι δι᾽ ὧν φησιν
λέξεων ‘‘ ταῦτα δὲ συμβέβηκεν Ἰουδαίοις κατ᾽
ἐκδίκησιν Ἰακώβου τοῦ δικαίου, ὃς ἦν ἀδελφὸς
Ἰησοῦ τοῦ λεγομένου Χριστοῦ, ἐπειδήπερ δικαιότατον αὐτὸν ὄντα οἱ Ἰουδαῖοι ἀπέκτειναν.’’

Ὁ δ᾽ αὐτὸς καὶ τὸν θάνατον αὐτοῦ ἐν εἰκοστῷ 21
Joseph. A.I.
20, 197. 199–
203
Joseph. A.I.
20, 197
Joseph. B.I.
2, 166
τῆς Ἀρχαιολογίας δηλοῖ διὰ τούτων· ‘‘ πέμπει
δὲ Καῖσαρ Ἀλβῖνον εἰς τὴν Ἰουδαίαν ἔπαρχον,
Φήστου τὴν τελευτὴν πυθόμενος. ὁ δὲ νεώτερος
Ἄνανος, ὃν τὴν ἀρχιερωσύνην εἴπαμεν παρειληφέναι, θρασὺς ἦν τὸν τρόπον καὶ τολμητὴς
διαφερόντως, αἵρεσιν δὲ μετῄει τὴν Σαδδουκαίων,
οἵπερ εἰσὶ περὶ τὰς κρίσεις ὠμοὶ παρὰ πάντας
τοὺς Ἰουδαίους, καθὼς ἤδη δεδηλώκαμεν. ἅτε 22
δὴ οὖν τοιοῦτος ὢν ὁ Ἄνανος, νομίσας ἔχειν
καιρὸν ἐπιτήδειον διὰ τὸ τεθνάναι μὲν Φῆστον,
Ἀλβῖνον δ᾽ ἔτι κατὰ τὴν ὁδὸν ὑπάρχειν, καθίζει
συνέδριον κριτῶν, καὶ παραγαγὼν εἰς αὐτὸ τὸν
ἀδελφὸν Ἰησοῦ, τοῦ Χριστοῦ λεγομένου, Ἰάκωβος
ὄνομα αὐτῷ, καί τινας ἑτέρους, ὡς παρανομη-
σάντων κατηγορίαν ποιησάμενος, παρέδωκεν λευ-
σθησομένους. ὅσοι δὲ ἐδόκουν ἐπιεικέστατοι τῶν 23
κατὰ τὴν πόλιν εἶναι καὶ τὰ περὶ τοὺς νόμους
176

This account is given at length by Hegesippus, but in agreement with Clement. Thus it seems that James was indeed a remarkable man and famous among all for righteousness, so that the wise even of the Jews thought that this was the cause of the siege of Jerusalem immediately after his martyrdom, and that it happened for no other reason than the crime which they had committed against him.

Of course Josephus did not shrink from giving written testimony to this, as follows : " And these things happened to the Jews to avenge James the Just, who was the brother of Jesus the so-called Christ, for the Jews killed him in spite of his great righteousness."[1] The same writer also narrates his death in the twentieth book of the *Antiquities* as follows : " Now when Caesar heard of the death of Festus he sent Albinus as governor to Judaea, but the younger Ananus, who, as we said, had received the High Priesthood, was bold in temperament and remarkably daring. He followed the sect of the Sadducees, who are cruel in their judgements beyond all the Jews, as we have already explained. Thus his character led Ananus to think that he had a suitable opportunity through the fact that Festus was dead and Albinus still on his way. He summoned a council of judges, brought before it the brother of Jesus, the so-called Christ, whose name was James, and some others, on the accusation of breaking the law and delivered them to be stoned. But all who were reputed the most reasonable of the citizens and strict observers of the law were

---

[1] This passage is not in the traditional text of Josephus.

ἀκριβεῖς, βαρέως ἤνεγκαν ἐπὶ τούτῳ, καὶ πέμ-
πουσι πρὸς τὸν βασιλέα κρύφα, παρακαλοῦντες
αὐτὸν ἐπιστεῖλαι τῷ Ἀνάνῳ μηκέτι τοιαῦτα
πράσσειν· μηδὲ γὰρ τὸ πρῶτον ὀρθῶς αὐτὸν
πεποιηκέναι. τινὲς δ' αὐτῶν καὶ τὸν Ἀλβῖνον
ὑπαντιάζουσιν ἀπὸ τῆς Ἀλεξανδρείας ὁδοιπο-
ροῦντα, καὶ διδάσκουσιν ὡς οὐκ ἐξὸν ἦν Ἀνάνῳ
χωρὶς αὐτοῦ γνώμης καθίσαι συνέδριον. Ἀλβῖνος 24
δὲ πεισθεὶς τοῖς λεγομένοις, γράφει μετ' ὀργῆς
τῷ Ἀνάνῳ, λήψεσθαι παρ' αὐτοῦ δίκας ἀπειλῶν,
καὶ ὁ βασιλεὺς Ἀγρίππας διὰ τοῦτο τὴν ἀρχιερωσύνην ἀφελόμενος αὐτοῦ ἄρξαντος μῆνας τρεῖς,
Ἰησοῦν τὸν τοῦ Δαμμαίου κατέστησεν." [1]

Τοιαῦτα καὶ τὰ κατὰ Ἰάκωβον, οὗ ἡ πρώτη
τῶν ὀνομαζομένων καθολικῶν ἐπιστολῶν εἶναι
λέγεται· ἰστέον δὲ ὡς νοθεύεται μέν, οὐ πολλοὶ 25
γοῦν τῶν παλαιῶν αὐτῆς ἐμνημόνευσαν, ὡς οὐδὲ
τῆς λεγομένης Ἰούδα, μιᾶς καὶ αὐτῆς οὔσης
τῶν ἑπτὰ λεγομένων καθολικῶν· ὅμως δ' ἴσμεν
καὶ ταύτας μετὰ τῶν λοιπῶν ἐν πλείσταις δεδη-
μοσιευμένας ἐκκλησίαις.

XXIV. Νέρωνος δὲ ὄγδοον ἄγοντος τῆς βασι- 1
λείας ἔτος, πρῶτος μετὰ Μάρκον τὸν εὐαγγελιστὴν τῆς ἐν Ἀλεξανδρείᾳ παροικίας Ἀννιανὸς τὴν
λειτουργίαν διαδέχεται.

XXV. Κραταιουμένης δ' ἤδη τῷ Νέρωνι τῆς 1
ἀρχῆς, εἰς ἀνοσίους ὀκείλας ἐπιτηδεύσεις, κατ' αὐτῆς ὡπλίζετο τῆς εἰς τὸν τῶν ὅλων θεὸν εὐσεβείας.
γράφειν μὲν οὖν οἷός τις οὗτος γεγένηται τὴν
μοχθηρίαν, οὐ τῆς παρούσης γένοιτ' ἂν σχολῆς·
πολλῶν γε μὴν τὰ κατ' αὐτὸν ἀκριβεστάταις 2
παραδεδωκότων διηγήσεσιν, πάρεστιν ὅτῳ φί-

angered at this and sent secretly to the Emperor,[1] begging him to write to Ananus to give up doing such things, for they said that he had not acted rightly from the very beginning. And some of them also went to meet Albinus as he journeyed from Alexandria, and explained that it was illegal for Ananus to assemble the council without his permission. Albinus was influenced by what was said and wrote angrily to Ananus threatening him with penalties, and for this reason King Agrippa deprived him of the High Priesthood when he had held it for three months, and appointed Jesus the son of Dammaeus." Such is the story of James, whose is said to be the first of the Epistles called Catholic. It is to be observed that its authenticity is denied, since few of the ancients quote it, as is also the case with the Epistle called Jude's, which is itself one of the seven called Catholic ; nevertheless we know that these letters have been used publicly with the rest in most churches.

XXIV. In the eighth year of the reign of Nero Annianus was the first after Mark the Evangelist to receive charge of the diocese[2] of Alexandria.

XXV. When the rule of Nero was now gathering strength for unholy objects he began to take up arms against the worship of the God of the universe. It is not part of the present work to describe his depravity: many indeed have related his story in accurate narrative, and from them he who wishes can study

---

[1] Or, possibly, to King Agrippa.
[2] Literally, colony or province.

---

[1] *Cf.* George Syncellus 641, 7–642, 9.

λον, ἐξ αὐτῶν τὴν σκαιότητα τῆς τἀνδρὸς ἐκτόπου
καταθεωρῆσαι μανίας, καθ᾿ ἣν οὐ μετὰ λογισμοῦ
μυρίων ὅσων ἀπωλείας διεξελθών, ἐπὶ τοσαύτην
ἤλασε μιαιφονίαν, ὡς μηδὲ τῶν οἰκειοτάτων τε
καὶ φιλτάτων ἐπισχεῖν, μητέρα δὲ ὁμοίως καὶ
ἀδελφοὺς καὶ γυναῖκα σὺν καὶ ἄλλοις μυρίοις
τῷ γένει προσήκουσιν τρόπον ἐχθρῶν καὶ πολεμίων ποικίλαις θανάτων ἰδέαις διαχρήσασθαι.
ἐνέδει δ᾿ ἄρα τοῖς πᾶσι καὶ τοῦτ᾿ ἐπιγραφῆναι 3
αὐτῷ, ὡς ἂν πρῶτος αὐτοκρατόρων τῆς εἰς τὸ
θεῖον εὐσεβείας πολέμιος ἀναδειχθείη. τούτου 4
πάλιν ὁ Ῥωμαῖος Τερτυλλιανὸς ὧδέ πως λέγων

Tert. Apol.
5

μνημονεύει "ἐντύχετε τοῖς ὑπομνήμασιν ὑμῶν,
ἐκεῖ εὑρήσετε πρῶτον Νέρωνα τοῦτο τὸ δόγμα,
ἡνίκα μάλιστα ἐν Ῥώμῃ, τὴν ἀνατολὴν πᾶσαν
ὑποτάξας, ὠμὸς ἦν εἰς πάντας, διώξαντα. τοιούτῳ τῆς κολάσεως ἡμῶν ἀρχηγῷ καυχώμεθα. ὁ
γὰρ εἰδὼς ἐκεῖνον νοῆσαι δύναται ὡς οὐκ ἄν, εἰ
μὴ μέγα τι ἀγαθὸν ἦν, ὑπὸ Νέρωνος κατακρι-
θῆναι.''

Ταύτῃ γοῦν οὗτος, θεομάχος ἐν τοῖς μάλιστα 5
πρῶτος ἀνακηρυχθείς, ἐπὶ τὰς κατὰ τῶν ἀποστόλων ἐπήρθη σφαγάς. Παῦλος δὴ οὖν ἐπ᾿
αὐτῆς Ῥώμης τὴν κεφαλὴν ἀποτμηθῆναι καὶ
Πέτρος ὡσαύτως ἀνασκολοπισθῆναι κατ᾿ αὐτὸν
ἱστοροῦνται, καὶ πιστοῦταί γε τὴν ἱστορίαν ἡ
Πέτρου καὶ Παύλου εἰς δεῦρο κρατήσασα ἐπὶ
τῶν αὐτόθι κοιμητηρίων πρόσρησις, οὐδὲν δὲ 6
ἧττον καὶ ἐκκλησιαστικὸς ἀνήρ, Γάϊος ὄνομα,
κατὰ Ζεφυρῖνον Ῥωμαίων γεγονὼς ἐπίσκοπον·
ὃς δὴ Πρόκλῳ τῆς κατὰ Φρύγας προϊσταμένῳ

---

[1] The Greek is scarcely translatable and is clearly a bad

the perversity of his degenerate madness, which made him compass the unreasonable destruction of so many thousands, until he reached that final guilt of sparing neither his nearest nor dearest, so that in various ways he did to death alike his mother, brothers, and wife, with thousands of others attached to his family, as though they were enemies and foes. But with all this there was still lacking to him this— that it should be attributed to him that he was the first of the emperors to be pointed out as a foe of divine religion. This again the Latin writer Tertullian mentions in one place as follows : " Look at your records : there you will find that Nero was the first to persecute this belief when, having overcome the whole East, he was specially cruel in Rome against all.[1] We boast that such a man was the author of our chastisement ; for he who knows him can understand that nothing would have been condemned by Nero had it not been great and good."

In this way then was he the first to be heralded as above all a fighter against God, and raised up to slaughter against the Apostles. It is related that in his time Paul was beheaded in Rome itself, and that Peter likewise was crucified, and the title of " Peter and Paul," which is still given to the cemeteries there, confirms the story, no less than does a writer of the Church named Caius, who lived when Zephyrinus was Bishop of Rome. Caius in a written discussion

rendering of Tertullian : " Consulite commentarios uestros, illic reperietis primum Neronem in hanc sectam cum maxime Romae orientem Caesariano gladio ferocisse " (" Consult your records : you will find that Nero was the first to let the imperial sword rage against this sect when it was just spring-ing up in Rome ").

181

γνώμης ἐγγράφως διαλεχθείς, αὐτὰ δὴ ταῦτα
περὶ τῶν τόπων, ἔνθα τῶν εἰρημένων ἀποστόλων
τὰ ἱερὰ σκηνώματα κατατέθειται, φησίν· " ἐγὼ 7
δὲ τὰ τρόπαια τῶν ἀποστόλων ἔχω δεῖξαι. ἐὰν γὰρ θελήσῃς ἀπελθεῖν ἐπὶ τὸν Βασι-
κανὸν ἢ ἐπὶ τὴν ὁδὸν τὴν Ὠστίαν, εὑρήσεις τὰ
τρόπαια τῶν ταύτην ἱδρυσαμένων τὴν ἐκκλησίαν."

Ὡς δὲ κατὰ τὸν αὐτὸν ἄμφω καιρὸν ἐμαρτύ- 8
ρησαν, Κορινθίων ἐπίσκοπος Διονύσιος ἐγγράφως
Ῥωμαίοις ὁμιλῶν, ὧδε παρίστησιν " ταῦτα καὶ
ὑμεῖς διὰ τῆς τοσαύτης νουθεσίας τὴν ἀπὸ Πέτρου
καὶ Παύλου φυτείαν γενηθεῖσαν Ῥωμαίων τε
καὶ Κορινθίων συνεκεράσατε. καὶ γὰρ ἄμφω
καὶ εἰς τὴν ἡμετέραν Κόρινθον φυτεύσαντες ἡμᾶς
ὁμοίως ἐδίδαξαν, ὁμοίως δὲ καὶ εἰς τὴν Ἰταλίαν
ὁμόσε διδάξαντες ἐμαρτύρησαν κατὰ τὸν αὐτὸν
καιρόν."[1] καὶ ταῦτα δέ, ὡς ἂν ἔτι μᾶλλον
πιστωθείη τὰ τῆς ἱστορίας.

Joseph. B.I.
2, 306–308
XXVI. Αὖθις δ᾽ ὁ Ἰώσηπος πλεῖστα ὅσα περὶ 1
τῆς τὸ πᾶν Ἰουδαίων ἔθνος καταλαβούσης διελθὼν
συμφορᾶς, δηλοῖ κατὰ λέξιν ἐπὶ πλείστοις ἄλλοις
μυρίους ὅσους τῶν παρὰ Ἰουδαίοις τετιμημένων
μάστιξιν αἰκισθέντας ἐν αὐτῇ τῇ Ἱερουσαλὴμ
Joseph. B.I.
2, 284; A.I.
20, 257
ἀνασταυρωθῆναι ὑπὸ Φλώρου· τοῦτον δὲ εἶναι
τῆς Ἰουδαίας ἐπίτροπον, ὁπηνίκα τὴν ἀρχὴν
ἀναρριπισθῆναι τοῦ πολέμου, ἔτους δωδεκάτου
Joseph. B.I.
2, 462. 465
τῆς Νέρωνος ἡγεμονίας, συνέβη. εἶτα δὲ καὶ 2
καθ᾽ ὅλην τὴν Συρίαν ἐπὶ τῇ τῶν Ἰουδαίων ἀποστάσει δεινήν φησι κατειληφέναι ταραχήν, πανταχόσε τῶν ἀπὸ τοῦ ἔθνους πρὸς τῶν κατὰ πόλιν

[1] Cf. George Syncellus 644, 8–645, 9.

with Proclus, the leader of the Montanists,[1] speaks as follows of the places where the sacred relics of the Apostles in question are deposited : " But I can point out the trophies of the Apostles, for if you will go to the Vatican or to the Ostian Way you will find the trophies of those who founded this Church." [2] And that they both were martyred at the same time Dionysius, bishop of Corinth, affirms in this passage of his correspondence with the Romans : " By so great an admonition you bound together the foundations of the Romans and Corinthians by Peter and Paul, for both of them taught together in our Corinth and were our founders, and together also taught in Italy in the same place and were martyred at the same time." And this may serve to confirm still further the facts narrated.

XXVI. Josephus in the course of his extremely detailed description of the catastrophe which overcame the whole Jewish race, in addition to many other things explains exactly how many thousand Jews of high rank in Jerusalem itself were outraged, scourged, and crucified by Florus, and that he was procurator of Judaea when it happened that the beginning of the war blazed up in the twelfth year of the reign of Nero. He next says that throughout Syria terrible disturbances followed the revolt of the Jews. Everywhere the Gentiles mercilessly attacked

---

[1] Literally, " the opinion among the Phrygians." Montanus was of Phrygian origin. His story is told by Eusebius in *Hist. Eccl.* v. 14-18. Proclus was one of his successors.

[2] According to the tradition that Peter was crucified on the Vatican (the exact spot is variously indicated), and Paul beheaded on the Via Ostia at Tre Fontane.

ἐνοίκων ὡς ἂν πολεμίων ἀνηλεῶς πορθουμένων,
ὥστε ὁρᾶν τὰς πόλεις μεστὰς ἀτάφων σωμάτων
καὶ νεκροὺς ἅμα νηπίοις γέροντας ἐρριμμένους
γύναιά τε μηδὲ τῆς ἐπ' αἰδῷ σκέπης μετειληφότα,
καὶ πᾶσαν μὲν τὴν ἐπαρχίαν μεστὴν ἀδιηγήτων
συμφορῶν, μείζονα δὲ τῶν ἑκάστοτε τολμωμένων
τὴν ἐπὶ τοῖς ἀπειλουμένοις ἀνάτασιν. ταῦτα κατὰ
λέξιν ὁ Ἰώσηπος. καὶ τὰ μὲν κατὰ Ἰουδαίους
ἐν τούτοις ἦν.

the Jews in the cities as though they were foes,
so that the cities could be seen full of unburied
bodies, thrown out dead, old men and children, and
women without covering for their nakedness; the
whole province was full of indescribable misery and
the strain of the threats for the future was worse
than the crimes of the present. This Josephus
narrates, and such was the condition of the Jews.

Γ

Τάδε καὶ ἡ γ̅ περιέχει βίβλος τῆς Ἐκκλησιαστικῆς ἱστορίας

Α̅ Ὅποι γῆς ἐκήρυξαν τὸν Χριστὸν οἱ ἀπόστολοι.

Β̅ Τίς πρῶτος τῆς Ῥωμαίων ἐκκλησίας προέστη.

Γ̅ Περὶ τῶν ἐπιστολῶν τῶν ἀποστόλων.

Δ̅ Περὶ τῆς πρώτης τῶν ἀποστόλων διαδοχῆς.

Ε̅ Περὶ τῆς μετὰ τὸν Χριστὸν ὑστάτης Ἰουδαίων πολιορκίας.

Ϛ̅ Περὶ τοῦ πιέσαντος αὐτοὺς λιμοῦ.

Ζ̅ Περὶ τῶν τοῦ Χριστοῦ προρρήσεων.

Η̅ Περὶ τῶν πρὸ τοῦ πολέμου σημείων.

Θ̅ Περὶ Ἰωσήπου καὶ ὧν κατέλιπεν συγγραμμάτων.

Ι̅ Ὅπως τῶν θείων μνημονεύει βιβλίων.

Ι̅Α̅ Ὡς μετὰ Ἰάκωβον ἡγεῖται Συμεὼν τῆς ἐν Ἱεροσολύμοις ἐκκλησίας.

Ι̅Β̅ Ὡς Οὐεσπασιανὸς τοὺς ἐκ Δαυὶδ ἀναζητεῖσθαι προστάττει.

Ι̅Γ̅ Ὡς δεύτερος Ἀλεξανδρέων ἡγεῖται Ἀβίλιος.

Ι̅Δ̅ Ὡς καὶ Ῥωμαίων δεύτερος Ἀνέγκλητος ἐπισκοπεῖ.

Ι̅Ε̅ Ὡς τρίτος μετ' αὐτὸν Κλήμης.

Ι̅Ϛ̅ Περὶ τῆς Κλήμεντος ἐπιστολῆς.

Ι̅Ζ̅ Περὶ τοῦ κατὰ Δομετιανὸν διωγμοῦ.

186

CONTENTS OF BOOK III

*The contents of the third book of the History
of the Church is as follows :*

I. The parts of the world in which the apostles
preached Christ.

II. Who was the first ruler of the church of the
Romans.

III. On the letters of the apostles.

IV. On the first successors of the apostles.

V. On the last siege of the Jews after Christ.

VI. On the famine that oppressed them.

VII. On the prophecies of Christ.

VIII. On the signs before the war.

IX. On Josephus and the writings which he left.

X. How he quotes the sacred books.

XI. How after James Simeon ruled the church at
Jerusalem.

XII. How Vespasian ordered the family of David
to be sought out.

XIII. How Abilius was the second ruler of the
Alexandrians.

XIV. How Anencletus was the second bishop of
the Romans.

XV. How, after him, Clement was the third.

XVI. On the epistle of Clement.

XVII. On the persecution under Domitian.

ΙΗ Περὶ Ἰωάννου τοῦ ἀποστόλου καὶ τῆς Ἀποκαλύψεως.

ΙΘ Ὡς Δομετιανὸς τοὺς ἀπὸ γένους Δαυὶδ ἀναιρεῖσθαι προστάττει.

Κ Περὶ τῶν πρὸς γένους τοῦ σωτῆρος ἡμῶν.

ΚΑ Ὡς τῆς Ἀλεξανδρέων ἐκκλησίας τρίτος ἡγεῖται Κέρδων.

ΚΒ Ὡς τῆς Ἀντιοχέων δεύτερος Ἰγνάτιος.

ΚΓ Ἱστορία περὶ Ἰωάννου τοῦ ἀποστόλου.

ΚΔ Περὶ τῆς τάξεως τῶν εὐαγγελίων.

ΚΕ Περὶ τῶν ὁμολογουμένων θείων γραφῶν καὶ τῶν μὴ τοιούτων.

ΚϚ Περὶ Μενάνδρου τοῦ γόητος.

ΚΖ Περὶ τῆς τῶν Ἐβιωναίων αἱρέσεως.

ΚΗ Περὶ Κηρίνθου αἱρεσιάρχου.

ΚΘ Περὶ Νικολάου καὶ τῶν ἐξ αὐτοῦ κεκλημένων.

Λ Περὶ τῶν ἐν συζυγίαις ἐξετασθέντων ἀποστόλων.

ΛΑ Περὶ τῆς Ἰωάννου καὶ Φιλίππου τελευτῆς.

ΛΒ Ὅπως Συμεὼν ὁ ἐν Ἱεροσολύμοις ἐπίσκοπος ἐμαρτύρησεν.

ΛΓ Ὅπως Τραϊανὸς ζητεῖσθαι Χριστιανοὺς ἐκώλυσεν.

ΛΔ Ὡς τῆς Ῥωμαίων ἐκκλησίας τέταρτος Εὐάρεστος ἡγεῖται.

ΛΕ Ὡς τρίτος τῆς ἐν Ἱεροσολύμοις Ἰοῦστος.

ΛϚ Περὶ Ἰγνατίου καὶ τῶν ἐπιστολῶν αὐτοῦ.

ΛΖ Περὶ τῶν εἰς ἔτι τότε διαπρεπόντων εὐαγγελιστῶν.

ΛΗ Περὶ τῆς Κλήμεντος ἐπιστολῆς καὶ τῶν ψευδῶς εἰς αὐτὸν ἀναφερομένων.

ΛΘ Περὶ τῶν Παπία συγγραμμάτων.

ECCLESIASTICAL HISTORY, III. CONTENTS

XVIII. On John the Apostle and the Apocalypse.

XIX. How Domitian commanded the family of David to be destroyed.

XX. On the family of our Saviour.

XXI. How Cerdo was the third to rule the church of the Alexandrians.

XXII. How Ignatius was the second of the Antiochians.

XXIII. A narrative about John the Apostle.

XXIV. On the order of the Gospels.

XXV. On the writings acknowledged as sacred and on those which are not.

XXVI. On Menander the Sorcerer.

XXVII. On the heresy of the Ebionites.

XXVIII. On Cerinthus the Heresiarch.

XXIX. On Nicholas and those called after him.

XXX. On the apostles who were tested by marriage.

XXXI. On the death of John and Philip.

XXXII. How Simeon, the bishop in Jerusalem, was martyred.

XXXIII. How Trajan forbade the Christians to be sought out.

XXXIV. How Evarestus was the fourth to rule the church of the Romans.

XXXV. How Justus was the third ruler of the church in Jerusalem.

XXXVI. On Ignatius and his letters.

XXXVII. On the evangelists who were still flourishing.

XXXVIII. On the letter of Clement and the writings falsely attributed to him.

XXXIX. On the writings of Papias.

III

I. Τὰ μὲν δὴ κατὰ Ἰουδαίους ἐν τούτοις ἦν· **1**
τῶν δὲ ἱερῶν τοῦ σωτῆρος ἡμῶν ἀποστόλων τε
καὶ μαθητῶν ἐφ' ἅπασαν κατασπαρέντων τὴν
οἰκουμένην, Θωμᾶς μέν, ὡς ἡ παράδοσις περιέχει,
τὴν Παρθίαν εἴληχεν, Ἀνδρέας δὲ τὴν Σκυθίαν,
Ἰωάννης τὴν Ἀσίαν, πρὸς οὓς καὶ διατρίψας ἐν
1 Pet. 1, 1 Ἐφέσῳ τελευτᾷ, Πέτρος δ' ἐν Πόντῳ καὶ Γαλατίᾳ **2**
καὶ Βιθυνίᾳ Καππαδοκίᾳ τε καὶ Ἀσίᾳ κεκηρυχέναι
τοῖς [ἐκ] διασπορᾶς Ἰουδαίοις ἔοικεν· ὃς καὶ ἐπὶ
τέλει ἐν Ῥώμῃ γενόμενος, ἀνεσκολοπίσθη κατὰ
κεφαλῆς, οὕτως αὐτὸς ἀξιώσας παθεῖν. τί δεῖ **3**
Rom. 15, 19 περὶ Παύλου λέγειν, ἀπὸ Ἰερουσαλὴμ μέχρι τοῦ
Ἰλλυρικοῦ πεπληρωκότος τὸ εὐαγγέλιον τοῦ Χριστοῦ καὶ ὕστερον ἐν τῇ Ῥώμῃ ἐπὶ Νέρωνος με-
μαρτυρηκότος; ταῦτα Ὠριγένει κατὰ λέξιν ἐν
τρίτῳ τόμῳ τῶν εἰς τὴν Γένεσιν ἐξηγητικῶν
εἴρηται.

II. Τῆς δὲ Ῥωμαίων ἐκκλησίας μετὰ τὴν **1**
Παύλου καὶ Πέτρου μαρτυρίαν πρῶτος κληροῦται
2 Tim. 4, 21 τὴν ἐπισκοπὴν Λίνος. μνημονεύει τούτου Τιμο-
θέῳ γράφων ἀπὸ Ῥώμης ὁ Παῦλος κατὰ τὴν ἐπὶ
τέλει τῆς ἐπιστολῆς πρόσρησιν.

III. Πέτρου μὲν οὖν ἐπιστολὴ μία, ἡ λεγομένη **1**
αὐτοῦ προτέρα, ἀνωμολόγηται, ταύτῃ δὲ καὶ οἱ
190

BOOK III

I. Such was the condition of things among the Jews, but the holy Apostles and disciples of our Saviour were scattered throughout the whole world. Thomas, as tradition relates, obtained by lot Parthia, Andrew Scythia, John Asia (and he stayed there and died in Ephesus), but Peter seems to have preached to the Jews of the Dispersion in Pontus and Galatia and Bithynia, Cappadocia, and Asia, and at the end he came to Rome and was crucified head downwards, for so he had demanded to suffer. What need be said of Paul, who fulfilled the gospel of Christ from Jerusalem to Illyria and afterward was martyred in Rome under Nero? This is stated exactly by Origen in the third volume of his commentary on Genesis.

II. After the martyrdom of Paul and Peter, Linus was the first appointed to the bishopric of the church of Rome. Paul mentions him when writing from Rome to Timothy in the salutation at the end of the Epistle.

III. Of Peter, one epistle, that which is called his first, is admitted, and the ancient presbyters used

πάλαι πρεσβύτεροι ὡς ἀναμφιλέκτῳ ἐν τοῖς σφῶν
αὐτῶν κατακέχρηνται συγγράμμασιν· τὴν δὲ φερομένην δευτέραν οὐκ ἐνδιάθηκον μὲν εἶναι παρειλήφαμεν, ὅμως δὲ πολλοῖς χρήσιμος φανεῖσα, μετὰ
τῶν ἄλλων ἐσπουδάσθη γραφῶν. τό γε μὴν τῶν 2
ἐπικεκλημένων αὐτοῦ Πράξεων καὶ τὸ κατ' αὐτὸν
ὠνομασμένον εὐαγγέλιον τό τε λεγόμενον αὐτοῦ
Κήρυγμα καὶ τὴν καλουμένην Ἀποκάλυψιν οὐδ'
ὅλως ἐν καθολικοῖς ἴσμεν παραδεδομένα, ὅτι μήτε
ἀρχαίων μήτε μὴν καθ' ἡμᾶς τις ἐκκλησιαστικὸς
συγγραφεὺς ταῖς ἐξ αὐτῶν συνεχρήσατο μαρτυρίαις. προϊούσης δὲ τῆς ἱστορίας προὔργου ποιή- 3
σομαι σὺν ταῖς διαδοχαῖς ὑποσημήνασθαι τίνες τῶν
κατὰ χρόνους ἐκκλησιαστικῶν συγγραφέων ὁποίαις
κέχρηνται τῶν ἀντιλεγομένων, τίνα τε περὶ τῶν
ἐνδιαθήκων καὶ ὁμολογουμένων γραφῶν καὶ ὅσα
περὶ τῶν μὴ τοιούτων αὐτοῖς εἴρηται. ἀλλὰ τὰ 4
μὲν ὀνομαζόμενα Πέτρου, ὧν μόνην μίαν γνησίαν
ἔγνων ἐπιστολὴν καὶ παρὰ τοῖς πάλαι πρεσβυτέροις ὁμολογουμένην, τοσαῦτα· τοῦ δὲ Παύλου
πρόδηλοι καὶ σαφεῖς αἱ δεκατέσσαρες· ὅτι γε μὴν 5
τινες ἠθετήκασι τὴν πρὸς Ἑβραίους, πρὸς τῆς
Ῥωμαίων ἐκκλησίας ὡς μὴ Παύλου οὖσαν αὐτὴν
ἀντιλέγεσθαι φήσαντες, οὐ δίκαιον ἀγνοεῖν· καὶ
τὰ περὶ ταύτης δὲ τοῖς πρὸ ἡμῶν εἰρημένα κατὰ
καιρὸν παραθήσομαι. οὐδὲ μὴν τὰς λεγομένας
Rom 16, 14 αὐτοῦ Πράξεις ἐν ἀναμφιλέκτοις παρείληφα. ἐπεὶ 6
δ' ὁ αὐτὸς ἀπόστολος ἐν ταῖς ἐπὶ τέλει προσρή-
σεσιν τῆς πρὸς Ῥωμαίους μνήμην πεποίηται μετὰ
τῶν ἄλλων καὶ Ἑρμᾶ, οὗ φασιν ὑπάρχειν τὸ τοῦ
Ποιμένος βιβλίον, ἰστέον ὡς καὶ τοῦτο πρὸς μέν
τινων ἀντιλέλεκται, δι' οὓς οὐκ ἂν ἐν ὁμολογου-
192

this in their own writings as unquestioned, but the so-called second Epistle we have not received as canonical, but nevertheless it has appeared useful to many, and has been studied with other Scriptures On the other hand, of the Acts bearing his name, and the Gospel named according to him and Preaching called his and the so-called Revelation, we have no knowledge at all in Catholic tradition, for no orthodox[1] writer of the ancient time or of our own has used their testimonies. As the narrative proceeds I will take pains to indicate successively which of the orthodox writers in each period used any of the doubtful books, and what they said about the canonical and accepted Scriptures and what about those which are not such. Now the above are the books bearing the name of Peter, of which I recognize only one as genuine and admitted by the presbyters of old. And the fourteen letters of Paul are obvious and plain, yet it is not right to ignore that some dispute the Epistle to the Hebrews, saying that it was rejected by the church of Rome as not being by Paul, and I will expound at the proper time what was said about it by our predecessors. Nor have I received his so-called Acts among undisputed books. But since the same Apostle in the salutations at the end of Romans has mentioned among others Hermas, whose, they say, is the Book of the Shepherd, it should be known that this also is rejected by some, and for their sake should not be placed among

---

[1] Gk. "ecclesiastic," that is, belonging to or recognized by the Church, as opposed to heretics, Jews, or heathen.

μένοις τεθείη, ὑφ' ἑτέρων δὲ ἀναγκαιότατον οἷς
μάλιστα δεῖ στοιχειώσεως εἰσαγωγικῆς, κέκριται·
ὅθεν ἤδη καὶ ἐν ἐκκλησίαις ἴσμεν αὐτὸ δεδημο-
σιευμένον, καὶ τῶν παλαιτάτων δὲ συγγραφέων
κεχρημένους τινὰς αὐτῷ κατείληφα. ταῦτα εἰς [7]
παράστασιν τῶν τε ἀναντιρρήτων καὶ τῶν μὴ παρὰ
πᾶσιν ὁμολογουμένων θείων γραμμάτων εἰρήσθω.

Rom. 15, 19 — IV. Ὅτι μὲν οὖν τοῖς ἐξ ἐθνῶν κηρύσσων ὁ [1]
Παῦλος τοὺς ἀπὸ Ἱερουσαλὴμ καὶ κύκλῳ μέχρι
τοῦ Ἰλλυρικοῦ τῶν ἐκκλησιῶν καταβέβλητο θεμελίους, δῆλον ἐκ τῶν αὐτοῦ γένοιτ' ἂν φωνῶν καὶ
ἀφ' ὧν ὁ Λουκᾶς ἐν ταῖς Πράξεσιν ἱστόρησεν· καὶ [2]
ἐκ τῶν Πέτρου δὲ λέξεων ἐν ὁπόσαις καὶ οὗτος
ἐπαρχίαις τοὺς ἐκ περιτομῆς τὸν Χριστὸν εὐαγγελιζόμενος τὸν τῆς καινῆς διαθήκης παρεδίδου

1 Pet. 1, 1 — λόγον, σαφὲς ἂν εἴη ἀφ' ἧς εἰρήκαμεν ὁμολογου-
μένης αὐτοῦ ἐπιστολῆς, ἐν ᾗ τοῖς ἐξ Ἑβραίων
οὖσιν ἐν διασπορᾷ Πόντου καὶ Γαλατίας Καππα-
δοκίας τε καὶ Ἀσίας καὶ Βιθυνίας γράφει. ὅσοι [3]
δὲ τούτων καὶ τίνες γνήσιοι ζηλωταὶ γεγονότες
τὰς πρὸς αὐτῶν ἱδρυθείσας ἱκανοὶ ποιμαίνειν
ἐδοκιμάσθησαν ἐκκλησίας, οὐ ῥᾴδιον εἰπεῖν, μὴ
ὅτι γε ὅσους ἄν τις ἐκ τῶν Παύλου φωνῶν ἀνα-
λέξοιτο· τούτου γὰρ οὖν μυρίοι συνεργοὶ καί, ὡς [4]
αὐτὸς ὠνόμασεν, συστρατιῶται γεγόνασιν, ὧν οἱ

Phil. 2, 25 — πλείους ἀλήστου πρὸς αὐτοῦ μνήμης ἠξίωνται,
Philem. 2 — διηνεκῆ τὴν περὶ αὐτῶν μαρτυρίαν ταῖς ἰδίαις
ἐπιστολαῖς ἐγκαταλέξαντος, οὐ μὴν ἀλλὰ καὶ ὁ
Λουκᾶς ἐν ταῖς Πράξεσιν τοὺς γνωρίμους αὐτοῦ
καταλέγων ἐξ ὀνόματος αὐτῶν μνημονεύει. Τιμό-

1 Tim. 1, 3 — θεός γε μὴν τῆς ἐν Ἐφέσῳ παροικίας ἱστορεῖται
Tit. 1, 5 — πρῶτος τὴν ἐπισκοπὴν εἰληχέναι, ὡς καὶ Τίτος

accepted books, but by others it has been judged most valuable, especially to those who need elementary instruction. For this reason we know that it has been used in public in churches, and I have found it quoted by some of the most ancient writers. Let this suffice for the establishment of the divine writings which are undisputed, and of those which are not received by all.

IV. Now it would be clear from Paul's own words and from the narrative of Luke in the Acts that Paul, in his preaching to the Gentiles, laid the foundations of the churches from Jerusalem round about unto Illyricum. And from the Epistle which we have spoken of as indisputably Peter's, in which he writes to those of the Hebrews in the Dispersion of Pontus and Galatia, Cappadocia, Asia, and Bithynia, it would be clear from his own words in how many provinces he delivered the word of the New Testament by preaching the Gospel of Christ to those of the circumcision. But it is not easy to say how many of these and which of them were genuinely zealous and proved their ability to be the pastors of the churches founded by the Apostles, except by making a list of those mentioned by Paul. For there were many thousands of his fellow-workers and, as he called them himself, fellow-soldiers, of whom the most were granted by him memorial past forgetting, for he recounts his testimony to them unceasingly in his own letters, and, moreover, Luke also in the Acts gives a list of those known to him and mentions them by name. Thus Timothy is related to have been the first appointed bishop of the diocese of Ephesus, as

τῶν ἐπὶ Κρήτης ἐκκλησιῶν. Λουκᾶς δὲ τὸ μὲν
γένος ὢν τῶν ἀπ' Ἀντιοχείας, τὴν ἐπιστήμην δὲ
ἰατρός, τὰ πλεῖστα συγγεγονὼς τῷ Παύλῳ, καὶ
τοῖς λοιποῖς δὲ οὐ παρέργως τῶν ἀποστόλων
ὡμιληκώς, ἧς ἀπὸ τούτων προσεκτήσατο ψυχῶν
θεραπευτικῆς ἐν δυσὶν ἡμῖν ὑποδείγματα θεο-
πνεύστοις κατέλιπεν βιβλίοις, τῷ τε εὐαγγελίῳ, ὃ

Luke 1, 2. 3 καὶ χαράξαι μαρτύρεται καθ' ἃ παρέδοσαν αὐτῷ
οἱ ἀπ' ἀρχῆς αὐτόπται καὶ ὑπηρέται γενόμενοι τοῦ
λόγου, οἷς καί φησιν ἔτ' ἄνωθεν ἅπασι παρηκο-
λουθηκέναι, καὶ ταῖς τῶν ἀποστόλων Πράξεσιν,
ἃς οὐκέτι δι' ἀκοῆς, ὀφθαλμοῖς δὲ παραλαβὼν συνετάξατο. φασὶν δ' ὡς ἄρα τοῦ κατ' αὐτὸν εὐαγγελίου μνημονεύειν ὁ Παῦλος εἴωθεν, ὁπηνίκα ὡς
περὶ ἰδίου τινὸς εὐαγγελίου γράφων ἔλεγεν '' κατὰ

Rom. 2, 16
2 Tim. 2, 8 τὸ εὐαγγέλιόν μου.'' τῶν δὲ λοιπῶν ἀκολούθων
2 Tim. 4, 10 τοῦ Παύλου Κρήσκης μὲν ἐπὶ τὰς Γαλλίας στειλά-
2 Tim. 4, 21 μενος ὑπ' αὐτοῦ μαρτυρεῖται, Λίνος δέ, οὗ μέμνηται
συνόντος ἐπὶ Ῥώμης αὐτῷ κατὰ τὴν δευτέραν
πρὸς Τιμόθεον ἐπιστολήν, πρῶτος μετὰ Πέτρον
τῆς Ῥωμαίων ἐκκλησίας τὴν ἐπισκοπὴν ἤδη πρό-

Phil. 4, 3 τερον κληρωθεὶς δεδήλωται· ἀλλὰ καὶ ὁ Κλήμης,
τῆς Ῥωμαίων καὶ αὐτὸς ἐκκλησίας τρίτος ἐπίσκοπος καταστάς, Παύλου συνεργὸς καὶ συναθλη-
τὴς γεγονέναι πρὸς αὐτοῦ μαρτυρεῖται. ἐπὶ τούτοις καὶ τὸν Ἀρεοπαγίτην ἐκεῖνον, Διονύσιος

Acts 17, 34 ὄνομα αὐτῷ, ὃν ἐν ταῖς Πράξεσι μετὰ τὴν ἐν
Ἀρείῳ πάγῳ πρὸς Ἀθηναίους Παύλου δημη-
γορίαν πρῶτον πιστεῦσαι ἀνέγραψεν ὁ Λουκᾶς,
τῆς ἐν Ἀθήναις ἐκκλησίας πρῶτον ἐπίσκοπον
ἀρχαίων τις ἕτερος Διονύσιος, τῆς Κορινθίων παροικίας ποιμήν, γεγονέναι ἱστορεῖ. ἀλλὰ γὰρ ὁδῷ

196

was Titus of the churches in Crete. Luke, who was by race an Antiochian and a physician by profession, was long a companion of Paul, and had careful conversation with the other Apostles, and in two books left us examples of the medicine for souls which he had gained from them—the Gospel, which he testifies that he had planned according to the tradition received by him by those who were from the beginning eyewitnesses and ministers of the word, all of whom he says,[1] moreover, he had followed from the beginning, and the Acts of the Apostles which he composed no longer on the evidence of hearing but of his own eyes. And they say that Paul was actually accustomed to quote from Luke's Gospel since when writing of some Gospel as his own he used to say, " According to my Gospel." Of the other followers of Paul there is evidence that Crescens was sent by him to Gaul, and Linus, who is mentioned in the second Epistle to Timothy as present with him in Rome has already been declared to have been the first after Peter to be appointed to the bishopric of the Church in Rome. Of Clement too, who was himself made the third bishop of the church of Rome, it is testified by Paul that he worked and strove in company with him. In addition to these Dionysius, one of the ancients, the pastor of the diocese of the Corinthians, relates that the first bishop of the Church at Athens was that member of the Areopagus, the other Dionysius, whose original conversion after Paul's speech to the Athenians in the Areopagus Luke described in the Acts. Now

[1] The translation obscures the difficulty of the Greek. Is it the tradition or the eyewitnesses which Luke (in the opinion of Eusebius) claims to have followed? The Greek is quite ambiguous.

προβαίνουσιν, ἐπὶ καιροῦ τὰ τῆς κατὰ χρόνους τῶν ἀποστόλων διαδοχῆς ἡμῖν εἰρήσεται· νῦν δ' ἐπὶ τὰ ἑξῆς ἴωμεν τῆς ἱστορίας.

Joseph. B.I.
4, 491 V. Μετὰ Νέρωνα δέκα πρὸς τρισὶν ἔτεσιν τὴν ἀρχὴν ἐπικρατήσαντα τῶν ἀμφὶ Γάλβαν καὶ Ὄθωνα ἐνιαυτὸν ἐπὶ μησὶν ἓξ διαγενομένων, Οὐεσπασιανός, ταῖς κατὰ Ἰουδαίων παρατάξεσιν λαμπρυνόμενος, βασιλεὺς ἐπ' αὐτῆς ἀναδείκνυται τῆς

Joseph. B.I.
4, 658 Ἰουδαίας, αὐτοκράτωρ πρὸς τῶν αὐτόθι στρατοπέδων ἀναγορευθείς. τὴν ἐπὶ Ῥώμης οὖν αὐτίκα στειλάμενος, Τίτῳ τῷ παιδὶ τὸν κατὰ Ἰουδαίων ἐγχειρίζει πόλεμον. μετά γε μὴν τὴν τοῦ σωτῆρος ἡμῶν ἀνάληψιν Ἰουδαίων πρὸς τῷ κατ' αὐτοῦ τολμήματι ἤδη καὶ κατὰ τῶν ἀποστόλων αὐτοῦ πλείστας ὅσας ἐπιβουλὰς μεμηχανημένων, πρώτου τε Στεφάνου λίθοις ὑπ' αὐτῶν ἀνῃρημένου, εἶτα δὲ μετ' αὐτὸν Ἰακώβου, ὃς ἦν Ζεβεδαίου μὲν παῖς, ἀδελφὸς δὲ Ἰωάννου, τὴν κεφαλὴν ἀποτμηθέντος, ἐπὶ πᾶσί τε Ἰακώβου, τοῦ τὸν αὐτόθι τῆς ἐπισκοπῆς θρόνον πρώτου μετὰ τὴν τοῦ σωτῆρος ἡμῶν ἀνάληψιν κεκληρωμένου, τὸν προδηλωθέντα τρόπον μεταλλάξαντος, τῶν τε λοιπῶν ἀποστόλων μυρία εἰς θάνατον ἐπιβεβουλευμένων καὶ τῆς μὲν Ἰουδαίας γῆς ἀπεληλαμένων, ἐπὶ δὲ τῇ τοῦ κηρύγματος διδασκαλίᾳ τὴν εἰς σύμπαντα τὰ ἔθνη στειλαμένων πορείαν σὺν δυνάμει τοῦ

Matt. 28, 19 Χριστοῦ, φήσαντος αὐτοῖς " πορευθέντες μαθητεύσατε πάντα τὰ ἔθνη ἐν τῷ ὀνόματί μου," οἱ

---

[1] Nero died June 9, A.D. 68.

[2] Eusebius accidentally omits Vitellius. Galba's reign was June 9, 68 to Jan. 15, 69. Otho's was Jan. 15 to April 20, 69. Vitellius was not killed until Dec. 20, 69 but Vespasian was proclaimed Emperor at Alexandria

198

as we go on our way the chronological details of the succession of the Apostles will be related, but at present let us go on to the next stage of the narrative.

V. After Nero had held the sovereignty for thirteen years [1] the affairs of Galba and Otho [2] occupied a year and six months, and then Vespasian, who had distinguished himself in the operations against the Jews, was proclaimed Imperator by the army there and appointed Emperor in Judaea itself. He at once set off for Rome and entrusted the war against the Jews to his son Titus. Now after the ascension of our Saviour in addition to their crime against him the Jews at once contrived numberless plots against his disciples. Stephen was first stoned to death by them and next after him James, the son of Zebedee and brother of John, was beheaded.[3] In addition to all, James, who was the first after the ascension of our Saviour to be appointed to the throne of the bishopric in Jerusalem, passed away in the manner described above and the other Apostles were driven from the land of Judaea by thousands of deadly plots. They went on their way to all the heathen teaching their message in the power of Christ for he had said to them, " Go and make disciples of all the heathen in my name." [4] On the other hand, the

July 1, 69 ; he was recognized by the Senate as soon as his soldiers had defeated Vitellius.

[3] *Cf.* Acts vi. 8 ff. and xii. 2.

[4] This is the form in which Eusebius usually quotes Matt. xxviii. 19, omitting the reference to baptism. It cannot be accidental, but there are no MSS. of the N.T. with this text. Some think that the Eusebian text is an earlier form, some that Eusebius wished to keep secret the formula of baptism.

μὴν ἀλλὰ καὶ τοῦ λαοῦ τῆς ἐν Ἱεροσολύμοις ἐκκλησίας κατά τινα χρησμὸν τοῖς αὐτόθι δοκίμοις
δι' ἀποκαλύψεως ἐκδοθέντα πρὸ τοῦ πολέμου μετ-
αναστῆναι τῆς πόλεως καί τινα τῆς Περαίας
πόλιν οἰκεῖν κεκελευσμένου, Πέλλαν αὐτὴν ὀνο-
μάζουσιν, [ἐν ᾗ] τῶν εἰς Χριστὸν πεπιστευκότων
ἀπὸ τῆς Ἱερουσαλὴμ μετῳκισμένων, ὡς ἂν παντελῶς ἐπιλελοιπότων ἁγίων ἀνδρῶν αὐτήν τε τὴν
Ἰουδαίων βασιλικὴν μητρόπολιν καὶ σύμπασαν τὴν
Ἰουδαίαν γῆν, ἡ ἐκ θεοῦ δίκη λοιπὸν αὐτοὺς ἅτε
τοσαῦτα εἴς τε τὸν Χριστὸν καὶ τοὺς ἀποστόλους
αὐτοῦ παρηνομηκότας μετῄει, τῶν ἀσεβῶν ἄρδην
τὴν γενεὰν αὐτὴν ἐκείνην ἐξ ἀνθρώπων ἀφανίζουσα.
ὅσα μὲν οὖν τηνικάδε κατὰ πάντα τόπον ὅλῳ τῷ
ἔθνει συνερρύη κακά, ὅπως τε μάλιστα οἱ τῆς
Ἰουδαίας οἰκήτορες εἰς ἔσχατα περιηλάθησαν
συμφορῶν, ὁπόσαι τε μυριάδες ἡβηδὸν γυναιξὶν
ἅμα καὶ παισὶ ξίφει καὶ λιμῷ καὶ μυρίοις ἄλλοις
εἴδεσι περιπεπτώκασιν θανάτου, πόλεών τε Ἰουδαϊκῶν ὅσαι τε καὶ οἷαι γεγόνασιν πολιορκίαι,
ἀλλὰ καὶ ὁπόσα οἱ ἐπ' αὐτὴν Ἱερουσαλὴμ ὡς ἂν
ἐπὶ μητρόπολιν ὀχυρωτάτην καταπεφευγότες δεινὰ
καὶ πέρα δεινῶν ἑοράκασι, τοῦ τε παντὸς πολέμου
τὸν τρόπον καὶ τῶν ἐν τούτῳ γεγενημένων ἐν

Dan. 9, 27 ; μέρει ἕκαστα, καὶ ὡς ἐπὶ τέλει τὸ πρὸς τῶν προφη-
12, 11
Matt. 24, 15 τῶν ἀνηγορευμένον βδέλυγμα τῆς ἐρημώσεως ἐν
Mark 13, 14 αὐτῷ κατέστη τῷ πάλαι τοῦ θεοῦ περιβοήτῳ νεῷ,
παντελῆ φθορὰν καὶ ἀφανισμὸν ἔσχατον τὸν διὰ
πυρὸς ὑπομείναντι, πάρεστιν ὅτῳ φίλον, ἐπ'
ἀκριβὲς ἐκ τῆς τῷ Ἰωσήπῳ γραφείσης ἀναλέ-
Joseph. B.I.
6, 425-428 ξασθαι ἱστορίας· ὡς δὲ ὁ αὐτὸς οὗτος τῶν ἀθροι-
σθέντων ἀπὸ τῆς Ἰουδαίας ἁπάσης ἐν ἡμέραις τῆς

people of the church in Jerusalem were commanded by an oracle given by revelation before the war to those in the city who were worthy of it to depart and dwell in one of the cities of Perea which they called Pella. To it those who believed on Christ migrated from Jerusalem, that when holy men had altogether deserted the royal capital of the Jews and the whole land of Judaea, the judgement of God might at last overtake them for all their crimes against the Christ and his Apostles, and all that generation of the wicked be utterly blotted out from among men. Those who wish can retrace accurately from the history written by Josephus how many evils at that time overwhelmed the whole nation in every place and especially how the inhabitants of Judaea were driven to the last point of suffering, how many thousands of youths, women, and children perished by the sword, by famine, and by countless other forms of death; they can read how many and what famous Jewish cities were besieged, and finally how terrors and worse than terrors were seen by those who fled to Jerusalem as if to a mighty capital; they can study the nature of the whole war, all the details of what happened in it, and how at the end the abomination of desolation spoken of by the prophets was set up in the very temple of God, for all its ancient fame, and it perished utterly and passed away in flames. But it is necessary to point out how the same writer estimates at three millions the

τοῦ πάσχα ἑορτῆς ὥσπερ ἐν εἱρκτῇ ῥήμασιν
αὐτοῖς ἀποκλεισθῆναι εἰς τὰ Ἱεροσόλυμα ἀμφὶ
τριακοσίας μυριάδας τὸ πλῆθος ἱστορεῖ, ἀναγκαῖον ὑποσημήνασθαι. χρῆν δ' οὖν ἐν αἷς ἡμέραις 6
τὸν πάντων σωτῆρα καὶ εὐεργέτην Χριστόν τε
τοῦ θεοῦ τὰ κατὰ τὸ πάθος διατέθεινται, ταῖς
αὐταῖς ὥσπερ ἐν εἱρκτῇ κατακλεισθέντας τὸν
μετελθόντα αὐτοὺς ὄλεθρον πρὸς τῆς θείας δίκης
καταδέξασθαι.

Παρελθὼν δὴ τὰ τῶν ἐν μέρει συμβεβηκότων 7
αὐτοῖς ὅσα διὰ ξίφους καὶ ἄλλῳ τρόπῳ κατ'
αὐτῶν ἐγκεχείρηται, μόνας τὰς διὰ τοῦ λιμοῦ
ἀναγκαῖον ἡγοῦμαι συμφορὰς παραθέσθαι, ὡς
ἂν ἐκ μέρους ἔχοιεν οἱ τῇδε τῇ γραφῇ ἐντυγχάνοντες εἰδέναι ὅπως αὐτοὺς τῆς εἰς τὸν Χριστὸν
τοῦ θεοῦ παρανομίας οὐκ εἰς μακρὸν ἡ ἐκ θεοῦ
μετῆλθεν τιμωρία. VI. φέρε δὴ οὖν, τῶν Ἱστο- 1
ριῶν τὴν πέμπτην τοῦ Ἰωσήπου μετὰ χεῖρας
αὖθις ἀναλαβών, τῶν τότε πραχθέντων δίελθε
Joseph. B. l.
5, 424–438 τὴν τραγῳδίαν· "τοῖς γε μὴν εὐπόροις" φησί
" καὶ τὸ μένειν πρὸς ἀπωλείας ἴσον ἦν· προφάσει
γὰρ αὐτομολίας ἀνῃρεῖτό τις διὰ τὴν οὐσίαν. τῷ
λιμῷ δ' ἡ ἀπόνοια τῶν στασιαστῶν συνήκμαζεν,
καὶ καθ' ἡμέραν ἀμφότερα προσεξεκάετο τὰ
δεινά. φανερὸς μέν γε οὐδαμοῦ σῖτος ἦν, ἐπ- 2
εισπηδῶντες δὲ διηρεύνων τὰς οἰκίας, ἔπειθ'
εὑρόντες μὲν ὡς ἀρνησαμένους ἠκίζοντο, μὴ εὑρόντες δὲ ὡς ἐπιμελέστερον κρύψαντας ἐβασάνιζον.
τεκμήριον δὲ τοῦ τ' ἔχειν καὶ μή, τὰ σώματα
τῶν ἀθλίων· ὧν οἱ μὲν ἔτι συνεστῶτες εὐπορεῖν
τροφῆς ἐδόκουν, οἱ τηκόμενοι δὲ ἤδη παρωδεύον-
το, καὶ κτείνειν ἄλογον ἐδόκει τοὺς ὑπ' ἐνδείας

number of those who in the days of the Feast of the Passover thronged Jerusalem from all Judaea and, to use his own words, were shut up as if in prison. It was indeed right that on the same day on which they had perpetrated the passion of the Saviour and benefactor of all men and the Christ of God they should be, as it were, shut up in prison and receive the destruction which pursued them from the sentence of God.

Omitting then the details of their misfortunes from the sword and otherwise, I think it necessary to adduce only their sufferings from famine in order that those who study this work may have some partial knowledge of how the punishment of God followed close after them for their crime against the Christ of God. VI. Come, then, take up again the fifth book of the history of Josephus and go through the tragedy of what was then done. " For the rich," he says, " to remain was equal to destruction, since for the sake of their property they were murdered on the charge of intended desertion. But the madness of the rebels grew with the famine, and the terror of both blazed more fiercely day by day. No corn was visible anywhere, but they burst into houses and searched them. Then, if they found any, they tormented the inmates for their denying ; if not, they tortured them for having hidden it too carefully. The bodies of the miserable creatures were evidence whether they had it or not. Those who were still in health seemed to be provided with food, while those who were already wasted away were passed by, and it seemed unreasonable to kill

τεθνηξομένους αὐτίκα. πολλοὶ δὲ λάθρα τὰς 3
κτήσεις ἑνὸς ἀντικατηλλάξαντο μέτρου, πυρῶν
μέν, εἰ πλουσιώτεροι τυγχάνοιεν ὄντες, οἱ δὲ
πενέστεροι κριθῆς· ἔπειτα κατακλείοντες ἑαυτοὺς
εἰς τὰ μυχαίτατα τῶν οἰκιῶν, τινὲς μὲν ὑπ' ἄκρας
ἐνδείας ἀνέργαστον τὸν σῖτον ἤσθιον, οἳ δ' ἔπεσσον
ὡς ἥ τε ἀνάγκη καὶ τὸ δέος παρήνει, καὶ τράπεζα 4
μὲν οὐδαμοῦ παρετίθετο, τοῦ δὲ πυρὸς ὑφέλκοντες
ἔτ' ὠμὰ τὰ σιτία διήρπαζον. ἐλεεινὴ δ' ἦν ἡ
τροφὴ καὶ δακρύων ἄξιος ἡ θέα, τῶν μὲν δυνα-
τωτέρων πλεονεκτούντων, τῶν δὲ ἀσθενῶν ὀδυ-
ρομένων. πάντων μὲν δὴ παθῶν ὑπερίσταται 5
λιμός, οὐδὲν δ' οὕτως ἀπόλλυσιν ὡς αἰδῶ[1]· τὸ
γὰρ ἄλλως ἐντροπῆς ἄξιον ἐν τούτῳ καταφρο-
νεῖται. γυναῖκες γοῦν ἀνδρῶν καὶ παῖδες πατέρων καί, τὸ οἰκτρότατον, μητέρες νηπίων ἐξ-
ήρπαζον ἐξ αὐτῶν τῶν στομάτων τὰς τροφάς,
καὶ τῶν φιλτάτων ἐν χερσὶ μαραινομένων οὐκ
ἦν φειδὼ τοὺς τοῦ ζῆν ἀφελέσθαι σταλαγμούς.
τοιαῦτα δ' ἐσθίοντες, ὅμως οὐ διελάνθανον, παντα- 6
χοῦ δ' ἐφίσταντο οἱ στασιασταὶ καὶ τούτων ταῖς
ἁρπαγαῖς. ὁπότε γὰρ κατίδοιεν ἀποκεκλεισμένην
οἰκίαν, σημεῖον ἦν τοῦτο τοὺς ἔνδον προσφέρεσθαι
τροφήν, εὐθέως δ' ἐξαράξαντες τὰς θύρας εἰσεπήδων, καὶ μόνον οὐκ ἐκ τῶν φαρύγγων ἀνα-
θλίβοντες τὰς ἀκόλους ἀνέφερον. ἐτύπτοντο δὲ 7
γέροντες ἀντεχόμενοι τῶν σιτίων, καὶ κόμης
ἐσπαράσσοντο γυναῖκες συγκαλύπτουσαι τὰ ἐν
χερσίν, οὐδέ τις ἦν οἶκτος πολιᾶς ἢ νηπίων,
ἀλλὰ συνεπαίροντες τὰ παιδία τῶν ψωμῶν ἐκ-
κρεμάμενα κατέσειον εἰς ἔδαφος. τοῖς δὲ φθάσασι

---

[1] The MSS. read αἰδώς, but αἰδῶ is necessary to the sense.

those who would soon die of need. Many secretly exchanged their property for a single measure of wheat, if they were richer, of barley, if they were poorer. Then, shutting themselves up in the inmost recesses of their houses, some, in the extremity of their want, would eat the grain unprepared, others would cook it as necessity and fear dictated. No table was set anywhere, but snatching it from the fire they tore in pieces the still uncooked food. Their living was pitiable, and their appearance worthy of tears ; the strong plundered and the weak wailed. Famine truly surpasses all sufferings, but it destroys nothing so much as shame [1] ; for what is at other times worthy of respect is despised in famine ; women took the food from the very mouths of their husbands, children from their fathers, and, most piteous of all, mothers from their children, and while their dearest were wasting away before them there was no scruple in taking away the last drop of life. Yet they did not escape detection when they thus ate, but everywhere the rioters arose to rob them even of this ; for whenever they saw a house shut up it was a sign that those within had obtained food and at once they tore down the doors, rushed in, and seized the morsels, almost squeezing them out of their throats. Old men were beaten for withholding food, and women were dragged by the hair for concealing it in their hands. There was no pity for grey-headed age or for little children, but they picked up babies clinging to crusts and dashed them on the floor.

[1] The Greek means rather more than this : it is almost a "sense of decency."

τὴν εἰσδρομὴν αὐτῶν καὶ προκαταπιοῦσιν τὸ
ἁρπαγησόμενον ὡς ἀδικηθέντες ἦσαν ὠμότεροι,
δεινὰς δὲ βασάνων ὁδοὺς ἐπενόουν πρὸς ἔρευναν
τροφῆς, ὀρόβοις μὲν ἐμφράττοντες τοῖς ἀθλίοις
τοὺς τῶν αἰδοίων πόρους, ῥάβδοις δ' ὀξείαις
ἀναπείροντες τὰς ἕδρας· τὰ φρικτὰ δὲ καὶ ἀκοαῖς
ἔπασχέ τις εἰς ἐξομολόγησιν ἑνὸς ἄρτου καὶ
ἵνα μηνύσῃ δράκα μίαν κεκρυμμένων ἀλφίτων.
οἱ βασανισταὶ δ' οὐδ' ἐπείνων (καὶ γὰρ ἧττον
ἂν ὠμὸν ἦν τὸ μετὰ ἀνάγκης), γυμνάζοντες δὲ
τὴν ἀπόνοιαν καὶ προπαρασκευάζοντες ἑαυτοῖς
εἰς τὰς ἑξῆς ἡμέρας ἐφόδια. τοῖς δ' ἐπὶ τὴν
Ῥωμαίων φρουρὰν νύκτωρ ἐξερπύσασιν ἐπὶ λα-
χάνων συλλογὴν ἀγρίων καὶ πόας ὑπαντῶντες,
ὅτ' ἤδη διαπεφευγέναι τοὺς πολεμίους ἐδόκουν,
ἀφήρπαζον τὰ κομισθέντα, καὶ πολλάκις ἱκετευ-
όντων καὶ τὸ φρικτότατον ἐπικαλουμένων ὄνομα
τοῦ θεοῦ μεταδοῦναί τι μέρος αὐτοῖς ὧν κινδυνεύ-
σαντες ἤνεγκαν, οὐδ' ὁτιοῦν μετέδοσαν, ἀγαπητὸν
δ' ἦν τὸ μὴ καὶ προσαπολέσθαι σεσυλημένον."

Joseph. B. I.
5, 512–519 Τούτοις μεθ' ἕτερα ἐπιφέρει λέγων· "'Ιουδαίοις
δὲ μετὰ τῶν ἐξόδων ἀπεκόπη πᾶσα σωτηρίας
ἐλπίς, καὶ βαθύνας ἑαυτὸν ὁ λιμὸς κατ' οἴκους
καὶ γενεὰς τὸν δῆμον ἐπεβόσκετο, καὶ τὰ μὲν
τέγη πεπλήρωτο γυναικῶν καὶ βρεφῶν λελυ-
μένων, οἱ στενωποὶ δὲ γερόντων νεκρῶν, παῖδες
δὲ καὶ νεανίαι διοιδοῦντες ὥσπερ εἴδωλα κατὰ
τὰς ἀγορὰς ἀνειλοῦντο καὶ κατέπιπτον ὅπῃ τινὰ
τὸ πάθος καταλαμβάνοι. θάπτειν δὲ τοὺς προσήκοντας οὔτε ἴσχυον οἱ κάμνοντες καὶ τὸ διευ-

---

[1] The MSS. read " swelling up," which is characteristic of

To those who had anticipated their entry, and had gulped down their expected prey, they were the more cruel, as though they had been injured by them. For the discovery of food they sought for terrible methods of torture, sewing up their victims and impaling them on sharp stakes. Men suffered things terrible even to hear to secure the confession of a single loaf, and to disclose a single pint of hidden barley. But the torturers suffered no hunger (and indeed their cruelty would have been less had it been from necessity) but there was method in their madness and they provided sustenance for themselves for days to come. When some crept out by night as far as the Roman lines to gather wild herbs and grass, they intercepted them when they thought that they had at last escaped the enemy, plundered them of what they were carrying, and for all their many entreaties and invocations of the awful name of God to give them some share of what they had brought at their own risk, they gave them nothing whatever, and he who was robbed was lucky not to be murdered too."

After some other details he continues : " Now when all hope of safety was cut off from the Jews by the closing of the exits from the city and famine deepening from house to house and family to family was eating up the people, the rooms were filled with dead women and children and the alley-ways with the corpses of old men. Boys and young men, wandering [1] like ghosts through the market-place, were seized by death and lay each where the blow had stricken him. The sick had no strength to bury

---

sufferers from famine, not of ghosts (and the text seems corrupt). Or it may be " swollen yet ghost-like " ?

τονοῦν ὤκνει διά τε τὸ πλῆθος τῶν νεκρῶν καὶ
τὸ κατὰ σφᾶς ἄδηλον· πολλοὶ γοῦν τοῖς ὑπ'
αὐτῶν θαπτομένοις ἐπαπέθνησκον, πολλοὶ δ' ἐπὶ
τὰς θήκας, πρὶν ἐπιστῆναι τὸ χρεών, προῆλθον.
οὔτε δὲ θρῆνος ἐν ταῖς συμφοραῖς οὔτε ὀλο-
φυρμὸς ἦν, ἀλλ' ὁ λιμὸς ἤλεγχε τὰ πάθη, ξηροῖς
δὲ τοῖς ὄμμασιν οἱ δυσθανατοῦντες ἐθεώρουν τοὺς
φθάσαντας ἀναπαύσασθαι, βαθεῖα δὲ τὴν πόλιν
περιεῖχεν σιγὴ καὶ νὺξ θανάτου γέμουσα. καὶ
τούτων οἱ λῃσταὶ χαλεπώτεροι. τυμβωρυχοῦν-
τες γοῦν τὰς οἰκίας, ἐσύλων τοὺς νεκρούς, καὶ
τὰ καλύμματα τῶν σωμάτων περισπῶντες, μετὰ
γέλωτος ἐξῄεσαν, τάς τε ἀκμὰς τῶν ξιφῶν ἐδοκί-
μαζον ἐν τοῖς πτώμασιν, καί τινας τῶν ἐρριμμέ-
νων ἔτι ζῶντας διήλαυνον ἐπὶ πείρᾳ τοῦ σιδήρου,
τοὺς δ' ἱκετεύοντας χρῆσαι σφίσιν δεξιὰν καὶ
ξίφος, τῷ λιμῷ κατέλιπον ὑπερηφανοῦντες, καὶ
τῶν ἐκπνεόντων ἕκαστος ἀτενὲς εἰς τὸν ναὸν
ἀφεώρα, τοὺς στασιαστὰς ζῶντας ἀπολιπών. οἱ
δὲ τὸ μὲν πρῶτον ἐκ τοῦ δημοσίου θησαυροῦ
τοὺς νεκροὺς θάπτειν ἐκέλευον, τὴν ὀσμὴν οὐ φέ-
ροντες· ἔπειθ' ὡς οὐ διήρκουν, ἀπὸ τῶν τειχῶν
ἐρρίπτουν εἰς τὰς φάραγγας. περιιὼν δὲ ταύτας
ὁ Τίτος ὡς ἐθεάσατο πεπλησμένας τῶν νεκρῶν καὶ
βαθὺν ἰχῶρα μυδώντων τὸν ὑπορρέοντα τῶν σωμάτων, ἐστέναξέν τε καὶ τὰς χεῖρας ἀνατείνας κατ-
εμαρτύρατο τὸν θεόν, ὡς οὐκ εἴη τὸ ἔργον αὐτοῦ.''

Joseph. B.I.
5, 566
Τούτοις ἐπειπών τινα μεταξὺ ἐπιφέρει λέγων·
''οὐκ ἂν ὑποστειλαίμην εἰπεῖν ἅ μοι κελεύει τὸ
πάθος· οἶμαι Ῥωμαίων βραδυνάντων ἐπὶ τοὺς ἀλι-
τηρίους, ἢ καταποθῆναι ἂν ὑπὸ χάσματος ἢ
κατακλυσθῆναι τὴν πόλιν ἢ τοὺς τῆς Σοδομηνῆς
208

their families and the strong hesitated for the number of the dead and their own doubtful fate. Many indeed fell in death on those whom they were burying and many went to their graves before the necessity arose. There was no lamentation or wailing at losses, but famine overcame emotion and those who were dying in misery looked with dry eyes on those who had found rest before them. Deep silence and night pregnant with death encompassed the city. Worse than these were the robbers. Breaking into houses like body-snatchers they robbed the dead, tearing the garments from their bodies, and went out with laughter. They tried the edge of their swords on the corpses, and to prove the steel ran through some of the fallen who were still alive, but those who begged for the kindliness of a mortal blow they left in contempt to the famine. These all died with eyes fixed on the temple and left the rebels to life. At first orders were given to bury the dead at the public expense because of the unbearable stench ; then afterwards when this was impracticable they were thrown from the walls into the trenches. When Titus, going round the trenches, saw them full of the dead and the thick gore oozing from the rotting bodies, he groaned, and raising his hands called God to witness that this was not his doing.''

After a little more he goes on : `` I cannot refrain from stating what emotion bids me. I think that had the Romans delayed their attack on the scoundrels the city would have been engulfed by the earth opening or overwhelmed by a flood or shared the

209

μεταλαβεῖν κεραυνούς· πολὺ γὰρ τῶν ταῦτα παθόν-
των ἤνεγκεν γενεὰν ἀθεωτέραν· τῇ γοῦν τούτων
ἀπονοίᾳ πᾶς ὁ λαὸς συναπώλετο."

Joseph. B.I.
6, 193–213

Καὶ ἐν τῷ ἕκτῳ δὲ βιβλίῳ οὕτως γράφει. "τῶν
δ' ὑπὸ τοῦ λιμοῦ φθειρομένων κατὰ τὴν πόλιν
ἄπειρον μὲν ἔπιπτε τὸ πλῆθος, ἀδιήγητα δὲ συνέβαινεν τὰ πάθη. καθ' ἑκάστην γὰρ οἰκίαν, εἴ
που τροφῆς παραφανείη σκιά, πόλεμος ἦν, καὶ
διὰ χειρῶν ἐχώρουν οἱ φίλτατοι πρὸς ἀλλήλους,
ἐξαρπάζοντες τὰ ταλαίπωρα τῆς ψυχῆς ἐφόδια,
πίστις δ' ἀπορίας οὐδὲ τοῖς θνήσκουσιν ἦν, ἀλλὰ
καὶ τοὺς ἐμπνέοντας οἱ λῃσταὶ διηρεύνων, μή τις
ὑπὸ κόλπον ἔχων τροφὴν, σκήπτοιτο τὸν θάνατον
αὑτῷ. οἳ δ' ὑπ' ἐνδείας κεχηνότες ὥσπερ λυσ-
σῶντες κύνες ἐσφάλλοντο καὶ παρεφέροντο ταῖς
τε θύραις ἐνσειόμενοι μεθυόντων τρόπον καὶ ὑπ'
ἀμηχανίας τοὺς αὐτοὺς οἴκους εἰσεπήδων δὶς
ἢ τρὶς ὥρᾳ μιᾷ. πάντα δ' ὑπ' ὀδόντας ἦγεν ἡ
ἀνάγκη, καὶ τὰ μηδὲ τοῖς ῥυπαρωτάτοις τῶν
ἀλόγων ζώων πρόσφορα συλλέγοντες ἐσθίειν ὑπέφερον. ζωστήρων γοῦν καὶ ὑποδημάτων τὸ τελευταῖον οὐκ ἀπέσχοντο καὶ τὰ δέρματα τῶν
θυρεῶν ἀποδέροντες ἐμασῶντο, τροφὴ δ' ἦν καὶ
χόρτου τισὶν παλαιοῦ σπαράγματα· τὰς γὰρ ἶνας
ἔνιοι συλλέγοντες, ἐλάχιστον σταθμὸν ἐπώλουν
Ἀττικῶν τεσσάρων.

"Καὶ τί δεῖ τὴν ἐπ' ἀψύχοις ἀναίδειαν τοῦ λιμοῦ
λέγειν; εἶμι γὰρ αὐτοῦ δηλώσων ὁγοῖον
μήτε παρ' Ἕλλησιν μήτε παρὰ βαρβάροις ἱστόρηται, φρικτὸν μὲν εἰπεῖν, ἄπιστον δ' ἀκοῦσαι.
καὶ ἔγωγε, μὴ δόξαιμι τερατεύεσθαι τοῖς αὖθις
ἀνθρώποις, κἂν παρέλιπον τὴν συμφορὰν ἡδέως,

thunderbolts of Sodom, for it had brought forth a generation far more ungodly than those who thus suffered. It was by their madness that the whole people perished."

In the sixth book he writes thus : " Of those who perished in the city from the famine the number which fell was countless and their sufferings indescribable. For in each house if there appeared the very shadow of food there was fighting, and the dearest friends wrestled together for it, snatching the miserable sustenance of life. Nor were even the dying believed to be destitute, but while they were still breathing the robbers searched them, lest any should feign death while having food on his person. Others, gaping from lack of food, stumbled and hurried along like mad dogs, beating at the doors like drunken men, and rushing two or three times in a single hour into the same houses from sheer incompetence. Necessity brought all things to men's teeth and they endured eating a collection of scraps unfit for the filthiest of brute beasts. At the last they abstained not even from belts and shoes and gnawed the hides stripped off their shields. Some fed on wisps of old straw, others collected stubble and sold a tiny portion for four Attic drachmae.[1]

" But what need is there to speak of the shamelessness of the famine towards inanimate things ? I purpose to relate a consequence of it such as has been narrated neither by the Greeks nor by the barbarians, horrible to tell, incredible to hear. I myself would have gladly omitted the tragedy to avoid

[1] About half a crown or sixty cents.

EUSEBIUS

εἰ μὴ τῶν κατ' ἐμαυτὸν εἶχον ἀπείρους μάρτυρας·
ἄλλως τε καὶ ψυχρὰν ἂν καταθείμην τῇ πατρίδι
χάριν, καθυφέμενος τὸν λόγον ὧν πέπονθε τὰ
ἔργα. γυνὴ τῶν ὑπὲρ Ἰορδάνην κατοικούντων, 2
Μαρία τοὔνομα, πατρὸς Ἐλεαζάρου, κώμης Βα-
θεζώρ (σημαίνει δὲ τοῦτο οἶκος ὑσσώπου), διὰ
γένος καὶ πλοῦτον ἐπίσημος, μετὰ τοῦ λοιποῦ
πλήθους εἰς τὰ Ἱεροσόλυμα καταφυγοῦσα συν-
επολιορκεῖτο. ταύτης τὴν μὲν ἄλλην κτῆσιν οἱ
τύραννοι διήρπασαν, ὅσην ἐκ τῆς Περαίας ἀνα-
σκευασαμένη μετήνεγκεν εἰς τὴν πόλιν, τὰ δὲ
λείψανα τῶν κειμηλίων καὶ¹ εἴ τι τροφῆς ἐπινοηθείη καθ' ἡμέραν εἰσπηδῶντες ἥρπαζον οἱ δορυ-
φόροι. δεινὴ δὲ τὸ γύναιον ἀγανάκτησις εἰσῄει,
καὶ πολλάκις λοιδοροῦσα καὶ καταρωμένη τοὺς
ἅρπαγας ἐφ' ἑαυτὴν ἠρέθιζεν. ὡς δ' οὔτε παρ- 3
οξυνόμενός τις οὔτ' ἐλεῶν αὐτὴν ἀνῄρει καὶ τὸ
μὲν εὑρεῖν τι σιτίον ἄλλοις ἐκοπία, πανταχόθεν
δ' ἄπορον ἦν ἤδη καὶ τὸ εὑρεῖν, ὁ λιμὸς δὲ διὰ
σπλάγχνων καὶ μυελῶν ἐχώρει καὶ τοῦ λιμοῦ
μᾶλλον ἐξέκαιον οἱ θυμοί, σύμβουλον λαβοῦσα
τὴν ὀργὴν μετὰ τῆς ἀνάγκης, ἐπὶ τὴν φύσιν ἐχώρει,
καὶ τὸ τέκνον, ἦν δ' αὐτῇ παῖς ὑπομάστιος, ἁρπα-
σαμένη, ' βρέφος,' εἶπεν, ' ἄθλιον, ἐν πολέμῳ καὶ
λιμῷ καὶ στάσει, τίνι σε τηρῶ; τὰ μὲν παρὰ
Ῥωμαίοις δουλεία κἂν ζήσωμεν ἐπ' αὐτούς,
φθάνει δὲ καὶ δουλείαν ὁ λιμός, οἱ στασιασταὶ
δὲ ἀμφοτέρων χαλεπώτεροι. ἴθι, γενοῦ μοι τροφὴ
καὶ τοῖς στασιασταῖς ἐρινὺς καὶ τῷ βίῳ μῦθος,
ὁ μόνος ἐλλείπων ταῖς Ἰουδαίων συμφοραῖς.'
καὶ ταῦθ' ἅμα λέγουσα κτείνει τὸν υἱόν, ἔπειτ'
ὀπτήσασα, τὸ μὲν ἥμισυ κατεσθίει, τὸ δὲ λοιπὸν
212

appearing to posterity to fabricate legend had I not had countless witnesses to it in my own generation. Certainly I should render cold comfort to my country were I to compromise the account of her sufferings. There was a woman among those who lived beyond Jordan named Mary whose father was Eliezer of the village Bathezor (which means " House of Hyssop "). She was famous for her family and wealth, and having fled with the rest of the population to Jerusalem was caught in the siege. The tyrants seized all her other possessions which she had brought from Peraea and carried into the city, and the guards rushed in daily and seized the remnants of her property and any food which they perceived. Fierce indignation seized the woman and by her frequent abuses and curses she tried to irritate the robbers against herself. But when no one killed her either in anger or pity and she wearied of finding food for others, and indeed it was now impossible to do so anywhere, famine entered into her heart and marrow, and rage burnt more fiercely than famine. Anger and necessity were her councillors : she turned against nature and seized her child, a boy whom she was suckling. ' Miserable infant,' she said, ' amid war, famine, and rebellion for what[1] am I keeping you ? Slavery among the Romans faces us if they give us our lives ; famine is overtaking slavery ; the rebels are worse than both. Come, be food for me, an avenging fury to the rebels, and the one story still lacking to the sufferings of the Jews to be told to the world.' With these words she killed her son, and then cooked him, ate half, and covered

---

[1] Or possibly " for whom."

---

[1] κἂν in most mss. and in Josephus, but it seems impossible.

κατακαλύψασα ἐφύλαττεν. εὐθέως δ᾽ οἱ στασιασταὶ παρῆσαν καὶ τῆς ἀθεμίτου κνίσης σπά-
σαντες, ἠπείλουν, εἰ μὴ δείξειεν τὸ παρα-
σκευασθέν, ἀποσφάξειν αὐτὴν εὐθέως· ἣ δὲ καὶ μοῖ-
ραν αὐτοῖς εἰποῦσα καλὴν τετηρηκέναι, τὰ λείψανα
τοῦ τέκνου διεκάλυψεν. τοὺς δ᾽ εὐθέως φρίκη καὶ 20
φρενῶν ἔκστασις ᾕρει, καὶ παρὰ τὴν ὄψιν ἐπεπή-
γεσαν. ἣ δ᾽, ‘ἐμόν,’ ἔφη, ‘τοῦτο τὸ τέκνον
γνήσιον, καὶ τὸ ἔργον ἐμόν. φάγετε, καὶ γὰρ
ἐγὼ βέβρωκα· μὴ γένησθε μήτε μαλακώτεροι
γυναικὸς μήτε συμπαθέστεροι μητρός. εἰ δ᾽
ὑμεῖς εὐσεβεῖς καὶ τὴν ἐμὴν ἀποστρέφεσθε θυσίαν,
ἐγὼ μὲν ὑμῖν βέβρωκα, καὶ τὸ λοιπὸν δ᾽ ἐμοὶ
μεινάτω.’ μετὰ ταῦθ᾽ οἱ μὲν τρέμοντες ἐξῄεσαν, 21
πρὸς ἓν τοῦτο δειλοὶ καὶ μόλις ταύτης τῆς τροφῆς
τῇ μητρὶ παραχωρήσαντες, ἀνεπλήσθη δ᾽ εὐθέως
ὅλη τοῦ μύσους ἡ πόλις, καὶ πρὸ ὀμμάτων ἕκαστος
τὸ πάθος λαμβάνων ὡς παρ᾽ αὐτῷ τολμηθέν,
ἔφριττεν. σπουδὴ δὲ τῶν λιμωττόντων ἐπὶ τὸν 22
θάνατον ἦν καὶ μακαρισμὸς τῶν φθασάντων
πρὶν ἀκοῦσαι καὶ θεάσασθαι κακὰ τηλικαῦτα.’’

VII. Τοιαῦτα τῆς Ἰουδαίων εἰς τὸν Χριστὸν 1
τοῦ θεοῦ παρανομίας τε καὶ δυσσεβείας τἀπίχειρα,
παραθεῖναι δ᾽ αὐτοῖς ἄξιον καὶ τὴν ἀψευδῆ τοῦ
σωτῆρος ἡμῶν πρόρρησιν, δι᾽ ἧς αὐτὰ ταῦτα
Matt. 24, 19–
21
δηλοῖ ὧδέ πως προφητεύων “οὐαὶ δὲ ταῖς ἐν
γαστρὶ ἐχούσαις καὶ ταῖς θηλαζούσαις ἐν ἐκείναις
ταῖς ἡμέραις· προσεύχεσθε δὲ ἵνα μὴ γένηται
ὑμῶν ἡ φυγὴ χειμῶνος μηδὲ σαββάτῳ. ἔσται
γὰρ τότε θλῖψις μεγάλη, οἵα οὐκ ἐγένετο ἀπ᾽
Joseph. B.I.
6, 420. 417.
418. 420, 435
ἀρχῆς κόσμου ἕως τοῦ νῦν, οὐδὲ μὴ γένηται.’’
συναγαγὼν δὲ πάντα τὸν τῶν ἀνῃρημένων ἀριθμὸν 23

up and kept the rest. At that moment the rebels came and smelling the horrible savour, threatened to kill her at once if they were not given what she had made ready. She told them that she had kept a good helping for them and uncovered the remains of the child. As for them, horror and amazement seized them at once, and they stood transfixed at the sight, but she said, ' This was my own child and the deed is mine. Eat, for I myself have eaten. Do not be more squeamish than a woman, or compassionate than a mother. But if you have scruples, and turn away from my sacrifice, what I have eaten was your share, let the rest remain for me.' At this they went out trembling, for only this made them cowards, and they scarcely yielded even this food to the mother ; but the whole city was at once filled with the horror, and each, holding the tragedy before his eyes, shuddered as if it had been his own crime. And the sufferers from the famine sought for death and pronounced those blessed whom it had reached before they heard or saw such awful evils."

VII. Such was the reward of the iniquity of the Jews and of their impiety against the Christ of God, but it is worth appending to it the infallible forecast of our Saviour in which he prophetically expounded these very things,—" Woe unto them that are with child and give suck in those days, but pray that your flight be not in the winter nor on a Sabbath day, for there shall then be great affliction such as was not from the beginning of the world until now, nor shall be." And the historian, estimating the whole number

ὁ συγγραφεὺς λιμῷ καὶ ξίφει μυριάδας ἑκατὸν
καὶ δέκα διαφθαρῆναί φησιν, τοὺς δὲ λοιποὺς
στασιώδεις καὶ ληστρικούς, ὑπ' ἀλλήλων μετὰ
τὴν ἅλωσιν ἐνδεικνυμένους, ἀνῃρῆσθαι, τῶν δὲ
νέων τοὺς ὑψηλοτάτους καὶ κάλλει σώματος
διαφέροντας τετηρῆσθαι θριάμβῳ, τοῦ δὲ λοιποῦ
πλήθους τοὺς ὑπὲρ ἑπτακαίδεκα ἔτη δεσμίους
εἰς τὰ κατ' Αἴγυπτον ἔργα παραπεμφθῆναι,
πλείους δὲ εἰς τὰς ἐπαρχίας διανενεμῆσθαι φθα-
ρησομένους ἐν τοῖς θεάτροις σιδήρῳ καὶ θηρίοις,
τοὺς δ' ἐντὸς ἑπτακαίδεκα ἐτῶν αἰχμαλώτους
ἀχθέντας διαπεπρᾶσθαι, τούτων δὲ μόνων τὸν
ἀριθμὸν εἰς ἐννέα μυριάδας ἀνδρῶν συναχθῆναι.

Ταῦτα δὲ τοῦτον ἐπράχθη τὸν τρόπον δευτέρῳ **3**
τῆς Οὐεσπασιανοῦ βασιλείας ἔτει ἀκολούθως ταῖς
προγνωστικαῖς τοῦ κυρίου καὶ σωτῆρος ἡμῶν
Ἰησοῦ Χριστοῦ προρρήσεσιν, θείᾳ δυνάμει ὥσπερ
ἤδη παρόντα προεορακότος αὐτὰ ἐπιδακρύσαντός
τε καὶ ἀποκλαυσαμένου κατὰ τὴν τῶν ἱερῶν
εὐαγγελιστῶν γραφήν, οἳ καὶ αὐτὰς αὐτοῦ παρα-
τέθεινται τὰς λέξεις, τοτὲ μὲν φήσαντος ὡς πρὸς
Luke 19, 42–44 αὐτὴν τὴν Ἰερουσαλήμ " εἰ ἔγνως καί γε σὺ ἐν τῇ **4**
ἡμέρᾳ ταύτῃ τὰ πρὸς εἰρήνην σου· νῦν δὲ ἐκρύβη
ἀπὸ ὀφθαλμῶν σου· ὅτι ἥξουσιν ἡμέραι ἐπὶ σέ,
καὶ περιβαλοῦσίν σοι οἱ ἐχθροί σου χάρακα, καὶ
περικυκλώσουσίν σε, καὶ συνέξουσίν σε πάντοθεν,
καὶ ἐδαφιοῦσίν σε καὶ τὰ τέκνα σου," τοτὲ δὲ **5**
Luke 21, 23–24 ὡς περὶ τοῦ λαοῦ " ἔσται γὰρ ἀνάγκη μεγάλη ἐπὶ
τῆς γῆς, καὶ ὀργὴ τῷ λαῷ τούτῳ· καὶ πεσοῦνται
ἐν στόματι μαχαίρας καὶ αἰχμαλωτισθήσονται
εἰς πάντα τὰ ἔθνη· καὶ Ἰερουσαλὴμ ἔσται πα-
τουμένη ὑπὸ ἐθνῶν, ἄχρις οὗ πληρωθῶσιν καιροὶ

of those who were destroyed, says that 1,100,000 perished by famine and the sword, and that the rest of the rebels and bandits were pointed out by one another after the capture of the city and killed. The tallest of the youths, and those distinguished for physical beauty, were kept for a triumph, and of the remaining population those above seventeen years old were sent as prisoners to hard labour in Egypt, but more were distributed throughout the provinces to be destroyed in the theatres by the sword and by wild beasts. Those below seventeen years old were sold into slavery and these alone were 90,000.

These things happened in this way in the second year of the reign of Vespasian in accordance with the prophetic utterances of our Lord and Saviour Jesus Christ, who foreseeing them by divine power as though already present, shed tears at them and mourned according to the writing of the sacred evangelist, who appends his actual words. For once he said to Jerusalem herself, " If thou hadst known, even thou, in this day the things which belong to thy peace : but now they are hid from thine eyes, for the days will come upon thee when thine enemy shall cast a trench around thee and compass thee round and keep thee in on every side, and shall lay thee and thy children even with the ground." And at another time, as if concerning the people, " For there shall be great distress on the earth and wrath upon this people, and they shall fall by the edge of the sword, and be sold into slavery to all the Gentiles, and Jerusalem shall be trodden down by the Gentiles until the times of the Gentiles

ἐθνῶν.'' καὶ πάλιν '' ὅταν δὲ ἴδητε κυκλουμένην ὑπὸ στρατοπέδων τὴν Ἱερουσαλήμ, τότε γνῶτε ὅτι ἤγγικεν ἡ ἐρήμωσις αὐτῆς.'' συγκρίνας δέ 6 τις τὰς τοῦ σωτῆρος ἡμῶν λέξεις ταῖς λοιπαῖς τοῦ συγγραφέως ἱστορίαις ταῖς περὶ τοῦ παντὸς πολέμου, πῶς οὐκ ἂν ἀποθαυμάσειεν, θείαν ὡς ἀληθῶς καὶ ὑπερφυῶς παράδοξον τὴν πρόγνωσιν ὁμοῦ καὶ πρόρρησιν τοῦ σωτῆρος ἡμῶν ὁμολογήσας;

Περὶ μὲν οὖν τῶν μετὰ τὸ σωτήριον πάθος καὶ 7 τὰς φωνὰς ἐκείνας ἐν αἷς ἡ τῶν Ἰουδαίων πληθὺς τὸν μὲν λῃστὴν καὶ φονέα τοῦ θανάτου παρῄτεται, τὸν δ' ἀρχηγὸν τῆς ζωῆς ἐξ αὐτῶν ἱκέτευσεν ἀρθῆναι, τῷ παντὶ συμβεβηκότων ἔθνει, οὐδὲν ἂν δέοι ταῖς ἱστορίαις ἐπιλέγειν, ταῦτα δ' ἂν εἴη δίκαιον ἐπιθεῖναι, ἃ γένοιτ' ἂν παραστατικὰ 8 φιλανθρωπίας τῆς παναγάθου προνοίας, τεσσαράκοντα ἐφ' ὅλοις ἔτεσιν μετὰ τὴν κατὰ τοῦ Χριστοῦ τόλμαν τὸν κατ' αὐτῶν ὄλεθρον ὑπερθεμένης, ἐν ὅσοις τῶν ἀποστόλων καὶ τῶν μαθητῶν πλείους Ἰάκωβός τε αὐτὸς ὁ τῇδε πρῶτος ἐπίσκοπος, τοῦ κυρίου χρηματίζων ἀδελφός, ἔτι τῷ βίῳ περιόντες καὶ ἐπ' αὐτῆς τῆς Ἱεροσολύμων πόλεως τὰς διατριβὰς ποιούμενοι, ἕρκος ὥσπερ ὀχυρώτατον παρέμενον τῷ τόπῳ, τῆς θείας ἐπισκοπῆς εἰς 9 ἔτι τότε μακροθυμούσης, εἰ ἄρα ποτὲ δυνηθεῖεν ἐφ' οἷς ἔδρασαν, μετανοήσαντες συγγνώμης καὶ σωτηρίας τυχεῖν, καὶ πρὸς τῇ τοσαύτῃ μακροθυμίᾳ παραδόξους θεοσημείας τῶν μελλόντων αὐτοῖς μὴ μετανοήσασι συμβήσεσθαι παρασχομένης· ἃ καὶ αὐτὰ μνήμης ἠξιωμένα πρὸς τοῦ δεδηλωμένου συγγραφέως οὐδὲν οἷον τοῖς τῇδε προσιοῦσιν τῇ γραφῇ παραθεῖναι.

218

Luke 21, 20
Luke 23, 18. 19
John 18, 40
Acts 3, 14

be fulfilled." And again, "And when ye see Jerusalem surrounded by armies then know that her desolation is at hand." If anyone compare the words of our Saviour with the other narratives of the historian concerning the whole war, how can he avoid surprise and a confession of the truly divine and supernaturally wonderful character both of the fore-knowledge and of the foretelling of our Saviour ?

There is no necessity to add to the narratives of what happened to the whole nation after the passion of the Saviour and those words in which the multitude of the Jews begged off from death the robber and murderer and besought that the author of Life should be taken from them ; but it would be right to add a possible confirmation of the kindliness of beneficent Providence. For forty whole years it suspended their destruction, after their crime against the Christ, and during all of them many of the apostles and disciples, and James himself, who is called the Lord's brother, the first bishop of the city, still survived in this world. By their dwelling in Jerusalem, they afforded, as it were, a strong protection to the place ; for the government of God had still patience, if haply they might at last by repenting of their deeds, be able to obtain pardon and salvation ; and in addition to such great long-suffering it sent wonderful tokens from God of what would happen to them if they did not repent. These things have been thought worthy of mention by the historian already quoted, and there is nothing better than to append them for the readers of this work.

VIII. Καὶ δὴ λαβὼν ἀνάγνωθι τὰ κατὰ τὴν ἕκτην 1
τῶν Ἱστοριῶν αὐτῷ δεδηλωμένα ἐν τούτοις.

Joseph. B.I.
6, 288-304

"Τὸν γοῦν ἄθλιον δῆμον οἱ μὲν ἀπατεῶνες
καὶ καταψευδόμενοι τοῦ θεοῦ τηνικαῦτα παρ-
έπειθον, τοῖς δ' ἐναργέσι καὶ προσημαίνουσι τὴν
μέλλουσαν ἐρημίαν τέρασιν οὔτε προσεῖχον οὔτ'
ἐπίστευον, ἀλλ' ὡς ἐμβεβροντημένοι καὶ μήτε
ὄμματα μήτε ψυχὴν ἔχοντες τῶν τοῦ θεοῦ κη-
ρυγμάτων παρήκουον, τοῦτο μὲν ὅθ' ὑπὲρ τὴν 2
πόλιν ἄστρον ἔστη ῥομφαίᾳ παραπλήσιον καὶ
παρατείνας ἐπ' ἐνιαυτὸν κομήτης, τοῦτο δ' ἡνίκα
πρὸ τῆς ἀποστάσεως καὶ τοῦ πρὸς τὸν πόλεμον
κινήματος, ἀθροιζομένου τοῦ λαοῦ πρὸς τὴν τῶν
ἀζύμων ἑορτήν, ὀγδόῃ Ξανθικοῦ μηνὸς κατὰ
νυκτὸς ἐνάτην ὥραν, τοσοῦτον φῶς περιέλαμψεν
τὸν βωμὸν καὶ τὸν ναόν, ὡς δοκεῖν ἡμέραν
εἶναι λαμπράν, καὶ τοῦτο παρέτεινεν ἐφ' ἡμίσειαν
ὥραν· ὃ τοῖς μὲν ἀπείροις ἀγαθὸν ἐδόκει εἶναι,
τοῖς δὲ ἱερογραμματεῦσι πρὸ τῶν ἀποβεβηκότων
εὐθέως ἐκρίθη. καὶ κατὰ τὴν αὐτὴν ἑορτὴν 3
βοῦς μὲν ἀχθεῖσα ὑπὸ τοῦ ἀρχιερέως πρὸς τὴν
θυσίαν ἔτεκεν ἄρνα ἐν τῷ ἱερῷ μέσῳ· ἡ δ' ἀνα- 4
τολικὴ πύλη τοῦ ἐνδοτέρω χαλκῆ μὲν οὖσα καὶ
στιβαρωτάτη, κλειομένη δὲ περὶ δείλην μόλις
ὑπ' ἀνθρώπων εἴκοσι, καὶ μοχλοῖς μὲν ἐπερει-
δομένη σιδηροδέτοις, καταπῆγας δ' ἔχουσα βα-
θυτάτους, ὤφθη κατὰ νυκτὸς ὥραν ἕκτην αὐτο-
μάτως ἠνοιγμένη. μετὰ δὲ τὴν ἑορτὴν ἡμέραις 5
οὐ πολλαῖς ὕστερον, μιᾷ καὶ εἰκάδι Ἀρτεμισίου
μηνός, φάσμα τι δαιμόνιον ὤφθη μεῖζον πίστεως,
τέρας δ' ἂν ἔδοξεν εἶναι τὸ ῥηθησόμενον, εἰ μὴ
καὶ παρὰ τοῖς θεασαμένοις ἱστόρητο καὶ τὰ

VIII. Take, then, and read what is related in the sixth book of the *Jewish War*. " Now at that time impostors and lying prophets perverted the miserable people, but they gave neither attention nor credence to the clear marvels which foretold approaching desolation, but as though they had been thunderstruck and had neither eyes nor soul, they neglected the declarations of God. At one time a star stood over the city like a sword, and a comet which lasted for a year. At another time, before the insurrection, and the disturbance which led to the war, when the people were assembled for the Feast of Unleavened Bread, on the eighth of April, at the ninth hour of the night, a light shone on the altar and on the temple so brightly that it seemed to be full day, and this lasted for half an hour. To the inexperienced this seemed a good sign, but was at once interpreted by the scribes before the events which actually followed. And at the same feast a cow, which had been led by the high-priest for the sacrifice, gave birth to a lamb in the middle of the temple. And the eastern gate of the inner building, which was of bronze and very massive and was closed at evening time with difficulty by twenty men, and rested on beams bound with iron and had bars sunk deep, was seen at night at the sixth hour to have opened of itself. And after the feast, not many days later, on the twenty-first of May, a demonic phantom appeared of incredible size, and what will be related would have seemed a fairy-tale had it not been told by those who saw it, and been attended by suffering

ἐπακολουθήσαντα πάθη τῶν σημείων ἦν ἄξια·
πρὸ γὰρ ἡλίου δύσεως ὤφθη μετέωρα περὶ πᾶσαν
τὴν χώραν ἅρματα καὶ φάλαγγες ἔνοπλοι δι-
ᾴττουσαι τῶν νεφῶν καὶ κυκλούμεναι τὰς πόλεις.
κατὰ δὲ τὴν ἑορτήν, ἣ πεντηκοστὴ καλεῖται, 6
νύκτωρ οἱ ἱερεῖς παρελθόντες εἰς τὸ ἱερόν, ὥσπερ
αὐτοῖς ἔθος ἦν, πρὸς τὰς λειτουργίας, πρῶτον
μὲν κινήσεως ἔφασαν ἀντιλαμβάνεσθαι καὶ κτύπου,
μετὰ δὲ ταῦτα φωνῆς ἀθρόας ' μεταβαίνομεν
ἐντεῦθεν.' [1] τὸ δὲ τούτων φοβερώτερον, Ἰησοῦς 7
γάρ τις ὄνομα, υἱὸς Ἀνανίου, τῶν ἰδιωτῶν,
ἄγροικος, πρὸ τεσσάρων ἐτῶν τοῦ πολέμου, τὰ
μάλιστα τῆς πόλεως εἰρηνευομένης καὶ εὐθηνού-
σης, ἐλθὼν ἐπὶ τὴν ἑορτήν, ἐπεὶ σκηνοποιεῖσθαι
πάντας ἔθος ἦν τῷ θεῷ, κατὰ τὸ ἱερὸν ἐξαπίνης
ἀναβοᾶν ἤρξατο ' φωνὴ ἀπ' ἀνατολῆς, φωνὴ ἀπὸ
δύσεως, φωνὴ ἀπὸ τῶν τεσσάρων ἀνέμων, φωνὴ
ἐπὶ Ἱεροσόλυμα καὶ τὸν ναόν, φωνὴ ἐπὶ νυμφίους
καὶ νύμφας, φωνὴ ἐπὶ πάντα τὸν λαόν.' τοῦτο
μεθ' ἡμέραν καὶ νύκτωρ κατὰ πάντας τοὺς στε-
νωποὺς περιῄει κεκραγώς. τῶν δ' ἐπισήμων 8
τινὲς δημοτῶν ἀγανακτήσαντες πρὸς τὸ κακό-
φημον, συλλαμβάνουσι τὸν ἄνθρωπον καὶ πολλαῖς
αἰκίζονται πληγαῖς· ὃ δ' οὔθ' ὑπὲρ ἑαυτοῦ φθεγ-
ξάμενος οὔτε ἰδίᾳ πρὸς τοὺς παρόντας, ἃς καὶ
πρότερον φωνὰς βοῶν διετέλει. νομίσαντες δ' 9
οἱ ἄρχοντες, ὅπερ ἦν, δαιμονιώτερον εἶναι τὸ
κίνημα τἀνδρός, ἀνάγουσιν αὐτὸν ἐπὶ τὸν παρὰ
Ῥωμαίοις ἔπαρχον· ἔνθα μάστιξιν μέχρις ὀστέων
ξαινόμενος οὔθ' ἱκέτευσεν οὔτ' ἐδάκρυσεν, ἀλλ'

---

[1] Cf. Eus. *Dem. evangel.* viii. 2. 121 and *Eccl. prophet.*
164. 2–6.

worthy of the portent. For before sunset there appeared in the air over the whole country chariots and armed troops coursing through the clouds and surrounding the cities. And at the feast called Pentecost the priests passed into the temple at night, as was their custom, for their services, and said that they first perceived movement and noise and after that a sudden cry, ' We go hence.' But what was more terrible a man of the people named Jesus, the son of Ananias, a countryman, four years before the war, when the city was in complete peace and prosperity, came to the feast when it was the custom for all to make booths for God, and began suddenly to cry out opposite the temple, ' A voice from the east, a voice from the west, a voice from the four winds, a voice against Jerusalem and the temple, a voice against bridegrooms and brides, a voice against all the people.' With this cry night and day he passed through all the narrow streets. But some of the notables of the people were annoyed at the ill omen, seized the man and abused him with many stripes. But he uttered no word in his own behalf, nor in private to those present, but went on with the same cry as before. But the rulers thought that the man's action was inspired by some demon, as it indeed was, and brought him to the Roman governor[1]; there, though he was flayed to the bone with scourges, he uttered no plea and shed no tear, but raising his

---

[1] That is, Albinus who was procurator from 61 to 64.

ὡς ἐνῆν μάλιστα τὴν φωνὴν ὀλοφυρτικῶς παρεγ-
κλίνων, πρὸς ἑκάστην ἀπεκρίνατο πληγήν ' αἶ αἶ
Ἱεροσολύμοις.¹ ''

Joseph. B.I.
6, 312. 313

Ἕτερον δ' ἔτι τούτου παραδοξότερον ὁ αὐτὸς
ἱστορεῖ, χρησμόν τινα φάσκων ἐν ἱεροῖς γράμμασιν
εὑρῆσθαι περιέχοντα ὡς κατὰ τὸν καιρὸν ἐκεῖνον
ἀπὸ τῆς χώρας τις αὐτῶν ἄρξει τῆς οἰκουμένης,
ὃν αὐτὸς μὲν ἐπὶ Οὐεσπασιανὸν πεπληρῶσθαι
ἐξείληφεν· ἀλλ' οὐχ ἁπάσης γε οὗτος ἀλλ' ἢ
μόνης ἦρξεν τῆς ὑπὸ Ῥωμαίους· δικαιότερον δ'
ἂν ἐπὶ τὸν Χριστὸν ἀναχθείη, πρὸς ὃν εἴρητο ὑπὸ

Ps. 2, 8

τοῦ πατρὸς '' αἴτησαι παρ' ἐμοῦ, καὶ δώσω σοι
ἔθνη τὴν κληρονομίαν σου, καὶ τὴν κατάσχεσίν
σου τὰ πέρατα τῆς γῆς,'' οὗ δὴ κατ' αὐτὸ δὴ

Ps. 18, 5

ἐκεῖνο τοῦ καιροῦ '' εἰς πᾶσαν τὴν γῆν ἐξῆλθεν ὁ
φθόγγος '' τῶν ἱερῶν ἀποστόλων '' καὶ εἰς τὰ
πέρατα τῆς οἰκουμένης τὰ ῥήματα αὐτῶν.''

IX. Ἐπὶ τούτοις ἅπασιν ἄξιον μηδ' αὐτὸν

---

¹ After Ἱεροσολύμοις the text of Josephus adds τοῦ δὲ ἀλβίνου
διερωτῶντοσ· οὗτος γὰρ ἔπαρχοσ ἦν· τίσ εἴη καὶ πόθεν καὶ διατί
ταῦτα φθέγγοιτο· πρὸς ταῦτα μὲν οὐδ' ὅτι οὖν ἀπεκρίνατο· τὸν
δὲ ἐπὶ τῇ πόλει θρῆνον εἴρων οὐ διέλιπεν μέχρι καταγνοὺς μανίαν
ὁ ἀλβίνος ἀπέλυσεν αὐτόν · ὁ δὲ τὸν μέχρι τοῦ πολέμου χρόνον·
οὔτε προσήει τινὶ τῶν πολιτῶν οὔτε ὤφθη λαλῶν· ἀλλὰ καθημέραν
ὥσπερ εὐχὴν μεμελετηκὼσ· αἶ αἶ ἱεροσολύμοισ ἐθρήνει· οὔτε δέ
τινι τῶν τυπτόντων αὐτῶν ὁσήμεραι κατηρᾶτο οὔτε τοὺς τροφῆσ
μεταδιδόντασ εὐλόγει. μία δὲ πρὸς πάντασ ἦν ἡ σκυθρωπὴ κληδὼν
ἀπόκρισισ. μάλιστα δὲ ἐν ταῖς ἑορταῖς ἐκεκράγει· καὶ τοῦτο
ἐφεπτὰ ἔτη καὶ μῆνασ πέντε εἴρων. οὔτε ἠμβλύνθη τὴν φωνὴν
οὔτε ἔκαμεν μέχρισ οὗ κατὰ τὴν πολιορκίαν ἔργωι τὰς κληδόνασ
ἰδὼν ἀνεπαύσατο. περιιὼν γὰρ ἐπὶ τοῦ τείχουσ αἶ αἶ πάλιν τῇ
πόλει καὶ τῷ λαῷ καὶ τῷ ναῷ διαπρύσιον ἐβόα. ὡς δὲ τελευταῖον
προσέθηκεν αἶ αἶ κἀμοὶ λίθοσ ἐκ τοῦ πετροβόλου σχασθεὶσ καὶ
πλήξασ αὐτόν, παραχρῆμα κτείνει. φθεγγομένην δὲ ἔτι τὰσ
κληδόνασ ἐκείνασ τὴν ψυχὴν ἀφῆκεν. This is also found in two
late mss. (ER) of Eusebius.

224

voice with all his power, answered to every blow, 'Woe, woe to Jerusalem.'"[1]

The same writer has a still more remarkable account in which he alleges that an oracle was found in "sacred script" to the effect that at that time one from their country should rule the world and he himself considered that this was fulfilled by Vespasian. Yet he did not reign over the whole world, but only such part as was subject to the Romans, and it would be more justly referred to Christ, to whom it was said by the Father, "Ask of me and I will give thee the heathen for thine inheritance and the ends of the earth for thy possession." And it was of his holy apostles at that very time that "the sound went forth into all the earth and their words unto the end of the earth."

IX. In addition to all this, it is right not to ignore

[1] Two late manuscripts make the following additions from Josephus. "And when Albinus, for he was governor, asked him who he was and whence he came and why he said these things, he made no answer but did not cease raising his lamentation against the city until Albinus considered him mad and let him go. Until the time of the war he neither approached any of the citizens nor was he seen talking, but daily, as though reciting a prayer, he wailed 'Woe, woe to Jerusalem.' He never cursed those who struck him daily, nor did he bless those who gave him food, but all received the same melancholy wail as an answer. He howled with especial vigour on feast days, and this he kept up for seven years and five months, nor did his voice fail or grow weary until at the siege he rested, seeing his lamentations fulfilled. For he went round on the wall with the piercing cry, 'Woe, woe to the people, to the city, and to the temple,' and as at last he added 'Woe, woe to me also,' a stone flew out from a catapult and hit him; he died at once, and gave up his soul still uttering those lamentations."

τὸν Ἰώσηπον, τοσαῦτα τῇ μετὰ χεῖρας συμβε-
βλημένον ἱστορίᾳ, ὁπόθεν τε καὶ ἀφ' οἵου γένους
ὡρμᾶτο, ἀγνοεῖν. δηλοῖ δὲ πάλιν αὐτὸς καὶ

Joseph. B.I.
1, 3 τοῦτο, λέγων ὧδε '' Ἰώσηπος Ματθίου παῖς,
ἐξ Ἱεροσολύμων ἱερεύς, αὐτός τε Ῥωμαίους
πολεμήσας τὰ πρῶτα καὶ τοῖς ὕστερον παρατυχὼν
ἐξ ἀνάγκης.'' μάλιστα δὲ τῶν κατ' ἐκεῖνο καιροῦ 2
Ἰουδαίων οὐ παρὰ μόνοις τοῖς ὁμοεθνέσιν, ἀλλὰ
καὶ παρὰ Ῥωμαίοις γέγονεν ἀνὴρ ἐπιδοξότατος,
ὡς αὐτὸν μὲν ἀναθέσει ἀνδριάντος ἐπὶ τῆς Ῥωμαίων τιμηθῆναι πόλεως, τοὺς δὲ σπουδασθέντας
αὐτῷ λόγους βιβλιοθήκης ἀξιωθῆναι. οὗτος δὴ 3
πᾶσαν τὴν Ἰουδαϊκὴν ἀρχαιολογίαν ἐν ὅλοις
εἴκοσι κατατέθειται συγγράμμασιν, τὴν δ' ἱστορίαν τοῦ κατ' αὐτὸν Ῥωμαϊκοῦ πολέμου ἐν ἑπτά,

Joseph. B.I.
1, 3 ἃ καὶ οὐ μόνον τῇ Ἑλλήνων, ἀλλὰ καὶ τῇ πατρίῳ
φωνῇ παραδοῦναι αὐτὸς ἑαυτῷ μαρτυρεῖ, ἄξιός
γε ὢν διὰ τὰ λοιπὰ πιστεύεσθαι· καὶ ἕτερα δ' 4
αὐτοῦ φέρεται σπουδῆς ἄξια δύο, τὰ Περὶ τῆς
Ἰουδαίων ἀρχαιότητος, ἐν οἷς καὶ ἀντιρρήσεις
πρὸς Ἀπίωνα τὸν γραμματικόν, κατὰ Ἰουδαίων
τηνικάδε συντάξαντα λόγον, πεποίηται καὶ πρὸς
ἄλλους, οἳ διαβάλλειν καὶ αὐτοὶ τὰ πάτρια τοῦ
Ἰουδαίων ἔθνους ἐπειράθησαν. τούτων ἐν τῷ 5
προτέρῳ τὸν ἀριθμὸν τῆς λεγομένης παλαιᾶς
τῶν ἐνδιαθήκων γραφῶν τίθησι, τίνα τὰ παρ'
Ἑβραίοις ἀναντίρρητα, ὡς ἂν ἐξ ἀρχαίας παραδόσεως αὐτοῖς ῥήμασι διὰ τούτων διδάσκων.

Joseph. C.
Apion. 1, 38–
42 X. '' Οὐ μυριάδες οὖν βιβλίων εἰσὶ παρ' ἡμῖν
ἀσυμφώνων καὶ μαχομένων, δύο δὲ μόνα πρὸς
τοῖς εἴκοσι βιβλία, τοῦ παντὸς ἔχοντα χρόνου
τὴν ἀναγραφήν, τὰ δικαίως θεῖα πεπιστευμένα.

226

the date and origin of the Josephus who collected so much material in the work just dealt with. He himself gives this information and says, " Josephus was a son of Matthias, a priest of Jerusalem, and at the beginning he fought against the Romans and was forced to take part in the later events." He was the most famous Jew of that time, not only among his fellow countrymen but also among the Romans, so that he was honoured by the erection of a statue in the city of Rome, and the inclusion of the works composed by him in its library   He compiled the whole ancient history of the Jews in twenty volumes,[1] and the history of the Roman War[2] in his own time in seven ; he testifies that he committed this not only to Greek but also to his native language, and he is for other reasons worthy of credence. Two other books of his, worthy of notice, are extant, entitled *On the ancientness of the Jews*,[3] in which he controverts Apion the Scribe, who had composed a treatise against the Jews, and others who had tried to calumniate the ancestral customs of the Jewish nation.   In the first of these he gives the number of the canonical scriptures of the so-called Old Testament, and showed as follows which are undisputed among the Hebrews as belonging to ancient tradition.

X. " We have no myriads of discordant and contradictory books, but only two and twenty, containing the narrative of all time, which have been justly believed to be divine.   Of these five are those of

---

[1] Usually quoted as " Antiquities," from the Latin rendering of ἀρχαιολογία by *antiquitates*.

[2] Usually known as the " Wars " or the " Jewish war " and often quoted as *B.I.* (*bellum iudaicum*).

[3] Usually known as *Contra Apionem*.

καὶ τούτων πέντε μέν ἐστιν Μωυσέως, ἃ τούς 2
τε νόμους περιέχει καὶ τὴν τῆς ἀνθρωπογονίας
παράδοσιν μέχρι τῆς αὐτοῦ τελευτῆς· οὗτος ὁ
χρόνος ἀπολείπει τρισχιλίων ὀλίγον ἐτῶν· ἀπὸ 3
δὲ τῆς Μωυσέως τελευτῆς μέχρι τῆς Ἀρταξέρξου
τοῦ μετὰ Ξέρξην Περσῶν βασιλέως οἱ μετὰ
Μωυσῆν προφῆται τὰ κατ' αὐτοὺς πραχθέντα
συνέγραψαν ἐν τρισὶν καὶ δέκα βιβλίοις· αἱ δὲ
λοιπαὶ τέσσαρες ὕμνους εἰς τὸν θεὸν καὶ τοῖς
ἀνθρώποις ὑποθήκας τοῦ βίου περιέχουσιν. ἀπὸ
δὲ Ἀρταξέρξου μέχρι τοῦ καθ' ἡμᾶς χρόνου
γέγραπται μὲν ἕκαστα, πίστεως δ' οὐχ ὁμοίας
ἠξίωται τοῖς πρὸ αὐτῶν διὰ τὸ μὴ γενέσθαι τὴν
τῶν προφητῶν ἀκριβῆ διαδοχήν. δῆλον δ' ἐστὶν
ἔργῳ πῶς ἡμεῖς πρόσιμεν τοῖς ἰδίοις γράμμασιν·
τοσούτου γὰρ αἰῶνος ἤδη παρῳχηκότος οὔτε
προσθεῖναί τις οὔτε ἀφελεῖν ἀπ' αὐτῶν οὔτε
μεταθεῖναι τετόλμηκεν, πᾶσι δὲ σύμφυτόν ἐστιν
εὐθὺς ἐκ πρώτης γενέσεως Ἰουδαίοις τὸ νομίζειν
αὐτὰ θεοῦ δόγματα καὶ τούτοις ἐπιμένειν καὶ
ὑπὲρ αὐτῶν, εἰ δέοι, θνήσκειν ἡδέως." καὶ
ταῦτα δὲ τοῦ συγγραφέως χρησίμως ὧδε παρα-
τεθείσθω. πεπόνηται δὲ καὶ ἄλλο οὐκ ἀγεννὲς
σπούδασμα τῷ ἀνδρί, Περὶ αὐτοκράτορος λογισμοῦ, ὅ τινες Μακκαβαϊκὸν ἐπέγραψαν τῷ τοὺς
ἀγῶνας τῶν ἐν τοῖς οὕτω καλουμένοις Μακκα-
βαϊκοῖς συγγράμμασιν ὑπὲρ τῆς εἰς τὸ θεῖον
εὐσεβείας ἀνδρισαμένων Ἑβραίων περιέχειν, καὶ
Joseph. A.I.
20, 268 πρὸς τῷ τέλει δὲ τῆς εἰκοστῆς Ἀρχαιολογίας
ἐπισημαίνεται ὁ αὐτὸς ὡς ἂν προῃρημένος ἐν
τέτταρσιν συγγράψαι βιβλίοις κατὰ τὰς πατρίους
δόξας τῶν Ἰουδαίων περὶ θεοῦ καὶ τῆς οὐσίας

Moses and contain the Law and the tradition of human history until his death. This period covers almost three thousand years. From the death of Moses to Artaxerxes who succeeded Xerxes, king of the Persians, the prophets after Moses wrote the account of the events contemporary with them in thirteen books.[1] The remaining four books contain hymns to God and precepts for the life of men. From the time of Artaxerxes to our own the details have been written,[2] but are not considered worthy of equal credence with the rest because there has not been an accurate succession of prophets. And facts show plainly how we approach our own literature, for though so long a time has elapsed no one has dared to make additions, omissions, or changes, but it is innate in Jews from their very birth to regard them as the decrees of God, to abide in them and, if it need be, to die for them gladly." This quotation from the author may be usefully appended.

Another work which is not without merit was produced by him on *The Supremacy of Reason*, which some entitled *Maccabees* [3] because it contains the conflicts of those Hebrews mentioned in the so-called books of the Maccabees, who strove valiantly for the worship of God. At the end of the twentieth book of the *Antiquities* the same writer announces that he had planned to compose four books on the ancestral belief of the Jews concerning God and his nature and

---

[1] Josephus does not state which these are. Probably he means Joshua, Judges and Ruth, 1 and 2 Sam., 1 and 2 Kings, 1 and 2 Chron., Ezra and Neh., Esther, Isaiah, Jer. and Lam., Ezek., Dan., the minor prophets, Job. The "remaining four books" would be Pss., Prov., Eccl., and the Song of Songs.

[2] He means 1 Maccabees and perhaps 2 Maccabees.

[3] 4 Maccabees.

αὐτοῦ καὶ περὶ τῶν νόμων, διὰ τί κατ' αὐτοὺς
τὰ μὲν ἔξεστι πράττειν, τὰ δὲ κεκώλυται, καὶ
ἄλλα δὲ αὐτῷ σπουδασθῆναι ὁ αὐτὸς ἐν τοῖς
ἰδίοις αὐτοῦ μνημονεύει λόγοις.   πρὸς τούτοις 8
εὔλογον καταλέξαι καὶ ἃς ἐπ' αὐτοῦ τῆς
'Αρχαιολογίας τοῦ τέλους φωνὰς παρατέθειται,
εἰς πίστωσιν τῆς τῶν ἐξ αὐτοῦ παραληφθέντων
ἡμῖν μαρτυρίας.   διαβάλλων δῆτα 'Ιοῦστον Τιβε-
ριέα, ὁμοίως αὐτῷ τὰ κατὰ τοὺς αὐτοὺς
ἱστορῆσαι χρόνους πεπειραμένον, ὡς μὴ τἀληθῆ
συγγεγραφότα, πολλάς τε ἄλλας εὐθύνας ἐπαγαγὼν
τῷ ἀνδρί, ταῦτα αὐτοῖς ῥήμασιν ἐπιλέγει " οὐ 9
μὴν ἐγώ σοι τὸν αὐτὸν τρόπον περὶ τῆς ἐμαυτοῦ
γραφῆς ἔδεισα, ἀλλ' αὐτοῖς ἐπέδωκα τοῖς αὐτοκρά-
τορσι τὰ βιβλία, μόνον οὐ τῶν ἔργων ἤδη βλεπομέ-
νων· συνήδειν γὰρ ἐμαυτῷ τετηρηκότι τὴν τῆς
ἀληθείας παράδοσιν, ἐφ' ᾗ μαρτυρίας τεύξεσθαι
προσδοκήσας οὐ διήμαρτον.   καὶ ἄλλοις δὲ πολλοῖς
ἐπέδωκα τὴν ἱστορίαν, ὧν ἔνιοι καὶ παρατετεύχεσαν
τῷ πολέμῳ, καθάπερ βασιλεὺς 'Αγρίππας καί τινες
αὐτοῦ τῶν συγγενῶν.   ὁ μὲν γὰρ αὐτοκράτωρ
Τίτος οὕτως ἐκ μόνων αὐτῶν ἐβουλήθη τὴν γνῶσιν
τοῖς ἀνθρώποις παραδοῦναι τῶν πράξεων, ὥστε
χαράξας τῇ αὐτοῦ χειρὶ τὰ βιβλία δημοσιῶσαι
προσέταξεν, ὁ δὲ βασιλεὺς 'Αγρίππας ξβ ἔγραψεν
ἐπιστολάς, τῇ τῆς ἀληθείας παραδόσει μαρτυρῶν."

'Αφ' ὧν καὶ δύο παρατίθησιν.   ἀλλὰ τὰ μὲν κατὰ
τοῦτον ταύτῃ πῃ δεδηλώσθω.

XI. "Ιωμεν δ' ἐπὶ τὰ ἑξῆς.   μετὰ τὴν 'Ιακώβου
μαρτυρίαν καὶ τὴν αὐτίκα γενομένην ἅλωσιν τῆς
'Ιερουσαλὴμ λόγος κατέχει τῶν ἀποστόλων καὶ τῶν
τοῦ κυρίου μαθητῶν τοὺς εἰς ἔτι τῷ βίῳ λειπομένους

Left margin notes:

Joseph. A.I.
1, 25. 29 ; 3,
94. 143 ; 4,
198 ; B.I. 5,
237. 247; A.I.
20, 267

Joseph. De
vita sua, 361-
364

concerning the Laws, why they allow some actions and forbid others. He also mentions in his own treatises that he had produced other works. Moreover, it is right to mention the words which he appends to the end of the *Antiquities* to confirm our quotation of the passages taken from him. Accusing of false statements Justus of Tiberias, who had undertaken to write a similar account of the same period, and bringing many other charges against him, he continues as follows : " I had no such fear as you with regard to my own writing, but I gave the books to the Emperors themselves while the events were still almost before their eyes. For I was conscious of having kept the tradition of the truth and I did not fail in my expectation of obtaining their testimony to that effect. I also gave the narrative to many others, of whom some had actually taken part in the war, such as King Agrippa and some of his relations. For the Emperor Titus was pleased that from these books alone should information be given the public as to the events, and, writing with his own hand, he ordered the books to be published, and King Agrippa wrote sixty-two letters testifying that they were handing on the truth." Of these letters he appends two, but let this suffice on the subject of Josephus and let us proceed.

XI. After the martyrdom of James and the capture of Jerusalem which immediately followed, the story goes that those of the Apostles and of the disciples of the Lord who were still alive came together from

ἐπὶ ταὐτὸν πανταχόθεν συνελθεῖν ἅμα τοῖς πρὸς
γένους κατὰ σάρκα τοῦ κυρίου (πλείους γὰρ καὶ
τούτων περιῆσαν εἰς ἔτι τότε τῷ βίῳ), βουλήν τε
ὁμοῦ τοὺς πάντας περὶ τοῦ τίνα χρὴ τῆς Ἰακώβου
διαδοχῆς ἐπικρῖναι ἄξιον, ποιήσασθαι, καὶ δὴ ἀπὸ
Luke 24, 18
John 19, 25
μιᾶς γνώμης τοὺς πάντας Συμεῶνα τὸν τοῦ Κλωπᾶ,
οὗ καὶ ἡ τοῦ εὐαγγελίου μνημονεύει γραφή, τοῦ τῆς
αὐτόθι παροικίας θρόνου ἄξιον εἶναι δοκιμάσαι,
ἀνεψιόν, ὥς γέ φασι, γεγονότα τοῦ σωτῆρος, τὸν γὰρ
οὖν Κλωπᾶν ἀδελφὸν τοῦ Ἰωσὴφ ὑπάρχειν Ἡγήσιππος ἱστορεῖ, XII. καὶ ἐπὶ τούτοις Οὐεσπα- 1
σιανὸν μετὰ τὴν τῶν Ἱεροσολύμων ἅλωσιν πάντας
τοὺς ἀπὸ γένους Δαυίδ, ὡς μὴ περιλειφθείη τις
παρὰ Ἰουδαίοις τῶν ἀπὸ τῆς βασιλικῆς φυλῆς,
ἀναζητεῖσθαι προστάξαι, μέγιστόν τε Ἰουδαίοις
αὖθις ἐκ ταύτης διωγμὸν ἐπαρτηθῆναι τῆς αἰτίας.

XIII. Ἐπὶ δέκα δὲ τὸν Οὐεσπασιανὸν ἔτεσιν 1
βασιλεύσαντα αὐτοκράτωρ Τίτος ὁ παῖς διαδέ-
χεται· οὗ κατὰ δεύτερον ἔτος τῆς βασιλείας Λίνος
ἐπίσκοπος τῆς Ῥωμαίων ἐκκλησίας δυοκαίδεκα τὴν
λειτουργίαν ἐνιαυτοῖς κατασχών, Ἀνεγκλήτῳ
ταύτην παραδίδωσιν.

Τίτον δὲ Δομετιανὸς ἀδελφὸς διαδέχεται, δύο
ἔτεσι καὶ μησὶ τοῖς ἴσοις βασιλεύσαντα. XIV.
τετάρτῳ μὲν οὖν ἔτει Δομετιανοῦ τῆς κατ' Ἀλεξάνδρειαν παροικίας ὁ πρῶτος Ἀννιανὸς δύο πρὸς τοῖς
εἴκοσι ἀποπλήσας ἔτη, τελευτᾷ, διαδέχεται δ' αὐτὸν
δεύτερος Ἀβίλιος. XV. δωδεκάτῳ δὲ ἔτει τῆς
αὐτῆς ἡγεμονίας τῆς Ῥωμαίων ἐκκλησίας Ἀνέγ-
κλητον ἔτεσιν ἐπισκοπεύσαντα δεκαδύο διαδέχεται
Κλήμης, ὃν συνεργὸν ἑαυτοῦ γενέσθαι Φιλιππησίοις
Phil. 4, 8
ἐπιστέλλων ὁ ἀπόστολος διδάσκει, λέγων '' μετὰ

every place with those who were, humanly speaking, of the family of the Lord, for many of them were then still alive, and they all took counsel together as to whom they ought to adjudge worthy to succeed James, and all unanimously decided that Simeon the son of Clopas, whom the scripture of the Gospel also mentions, was worthy of the throne of the diocese there. He was, so it is said, a cousin of the Saviour, for Hegesippus relates that Clopas was the brother of Joseph, (XII.) and in addition that Vespasian, after the capture of Jerusalem, ordered a search to be made for all who were of the family of David, that there might be left among the Jews no one of the royal family and, for this reason, a very great persecution was again inflicted on the Jews.

XIII. When Vespasian had reigned for ten years, his son Titus succeeded him as emperor,[1] and in the second year of his reign, Linus, bishop of the church of the Romans, after holding his office for twelve years, handed it on to Anencletus. After Titus had reigned for two years and as many months Domitian, his brother, succeeded him.[2] XIV. Now in the fourth year of Domitian, Annianus, the first of the see of Alexandria, died after completing twenty-two years, and Abilius succeeded him as the second. XV. And in the twelfth year of the same reign, Clement succeeded Anencletus after he had been bishop of the church of the Romans for twelve years. The apostle states that he had been his fellow-worker in his epistle to the Philippians saying, " With Clement and

---

[1] June 24, A.D. 79.
[2] Dec. 13, A.D. 81.

καὶ Κλήμεντος καὶ τῶν λοιπῶν συνεργῶν μου, ὧν τὰ ὀνόματα ἐν βίβλῳ ζωῆς."

XVI. Τούτου δὴ οὖν ὁμολογουμένη μία ἐπιστολὴ 1 φέρεται, μεγάλη τε καὶ θαυμασία, ἣν ὡς ἀπὸ τῆς Ῥωμαίων ἐκκλησ'ας τῇ Κορινθίων διετυπώσατο, στάσεως τηνικάδε κατὰ τὴν Κόρινθον γενομένης. ταύτην δὲ καὶ ἐν πλείσταις ἐκκλησίαις ἐπὶ τοῦ κοινοῦ δεδημοσιευμένην πάλαι τε καὶ καθ' ἡμᾶς αὐτοὺς ἔγνωμεν. καὶ ὅτι γε κατὰ τὸν δηλούμενον τὰ τῆς Κορινθίων κεκίνητο στάσεως, ἀξιόχρεως μάρτυς ὁ Ἡγήσιππος.

XVII. Πολλήν γε μὴν εἰς πολλοὺς ἐπιδειξάμενος ὁ 1 Δομετιανὸς ὠμότητα οὐκ ὀλίγον τε τῶν ἐπὶ Ῥώμης εὐπατριδῶν τε καὶ ἐπισήμων ἀνδρῶν πλῆθος οὐ μετ' εὐλόγου κρίσεως κτείνας μυρίους τε ἄλλους ἐπιφανεῖς ἄνδρας ταῖς ὑπὲρ τὴν ἐνορίαν ζημιώσας φυγαῖς καὶ ταῖς τῶν οὐσιῶν ἀποβολαῖς ἀναιτίως, τελευτῶν τῆς Νέρωνος θεοεχθρίας τε καὶ θεομαχίας διάδοχον ἑαυτὸν κατεστήσατο. δεύτερος δῆτα τὸν καθ' ἡμῶν ἀνεκίνει διωγμόν, καίπερ τοῦ πατρὸς αὐτῷ Οὐεσπασιανοῦ μηδὲν καθ' ἡμῶν ἄτοπον ἐπινοήσαντος.

XVIII. Ἐν τούτῳ κατέχει λόγος τὸν ἀπόστολον 1 ἅμα καὶ εὐαγγελιστὴν Ἰωάννην ἔτι τῷ βίῳ ἐνδιατρίβοντα, τῆς εἰς τὸν θεῖον λόγον ἕνεκεν μαρτυρίας Πάτμον οἰκεῖν καταδικασθῆναι τὴν νῆσον. γράφων 2 γέ τοι ὁ Εἰρηναῖος περὶ τῆς ψήφου τῆς κατὰ τὸν ἀντίχριστον προσηγορίας φερομένης ἐν τῇ Ἰωάννου λεγομένῃ Ἀποκαλύψει, αὐταῖς συλλαβαῖς ἐν πέμπτῳ τῶν πρὸς τὰς αἱρέσεις ταῦτα περὶ τοῦ Ἰωάννου φησίν " εἰ δὲ ἔδει ἀναφανδὸν ἐν τῷ νῦν καιρῷ 3 κηρύττεσθαι τοὔνομα αὐτοῦ, δι' ἐκείνου ἂν ἐρρέθη

Rev. 13, 18

Iren. 5, 30. 3

my other fellow-workers whose names are in the book of Life."

XVI. There is one recognized epistle of Clement, long and wonderful, which he drew up for the church of the Corinthians in the name of the church of the Romans when there had been dissension in Corinth. We have ascertained that this letter was publicly read in the common assembly in many churches both in the days of old and in our own time ; and that the affairs of Corinth were disturbed by dissension in his day is adequately testified to by Hegesippus.

XVII. When Domitian had given many proofs of his great cruelty and had put to death without any reasonable trial no small number of men distinguished at Rome by family and career, and had punished without a cause myriads of other notable men by banishment and confiscation of their property, he finally showed himself the successor of Nero's campaign of hostility to God. He was the second to promote persecution against us, though his father, Vespasian, had planned no evil against us.

XVIII. At this time, the story goes, the Apostle and Evangelist John was still alive, and was condemned to live in the island of Patmos for his witness to the divine word. At any rate Irenaeus, writing about the number of the name ascribed to the anti-Christ in the so-called Apocalypse of John, states this about John in so many words in the fifth book against Heresies. " But if it had been necessary to announce his name plainly at the present time, it would have

τοῦ καὶ τὴν ἀποκάλυψιν ἑορακότος. οὐδὲ γὰρ πρὸ
πολλοῦ χρόνου ἑωράθη, ἀλλὰ σχεδὸν ἐπὶ τῆς ἡμετέρας γενεᾶς, πρὸς τῷ τέλει τῆς Δομετιανοῦ ἀρχῆς.''

Εἰς τοσοῦτον δὲ ἄρα κατὰ τοὺς δηλουμένους ἡ τῆς 4
ἡμετέρας πίστεως διέλαμπεν διδασκαλία, ὡς καὶ
τοὺς ἄποθεν τοῦ καθ' ἡμᾶς λόγου συγγραφεῖς μὴ
ἀποκνῆσαι ταῖς αὐτῶν ἱστορίαις τόν τε διωγμὸν καὶ
τὰ ἐν αὐτῷ μαρτύρια παραδοῦναι, οἵ γε καὶ τὸν
καιρὸν ἐπ' ἀκριβὲς ἐπεσημήναντο, ἐν ἔτει πεντεκαιδεκάτῳ Δομετιανοῦ μετὰ πλείστων ἑτέρων καὶ
Φλαυίαν Δομέτιλλαν ἱστορήσαντες, ἐξ ἀδελφῆς
γεγονυῖαν Φλαυίου Κλήμεντος, ἑνὸς τῶν τηνικάδε
ἐπὶ Ῥώμης ὑπάτων, τῆς εἰς Χριστὸν μαρτυρίας
ἕνεκεν εἰς νῆσον Ποντίαν κατὰ τιμωρίαν δεδόσθαι.

XIX. Τοῦ δ' αὐτοῦ Δομετιανοῦ τοὺς ἀπὸ γένους 1
Δαυὶδ ἀναιρεῖσθαι προστάξαντος, παλαιὸς κατέχει
λόγος τῶν αἱρετικῶν τινας κατηγορῆσαι τῶν ἀπογόνων Ἰούδα (τοῦτον δ' εἶναι ἀδελφὸν κατὰ σάρκα
τοῦ σωτῆρος) ὡς ἀπὸ γένους τυγχανόντων Δαυὶδ
καὶ ὡς αὐτοῦ συγγένειαν τοῦ Χριστοῦ φερόντων.
ταῦτα δὲ δηλοῖ κατὰ λέξιν ὧδέ πως λέγων ὁ
Ἡγήσιππος. XX. "ἔτι δὲ περιῆσαν οἱ ἀπὸ γένους 1
τοῦ κυρίου υἱωνοὶ Ἰούδα τοῦ κατὰ σάρκα λεγομένου
αὐτοῦ ἀδελφοῦ· οὓς ἐδηλατόρευσαν[1] ὡς ἐκ γένους
ὄντας Δαυίδ. τούτους ὁ ἠουοκᾶτος ἤγαγεν πρὸς
Δομετιανὸν Καίσαρα. ἐφοβεῖτο γὰρ τὴν παρουσίαν τοῦ Χριστοῦ ὡς καὶ Ἡρώδης. καὶ ἐπηρώ- 2
τησεν αὐτοὺς εἰ ἐκ Δαυίδ εἰσιν, καὶ ὡμολόγησαν.
τότε ἠρώτησεν αὐτοὺς πόσας κτήσεις ἔχουσιν ἢ

Matt. 13, 55
Mark 6, 3

---

[1] A Latinism made out of *delatus*.

---

[1] A.D. 96. *Cf.* Suetonius, *Dom.* 15, who however says that
Domitilla was the wife of Clemens. Some think that

been spoken by him who saw the apocalypse. For it was not seen long ago but almost in our own time, at the end of the reign of Domitian."

The teaching of our faith shone so brilliantly in the days described that even writers foreign to our belief did not hesitate to commit to their narratives the persecutions and the martyrdoms in it, and they even indicated the time accurately, relating that in the fifteenth year[1] of Domitian, Flavia Domitilla, who was the niece of Flavius Clemens, one of the consuls at Rome at that time, was banished with many others to the island of Pontia as testimony to Christ.

XIX. The same Domitian gave orders for the execution of those of the family of David and an ancient story goes that some heretics accused the grandsons of Judas (who is said to have been the brother, according to the flesh, of the Saviour) saying that they were of the family of David and related to the Christ himself. Hegesippus relates this exactly as follows. XX. " Now there still survived of the family of the Lord grandsons of Judas, who was said to have been his brother according to the flesh, and they were delated as being of the family of David. These the officer[2] brought to Domitian Caesar, for, like Herod, he was afraid of the coming of the Christ. He asked them if they were of the house of David and they admitted it. Then he asked them how much property they had, or how

there were two Domitillas. Suetonius does not mention that she was a Christian.

[2] The Greek represents the Latin *evocatus*, apparently the name of an official, but even Rufinus did not fully understand it and made out of it a proper name *Revocatus quidam.*

πόσων χρημάτων κυριεύουσιν. οἱ δὲ εἶπαν ἀμφοτέ-
ροις ἐννακισχίλια δηνάρια ὑπάρχειν αὐτοῖς μόνα,
ἑκάστῳ αὐτῶν ἀνήκοντος τοῦ ἡμίσεος, καὶ ταῦτα
οὐκ ἐν ἀργυρίοις ἔφασκον ἔχειν, ἀλλ' ἐν διατιμήσει
γῆς πλέθρων λθ' μόνων, ἐξ ὧν καὶ τοὺς φόρους ἀνα-
φέρειν καὶ αὐτοὺς αὐτουργοῦντας διατρέφεσθαι.'' [1]
εἶτα δὲ καὶ τὰς χεῖρας τὰς ἑαυτῶν ἐπιδεικνύναι, 3
μαρτύριον τῆς αὐτουργίας τὴν τοῦ σώματος σκλη-
ρίαν καὶ τοὺς ἀπὸ τῆς συνεχοῦς ἐργασίας ἐναποτυ-
πωθέντας ἐπὶ τῶν ἰδίων χειρῶν τύλους παριστάντας.
ἐρωτηθέντας δὲ περὶ τοῦ Χριστοῦ καὶ τῆς βασιλείας 4
αὐτοῦ ὁποία τις εἴη καὶ ποῖ καὶ πότε φανησομένη,
λόγον δοῦναι ὡς οὐ κοσμικὴ μὲν οὐδ' ἐπίγειος,
Matt. 16, 27
Acts 10, 42
Rom. 2, 6
2 Tim. 4, 1
ἐπουράνιος δὲ καὶ ἀγγελικὴ τυγχάνοι, ἐπὶ συντελείᾳ
τοῦ αἰῶνος γενησομένη, ὁπηνίκα ἐλθὼν ἐν δόξῃ
κρινεῖ ζῶντας καὶ νεκροὺς καὶ ἀποδώσει ἑκάστῳ
κατὰ τὰ ἐπιτηδεύματα αὐτοῦ· ἐφ' οἷς μηδὲν αὐτῶν 5
κατεγνωκότα τὸν Δομετιανόν, ἀλλὰ καὶ ὡς εὐτελῶν
καταφρονήσαντα, ἐλευθέρους μὲν αὐτοὺς ἀνεῖναι,
καταπαῦσαι δὲ διὰ προστάγματος τὸν κατὰ τῆς
ἐκκλησίας διωγμόν.[2] τοὺς δὲ ἀπολυθέντας ἡγήσα- 6
σθαι τῶν ἐκκλησιῶν, ὡς ἂν δὴ μάρτυρας ὁμοῦ καὶ
ἀπὸ γένους ὄντας τοῦ κυρίου, γενομένης τε εἰρήνης
μέχρι Τραϊανοῦ παραμεῖναι αὐτοὺς τῷ βίῳ. ταῦτα 7
μὲν ὁ Ἡγήσιππος· οὐ μὴν ἀλλὰ καὶ ὁ Τερτυλλιανὸς
Tert. Apol.
5
τοῦ Δομετιανοῦ τοιαύτην πεποίηται μνήμην '' πεπει-
ράκει ποτὲ καὶ Δομετιανὸς ταὐτὸ ποιεῖν ἐκείνῳ,
μέρος ὢν τῆς Νέρωνος ὠμότητος. ἀλλ', οἶμαι,
ἅτε ἔχων τι συνέσεως, τάχιστα ἐπαύσατο, ἀνακαλε-
σάμενος καὶ οὓς ἐξηλάκει.''

[1] Cf. George Syncellus 652. 5-14.
[2] Cf. Zonaras 362. 2-20.

238

much money they controlled, and they said that all they possessed was nine thousand denarii[1] between them, the half belonging to each, and they stated that they did not possess this in money but that it was the valuation of only thirty-nine plethra[2] of ground on which they paid taxes and lived on it by their own work." They then showed him their hands, adducing as testimony of their labour the hardness of their bodies, and the tough skin which had been embossed on their hands from their incessant work. They were asked concerning the Christ and his kingdom, its nature, origin, and time of appearance, and explained that it was neither of the world nor earthly, but heavenly and angelic, and it would be at the end of the world, when he would come in glory to judge the living and the dead and to reward every man according to his deeds. At this Domitian did not condemn them at all, but despised them as simple folk, released them, and decreed an end to the persecution against the church. But when they were released they were the leaders of the churches, both for their testimony and for their relation to the Lord, and remained alive in the peace which ensued until Trajan. Hegesippus tells this; moreover, Tertullian also has made similar mention of Domitian. " Domitian also once tried to do the same as he, for he was a Nero in cruelty, but, I believe, inasmuch as he had some sense, he stopped at once and recalled those whom he had banished."

[1] About £35.
[2] The Greek plethron is not quite a quarter of an acre, but is used to represent the Latin *iugerum* = more than half an acre.

Μετὰ δὲ τὸν Δομετιανὸν πεντεκαίδεκα ἔτεσιν 8
κρατήσαντα Νερούα τὴν ἀρχὴν διαδεξαμένου,
καθαιρεθῆναι μὲν τὰς Δομετιανοῦ τιμάς, ἐπανελθεῖν
δ' ἐπὶ τὰ οἰκεῖα μετὰ τοῦ καὶ τὰς οὐσίας ἀπολαβεῖν
τοὺς ἀδίκως ἐξεληλαμένους ἡ Ῥωμαίων σύγκλητος
βουλὴ ψηφίζεται· ἱστοροῦσιν οἱ γραφῇ τὰ κατὰ
τοὺς χρόνους παραδόντες. τότε δὴ οὖν καὶ τὸν 9
ἀπόστολον Ἰωάννην ἀπὸ τῆς κατὰ τὴν νῆσον φυγῆς
τὴν ἐπὶ τῆς Ἐφέσου διατριβὴν ἀπειληφέναι ὁ τῶν
παρ' ἡμῖν ἀρχαίων παραδίδωσι λόγος.

XXI. Μικρῷ δὲ πλέον ἐνιαυτοῦ βασιλεύσαντα 1
Νερούαν διαδέχεται Τραϊανός· οὗ δὴ πρῶτον ἔτος ἦν
ἐν ᾧ τῆς κατ' Ἀλεξάνδρειαν παροικίας Ἀβίλιον δέκα
πρὸς τρισὶν ἔτεσιν ἡγησάμενον διαδέχεται Κέρδων·
τρίτος οὗτος τῶν αὐτόθι μετὰ τὸν πρῶτον Ἀννιανὸν
προέστη. ἐν τούτῳ δὲ Ῥωμαίων εἰς ἔτι Κλήμης
ἡγεῖτο, τρίτον καὶ αὐτὸς ἐπέχων τῶν τῇδε μετὰ
Παῦλόν τε καὶ Πέτρον ἐπισκοπευσάντων βαθμόν·
Λίνος δὲ ὁ πρῶτος ἦν καὶ μετ' αὐτὸν Ἀνέγκλητος.

XXII. ἀλλὰ καὶ τῶν ἐπ' Ἀντιοχείας Εὐοδίου πρώ- 1
του κατασταντος δεύτερος ἐν τοῖς δηλουμένοις Ἰγνάτιος ἐγνωρίζετο. Συμεὼν ὁμοίως δεύτερος μετὰ τὸν
τοῦ σωτῆρος ἡμῶν ἀδελφὸν τῆς ἐν Ἱεροσολύμοις
ἐκκλησίας κατὰ τούτους τὴν λειτουργίαν εἶχεν.

XXIII. Ἐπὶ τούτοις κατὰ τὴν Ἀσίαν ἔτι τῷ βίῳ 1
περιλειπόμενος αὐτὸς ἐκεῖνος ὃν ἠγάπα ὁ Ἰησοῦς,

John 13, 23;
19, 26; 21, 7.
20

ἀπόστολος ὁμοῦ καὶ εὐαγγελιστὴς Ἰωάννης τὰς
αὐτόθι διεῖπεν ἐκκλησίας, ἀπὸ τῆς κατὰ τὴν νῆσον
μετὰ τὴν Δομετιανοῦ τελευτὴν ἐπανελθὼν φυγῆς.
ὅτι δὲ εἰς τούτους τῷ βίῳ περιῆν, ἀπόχρη διὰ δύο 2
πιστώσασθαι τὸν λόγον μαρτύρων, πιστοὶ δ' ἂν εἶεν
οὗτοι, τῆς ἐκκλησιαστικῆς πρεσβεύσαντες ὀρθο-

After Domitian had reigned fifteen years, Nerva
succeeded.[1]   The sentences of Domitian were an-
nulled, and the Roman Senate decreed the return
of those who had been unjustly banished and the
restoration of their property.   Those who committed
the story of those times to writing relate it.   At
that time, too, the story of the ancient Christians
relates that the Apostle John, after his banishment
to the island, took up his abode at Ephesus.

XXI. After Nerva had reigned a little more than
a year he was succeeded by Trajan,[2] in whose first
year Abilius, after leading the diocese of Alexandria
for thirteen years, was succeeded by Cerdo ; he
was the third in charge of that see after the first,
Annianus.   At this time Clement was still governing
the Romans and he, also, occupied the third place
in the list of bishops in Rome after Paul and Peter ;
Linus was the first and after him Anencletus.
XXII. Moreover, at the time mentioned, Ignatius
was famous as the second bishop at Antioch where
Evodius had been the first.   Likewise at this time,
Simeon was second after the brother of our Saviour
to hold the ministry of the church in Jerusalem.

XXIII. At this time that very disciple whom Jesus
loved, John, at once Apostle and Evangelist, still
remained alive in Asia and administered the churches
there, for after the death of Domitian, he had returned from his banishment on the island.   And that
he remained alive until this time may fully be confirmed by two witnesses, and these ought to be
trustworthy for they represent the orthodoxy of the

---

[1] Sept. 18, A.D. 96.   [2] Jan. 27, A.D. 98.

δοξίας, εἰ δὴ τοιοῦτοι Εἰρηναῖος καὶ Κλήμης ὁ
Ἀλεξανδρεύς· ὧν ὁ μὲν πρότερος ἐν δευτέρῳ τῶν 3
Iren. 2, 22. 5 πρὸς τὰς αἱρέσεις ὧδέ πως γράφει κατὰ λέξιν· "καὶ.
πάντες οἱ πρεσβύτεροι μαρτυροῦσιν οἱ κατὰ τὴν
Ἀσίαν Ἰωάννῃ τῷ τοῦ κυρίου μαθητῇ συμβεβλη-
κότες παραδεδωκέναι τὸν Ἰωάννην. παρέμεινεν
γὰρ αὐτοῖς μέχρι τῶν Τραϊανοῦ χρόνων."[1] καὶ ἐν 4
τρίτῳ δὲ τῆς αὐτῆς ὑποθέσεως ταὐτὸ τοῦτο δηλοῖ
Iren. 3, 3. 4 διὰ τούτων· "ἀλλὰ καὶ ἡ ἐν Ἐφέσῳ ἐκκλησία ὑπὸ
Παύλου μὲν τεθεμελιωμένη, Ἰωάννου δὲ παραμείναντος αὐτοῖς μέχρι τῶν Τραϊανοῦ χρόνων, μάρτυς
ἀληθής ἐστιν τῆς τῶν ἀποστόλων παραδόσεως."

Ὁ δὲ Κλήμης ὁμοῦ τὸν χρόνον ἐπισημηνάμενος, 5
καὶ ἱστορίαν ἀναγκαιοτάτην οἷς τὰ καλὰ καὶ
ἐπωφελῆ φίλον ἀκούειν, προστίθησιν ἐν ᾧ "Τίς ὁ
σῳζόμενος πλούσιος" ἐπέγραψεν αὐτοῦ συγγράμ-
ματι· λαβὼν δὲ ἀνάγνωθι ὧδέ πως ἔχουσαν καὶ
Clem. De di-
vite serv. 42 αὐτοῦ τὴν γραφήν· "ἄκουσον μῦθον οὐ μῦθον ἀλλὰ 6
ὄντα λόγον περὶ Ἰωάννου τοῦ ἀποστόλου παραδεδο-
μένον καὶ μνήμῃ πεφυλαγμένον. ἐπειδὴ γὰρ τοῦ
τυράννου τελευτήσαντος ἀπὸ τῆς Πάτμου τῆς νήσου
μετῆλθεν ἐπὶ τὴν Ἔφεσον, ἀπῄει παρακαλούμενος
καὶ ἐπὶ τὰ πλησιόχωρα τῶν ἐθνῶν, ὅπου μὲν
ἐπισκόπους καταστήσων, ὅπου δὲ ὅλας ἐκκλησίας
ἁρμόσων, ὅπου δὲ κλῆρον ἕνα γέ τινα κληρώσων τῶν
ὑπὸ τοῦ πνεύματος σημαινομένων. ἐλθὼν οὖν καὶ 7
ἐπί τινα τῶν οὐ μακρὰν πόλεων,[2] ἧς καὶ τοὔνομα
λέγουσιν ἔνιοι, καὶ τἆλλα ἀναπαύσας τοὺς ἀδελφούς,
ἐπὶ πᾶσι τῷ καθεστῶτι προσβλέψας ἐπισκόπῳ,
νεανίσκον ἱκανὸν τῷ σώματι καὶ τὴν ὄψιν ἀστεῖον
καὶ θερμὸν τὴν ψυχὴν ἰδών, 'τοῦτον' ἔφη 'σοὶ

[1] Cf. George Syncellus 653. 9-11. [2] Cf. Chron. Pasc. 470. 9.

church, no less persons than Irenaeus and Clement of Alexandria. The former of these writes in one place in the second of his books *Against the Heresies,* as follows : " And all the presbyters who had been associated in Asia with John, the disciple of the Lord, bear witness to his tradition, for he remained with them until the times of Trajan." And in the third book of the same work he makes the same statement as follows : " Now the church at Ephesus was founded by Paul, but John stayed there until the times of Trajan, and it is a true witness of the tradition of the Apostles."

Clement indicates the same time, and in the treatise to which he gave the title *Who is the rich man that is saved,* adds a narrative most acceptable to those who enjoy hearing what is fine and edifying. Take and read here what he wrote. " Listen to a story which is not a story but a true tradition of John the Apostle preserved in memory. For after the death of the tyrant he passed from the island of Patmos to Ephesus, and used also to go, when he was asked, to the neighbouring districts of the heathen,[1] in some places to appoint bishops, in others to reconcile whole churches, and in others to ordain some one of those pointed out by the Spirit. He came to one of the cities which were near by (and some tell even its name),[2] and gave rest in general to the brethren ; then, while looking before them all at the bishop who had been appointed, he saw a young man of strong body, beautiful appearance, and warm heart. ' I commend this man,' he said,

---

[1] 'ἐθνῶν possibly means " country-people " as opposed to " town-folk."

[2] According to the *Chronicon Paschale* it was Smyrna.

παρακατατίθεμαι μετὰ πάσης σπουδῆς ἐπὶ τῆς
ἐκκλησίας καὶ τοῦ Χριστοῦ μάρτυρος.' τοῦ δὲ
δεχομένου καὶ πάνθ' ὑπισχνουμένου, καὶ πάλιν τὰ
αὐτὰ διελέγετο καὶ διεμαρτύρετο. εἶτα ὁ μὲν ἀπ-
ῆρεν ἐπὶ τὴν Ἔφεσον, ὁ δὲ πρεσβύτερος ἀναλαβὼν
οἴκαδε τὸν παραδοθέντα νεανίσκον ἔτρεφεν, συνεῖχεν,
ἔθαλπεν, τὸ τελευταῖον ἐφώτισεν. καὶ μετὰ τοῦτο
ὑφῆκεν τῆς πλείονος ἐπιμελείας καὶ παραφυλακῆς,
ὡς τὸ τέλειον αὐτῷ φυλακτήριον ἐπιστήσας τὴν
σφραγῖδα κυρίου. τῷ δὲ ἀνέσεως πρὸ ὥρας
λαβομένῳ προσφθείρονταί τινες ἥλικες ἀργοὶ καὶ
ἀπερρωγότες, ἐθάδες κακῶν, καὶ πρῶτον μὲν δι'
ἑστιάσεων πολυτελῶν αὐτὸν ἐπάγονται, εἶτά που
καὶ νύκτωρ ἐπὶ λωποδυσίαν ἐξιόντες συνεπάγονται,
εἶτά τι καὶ μεῖζον συμπράττειν ἠξίουν· ὁ δὲ κατ'
ὀλίγον προσειθίζετο, καὶ διὰ μέγεθος φύσεως
ἐκστὰς ὥσπερ ἄστομος καὶ εὔρωστος ἵππος ὀρθῆς
ὁδοῦ καὶ τὸν χαλινὸν ἐνδακών, μειζόνως κατὰ τῶν
βαράθρων ἐφέρετο. ἀπογνοὺς δὲ τελέως τὴν ἐν θεῷ
σωτηρίαν, οὐδὲν ἔτι μικρὸν διενοεῖτο, ἀλλὰ μέγα τι
πράξας, ἐπειδήπερ ἅπαξ ἀπολώλει, ἴσα τοῖς ἄλλοις
παθεῖν ἠξίου. αὐτοὺς δὴ τούτους ἀναλαβὼν καὶ
λῃστήριον συγκροτήσας, ἕτοιμος λήσταρχος ἦν,
βιαιότατος μιαιφονώτατος χαλεπώτατος. χρόνος
ἐν μέσῳ, καί τινος ἐπιπεσούσης χρείας ἀνακαλοῦσι
τὸν Ἰωάννην. ὁ δὲ ἐπεὶ τὰ ἄλλα ὧν χάριν ἧκεν
κατεστήσατο, 'ἄγε δή' ἔφη 'ὦ ἐπίσκοπε, τὴν
παραθήκην ἀπόδος ἡμῖν, ἣν ἐγώ τε καὶ ὁ Χριστός
σοι παρακατεθέμεθα ἐπὶ τῆς ἐκκλησίας, ἧς προ-
καθέζῃ, μάρτυρος.' ὁ δὲ τὸ μὲν πρῶτον ἐξεπλάγη,
χρήματα οἰόμενος, ἅπερ οὐκ ἔλαβεν, συκοφαντεῖ-
σθαι, καὶ οὔτε πιστεύειν εἶχεν ὑπὲρ ὧν οὐκ εἶχεν,

' to you with all diligence in the face of the church, and with Christ as my witness.' The bishop received him, and promised everything, and the same conversations and protestations were used. John then returned to Ephesus and the presbyter[1] took to his house the young man entrusted to him, brought him up, looked after him, and finally baptized him. After this he relaxed his great care and watchfulness, because he had set upon him the seal of the Lord as the perfect safeguard. But some idle and dissolute youths, familiar with evil, corrupted him in his premature freedom. First they led him on by expensive feasts, then they started out at night for robbery and took him with them, then they urged him to greater crimes. He gradually became accustomed to this, and like an unbroken and powerful horse starting from the straight way and tearing at the bit, rushed all the more to the precipice because of his natural vigour. Finally he renounced salvation from God; and now he planned nothing small, but, having perpetrated some great crime, since he was ruined once for all, accepted the same lot as the others. He collected them and formed a band of brigands and was himself a born chief, excelling in violence, in murder, and in cruelty. Time went on and some necessity arose to summon John. When he had arranged the rest of his mission John said, ' Come now, bishop, pay me back the deposit which Christ and I left with you, with the church, over which you preside, as witness.' The bishop was at first amazed, thinking that he was being blackmailed for money which he had not received. He could neither show his faithfulness in

---

[1] Immediately above he is called a bishop.

οὔτε ἀπιστεῖν Ἰωάννῃ· ὡς δέ ʽτὸν νεανίσκονʼ
εἶπεν ʽἀπαιτῶ καὶ τὴν ψυχὴν τοῦ ἀδελφοῦ,ʼ
στενάξας κάτωθεν ὁ πρεσβύτης καί τι καὶ ἐπι-
δακρύσας, ʽἐκεῖνοςʼ ἔφη ʽτέθνηκεν.ʼ ʽπῶς καὶ
τίνα θάνατον ;ʼ ʽθεῷ τέθνηκενʼ εἶπεν· ʽἀπέβη γὰρ
πονηρὸς καὶ ἐξώλης καί, τὸ κεφάλαιον, λῃστής, καὶ
νῦν ἀντὶ τῆς ἐκκλησίας τὸ ὄρος κατείληφεν μεθʼ
ὁμοίου στρατιωτικοῦ.ʼ καταρρηξάμενος τὴν ἐσθῆ- 14
τα ὁ ἀπόστολος καὶ μετὰ μεγάλης οἰμωγῆς πληξά-
μενος τὴν κεφαλήν, ʽκαλόν γεʼ ἔφη ʽφύλακα
τῆς τἀδελφοῦ ψυχῆς κατέλιπον. ἀλλʼ ἵππος ἤδη
μοι παρέστω, καὶ ἡγεμὼν γενέσθω μοί τις τῆς
ὁδοῦ.ʼ ἤλαυνεν, ὥσπερ εἶχεν, αὐτόθεν ἀπὸ τῆς
ἐκκλησίας. ἐλθὼν δὲ εἰς τὸ χωρίον, ὑπὸ τῆς
προφυλακῆς τῶν λῃστῶν ἁλίσκεται, μήτε φεύγων
μήτε παραιτούμενος, ἀλλὰ βοῶν ʽἐπὶ τοῦτʼ ἐλή-
λυθα, ἐπὶ τὸν ἄρχοντα ὑμῶν ἀγάγετέ με·ʼ ὃς τέως,
ὥσπερ ὥπλιστο, ἀνέμενεν, ὡς δὲ προσιόντα ἐγνώ-
ρισε τὸν Ἰωάννην, εἰς φυγὴν αἰδεσθεὶς ἐτράπετο.
ὁ δὲ ἐδίωκεν ἀνὰ κράτος, ἐπιλαθόμενος τῆς ἡλικίας
τῆς ἑαυτοῦ, κεκραγώς ʽτί με φεύγεις, τέκνον, τὸν
σαυτοῦ πατέρα, τὸν γυμνόν, τὸν γέροντα; ἐλέησόν
με, τέκνον, μὴ φοβοῦ· ἔχεις ἔτι ζωῆς ἐλπίδας.
ἐγὼ Χριστῷ λόγον δώσω ὑπὲρ σοῦ· ἂν δέῃ, τὸν
σὸν θάνατον ἑκὼν ὑπομενῶ, ὡς ὁ κύριος τὸν ὑπὲρ
ἡμῶν· ὑπὲρ σοῦ τὴν ψυχὴν ἀντιδώσω τὴν ἐμήν.
στῆθι, πίστευσον· Χριστός με ἀπέστειλεν.ʼ ὁ δὲ
ἀκούσας, πρῶτον ἔστη μὲν κάτω βλέπων, εἶτα
ἔρριψεν τὰ ὅπλα, εἶτα τρέμων ἔκλαιεν πικρῶς·
προσελθόντα δὲ τὸν γέροντα περιέλαβεν, ἀπολογούμενος ταῖς οἰμωγαῖς ὡς ἐδύνατο καὶ τοῖς δάκρυσι
βαπτιζόμενος ἐκ δευτέρου, μόνην ἀποκρύπτων τὴν

what he had never had, nor could he fail John. But when John said, 'I ask back the young man and the soul of the brother,' the old man groaned deeply and shedding tears, said, 'He has died.' 'How and with what death?' 'He has died to God,' he said, 'for he turned out wicked and abandoned and finally a brigand, and now instead of the church he has taken to the mountains with an armed band of men like himself.' Then the apostle rent his garments and beat his head with great lamentation. 'Well,' he said, 'it was a fine guardian whom I left for the soul of our brother. But let me have a horse and some one to show me the way.' So he rode, just as he was, straight from the church. When he came to the place he was seized by the sentinel of the brigands and neither fled nor made excuses, but called out, 'This is why I am come; take me to your leader.' The leader waited for him, armed as he was, but when he recognized John on his approach, he turned and fled in shame. But John pursued with all his might, forgetting his age and calling out, 'Why do you run away from me, child, your own father, unarmed and old? Pity me, child, do not fear me! You have still hope of life. I will account to Christ for you. If it must be, I will willingly suffer your death, as the Lord suffered for us; for your life, I will give my own. Stay, believe; Christ sent me.' When he heard this he first stood looking down, then he tore off his weapons, then he began to tremble and to weep bitterly. He embraced the old man when he came up, pleading for himself with lamentations as best he could, baptized a second time in his tears, but his right

δεξιάν· ὃ δ' ἐγγυώμενος, ἐπομνύμενος ὡς ἄφεσιν 19
αὐτῷ παρὰ τοῦ σωτῆρος ηὕρηται, δεόμενος, γονυ-
πετῶν, αὐτὴν τὴν δεξιὰν ὡς ὑπὸ τῆς μετανοίας
κεκαθαρμένην καταφιλῶν, ἐπὶ τὴν ἐκκλησίαν ἐπ-
ανήγαγεν, καὶ δαψιλέσι μὲν εὐχαῖς ἐξαιτούμενος,
συνεχέσι δὲ νηστείαις συναγωνιζόμενος, ποικίλαις δὲ
σειρῆσι λόγων κατεπᾴδων αὐτοῦ τὴν γνώμην, οὐ
πρότερον ἀπῆλθεν, ὥς φασιν, πρὶν αὐτὸν ἐπιστῆσαι
τῇ ἐκκλησίᾳ, διδοὺς μέγα παράδειγμα μετανοίας
ἀληθινῆς καὶ μέγα γνώρισμα παλιγγενεσίας, τρό-
παιον ἀναστάσεως βλεπομένης.''[1]   ταῦτα τοῦ
Κλήμεντος, ἱστορίας ὁμοῦ καὶ ὠφελείας τῆς τῶν
ἐντευξομένων ἕνεκεν, ἐνταῦθά μοι κείσθω.

XXIV. Φέρε δέ, καὶ τοῦδε τοῦ ἀποστόλου τὰς 1
ἀναντιρρήτους ἐπισημηνώμεθα γραφάς.   καὶ δὴ 2
τὸ κατ' αὐτὸν εὐαγγέλιον ταῖς ὑπὸ τὸν οὐρανὸν
διεγνωσμένον ἐκκλησίαις, πρῶτον ἀνωμολογήσθω·
ὅτι γε μὴν εὐλόγως πρὸς τῶν ἀρχαίων ἐν τετάρτῃ
μοίρᾳ τῶν ἄλλων τριῶν κατείλεκται, ταύτῃ ἂν
γένοιτο δῆλον.   οἱ θεσπέσιοι καὶ ὡς ἀληθῶς 3
θεοπρεπεῖς, φημὶ δὲ τοῦ Χριστοῦ τοὺς ἀποστόλους,
τὸν βίον ἄκρως κεκαθαρμένοι καὶ ἀρετῇ πάσῃ τὰς
Acts 4, 13
2 Cor. 11ψυχὰς κεκοσμημένοι, τὴν δὲ γλῶτταν ἰδιωτεύοντες,
τῇ γε μὴν πρὸς τοῦ σωτῆρος αὐτοῖς δεδωρημένῃ
θείᾳ καὶ παραδοξοποιῷ δυνάμει θαρσοῦντες, τὸ μὲν
1 Cor. 2, 4 ἐν πειθοῖ καὶ τέχνῃ λόγων τὰ τοῦ διδασκάλου
μαθήματα πρεσβεύειν οὔτε ᾔδεσαν οὔτε ἐνεχείρουν,
τῇ δὲ τοῦ θείου πνεύματος τοῦ συνεργοῦντος αὐτοῖς
ἀποδείξει καὶ τῇ δι' αὐτῶν συντελουμένῃ θαυμα-
τουργῷ τοῦ Χριστοῦ δυνάμει μόνῃ χρώμενοι, τῆς
τῶν οὐρανῶν βασιλείας τὴν γνῶσιν ἐπὶ πᾶσαν

[1] Cf. George Syncellus 653. 12-654. 16.

hand he kept back. But John assured him by pledges and protestations that he had found forgiveness for him with the Saviour, led him back, prayed and kneeled and kissed that right hand as though cleansed by his repentance. He brought him to the church, he prayed with many supplications, he joined with him in the struggle of continuous fasting, he worked on his mind by varied addresses and did not leave him, so they say, until he had restored him to the church, and thus gave a great example of true repentance and a great testimony of regeneration, the trophy of a visible resurrection." These remarks of Clement may be quoted both for the sake of the narrative and the edification of those who shall read them.

XXIV. But come, let us indicate the undoubted writings of this Apostle.[1] Let the Gospel according to him be first recognized, for it is read in all the churches under heaven. Moreover, that it was reasonable for the ancients to reckon it in the fourth place after the other three may be explained thus. Those inspired and venerable ancients, I mean Christ's Apostles, had completely purified their life and adorned their souls with every virtue, yet were but simple men in speech. Though they were indeed bold in the divine and wonder-working power given them by the Saviour, they had neither the knowledge nor the desire to represent the teachings of the Master in persuasive or artistic language, but they used only the proof of the Spirit of God which worked with them, and the wonder-working power of Christ which was consummated through them. Thus they announced the knowledge of the Kingdom of Heaven

[1] John.

κατήγγελλον τὴν οἰκουμένην, σπουδῆς τῆς περὶ τὸ
λογογραφεῖν μικρὰν ποιούμενοι φροντίδα. καὶ 4
τοῦτ' ἔπραττον ἅτε μείζονι καὶ ὑπὲρ ἄνθρωπον
ἐξυπηρετούμενοι διακονίᾳ. ὁ γοῦν Παῦλος πάντων ἐν παρασκευῇ λόγων δυνατώτατος νοήμασίν τε
ἱκανώτατος γεγονώς, οὐ πλέον τῶν βραχυτάτων
ἐπιστολῶν γραφῇ παραδέδωκεν, καίτοι μυρία γε καὶ
2 Cor. 12, 2-4 ἀπόρρητα λέγειν ἔχων, ἅτε τῶν μέχρις οὐρανοῦ
τρίτου θεωρημάτων ἐπιψαύσας ἐπ' αὐτόν τε τὸν
θεοπρεπῆ παράδεισον ἀναρπασθεὶς καὶ τῶν ἐκεῖσε
ῥημάτων ἀρρήτων ἀξιωθεὶς ἐπακοῦσαι. οὐκ 5
ἄπειροι μὲν οὖν ὑπῆρχον τῶν αὐτῶν καὶ οἱ λοιποὶ
τοῦ σωτῆρος ἡμῶν φοιτηταί, δώδεκα μὲν ἀπόστολοι,
ἑβδομήκοντα δὲ μαθηταί, ἄλλοι τε ἐπὶ τούτοις
μυρίοι· ὅμως δ' οὖν ἐξ ἁπάντων τῶν τοῦ κυρίου
διατριβῶν ὑπομνήματα Ματθαῖος ἡμῖν καὶ Ἰωάννης μόνοι καταλελοίπασιν· οὓς καὶ ἐπάναγκες ἐπὶ
τὴν γραφὴν ἐλθεῖν κατέχει λόγος. Ματθαῖός τε 6
γὰρ πρότερον Ἑβραίοις κηρύξας, ὡς ἤμελλεν καὶ ἐφ'
ἑτέρους ἰέναι, πατρίῳ γλώττῃ γραφῇ παραδοὺς τὸ
κατ' αὐτὸν εὐαγγέλιον, τὸ λεῖπον τῇ αὑτοῦ παρουσίᾳ
τούτοις ἀφ' ὧν ἐστέλλετο, διὰ τῆς γραφῆς ἀπεπλή-
ρου· ἤδη δὲ Μάρκου καὶ Λουκᾶ τῶν κατ' αὐτοὺς 7
εὐαγγελίων τὴν ἔκδοσιν πεποιημένων, Ἰωάννην
φασὶ τὸν πάντα χρόνον ἀγράφῳ κεχρημένον κηρύγματι, τέλος καὶ ἐπὶ τὴν γραφὴν ἐλθεῖν τοιᾶσδε χάριν
αἰτίας. τῶν προαναγραφέντων τριῶν εἰς πάντας
ἤδη καὶ εἰς αὐτὸν διαδεδομένων, ἀποδέξασθαι μέν
φασιν, ἀλήθειαν αὐτοῖς ἐπιμαρτυρήσαντα, μόνην δὲ
ἄρα λείπεσθαι τῇ γραφῇ τὴν περὶ τῶν ἐν πρώτοις
καὶ κατ' ἀρχὴν τοῦ κηρύγματος ὑπὸ τοῦ Χριστοῦ
πεπραγμένων διήγησιν. καὶ ἀληθής γε ὁ λόγος. 8

to all the world and cared but little for attention to their style. And this they did inasmuch as they were serving a greater, superhuman ministry. Thus Paul, the most powerful of all in the preparation of argument and the strongest thinker, committed to writing no more than short epistles, though he had ten thousand ineffable things to say, seeing that he had touched the vision of the third heaven, had been caught up to the divine paradise itself, and was there granted the hearing of ineffable words. Nor were the other pupils of our Saviour without experience of the same things,—the twelve Apostles and the seventy disciples and ten thousand others in addition to them. Yet nevertheless of all those who had been with the Lord only Matthew and John have left us their recollections, and tradition says that they took to writing perforce. Matthew had first preached to Hebrews, and when he was on the point of going to others he transmitted in writing in his native language the Gospel according to himself, and thus supplied by writing the lack of his own presence to those from whom he was sent, and Mark and Luke had already published the Gospels according to them, but John, it is said, used all the time a message which was not written down, and at last took to writing for the following cause. The three gospels which had been written down before were distributed to all including himself ; it is said that he welcomed them and testified to their truth but said that there was only lacking to the narrative the account of what was done by Christ at first and at the beginning of the preaching. The story is

τοὺς τρεῖς γοῦν εὐαγγελιστὰς συνιδεῖν πάρεστιν
μόνα τὰ μετὰ τὴν ἐν τῷ δεσμωτηρίῳ Ἰωάννου τοῦ
βαπτιστοῦ κάθειρξιν ἐφ' ἕνα ἐνιαυτὸν πεπραγμένα
τῷ σωτῆρι συγγεγραφότας αὐτό τε τοῦτ' ἐπισημη-
ναμένους κατ' ἀρχὰς τῆς αὐτῶν ἱστορίας· μετὰ 9
γοῦν τὴν τεσσαρακονταήμερον νηστείαν καὶ τὸν ἐπὶ
ταύτῃ πειρασμὸν τὸν χρόνον τῆς ἰδίας γραφῆς ὁ μὲν

Matt. 14, 12

Ματθαῖος δηλοῖ λέγων " ἀκούσας δὲ ὅτι Ἰωάννης
παρεδόθη, ἀνεχώρησεν " ἀπὸ τῆς Ἰουδαίας " εἰς

Mark 1, 14

τὴν Γαλιλαίαν," ὁ δὲ Μάρκος ὡσαύτως " μετὰ δὲ 10
τὸ παραδοθῆναι " φησίν " Ἰωάννην ἦλθεν Ἰησοῦς

Luke 3, 19.
20

εἰς τὴν Γαλιλαίαν," καὶ ὁ Λουκᾶς δὲ πρὶν ἄρξασθαι
τῶν τοῦ Ἰησοῦ πράξεων, παραπλησίως ἐπιτηρεῖ,
φάσκων ὡς ἄρα προσθεὶς Ἡρῴδης οἷς διεπράξατο
πονηροῖς, " κατέκλεισε τὸν Ἰωάννην ἐν φυλακῇ."
παρακληθέντα δὴ οὖν τούτων ἕνεκά φασι τὸν 11
ἀπόστολον Ἰωάννην τὸν ὑπὸ τῶν προτέρων εὐαγγελιστῶν παρασιωπηθέντα χρόνον καὶ τὰ κατὰ τοῦτον πεπραγμένα τῷ σωτῆρι (ταῦτα δ' ἦν τὰ πρὸ
τῆς τοῦ βαπτιστοῦ καθείρξεως) τῷ κατ' αὐτὸν
εὐαγγελίῳ παραδοῦναι, αὐτό τε τοῦτ' ἐπιση-

John 2, 11

μήνασθαι, τοτὲ μὲν φήσαντα " ταύτην ἀρχὴν

John 3, 23.
24

ἐποίησεν τῶν παραδόξων ὁ Ἰησοῦς," τοτὲ δὲ
μνημονεύσαντα τοῦ βαπτιστοῦ μεταξὺ τῶν Ἰησοῦ
πράξεων ὡς ἔτι τότε βαπτίζοντος ἐν Αἰνὼν ἐγγὺς
τοῦ Σαλείμ, σαφῶς τε τοῦτο δηλοῦν ἐν τῷ λέγειν
" οὔπω γὰρ ἦν Ἰωάννης βεβλημένος εἰς φυλακήν,"
οὐκοῦν ὁ μὲν Ἰωάννης τῇ τοῦ κατ' αὐτὸν εὐαγ- 12
γελίου γραφῇ τὰ μηδέπω τοῦ βαπτιστοῦ εἰς φυλακὴν
βεβλημένου πρὸς τοῦ Χριστοῦ πραχθέντα παραδίδωσιν, οἱ δὲ λοιποὶ τρεῖς εὐαγγελισταὶ τὰ μετὰ
τὴν εἰς τὸ δεσμωτήριον κάθειρξιν τοῦ βαπτιστοῦ

surely true. It is at least possible to see that the three evangelists related only what the Saviour did during one year after John the Baptist had been put in prison and that they stated this at the beginning of their narrative. At any rate, after the forty days' fast, and the temptation which followed Matthew fixes the time described in his own writing by saying that " hearing that John had been betrayed, he retreated " from Judaea " into Galilee." Similarly Mark says, " and after John was betrayed Jesus came into Galilee." And Luke, too, makes a similar observation before beginning the acts of Jesus saying that Herod added to the evil deeds which he had done by " shutting up John in prison." They say accordingly that for this reason the apostle John was asked to relate in his own gospel the period passed over in silence by the former evangelists and the things done during it by the Saviour (that is to say, the events before the imprisonment of the Baptist), and that he indicated this at one time by saying, " this beginning of miracles did Jesus," at another by mentioning the Baptist in the midst of the acts of Jesus as at that time still baptizing at Aenon near Salem, and that he makes this plain by saying, " for John was not yet cast into prison." Thus John in the course of his gospel relates what Christ did before the Baptist had been thrown into prison, but the other three evangelists narrate the events after the imprisonment of the Baptist. If

μνημονεύουσιν· οἷς καὶ ἐπιστήσαντι οὐκέτ᾽ ἂν 13
δόξαι διαφωνεῖν ἀλλήλοις τὰ εὐαγγέλια τῷ τὸ μὲν
κατὰ Ἰωάννην τὰ πρῶτα τῶν τοῦ Χριστοῦ πράξεων
περιέχειν, τὰ δὲ λοιπὰ τὴν ἐπὶ τέλει τοῦ χρόνου
αὐτῷ γεγενημένην ἱστορίαν· εἰκότως δ᾽ οὖν τὴν μὲν
τῆς σαρκὸς τοῦ σωτῆρος ἡμῶν γενεαλογίαν ἅτε
Ματθαίῳ καὶ Λουκᾷ προγραφεῖσαν ἀποσιωπῆσαι
τὸν Ἰωάννην, τῆς δὲ θεολογίας ἀπάρξασθαι ὡς ἂν
αὐτῷ πρὸς τοῦ θείου πνεύματος οἷα κρείττονι
παραπεφυλαγμένης.

Ταῦτα μὲν οὖν ἡμῖν περὶ τῆς τοῦ κατὰ Ἰωάννην 14
εὐαγγελίου γραφῆς εἰρήσθω, καὶ τῆς κατὰ Μάρκον
δὲ ἡ γενομένη αἰτία ἐν τοῖς πρόσθεν ἡμῖν δεδήλωται·
ὁ δὲ Λουκᾶς ἀρχόμενος καὶ αὐτὸς τοῦ κατ᾽ αὐτὸν 15

Luke 1 1–4 συγγράμματος τὴν αἰτίαν προύθηκεν δι᾽ ἣν πεποίηται
τὴν σύνταξιν, δηλῶν ὡς ἄρα πολλῶν καὶ ἄλλων
προπετέστερον ἐπιτετηδευκότων διήγησιν ποιήσασθαι ὧν αὐτὸς πεπληροφόρητο λόγων, ἀναγκαίως
ἀπαλλάττων ἡμᾶς τῆς περὶ τοὺς ἄλλους ἀμφηρίστου
ὑπολήψεως, τὸν ἀσφαλῆ λόγον ὧν αὐτὸς ἱκανῶς τὴν
ἀλήθειαν κατειλήφει ἐκ τῆς ἅμα Παύλῳ συνουσίας
τε καὶ διατριβῆς καὶ τῆς τῶν λοιπῶν ἀποστόλων
ὁμιλίας ὠφελημένος, διὰ τοῦ ἰδίου παρέδωκεν
εὐαγγελίου. καὶ ταῦτα μὲν ἡμεῖς περὶ τούτων· 16
οἰκειότερον δὲ κατὰ καιρὸν διὰ τῆς τῶν ἀρχαίων
παραθέσεως τὰ καὶ τοῖς ἄλλοις περὶ αὐτῶν εἰρημένα
πειρασόμεθα δηλῶσαι.

Τῶν δὲ Ἰωάννου γραμμάτων πρὸς τῷ εὐαγγελίῳ 17
καὶ ἡ προτέρα τῶν ἐπιστολῶν παρά τε τοῖς νῦν καὶ
τοῖς ἔτ᾽ ἀρχαίοις ἀναμφίλεκτος ὡμολόγηται, ἀντιλέ- 18
γονται δὲ αἱ λοιπαὶ δύο, τῆς δ᾽ Ἀποκαλύψεως εἰς

---

[1] The exact meaning of this word in Luke's preface was

this be understood the gospels no longer appear to disagree, because that according to John contains the first of the acts of Christ and the others the narrative of what he did at the end of the period, and it will seem probable that John passed over the genealogy of our Saviour according to the flesh, because it had been already written out by Matthew and Luke, and began with the description of his divinity since this had been reserved for him by the Divine Spirit as for one greater than they

The above must suffice us concerning the writing of the Gospel according to John, and the cause for that according to Mark has been explained above. Luke himself at the beginning of his treatise prefixed an account of the cause for which he had made his compilation, explaining that while many others had somewhat rashly attempted to make a narrative of the things of which he had himself full knowledge,[1] he felt obliged to release us from the doubtful propositions of the others and related in his own gospel the accurate account of the things of which he had himself firmly learnt the truth from his profitable intercourse and life with Paul and his conversation with the other apostles. This must suffice us for the present, but at the proper time we will endeavour to explain by citation from the ancients what has been said on the point by others.

Of the writings of John in addition to the gospel the first of his epistles has been accepted without controversy by ancients and moderns alike but the other two are disputed, and as to the Revelation there

---

probably as obscure in the fourth century as it is to us; but the "himself" in the Greek seems to imply that Eusebius thought that Luke was contrasting his own "full" knowledge with the imperfect efforts of his predecessors.

ἑκάτερον ἔτι νῦν παρὰ τοῖς πολλοῖς περιέλκεται ἡ δόξα· ὁμοίως γε μὴν ἐκ τῆς τῶν ἀρχαίων μαρτυρίας ἐν οἰκείῳ καιρῷ τὴν ἐπίκρισιν δέξεται καὶ αὐτή.

XXV. Εὔλογον δ' ἐνταῦθα γενομένους ἀνακεφαλαιώσασθαι τὰς δηλωθείσας τῆς καινῆς διαθήκης γραφάς. καὶ δὴ τακτέον ἐν πρώτοις τὴν ἁγίαν τῶν εὐαγγελίων τετρακτύν, οἷς ἕπεται ἡ τῶν Πράξεων τῶν ἀποστόλων γραφή· μετὰ δὲ ταύτην τὰς Παύλου 2 καταλεκτέον ἐπιστολάς, αἷς ἑξῆς τὴν φερομένην Ἰωάννου προτέραν καὶ ὁμοίως τὴν Πέτρου κυρωτέον ἐπιστολήν· ἐπὶ τούτοις τακτέον, εἴ γε φανείη, τὴν Ἀποκάλυψιν Ἰωάννου, περὶ ἧς τὰ δόξαντα κατὰ καιρὸν ἐκθησόμεθα. καὶ ταῦτα μὲν ἐν ὁμολογουμένοις· τῶν δ' ἀντιλεγομένων, γνωρίμων δ' οὖν ὅμως τοῖς πολλοῖς, ἡ λεγομένη Ἰακώβου φέρεται καὶ ἡ Ἰούδα ἥ τε Πέτρου δευτέρα ἐπιστολὴ καὶ ἡ ὀνομαζομένη δευτέρα καὶ τρίτη Ἰωάννου, εἴτε τοῦ εὐαγγελιστοῦ τυγχάνουσαι εἴτε καὶ ἑτέρου ὁμωνύμου ἐκείνῳ. ἐν τοῖς νόθοις κατατετάχθω καὶ τῶν 4 Παύλου Πράξεων ἡ γραφὴ ὅ τε λεγόμενος Ποιμὴν καὶ ἡ Ἀποκάλυψις Πέτρου καὶ πρὸς τούτοις ἡ φερομένη Βαρναβᾶ ἐπιστολὴ καὶ τῶν ἀποστόλων αἱ λεγόμεναι Διδαχαὶ ἔτι τε, ὡς ἔφην, ἡ Ἰωάννου Ἀποκάλυψις, εἰ φανείη· ἥν τινες, ὡς ἔφην, ἀθετοῦσιν, ἕτεροι δὲ ἐγκρίνουσιν τοῖς ὁμολογουμένοις. ἤδη δ' ἐν τούτοις τινὲς καὶ τὸ καθ' Ἑβραίους εὐαγγέλιον κατέλεξαν, ᾧ μάλιστα Ἑβραίων οἱ τὸν Χριστὸν παραδεξάμενοι χαίρουσιν. ταῦτα δὲ πάντα τῶν ἀντιλεγομένων ἂν εἴη, ἀναγκαίως δὲ καὶ τούτων ὅμως τὸν κατάλογον πεποιήμεθα, διακρίνοντες τάς τε κατὰ τὴν ἐκκλησιαστικὴν παράδοσιν

have been many advocates of either opinion up to the present. This, too, shall be similarly illustrated by quotations from the ancients at the proper time.

XXV. At this point it seems reasonable to summarize the writings of the New Testament which have been quoted. In the first place should be put the holy tetrad of the Gospels. To them follows the writing of the Acts of the Apostles. After this should be reckoned the Epistles of Paul. Following them the Epistle of John called the first, and in the same way should be recognized the Epistle of Peter. In addition to these should be put, if it seem desirable, the Revelation of John, the arguments concerning which we will expound at the proper time. These belong to the Recognized Books. Of the Disputed Books which are nevertheless known to most are the Epistle called of James, that of Jude, the second Epistle of Peter, and the so-called second and third Epistles of John which may be the work of the evangelist or of some other with the same name. Among the books which are not genuine must be reckoned the Acts of Paul, the work entitled the Shepherd, the Apocalypse of Peter, and in addition to them the letter called of Barnabas and the so-called Teachings of the Apostles. And in addition, as I said, the Revelation of John, if this view prevail. For, as I said, some reject it, but others count it among the Recognized Books. Some have also counted the Gospel according to the Hebrews in which those of the Hebrews who have accepted Christ take a special pleasure. These would all belong to the disputed books, but we have nevertheless been obliged to make a list of them, distinguishing between those writings which, according to the tradition of

ἀληθεῖς καὶ ἀπλάστους καὶ ἀνωμολογημένας γραφὰς
καὶ τὰς ἄλλως παρὰ ταύτας, οὐκ ἐνδιαθήκους μὲν
ἀλλὰ καὶ ἀντιλεγομένας, ὅμως δὲ παρὰ πλείστοις
τῶν ἐκκλησιαστικῶν γινωσκομένας, ἵν᾽ εἰδέναι
ἔχοιμεν αὐτάς τε ταύτας καὶ τὰς ὀνόματι τῶν
ἀποστόλων πρὸς τῶν αἱρετικῶν προφερομένας ἤτοι
ὡς Πέτρου καὶ Θωμᾶ καὶ Ματθία ἢ καί τινων παρὰ
τούτους ἄλλων εὐαγγέλια περιεχούσας ἢ ὡς
Ἀνδρέου καὶ Ἰωάννου καὶ τῶν ἄλλων ἀποστόλων
πράξεις· ὧν οὐδὲν οὐδαμῶς ἐν συγγράμματι τῶν
κατὰ τὰς διαδοχὰς ἐκκλησιαστικῶν τις ἀνὴρ εἰς
μνήμην ἀγαγεῖν ἠξίωσεν, πόρρω δέ που καὶ ὁ τῆς 7
φράσεως παρὰ τὸ ἦθος τὸ ἀποστολικὸν ἐναλλάττει
χαρακτήρ, ἥ τε γνώμη καὶ ἡ τῶν ἐν αὐτοῖς φερομένων προαίρεσις πλεῖστον ὅσον τῆς ἀληθοῦς
ὀρθοδοξίας ἀπάδουσα, ὅτι δὴ αἱρετικῶν ἀνδρῶν
ἀναπλάσματα τυγχάνει, σαφῶς παρίστησιν· ὅθεν
οὐδ᾽ ἐν νόθοις αὐτὰ κατατακτέον, ἀλλ᾽ ὡς ἄτοπα
πάντῃ καὶ δυσσεβῆ παραιτητέον.

Iren. 1, 23. 5 XXVI. Ἴωμεν δὴ λοιπὸν καὶ ἐπὶ τὴν ἑξῆς 1
ἱστορίαν. Σίμωνα τὸν μάγον Μένανδρος διαδεξάμενος, ὅπλον δεύτερον οὐ χεῖρον τοῦ προτέρου τῆς
διαβολικῆς ἐνεργείας ἀποδείκνυται τὸν τρόπον. ἦν
καὶ οὗτος Σαμαρεύς, εἰς ἄκρον δὲ γοητείας οὐκ
ἔλαττον τοῦ διδασκάλου προελθών, μείζοσιν ἐπιδαψι-
λεύεται τερατολογίαις, ἑαυτὸν μὲν ὡς ἄρα εἴη,
λέγων, ὁ σωτὴρ ἐπὶ τῇ τῶν ἀνθρώπων ἄνωθέν
ποθεν ἐξ ἀοράτων αἰώνων ἀπεσταλμένος σωτηρίᾳ,
διδάσκων δὲ μὴ ἄλλως δύνασθαί τινα καὶ αὐτῶν τῶν 2
κοσμοποιῶν ἀγγέλων περιγενήσεσθαι, μὴ πρότερον
διὰ τῆς πρὸς αὐτοῦ παραδιδομένης μαγικῆς ἐμπει-
ρίας ἀχθέντα καὶ διὰ τοῦ μεταδιδομένου πρὸς αὐτοῦ

the Church, are true, genuine, and recognized, and those which differ from them in that they are not canonical but disputed, yet nevertheless are known to most of the writers of the Church, in order that we might know them and the writings which are put forward by heretics under the name of the apostles containing gospels such as those of Peter, and Thomas, and Matthias, and some others besides, or Acts such as those of Andrew and John and the other apostles. To none of these has any who belonged to the succession of the orthodox ever thought it right to refer in his writings. Moreover, the type of phraseology differs from apostolic style, and the opinion and tendency of their contents is widely dissonant from true orthodoxy and clearly shows that they are the forgeries of heretics. They ought, therefore, to be reckoned not even among spurious books but shunned as altogether wicked and impious.

XXVI. Let us now continue the narrative. Menander succeeded Simon Magus and showed himself as a weapon of the devil's power not inferior to his predecessor. He, too, was a Samaritan, progressed to the highest point of sorcery not less than his master, and abounded in greater wonders. He said of himself that he was the saviour who had been sent from above for the salvation of men from invisible aeons [1] and taught that no one, not even of the angels who made the world, could survive unless they were first rescued through the magic art which was transmitted by him and through the baptism

---

[1] The Greek word literally means " age," but in ecclesiastical Greek is sometimes used, as here, of the supernatural beings who form part of Gnostic theology.

βαπτίσματος, οὗ τοὺς καταξιουμένους ἀθανασίαν
ἀΐδιον ἐν αὐτῷ τούτῳ μεθέξειν τῷ βίῳ, μηκέτι
θνήσκοντας, αὐτοῦ δὲ παραμένοντας εἰς τὸ ἀεὶ
ἀγήρως τινὰς καὶ ἀθανάτους ἐσομένους. ταῦτα
μὲν οὖν καὶ ἐκ τῶν Εἰρηναίου διαγνῶναι ῥᾴδιον·
καὶ ὁ Ἰουστῖνος δὲ κατὰ τὸ αὐτὸ τοῦ Σίμωνος μνημονεύσας, καὶ τὴν περὶ τούτου διήγησιν ἐπιφέρει,

Justin, Apol.
1, 26 λέγων· " Μένανδρον δέ τινα καὶ αὐτὸν Σαμαρέα,
τὸν ἀπὸ κώμης Καπαρατταίας, γενόμενον μαθητὴν
τοῦ Σίμωνος, οἰστρηθέντα καὶ αὐτὸν ὑπὸ τῶν
δαιμόνων καὶ ἐν Ἀντιοχείᾳ γενόμενον, πολλοὺς
ἐξαπατῆσαι διὰ μαγικῆς τέχνης οἴδαμεν· ὃς καὶ
τοὺς αὐτῷ ἑπομένους ὡς μὴ ἀποθνήσκοιεν, ἔπεισεν,
καὶ νῦν τινές εἰσιν, ἀπ' ἐκείνου τοῦτο ὁμολογοῦντες."

Ἦν δ' ἄρα διαβολικῆς ἐνεργείας διὰ τοιῶνδε
γοήτων τὴν Χριστιανῶν προσηγορίαν ὑποδυομένων
τὸ μέγα τῆς θεοσεβείας μυστήριον ἐπὶ μαγείᾳ σπου-
δάσαι διαβαλεῖν διασῦραί τε δι' αὐτῶν τὰ περὶ ψυχῆς
ἀθανασίας καὶ νεκρῶν ἀναστάσεως ἐκκλησιαστικὰ
δόγματα. ἀλλ' οὗτοι μὲν τούτους σωτῆρας ἐπι-
γραψάμενοι τῆς ἀληθοῦς ἀποπεπτώκασιν ἐλπίδος·
XXVII. ἄλλους δ' ὁ πονηρὸς δαίμων, τῆς περὶ τὸν
Χριστὸν τοῦ θεοῦ διαθέσεως ἀδυνατῶν ἐκσεῖσαι,
θατεραλήπτους εὑρὼν ἐσφετερίζετο· Ἐβιωναίους
τούτους οἰκείως ἐπεφήμιζον οἱ πρῶτοι, πτωχῶς καὶ
ταπεινῶς τὰ περὶ τοῦ Χριστοῦ δοξάζοντας. λιτὸν
μὲν γὰρ αὐτὸν καὶ κοινὸν ἡγοῦντο, κατὰ προκοπὴν
ἤθους αὐτὸ μόνον ἄνθρωπον δεδικαιωμένον ἐξ ἀνδρός
τε κοινωνίας καὶ τῆς Μαρίας γεγεννημένον· δεῖν δὲ
πάντως αὐτοῖς τῆς νομικῆς θρησκείας ὡς μὴ ἂν διὰ
μόνης τῆς εἰς τὸν Χριστὸν πίστεως καὶ τοῦ κατ'
αὐτὴν βίου σωθησομένοις. ἄλλοι δὲ παρὰ τού-

which he delivered, for those who were vouchsafed it would obtain a share of eternal immortality in this life itself, no longer mortal but remaining here, destined to everlasting and ageless immortality. This point can also be easily studied from the writings of Irenaeus. Justin, too, in the same way after mentioning Simon continues his account of him by saying, "We also know that a certain Menander, who also was a Samaritan from the village of Caparattaea, became a disciple of Simon and being similarly stimulated by the demons appeared in Antioch and deceived many by magical arts. He persuaded those who followed him that they would not die, and there are still some of his followers who believe this."

It was assuredly at the instigation of the devil that the name of Christian was adopted by such sorcerers to calumniate by magic the great mystery of religion and through them to destroy the teaching of the Church on the immortality of the soul and the resurrection of the dead. Those who termed these Saviours fell from the true hope. XXVII. But others the wicked demon, when he could not alienate them from God's plan in Christ, made his own, when he found them by a different snare. The first Christians gave these the suitable name of Ebionites because they had poor and mean opinions concerning Christ. They held him to be a plain and ordinary man who had achieved righteousness merely by the progress of his character and had been born naturally from Mary and her husband. They insisted on the complete observation of the Law, and did not think that they would be saved by faith in Christ alone and by a life in accordance with it. But there were others besides these

261

τους τῆς αὐτῆς ὄντες προσηγορίας, τὴν μὲν τῶν
εἰρημένων ἔκτοπον διεδίδρασκον ἀτοπίαν, ἐκ παρθένου καὶ ἁγίου πνεύματος μὴ ἀρνούμενοι γεγονέναι τὸν κύριον, οὐ μὴν ἔθ᾽ ὁμοίως καὶ οὗτοι
προϋπάρχειν αὐτὸν θεὸν λόγον ὄντα καὶ σοφίαν
ὁμολογοῦντες, τῇ τῶν προτέρων περιετρέποντο
δυσσεβείᾳ, μάλιστα ὅτε καὶ τὴν σωματικὴν περὶ
τὸν νόμον λατρείαν ὁμοίως ἐκείνοις περιέπειν
ἐσπούδαζον. οὗτοι δὲ τοῦ μὲν ἀποστόλου πάμπαν τὰς ἐπιστολὰς ἀρνητέας ἡγοῦντο εἶναι δεῖν,
ἀποστάτην ἀποκαλοῦντες αὐτὸν τοῦ νόμου, εὐαγγελίῳ δὲ μόνῳ τῷ καθ᾽ Ἑβραίους λεγομένῳ
χρώμενοι, τῶν λοιπῶν σμικρὸν ἐποιοῦντο λόγον·
καὶ τὸ μὲν σάββατον καὶ τὴν ἄλλην Ἰουδαϊκὴν
ἀγωγὴν ὁμοίως ἐκείνοις παρεφύλαττον, ταῖς δ᾽
αὖ κυριακαῖς ἡμέραις ἡμῖν τὰ παραπλήσια εἰς
μνήμην τῆς σωτηρίου ἀναστάσεως ἐπετέλουν·
ὅθεν παρὰ τὴν τοιαύτην ἐγχείρησιν τῆς τοιᾶσδε
λελόγχασι προσηγορίας, τοῦ Ἐβιωναίων ὀνόματος
τὴν τῆς διανοίας πτωχείαν αὐτῶν ὑποφαίνοντος·
ταύτῃ γὰρ ἐπίκλην ὁ πτωχὸς παρ᾽ Ἑβραίοις
ὀνομάζεται.

XXVIII. Κατὰ τοὺς δηλουμένους χρόνους ἑτέρας αἱρέσεως ἀρχηγὸν γενέσθαι Κήρινθον παρει-
λήφαμεν· Γάϊος, οὗ φωνὰς ἤδη πρότερον παρα-
τέθειμαι, ἐν τῇ φερομένῃ αὐτοῦ ζητήσει ταῦτα
περὶ αὐτοῦ γράφει·

Rev. 1, 2.22,8
Rev. 20. 4-6
Rev. 21, 2.
10. 22, 1. 2.
14. 17
Rev. 20, 3. 6
Rev. 19, 7. 9.
21, 2.9.22,17
"'Ἀλλὰ καὶ Κήρινθος ὁ δι᾽ ἀποκαλύψεων ὡς ὑπὸ
ἀποστόλου μεγάλου γεγραμμένων τερατολογίας
ἡμῖν ὡς δι᾽ ἀγγέλων αὐτῷ δεδειγμένας ψευδόμενος
ἐπεισάγει, λέγων μετὰ τὴν ἀνάστασιν ἐπίγειον
εἶναι τὸ βασίλειον τοῦ Χριστοῦ καὶ πάλιν ἐπι-

who have the same name. These escaped the absurd folly of the first mentioned, and did not deny that the Lord was born of a Virgin and the Holy Spirit, but nevertheless agreed with them in not confessing his pre-existence as God, being the Logos and Wisdom. Thus they shared in the impiety of the former class, especially in that they were equally zealous to insist on the literal observance of the Law. They thought that the letters of the Apostle[1] ought to be wholly rejected and called him an apostate from the Law. They used only the Gospel called according to the Hebrews and made little account of the rest. Like the former they used to observe the sabbath and the rest of the Jewish ceremonial, but on Sundays celebrated rites like ours in commemoration of the Saviour's resurrection. Wherefore from these practices they have obtained their name, for the name of Ebionites indicates the poverty of their intelligence, for this name means " poor " in Hebrew.[2]

XXVIII. We have received the tradition that at the time under discussion Cerinthus founded another heresy. Gaius, whose words I have quoted before, in the inquiry attributed to him writes as follows about Cerinthus. " Moreover, Cerinthus, who through revelations attributed to the writing of a great apostle, lyingly introduces portents to us as though shown him by angels, and says that after the resurrection the kingdom of Christ will be on earth and that

---

[1] That is, Paul.
[2] The word does mean "poor" in Hebrew; but it is not known why it was applied to the Jewish Christians. One guess is as good as another.

θυμίαις καὶ ἡδοναῖς ἐν Ἱερουσαλὴμ τὴν σάρκα
πολιτευομένην δουλεύειν. καὶ ἐχθρὸς ὑπάρχων
ταῖς γραφαῖς τοῦ θεοῦ, ἀριθμὸν χιλιονταετίας ἐν
γάμῳ ἑορτῆς, θέλων πλανᾶν, λέγει γίνεσθαι.''

Καὶ Διονύσιος δέ, ὁ τῆς κατὰ Ἀλεξάνδρειαν **3**
παροικίας καθ᾽ ἡμᾶς τὴν ἐπισκοπὴν εἰληχώς, ἐν
δευτέρῳ τῶν Ἐπαγγελιῶν περὶ τῆς Ἰωάννου
Ἀποκαλύψεως εἰπών τινα ὡς ἐκ τῆς ἀνέκαθεν
παραδόσεως, τοῦ αὐτοῦ μέμνηται ἀνδρὸς τούτοις
τοῖς ῥήμασιν·

'' Κήρινθον δέ, τὸν καὶ τὴν ἀπ᾽ ἐκείνου κληθεῖ- **4**
σαν Κηρινθιανὴν αἵρεσιν συστησάμενον, ἀξιόπιστον ἐπιφημίσαι θελήσαντα τῷ ἑαυτοῦ πλάσματι
ὄνομα. τοῦτο γὰρ εἶναι τῆς διδασκαλίας αὐτοῦ **5**
τὸ δόγμα, ἐπίγειον ἔσεσθαι τὴν τοῦ Χριστοῦ
βασιλείαν, καὶ ὧν αὐτὸς ὠρέγετο, φιλοσώματος
ὢν καὶ πάνυ σαρκικός, ἐν τούτοις ὀνειροπολεῖν
ἔσεσθαι, γαστρὸς καὶ τῶν ὑπὸ γαστέρα πλησμο-
ναῖς, τοῦτ᾽ ἐστὶ σιτίοις καὶ πότοις καὶ γάμοις καὶ
δι᾽ ὧν εὐφημότερον ταῦτα ᾠήθη ποριεῖσθαι,
ἑορταῖς καὶ θυσίαις καὶ ἱερείων σφαγαῖς.''

Iren. 1, 26. 1 Ταῦτα Διονύσιος· ὁ δὲ Εἰρηναῖος ἀπορρητοτέ- **6**
ρας δή τινας τοῦ αὐτοῦ ψευδοδοξίας ἐν πρώτῳ
συγγράμματι τῶν πρὸς τὰς αἱρέσεις προθείς, ἐν
τῷ τρίτῳ καὶ ἱστορίαν οὐκ ἀξίαν λήθης τῇ γραφῇ
Iren. 3, 3. 4 παραδέδωκεν, ὡς ἐκ παραδόσεως Πολυκάρπου
φάσκων Ἰωάννην τὸν ἀπόστολον εἰσελθεῖν ποτε
ἐν βαλανείῳ, ὥστε λούσασθαι, γνόντα δὲ ἔνδον
ὄντα τὸν Κήρινθον, ἀποπηδῆσαί τε τοῦ τόπου καὶ
ἐκφυγεῖν θύραζε, μηδ᾽ ὑπομείναντα τὴν αὐτὴν
αὐτῷ ὑποδῦναι στέγην, ταὐτὸ δὲ τοῦτο καὶ τοῖς
σὺν αὐτῷ παραινέσαι, φήσαντα '' φύγωμεν, μὴ

humanity living in Jerusalem will again be the slave of lust and pleasure He is the enemy of the scriptures of God and in his desire to deceive says that the marriage feast [1] will last a thousand years." Dionysius, too, who held the bishopric of the diocese of Alexandria in our time, in the second book of his Promises makes some remarks about the Apocalypse of John as though from ancient tradition and refers to the same Cerinthus in these words, " Cerinthus too, who founded the Cerinthian heresy named after him, wished to attach a name worthy of credit to his own invention, for the doctrine of his teaching was this, that the kingdom of Christ would be on earth, and being fond of his body and very carnal he dreamt of a future according to his own desires, given up to the indulgence of the flesh, that is, eating and drinking and marrying, and to those things which seem a euphemism for these things, feasts and sacrifices and the slaughter of victims."

Dionysius said this and Irenaeus in his first book *Against Heresies* quoted some of his more abominable errors, and in the third book has committed to writing a narrative, which deserves not to be forgotten, stating how, according to the tradition of Polycarp, the apostle John once went into a bath-house to wash, but when he knew that Cerinthus was within leapt out of the place and fled from the door, for he did not endure to be even under the same roof with him, and enjoined on those who were with him to do the same, saying, " Let us flee, lest the bath-house

---

[1] This is the obvious sense of the Greek which is, however, clearly corrupt. It would appear that Gaius thought that Cerinthus was the writer of the Apocalypse.

καὶ τὸ βαλανεῖον συμπέσῃ, ἔνδον ὄντος
τοῦ τῆς ἀληθείας ἐχθροῦ."

XXIX. Ἐπὶ τούτων δῆτα καὶ ἡ λεγομένη τῶν 1
Νικολαϊτῶν αἵρεσις ἐπὶ σμικρότατον συνέστη
χρόνον, ἧς δὴ καὶ ἡ τοῦ Ἰωάννου Ἀποκάλυψις
μνημονεύει· οὗτοι Νικόλαον ἕνα τῶν ἀμφὶ τὸν
Στέφανον διακόνων πρὸς τῶν ἀποστόλων ἐπὶ τῇ
τῶν ἐνδεῶν θεραπείᾳ προκεχειρισμένων ηὔχουν.
ὅ γε μὴν Ἀλεξανδρεὺς Κλήμης ἐν τρίτῳ Στρωματεῖ ταῦτα περὶ αὐτοῦ κατὰ λέξιν ἱστορεῖ·
"'Ὡραίαν, φασί, γυναῖκα ἔχων οὗτος, μετὰ τὴν 2
ἀνάληψιν τὴν τοῦ σωτῆρος πρὸς τῶν ἀποστόλων
ὀνειδισθεὶς ζηλοτυπίαν, εἰς μέσον ἀγαγὼν τὴν
γυναῖκα γῆμαι τῷ βουλομένῳ ἐπέτρεψεν. ἀκόλουθον γὰρ εἶναί φασι τὴν πρᾶξιν ταύτην ἐκείνῃ
τῇ φωνῇ τῇ ὅτι 'παραχρᾶσθαι τῇ σαρκὶ δεῖ,'
καὶ δὴ κατακολουθήσαντες τῷ γεγενημένῳ τῷ
τε εἰρημένῳ ἁπλῶς καὶ ἀβασανίστως, ἀνέδην
ἐκπορνεύουσιν οἱ τὴν αἵρεσιν αὐτοῦ μετιόντες.
πυνθάνομαι δ' ἐγὼ τὸν Νικόλαον μηδεμιᾷ ἑτέρᾳ 3
παρ' ἣν ἔγημε κεχρῆσθαι γυναικί, τῶν τε ἐκείνου
τέκνων τὰς μὲν θηλείας καταγηρᾶσαι παρθένους,
ἄφθορον δὲ διαμεῖναι τὸν υἱόν· ὧν οὕτως ἐχόντων
ἀποβολὴ πάθους ἦν ἡ εἰς μέσον τῶν ἀποστόλων
τῆς ζηλοτυπουμένης ἐκκύκλησις γυναικός, καὶ ἡ
ἐγκράτεια τῶν περισπουδάστων ἡδονῶν τὸ 'παραχρᾶσθαι τῇ σαρκὶ' ἐδίδασκεν. οὐ γάρ, οἶμαι,
ἐβούλετο κατὰ τὴν τοῦ σωτῆρος ἐντολὴν 'δυσὶ
κυρίοις δουλεύειν,' ἡδονῇ καὶ κυρίῳ. λέγουσι 4
δ' οὖν καὶ τὸν Ματθίαν οὕτω διδάξαι, σαρκὶ μὲν
μάχεσθαι καὶ παραχρᾶσθαι μηδὲν αὐτῇ πρὸς
ἡδονὴν ἐνδιδόντα, ψυχὴν δὲ αὔξειν διὰ πίστεως καὶ

Rev. 2, 6. 15
Acts 6, 5
Clem. Strom.
3, 25. 26
Clem. Strom.
2, 118
Matt. 6, 24
Luke 16, 13

fall in, for Cerinthus, the enemy of the truth, is within."

XXIX. At this time, too, there existed for a short time the heresy of the Nicolaïtans of which the Apocalypse of John also makes mention. These claimed Nicolas, one of the deacons in the company of Stephen who were appointed by the Apostles for the service of the poor. Clement of Alexandria in the third book of the *Stromata* gives the following account of him. " He had, they say, a beautiful wife ; but after the ascension of the Saviour he was accused of jealousy by the apostles, and brought her forward and commanded her to be mated to anyone who wished. They say that this action was in consequence of the injunction ' it is necessary to abuse the flesh,' and that by following up what had been done and said with simplicity and without perversion those who follow his heresy lead a life of unrestrained license. But I have learned that Nicolas had nothing to do with any other woman beside her whom he married, and that of his children the daughters reached old age as virgins, and that the son remained uncorrupted. Since this is the case it is clear that the exposure of the wife of whom he was jealous in the midst of the disciples was the abandonment of passion, and that teaching the abuse of the flesh was continence from the pleasures which he had sought. For I think that according to the command of the Saviour he did not wish to serve two masters —pleasure and the Lord. They also say that this was the teaching of Matthias, to slight the flesh and abuse it, yielding nothing to it for pleasure, but to make the soul grow through faith and knowledge."

γνώσεως." ταῦτα μὲν οὖν περὶ τῶν κατὰ τοὺς δηλουμένους χρόνους παραβραβεῦσαι τὴν ἀλήθειαν ἐγκεχειρηκότων, λόγου γε μὴν θᾶττον εἰς τὸ παντελὲς ἀπεσβηκότων εἰρήσθω.

XXX. Ὁ μέντοι Κλήμης, οὗ τὰς φωνὰς ἀρτίως 1 ἀνέγνωμεν, τοῖς προειρημένοις ἑξῆς διὰ τοὺς ἀθετοῦντας τὸν γάμον τοὺς τῶν ἀποστόλων ἐξ-

Clem. Strom.
3, 52. 53 ετασθέντας ἐν συζυγίαις καταλέγει, φάσκων· " ἢ καὶ τοὺς ἀποστόλους ἀποδοκιμάσουσιν; Πέτρος μὲν γὰρ καὶ Φίλιππος ἐπαιδοποιήσαντο, Φίλιππος δὲ καὶ τὰς θυγατέρας ἀνδράσιν ἐξέδωκεν, καὶ ὅ γε

Phil. 4, 3
1 Cor. 9, 5.
12 Παῦλος οὐκ ὀκνεῖ ἔν τινι ἐπιστολῇ τὴν αὑτοῦ προσαγορεῦσαι σύζυγον, ἣν οὐ περιεκόμιζεν διὰ τὸ τῆς ὑπηρεσίας εὐσταλές." ἐπεὶ δὲ τούτων 2 ἐμνήσθημεν, οὐ λυπεῖ καὶ ἄλλην ἀξιοδιήγητον ἱστορίαν τοῦ αὐτοῦ παραθέσθαι, ἣν ἐν τῷ ἑβδόμῳ Στρωματεῖ τοῦτον ἱστορῶν ἀνέγραψεν τὸν τρόπον·

Clem. Strom.
7, 63. 64 " φασὶ γοῦν τὸν μακάριον Πέτρον θεασάμενον τὴν ἑαυτοῦ γυναῖκα ἀπαγομένην τὴν ἐπὶ θανάτῳ, ἡσθῆναι μὲν τῆς κλήσεως χάριν καὶ τῆς εἰς οἶκον ἀνακομιδῆς, ἐπιφωνῆσαι δὲ εὖ μάλα προτρεπτι- κῶς καὶ παρακλητικῶς, ἐξ ὀνόματος προσειπόντα ' μέμνησο, ὦ αὕτη, τοῦ κυρίου.' τοιοῦτος ἦν ὁ τῶν μακαρίων γάμος καὶ ἡ τῶν φιλτάτων τελεία διάθεσις." καὶ ταῦτα δ', οἰκεῖα ὄντα τῇ μετὰ χεῖρας ὑποθέσει, ἐνταῦθά μοι κατὰ καιρὸν κείσθω.

XXXI. Παύλου μὲν οὖν καὶ Πέτρου τῆς 1 τελευτῆς ὅ τε χρόνος καὶ ὁ τρόπος καὶ πρὸς ἔτι τῆς μετὰ τὴν ἀπαλλαγὴν τοῦ βίου τῶν σκηνω- μάτων αὐτῶν καταθέσεως ὁ χῶρος ἤδη πρότερον ἡμῖν δεδήλωται· τοῦ δὲ Ἰωάννου τὰ μὲν τοῦ 2

Let this suffice concerning the attempts made during this period to triumph against the truth which were, nevertheless, extinguished for ever more quickly than it takes to tell.

XXX. Clement, whose words we cited recently in the context of the previous quotation, enumerates, on account of those who reject marriage, those of the Apostles who were married, saying, " Or will they disapprove even of the Apostles ? For Peter and Philip begat children, and Philip even gave his daughters to husbands, while Paul himself does not hesitate in one of his letters to address[1] his wife whom he did not take about with him in order to facilitate his mission." Since we have made these quotations there is no harm in adducing another memorable narrative of Clement which he wrote down in the seventh book of the *Stromata*, and narrates as follows : " They say that the blessed Peter when he saw his own wife led out to death rejoiced at her calling and at her return home, and called out to her in true warning and comfort, addressing her by her name, ' Remember the Lord.' Such was the marriage of the blessed and the perfect disposition of those dearest to them." Let this, cognate to the present subject, suffice for the moment.

XXXI. The time and manner of the death of Paul and of Peter, and the place where their corpses were laid after their departure from this life, have been already described by us. The date of the death of

---

[1] Philipp. iv. 3 γνήσιε σύζυγε, ' true yoke-fellow ' or ' wife.'

χρόνου ἤδη πως εἴρηται, τὸ δέ γε τοῦ σκηνώματος αὐτοῦ χωρίον ἐξ ἐπιστολῆς Πολυκράτους (τῆς δ' ἐν Ἐφέσῳ παροικίας ἐπίσκοπος οὗτος ἦν) ἐπιδείκνυται, ἣν Οὐίκτορι Ῥωμαίων ἐπισκόπῳ γράφων, ὁμοῦ τε αὐτοῦ καὶ Φιλίππου μνημονεύει τοῦ ἀποστόλου τῶν τε τούτου θυγατέρων ὧδέ πως· "καὶ γὰρ κατὰ τὴν Ἀσίαν μεγάλα στοιχεῖα 3 κεκοίμηται· ἅτινα ἀναστήσεται τῇ ἐσχάτῃ ἡμέρᾳ τῆς παρουσίας τοῦ κυρίου, ἐν ᾗ ἔρχεται μετὰ δόξης ἐξ οὐρανοῦ καὶ ἀναζητήσει πάντας τοὺς ἁγίους, Φίλιππον τῶν δώδεκα ἀποστόλων, ὃς κεκοίμηται ἐν Ἱεραπόλει καὶ δύο θυγατέρες αὐτοῦ γεγηρακυῖαι παρθένοι καὶ ἡ ἑτέρα αὐτοῦ
John 13, 25.
21, 20 θυγάτηρ ἐν ἁγίῳ πνεύματι πολιτευσαμένη ἐν Ἐφέσῳ ἀναπαύεται· ἔτι δὲ καὶ Ἰωάννης, ὁ ἐπὶ τὸ στῆθος τοῦ κυρίου ἀναπεσών, ὃς ἐγενήθη
Exod. 28, 32-
34
Lev. 8, 9
Matt. 18, 18 ἱερεὺς τὸ πέταλον πεφορεκὼς καὶ μάρτυς καὶ διδάσκαλος, οὗτος ἐν Ἐφέσῳ κεκοίμηται." ταῦτα 4 καὶ περὶ τῆς τῶνδε τελευτῆς· καὶ ἐν τῷ Γαΐου δέ, οὗ μικρῷ πρόσθεν ἐμνήσθημεν, διαλόγῳ Πρόκλος, πρὸς ὃν ἐποιεῖτο τὴν ζήτησιν, περὶ τῆς Φιλίππου καὶ τῶν θυγατέρων αὐτοῦ τελευτῆς, συνᾴδων τοῖς ἐκτεθεῖσιν, οὕτω φησίν· "μετὰ τοῦτον προφήτιδες τέσσαρες αἱ Φιλίππου γεγένηνται ἐν Ἱεραπόλει τῇ κατὰ τὴν Ἀσίαν· ὁ τάφος αὐτῶν ἔστιν ἐκεῖ καὶ ὁ τοῦ πατρὸς αὐτῶν." ταῦτα 5 μὲν οὗτος· ὁ δὲ Λουκᾶς ἐν ταῖς Πράξεσιν τῶν ἀποστόλων τῶν Φιλίππου θυγατέρων ἐν Καισαρείᾳ τῆς Ἰουδαίας ἅμα τῷ πατρὶ τότε διατριβουσῶν προφητικοῦ τε χαρίσματος ἠξιωμένων

---

¹ Bk. iii. 23. 4, where Irenaeus, *Haer.* ii. 22. 5 is quoted to show that John lived until the reign of Trajan.

John has also been already[1] mentioned, and the place of his body is shown by a letter of Polycrates (he was bishop of the diocese of Ephesus) which he wrote to Victor, bishop of Rome. In this he mentions both John, Philip the apostle,[2] and Philip's daughters as follows: " For great luminaries sleep in Asia, and they will rise again at the last day of the advent of the Lord, when he shall come with glory from heaven and call back all the saints, such as was Philip, one of the twelve apostles, who sleeps at Hierapolis with his two daughters who grew old as virgins and his third daughter[3] who lived in the Holy Spirit and rests in Ephesus. And there is also John, who leaned on the Lord's breast, who was a priest wearing the mitre,[4] and martyr and teacher, and he sleeps at Ephesus." So far concerning their deaths. And in the dialogue of Gaius, which we mentioned a little earlier, Proclus, with whom he was disputing, speaks thus about the death of Philip and his daughters and agrees with what has been stated. " After him the four daughters of Philip who were prophetesses were at Hierapolis in Asia. Their grave is there and so is their father's." So he says. And Luke in the Acts of the Apostles mentions the daughters of Philip who were then living with their father at Caesarea in Judaea and were vouchsafed the gift of prophecy. He says as

[2] Possibly Polycrates has confused Philip the Apostle and Philip the Deacon, and Eusebius did not notice it.

[3] This must be the meaning unless the text be corrupt. The Greek word translated " third " ought to mean " the second of two."

[4] The word πέταλον is used in the LXX. of the " plate " or " diadem " of the High Priest (cf. Exod. xxviii.), but what it means here has never been discovered.

Acts 21, 8. 9 μνημονεύει, κατὰ λέξιν ὧδέ πως λέγων· '' ἤλθομεν εἰς Καισάρειαν, καὶ εἰσελθόντες εἰς τὸν οἶκον Φιλίππου τοῦ εὐαγγελιστοῦ, ὄντος ἐκ τῶν ἑπτά, ἐμείναμεν παρ' αὐτῷ. τούτῳ δὲ ἦσαν παρθένοι θυγατέρες τέσσαρες προφητεύουσαι.''

Τὰ μὲν οὖν εἰς ἡμετέραν ἐλθόντα γνῶσιν περί 6 τε τῶν ἀποστόλων καὶ τῶν ἀποστολικῶν χρόνων ὧν τε καταλελοίπασιν ἡμῖν ἱερῶν γραμμάτων καὶ τῶν ἀντιλεγομένων μέν, ὅμως δ' ἐν πλείσταις ἐκκλησίαις παρὰ πολλοῖς δεδημοσιευμένων τῶν τε παντελῶς νόθων καὶ τῆς ἀποστολικῆς ὀρθοδοξίας ἀλλοτρίων ἐν τούτοις διειληφότες, ἐπὶ τὴν τῶν ἑξῆς προΐωμεν ἱστορίαν.

XXXII. Μετὰ Νέρωνα καὶ Δομετιανὸν κατὰ 1 τοῦτον οὗ νῦν τοὺς χρόνους ἐξετάζομεν, μερικῶς καὶ κατὰ πόλεις ἐξ ἐπαναστάσεως δήμων τὸν καθ' ἡμῶν κατέχει λόγος ἀνακινηθῆναι διωγμόν· ἐν ᾧ Συμεῶνα τὸν τοῦ Κλωπᾶ, ὃν δεύτερον κατα- στῆναι τῆς ἐν Ἱεροσολύμοις ἐκκλησίας ἐπίσκοπον ἐδηλώσαμεν, μαρτυρίῳ τὸν βίον ἀναλῦσαι παρ- ειλήφαμεν. καὶ τούτου μάρτυς αὐτὸς ἐκεῖνος, 2 οὗ διαφόροις ἤδη πρότερον ἐχρησάμεθα φωναῖς, Ἡγήσιππος· ὃς δὴ περί τινων αἱρετικῶν ἱστορῶν, ἐπιφέρει δηλῶν ὡς ἄρα ὑπὸ τούτων κατὰ τόνδε τὸν χρόνον ὑπομείνας κατηγορίαν, πολυτρόπως ὁ δηλούμενος ὡς ἂν Χριστιανὸς ἐπὶ πλείσταις αἰκισθεὶς ἡμέραις αὐτόν τε τὸν δικαστὴν καὶ τοὺς ἀμφ' αὐτὸν εἰς τὰ μέγιστα καταπλήξας, τῷ τοῦ κυρίου πάθει παραπλήσιον τέλος ἀπηνέγκατο· οὐδὲν δὲ οἷον καὶ τοῦ συγγραφέως ἐπακοῦσαι, 3 αὐτὰ δὴ ταῦτα κατὰ λέξιν ὧδέ πως ἱστοροῦντος '' ἀπὸ τούτων δηλαδὴ τῶν αἱρετικῶν κατηγοροῦσί

follows : " We came to Caesarea and entered into
the house of Philip the Evangelist, one of the seven,
and remained with him. And he had four daughters
who were prophetesses."

We have now described the facts which have come
to our knowledge concerning the Apostles and their
times, the sacred writings which they have left us,
those books which are disputed yet nevertheless are
used openly by many in most churches, and those
which are altogether fictitious and foreign to our
historic orthodoxy. Let us now continue the
narrative.

XXXII. After Nero and Domitian tradition says
that under the Emperor whose times we are now describing persecution was raised against us sporadi-
cally, in some cities, from popular risings. We have
learnt that in it Symeon, the son of Clopas, whom
we showed to have been the second bishop of the
church at Jerusalem, ended his life in martyrdom.
The witness for this is that same Hegesippus, of
whom we have already quoted several passages.
After speaking of certain heretics he goes on to
explain how Symeon was at this time accused by
them and for many days was tortured in various
manners for being a Christian, to the great astonish-
ment of the judge and those with him, until he
suffered an end like that of the Lord. But there is
nothing better than to listen to the historian who
tells these facts as follows. " Some of these (that

τινες Σίμωνος τοῦ Κλωπᾶ ὡς ὄντος ἀπὸ Δαυὶδ
καὶ Χριστιανοῦ, καὶ οὕτως μαρτυρεῖ ἐτῶν ὢν ρκ
ἐπὶ Τραϊανοῦ Καίσαρος καὶ ὑπατικοῦ Ἀττικοῦ.''
φησὶν δὲ ὁ αὐτὸς ὡς ἄρα καὶ τοὺς κατηγόρους 4
αὐτοῦ, ζητουμένων τότε τῶν ἀπὸ τῆς βασιλικῆς
Ἰουδαίων φυλῆς, ὡς ἂν ἐξ αὐτῶν ὄντας ἁλῶναι
συνέβη. λογισμῷ δ' ἂν καὶ τὸν Συμεῶνα τῶν
αὐτοπτῶν καὶ αὐτηκόων εἴποι ἄν τις γεγονέναι
τοῦ κυρίου, τεκμηρίῳ τῷ μήκει τοῦ χρόνου τῆς
αὐτοῦ ζωῆς χρώμενος καὶ τῷ μνημονεύειν τὴν
John 19. 25 τῶν εὐαγγελίων γραφὴν Μαρίας τῆς τοῦ Κλωπᾶ,
Eus. H.E.
iii. 11. 1 οὗ γεγονέναι αὐτὸν καὶ πρότερον ὁ λόγος ἐδήλωσεν.

Ὁ δ' αὐτὸς συγγραφεὺς καὶ ἑτέρους ἀπογόνους 5
ἑνὸς τῶν φερομένων ἀδελφῶν τοῦ σωτῆρος, ᾧ
ὄνομα Ἰούδας, φησὶν εἰς τὴν αὐτὴν ἐπιβιῶναι
βασιλείαν μετὰ τὴν ἤδη πρότερον ἱστορηθεῖσαν
αὐτῶν ὑπὲρ τῆς εἰς τὸν Χριστὸν πίστεως ἐπὶ
Δομετιανοῦ μαρτυρίαν, γράφει δὲ οὕτως· '' ἔρχονται 6
οὖν καὶ προηγοῦνται πάσης ἐκκλησίας ὡς μάρτυρες
καὶ ἀπὸ γένους τοῦ κυρίου, καὶ γενομένης εἰρήνης
βαθείας ἐν πάσῃ ἐκκλησίᾳ, μένουσι μέχρι Τραϊανοῦ
Καίσαρος, μέχρις οὗ ὁ ἐκ θείου τοῦ κυρίου, ὁ
προειρημένος Σίμων υἱὸς Κλωπᾶ, συκοφαντηθεὶς
ὑπὸ τῶν αἱρέσεων ὡσαύτως κατηγορήθη καὶ
αὐτὸς ἐπὶ τῷ αὐτῷ λόγῳ ἐπὶ Ἀττικοῦ τοῦ ὑπατικοῦ.
καὶ ἐπὶ πολλαῖς ἡμέραις αἰκιζόμενος ἐμαρτύρησεν,
ὡς πάντας ὑπερθαυμάζειν καὶ τὸν ὑπατικὸν πῶς
ρκ τυγχάνων ἐτῶν ὑπέμεινεν, καὶ ἐκελεύσθη
σταυρωθῆναι.''

Ἐπὶ τούτοις ὁ αὐτὸς ἀνὴρ διηγούμενος τὰ κατὰ 7

---

[1] The date of Atticus is unknown, but in the *Chronicon*

is to say the heretics) accused Simon the son of Clopas of being descended from David and a Christian and thus he suffered martyrdom, being a hundred and twenty years old, when Trajan was emperor and Atticus was Consular.[1]" The same writer says that his accusers also suffered arrest for being of the royal house of the Jews when search was made at that time for those of that family. And one would reasonably say that Symeon was one of the eyewitnesses and actual hearers of the Lord on the evidence of the length of his life and the reference in the Gospels to Mary the wife of Clopas whose son the narrative has already shown him to be.

The same writer says that other grandsons of one of the so-called brethren of the Saviour named Judas survived to the same reign after they had given in the time of Domitian the testimony already recorded of them in behalf of the faith in Christ. He writes thus : " They came therefore and presided over every church as witnesses belonging to the Lord's family, and when there was complete peace in every church they survived until the reign of the Emperor Trajan, until the time when the son of the Lord's uncle,[2] the aforesaid Simon the son of Clopas, was similarly accused by the sects on the same charge before Atticus the Consular. He was tortured for many days and gave his witness, so that all, even the consular, were extremely surprised how, at the age of one hundred and twenty, he endured, and he was commanded to be crucified." Besides this the same writer, explaining the events

Eusebius dates the martyrdom of Symeon in the ninth or tenth year of Trajan (A.D. 106 or 107).
[2] He was the brother of Joseph; see iii. 11. 1.

τοὺς δηλουμένους, ἐπιλέγει ὡς ἄρα μέχρι τῶν
τότε χρόνων παρθένος καθαρὰ καὶ ἀδιάφθορος
ἔμεινεν ἡ ἐκκλησία, ἐν ἀδήλῳ που σκότει ὡς εἰ
φωλευόντων εἰς ἔτι τότε τῶν, εἰ καί τινες ὑπῆρχον,
παραφθείρειν ἐπιχειρούντων τὸν ὑγιῆ κανόνα τοῦ
σωτηρίου κηρύγματος· ὡς δ' ὁ ἱερὸς τῶν ἀποστόλων χορὸς διάφορον εἰλήφει τοῦ βίου τέλος παρ-
εληλύθει τε ἡ γενεὰ ἐκείνη τῶν αὐταῖς ἀκοαῖς
τῆς ἐνθέου σοφίας ἐπακοῦσαι κατηξιωμένων, τηνικαῦτα τῆς ἀθέου πλάνης ἀρχὴν ἐλάμβανεν ἡ
σύστασις διὰ τῆς τῶν ἑτεροδιδασκάλων ἀπάτης,
οἳ καὶ ἅτε μηδενὸς ἔτι τῶν ἀποστόλων λειπο-
1 Tim. 6 20 μένου, γυμνῇ λοιπὸν ἤδη κεφαλῇ τῷ τῆς ἀληθείας
κηρύγματι τὴν ψευδώνυμον γνῶσιν ἀντικηρύττειν
ἐπεχείρουν.

XXXIII. Τοσοῦτός γε μὴν ἐν πλείοσι τόποις
ὁ καθ' ἡμῶν ἐπετάθη τότε διωγμός, ὡς Πλίνιον
Σεκοῦνδον, ἐπισημότατον ἡγεμόνων, ἐπὶ τῷ πλήθει
τῶν μαρτύρων κινηθέντα, βασιλεῖ κοινώσασθαι
περὶ τοῦ πλήθους τῶν ὑπὲρ τῆς πίστεως ἀναιρου-
μένων, ἅμα δ' ἐν ταὐτῷ μηνῦσαι μηδὲν ἀνόσιον
μηδὲ παρὰ τοὺς νόμους πράττειν αὐτοὺς κατειληφέναι, πλὴν τό γε ἅμα τῇ ἕῳ διεγειρομένους
τὸν Χριστὸν θεοῦ δίκην ὑμνεῖν, τὸ δὲ μοιχεύειν
καὶ φονεύειν καὶ τὰ συγγενῆ τούτοις ἀθέμιτα
πλημμελήματα καὶ αὐτοὺς ἀπαγορεύειν πάντα
τε πράττειν ἀκολούθως τοῖς νόμοις· πρὸς ἃ τὸν
Τραϊανὸν δόγμα τοιόνδε τεθεικέναι, τὸ Χριστιανῶν·
φῦλον μὴ ἐκζητεῖσθαι μέν, ἐμπεσὸν δὲ κολάζεσθαι·
δι' οὗ ποσῶς μὲν τοῦ διωγμοῦ σβεσθῆναι τὴν
ἀπειλὴν σφοδρότατα ἐγκειμένην, οὐ χεῖρόν γε
μὴν τοῖς κακουργεῖν περὶ ἡμᾶς ἐθέλουσιν λείπεσθαι
276

of these times, adds that until then the church remained a pure and uncorrupted virgin, for those who attempted to corrupt the healthful rule of the Saviour's preaching, if they existed at all, lurked in obscure darkness. But when the sacred band of the Apostles and the generation of those to whom it had been vouchsafed to hear with their own ears the divine wisdom had reached the several ends of their lives, then the federation of godless error took its beginning through the deceit of false teachers who, seeing that none of the Apostles still remained, barefacedly tried against the preaching of the truth the counter-proclamation of " knowledge falsely so-called."

XXXIII. The persecution which at that time was extended against us in many places was so great that Plinius Secundus, one of the most distinguished governors, was disturbed at the number of the martyrs, and reported to the Emperor the number of those being put to death for the faith, and in the same document mentioned that he understood them to do nothing wicked or illegal except that they rose at dawn to sing to Christ as though a God, and that they themselves forbade adultery, murder and similar terrible crimes, and that they did everything in obedience to the law. In answer to this Trajan issued a decree to the effect that the tribe of Christians should not be sought for but punished when it was met with. By this means the imminent threat of persecution was extinguished to some extent, but none the less opportunities remained to those who wished to harm

προφάσεις, ἔσθ' ὅπῃ μὲν τῶν δήμων, ἔσθ' ὅπῃ
δὲ καὶ τῶν κατὰ χώρας ἀρχόντων τὰς καθ' ἡμῶν
συσκευαζομένων ἐπιβουλάς, ὡς καὶ ἄνευ προ-
φανῶν διωγμῶν μερικοὺς κατ' ἐπαρχίαν ἐξάπτεσθαι
πλείους τε τῶν πιστῶν διαφόροις ἐναγωνίζεσθαι
μαρτυρίοις. εἴληπται δ' ἡ ἱστορία ἐξ ἧς ἀνώτερον
δεδηλώκαμεν τοῦ Τερτυλλιανοῦ Ῥωμαϊκῆς ἀπολογίας, ἧς ἡ ἑρμηνεία τοῦτον ἔχει τὸν τρόπον·

Tert. Apol. 2 "καίτοι εὑρήκαμεν καὶ τὴν εἰς ἡμᾶς ἐπιζήτησιν
κεκωλυμένην. Πλίνιος γὰρ Σεκοῦνδος ἡγούμενος
ἐπαρχίου κατακρίνας Χριστιανούς τινας καὶ τῆς
ἀξίας ἐκβαλών, ταραχθεὶς τῷ πλήθει, διὸ ἠγνόει

Plin. et Tra- τί αὐτῷ λοιπὸν εἴη πρακτέον, Τραϊανῷ τῷ βασιλεῖ
ian. Epist.
96,7 ἀνεκοινώσατο λέγων ἔξω τοῦ μὴ βούλεσθαι αὐτοὺς
εἰδωλολατρεῖν οὐδὲν ἀνόσιον ἐν αὐτοῖς εὑρηκέναι·
ἐμήνυεν δὲ καὶ τοῦτο, ἀνίστασθαι ἕωθεν τοὺς
Χριστιανοὺς καὶ τὸν Χριστὸν θεοῦ δίκην ὑμνεῖν
καὶ πρὸς τὸ τὴν ἐπιστήμην αὐτῶν διαφυλάσσειν
κωλύεσθαι φονεύειν, μοιχεύειν, πλεονεκτεῖν, ἀπο-
στερεῖν καὶ τὰ τούτοις ὅμοια. πρὸς ταῦτα

Plin. et Tra- ἀντέγραψεν Τραϊανὸς τὸ τῶν Χριστιανῶν φῦλον
ian. Epist.
97,2 μὴ ἐκζητεῖσθαι μέν, ἐμπεσὸν δὲ κολάζεσθαι."
καὶ ταῦτα μὲν ἐν τούτοις ἦν.

XXXIV. Τῶν δ' ἐπὶ Ῥώμης ἐπισκόπων ἔτει
τρίτῳ τῆς τοῦ προειρημένου βασιλέως ἀρχῆς
Κλήμης Εὐαρέστῳ παραδοὺς τὴν λειτουργίαν
ἀναλύει τὸν βίον, τὰ πάντα προστὰς ἔτεσιν ἐννέα
τῆς τοῦ θείου λόγου διδασκαλίας.

XXXV. Ἀλλὰ καὶ τοῦ Συμεῶνος τὸν δηλωθέντα
τελειωθέντος τρόπον, τῆς ἐν Ἱεροσολύμοις ἐπισκοπῆς τὸν θρόνον Ἰουδαῖός τις ὄνομα Ἰοῦστος,
μυρίων ὅσων ἐκ περιτομῆς εἰς τὸν Χριστὸν τηνι-

278

us. Sometimes the populace, sometimes even the local authorities contrived plots against us, so that with no open persecution partial attacks broke out in various provinces and many of the faithful endured martyrdom in various ways. The narrative has been taken from the Latin apology of Tertullian mentioned above of which the translation is as follows : " Yet we found that this attempt against us was also prevented, for the governor of the province, Pliny Secundus, after condemning certain Christians and depriving them of their rank, was troubled at their number and, not knowing what to do in the future, communicated with the Emperor Trajan, saying that beyond their unwillingness to offer sacrifice to idols, he had found nothing wicked in them. He also mentioned this, that the Christians arose at dawn and sang a hymn to Christ as a God, and in order to preserve their teaching [1] forbade murder, adultery, covetousness, robbery, and suchlike. To this Trajan sent a rescript that the tribe of Christians should not be sought out but punished if met with." Such were the events at that time.

XXXIV. In the third year of the afore-mentioned emperor, Clement handed over the ministry of the bishops of Rome to Evarestos and departed this life, having been in charge of the teaching of the divine word for nine years.

XXXV. Moreover, when Symeon suffered martyrdom in the manner already described a certain Jew named Justus, who was one of the many thousands of the circumcision who by that time had believed on

---

[1] The Greek word means *knowledge* which is meaningless and clearly a mistaken translation of the Latin. Tertullian wrote *disciplinam.*

καῦτα πεπιστευκότων εἷς καὶ αὐτὸς ὤν, διαδέχεται.

XXXVI. Διέπρεπέν γε μὴν κατὰ τούτους ἐπὶ 1
τῆς Ἀσίας τῶν ἀποστόλων ὁμιλητὴς Πολύκαρπος,
τῆς κατὰ Σμύρναν ἐκκλησίας πρὸς τῶν αὐτοπτῶν
καὶ ὑπηρετῶν τοῦ κυρίου τὴν ἐπισκοπὴν ἐγκε-
χειρισμένος· καθ᾽ ὃν ἐγνωρίζετο Παπίας, τῆς ἐν 2
Ἱεραπόλει παροικίας καὶ αὐτὸς ἐπίσκοπος, ὅ τε
παρὰ πλείστοις εἰς ἔτι νῦν διαβόητος Ἰγνάτιος,
τῆς κατὰ Ἀντιόχειαν Πέτρου διαδοχῆς δεύτερος
τὴν ἐπισκοπὴν κεκληρωμένος. λόγος δ᾽ ἔχει 3
τοῦτον ἀπὸ Συρίας ἐπὶ τὴν Ῥωμαίων πόλιν
ἀναπεμφθέντα, θηρίων γενέσθαι βορὰν τῆς εἰς
Χριστὸν μαρτυρίας ἕνεκεν· καὶ δὴ τὴν δι᾽ Ἀσίας 4
ἀνακομιδὴν μετ᾽ ἐπιμελεστάτης φρουρῶν φυλακῆς
ποιούμενος, τὰς κατὰ πόλιν αἷς ἐπεδήμει, παροικίας
ταῖς διὰ λόγων ὁμιλίαις τε καὶ προτροπαῖς ἐπιρ-
ρωννύς, ἐν πρώτοις μάλιστα προφυλάττεσθαι τὰς
αἱρέσεις ἄρτι τότε πρῶτον ἐπιπολαζούσας παρῄνει
προύτρεπέν τε ἀπρὶξ ἔχεσθαι τῆς τῶν ἀποστόλων
παραδόσεως, ἣν ὑπὲρ ἀσφαλείας καὶ ἐγγράφως
ἤδη μαρτυρόμενος διατυποῦσθαι ἀναγκαῖον ἡγεῖτο.

Ign. Eph. 21
Ign. Eph. 1.
2. 6
Ign. Magn.
2. 15
Ign. Trall. 1.
12
Ign. Rom. 5
οὕτω δῆτα ἐν Σμύρνῃ γενόμενος, ἔνθα ὁ Πολύκαρπος 5
ἦν, μίαν μὲν τῇ κατὰ τὴν Ἔφεσον ἐπιστολὴν
ἐκκλησίᾳ γράφει, ποιμένος αὐτῆς μνημονεύων
Ὀνησίμου, ἑτέραν δὲ τῇ ἐν Μαγνησίᾳ τῇ πρὸς
Μαιάνδρῳ, ἔνθα πάλιν ἐπισκόπου Δαμᾶ μνήμην
πεποίηται, καὶ τῇ ἐν Τράλλεσι δὲ ἄλλην, ἧς
ἄρχοντα τότε ὄντα Πολύβιον ἱστορεῖ. πρὸς ταύ- 6
ταις καὶ τῇ Ῥωμαίων ἐκκλησίᾳ γράφει, ᾗ καὶ
παράκλησιν προτείνει ὡς μὴ παραιτησάμενοι τοῦ
μαρτυρίου τῆς ποθουμένης αὐτὸν ἀποστερήσαιεν
280

Christ, succeeded to the throne of the bishopric of Jerusalem.

XXXVI. At this time there flourished in Asia Polycarp, the companion of the Apostles, who had been appointed to the bishopric of the church in Smyrna by the eyewitnesses and ministers of the Lord. Distinguished men at the same time were Papias, who was himself bishop of the diocese of Hierapolis, and Ignatius, still a name of note to most men, the second after Peter to succeed to the bishopric of Antioch. The story goes that he was sent from Syria to Rome to be eaten by beasts in testimony to Christ. He was taken through Asia under most careful guard, and strengthened by his speech and exhortation the diocese of each city in which he stayed. He particularly warned them to be on their guard against the heresies which then for the first time were beginning to obtain, and exhorted them to hold fast to the tradition of the Apostles, to which he thought necessary, for safety's sake, to give the form of written testimony. Thus while he was in Smyrna where Polycarp was, he wrote one letter to the church at Ephesus, mentioning their pastor Onesimus, and another to the church at Magnesia on the Meander (and here, too, he mentioned the bishop Damas), and another to the church in Tralles, of which he relates that Polybius was then the ruler. In addition to these he also wrote to the church at Rome, and to it he extended the request that they should not deprive him of the hope for which he longed by begging him off from his martyrdom. It

281

ἐλπίδος· ἐξ ὧν καὶ βραχύτατα εἰς ἐπίδειξιν τῶν
εἰρημένων παραθέσθαι ἄξιον. γράφει δὴ οὖν
κατὰ λέξιν· '' ἀπὸ Συρίας μέχρι Ῥώμης θηριο- 7
μαχῶ διὰ γῆς καὶ θαλάσσης, νυκτὸς καὶ ἡμέρας, ἐν-
δεδεμένος δέκα λεοπάρδοις, ὅ ἐστιν στρατιωτικὸν
τάγμα, οἳ καὶ εὐεργετούμενοι χείρονες γίνονται,
ἐν δὲ τοῖς ἀδικήμασιν αὐτῶν μᾶλλον μαθητεύομαι·
ἀλλ' οὐ παρὰ τοῦτο δεδικαίωμαι. ὀναίμην τῶν 8
θηρίων τῶν ἐμοὶ ἑτοίμων, ἃ καὶ εὔχομαι σύντομά
μοι εὑρεθῆναι· ἃ καὶ κολακεύσω συντόμως με
καταφαγεῖν, οὐχ ὥσπερ τινῶν δειλαινόμενα οὐχ
ἥψαντο, κἂν αὐτὰ δὲ ἄκοντα μὴ θέλῃ, ἐγὼ προσ-
βιάσομαι. συγγνώμην. μοι ἔχετε· τί μοι συμ- 9
φέρει, ἐγὼ γινώσκω, νῦν ἄρχομαι μαθητὴς εἶναι.
μηδέν με ζηλώσαι τῶν ὁρατῶν καὶ ἀοράτων,
ἵνα 'Ιησοῦ Χριστοῦ ἐπιτύχω· πῦρ καὶ σταυρὸς
θηρίων τε συστάσεις, σκορπισμοὶ ὀστέων, συγκοπαὶ
μελῶν, ἀλεσμοὶ ὅλου τοῦ σώματος, κολάσεις τοῦ
διαβόλου εἰς ἐμὲ ἐρχέσθωσαν, μόνον ἵνα 'Ιησοῦ
Χριστοῦ ἐπιτύχω.''

1 Cor. 4, 4

Καὶ ταῦτα μὲν ἀπὸ τῆς δηλωθείσης πόλεως 10
ταῖς καταλεχθείσαις ἐκκλησίαις διετυπώσατο· ἤδη
δ' ἐπέκεινα τῆς Σμύρνης γενόμενος, ἀπὸ Τρωάδος
τοῖς τε ἐν Φιλαδελφίᾳ αὖθις διὰ γραφῆς ὁμιλεῖ
καὶ τῇ Σμυρναίων ἐκκλησίᾳ ἰδίως τε τῷ ταύτης
προηγουμένῳ Πολυκάρπῳ· ὃν οἷα δὴ ἀποστολικὸν
ἄνδρα εὖ μάλα γνωρίζων, τὴν κατ' 'Αντιόχειαν
αὐτῷ ποίμνην οἷα γνήσιος καὶ ἀγαθὸς ποιμὴν
παρατίθεται, τὴν περὶ αὐτῆς φροντίδα διὰ σπουδῆς
ἔχειν αὐτὸν ἀξιῶν. ὁ δ' αὐτὸς Σμυρναίοις 11
γράφων, οὐκ οἶδ' ὁπόθεν ῥητοῖς συγκέχρηται,
τοιαῦτά τινα περὶ τοῦ Χριστοῦ διεξιών· '' ἐγὼ δὲ

Ign. Philad.
11
Ign. Smyrn.
12
Ign. To Poly-
carp 8
Ign. To Poly-
carp 7

Ign. Smyrn.

is worth while appending a short extract from this in support of what has been said. He writes as follows : " From Syria to Rome I am fighting with wild beasts, by land and sea, by night and day, bound to ten ' leopards ' (that is, a company of soldiers), and they become worse for kind treatment. Now I become the more a disciple for their ill deeds, ' but not by this am I justified.' I long for the beasts that are prepared for me ; and I pray that they may be found prompt for me ; I will even entice them to devour me promptly ; not as has happened to some whom they have not touched from fear ; even if they be unwilling of themselves, I will force them to it. Grant me this favour. I know what is expedient for me ; now I am beginning to be a disciple. May I envy nothing of things seen or unseen that I may attain to Jesus Christ. Let there come on me fire, and cross, and struggles with wild beasts, cutting, and tearing asunder, rackings of bones, mangling of limbs, crushing of my whole body, cruel tortures of the devil, may I but attain to Jesus Christ ! "

This he put into words from the city mentioned to the churches named. When he had already passed beyond Smyrna he also again conversed in writing from Troas with those in Philadelphia and with the church of the Smyrnaeans, and especially with Polycarp who was then the head of this church. He knew well that Polycarp was an apostolic man and like a true and good shepherd commends the flock at Antioch to him, asking him to be zealous in his care for it. He also wrote to the Smyrnaeans quoting words from I know not what source and discoursing thus about Christ : " For I know and believe that

283

καὶ μετὰ τὴν ἀνάστασιν ἐν σαρκὶ αὐτὸν οἶδα καὶ πιστεύω ὄντα. καὶ ὅτε πρὸς τοὺς περὶ Πέτρον ἐλήλυθεν, ἔφη αὐτοῖς· ʻλάβετε, ψηλαφήσατέ με καὶ ἴδετε ὅτι οὐκ εἰμὶ δαιμόνιον ἀσώματον·' καὶ εὐθὺς αὐτοῦ ἥψαντο καὶ ἐπίστευσαν."

Οἶδεν δὲ αὐτοῦ τὸ μαρτύριον καὶ ὁ Εἰρηναῖος, 12 καὶ τῶν ἐπιστολῶν αὐτοῦ μνημονεύει, λέγων Iren. 5, 28. 4 οὕτως· " ὡς εἶπέν τις τῶν ἡμετέρων, διὰ τὴν πρὸς θεὸν μαρτυρίαν κατακριθεὶς πρὸς θηρία, Ign. Rom. 4 ὅτι ʻσῖτός εἰμι θεοῦ καὶ δι' ὀδόντων θηρίων ἀλήθομαι, ἵνα καθαρὸς ἄρτος εὑρεθῶ.' "

Καὶ ὁ Πολύκαρπος δὲ τούτων αὐτῶν μέμνηται 13 ἐν τῇ φερομένῃ αὐτοῦ πρὸς Φιλιππησίους ἐπιστολῇ Polycarp, Philipp. 9 φάσκων αὐτοῖς ῥήμασιν· " παρακαλῶ οὖν πάντας ὑμᾶς πειθαρχεῖν καὶ ἀσκεῖν πᾶσαν ὑπομονήν, ἣν εἴδετε κατ' ὀφθαλμοὺς οὐ μόνον ἐν τοῖς μακαρίοις Ἰγνατίῳ καὶ Ῥούφῳ καὶ Ζωσίμῳ, ἀλλὰ καὶ ἐν ἄλλοις τοῖς ἐξ ὑμῶν καὶ ἐν αὐτῷ Παύλῳ καὶ τοῖς λοιποῖς ἀποστόλοις, πεπεισμένους ὅτι οὗτοι Phil. 2, 16 πάντες οὐκ εἰς κενὸν ἔδραμον, ἀλλ' ἐν πίστει καὶ δικαιοσύνῃ, καὶ ὅτι εἰς τὸν ὀφειλόμενον αὐτοῖς 1 Clem. 5 τόπον εἰσὶν παρὰ κυρίῳ, ᾧ καὶ συνέπαθον. οὐ 2 Tim. 4, 10 γὰρ τὸν νῦν ἠγάπησαν αἰῶνα, ἀλλὰ τὸν ὑπὲρ ἡμῶν ἀποθανόντα καὶ δι' ἡμᾶς ὑπὸ τοῦ θεοῦ Polycarp, Philipp. 13 ἀναστάντα." καὶ ἑξῆς ἐπιφέρει· " ἐγράψατέ μοι 14 καὶ ὑμεῖς καὶ Ἰγνάτιος, ἵν' ἐάν τις ἀπέρχηται εἰς Συρίαν, καὶ τὰ παρ' ὑμῶν ἀποκομίσῃ γράμματα· ὅπερ ποιήσω, ἐὰν λάβω καιρὸν εὔθετον, εἴτε ἐγὼ εἴτε ὃν πέμπω πρεσβεύσοντα καὶ περὶ ὑμῶν. τὰς ἐπιστολὰς Ἰγνατίου τὰς πεμφθείσας ἡμῖν 15 ὑπ' αὐτοῦ καὶ ἄλλας ὅσας εἴχομεν παρ' ἡμῖν, ἐπέμψαμεν ὑμῖν, καθὼς ἐνετείλασθε· αἵτινες ὑπο-

he was in the flesh even after the Resurrection And when he came to those with Peter he said to them : ' Take, handle me and see that I am not a phantom without a body.' And they immediately touched him and believed."

Irenaeus also knew of his martyrdom and quotes his letters saying thus : " As one of the Christians said when he was condemned to the beasts as testimony for God, ' I am the wheat of God and I am ground by the teeth of beasts that I may be found pure bread.' "

Polycarp, too, mentions these same things in the letter to the Philippians bearing his name and says : " Now I beseech you all to obey the word of righteousness, and to practise all the endurance which you also saw before your eyes, not only in the blessed Ignatius, and Zosimus, and Rufus, but also in others among yourselves, and in Paul himself, and in the other Apostles ; being persuaded that all of these ' ran not in vain,' but in faith and righteousness, and that they are with the Lord in the ' place which is their due,' with whom they also suffered. For they did not ' love this present world ' but him who died on our behalf, and was raised by God for our sakes." And he continues later, " Both you and Ignatius wrote to me that if anyone was going to Syria he should also take your letters. I will do this if I have a convenient opportunity, either myself or the man whom I am sending as a representative for you and me. We send you, as you asked, the letters of Ignatius, which were sent to us by him, and others which we had by us. These are subjoined

τεταγμέναι εἰσὶν τῇ ἐπιστολῇ ταύτῃ· ἐξ ὧν
μεγάλα ὠφεληθῆναι δυνήσεσθε. περιέχουσι γὰρ
πίστιν καὶ ὑπομονὴν καὶ πᾶσαν οἰκοδομὴν τὴν
εἰς τὸν κύριον ἡμῶν ἀνήκουσαν." καὶ τὰ μὲν
περὶ τὸν Ἰγνάτιον τοιαῦτα· διαδέχεται δὲ μετ'
αὐτὸν τὴν Ἀντιοχείας ἐπισκοπὴν Ἥρως.

XXXVII. Τῶν δὲ κατὰ τούτους διαλαμψάντων 1
καὶ Κοδρᾶτος ἦν, ὃν ἅμα ταῖς Φιλίππου θυγατράσιν
προφητικῷ χαρίσματι λόγος ἔχει διαπρέψαι, καὶ
ἄλλοι δ' ἐπὶ τούτοις πλείους ἐγνωρίζοντο κατὰ
τούσδε, τὴν πρώτην τάξιν τῆς τῶν ἀποστόλων
ἐπέχοντες διαδοχῆς· οἳ καί, ἅτε τηλικῶνδε ὄντες
θεοπρεπεῖς μαθηταί, τοὺς κατὰ πάντα τόπον τῶν
1 Cor. 3, 10 ἐκκλησιῶν προκαταβληθέντας ὑπὸ τῶν ἀποστόλων
θεμελίους ἐπῳκοδόμουν, αὔξοντες εἰς πλέον τὸ
κήρυγμα καὶ τὰ σωτήρια σπέρματα τῆς τῶν
οὐρανῶν βασιλείας ἀνὰ πᾶσαν εἰς πλάτος ἐπι-
σπείροντες τὴν οἰκουμένην. καὶ γὰρ δὴ πλεῖστοι 2
τῶν τότε μαθητῶν σφοδροτέρῳ φιλοσοφίας ἔρωτι
πρὸς τοῦ θείου λόγου τὴν ψυχὴν πληττόμενοι,
Matt. 10, 9
Mark 6, 8
Luke 9, 3 τὴν σωτήριον πρότερον ἀπεπλήρουν παρακέλευσιν,
ἐνδεέσιν νέμοντες τὰς οὐσίας, εἶτα δὲ ἀποδημίας
Rom. 15, 20.
21 στελλόμενοι ἔργον ἐπετέλουν εὐαγγελιστῶν, τοῖς
ἔτι πάμπαν ἀνηκόοις τοῦ τῆς πίστεως λόγου
κηρύττειν φιλοτιμούμενοι καὶ τὴν τῶν θείων
Eph. 2, 19.
20 εὐαγγελίων παραδιδόναι γραφήν. οὗτοι δὲ θε- 3
μελίους τῆς πίστεως ἐπὶ ξένοις τισὶ τόποις αὐτὸ
μόνον καταβαλλόμενοι ποιμένας τε καθιστάντες
ἑτέρους τούτοις τε αὐτοῖς ἐγχειρίζοντες τὴν τῶν
ἀρτίως εἰσαχθέντων γεωργίαν, ἑτέρας αὐτοὶ πάλιν
χώρας τε καὶ ἔθνη μετῄεσαν σὺν τῇ ἐκ θεοῦ χάριτι
καὶ συνεργίᾳ, ἐπεὶ καὶ τοῦ θείου πνεύματος εἰς

to this letter, and you will be able to benefit greatly from them. For they contain faith, patience, and all the edification which pertains to our Lord." Such is the story concerning Ignatius, and Heros succeeded to the bishopric of Antioch after him.

XXXVII. Among those who were famous at this time was also Quadratus, of whom tradition says that he shared with the daughters of Philip the distinction of a prophetic gift. And many others besides them were well known at this time and take the first rank in the Apostolic succession. These pious disciples of great men built in every place on the foundations of the churches laid by the Apostles. They spread the preaching and scattered the saving seeds of the kingdom of Heaven, sowing them broadcast through the whole world. Many of those then disciples, smitten in the soul by the divine Logos with an ardent passion for the love of wisdom,[1] first fulfilled the Saviour's command and distributed their property to the needy, then, starting on their journey, took up the work of evangelists and were zealous to preach to all who had not yet heard the word of the faith, and to transmit the writing of the divine Gospels As soon as they had no more than laid the foundations of the faith in some strange place, they appointed others as shepherds and committed to them the task of tending those who had been just brought in, but they themselves passed on again to other lands and peoples, helped by the grace and co-operation of God, seeing that

[1] The Greek word is " philosophy " ; but Eusebius does not mean metaphysics.

ἔτι τότε δι' αὐτῶν πλεῖσται παράδοξοι δυνάμεις ἐνήργουντο,[1] ὥστε ἀπὸ πρώτης ἀκροάσεως ἀθρόως αὔτανδρα πλήθη προθύμως τὴν εἰς τὸν τῶν ὅλων δημιουργὸν εὐσέβειαν ἐν ταῖς αὐτῶν ψυχαῖς καταδέχεσθαι.

Ἀδυνάτου δ' ὄντος ἡμῖν ἅπαντας ἐξ ὀνόματος 4 ἀπαριθμεῖσθαι ὅσοι ποτὲ κατὰ τὴν πρώτην τῶν ἀποστόλων διαδοχὴν ἐν ταῖς κατὰ τὴν οἰκουμένην ἐκκλησίαις γεγόνασιν ποιμένες ἢ καὶ εὐαγγελισταί, τούτων εἰκότως ἐξ ὀνόματος γραφῇ μόνων τὴν μνήμην κατατεθείμεθα, ὧν ἔτι καὶ νῦν εἰς ἡμᾶς δι' ὑπομνημάτων τῆς ἀποστολικῆς διδασκαλίας ἡ παράδοσις φέρεται, XXXVIII. ὥσπερ οὖν 1 ἀμέλει τοῦ Ἰγνατίου ἐν αἷς κατελέξαμεν ἐπιστολαῖς, καὶ τοῦ Κλήμεντος ἐν τῇ ἀνωμολογημένῃ παρὰ πᾶσιν, ἣν ἐκ προσώπου τῆς Ῥωμαίων ἐκκλησίας τῇ Κορινθίων διετυπώσατο· ἐν ᾗ τῆς πρὸς Ἑβραίους πολλὰ νοήματα παραθείς, ἤδη δὲ καὶ αὐτολεξεὶ ῥητοῖς τισιν ἐξ αὐτῆς χρησάμενος, σαφέστατα παρίστησιν ὅτι μὴ νέον ὑπάρχει τὸ 2 σύγγραμμα, ὅθεν δὴ καὶ εἰκότως ἔδοξεν αὐτὸ τοῖς λοιποῖς ἐγκαταλεχθῆναι γράμμασι τοῦ ἀποστόλου. Ἑβραίοις γὰρ διὰ τῆς πατρίου γλώττης ἐγγράφως ὡμιληκότος τοῦ Παύλου, οἱ μὲν τὸν εὐαγγελιστὴν Λουκᾶν, οἱ δὲ τὸν Κλήμεντα τοῦτον αὐτὸν ἑρμηνεῦσαι λέγουσι τὴν γραφήν· ὃ καὶ 3 μᾶλλον ἂν εἴη ἀληθὲς τῷ τὸν ὅμοιον τῆς φράσεως χαρακτῆρα τήν τε τοῦ Κλήμεντος ἐπιστολὴν καὶ τὴν πρὸς Ἑβραίους ἀποσῴζειν καὶ τῷ μὴ πόρρω τὰ ἐν ἑκατέροις τοῖς συγγράμμασι νοήματα καθεστάναι.

Ἰστέον δ' ὡς καὶ δευτέρα τις εἶναι λέγεται τοῦ 4

1 Clem. 17
[=Heb. 11,
37]. 21 [=
Heb. 4, 12].
27 [=Heb.
10, 23]
36 [=Heb. 2,
17. 18. 4, 14.
15. 8, 3. 1, 3.
4, 7. 5, 13]

many strange miracles of the divine spirit were at that time still being wrought by them, so that whole crowds of men at the first hearing eagerly received in their souls the religion of the Creator of the universe.

It is impossible for us to give the number and the names of all who first succeeded the Apostles, and were shepherds or evangelists in the churches throughout the world. It was, therefore, natural for us to record by name the memory only of those of whom the tradition still survives to our time by their treatises on the Apostolic teaching. XXXVIII. Such writings, of course, were the letters of Ignatius cf which we gave the list, and the Epistle of Clement which is recognized by all, which he wrote in the name of the church of the Romans to that of the Corinthians. In this he has many thoughts parallel to the Epistle to the Hebrews, and actually makes some verbal quotations from it showing clearly that it was not a recent production, and for this reason, too, it has seemed natural to include it among the other writings of the Apostle. For Paul had spoken in writing to the Hebrews in their native language, and some say that the evangelist Luke, others that this same Clement translated the writing. And the truth of this would be supported by the similarity of style preserved by the Epistle of Clement and that to the Hebrews, and by the little difference between the thoughts in both writings.

It must be known that there is also a second

---

¹ So Wendland: the MSS. read ἐνήργουν.

Κλήμεντος ἐπιστολή, οὐ μὴν ἔθ᾽ ὁμοίως τῇ προτέρᾳ
καὶ ταύτην γνώριμον ἐπιστάμεθα, ὅτι μηδὲ τοὺς
ἀρχαίους αὐτῇ κεχρημένους ἴσμεν. ἤδη δὲ καὶ 5
ἕτερα πολυεπῆ καὶ μακρὰ συγγράμματα ὡς τοῦ
αὐτοῦ χθὲς καὶ πρώην τινὲς προήγαγον, Πέτρου
δὴ καὶ Ἀπίωνος διαλόγους περιέχοντα· ὧν οὐδ᾽
ὅλως μνήμη τις παρὰ τοῖς παλαιοῖς φέρεται,
οὐδὲ γὰρ καθαρὸν τῆς ἀποστολικῆς ὀρθοδοξίας
ἀποσῴζει τὸν χαρακτῆρα.

XXXIX. Ἡ μὲν οὖν τοῦ Κλήμεντος ὁμολογου- 1
μένη γραφὴ πρόδηλος, εἴρηται δὲ καὶ τὰ Ἰγνατίου
καὶ Πολυκάρπου· τοῦ δὲ Παπία συγγράμματα
πέντε τὸν ἀριθμὸν φέρεται, ἃ καὶ ἐπιγέγραπται
Λογίων κυριακῶν ἐξηγήσεως. τούτων καὶ Εἰρηναῖος ὡς μόνων αὐτῷ γραφέντων μνημονεύει,
Iren. 5, 33, 4 ὧδέ πως λέγων· "ταῦτα δὲ καὶ Παπίας ὁ Ἰωάννου
μὲν ἀκουστής, Πολυκάρπου δὲ ἑταῖρος γεγονώς,
ἀρχαῖος ἀνήρ, ἐγγράφως ἐπιμαρτυρεῖ ἐν τῇ τετάρτῃ τῶν ἑαυτοῦ βιβλίων. ἔστιν γὰρ αὐτῷ
πέντε βιβλία συντεταγμένα." καὶ ὁ μὲν Εἰρηναῖος 2
ταῦτα· αὐτός γε μὴν ὁ Παπίας κατὰ τὸ προοίμιον
τῶν αὐτοῦ λόγων ἀκροατὴν μὲν καὶ αὐτόπτην
οὐδαμῶς ἑαυτὸν γενέσθαι τῶν ἱερῶν ἀποστόλων
ἐμφαίνει, παρειληφέναι δὲ τὰ τῆς πίστεως παρὰ
τῶν ἐκείνοις γνωρίμων διδάσκει δι᾽ ὧν φησιν
λέξεων· "οὐκ ὀκνήσω δέ σοι καὶ ὅσα ποτὲ παρὰ 3
τῶν πρεσβυτέρων καλῶς ἔμαθον καὶ καλῶς ἐμνη-
μόνευσα, συγκατατάξαι ταῖς ἑρμηνείαις, διαβε-
βαιούμενος ὑπὲρ αὐτῶν ἀλήθειαν. οὐ γὰρ τοῖς
τὰ πολλὰ λέγουσιν ἔχαιρον ὥσπερ οἱ πολλοί,
ἀλλὰ τοῖς τἀληθῆ διδάσκουσιν, οὐδὲ τοῖς τὰς

---

[1] This may refer to the Clementine Homilies.

letter ascribed to Clement, but we have not the same knowledge of its recognition as we have of the former, for we do not even know if the primitive writers used it. Some have also quite recently put forward other verbose and long treatises, purporting to be Clement's, containing dialogues with Peter and Apion,[1] but there is absolutely no mention of them among the ancient writers nor do they preserve the pure type of apostolic orthodoxy.

XXXIX. Thus the recognized writing of Clement is well known and the works of Ignatius and Polycarp have been spoken of, and of Papias five treatises are extant which have also the title of " Interpretation of the Oracles of the Lord." These are also mentioned by Irenaeus as though his only writing, for he says in one place, " To these things also Papias, the hearer of John, who was a companion of Polycarp and one of the ancients,[2] bears witness in writing in the fourth of his books, for five books were composed by him." So says Irenaeus. Yet Papias himself, according to the preface of his treatises, makes plain that he had in no way been a hearer and eyewitness of the sacred Apostles, but teaches that he had received the articles of the faith from those who had known them, for he speaks as follows : " And I shall not hesitate to append to the interpretations all that I ever learnt well from the presbyters and remember well, for of their truth I am confident. For unlike most I did not rejoice in them who say much, but in them who teach the truth, nor in

---

[2] " Primitive " would perhaps be a better rendering for the Greek, which at least sometimes seems to mean a man who belonged to " the beginning," cf. the application of the adjective to Mnason (ἀρχαίῳ μαθητῇ) in Acts xxi. 16.

ἀλλοτρίας ἐντολὰς μνημονεύουσιν, ἀλλὰ τοῖς τὰς
παρὰ τοῦ κυρίου τῇ πίστει δεδομένας καὶ ἀπ'
αὐτῆς παραγινομένας τῆς ἀληθείας· εἰ δέ που
Luke i. 3 καὶ παρηκολουθηκώς τις τοῖς πρεσβυτέροις ἔλθοι,
τοὺς τῶν πρεσβυτέρων ἀνέκρινον λόγους, τί
Ἀνδρέας ἢ τί Πέτρος εἶπεν ἢ τί Φίλιππος ἢ τί
Θωμᾶς ἢ Ἰάκωβος ἢ τί Ἰωάννης ἢ Ματθαῖος
ἤ τις ἕτερος τῶν τοῦ κυρίου μαθητῶν ἅ τε Ἀρι-
στίων καὶ ὁ πρεσβύτερος Ἰωάννης, τοῦ κυρίου
μαθηταί, λέγουσιν. οὐ γὰρ τὰ ἐκ τῶν βιβλίων
τοσοῦτόν με ὠφελεῖν ὑπελάμβανον ὅσον τὰ παρὰ
ζώσης φωνῆς καὶ μενούσης.''

Ἔνθα καὶ ἐπιστῆσαι ἄξιον δὶς καθαρθμιοῦντι
αὐτῷ τὸ Ἰωάννου ὄνομα, ὧν τὸν μὲν πρότερον
Πέτρῳ καὶ Ἰακώβῳ καὶ Ματθαίῳ καὶ τοῖς
λοιποῖς ἀποστόλοις συγκαταλέγει, σαφῶς δηλῶν
τὸν εὐαγγελιστήν, τὸν δ' ἕτερον Ἰωάννην, δια-
στείλας τὸν λόγον, ἑτέροις παρὰ τὸν τῶν ἀποστόλων
ἀριθμὸν κατατάσσει, προτάξας αὐτοῦ τὸν Ἀρι-
στίωνα, σαφῶς τε αὐτὸν πρεσβύτερον ὀνομάζει·[1]
ὡς καὶ διὰ τούτων ἀποδείκνυσθαι τὴν ἱστορίαν
ἀληθῆ τῶν δύο κατὰ τὴν Ἀσίαν ὁμωνυμίᾳ κεχρῆσθαι εἰρηκότων δύο τε ἐν Ἐφέσῳ γενέσθαι·
μνήματα καὶ ἑκάτερον Ἰωάννου ἔτι νῦν λέγεσθαι·
οἷς καὶ ἀναγκαῖον προσέχειν τὸν νοῦν, εἰκὸς γὰρ
τὸν δεύτερον, εἰ μή τις ἐθέλοι τὸν πρῶτον, τὴν
ἐπ' ὀνόματος φερομένην Ἰωάννου ἀποκάλυψιν
ἑορακέναι. καὶ ὁ νῦν δὲ ἡμῖν δηλούμενος Παπίας
τοὺς μὲν τῶν ἀποστόλων λόγους παρὰ τῶν αὐτοῖς
παρηκολουθηκότων ὁμολογεῖ παρειληφέναι, Ἀρι-
στίωνος δὲ καὶ τοῦ πρεσβυτέρου Ἰωάννου αὐτήκοον
ἑαυτὸν φησι γενέσθαι· ὀνομαστὶ γοῦν πολλάκις

them who recount the commandments of others, but in them who repeated those given to the faith by the Lord and derived from truth itself; but if ever anyone came who had followed[1] the presbyters, I inquired into the words of the presbyters, what Andrew or Peter or Philip or Thomas or James or John or Matthew, or any other of the Lord's disciples, had said, and what Aristion and the presbyter John, the Lord's disciples, were saying. For I did not suppose that information from books would help me so much as the word of a living and surviving voice."

It is here worth noting that he twice counts the name of John, and reckons the first John with Peter and James and Matthew and the other Apostles, clearly meaning the evangelist, but by changing his statement places the second with the others outside the number of the Apostles, putting Aristion before him and clearly calling him a presbyter. This confirms the truth of the story of those who have said that there were two of the same name in Asia, and that there are two tombs at Ephesus both still called John's. This calls for attention: for it is probable that the second (unless anyone prefer the former) saw the revelation which passes under the name of John. The Papias whom we are now treating confesses that he had received the words of the Apostles from their followers, but says that he had actually heard Aristion and the presbyter John. He often quotes them by name and gives

---

[1] The meaning of the Greek is doubtful; see Jackson and Lake, *Beginnings of Christianity*, vol. ii. p. 501.

---

[1] *Cf.* vii. 25. 16 (excerpt from Dionysios).

αὐτῶν μνημονεύσας ἐν τοῖς αὐτοῦ συγγράμμασιν
τίθησιν αὐτῶν παραδόσεις. καὶ ταῦτα δ᾽ ἡμῖν
οὐκ εἰς τὸ ἄχρηστον εἰρήσθω· ἄξιον δὲ ταῖς
ἀποδοθείσαις τοῦ Παπία φωναῖς προσάψαι λέξεις
ἑτέρας αὐτοῦ, δι᾽ ὧν παράδοξά τινα ἱστορεῖ καὶ
ἄλλα ὡς ἂν ἐκ παραδόσεως εἰς αὐτὸν ἐλθόντα.
τὸ μὲν οὖν κατὰ τὴν Ἱεράπολιν Φίλιππον τὸν
ἀπόστολον ἅμα ταῖς θυγατράσιν διατρῖψαι διὰ
τῶν πρόσθεν δεδήλωται· ὡς δὲ κατὰ τοὺς αὐτοὺς
ὁ Παπίας γενόμενος, διήγησιν παρειληφέναι θαυ-
μασίαν ὑπὸ τῶν τοῦ Φιλίππου θυγατέρων μνημονεύει, τὰ νῦν σημειωτέον· νεκροῦ γὰρ ἀνάστασιν
κατ᾽ αὐτὸν γεγονυῖαν ἱστορεῖ καὶ αὖ πάλιν ἕτερον
παράδοξον περὶ Ἰοῦστον τὸν ἐπικληθέντα Βαρσαβᾶν γεγονός, ὡς δηλητήριον φάρμακον ἐμπιόντος
καὶ μηδὲν ἀηδὲς διὰ τὴν τοῦ κυρίου χάριν ὑπο-
μείναντος.[1] τοῦτον δὲ τὸν Ἰοῦστον μετὰ τὴν τοῦ
σωτῆρος ἀνάλημψιν τοὺς ἱεροὺς ἀποστόλους μετὰ
Ματθία στῆσαί τε καὶ ἐπεύξασθαι ἀντὶ τοῦ προδότου Ἰούδα ἐπὶ τὸν κλῆρον τῆς ἀναπληρώσεως
τοῦ αὐτῶν ἀριθμοῦ ἡ τῶν Πράξεων ὧδέ πω
Acts 1, 23, 24 ἱστορεῖ γραφή· " καὶ ἔστησαν δύο, Ἰωσὴφ τὸν
καλούμενον Βαρσαβᾶν, ὃς ἐπεκλήθη Ἰοῦστος
καὶ Ματθίαν· καὶ προσευξάμενοι εἶπαν." κα
ἄλλα δὲ ὁ αὐτὸς ὡς ἐκ παραδόσεως ἀγράφου εἰς
αὐτὸν ἥκοντα παρατέθειται ξένας τέ τινας παρα-
βολὰς τοῦ σωτῆρος καὶ διδασκαλίας αὐτοῦ κα
τινα ἄλλα μυθικώτερα· ἐν οἷς καὶ χιλιάδα τινα
φησιν ἐτῶν ἔσεσθαι μετὰ τὴν ἐκ νεκρῶν ἀνάστασιν
σωματικῶς τῆς Χριστοῦ βασιλείας ἐπὶ ταυτησ
τῆς γῆς ὑποστησομένης· ἃ καὶ ἡγοῦμαι τὰ
ἀποστολικὰς παρεκδεξάμενον διηγήσεις ὑπολαβεῖν
294

their traditions in his writings. Let this suffice to
good purpose. But it is worth while to add to the
words of Papias already given other sayings of his,
in which he tells certain marvels and other details
which apparently reached him by tradition. It has
already been mentioned that Philip the Apostle
lived at Hierapolis with his daughters, but it must
now be shown how Papias was with them and received
a wonderful story from the daughters of Philip; for
he relates the resurrection of a corpse in his time
and in another place another miracle connected with
Justus surnamed Barsabas, for he drank poison but
by the Lord's grace suffered no harm. Of this
Justus the Acts relates that the sacred Apostles
set him up and prayed over him together with
Matthias after the ascension of the Lord for the
choice of one to fill up their number in place of the
traitor Judas, " and they set forth two, Joseph
called Barsabas, who was called Justus, and Matthias;
and they prayed and said." The same writer
adduces other accounts, as though they came to
him from unwritten tradition, and some strange
parables and teachings of the Saviour, and some
other more mythical accounts. Among them he
says that there will be a millennium after the resurrection of the dead, when the kingdom of Christ
will be set up in material form on this earth. I
suppose that he got these notions by a perverse

---

¹ *Cf.* C. de Boor's fragments of Papias in *Texte und
Untersuchungen*, v. 2. 170.

τὰ ἐν ὑποδείγμασι πρὸς αὐτῶν μυστικῶς εἰρημένα
μὴ συνεορακότα. σφόδρα γάρ τοι σμικρὸς ὢν 1
τὸν νοῦν, ὡς ἂν ἐκ τῶν αὐτοῦ λόγων τεκμη-
ράμενον εἰπεῖν, φαίνεται, πλὴν καὶ τοῖς μετ᾽
αὐτὸν πλείστοις ὅσοις τῶν ἐκκλησιαστικῶν τῆς
ὁμοίας αὐτῷ δόξης παραίτιος γέγονεν τὴν
ἀρχαιότητα τἀνδρὸς προβεβλημένοις, ὥσπερ οὖν
Εἰρηναίῳ καὶ εἴ τις ἄλλος τὰ ὅμοια φρονῶν ἀνα-
πέφηνεν.

Καὶ ἄλλας δὲ τῇ ἰδίᾳ γραφῇ παραδίδωσιν Ἀρι- 1
στίωνος τοῦ πρόσθεν δεδηλωμένου τῶν τοῦ κυρίου
λόγων διηγήσεις καὶ τοῦ πρεσβυτέρου Ἰωάννου
παραδόσεις· ἐφ᾽ ἃς τοὺς φιλομαθεῖς ἀναπέμ-
ψαντες, ἀναγκαίως νῦν προσθήσομεν ταῖς προ-
εκτεθείσαις αὐτοῦ φωναῖς παράδοσιν ἣν περὶ
Μάρκου τοῦ τὸ εὐαγγέλιον γεγραφότος ἐκτέθειται
διὰ τούτων· "καὶ τοῦθ᾽ ὁ πρεσβύτερος ἔλεγεν· 1
Μάρκος μὲν ἑρμηνευτὴς Πέτρου γενόμενος, ὅσα
ἐμνημόνευσεν, ἀκριβῶς ἔγραψεν, οὐ μέντοι τάξει,
τὰ ὑπὸ τοῦ κυρίου ἢ λεχθέντα ἢ πραχθέντα.
οὔτε γὰρ ἤκουσεν τοῦ κυρίου οὔτε παρηκολούθησεν
αὐτῷ, ὕστερον δέ, ὡς ἔφην, Πέτρῳ· ὃς πρὸς
τὰς χρείας ἐποιεῖτο τὰς διδασκαλίας, ἀλλ᾽ οὐχ
ὥσπερ σύνταξιν τῶν κυριακῶν ποιούμενος λογίων,
ὥστε οὐδὲν ἥμαρτεν Μάρκος οὕτως ἔνια γράψας
ὡς ἀπεμνημόνευσεν. ἑνὸς γὰρ ἐποιήσατο πρό-
νοιαν, τοῦ μηδὲν ὧν ἤκουσεν παραλιπεῖν ἢ ψεύσα-
σθαί τι ἐν αὐτοῖς." ταῦτα μὲν οὖν ἱστόρηται 1
τῷ Παπίᾳ περὶ τοῦ Μάρκου· περὶ δὲ τοῦ Ματθαίου
ταῦτ᾽ εἴρηται· "Ματθαῖος μὲν οὖν Ἑβραΐδι διαλέκτῳ τὰ λόγια συνετάξατο, ἡρμήνευσεν δ᾽ αὐτὰ
ὡς ἦν δυνατὸς ἕκαστος."

reading of the apostolic accounts, not realizing that they had spoken mystically and symbolically. For he was a man of very little intelligence, as is clear from his books. But he is responsible for the fact that so many Christian writers after him held the same opinion, relying on his antiquity, for instance Irenaeus and whoever else appears to have held the same views.

In the same writing he also quotes other interpretations of the words of the Lord given by the Aristion mentioned above and traditions of John the presbyter. To them we may dismiss the studious ; but we are now obliged to append to the words already quoted from him a tradition about the Mark who wrote the Gospel, which he expounds as follows. " And the Presbyter used to say this, ' Mark became Peter's interpreter and wrote accurately all that he remembered, not, indeed, in order, of the things said or done by the Lord. For he had not heard the Lord, nor had he followed him, but later on, as I said, followed Peter, who used to give teaching as necessity demanded but not making, as it were, an arrangement of the Lord's oracles, so that Mark did nothing wrong in thus writing down single points as he remembered them. For to one thing he gave attention, to leave out nothing of what he had heard and to make no false statements in them.' " This is related by Papias about Mark, and about Matthew this was said, " Matthew collected the oracles in the Hebrew language, and each interpreted them as best he could."

EUSEBIUS

Κέχρηται δ' ὁ αὐτὸς μαρτυρίαις ἀπὸ τῆς Ἰωάννου 17
προτέρας ἐπιστολῆς καὶ ἀπὸ τῆς Πέτρου ὁμοίως,
ἐκτέθειται δὲ καὶ ἄλλην ἱστορίαν περὶ γυναικὸς
ἐπὶ πολλαῖς ἁμαρτίαις διαβληθείσης ἐπὶ τοῦ
κυρίου, ἣν τὸ καθ' Ἑβραίους εὐαγγέλιον περιέχει.
καὶ ταῦτα δ' ἡμῖν ἀναγκαίως πρὸς τοῖς ἐκτεθεῖσιν
ἐπιτετηρήσθω.

The same writer used quotations from the first
Epistle of John, and likewise also from that of
Peter, and has expounded another story about a
woman who was accused before the Lord of many
sins, which the Gospel according to the Hebrews
contains. Let this suffice us in addition to the
extracts made.

Δ

Τάδε καὶ ἡ τετάρτη περιέχει βίβλος τῆς
Ἐκκλησιαστικῆς ἱστορίας

Ā Τίνες ἐπὶ τῆς Τραϊανοῦ βασιλείας Ῥωμαίων
γεγόνασι καὶ Ἀλεξανδρέων ἐπίσκοποι.

B̄ Ὁποῖα Ἰουδαῖοι κατ' αὐτὸν πεπόνθασιν.

Γ̄ Οἱ κατὰ Ἀδριανὸν ὑπὲρ τῆς πίστεως ἀπο-
λογησάμενοι.

Δ̄ Οἱ κατ' αὐτὸν Ῥωμαίων καὶ Ἀλεξανδρέων
ἐπίσκοποι.

Ē Οἱ ἀνέκαθεν ἀπὸ τοῦ σωτῆρος καὶ ἐπὶ τοὺς
δηλουμένους Ἱεροσολύμων ἐπίσκοποι.

Ϛ Ἡ κατὰ Ἀδριανὸν ὑστάτη Ἰουδαίων πολιορκία.

Z̄ Τίνες κατ' ἐκεῖνο καιροῦ γεγόνασιν ψευδωνύμου γνώσεως ἀρχηγοί.

H̄ Τίνες ἐκκλησιαστικοὶ συγγραφεῖς.

Θ̄ Ἐπιστολὴ Ἀδριανοῦ ὑπὲρ τοῦ μὴ δεῖν
ἀκρίτως ἡμᾶς ἐλαύνειν.

Ī Τίνες ἐπὶ τῆς Ἀντωνίνου βασιλείας ἐπίσκοποι
Ῥωμαίων καὶ Ἀλεξανδρέων γεγόνασιν.

ĪĀ Περὶ τῶν κατ' αὐτοὺς αἱρεσιαρχῶν.

ĪB̄ Περὶ τῆς Ἰουστίνου πρὸς Ἀντωνῖνον ἀπολογίας.

ĪΓ̄ Ἀντωνίνου πρὸς τὸ κοινὸν τῆς Ἀσίας ἐπιστολὴ περὶ τοῦ καθ' ἡμᾶς λόγου.

CONTENTS OF BOOK IV

*The contents of the fourth book of the History
of the Church is as follows :*

I. Who were the bishops of Rome and Alexandria in the reign of Trajan.

II. What the Jews suffered in his time.

III. The apologists for Christianity in the time of Hadrian.

IV. The bishops of Rome and Alexandria in his time.

V. The bishops of Jerusalem, beginning from the Saviour down to the time mentioned.

VI. The last siege of the Jews under Hadrian.

VII. Who were the leaders of Knowledge, falsely so-called, at that time.

VIII. Who are the writers of the church.

IX. A letter of Hadrian to the effect that we must not be persecuted without being tried.

X. Who were the bishops of Rome and Alexandria in the reign of Antoninus.

XI. On the leaders of heresy in their times.

XII. On the apology of Justin to Antoninus.

XIII. A letter of Antoninus to the Council of Asia on our religion.

ΙΔ Τὰ περὶ Πολυκάρπου τοῦ τῶν ἀποστόλων
γνωρίμου μνημονευόμενα.

ΙΕ Ὅπως κατὰ Οὐῆρον ὁ Πολύκαρπος ἅμ᾽
ἑτέροις ἐμαρτύρησεν ἐπὶ τῆς Σμυρναίων
πόλεως.

ΙϚ Ὅπως Ἰουστῖνος ὁ φιλόσοφος τὸν Χριστοῦ
λόγον ἐπὶ τῆς Ῥωμαίων πόλεως πρεσβεύων
ἐμαρτύρησεν.

ΙΖ Περὶ ὧν Ἰουστῖνος ἐν ἰδίῳ συγγράμματι
μνημονεύει μαρτύρων.

ΙΗ Τίνες εἰς ἡμᾶς ἦλθον τῶν Ἰουστίνου λόγων.

ΙΘ Τίνες ἐπὶ τῆς Οὐήρου βασιλείας τῆς Ῥωμαίων
καὶ Ἀλεξανδρέων ἐκκλησίας προέστησαν.

Κ Τίνες οἱ τῆς Ἀντιοχέων.

ΚΑ Περὶ τῶν κατὰ τούτους διαλαμψάντων ἐκκλησιαστικῶν συγγραφέων.

ΚΒ Περὶ Ἡγησίππου καὶ ὧν αὐτὸς μνημονεύει.

ΚΓ Περὶ Διονυσίου Κορινθίων ἐπισκόπου καὶ ὧν
ἔγραψεν ἐπιστολῶν.

ΚΔ Περὶ Θεοφίλου Ἀντιοχέων ἐπισκόπου.

ΚΕ Περὶ Φιλίππου καὶ Μοδέστου.

ΚϚ Περὶ Μελίτωνος καὶ ὧν αὐτὸς ἐμνημόνευσεν.

ΚΖ Περὶ Ἀπολιναρίου.

ΚΗ Περὶ Μουσανοῦ.

ΚΘ Περὶ τῆς κατὰ Τατιανὸν αἱρέσεως.

Λ Περὶ Βαρδησάνου τοῦ Σύρου καὶ τῶν φερομένων αὐτοῦ λόγων.

ECCLESIASTICAL HISTORY, IV. CONTENTS

XIV. The story of Polycarp who had known the apostles.

XV. How in the time of Verus Polycarp with others was martyred in the city of Smyrna.

XVI. How Justin the philosopher was martyred in the city of Rome as an ambassador for the word of Christ.

XVII. On the martyrs whom Justin mentions in his own writings.

XVIII. What writings of Justin have come down to us.

XIX. Who were the leaders of the churches of Rome and Alexandria in the reign of Verus.

XX. Who were the bishops of Antioch.

XXI. On the ecclesiastical writers who were famous in their time.

XXII. On Hegesippus and what he relates.

XXIII. On Dionysius, the bishop of Corinth, and the letters which he wrote.

XXIV. On Theophilus, bishop of Antioch.

XXV. On Philip and Modestus.

XXVI. On Melito and the statements which he makes.

XXVII. On Apolinarius.

XXVIII. On Musanus.

XXIX. On the heresy of Tatian.

XXX. On Bardesanes the Syrian and his extant books.

Δ

I. Ἀμφὶ δὲ τὸ δωδέκατον ἔτος τῆς Τραϊανοῦ βασιλείας ὁ μικρῷ πρόσθεν ἡμῖν τῆς ἐν Ἀλεξανδρείᾳ παροικίας δηλωθεὶς ἐπίσκοπος τὴν ζωὴν μεταλλάττει, τέταρτος δ᾿ ἀπὸ τῶν ἀποστόλων τὴν τῶν αὐτόθι λειτουργίαν κληροῦται Πρῖμος. ἐν τούτῳ καὶ Ἀλέξανδρος ἐπὶ Ῥώμης, ὄγδοον ἔτος ἀποπλήσαντος Εὐαρέστου, πέμπτην ἀπὸ Πέτρου καὶ Παύλου κατάγων διαδοχήν, τὴν ἐπισκοπὴν ὑπολαμβάνει.

II. Καὶ τὰ μὲν τῆς τοῦ σωτῆρος ἡμῶν διδασκαλίας τε καὶ ἐκκλησίας ὁσημέραι ἀνθοῦντα ἐπὶ μεῖζον ἐχώρει προκοπῆς, τὰ δὲ τῆς Ἰουδαίων συμφορᾶς κακοῖς ἐπαλλήλοις ἤκμαζεν. ἤδη γοῦν τοῦ αὐτοκράτορος εἰς ἐνιαυτὸν ὀκτωκαιδέκατον ἐλαύνοντος, αὖθις Ἰουδαίων κίνησις ἐπαναστᾶσα πάμπολυ πλῆθος αὐτῶν διαφθείρει. ἔν τε γὰρ Ἀλεξανδρείᾳ καὶ τῇ λοιπῇ Αἰγύπτῳ καὶ προσέτι κατὰ Κυρήνην, ὥσπερ ὑπὸ πνεύματος δεινοῦ τινος καὶ στασιώδους ἀναρριπισθέντες, ὥρμηντο πρὸς τοὺς συνοίκους Ἕλληνας στασιάζειν, αὐξήσαντές τε εἰς μέγα τὴν στάσιν, τῷ ἐπιόντι ἐνιαυτῷ πόλεμον οὐ σμικρὸν . συνῆψαν, ἡγουμένου τηνικαῦτα Λούπου τῆς ἁπάσης Αἰγύπτου. καὶ δὴ ἐν τῇ πρώτῃ συμβολῇ ἐπικρατῆσαι αὐτοὺς συνέβη τῶν Ἑλλήνων·

BOOK IV

I. About the twelfth year of the reign of Trajan[1] the bishop[2] of the diocese of Alexandria, whom we mentioned a little earlier, passed away, and Primus, the fourth from the Apostles, received the charge of those in that place. At this time, too, at Rome Alexander, when Evarestus had completed his eighth year, was the fifth to succeed Peter and Paul, and took up the bishopric.

II. While the teaching of our Saviour and the church were flourishing daily and moving on to further progress the tragedy of the Jews was reaching the climax of successive woes. In the course of the eighteenth year[3] of the reign of the Emperor a rebellion of the Jews again broke out and destroyed a great multitude of them. For both in Alexandria and in the rest of Egypt and especially in Cyrene, as though they had been seized by some terrible spirit of rebellion, they rushed into sedition against their Greek fellow citizens, and increasing the scope of the rebellion in the following year started a great war while Lupus was governor of all Egypt.[4] In the first engagement they happened to overcome

---

[1] A.D. 109.   [2] Cerdo, cf. iii. 21.   [3] A.D. 115.
    [4] Cf. Dio Cassius, lxviii. 32 and lxix. 12 f.

οἳ καὶ καταφυγόντες εἰς τὴν Ἀλεξάνδρειαν τοὺς
ἐν τῇ πόλει Ἰουδαίους ἐζώγρησάν τε καὶ ἀπέκτειναν,
τῆς δὲ παρὰ τούτων συμμαχίας ἀποτυχόντες οἱ
κατὰ Κυρήνην τὴν χώραν τῆς Αἰγύπτου λεη-
λατοῦντες καὶ τοὺς ἐν αὐτῇ νομοὺς φθείροντες
διετέλουν, ἡγουμένου αὐτῶν Λουκούα· ἐφ' οὓς ὁ
αὐτοκράτωρ ἔπεμψεν Μάρκιον Τούρβωνα σὺν
δυνάμει πεζῇ τε καὶ ναυτικῇ, ἔτι δὲ καὶ ἱππικῇ.
ὁ δὲ πολλαῖς μάχαις οὐκ ὀλίγῳ τε χρόνῳ τὸν 4
πρὸς αὐτοὺς διαπονήσας πόλεμον, πολλὰς μυριάδας
Ἰουδαίων, οὐ μόνον τῶν ἀπὸ Κυρήνης, ἀλλὰ καὶ
τῶν ἀπ' Αἰγύπτου συναιρομένων Λουκούα τῷ
βασιλεῖ αὐτῶν, ἀναιρεῖ.   ὁ δὲ αὐτοκράτωρ ὑπ- 5
οπτεύσας καὶ τοὺς ἐν Μεσοποταμίᾳ Ἰουδαίους
ἐπιθήσεσθαι τοῖς αὐτόθι, Λουσίῳ Κυήτῳ προσέταξεν ἐκκαθᾶραι τῆς ἐπαρχίας αὐτούς· ὃς καὶ
παραταξάμενος, πάμπολυ πλῆθος τῶν αὐτόθι
φονεύει, ἐφ' ᾧ κατορθώματι Ἰουδαίας ἡγεμὼν
ὑπὸ τοῦ αὐτοκράτορος ἀνεδείχθη.   ταῦτα καὶ
Ἑλλήνων οἱ τὰ κατὰ τοὺς αὐτοὺς χρόνους γραφῇ
παραδόντες αὐτοῖς ἱστόρησαν ῥήμασιν.

III. Τραϊανοῦ δὲ ἐφ' ὅλοις ἔτεσιν εἴκοσι τὴν 1
ἀρχὴν μησὶν ἓξ δέουσιν κρατήσαντος, Αἴλιος Ἀδριανὸς διαδέχεται τὴν ἡγεμονίαν.   τούτῳ Κοδρᾶτος
λόγον προσφωνήσας ἀναδίδωσιν, ἀπολογίαν συντάξας ὑπὲρ τῆς καθ' ἡμᾶς θεοσεβείας, ὅτι δή τινες
πονηροὶ ἄνδρες τοὺς ἡμετέρους ἐνοχλεῖν ἐπειρῶντο·
εἰς ἔτι δὲ φέρεται παρὰ πλείστοις τῶν ἀδελφῶν,
ἀτὰρ καὶ παρ' ἡμῖν τὸ σύγγραμμα· ἐξ οὗ κατιδεῖν
ἔστιν λαμπρὰ τεκμήρια τῆς τε τοῦ ἀνδρὸς διανοίας
καὶ τῆς ἀποστολικῆς ὀρθοτομίας.   ὁ δ' αὐτὸς τὴν 2
καθ' ἑαυτὸν ἀρχαιότητα παραφαίνει δι' ὧν ἱστορεῖ
306

the Greeks, who fled to Alexandria and captured and killed the Jews in the city, but though thus losing the help of the townsmen, the Jews of Cyrene continued to plunder the country of Egypt and to ravage the districts in it under their leader Lucuas. The Emperor sent against them Marcius Turbo with land and sea forces including cavalry. He waged war vigorously against them in many battles for a considerable time and killed many thousands of Jews, not only those of Cyrene but also those of Egypt who had rallied to Lucuas,[1] their king. The Emperor suspected that the Jews in Mesopotamia would also attack the inhabitants and ordered Lusius Quietus to clean them out of the province. He organized a force and murdered a great multitude of the Jews there, and for this reform was appointed governor of Judaea by the Emperor. The Greek authors [2] who chronicle the same period have related this narrative in these very words.

III. When Trajan had reigned for nineteen and a half years Aelius Hadrian succeeded [3] to the sovereignty. To him Quadratus addressed a treatise, composing a defence for our religion because some wicked men were trying to trouble the Christians. It is still extant among many of the brethren and we have a copy ourselves. From it can be seen the clear proof of his intellect and apostolic orthodoxy. He shows his early date by what he says as follows

[1] Dio Cassius (lxviii. 32) gives his name as Andreas.
[2] Except for Dio Cassius these cannot be identified.
[3] A.D. 117.

ταῦτα ἰδίαις φωναῖς· '' τοῦ δὲ σωτῆρος ἡμῶν τὰ
ἔργα ἀεὶ παρῆν ἀληθῆ γὰρ ἦν, οἱ θεραπευθέντες, οἱ
ἀναστάντες ἐκ νεκρῶν, οἳ οὐκ ὤφθησαν μόνον
θεραπευόμενοι καὶ ἀνιστάμενοι, ἀλλὰ καὶ ἀεὶ
παρόντες, οὐδὲ ἐπιδημοῦντος μόνον τοῦ σωτῆρος,
ἀλλὰ καὶ ἀπαλλαγέντος ἦσαν ἐπὶ χρόνον ἱκανόν,
ὥστε καὶ εἰς τοὺς ἡμετέρους χρόνους τινὲς αὐτῶν
ἀφίκοντο.''[1] τοιοῦτος μὲν οὗτος· καὶ Ἀριστείδης
δέ, πιστὸς ἀνὴρ τῆς καθ' ἡμᾶς ὁρμώμενος εὐσεβείας,
τῷ Κοδράτῳ παραπλησίως ὑπὲρ τῆς πίστεως
ἀπολογίαν ἐπιφωνήσας Ἀδριανῷ καταλέλοιπεν·
σῴζεται δέ γε εἰς δεῦρο παρὰ πλείστοις καὶ ἡ
τούτου γραφή.

IV. Ἔτει δὲ τρίτῳ τῆς αὐτῆς ἡγεμονίας Ἀλέξανδρος Ῥωμαίων ἐπίσκοπος τελευτᾷ, δέκατον τῆς
οἰκονομίας ἀποπλήσας ἔτος· Ξύστος ἦν τούτῳ
διάδοχος. καὶ τῆς Ἀλεξανδρέων δὲ παροικίας
ἀμφὶ τὸν αὐτὸν χρόνον Πρῖμον μεταλλάξαντα δωδεκάτῳ τῆς προστασίας ἔτει διαδέχεται Ἰοῦστος.

V. Τῶν γε μὴν ἐν Ἱεροσολύμοις ἐπισκόπων τοὺς
χρόνους γραφῇ σῳζομένους οὐδαμῶς εὑρών (κομιδῇ
γὰρ οὖν βραχυβίους αὐτοὺς λόγος κατέχει γενέσθαι),
τοσοῦτον ἐξ ἐγγράφων παρείληφα, ὡς μέχρι τῆς
κατὰ Ἀδριανὸν Ἰουδαίων πολιορκίας πεντεκαίδεκα
τὸν ἀριθμὸν αὐτόθι γεγόνασιν ἐπισκόπων διαδοχαί,
οὓς πάντας Ἑβραίους φασὶν ὄντας ἀνέκαθεν, τὴν
γνῶσιν τοῦ Χριστοῦ γνησίως καταδέξασθαι, ὥστ'
ἤδη πρὸς τῶν τὰ τοιάδε ἐπικρίνειν δυνατῶν καὶ
τῆς τῶν ἐπισκόπων λειτουργίας ἀξίους δοκιμα-
σθῆναι· συνεστάναι γὰρ αὐτοῖς τότε τὴν πᾶσαν
ἐκκλησίαν ἐξ Ἑβραίων πιστῶν ἀπὸ τῶν ἀπο-

---

[1] *Cf.* George Syncellus, 658. 8-13.

in his own words: " But the works of our Saviour were always present, for they were true, those who were cured, those who rose from the dead, who not merely appeared as cured and risen, but were constantly present, not only while the Saviour was living, but even for some time after he had gone, so that some of them survived even till our own time." Such was he. Aristides too, a man of faith and devoted to our religion, has, like Quadratus, left behind a defence of the faith addressed to Hadrian. His writing, too, is still preserved by many.[1]

IV. In the third year of the same reign [2] Alexander, the bishop of the Romans, died after completing the tenth year of his ministry ; Xystus was his successor. And at the same time, in the diocese of the Alexandrians, Justus succeeded Primus, who died in the twelfth year of his rule.

V. I have not found any written statement of the dates of the bishops in Jerusalem, for tradition says that they were extremely short-lived, but I have gathered from documents this much—that up to the siege of the Jews by Hadrian the successions of bishops were fifteen in number. It is said that they were all Hebrews by origin who had nobly accepted the knowledge of Christ, so that they were counted worthy even of the episcopal ministry by those who had the power to judge such questions. For their whole church at that time consisted of Hebrews who

---

[1] The Syriac text was discovered by J. Rendel Harris on Mt. Sinai and published by him in *Texts and Studies*, i. 1. See Introduction p. xlix.

[2] A.D. 120.

στόλων καὶ εἰς τὴν τότε διαρκεσάντων πολιορκίαν, καθ' ἣν Ἰουδαῖοι Ῥωμαίων αὖθις ἀποστάντες, οὐ μικροῖς πολέμοις ἥλωσαν. διαλελοιπότων δ' οὖν τηνικαῦτα τῶν ἐκ περιτομῆς ἐπισκόπων, τοὺς ἀπὸ πρώτου νῦν ἀναγκαῖον ἂν εἴη καταλέξαι. πρῶτος τοιγαροῦν Ἰάκωβος ὁ τοῦ κυρίου λεγόμενος ἀδελφός ἦν· μεθ' ὃν δεύτερος Συμεών· τρίτος Ἰοῦστος· Ζακχαῖος τέταρτος· πέμπτος Τωβίας· ἕκτος Βενιαμίν· Ἰωάννης ἕβδομος· ὄγδοος Ματθίας· ἔνατος Φίλιππος· δέκατος Ζενέκας· ἑνδέκατος Ἰοῦστος· Λευὶς δωδέκατος· Ἐφρῆς τρισκαιδέκατος· τεσσαρεσκαιδέκατος Ἰωσήφ· ἐπὶ πᾶσι πεντεκαιδέκατος Ἰούδας. τοσοῦτοι καὶ οἱ ἐπὶ τῆς Ἱεροσολύμων πόλεως ἐπίσκοποι ἀπὸ τῶν ἀποστόλων εἰς τὸν δηλούμενον διαγενόμενοι χρόνον, οἱ πάντες ἐκ περιτομῆς. ἤδη δὲ δωδέκατον ἐχούσης ἔτος τῆς ἡγεμονίας, Ξύστον δεκαέτη χρόνον ἀποπλήσαντα ἐπὶ τῆς Ῥωμαίων ἐπισκοπῆς ἕβδομος ἀπὸ τῶν ἀποστόλων διαδέχεται Τελεσφόρος· ἐνιαυτοῦ δὲ μεταξὺ καὶ μηνῶν διαγενομένου, τῆς Ἀλεξανδρέων παροικίας τὴν προστασίαν Εὐμένης ἕκτῳ κλήρῳ διαδέχεται, τοῦ πρὸ αὐτοῦ ἔτεσιν ἕνδεκα διαρκέσαντος.

VI. Καὶ δῆτα τῆς Ἰουδαίων ἀποστασίας αὖθις εἰς μέγα καὶ πολὺ προελθούσης, Ῥοῦφος ἔπαρχων τῆς Ἰουδαίας, στρατιωτικῆς αὐτῷ συμμαχίας ὑπὸ βασιλέως πεμφθείσης, ταῖς ἀπονοίαις αὐτῶν ἀφειδῶς χρώμενος ἐπεξῄει, μυριάδας ἀθρόως ἀνδρῶν ὁμοῦ καὶ παίδων καὶ γυναικῶν διαφθείρων πολέμου τε νόμῳ τὰς χώρας αὐτῶν ἐξανδραποδιζόμενος. ἐστρατήγει δὲ τότε Ἰουδαίων Βαρχωχεβας ὄνομα, ὃ δὴ ἀστέρα δηλοῖ, τὰ μὲν ἄλλα

had continued Christian from the Apostles down to the siege at the time when the Jews again rebelled from the Romans and were beaten in a great war. Since the Jewish bishops then ceased, it is now necessary to give their names from the beginning. The first then was James who was called the Lord's brother, and after him Simeon was the second. The third was Justus, Zacchaeus was the fourth, Tobias the fifth, the sixth Benjamin, the seventh John, the eighth Matthias, the ninth Philip, the tenth Seneca, the eleventh Justus, the twelfth Levi, the thirteenth Ephres, the fourteenth Joseph, and last of all the fifteenth Judas. Such were the bishops in the city of Jerusalem, from the Apostles down to the time mentioned, and they were all Jews. Now during the twelfth year of the reign of Hadrian, Telesphorus, the seventh from the Apostles, succeeded Xystus who had completed ten years in the bishopric of the Romans, and one year and some months later Eumenes succeeded to the government of the diocese of Alexandria as the sixth bishop, when his predecessor had completed eleven years.

VI. The rebellion of the Jews [1] once more progressed in character and extent, and Rufus, the governor of Judaea, when military aid had been sent him by the Emperor, moved out against them, treating their madness without mercy. He destroyed in heaps thousands of men, women, and children, and, under the law of war, enslaved their land. The Jews were at that time led by a certain Bar Chochebas, [2] which means " star," a man who was

[1] *Cf.* Dio Cassius, lxix. 12-14.

[2] Literally " son of a star," with a probable reference to Numbers xxiv. 17. After his defeat the Jews called him Bar Choziba, " son of a lie."

φονικὸς καὶ λῃστρικός τις ἀνήρ, ἐπὶ δὲ τῇ προσηγορίᾳ, οἷα ἐπ' ἀνδραπόδων, ὡς δὴ ἐξ οὐρανοῦ φωστὴρ αὐτοῖς κατεληλυθὼς κακουμένοις τε ἐπιλάμψαι τερατευόμενος. ἀκμάσαντος δὲ τοῦ πο- 3 λέμου ἔτους ὀκτωκαιδεκάτου τῆς ἡγεμονίας κατὰ Βηθθηρα (πολίχνη τις ἦν ὀχυρωτάτη, τῶν Ἱεροσολύμων οὐ σφόδρα πόρρω διεστῶσα) τῆς τε ἔξωθεν πολιορκίας χρονίου γενομένης λιμῷ τε καὶ δίψει τῶν νεωτεροποιῶν εἰς ἔσχατον ὀλέθρου περιελαθέντων καὶ τοῦ τῆς ἀπονοίας αὐτοῖς αἰτίου τὴν ἀξίαν ἐκτίσαντος δίκην, τὸ πᾶν ἔθνος ἐξ ἐκείνου καὶ τῆς περὶ τὰ Ἱεροσόλυμα γῆς πάμπαν ἐπιβαίνειν εἴργεται νόμου δόγματι καὶ διατάξεσιν Ἀδριανοῦ, ὡς ἂν μηδ' ἐξ ἀπόπτου θεωροῖεν τὸ πατρῷον ἔδαφος, ἐγκελευσαμένου· Ἀρίστων ὁ Πελλαῖος ἱστορεῖ. οὕτω δὴ τῆς πόλεως εἰς 4 ἐρημίαν τοῦ Ἰουδαίων ἔθνους παντελῆ τε φθορὰν τῶν πάλαι οἰκητόρων ἐλθούσης ἐξ ἀλλοφύλων τε γένους συνοικισθείσης, ἡ μετέπειτα συστᾶσα Ῥωμαϊκὴ πόλις τὴν ἐπωνυμίαν ἀμείψασα, εἰς τὴν τοῦ κρατοῦντος Αἰλίου Ἀδριανοῦ τιμὴν Αἰλία προσαγορεύεται. καὶ δὴ τῆς αὐτόθι ἐκκλησίας ἐξ ἐθνῶν συγκροτηθείσης, πρῶτος μετὰ τοὺς ἐκ περιτομῆς ἐπισκόπους τὴν τῶν ἐκεῖσε λειτουργίαν ἐγχειρίζεται Μάρκος.

VII. Ἤδη δὲ λαμπροτάτων δίκην φωστήρων τῶν 1 ἀνὰ τὴν οἰκουμένην ἀποστιλβουσῶν ἐκκλησιῶν ἀκμαζούσης τε εἰς ἅπαν τὸ τῶν ἀνθρώπων γένος τῆς εἰς τὸν σωτῆρα καὶ κύριον ἡμῶν Ἰησοῦν Χριστὸν πίστεως, ὁ μισόκαλος δαίμων οἷα τῆς ἀληθείας ἐχθρὸς καὶ τῆς τῶν ἀνθρώπων σωτηρίας ἀεὶ τυγχάνων πολεμιώτατος, πάσας στρέφων κατὰ

murderous and a bandit, but relied on his name, as if dealing with slaves, and claimed to be a luminary who had come down to them from heaven and was magically enlightening those who were in misery. The war reached its height in the eighteenth year of the reign of Hadrian in Beththera,[1] which was a strong citadel not very far from Jerusalem; the siege lasted a long time before the rebels were driven to final destruction by famine and thirst and the instigator of their madness paid the penalty he deserved. Hadrian then commanded that by a legal decree and ordinances the whole nation should be absolutely prevented from entering from thenceforth even the district round Jerusalem, so that not even from a distance could it see its ancestral home. Ariston of Pella tells the story.[2] Thus when the city came to be bereft of the nation of the Jews, and its ancient inhabitants had completely perished, it was colonized by foreigners, and the Roman city which afterwards arose changed its name, and in honour of the reigning emperor Aelius Hadrian was called Aelia. The church, too, in it was composed of Gentiles, and after the Jewish bishops the first who was appointed to minister to those there was Marcus.

VII. Like brilliant lamps the churches were now shining throughout the world, and faith in our Saviour and Lord Jesus Christ was flourishing among all mankind, when the devil who hates what is good, as the enemy of truth, ever most hostile to man's salvation, turned all his devices against the church.

---

[1] It has not been identified.
[2] The book is not extant.

τῆς ἐκκλησίας μηχανάς, πάλαι μὲν τοῖς ἔξωθεν
διωγμοῖς κατ' αὐτῆς ὡπλίζετο, τότε γε μὴν 2
τούτων ἀποκεκλεισμένος, πονηροῖς καὶ γόησιν
ἀνδράσιν ὥσπερ τισὶν ὀλεθρίοις ψυχῶν ὀργάνοις
διακόνοις τε ἀπωλείας χρώμενος, ἑτέραις κατ-
εστρατήγει μεθόδοις, πάντα πόρον ἐπινοῶν, ὡς
ἂν ὑποδύντες γόητες καὶ ἀπατηλοὶ τὴν αὐτὴν τοῦ
δόγματος ἡμῖν προσηγορίαν, ὁμοῦ μὲν τῶν πιστῶν
τοὺς πρὸς αὐτῶν ἁλισκομένους εἰς βυθὸν ἀπωλείας
ἄγοιεν, ὁμοῦ δὲ τοὺς τῆς πίστεως ἀγνῶτας δι' ὧν
αὐτοὶ δρῶντες ἐπιχειροῖεν, ἀποτρέποιντο τῆς ἐπὶ
τὸν σωτήριον λόγον παρόδου. ἀπὸ γοῦν τοῦ 3
Μενάνδρου, ὃν διάδοχον τοῦ Σίμωνος ἤδη πρότερον
παραδεδώκαμεν, ἀμφίστομος ὥσπερ καὶ δικέφαλος
ὀφιώδης τις προελθοῦσα δύναμις δυεῖν αἱρέσεων
διαφόρων ἀρχηγοὺς κατεστήσατο, Σατορνῖνόν τε
Ἀντιοχέα τὸ γένος καὶ Βασιλείδην Ἀλεξανδρέα·
ὧν ὁ μὲν κατὰ Συρίαν, ὁ δὲ κατ' Αἴγυπτον συν-
εστήσαντο θεομισῶν αἱρέσεων διδασκαλεῖα. τὰ μὲν 4
οὖν πλεῖστα τὸν Σατορνῖνον τὰ αὐτὰ τῷ Μενάνδρῳ
ψευδολογῆσαι ὁ Εἰρηναῖος δηλοῖ, προσχήματι δὲ
ἀπορρητοτέρων τὸν Βασιλείδην εἰς τὸ ἄπειρον
τεῖναι τὰς ἐπινοίας, δυσσεβοῦς αἱρέσεως ἑαυτῷ
τερατώδεις ἀναπλάσαντα μυθοποιίας. πλείστων
οὖν ἐκκλησιαστικῶν ἀνδρῶν κατ' ἐκεῖνο καιροῦ
τῆς ἀληθείας ὑπεραγωνιζομένων λογικώτερόν τε
τῆς ἀποστολικῆς καὶ ἐκκλησιαστικῆς δόξης ὑπερ-
μαχούντων, ἤδη τινὲς καὶ διὰ συγγραμμάτων τοῖς
μετέπειτα προφυλακτικὰς αὐτῶν δὴ τούτων τῶν
δηλωθεισῶν αἱρέσεων παρεῖχον ἐφόδους· ὧν εἰς
ἡμᾶς κατῆλθεν ἐν τοῖς τότε γνωριμωτάτου συγγραφέως Ἀγρίππα Κάστορος ἱκανώτατος κατὰ

Iren. 1, 24, 1
Iren. 1, 24, 3

314

Formerly he had used persecutions from without as his weapon against her, but now that he was excluded from this he employed wicked men and sorcerers, like baleful weapons and ministers of destruction against the soul, and conducted his campaign by other measures, plotting by every means that sorcerers and deceivers might assume the same name as our religion and at one time lead to the depth of destruction those of the faithful whom they caught, and at others, by the deeds which they undertook, might turn away from the path to the saving word those who were ignorant of the faith. Thus from Menander, whom we have already mentioned as the successor of Simon, there proceeded a certain snake-like power with two mouths and double head, and established the leaders of two heresies, Saturninus, an Antiochian by race, and Basilides of Alexandria. The first established schools of impious heresy in Syria, the latter in Egypt. Irenaeus makes it plain that Saturninus uttered for the most part the same falsehoods as Menander, but Basilides, under the pretext of secret doctrine, stretched fancy infinitely far, fabricating monstrous myths for his impious heresy. Now while most of the orthodox at that time were struggling for the truth, and fighting with great eloquence[1] for the glory of the Apostles and of the Church, some also by their writings provided for their successors methods of defence against the heresies which have been mentioned. Of these a most powerful refutation of Basilides[2] has reached us from Agrippa Castor, a most famous

---

[1] The Greek might naturally mean "logically," but the antithesis with written defences shows what is intended.
[2] Not extant.

Βασιλείδου ἔλεγχος, τὴν δεινότητα τῆς τἀνδρὸς 7
ἀποκαλύπτων γοητείας. ἐκφαίνων δ' οὖν αὐτοῦ
τὰ ἀπόρρητα, φησὶν αὐτὸν εἰς μὲν τὸ εὐαγγέλιον
τέσσαρα πρὸς τοῖς εἴκοσι συντάξαι βιβλία, προφήτας δὲ ἑαυτῷ ὀνομάσαι Βαρκαββᾶν καὶ Βαρκωφ
καὶ ἄλλους ἀνυπάρκτους τινὰς ἑαυτῷ συστησάμενον, βαρβάρους τε αὐτοῖς εἰς κατάπληξιν τῶν
τὰ τοιαῦτα τεθηπότων ἐπιφημίσαι προσηγορίας,
διδάσκειν τε ἀδιαφορεῖν εἰδωλοθύτων ἀπογευο-
μένους καὶ ἐξομνυμένους ἀπαραφυλάκτως τὴν
πίστιν κατὰ τοὺς τῶν διωγμῶν καιρούς, Πυθα-
γορικῶς τε τοῖς προσιοῦσιν αὐτῷ πενταετῆ σιωπὴν
παρακελεύεσθαι· καὶ ἕτερα δὲ τούτοις παραπλήσια 8
ἀμφὶ τοῦ Βασιλείδου καταλέξας ὁ εἰρημένος
οὐκ ἀγεννῶς τῆς δηλωθείσης αἱρέσεως εἰς πρὸῦπτον

Iren. 1, 25. 1,
6, 3, 4

ἐφώρασε τὴν πλάνην. γράφει δὲ καὶ Εἰρηναῖος 9
συγχρονίσαι τούτοις Καρποκράτην, ἑτέρας αἱρέσεως
τῆς τῶν Γνωστικῶν ἐπικληθείσης πατέρα· οἳ καὶ
τοῦ Σίμωνος οὐχ ὡς ἐκεῖνος κρύβδην, ἀλλ' ἤδη καὶ
εἰς φανερὸν τὰς μαγείας παραδιδόναι ἠξίουν, ὡς
ἐπὶ μεγάλοις δή, μόνον οὐχὶ καὶ σεμνυνόμενοι τοῖς
κατὰ περιεργίαν πρὸς αὐτῶν ἐπιτελουμένοις φίλ-
τροις ὀνειροπομποῖς τε καὶ παρέδροις τισὶ δαίμοσιν
καὶ ἄλλαις ὁμοιοτρόποις τισὶν ἀγωγαῖς· τούτοις
τε ἀκολούθως πάντα δρᾶν χρῆναι διδάσκειν τὰ
αἰσχρουργότατα τοὺς μέλλοντας εἰς τὸ τέλειον τῆς
κατ' αὐτοὺς μυσταγωγίας ἢ καὶ μᾶλλον μυσαρο-
ποιίας ἐλεύσεσθαι, ὡς μὴ ἂν ἄλλως ἐκφευξομένους
τοὺς κοσμικούς, ὡς ἂν ἐκεῖνοι φαῖεν, ἄρχοντας,
μὴ οὐχὶ πᾶσιν τὰ δι' ἀρρητοποιίας ἀπονείμαντας
χρέα. τούτοις δῆτα συνέβαινεν διακόνοις χρώμενον 10
τὸν ἐπιχαιρεσίκακον δαίμονα τοὺς μὲν πρὸς αὐτῶν

writer of that time, revealing the cleverness of the man's deception. In expounding his mysteries he says that he compiled twenty-four books on the gospel, and that he named his own prophets Bar Cabbas and Bar Coph,[1] and that he set up some others for himself who had never existed, but that he invented barbarous names for them to astonish those who were influenced by such things. He taught that there was no harm in eating things offered to idols, or in light-heartedly denying the faith in times of persecution. Like Pythagoras he enjoined those who came to him to keep silence for five years. The same writer tells other similar things about Basilides, and offers a magnificent refutation of the error of the heresy described. Irenaeus also writes that Carpocrates was a contemporary of these, the father of another heresy which was called that of the Gnostics. These did not, like Basilides, desire to transmit the magic of Simon secretly but openly, as though it was some great thing, speaking almost with awe of their magical ceremonies, of love charms, of the bringers of dreams and familiar spirits, and of other similar performances. In accordance with this they teach that those who purpose coming to initiation in their mysteries, or rather in their obscenities, must perform all the shocking deeds because in no other way can they escape the " rulers of the world," as they would say, except by fulfilling to all of them what was necessary through their mysteries. By using these ministers the demon who rejoices in evil accomplished the piteous enslavement

[1] Nothing is known of these persons, but for a suggested connexion of Gnostic prophecy with Zoroastrian writings see Hort's article on Barcabbas in the *Dictionary of Christian Biography*.

ἀπατωμένους οἰκτρῶς οὕτως εἰς ἀπώλειαν ἀνδρα-
ποδίζεσθαι, τοῖς δ' ἀπίστοις ἔθνεσιν πολλὴν
παρέχειν κατὰ τοῦ θείου λόγου δυσφημίας περι-
ουσίαν, τῆς ἐξ αὐτῶν φήμης εἰς τὴν τοῦ παντὸς
Χριστιανῶν ἔθνους διαβολὴν καταχεομένης. ταύτῃ 11
δ' οὖν ἐπὶ πλεῖστον συνέβαινεν τὴν περὶ ἡμῶν
παρὰ τοῖς τότε ἀπίστοις ὑπόνοιαν δυσσεβῆ καὶ
ἀτοπωτάτην διαδίδοσθαι, ὡς δὴ ἀθεμίτοις πρὸς
μητέρας καὶ ἀδελφὰς μίξεσιν ἀνοσίαις τε τροφαῖς
χρωμένων. οὐκ εἰς μακρόν γε μὴν αὐτῷ ταῦτα 12
προυχώρει, τῆς ἀληθείας αὐτῆς ἑαυτὴν συνιστώσης
ἐπὶ μέγα τε φῶς κατὰ τὸν προϊόντα χρόνον δια-
λαμπούσης. ἔσβεστο μὲν γὰρ αὐτίκα πρὸς αὐτῆς 13
ἐνεργείας ἀπελεγχόμενα τὰ τῶν ἐχθρῶν ἐπιτεχνή-
ματα, ἄλλων ἐπ' ἄλλαις αἱρέσεων καινοτομουμένων
ὑπορρεουσῶν ἀεὶ τῶν προτέρων καὶ εἰς πολυτρόπους
καὶ πολυμόρφους ἰδέας ἄλλοτε ἄλλως φθειρομένων·
προήει δ' εἰς αὔξην καὶ μέγεθος, ἀεὶ κατὰ τὰ αὐτὰ
καὶ ὡσαύτως ἔχουσα, ἡ τῆς καθόλου καὶ μόνης
ἀληθοῦς ἐκκλησίας λαμπρότης, τὸ σεμνὸν καὶ
εἰλικρινὲς καὶ ἐλευθέριον τό τε σῶφρον καὶ καθαρὸν
τῆς ἐνθέου πολιτείας τε καὶ φιλοσοφίας εἰς ἅπαν
γένος Ἑλλήνων τε καὶ βαρβάρων ἀποστίλβουσα.
συναπέσβη δ' οὖν ἅμα τῷ χρόνῳ καὶ ἡ κατὰ παντὸς 14
τοῦ δόγματος διαβολή, ἔμενεν δὲ ἄρα μόνη παρὰ
πᾶσι κρατοῦσα καὶ ἀνομολογουμένη τὰ μάλιστα
διαπρέπειν ἐπὶ σεμνότητι καὶ σωφροσύνῃ θείοις τε
καὶ φιλοσόφοις δόγμασιν ἡ καθ' ἡμᾶς διδασκαλία,
ὡς μηδένα τῶν εἰς νῦν αἰσχρὰν ἐπιφέρειν τολμᾶν

---

[1] The reference is to the story which was at that time told
by the heathen of the Christians and has since been told among
Christians of the Jews that they kill and eat small children.

to perdition of those who were thus deceived by them, and brought much weight of discredit upon the divine word among the unbelieving Gentiles, because the report which started from them was scattered calumniously on the whole race of Christians. It was especially in this way that it came to pass that a blasphemous and wicked suspicion concerning us was spread among the heathen of those days, to the effect that we practised unspeakable incest with mothers and sisters and took part in wicked food.[1] Yet this did not long succeed, for the truth vindicated itself and as time went on shone ever more brightly. For by its power the machinations of its enemies were refuted ; though new heresies were invented one after another, the earlier ones flowed into strange multiple and multifarious forms and perished in different ways at different times. But the brightness of the universal and only true church proceeded to increase in greatness, for it ever held to the same points in the same way, and radiated forth to all the race of Greeks and barbarians the reverent, sincere, and free nature, and the sobriety and purity of the divine teaching as to conduct and thought. Thus with the lapse of time the calumnies against the whole teaching were extinguished, and our doctrine remained as the only one which had power among all and was admitted to excel in its godliness and sobriety,[2] and its divine and wise doctrines. So that no one has dared to

---

[2] These two words are peculiarly difficult to translate. The first means the quality which demands reverence from others. The second is the moderation, self-restraint, and sobriety which are essential to a good life. There is no word in English which adequately translates either.

κατὰ τῆς πίστεως ἡμῶν δυσφημίαν μηδέ τινα τοιαύτην διαβολὴν οἵαις πάλαι πρότερον φίλον ἦν χρῆσθαι τοῖς καθ' ἡμῶν ἐπισυνισταμένοις.

Ὅμως δ' οὖν κατὰ τοὺς δηλουμένους αὖθις 1 παρῆγεν εἰς μέσον ἡ ἀλήθεια πλείους ἑαυτῆς ὑπερμάχους, οὐ δι' ἀγράφων αὐτὸ μόνον ἐλέγχων, ἀλλὰ καὶ δι' ἐγγράφων ἀποδείξεων κατὰ τῶν ἀθέων αἱρέσεων στρατευομένους· VIII. ἐν τούτοις 1 ἐγνωρίζετο Ἡγήσιππος, οὗ πλείσταις ἤδη πρότερον κεχρήμεθα φωναῖς, ὡς ἂν ἐκ τῆς αὐτοῦ παραδόσεως τινὰ τῶν κατὰ τοὺς ἀποστόλους παραθέμενοι. ἐν πέντε δ' οὖν συγγράμμασιν οὗτος τὴν ἀπλανῆ 2 παράδοσιν τοῦ ἀποστολικοῦ κηρύγματος ἁπλουστάτῃ συντάξει γραφῆς ὑπομνηματισάμενος, καθ' ὃν ἐγνωρίζετο σημαίνει χρόνον, περὶ τῶν ἀρχῆθεν ἱδρυσάντων τὰ εἴδωλα οὕτω πως γράφων· "οἷς κενοτάφια καὶ ναοὺς ἐποίησαν ὡς μέχρι νῦν· ὧν ἐστιν καὶ Ἀντίνοος, δοῦλος Ἀδριανοῦ Καίσαρος, οὗ καὶ ἀγὼν ἄγεται Ἀντινόειος, ὁ ἐφ' ἡμῶν γενόμενος. καὶ γὰρ πόλιν ἔκτισεν ἐπώνυμον Ἀντινόου καὶ προφήτας." κατ' αὐτὸν δὲ καὶ Ἰου- 3 στῖνος, γνήσιος τῆς ἀληθοῦς φιλοσοφίας ἐραστής, ἔτι τοῖς παρ' Ἕλλησιν ἀσκούμενος ἐνδιέτριβεν λόγοις· σημαίνει δὲ καὶ αὐτὸς τουτονὶ τὸν χρόνον ἐν τῇ πρὸς Ἀντωνῖνον ἀπολογίᾳ ὧδε γράφων· "οὐκ ἄτοπον δὲ ἐπιμνησθῆναι ἐν τούτοις ἡγούμεθα καὶ Ἀντινόου τοῦ νῦν γενομένου, ὃν καὶ ἅπαντες ὡς θεὸν διὰ φόβον σέβειν ὥρμηντο, ἐπιστάμενοι τίς τε ἦν καὶ πόθεν ὑπῆρχεν."

Justin, Apol. 1, 29

---

[1] The word ὑπομνήματα, which was translated in Latin by *commentarii*, means a report made by an official to the emperor or other authority, and so came to be used of an

continue the base implications of calumny against our faith, such as those who were opposed to us were formerly accustomed to use.

Nevertheless, at the time spoken of, the truth again brought forward for itself more champions who campaigned against the godless heresies not only by unwritten arguments but also in written demonstrations. VIII. Among these Hegesippus was famous and of his words we have already made much use, for from his tradition we have quoted details as to the apostolic age. He collected his material [1] in five books, giving in the simplest style of writing the unerring tradition of the apostolic preaching. He indicates the time in which he flourished by writing thus about those who had made idols: "To them they made cenotaphs [2] and shrines until now, and among them is Antinous, a slave of the Emperor Hadrian, in whose honour the Antinoian games are held, though he was our contemporary. For he also built a city called after Antinous, and instituted prophets for him." [3] At the same time too, Justin, a genuine lover of true philosophy, was still continuing to practise the learning of the Greeks. And he also himself indicates this period in his Apology to Antoninus by writing thus, "And we thought it not out of place to mention at this point Antinous of the present day whom all were intimidated to worship as a god, though they knew his nature and origin."

historical work which had not yet been put into literary form. As to Hegesippus see Introduction, pp. xlvi sq.

[2] A cenotaph is a monument in the form of a tomb but with no body in it.

[3] The sentence seems to break off in the middle, but the subject of the verb, though not expressed, is doubtless Hadrian.

ὁ δ' αὐτὸς καὶ τοῦ τότε κατὰ Ἰουδαίων πολέμου 4
μνημονεύων ταῦτα παρατίθεται· " καὶ γὰρ ἐν τῷ
νῦν γενομένῳ Ἰουδαϊκῷ πολέμῳ Βαρχωχεβας, ὁ
τῆς Ἰουδαίων ἀποστάσεως ἀρχηγέτης, Χριστιανοὺς μόνους εἰς τιμωρίας δεινάς, εἰ μὴ ἀρνοῖντο
Ἰησοῦν τὸν Χριστὸν καὶ βλασφημοῖεν, ἐκέλευεν
ἄγεσθαι."

Ἐν ταὐτῷ δὲ καὶ τὴν ἀπὸ τῆς Ἑλληνικῆς 5
φιλοσοφίας ἐπὶ τὴν θεοσέβειαν μεταβολὴν αὐτοῦ,
ὅτι μὴ ἀλόγως, μετὰ κρίσεως δὲ αὐτῷ γεγόνει,
δηλῶν, ταῦτα γράφει· " καὶ γὰρ αὐτὸς ἐγώ, τοῖς
Πλάτωνος χαίρων διδάγμασι, διαβαλλομένους
ἀκούων Χριστιανούς, ὁρῶν δὲ καὶ ἀφόβους πρὸς
θάνατον καὶ πάντα τὰ νομιζόμενα φοβερά, ἐν-
ενόουν ἀδύνατον εἶναι ἐν κακίᾳ καὶ φιληδονίᾳ
ὑπάρχειν αὐτούς· τίς γὰρ φιλήδονος ἢ ἀκρατὴς
καὶ ἀνθρωπείων σαρκῶν βορὰν ἡγούμενος ἀγαθόν,
δύναιτ' ἂν θάνατον ἀσπάζεσθαι, ὅπως τῶν ἑαυτοῦ
στερηθείη ἐπιθυμιῶν, ἀλλ' οὐκ ἐκ παντὸς ζῆν ἀεὶ
τὴν ἐνθάδε βιοτὴν καὶ λανθάνειν τοὺς ἄρχοντας
ἐπειρᾶτο, οὐχ ὅτι ἑαυτὸν κατήγγελλεν φονευθησό-
μενον;"

Ἔτι δ' ὁ αὐτὸς ἱστορεῖ δεξάμενον τὸν Ἀδριανὸν
παρὰ Σερεννίου Γρανιανοῦ, λαμπροτάτου ἡγουμένου, γράμματα ὑπὲρ Χριστιανῶν περιέχοντα ὡς
οὐ δίκαιον εἴη ἐπὶ μηδενὶ ἐγκλήματι βοαῖς δήμου
χαριζομένους ἀκρίτως κτείνειν αὐτούς, ἀντιγράψαι
Μινουκίῳ Φουνδανῷ, ἀνθυπάτῳ τῆς Ἀσίας, προστάττοντα μηδένα κρίνειν ἄνευ ἐγκλήματος καὶ
εὐλόγου κατηγορίας· καὶ τῆς ἐπιστολῆς δὲ ἀντί- 7
γραφον παρατέθειται, τὴν Ῥωμαϊκὴν φωνήν, ὡς
εἶχεν, διαφυλάξας, προλέγει δ' αὐτῆς ταῦτα· " καὶ

Justin, Apol.
1, 31

Justin, Apol.
2, 12

The same writer mentions the war of that time against the Jews and makes this observation, "For in the present Jewish war it was only Christians whom Bar Chocheba, the leader of the rebellion of the Jews, commanded to be punished severely, if they did not deny Jesus as the Messiah and blaspheme him."

In the same book he shows that his conversion from Greek philosophy to true religion did not take place irrationally, but as an act of deliberate judgment ; for he writes thus : " For I myself, while I was rejoicing in the teaching of Plato, heard the Christians abused. But I saw that they were afraid neither of death, nor of anything usually thought fearful, and I considered it was impossible that they were living in wickedness and libertinism. For what libertine or incontinent person, or one who finds good in the eating of human flesh, could greet death, that it might take away all his lusts, and would not try to prolong by all means his present life and to avoid the notice of the rulers, and not give himself up to be murdered ? "

Moreover, the same writer relates that Hadrian received a dispatch in favour of the Christians from Serennius Granianus, a most distinguished governor, to the effect that it was not just to put them to death, without accusation or trial, to appease popular clamour, and that he wrote an answer to Minucius Fundanus, proconsul of Asia, ordering him to try no one without indictment and reasonable accusation, and Justin appends a copy of the letter, preserving the original Latin [1] as he had it, and prefixing these

[1] This is not so in the extant MS. of Justin, which has replaced the Latin by the Greek of Eusebius. The authenticity of the document has been warmly disputed, and there is not yet any agreement on the point among critics.

Justin, Apol.
1, 68 ἐξ ἐπιστολῆς δὲ τοῦ μεγίστου καὶ ἐπιφανεστά
του Καίσαρος Ἀδριανοῦ τοῦ πατρὸς ὑμῶν ἔχοντες
ἀπαιτεῖν ὑμᾶς, καθὰ ἠξιώσαμεν, κελεῦσαι τὰς
κρίσεις γίνεσθαι, τοῦτο οὐχ ὡς ὑπὸ Ἀδριανοῦ
κελευσθὲν μᾶλλον ἠξιώσαμεν, ἀλλ' ἐκ τοῦ ἐπί
στασθαι δικαίαν ἀξιοῦν τὴν προσφώνησιν. ὑπ
ετάξαμεν δὲ καὶ τῆς ἐπιστολῆς Ἀδριανοῦ τὸ
ἀντίγραφον, ἵνα καὶ τοῦτο ἀληθεύειν ἡμᾶς γνωρί
ζητε, καὶ ἔστιν τόδε."

Τούτοις ὁ μὲν δηλωθεὶς ἀνὴρ αὐτὴν παρατέθειται
τὴν Ῥωμαϊκὴν ἀντιγραφήν, ἡμεῖς δ' ἐπὶ τὸ
Ἑλληνικὸν κατὰ δύναμιν αὐτὴν μετειλήφαμεν,
ἔχουσαν ὧδε·

Justin, Apol.
1, 68 IX. "Μινουκίῳ Φουνδανῷ. ἐπιστολὴν ἐδεξάμην
γραφεῖσάν μοι ἀπὸ Σερεννίου Γρανιανοῦ, λαμ
προτάτου ἀνδρός, ὅντινα σὺ διεδέξω. οὐ δοκεῖ
μοι οὖν τὸ πρᾶγμα ἀζήτητον καταλιπεῖν, ἵνα μήτε
οἱ ἄνθρωποι ταράττωνται καὶ τοῖς συκοφάνταις
χορηγία κακουργίας παρασχεθῇ. εἰ οὖν σαφῶς
εἰς ταύτην τὴν ἀξίωσιν οἱ ἐπαρχιῶται δύνανται
διισχυρίζεσθαι κατὰ τῶν Χριστιανῶν, ὡς καὶ πρὸ
βήματος ἀποκρίνασθαι, ἐπὶ τοῦτο μόνον τραπῶσιν,
ἀλλ' οὐκ ἀξιώσεσιν οὐδὲ μόναις βοαῖς. πολλῷ
γὰρ μᾶλλον προσῆκεν, εἴ τις κατηγορεῖν βούλοιτο,
τοῦτό σε διαγινώσκειν. εἴ τις οὖν κατηγορεῖ καὶ
δείκνυσίν τι παρὰ τοὺς νόμους πράττοντας, οὕτως
ὅριζε κατὰ τὴν δύναμιν τοῦ ἁμαρτήματος· ὡς μὰ
τὸν Ἡρακλέα εἴ τις συκοφαντίας χάριν τοῦτο
προτείνοι, διαλάμβανε ὑπὲρ τῆς δεινότητος καὶ
φρόντιζε ὅπως ἂν ἐκδικήσειας." καὶ τὰ μὲν τῆς
Ἀδριανοῦ ἀντιγραφῆς τοιαῦτα.

remarks: "Though we might have begged you to order trials to be held, as we desired, on the strength of a letter from the great and glorious Emperor Hadrian, we preferred to rest our request not on the command of Hadrian but on our knowledge that we are making a righteous request. However, we also append a copy of the letter of Hadrian, that you may know that we are speaking the truth on this point, and here it is."

The author quoted then appends the Latin rescript itself, but we have translated it to the best of our power into Greek as follows:

IX. "To Minucius Fundanus. I received a letter written to me from his Excellency Serennius Granianus, your predecessor. I think that the matter ought not to remain without inquiry, to prevent men from being harassed or helping the rascality of informers. If then the provincials can make out a clear case on these lines against the Christians so as to plead it in open court, let them be influenced by this alone and not by opinions or mere outcries. For it is far more correct if anyone wishes to make an accusation for you to examine this point. If then anyone accuses them, and shows that they are acting illegally, decide the point according to the nature of the offence, but by Hercules, if anyone brings the matter forward for the purpose of blackmail, investigate strenuously and be careful to inflict penalties adequate to the crime."[1] Such was the rescript of Hadrian.

[1] The Latin of Rufinus (see Introduction, p. xxviii) may be the original: "in hunc pro sui nequitia suppliciis severioribus vindices".

X. Τούτου δὲ τὸ χρεὼν μετὰ πρῶτον καὶ εἰκοστὸν ἔτος ἐκτίσαντος, Ἀντωνῖνος ὁ κληθεὶς Εὐσεβὴς τὴν Ῥωμαίων ἀρχὴν διαδέχεται. τούτου δὲ
ἐν ἔτει πρώτῳ Τελεσφόρου τὸν βίον ἐνδεκάτῳ τῆς
λειτουργίας ἐνιαυτῷ μεταλλάξαντος, Ὑγῖνος τὸν
κλῆρον τῆς Ῥωμαίων ἐπισκοπῆς παραλαμβάνει.

Iren. 3, 8, 3
[= Eus. 5, 6,
4] ἱστορεῖ γε μὴν ὁ Εἰρηναῖος τὸν Τελεσφόρου
μαρτυρίῳ τὴν τελευτὴν διαπρέψαι, δηλῶν ἐν
ταὐτῷ κατὰ τὸν δηλούμενον Ῥωμαίων ἐπίσκοπον
Ὑγῖνον Οὐαλεντῖνον ἰδίας αἱρέσεως εἰσηγητὴν καὶ
Κέρδωνα τῆς κατὰ Μαρκίωνα πλάνης ἀρχηγὸν
ἐπὶ τῆς Ῥώμης ἄμφω γνωρίζεσθαι, γράφει δὲ
οὕτως·

Iren. 3, 4, 3 **XI.** "Οὐαλεντῖνος μὲν γὰρ ἦλθεν εἰς Ῥώμην
ἐπὶ Ὑγίνου, ἤκμασεν δὲ ἐπὶ Πίου, καὶ παρέμεινεν
ἕως Ἀνικήτου· Κέρδων δ᾽ ὁ πρὸ Μαρκίωνος καὶ
αὐτὸς ἐπὶ Ὑγίνου, ὃς ἦν ἔνατος ἐπίσκοπος, εἰς
τὴν ἐκκλησίαν ἐλθὼν καὶ ἐξομολογούμενος, οὕτως
διετέλεσεν, ποτὲ μὲν λαθροδιδασκαλῶν, ποτὲ δὲ
πάλιν ἐξομολογούμενος, ποτὲ δὲ ἐλεγχόμενος ἐφ᾽
οἷς ἐδίδασκεν κακῶς, καὶ ἀφιστάμενος τῆς τῶν
ἀδελφῶν συνοδίας." ταῦτα δέ φησιν ἐν τρίτῳ τῶν
πρὸς τὰς αἱρέσεις· ἕν γε μὴν τῷ πρώτῳ αὖθις περὶ
Iren. 1, 27,
1. 2 τοῦ Κέρδωνος ταῦτα διέξεισιν· "Κέρδων δέ τις
ἀπὸ τῶν περὶ τὸν Σίμωνα τὰς ἀφορμὰς λαβὼν
καὶ ἐπιδημήσας ἐν τῇ Ῥώμῃ ἐπὶ Ὑγίνου ἔνατον
κλῆρον τῆς ἐπισκοπικῆς διαδοχῆς ἀπὸ τῶν ἀποστόλων ἔχοντος, ἐδίδαξεν τὸν ὑπὸ τοῦ νόμου καὶ
προφητῶν κεκηρυγμένον θεὸν μὴ εἶναι πατέρα
τοῦ κυρίου ἡμῶν Ἰησοῦ Χριστοῦ· τὸν μὲν γὰρ
γνωρίζεσθαι, τὸν δὲ ἀγνῶτα εἶναι, καὶ τὸν μὲν
δίκαιον, τὸν δὲ ἀγαθὸν ὑπάρχειν. διαδεξάμενος

X. After twenty-one years Hadrian paid the debt of nature, and Antoninus, called Pius, received the sovereignty of Rome. In his first year Telesphorus passed away in the eleventh year of his ministry, and Hyginus received the lot of the bishopric of the Romans. Irenaeus relates that Telesphorus gained renown in his death by martyrdom, and states in the same place that in the time of Hyginus, the afore-mentioned bishop of Rome, Valentinus, the founder of a special heresy, and Cerdo, the founder of the Marcionite error, were both famous in Rome. He writes thus :

XI. " Valentinus came to Rome in the time of Hyginus, but he flourished under Pius, and remained until Anicetus, and Cerdo, who before the time of Marcion, in the days of Hyginus, the ninth bishop, had come to the church and confessed, went on in the same way, sometimes teaching heresy, some-times confessing again, and sometimes convicted by his evil teaching and separated from the assembly of the brethren." This he says in the third book against the heresies. Moreover, in the first book he makes the following statement about Cerdo : " A certain Cerdo had come originally from the circle of Simon and settled in Rome in the time of Hyginus, who held the ninth place in the apostolic succession from the apostles. He taught that the God preached by the Law and the Prophets was not the father of our Lord Jesus Christ, for the one was known, the other unknown, the one was righteous and the other

δὲ αὐτὸν Μαρκίων ὁ Ποντικὸς ηὔξησεν τὸ διδασκαλεῖον, ἀπηρυθριασμένως βλασφημῶν.''

Iren. 1, 1-9 Ὁ δ' αὐτὸς Εἰρηναῖος τὸν ἄπειρον βυθὸν τῆς **3**
Οὐαλεντίνου πολυπλανοῦς ὕλης εὐτονώτατα δια-
πλώσας, ἑρπετοῦ δίκην φωλεύοντος ἀπόκρυφον
οὖσαν αὐτοῦ καὶ λεληθυῖαν ἀπογυμνοῖ τὴν κακίαν·

Iren. 1, 13, 1 πρὸς τούτοις καὶ ἄλλον τινά, Μάρκος αὐτῷ ὄνομα, **4**
κατ' αὐτοὺς γενέσθαι λέγει μαγικῆς κυβείας
ἐμπειρότατον, γράφει δὲ καὶ τὰς ἀτελέστους
αὐτῶν τελετὰς μυσεράς τε μυσταγωγίας ἐκφαίνων

Iren. 1, 21, 3
=Epiphan.
34, 20 αὐτοῖς δὴ τούτοις τοῖς γράμμασιν· '' οἳ μὲν γὰρ **5**
αὐτῶν νυμφῶνα κατασκευάζουσιν καὶ μυστ-
αγωγίαν ἐπιτελοῦσιν μετ' ἐπιρρήσεών τινων τοῖς
τελουμένοις καὶ πνευματικὸν γάμον φάσκουσιν
εἶναι τὸ ὑπ' αὐτῶν γινόμενον κατὰ τὴν ὁμοιότητα
τῶν ἄνω συζυγιῶν, οἳ δὲ ἄγουσιν ἐφ' ὕδωρ καὶ
βαπτίζοντες οὕτως ἐπιλέγουσιν· ' εἰς ὄνομα ἀ-
γνώστου πατρὸς τῶν ὅλων, εἰς ἀλήθειαν μητέρα
τῶν πάντων, εἰς τὸν κατελθόντα εἰς τὸν Ἰησοῦν.'
ἄλλοι δὲ Ἑβραϊκὰ ὀνόματα ἐπιλέγουσιν πρὸς τὸ
μᾶλλον καταπλήξασθαι τοὺς τελουμένους.''

Ἀλλὰ γὰρ μετὰ τέταρτον τῆς ἐπισκοπῆς ἔτος **6**
Ὑγίνου τελευτήσαντος, Πίος ἐπὶ Ῥώμης ἐγχειρίζεται τὴν λειτουργίαν. κατά γε μὴν τὴν
Ἀλεξάνδρειαν Μάρκος ἀναδείκνυται ποιμὴν Εὐ-
μένους ἔτη τὰ πάντα δέκα πρὸς τρισὶν ἐκπλήσαντος,
τοῦ τε Μάρκου ἐπὶ δέκα ἔτη τῆς λειτουργίας
ἀναπαυσαμένου, Κελαδίων τῆς Ἀλεξανδρέων ἐκκλησίας τὴν λειτουργίαν παραλαμβάνει. καὶ κατὰ **7**
τὴν Ῥωμαίων δὲ πόλιν πεντεκαιδεκάτῳ τῆς
ἐπισκοπῆς ἐνιαυτῷ Πίου μεταλλάξαντος, Ἀνίκητος
τῶν ἐκεῖσε προΐσταται· καθ' ὃν Ἡγήσιππος
328

good. Marcion of Pontus succeeded him and increased the school, blaspheming unblushingly."

The same Irenaeus powerfully exposed the bottomless pit of the system of Valentinus with its many errors, and unbared his secret and latent wickedness while he was lurking like a reptile. Furthermore he says that there was in their time [1] another named Marcus, most experienced in the magic arts, and he writes of his initiations, which could not initiate, and of his foul mysteries,[2] expounding them in these words : " Some of them construct a bride-chamber, and celebrate a mystery with certain invocations on their initiate, and say that what they do is a spiritual marriage, according to the likeness of the unions above ; others bring them to water and baptize them with this invocation, ' To the name of the unknown Father of the universe, to Truth, the mother of all things, to him who descended into Jesus,' and others invoke Hebrew words in order more fully to amaze the initiate."

After the fourth year of his episcopate Hyginus died and Pius undertook the ministry of Rome. In Alexandria Marcus was appointed after Eumenes had completed thirteen years, and when Marcus rested from the ministry after ten years, Celadion received the ministry of the church of the Alexandrians. In the city of the Romans Pius passed away in the fifteenth year of his ministry and Anicetus presided over those there. In his time

---

[1] Apparently "in the time of Valentinus and Cerdo."
[2] The play on the words in the Greek is untranslatable.

ἱστορεῖ ἑαυτὸν ἐπιδημῆσαι τῇ ᾿Ρώμῃ παραμεῖναί
τε αὐτόθι μέχρι τῆς ἐπισκοπῆς ᾿Ελευθέρου. μά- 8
λιστα δ᾿ ἤκμαζεν ἐπὶ τῶνδε ᾿Ιουστῖνος, ἐν φιλοσόφου σχήματι πρεσβεύων τὸν θεῖον λόγον καὶ
τοῖς ὑπὲρ τῆς πίστεως ἐναγωνιζόμενος συγγράμ-
μασιν· ὃς δὴ καὶ γράψας κατὰ Μαρκίωνος σύγγραμμα, μνημονεύει ὡς καθ᾿ ὃν συνέταττε καιρὸν
γνωριζομένου τῷ βίῳ τἀνδρός, φησὶν δὲ οὕτως·

Justin, *Apol.*
1, 26

"Μαρκίωνα δέ τινα Ποντικόν, ὃς καὶ νῦν ἔτι 9
ἐστὶν διδάσκων τοὺς πειθομένους ἄλλον τινὰ
νομίζειν μείζονα τοῦ δημιουργοῦ θεόν· ὃς καὶ
κατὰ πᾶν γένος ἀνθρώπων διὰ τῆς τῶν δαιμόνων
συλλήψεως πολλοὺς πεποίηκε βλάσφημα λέγειν
καὶ ἀρνεῖσθαι τὸν ποιητὴν τοῦδε τοῦ παντὸς
πατέρα εἶναι τοῦ Χριστοῦ, ἄλλον δέ τινα ὡς ὄντα
μείζονα παρὰ τοῦτον ὁμολογεῖν [πεποιηκέναι].
καὶ πάντες οἱ ἀπὸ τούτων ὡρμημένοι, ὡς ἔφαμεν,
Χριστιανοὶ καλοῦνται, ὃν τρόπον καὶ οὐ κοινῶν
ὄντων δογμάτων τοῖς φιλοσόφοις τὸ ἐπικαλούμενον
ὄνομα τῆς φιλοσοφίας κοινόν ἐστιν." τούτοις 10
ἐπιφέρει λέγων "ἔστιν δὲ ἡμῖν καὶ σύνταγμα κατὰ
πασῶν τῶν γεγενημένων αἱρέσεων, ᾧ εἰ βούλεσθε
ἐντυχεῖν, δώσομεν."

᾿Ο δ᾿ αὐτὸς οὗτος ᾿Ιουστῖνος καὶ πρὸς ῞Ελληνας 11
ἱκανώτατα πονήσας, καὶ ἑτέρους λόγους ὑπὲρ τῆς
ἡμετέρας πίστεως ἀπολογίαν ἔχοντας βασιλεῖ
᾿Αντωνίνῳ τῷ δὴ ἐπικληθέντι Εὐσεβεῖ καὶ τῇ
᾿Ρωμαίων συγκλήτῳ βουλῇ προσφωνεῖ· καὶ γὰρ
ἐπὶ τῆς ᾿Ρώμης τὰς διατριβὰς ἐποιεῖτο. ἐμφαίνει
δ᾿ ἑαυτὸν ὅστις καὶ πόθεν ἦν, διὰ τῆς ἀπολογίας ἐν

Justin, *Apol.*
1, 1

τούτοις· XII. "Αὐτοκράτορι Τίτῳ Αἰλίῳ ᾿Αδριανῷ 1
᾿Αντωνίνῳ Εὐσεβεῖ Καίσαρι Σεβαστῷ καὶ Οὐη-

Hegesippus states that he stayed in Rome and remained there until the episcopate of Eleutherus. In their time Justin was at the height of his fame ; in the garb of philosopher he served as ambassador of the word of God and contended in his writings for the faith. He wrote a treatise against Marcion and mentions that at the time he was writing the heretic was alive and notorious. He speaks thus : " And there was a certain Marcion of Pontus who even now is still teaching those who believe him to think that there is another God greater than the creator. Throughout the whole race of men by the instigation of demons he has made many to speak blasphemously and to deny that the Maker of this universe is the Father of Christ, and to confess that there is another greater than He. All those who begin from them, as we said, are called Christians just as the name of philosophy is common to philosophers though their doctrines vary." He goes on to say, " And we have a treatise against all the heresies which have arisen which we will give to any who wish to study it."

The same Justin laboured powerfully against the Gentiles, and addressed other arguments, affording a defence for our faith, to the Emperor Antoninus, called Pius, and to the Senate of the Romans, for he was living in Rome. In his Apology he explains his position and origin as follows : XII. " To the Emperor Titus Aelius Hadrian Antoninus Pius, Caesar Augustus, and to Verissimus, his son the philosopher,

ρισσίμῳ υἱῷ φιλοσόφῳ καὶ Λουκίῳ φιλοσόφου
Καίσαρος φύσει υἱῷ καὶ Εὐσεβοῦς εἰσποιητῷ,
ἐραστῇ παιδείας, ἱερᾷ τε συγκλήτῳ καὶ παντὶ
δήμῳ Ῥωμαίων ὑπὲρ τῶν ἐκ παντὸς γένους
ἀνθρώπων ἀδίκως μισουμένων καὶ ἐπηρεαζομένων
Ἰουστῖνος Πρίσκου τοῦ Βακχείου τῶν ἀπὸ Φλαυίας
Νέας πόλεως τῆς Συρίας Παλαιστίνης, εἷς αὐτῶν,
τὴν προσφώνησιν καὶ ἔντευξιν πεποίημαι.''

Ἐντευχθεὶς δὲ καὶ ὑφ' ἑτέρων ὁ αὐτὸς βασιλεὺς
ἐπὶ τῆς Ἀσίας ἀδελφῶν παντοίαις ὕβρεσιν πρὸς
τῶν ἐπιχωρίων δήμων καταπονουμένων, τοιαύτης
ἠξίωσεν τὸ κοινὸν τῆς Ἀσίας διατάξεως· XIII. 1
'' Αὐτοκράτωρ Καῖσαρ Μάρκος Αὐρήλιος Ἀντωνῖνος Σεβαστός, Ἀρμένιος, ἀρχιερεὺς μέγιστος,
δημαρχικῆς ἐξουσίας τὸ πέμπτον καὶ τὸ δέκατον,
ὕπατος τὸ τρίτον, τῷ κοινῷ τῆς Ἀσίας χαίρειν.
ἐγὼ μὲν οἶδ' ὅτι καὶ τοῖς θεοῖς ἐπιμελές ἐστι μὴ 2
λανθάνειν τοὺς τοιούτους· πολὺ γὰρ μᾶλλον ἐκεῖνοι
κολάσαιεν ἂν τοὺς μὴ βουλομένους αὐτοῖς προσκυνεῖν
ἢ ὑμεῖς. οὓς εἰς ταραχὴν ἐμβάλλετε, βεβαιοῦντες 3
τὴν γνώμην αὐτῶν ἥνπερ ἔχουσιν, ὡς ἀθέων
κατηγοροῦντες· εἴη δ' ἂν κἀκείνοις αἱρετὸν τῷ
δοκεῖν κατηγορουμένοις τεθνάναι μᾶλλον ἢ ζῆν
ὑπὲρ τοῦ οἰκείου θεοῦ· ὅθεν καὶ νικῶσι, προϊέμενοι
τὰς ἑαυτῶν ψυχὰς ἤπερ πειθόμενοι οἷς ἀξιοῦτε

---

[1] The Council of Asia was one of the provincial councils to
the emperor. It consisted of deputies from the various states
and provinces. Among other things they were responsible
for the religious life of the province. The Council of Asia met
originally in the temple of the emperor and city of Rome at
Pergamon; later on it met in various other centres, Ephesus,
Sardis, Smyrna, Laodicaea, Philadelphia and Cyzicus.
Cf. Guiraud, *Assemblées provinciales dans l'Empire romain.*

and to Lucius, the lover of instruction, the son by nature of the philosopher-emperor, and by adoption of Pius, and to the holy Senate and to the whole people of Rome, on behalf of those men of every race who are unjustly hated and abused, I, Justin, the son of Priscus, the son of Baccheius, of Flavia Neapolis in Palestinian Syria, myself a Christian, offer an address and entreaty."

The same Emperor was entreated by other Asiatic Christians who had suffered all manner of injury from the local population and he thought fit to send the following decree to the Council of Asia.[1] XIII. " The Emperor Caesar Marcus Aurelius Antoninus Augustus Armenicus, Pontifex Maximus, Tribune for the fifteenth time, Consul for the third time, to the Council of Asia, greeting.[2] I know that the gods also take care that such men should not escape notice, for they would be far more likely to punish those who are unwilling to worship them than you are. But you drive them into tumult, for you confirm them in the opinion which they hold by accusing them as atheists, and they too when so accused might well prefer apparent[3] death rather than life for the sake of their own God. Wherefore they are also conquerors because they sacrifice their lives rather

---

[2] The date indicated is between March 7 and December 9, A.D. 161. This rescript is usually regarded as spurious, but Harnack, *Texte und Untersuchungen* xiii. 4, has tried to explain it as a genuine document with Christian interpolations. Schwartz thinks it is a translation of a Latin forgery. It is found in cod. Paris. 450 after the *Apology* of Justin, and is there attributed to Antoninus Pius when tribune for the 24th time, *i.e.* between Dec. 10, A.D. 160 and March 7, A.D. 161.

[3] This translation would better suit τὸ δοκεῖν, but τῷ δοκεῖν may be a phrase qualifying τεθνάναι. It is not improbable that it is a gloss.

πράττειν αὐτούς. περὶ δὲ τῶν σεισμῶν τῶν 4
γεγονότων καὶ γινομένων, οὐκ ἄτοπον ὑμᾶς
ὑπομνῆσαι ἀθυμοῦντας μὲν ὅταν περ ὦσιν, παρα-
βάλλοντας δὲ τὰ ἡμέτερα πρὸς τὰ ἐκείνων. οἳ 5
μὲν οὖν εὐπαρρησιαστότεροι γίνονται πρὸς τὸν
θεόν, ὑμεῖς δὲ παρὰ πάντα τὸν χρόνον καθ᾿ ὃν
ἀγνοεῖν δοκεῖτε, τῶν τε θεῶν τῶν ἄλλων ἀμελεῖτε
καὶ τῆς θρησκείας τῆς περὶ τὸν ἀθάνατον· ὃν δὴ
τοὺς Χριστιανοὺς θρησκεύοντας ἐλαύνετε καὶ
διώκετε ἕως θανάτου. ὑπὲρ δὲ τῶν τοιούτων 6
ἤδη καὶ πολλοὶ τῶν περὶ τὰς ἐπαρχίας ἡγεμόνων
καὶ τῷ θειοτάτῳ ἡμῶν ἔγραψαν πατρί, οἷς καὶ
ἀντέγραψεν μηδὲν ἐνοχλεῖν τοῖς τοιούτοις, εἰ μὴ
ἐμφαίνοιντό τι περὶ τὴν Ῥωμαίων ἡγεμονίαν
ἐγχειροῦντες. καὶ ἐμοὶ δὲ περὶ τῶν τοιούτων
πολλοὶ ἐσήμαναν· οἷς δὴ καὶ ἀντέγραψα κατα-
ακολουθῶν τῇ τοῦ πατρὸς γνώμῃ. εἰ δέ τις ἐπιμένοι 7
τινὰ τῶν τοιούτων εἰς πράγματα φέρων ὡς δὴ
τοιοῦτον, ἐκεῖνος ὁ καταφερόμενος ἀπολελύσθω
τοῦ ἐγκλήματος καὶ ἐὰν φαίνηται τοιοῦτος ὤν,
ὁ δὲ καταφέρων ἔνοχος ἔσται δίκης. προετέθη ἐν
Ἐφέσῳ ἐν τῷ κοινῷ τῆς Ἀσίας.''

Τούτοις οὕτω χωρήσασιν ἐπιμαρτυρῶν Μελίτων, 8
τῆς ἐν Σάρδεσιν ἐκκλησίας ἐπίσκοπος κατ᾿ αὐτὸ
γνωριζόμενος τοῦ χρόνου, δῆλός ἐστιν ἐκ τῶν
εἰρημένων αὐτῷ ἐν ᾗ πεποίηται πρὸς αὐτοκράτορα
Οὐῆρον ὑπὲρ τοῦ καθ᾿ ἡμᾶς δόγματος ἀπολογίᾳ.

XIV. Ἐπὶ δὲ τῶν δηλουμένων, Ἀνικήτου τῆς 1
Ῥωμαίων ἐκκλησίας ἡγουμένου, Πολύκαρπον ἔτι
περιόντα τῷ βίῳ γενέσθαι τε ἐπὶ Ῥώμης καὶ εἰς
ὁμιλίαν τῷ Ἀνικήτῳ ἐλθεῖν διά τι ζήτημα περὶ

than obey and do what you command. With regard to the earthquakes which have taken place and are still going on it is not out of place to remind you that when they happen you are depressed, and so set up a comparison between our position and theirs. They obtain increased confidence towards God, but you the whole of the time neglect the other gods and the worship of the immortal.[1] But when the Christians worship him you harry and persecute them to death. And many of the provincial governors wrote formerly on behalf of such men to our divine father, and he replied that they were not to be interfered with unless they appeared to be plotting against the Roman government. And to me also many reported about such men, and to them I too replied consistently with my father's opinion. But if anyone persist in taking action against any one of such persons, on the ground that he is so, let that one who is accused be released from the charge, even if it appear that he is such, but the accuser shall be liable to penalty. Published at Ephesus in the Council of Asia."

Further testimony to these events is given by Melito, the famous bishop of the church in Sardis at that time, as is clear from what he says in the Apology which he made to the Emperor Verus on behalf of our faith.

XIV. During the time of the emperors referred to, while Anicetus was ruling the church of Rome, Irenaeus relates that Polycarp was still alive and came to Rome and conversed with Anicetus about

---

[1] The text as it stands in the Greek is hopeless. Possibly καθ' ὃν ἀγνοεῖν δοκεῖτε have been displaced and refer to the "immortal" or the emendation of καθ' ὃν to καὶ θεὸν might be accepted.

τῆς κατὰ τὸ πάσχα ἡμέρας. Εἰρηναῖος ἱστορεῖ. καὶ ἄλλην δὲ ὁ αὐτὸς περὶ τοῦ Πολυκάρπου παρα- 2 δίδωσιν διήγησιν, ἣν ἀναγκαῖον τοῖς περὶ αὐτοῦ δηλουμένοις ἐπισυνάψαι, οὕτως ἔχουσαν·

ΑΠΟ ΤΟΥ ΤΡΙΤΟΥ ΤΩΝ ΠΡΟΣ ΤΑΣ ΑΙΡΕΣΕΙΣ ΕΙΡΗΝΑΙΟΥ

Iren. 3, 3, 4   '' Καὶ Πολύκαρπος δὲ οὐ μόνον ὑπὸ ἀποστόλων 3 μαθητευθεὶς καὶ συναναστραφεὶς πολλοῖς τοῖς τὸν κύριον ἑορακόσιν, ἀλλὰ καὶ ὑπὸ ἀποστόλων κατα- σταθεὶς εἰς τὴν Ἀσίαν ἐν τῇ ἐν Σμύρνῃ ἐκκλησίᾳ ἐπίσκοπος, ὃν καὶ ἡμεῖς ἑοράκαμεν ἐν τῇ πρώτῃ 4 ἡμῶν ἡλικίᾳ (ἐπὶ πολὺ γὰρ παρέμεινεν καὶ πάνυ γηραλέος ἐνδόξως καὶ ἐπιφανέστατα μαρτυρήσας ἐξῆλθεν τοῦ βίου), ταῦτα διδάξας ἀεὶ ἃ καὶ παρὰ τῶν ἀποστόλων ἔμαθεν, ἃ καὶ ἡ ἐκκλησία παρα- δίδωσιν, ἃ καὶ μόνα ἐστὶν ἀληθῆ. μαρτυροῦσι 5 τούτοις αἱ κατὰ τὴν Ἀσίαν ἐκκλησίαι πᾶσαι καὶ οἱ μέχρι νῦν διαδεδεγμένοι τὸν Πολύκαρπον, πολλῷ ἀξιοπιστότερον καὶ βεβαιότερον ἀληθείας μάρτυρα ὄντα Οὐαλεντίνου καὶ Μαρκίωνος καὶ τῶν λοιπῶν κακογνωμόνων· ὃς καὶ ἐπὶ Ἀνικήτου ἐπιδημήσας τῇ Ῥώμῃ, πολλοὺς ἀπὸ τῶν προ- ειρημένων αἱρετικῶν ἐπέστρεψεν εἰς τὴν ἐκκλησίαν τοῦ θεοῦ, μίαν καὶ μόνην ταύτην ἀλήθειαν κηρύξας ὑπὸ τῶν ἀποστόλων παρειληφέναι τὴν ὑπὸ τῆς ἐκκλησίας παραδεδομένην. καὶ εἰσὶν οἱ ἀκηκοότες 6 αὐτοῦ ὅτι Ἰωάννης ὁ τοῦ κυρίου μαθητὴς ἐν τῇ Ἐφέσῳ πορευθεὶς λούσασθαι καὶ ἰδὼν ἔσω Κή- ρινθον ἐξήλατο τοῦ βαλανείου μὴ λουσάμενος, ἀλλ' ἐπειπὼν ' φύγωμεν, μὴ καὶ τὸ βαλανεῖον συμπέσῃ, ἔνδον ὄντος Κηρίνθου τοῦ τῆς ἀληθείας ἐχθροῦ.'

336

some difficulty as to the day of the Passover. The same writer tells another story about Polycarp which it is necessary to add to what has been said about him. It runs as follows :

From the third book of Irenaeus against Heresies

" And Polycarp also was not only instructed by apostles and conversed with many who had seen the Lord, but was also appointed bishop by apostles in Asia in the church in Smyrna. We also saw him in our childhood, for he lived a long time and in extreme old age passed from life, a splendid and glorious martyr. He constantly taught those things which he had learnt from the apostles, which also are the tradition of the church, which alone are true. To these facts all the churches in Asia bear witness, and the present successors of Polycarp, and he is a far more trustworthy and reliable witness of the truth than Valentinus and Marcion and the others who hold wrong opinions. In the time of Anicetus he visited Rome and converted many of the above-mentioned heretics to the church of God, preaching that the one and only truth which he had received from the apostles was that which is the tradition of the church. And there are those who heard him tell that John the disciple of the Lord went in Ephesus to bathe and seeing Cerinthus within, sprang out of the baths without bathing calling out, ' Let us fly lest the baths fall in, since Cerinthus, the enemy of

337

καὶ αὐτὸς δὲ ὁ Πολύκαρπος Μαρκίωνί ποτε εἰς
ὄψιν αὐτῷ ἐλθόντι καὶ φήσαντι 'ἐπιγίνωσκε
ἡμᾶς' ἀπεκρίθη 'ἐπιγινώσκω· ἐπιγινώσκω τὸν
πρωτότοκον τοῦ σατανᾶ.' τοσαύτην οἱ ἀπόστολοι
καὶ οἱ μαθηταὶ αὐτῶν ἔσχον εὐλάβειαν πρὸς τὸ
μηδὲ μέχρι λόγου κοινωνεῖν τινι τῶν παραχαρασ-
Tit. 8, 10. 11 σόντων τὴν ἀλήθειαν, ὡς καὶ Παῦλος ἔφησεν
'αἱρετικὸν ἄνθρωπον μετὰ μίαν καὶ δευτέραν
νουθεσίαν παραιτοῦ, εἰδὼς ὅτι ἐξέστραπται ὁ
τοιοῦτος καὶ ἁμαρτάνει ὢν αὐτοκατάκριτος.' ἔστιν 8
δὲ καὶ ἐπιστολὴ Πολυκάρπου πρὸς Φιλιππησίους
γεγραμμένη ἱκανωτάτη, ἐξ ἧς καὶ τὸν χαρακτῆρα
τῆς πίστεως αὐτοῦ καὶ τὸ κήρυγμα τῆς ἀληθείας
οἱ βουλόμενοι καὶ φροντίζοντες τῆς ἑαυτῶν σωτηρίας δύνανται μαθεῖν.'' ταῦτα ὁ Εἰρηναῖος· ὁ 9
γέ τοι Πολύκαρπος ἐν τῇ δηλωθείσῃ πρὸς Φιλιππησίους αὐτοῦ γραφῇ, φερομένῃ εἰς δεῦρο, κέχρηταί
τισιν μαρτυρίαις ἀπὸ τῆς Πέτρου προτέρας ἐπιστολῆς.

Ἀντωνῖνον μὲν δὴ τὸν Εὐσεβῆ κληθέντα, εἰκοστὸν 1
καὶ δεύτερον ἔτος τῆς ἀρχῆς διανύσαντα, Μάρκος
Αὐρήλιος Οὐῆρος, ὁ καὶ Ἀντωνῖνος, υἱὸς αὐτοῦ,
σὺν καὶ Λουκίῳ ἀδελφῷ διαδέχεται. XV. ἐν τούτῳ 1
δὲ ὁ Πολύκαρπος μεγίστων τὴν Ἀσίαν ἀναθορυ-
βησάντων διωγμῶν μαρτυρίῳ τελειοῦται, ἀναγκαιότατον δ' αὐτοῦ τὸ τέλος ἐγγράφως ἔτι φερό-
μενον ἡγοῦμαι δεῖν μνήμῃ τῆσδε τῆς ἱστορίας
καταθέσθαι. ἔστιν δὲ ἡ γραφὴ ἐκ προσώπου ἧς 2
αὐτὸς ἐκκλησίας ἡγεῖτο, ταῖς κατὰ τόπον παροικίαις
338

the truth, is within.' And Polycarp himself when Marcion once met him and said, ' Recognize us,' answered, ' I do, I recognize the first-born of Satan.' Such care did the apostles and their disciples take not even to join in conversation with any of those who mutilate the truth, as Paul also said, ' A man that is heretical after a first and second exhortation, refuse, knowing such a one is perverted and sinneth, being self-condemned.' There is also a most powerful letter of Polycarp's written to the Philippians, from which those who wish and care for their own salvation can learn both the character of his faith and the preaching of the truth." So says Irenaeus. Moreover, Polycarp, in his above-mentioned letter to the Philippians, which is still extant, has made some quotations from the first Epistle of Peter.[1]

Antoninus, called Pius, held the sovereignty for twenty-two years [2] and was succeeded by Marcus Aurelius Verus, also called Antoninus, his son, together with his brother Lucius. XV. At this time [3] Polycarp was consecrated by martyrdom when great persecutions again disturbed Asia, and I think it most necessary to give in this history the account of his end, which is still extant in writing. The document purports to be from the church of which he was the leader, and gives to the neighbouring

---

[1] The references to 1 Peter in Polycarp's Epistle are: i. 3 = 1 Pet. i. 8; ii. 1 = 1 Pet. i. 13, 21; ii. 2 = 1 Pet. iii. 9; v. 3 = 1 Pet. ii. 11; vii. 2 = 1 Pet. iv. 7; viii. 1 = 1 Pet. ii. 24, 22; x. 2 = 1 Pet. ii. 12.

[2] Antoninus Pius died March 7, A.D. 161. Marcus Aurelius and Lucius were two adopted sons.

[3] This seems to be a mistake. It is almost certain that the death of Polycarp was in A.D. 156. See *Studia Biblica*, ii. pp. 105 ff.

EUSEBIUS

Mart. Polyc.
1

τὰ κατ᾽ αὐτὸν ἀποσημαίνουσα διὰ τούτων· " Ἡ **3**
ἐκκλησία τοῦ θεοῦ ἡ παροικοῦσα Σμύρναν τῇ
ἐκκλησίᾳ τοῦ θεοῦ τῇ παροικούσῃ ἐν Φιλομηλίῳ
καὶ πάσαις ταῖς κατὰ πάντα τόπον τῆς ἁγίας
καθολικῆς ἐκκλησίας παροικίαις ἔλεος εἰρήνη καὶ
ἀγάπη θεοῦ πατρὸς καὶ κυρίου ἡμῶν Ἰησοῦ
Χριστοῦ πληθυνθείη. ἐγράψαμεν ὑμῖν, ἀδελφοί,
τὰ κατὰ τοὺς μαρτυρήσαντας καὶ τὸν μακάριον
Πολύκαρπον, ὅστις ὥσπερ ἐπισφραγίσας διὰ τῆς
μαρτυρίας αὐτοῦ κατέπαυσε τὸν διωγμόν."

Mart. Polyc.
2-7

Τούτοις ἑξῆς πρὸ τῆς ἀμφὶ τοῦ Πολυκάρπου **4**
διηγήσεως τὰ κατὰ τοὺς λοιποὺς ἀνιστοροῦσι
μάρτυρας, οἵας ἐνστάσεις πρὸς τὰς ἀλγηδόνας
ἐνεδείξαντο, διαγράφοντες. καταπλῆξαι γάρ φασι
τοὺς ἐν κύκλῳ περιεστῶτας, θεωμένους τοτὲ μὲν
μάστιξι μέχρι καὶ τῶν ἐνδοτάτω φλεβῶν καὶ
ἀρτηριῶν καταξαινομένους, ὡς ἤδη καὶ τὰ ἐν μυχοῖς
ἀπόρρητα τοῦ σώματος σπλάγχνα τε αὐτῶν καὶ
μέλη κατοπτεύεσθαι, τοτὲ δὲ τοὺς ἀπὸ θαλάττης
κήρυκας καί τινας ὀξεῖς ὀβελίσκους ὑποστρων-
νυμένους, καὶ διὰ παντὸς εἴδους κολάσεων καὶ
βασάνων προϊόντας καὶ τέλος θηρσὶν εἰς βορὰν
παραδιδομένους. μάλιστα δὲ ἱστοροῦσιν διαπρέψαι **5**
τὸν γενναιότατον Γερμανικόν, ὑπορρωννύντα σὺν
θείᾳ χάριτι τὴν ἔμφυτον περὶ τὸν θάνατον τοῦ
σώματος δειλίαν. βουλομένου γέ τοι τοῦ ἀνθυπάτου πείθειν αὐτὸν προβαλλομένου τε τὴν ἡλικίαν
καὶ ἀντιβολοῦντος κομιδῇ νέον ὄντα καὶ ἀκμαῖον

---

[1] Literally " place of sojourn." The word probably
embodies the recognition that Christians are those whose
citizenship is above. It seems to have been used originally
340

dioceses[1] the following account of what happened to him. " The Church of God which sojourns in Smyrna, to the Church of God which sojourns in Philomelium,[2] and to all the sojournings of the Holy Catholic Church in every place. Mercy, peace, and love of God the Father, and our Lord Jesus Christ be multiplied. We write to you, brethren, the story of the martyrs and of the blessed Polycarp, who put an end to the persecution by his martyrdom as though adding the seal."

They then go on, before the narrative about Polycarp, to give the story of the other martyrs, describing the constancy which they showed against torture, for they say that those who were standing around were amazed when they saw that at one time they were torn by scourges down to deep-seated veins and arteries, so that the hidden contents of the recesses of their bodies, their entrails and organs, were exposed to sight. At another time they were stretched on seashells and on sharp points, were taken through all kinds of punishment and torture, and finally were given to be eaten by wild beasts. They say that the noble Germanicus was especially distinguished, being strengthened by the grace of God to overcome the natural cowardice of the body for death. Even when the proconsul wished to dissuade him, urging his youth and entreating him as he was still just in the flower of his youth

of the district dominated by some great church and corresponds roughly to the modern use of the word diocese, but its meaning was gradually restricted to smaller districts and it is etymologically still current in the word parish.

[2] In Phrygia, not far from Pisidian Antioch. This letter is usually called the *Martyrdom of Polycarp*. It is published in L.C.L., *The Apostolic Fathers*, vol. ii. pp. 309 ff.

οἶκτον ἑαυτοῦ λαβεῖν, μὴ μελλῆσαι, προθύμως δ'
ἐπισπάσασθαι εἰς ἑαυτὸν τὸ θηρίον, μόνον οὐχὶ
βιασάμενον καὶ παροξύναντα, ὡς ἂν τάχιον τοῦ
ἀδίκου καὶ ἀνόμου βίου αὐτῶν ἀπαλλαγείη. τούτου 6
δ' ἐπὶ τῷ διαπρεπεῖ θανάτῳ τὸ πᾶν πλῆθος ἀπο-
θαυμάσαν τῆς ἀνδρείας τὸν θεοφιλῆ μάρτυρα καὶ
τὴν καθόλου τοῦ γένους τῶν Χριστιανῶν ἀρετήν,
ἀθρόως ἐπιβοᾶν ἄρξασθαι '' αἶρε τοὺς ἀθέους·
ζητείσθω Πολύκαρπος.'' καὶ δὴ πλείστης ἐπὶ 7
ταῖς βοαῖς γενομένης ταραχῆς, Φρύγα τινὰ τὸ
γένος, Κόϊντον τοὔνομα, νεωστὶ ἐκ τῆς Φρυγίας
ἐπιστάντα, ἰδόντα τοὺς θῆρας καὶ τὰς ἐπὶ τούτοις
ἀπειλάς, καταπτῆξαι τὴν ψυχὴν μαλακισθέντα
καὶ τέλος τῆς σωτηρίας ἐνδοῦναι. ἐδήλου δὲ 8
τοῦτον ὁ τῆς προειρημένης γραφῆς λόγος προπετέστερον ἀλλ' οὐ κατ' εὐλάβειαν ἐπιπηδῆσαι
τῷ δικαστηρίῳ σὺν ἑτέροις, ἁλόντα δ' οὖν ὅμως
καταφανὲς ὑπόδειγμα τοῖς πᾶσιν παρασχεῖν, ὅτι
μὴ δέοι τοῖς τοιούτοις ῥιψοκινδύνως καὶ ἀνευλαβῶς
ἐπιτολμᾶν. ἀλλὰ ταύτῃ μὲν εἶχεν πέρας τὰ κατὰ
τούτους· τόν γε μὴν θαυμασιώτατον Πολύκαρπον 9
τὰ μὲν πρῶτα τούτων ἀκούσαντα ἀτάραχον μεῖναι,
εὐσταθὲς τὸ ἦθος καὶ ἀκίνητον φυλάξαντα, βού-
λεσθαί τε αὐτοῦ κατὰ πόλιν περιμένειν· πεισθέντα
γε μὴν ἀντιβολοῦσι τοῖς ἀμφ' αὐτὸν καὶ ὡς ἂν
ὑπεξέλθοι παρακαλοῦσι, προελθεῖν εἰς οὐ πόρρω
διεστῶτα τῆς πόλεως ἀγρὸν διατρίβειν τε σὺν
ὀλίγοις ἐνταῦθα, νύκτωρ καὶ μεθ' ἡμέραν οὔτι
ἕτερον πράττοντα ἢ ταῖς πρὸς τὸν κύριον δια-
καρτεροῦντα εὐχαῖς· δι' ὧν δεῖσθαι καὶ ἱκετεύειν
εἰρήνην ἐξαιτούμενον ταῖς ἀνὰ πᾶσαν τὴν οἰκουμένην ἐκκλησίαις, τοῦτο γὰρ καὶ εἶναι ἐκ τοῦ

to have pity on himself, he did not hesitate, but took pains to drag the beast to himself, almost forcing him and provoking him in order that he might be the sooner free from an unjust and wicked life. At his glorious death the whole crowd was amazed at the God-loving martyr for his bravery, and at the courage of the whole race of Christians, and began to howl out together, " Kill the atheists ! Let Polycarp be sent for." When a great uproar arose at this cry, a certain native of Phrygia named Quintus, lately arrived from Phrygia, seeing the beasts and the other threats, was overcome in his mind and weakened and finally abandoned his salvation. The narrative of the above-mentioned document shows that this man had rushed to the tribunal with the others in a headstrong but irreligious spirit ; but that nevertheless when he was convicted he gave manifest proofs to all that such men ought not to make foolhardy ventures which do not spring from religion. Such was the fate of these men. Yet the wonderful Polycarp, when he first heard this, remained undisturbed, keeping his mind steadfast and unmoved, and wished to stay there in the city. But the urgency of his friends and their entreaty that he should go out persuaded him, and he departed to a farm not far from the city where he stayed with a few others, and night and day did nothing but persevere in prayers to the Lord. In them he entreated and supplicated for peace, begging that it be given the churches throughout the world, for this was his invariable custom.

παντὸς αὐτῷ σύνηθες. καὶ δὴ εὐχόμενον, ἐν 10
ὀπτασίᾳ τριῶν πρότερον ἡμερῶν τῆς συλλήψεως
νύκτωρ ἰδεῖν τὸ ὑπὸ κεφαλῆς αὐτῷ στρῶμα ἀθρόως
οὕτως ὑπὸ πυρὸς φλεχθὲν δεδαπανῆσθαι, ἔξυπνον
δ᾽ ἐπὶ τούτῳ γενόμενον, εὐθὺς ὑφερμηνεῦσαι τοῖς
παροῦσι τὸ φανέν, μόνον οὐχὶ τὸ μέλλον προ-
θεσπίσαντα σαφῶς τε ἀνειπόντα τοῖς ἀμφ᾽ αὐτὸν
ὅτι δέοι αὐτὸν διὰ Χριστὸν πυρὶ τὴν ζωὴν μεταλ-
λάξαι. ἐπικειμένων δὴ οὖν σὺν πάσῃ σπουδῇ τῶν 11
ἀναζητούντων αὐτόν, αὖθις ὑπὸ τῆς τῶν ἀδελφῶν
διαθέσεως καὶ στοργῆς ἐκβεβιασμένον μεταβῆναί
φασιν ἐφ᾽ ἕτερον ἀγρόν· ἔνθα μετ᾽ οὐ πλεῖστον
τοὺς συνελαύνοντας ἐπελθεῖν, δύο δὲ τῶν αὐτόθι
συλλαβεῖν παίδων· ὧν θάτερον αἰκισαμένους ἐπιστῆναι δι᾽ αὐτοῦ τῇ τοῦ Πολυκάρπου καταγωγῇ, 12
ὀψὲ δὲ τῆς ὥρας ἐπελθόντας, αὐτὸν μὲν εὑρεῖν ἐν
ὑπερῴῳ κατακείμενον, ὅθεν δυνατὸν ὂν αὐτῷ ἐφ᾽
ἑτέραν μεταστῆναι οἰκίαν, μὴ βεβουλῆσθαι, εἰπόντα
Acts 21, 14 "τὸ θέλημα τοῦ θεοῦ γινέσθω." καὶ δὴ μαθὼν 13
παρόντας, ὡς ὁ λόγος φησί, καταβὰς αὐτοῖς
διελέξατο εὖ μάλα φαιδρῷ καὶ πραοτάτῳ προσώπῳ,
ὡς καὶ θαῦμα δοκεῖν ὁρᾶν τοὺς πάλαι τοῦ ἀνδρὸς
ἀγνῶτας, ἐναποβλέποντας τῷ τῆς ἡλικίας αὐτοῦ
παλαιῷ καὶ τῷ σεμνῷ καὶ εὐσταθεῖ τοῦ τρόπου,
καὶ εἰ τοσαύτη γένοιτο σπουδὴ ὑπὲρ τοῦ τοιούτου
συλληφθῆναι πρεσβύτην. ὃ δ᾽ οὐ μελλήσας εὐθέως 14
τράπεζαν αὐτοῖς παρατεθῆναι προστάττει, εἶτα
τροφῆς ἀφθόνου μεταλαβεῖν ἀξιοῖ, μίαν τε ὥραν,
ὡς ἂν προσεύξοιτο ἀδεῶς, παρ᾽ αὐτῶν αἰτεῖται·
ἐπιτρεψάντων δὲ ἀναστὰς ηὔχετο, ἔμπλεως τῆς
χάριτος ὢν τοῦ κυρίου, ὡς ἐκπλήττεσθαι τοὺς
παρόντας εὐχομένου αὐτοῦ ἀκροωμένους πολλούς
344

While he was praying, in a vision at night three days before his capture, he saw the pillow under his head suddenly flaming with fire and so destroyed, and when he woke up at this he at once interpreted what he had seen to those present, all but foretelling the future and clearly announcing to his friends that in fire he must give up his life for Christ's sake. While those who were seeking for him were pressing on with great zeal, he was again constrained by the affection and love of the brethren to move to another farm. Shortly after the pursuers came up and arrested two of the slaves there. They tortured one of them and were brought by him to the abode of Polycarp. They entered in the evening and found him lying in an upper chamber. It was possible for him to have moved thence to another house, but he was not willing and said, " The Lord's will be done." When he heard that they had come, so the story says, he went down and conversed with them with a bright and gentle countenance, so that those who did not know him before thought that they saw a marvel when they regarded his old age and his venerable and steadfast behaviour, and they wondered that there should be such activity for the arrest of an old man of such character. He did not delay but immediately ordered a table to be set for them and invited them to partake of plentiful food, asking from them a single hour that he might pray undisturbed. They gave him leave, and he arose and prayed, filled with the grace of the Lord, so that those who were present were astonished when they heard his prayer, and many of them already began

τε αὐτῶν μετανοεῖν ἤδη ἐπὶ τῷ τοιοῦτον ἀναιρεῖσθαι μέλλειν σεμνὸν καὶ θεοπρεπῆ πρεσβύτην.

Ἐπὶ τούτοις ἡ περὶ αὐτοῦ γραφὴ κατὰ λέξιν 15 ὧδέ πως τὰ ἑξῆς τῆς ἱστορίας ἔχει· '' ἐπεὶ δέ ποτε

Mart. Polyc.
8-19

κατέπαυσε τὴν προσευχὴν μνημονεύσας ἁπάντων καὶ τῶν πώποτε συμβεβληκότων αὐτῷ, μικρῶν τε καὶ μεγάλων, ἐνδόξων τε καὶ ἀδόξων, καὶ πάσης τῆς κατὰ τὴν οἰκουμένην καθολικῆς ἐκκλησίας, τῆς ὥρας ἐλθούσης τοῦ ἐξιέναι, ὄνῳ καθίσαντες αὐτὸν ἤγαγον εἰς τὴν πόλιν, ὄντος σαββάτου μεγάλου. καὶ ὑπήντα αὐτῷ ὁ εἰρήναρχος Ἡρῴδης καὶ ὁ πατὴρ αὐτοῦ Νικήτης· οἳ καὶ μεταθέντες αὐτὸν εἰς τὸ ὄχημα, ἔπειθον παρακαθεζόμενοι καὶ λέγοντες ʿ τί γὰρ κακόν ἐστιν εἰπεῖν, κύριος Καῖσαρ, καὶ θῦσαι καὶ διασῴζεσθαι;ʾ ὃ δὲ τὰ μὲν πρῶτα οὐκ ἀπεκρίνατο, ἐπιμενόντων 16 δὲ αὐτῶν, ἔφη ʿ οὐ μέλλω πράττειν ὃ συμβουλεύετέ μοι.ʾ οἱ δὲ ἀποτυχόντες τοῦ πεῖσαι αὐτόν, δεινὰ ῥήματα ἔλεγον καὶ μετὰ σπουδῆς καθῄρουν, ὡς κατιόντα ἀπὸ τοῦ ὀχήματος ἀποσῦραι τὸ ἀντικνήμιον· ἀλλὰ γὰρ μὴ ἐπιστραφείς, οἷα μηδὲν πεπονθώς, προθύμως μετὰ σπουδῆς ἐπορεύετο, ἀγόμενος εἰς τὸ στάδιον. θορύβου δὲ τηλικούτου 17 ὄντος ἐν τῷ σταδίῳ, ὡς μηδὲ πολλοῖς ἀκουσθῆναι,

Josh. 1, 9
Acts 9, 7

τῷ Πολυκάρπῳ εἰσιόντι εἰς τὸ στάδιον φωνὴ ἐξ οὐρανοῦ γέγονεν ʿ ἴσχυε, Πολύκαρπε, καὶ ἀνδρίζου.ʾ καὶ τὸν μὲν εἰπόντα οὐδεὶς εἶδεν, τὴν δὲ φωνὴν τῶν ἡμετέρων πολλοὶ ἤκουσαν. προσαχθέντος οὖν 18 αὐτοῦ, θόρυβος ἦν μέγας ἀκουσάντων ὅτι Πολύκαρπος συνείληπται. λοιπὸν οὖν προσελθόντα ἀν-

---

[1] The preceding paragraphs are all based on the *Martyrdom of Polycarp*, but Eusebius has abbreviated it.

to repent that so venerable and godlike an old man was going to be killed.

After this the document concerning him continues as follows[1]: " Now when he had at last finished his prayer, after remembering all who had ever even come his way, both small and great, high and low, and the whole Catholic Church throughout the world, the hour came for departure, and they set him on an ass, and led him into the city, on a ' great Sabbath day.'[2]   And the police captain Herod and his father Niketas met him and removed him into the wagon, and sat by his side trying to persuade him and saying : ' But what harm is it to say, " Lord Caesar," and to offer sacrifice, and to be saved ? '   But he at first did not answer them, but when they continued he said : ' I am not going to do what you counsel me.' And they gave up the attempt to persuade him, and began to speak fiercely, and turned him out in such a hurry that in getting down from the wagon he scraped his shin ; and without turning round, as though he had suffered nothing, he walked on promptly and quickly, and was taken to the arena, while the uproar in the arena was so great that no one could even be heard.   Now when Polycarp entered into the arena there came a voice from heaven : ' Be strong, Polycarp, and play the man.' And no one saw the speaker, but many of our friends who were there heard the voice.   And when he was brought forward, there was a great uproar of those who heard that Polycarp had been arrested.   Next

[2] The traditional date of Polycarp's martyrdom was Feb. 23.   If so, " a great Sabbath " may mean the feast of Purim, or it may mean the Sabbath after the Passover.   See C. H. Turner in *Stud. Bib.* ii. pp. 105, and E. Schwartz in *Abhandl. der k. Ges. der Wiss. zu Gött.* viii. (1905) 6, pp. 125 ff.

ηρώτα ὁ ἀνθύπατος εἰ αὐτὸς εἴη Πολύκαρπος,
καὶ ὁμολογήσαντος, ἔπειθεν ἀρνεῖσθαι, λέγων
'αἰδέσθητί σου τὴν ἡλικίαν' καὶ ἕτερα τούτοις
ἀκόλουθα, ἃ σύνηθες αὐτοῖς ἐστι λέγειν, 'ὄμοσον
τὴν Καίσαρος τύχην, μετανόησον, εἰπόν, αἶρε τοὺς
ἀθέους.' ὁ δὲ Πολύκαρπος ἐμβριθεῖ τῷ προσώπῳ 19
εἰς πάντα τὸν ὄχλον τὸν ἐν τῷ σταδίῳ ἐμβλέψας,
ἐπισείσας αὐτοῖς τὴν χεῖρα στενάξας τε καὶ
ἀναβλέψας εἰς τὸν οὐρανόν, εἶπεν 'αἶρε τοὺς
ἀθέους.' ἐγκειμένου δὲ τοῦ ἡγουμένου καὶ λέ- 20
γοντος 'ὄμοσον, καὶ ἀπολύσω σε, λοιδόρησον τὸν
Χριστόν,' ἔφη ὁ Πολύκαρπος 'ὀγδοήκοντα καὶ
ἓξ ἔτη δουλεύω αὐτῷ, καὶ οὐδέν με ἠδίκησεν·
καὶ πῶς δύναμαι βλασφημῆσαι τὸν βασιλέα μου,
τὸν σώσαντά με;' ἐπιμένοντος δὲ πάλιν αὐτοῦ 21
καὶ λέγοντος 'ὄμοσον τὴν Καίσαρος τύχην,' ὁ
Πολύκαρπος 'εἰ κενοδοξεῖς,' φησίν, 'ἵνα ὁμόσω
τὴν Καίσαρος τύχην, ὡς λέγεις προσποιούμενος
ἀγνοεῖν ὅστις εἰμί, μετὰ παρρησίας ἄκουε· Χριστιανός εἰμι. εἰ δὲ θέλεις τὸν τοῦ Χριστιανισμοῦ
μαθεῖν λόγον, δὸς ἡμέραν καὶ ἄκουσον.' ἔφη ὁ 22
ἀνθύπατος 'πεῖσον τὸν δῆμον.' Πολύκαρπος ἔφη,
Rom. 13, 1 'σὲ μὲν καὶ λόγου ἠξίωκα, δεδιδάγμεθα γὰρ
ἀρχαῖς καὶ ἐξουσίαις ὑπὸ θεοῦ τεταγμέναις τιμὴν
κατὰ τὸ προσῆκον τὴν μὴ βλάπτουσαν ἡμᾶς
ἀπονέμειν· ἐκείνους δὲ οὐκ ἀξίους ἡγοῦμαι τοῦ
ἀπολογεῖσθαι αὐτοῖς.' ὁ δ' ἀνθύπατος εἶπεν 'θηρία 23
ἔχω· τούτοις σε παραβαλῶ, ἐὰν μὴ μετανοήσῃς.'
ὁ δὲ εἶπεν 'κάλει· ἀμετάθετος γὰρ ἡμῖν ἡ ἀπὸ
τῶν κρειττόνων ἐπὶ τὰ χείρω μετάνοια, καλὸν δὲ
μετατίθεσθαι ἀπὸ τῶν χαλεπῶν ἐπὶ τὰ δίκαια.'
ὁ δὲ πάλιν πρὸς αὐτόν 'πυρί σε ποιήσω δαμασθῆναι, 24
348

when he approached the proconsul asked him if he were Polycarp, and when he admitted it he tried to persuade him to deny, saying : ' Respect your age,' and so forth, as they are accustomed to say : ' Swear by the genius of Caesar, repent, say : " Away with the Atheists " ' ; but Polycarp, with a stern countenance looked on all the crowd in the arena, and waving his hand at them, he groaned and looked up to heaven and said : ' Away with the Atheists.' But when the Governor pressed him and said : ' Take the oath and I will let you go, revile Christ,' Polycarp said : ' For eighty and six years have I been his servant, and he has done me no wrong, and how can I blaspheme my King who saved me ? ' But when he persisted again, and said : ' Swear by the genius[1] of Caesar,' he said : ' If you vainly suppose that I will swear by the genius of Caesar, as you say, and pretend that you are ignorant who I am, listen plainly : I am a Christian. And if you wish to learn the doctrine of Christianity fix a day and listen.' The proconsul said : ' Persuade the people.' And Polycarp said : ' You I should have held worthy of discussion, for we have been taught to render honour, as is meet, if it hurt us not, to princes and authorities appointed by God ; but as for those, I do not count them worthy that a defence should be made to them.' And the proconsul said : ' I have wild beasts, I will deliver you to them, unless you change your mind.' And he said : ' Call for them, for change of mind from better to worse is a change we may not make ; but it is good to change from evil to righteousness.' And he said again to him : ' I

[1] Literally " fortune " ; but the Greeks thus translated the Latin oath, " per genium Caesaris," or " per genios Caesarum," which was introduced at the beginning of the Empire.

ἐὰν τῶν θηρίων καταφρονῇς, ἐὰν μὴ μετανοήσῃς.'
Πολύκαρπος εἶπεν ' πῦρ ἀπειλεῖς πρὸς ὥραν
καιόμενον καὶ μετ' ὀλίγον σβεννύμενον· ἀγνοεῖς
γὰρ τὸ τῆς μελλούσης κρίσεως καὶ αἰωνίου κολάσεως τοῖς ἀσεβέσι τηρούμενον πῦρ. ἀλλὰ τί
βραδύνεις; φέρε ὃ βούλει.' ταῦτα δὲ καὶ ἕτερα 25
πλείονα λέγων, θάρσους καὶ χαρᾶς ἐνεπίμπλατο
καὶ τὸ πρόσωπον αὐτοῦ χάριτος ἐπληροῦτο, ὥστε
μὴ μόνον μὴ συμπεσεῖν ταραχθέντα ὑπὸ τῶν
λεγομένων πρὸς αὐτόν, ἀλλὰ τοὐναντίον τὸν
ἀνθύπατον ἐκστῆναι πέμψαι τε τὸν κήρυκα καὶ
ἐν μέσῳ τῷ σταδίῳ κηρῦξαι 'τρὶς Πολύκαρπος
ὡμολόγησεν ἑαυτὸν Χριστιανὸν εἶναι.' τούτου 26
λεχθέντος ὑπὸ τοῦ κήρυκος, πᾶν τὸ πλῆθος ἐθνῶν
τε καὶ Ἰουδαίων τῶν τὴν Σμύρναν κατοικούντων
ἀκατασχέτῳ θυμῷ καὶ μεγάλῃ φωνῇ ἐβόα 'οὗτός
ἐστιν ὁ τῆς Ἀσίας διδάσκαλος, ὁ πατὴρ τῶν
Χριστιανῶν, ὁ τῶν ἡμετέρων θεῶν καθαιρέτης, ὁ
πολλοὺς διδάσκων μὴ θύειν μηδὲ προσκυνεῖν.'
ταῦτα λέγοντες, ἐπεβόων καὶ ἠρώτων τὸν ἀσιάρχην 27
Φίλιππον ἵνα ἐπαφῇ τῷ Πολυκάρπῳ λέοντα· ὁ δὲ
ἔφη μὴ εἶναι ἐξὸν αὐτῷ ἐπειδὴ πεπληρώκει τὰ
κυνηγέσια. τότε ἔδοξεν αὐτοῖς ὁμοθυμαδὸν ἐπι-
βοῆσαι ὥστε ζῶντα τὸν Πολύκαρπον κατακαῦσαι.
ἔδει γὰρ τὸ τῆς φανερωθείσης αὐτῷ ἐπὶ τοῦ 28
προσκεφαλαίου ὀπτασίας πληρωθῆναι, ὅτε ἰδὼν
αὐτὸ καιόμενον προσευχόμενος, εἶπεν ἐπιστραφεὶς
τοῖς μετ' αὐτοῦ πιστοῖς προφητικῶς 'δεῖ με
ζῶντα καῆναι.' ταῦτα οὖν μετὰ τοσούτου τάχους 29
ἐγένετο θᾶττον ἢ ἐλέγετο, τῶν ὄχλων παραχρῆμα
συναγόντων ἐκ τῶν ἐργαστηρίων καὶ ἐκ τῶν
βαλανείων ξύλα καὶ φρύγανα, μάλιστα Ἰουδαίων

will cause you to be consumed by fire, if you despise
the beasts, unless you repent.' But Polycarp said :
' You threaten with the fire that burns for a time,
and is quickly quenched, for you do not know the
fire which awaits the wicked in the judgement to
come and in everlasting punishment. But why are
you waiting ? Come, do what you will.' And with
these and many other words he was filled with
courage and joy, and his face was full of grace, so
that it not only did not fall with trouble at the
things said to him, but that the proconsul, on the
other hand, was astounded and sent his herald into
the midst of the arena to announce three times :
' Polycarp has confessed that he is a Christian.'
When this had been said by the herald, all the
multitude of heathen and Jews living in Smyrna
cried out with uncontrollable wrath and a loud
shout : ' This is the teacher of Asia, the father of
the Christians, the destroyer of our Gods, who
teaches many neither to offer sacrifice nor to worship.'
And when they said this, they cried out and asked
Philip the Asiarch to let loose a lion on Polycarp.
But he said he could not legally do this, since he
had closed the sports. Then they found it good to
cry out with one mind that he should burn Polycarp
alive, for the vision which had appeared to him on
his pillow must be fulfilled, when he saw it burning,
while he was praying and he turned and said prophetically to those of the faithful who were with
him, ' I must be burnt alive.' These things then
happened with so great speed, quicker than it takes
to tell, and the crowd came together immediately,
and prepared wood and faggots from the workshops
and baths and the Jews were extremely zealous, as

προθύμως, ὡς ἔθος αὐτοῖς, εἰς ταῦτα ὑπουργούντων. ἀλλ' ὅτε ἡ πυρὰ ἡτοιμάσθη, ἀποθέμενος ἑαυτῷ 30 πάντα τὰ ἱμάτια καὶ λύσας τὴν ζώνην, ἐπειρᾶτο καὶ ὑπολύειν ἑαυτόν, μὴ πρότερον τοῦτο ποιῶν διὰ τὸ ἀεὶ ἕκαστον τῶν πιστῶν σπουδάζειν ὅστις τάχιον τοῦ χρωτὸς αὐτοῦ ἐφάψηται· ἐν παντὶ γὰρ ἀγαθῆς ἕνεκεν πολιτείας καὶ πρὸ τῆς πολιᾶς ἐκεκόσμητο. εὐθέως οὖν αὐτῷ περιετίθετο τὰ 31 πρὸς τὴν πυρὰν ἡρμοσμένα ὄργανα· μελλόντων δὲ αὐτῶν καὶ προσηλοῦν αὐτόν, εἶπεν 'ἄφετέ με οὕτως· ὁ γὰρ διδοὺς ὑπομεῖναι τὸ πῦρ δώσει καὶ χωρὶς τῆς ὑμετέρας ἐκ τῶν ἥλων ἀσφαλείας ἀσκύλτως ἐπιμεῖναι τῇ πυρᾷ.' οἱ δὲ οὐ καθήλωσαν, προσέδησαν δὲ αὐτόν. ὁ δ' ὀπίσω τὰς χεῖρας 32 ποιήσας καὶ προσδεθεὶς ὥσπερ κριὸς ἐπίσημος, Wisd. 3, 6   ἀναφερόμενος ἐκ μεγάλου ποιμνίου ὁλοκαύτωμα δεκτὸν θεῷ παντοκράτορι, εἶπεν 'ὁ τοῦ ἀγαπητοῦ 33 καὶ εὐλογητοῦ παιδός σου Ἰησοῦ Χριστοῦ πατήρ, δι' οὗ τὴν περὶ σὲ ἐπίγνωσιν εἰλήφαμεν, ὁ θεὸς ἀγγέλων καὶ δυνάμεων καὶ πάσης κτίσεως παντός τε τοῦ γένους τῶν δικαίων οἳ ζῶσιν ἐνώπιόν σου, εὐλογῶ σε ὅτι ἠξίωσάς με τῆς ἡμέρας καὶ ὥρας ταύτης, τοῦ λαβεῖν μέρος ἐν ἀριθμῷ τῶν μαρτύρων ἐν τῷ ποτηρίῳ τοῦ Χριστοῦ σου εἰς ἀνάστασιν ζωῆς αἰωνίου ψυχῆς τε καὶ σώματος ἐν ἀφθαρσίᾳ πνεύματος ἁγίου· ἐν οἷς προσδεχθείην ἐνώπιόν σου 34 σήμερον ἐν θυσίᾳ πίονι καὶ προσδεκτῇ, καθὼς προητοίμασας, προφανερώσας καὶ πληρώσας ὁ ἀψευδὴς καὶ ἀληθινὸς θεός. διὰ τοῦτο καὶ περὶ 35 πάντων σὲ αἰνῶ, σὲ εὐλογῶ, σὲ δοξάζω διὰ τοῦ αἰωνίου ἀρχιερέως Ἰησοῦ Χριστοῦ τοῦ ἀγαπητοῦ

is their custom, in assisting at this. Now when the fire was ready he put off all his clothes, and loosened his girdle and tried also to take off his shoes, a thing he was not used to doing, because each of the faithful was always zealous, which of them might the more quickly touch his flesh. For he had been treated with all respect because of his noble life, even before his old age. Immediately, therefore, he was fastened to the instruments which had been prepared for the fire, but when they were going to nail him as well he said : ' Leave me thus, for He who gives me power to endure the fire, will grant me to remain in the flames unmoved even without the security you will give by the nails.' So they did not nail him, but bound him, and he put his hands behind him and was bound, as a noble ram that is offered out of a great flock as a whole burnt offering acceptable to Almighty God ; and he said : ' O Father of thy beloved and blessed Child, Jesus Christ, through whom we have received full knowledge of thee, the God of angels and powers, and of all creation, and of the whole family of the righteous, who live before thee ! I bless thee, that Thou hast granted me this day and hour, that I may share, among the number of the martyrs, in the cup of thy Christ, for the Resurrection to everlasting life, both of soul and body in the immortality of the Holy Spirit. And may I, to-day, be received among them before Thee, as a rich and acceptable sacrifice, as Thou, the God who lies not and is truth, hast prepared beforehand, and shown forth, and fulfilled. For this reason I also praise Thee for all things, I bless Thee, I glorify Thee through the everlasting and heavenly high priest, Jesus Christ, thy beloved Child, through

σου παιδός, δι' οὗ σοι σὺν αὐτῷ ἐν πνεύματι ἁγίῳ
δόξα καὶ νῦν καὶ εἰς τοὺς μέλλοντας αἰῶνας, ἀμήν.'
ἀναπέμψαντος δὲ αὐτοῦ τὸ ἀμὴν καὶ πληρώσαντος 3
τὴν προσευχήν, οἱ τοῦ πυρὸς ἄνθρωποι ἐξῆψαν τὸ
πῦρ, μεγάλης δὲ ἐκλαμψάσης φλογὸς θαῦμα εἴδομεν
οἷς ἰδεῖν ἐδόθη, οἳ καὶ ἐτηρήθησαν εἰς τὸ ἀν-
αγγεῖλαι τοῖς λοιποῖς τὰ γενόμενα. τὸ γὰρ πῦρ 3
καμάρας εἶδος ποιῆσαν ὥσπερ ὀθόνης πλοίου ὑπὸ
πνεύματος πληρουμένης, κύκλῳ περιετείχισε τὸ
σῶμα τοῦ μάρτυρος, καὶ ἦν μέσον οὐχ ὡς σὰρξ
Wisd. 3, 6 καιομένη, ἀλλ' ὡς χρυσὸς καὶ ἄργυρος ἐν καμίνῳ
πυρούμενος· καὶ γὰρ εὐωδίας τοσαύτης ἀντελαβό-
μεθα ὡς λιβανωτοῦ πνέοντος ἢ ἄλλου τινὸς τῶν
τιμίων ἀρωμάτων. πέρας γοῦν ἰδόντες οἱ ἄνομοι 3
μὴ δυνάμενον τὸ σῶμα ὑπὸ τοῦ πυρὸς δαπανηθῆναι,
ἐκέλευσαν προσελθόντα αὐτῷ κομφέκτορα παρα-
βῦσαι ξίφος, καὶ τοῦτο ποιήσαντος, ἐξῆλθεν πλῆθος 3
αἵματος, ὥστε κατασβέσαι τὸ πῦρ καὶ θαυμάσαι
πάντα τὸν ὄχλον εἰ τοσαύτη τις διαφορὰ μεταξὺ
τῶν τε ἀπίστων καὶ τῶν ἐκλεκτῶν· ὧν εἷς καὶ
οὗτος γέγονεν ὁ θαυμασιώτατος ἐν τοῖς καθ' ἡμᾶς
χρόνοις διδάσκαλος ἀποστολικὸς καὶ προφητικὸς
γενόμενος ἐπίσκοπος τῆς ἐν Σμύρνῃ καθολικῆς
ἐκκλησίας· πᾶν γὰρ ῥῆμα ὃ ἀφῆκεν ἐκ τοῦ στόματος
αὐτοῦ, καὶ ἐτελειώθη καὶ τελειωθήσεται.

" Ὁ δὲ ἀντίζηλος καὶ βάσκανος πονηρός, ὁ 4
ἀντικείμενος τῷ γένει τῶν δικαίων, ἰδὼν τὸ
μέγεθος αὐτοῦ τῆς μαρτυρίας καὶ τὴν ἀπ' ἀρχῆς
ἀνεπίληπτον πολιτείαν ἐστεφανωμένον τε τὸν τῆς
ἀφθαρσίας στέφανον καὶ βραβεῖον ἀναντίρρητον
ἀπενηνεγμένον, ἐπετήδευσεν ὡς μηδὲ τὸ σωμάτιον
αὐτοῦ ὑφ' ἡμῶν ληφθείη, καίπερ πολλῶν ἐπι-

whom be glory to Thee with Him and the Holy Spirit, both now and for the ages that are to come, Amen.' Now when he had uttered his Amen and finished his prayer, the men in charge of the fire lit it, and a great flame blazed up and we, to whom it was given to see, saw a marvel. And we have been preserved to report to others what befell. For the fire made the likeness of a room, like the sail of a vessel filled with wind, and surrounded the body of the martyr as with a wall, and he was within it not as burning flesh, but as gold and silver being refined in a furnace. And we perceived such a fragrant smell as the scent of incense or other costly spices. At length the lawless men, seeing that his body could not be consumed by the fire, commanded an executioner to go up and stab him with a dagger, and when he did this, there came out much blood, so that the fire was quenched, and all the crowd marvelled that there was such a difference between the unbelievers and the elect. And of the elect was he indeed one, the wonderful martyr, Polycarp, who in our days was an apostolic and prophetic teacher, bishop of the Catholic Church in Smyrna. For every word which he uttered from his mouth both was fulfilled and will be fulfilled.

But the jealous and envious evil one who resists the family of the righteous, when he saw the greatness of his martyrdom, and his blameless career from the beginning, and that he was crowned with the crown of immortality, and had carried off the unspeakable prize, took care that not even his poor body should be taken away by us, though many

θυμούντων τοῦτο ποιῆσαι καὶ κοινωνῆσαι τῷ ἁγίῳ
αὐτοῦ σαρκίῳ. ὑπέβαλον γοῦν τινες Νικήτην, τὸν
τοῦ Ἡρῴδου πατέρα, ἀδελφὸν δ' Ἄλκης, ἐντυχεῖν
τῷ ἡγεμόνι ὥστε μὴ δοῦναι αὐτοῦ τὸ σῶμα,
'μή,' φησίν, 'ἀφέντες τὸν ἐσταυρωμένον, τοῦτον
ἄρξωνται σέβειν.' καὶ ταῦτα εἶπον ὑποβαλόντων
καὶ ἐνισχυσάντων τῶν Ἰουδαίων· οἳ καὶ ἐτήρησαν
μελλόντων ἡμῶν ἐκ τοῦ πυρὸς αὐτὸν λαμβάνειν,
ἀγνοοῦντες ὅτι οὔτε τὸν Χριστόν ποτε καταλιπεῖν
δυνησόμεθα, τὸν ὑπὲρ τῆς τοῦ παντὸς κόσμου τῶν
σῳζομένων σωτηρίας παθόντα, οὔτε ἕτερόν τινα
σέβειν. τοῦτον μὲν γὰρ υἱὸν ὄντα τοῦ θεοῦ προσ-
κυνοῦμεν, τοὺς δὲ μάρτυρας ὡς μαθητὰς καὶ
μιμητὰς τοῦ κυρίου ἀγαπῶμεν ἀξίως ἕνεκα εὐνοίας
ἀνυπερβλήτου τῆς εἰς τὸν ἴδιον βασιλέα καὶ
διδάσκαλον· ὧν γένοιτο καὶ ἡμᾶς συγκοινωνούς
τε καὶ συμμαθητὰς γενέσθαι. ἰδὼν οὖν ὁ ἑκατοντ-
άρχης τὴν τῶν Ἰουδαίων γενομένην φιλονεικίαν,
θεὶς αὐτὸν ἐν μέσῳ, ὡς ἔθος αὐτοῖς, ἔκαυσεν,
οὕτως τε ἡμεῖς ὕστερον ἀνελόμενοι τὰ τιμιώτερα
λίθων πολυτελῶν καὶ δοκιμώτερα ὑπὲρ χρυσίον
ὀστᾶ αὐτοῦ ἀπεθέμεθα ὅπου καὶ ἀκόλουθον ἦν.
ἔνθα, ὡς δυνατόν, ἡμῖν συναγομένοις ἐν ἀγαλλιάσει
καὶ χαρᾷ παρέξει ὁ κύριος ἐπιτελεῖν τὴν τοῦ
μαρτυρίου αὐτοῦ ἡμέραν γενέθλιον εἴς τε τὴν τῶν
προηθληκότων μνήμην καὶ τῶν μελλόντων ἄσκησίν
τε καὶ ἑτοιμασίαν. τοιαῦτα τὰ κατὰ τὸν μακάριον
Πολύκαρπον· σὺν τοῖς ἀπὸ Φιλαδελφείας δωδεκάτου ἐν Σμύρνῃ μαρτυρήσαντος, [ὃς] μόνος ὑπὸ
πάντων μᾶλλον μνημονεύεται, ὡς καὶ ὑπὸ τῶν
ἐθνῶν ἐν παντὶ τόπῳ λαλεῖσθαι."

Τὰ μὲν δὴ κατὰ τὸν θαυμάσιον καὶ ἀποστολικὸν

desired to do so, and to have fellowship with his holy flesh. Therefore he put forward Niketas, the father of Herod, and the brother of Alce, to ask the Governor not to give his body, ' lest,' he said, ' they leave the crucified one and begin to worship this man.' And they said this owing to the suggestions and pressure of the Jews, who also watched when we were going to take it from the fire, for they do not know that we shall not ever be able either to abandon Christ, who suffered for the salvation of those who are being saved in the whole world, or to worship any other. For him we worship as the Son of God, but the martyrs we love as disciples and imitators of the Lord ; and rightly, because of their unsurpassable affection toward their own King and Teacher. God grant that we too may be their companions and fellow-disciples. When therefore the centurion saw the contentiousness caused by the Jews, he put the body in the midst, as was their custom, and burnt it. Thus we, at last, took up his bones, more precious than precious stones, and finer than gold, and put them where it was meet. There the Lord will permit us to come together according to our power in gladness and joy, and celebrate the birthday of his martyrdom, both in memory of those who have already contested, and for the practice and training of those whose fate it shall be. Such was the lot of the blessed Polycarp, who though he was, together with those from Philadelphia, the twelfth martyr in Smyrna, is alone especially remembered by all, so that he is spoken of in every place, even by the heathen.''

This great end was vouchsafed to the life of the

EUSEBIUS

Πολύκαρπον τοιούτου κατηξίωτο τέλους, τῶν κατὰ τὴν Σμυρναίων ἐκκλησίαν ἀδελφῶν τὴν ἱστορίαν ἐν ᾗ δεδηλώκαμεν αὐτῶν ἐπιστολῇ κατατεθειμένων· ἐν τῇ αὐτῇ δὲ περὶ αὐτοῦ γραφῇ καὶ ἄλλα μαρτύρια συνῆπτο κατὰ τὴν αὐτὴν Σμύρναν πεπραγμένα ὑπὸ τὴν αὐτὴν περίοδον τοῦ χρόνου τῆς τοῦ Πολυκάρπου μαρτυρίας, μεθ' ὧν καὶ Μητρόδωρος τῆς κατὰ Μαρκίωνα πλάνης πρεσβύτερος δὴ εἶναι δοκῶν πυρὶ παραδοθεὶς ἀνῄρηται. τῶν γε μὴν τότε περιβόητος μάρτυς εἷς τις ἐγνωρίζετο Πιόνιος· οὗ τὰς κατὰ μέρος ὁμολογίας τὴν τε τοῦ λόγου παρρησίαν καὶ τὰς ὑπὲρ τῆς πίστεως ἐπὶ τοῦ δήμου καὶ τῶν ἀρχόντων ἀπολογίας διδασκαλικάς τε δημηγορίας καὶ ἔτι τὰς πρὸς τοὺς ὑποπεπτωκότας τῷ κατὰ τὸν διωγμὸν πειρασμῷ δεξιώσεις παραμυθίας τε ἃς ἐπὶ τῆς εἱρκτῆς τοῖς παρ' αὐτὸν εἰσαφικνουμένοις ἀδελφοῖς παρετίθετο, ἅς τε ἐπὶ τούτοις ὑπέμεινεν βασάνους, καὶ τὰς ἐπὶ ταύταις ἀλγηδόνας καθηλώσεις τε καὶ τὴν ἐπὶ τῆς πυρᾶς καρτερίαν τήν τε ἐφ' ἅπασιν τοῖς παραδόξοις αὐτοῦ τελευτὴν πληρέστατα τῆς περὶ αὐτοῦ γραφῆς περιεχούσης, τοὺς οἷς φίλον ἐπὶ ταύτην ἀναπέμψομεν τοῖς τῶν ἀρχαίων συναχθεῖσιν ἡμῖν μαρτυρίοις ἐντεταγμένην. ἑξῆς δὲ καὶ ἄλλων ἐν Περγάμῳ πόλει τῆς Ἀσίας ὑπομνήματα μεμαρτυρηκότων φέρεται, Κάρπου καὶ Παπύλου καὶ γυναικὸς Ἀγαθονίκης, μετὰ πλείστας καὶ διαπρεπεῖς ὁμολογίας ἐπιδόξως τετελειωμένων.

XVI. Κατὰ τούτους δὲ καὶ ὁ μικρῷ πρόσθεν ἡμῖν δηλωθεὶς Ἰουστῖνος δεύτερον ὑπὲρ τῶν καθ' ἡμᾶς δογμάτων βιβλίον ἀναδοὺς τοῖς δεδηλωμένοις ἄρχουσιν, θείῳ κατακοσμεῖται μαρτυρίῳ, φιλοσόφου

marvellous and apostolic Polycarp, as the Christians of the church at Smyrna have given the story in their letter which we have quoted. In the same document concerning him other martyrdoms are appended which took place in the same Smyrna at the same time as the martyrdom of Polycarp, and among them Metrodorus, who seems to have been a presbyter of the Marcionite error, was given to the fire and put to death. A famous martyr of those at that time was Pionius. The document concerning him gives a full account of his special confession, his boldness of speech, the instructive apologies for the faith and popular addresses before the people and magistrates, as well as the correction and comfort to those who had succumbed to temptation in the persecution, which he addressed during his imprisonment to the brethren who visited him, in addition to this the tortures which he underwent, added to pain, nailing, the enduring of the flame, and, after all his marvellous deeds, his death ; and to it we will refer those interested, for it is included in the martyrdoms of the ancients collected by us.[1] There are also memoirs extant of others who were martyred in the city of Pergamon in Asia, Carpus and Papylas, and a woman, Agathonice, who died after many glorious confessions.

XVI. In their time too Justin,[2] whom we mentioned a little earlier, after delivering to the rulers mentioned a second book in behalf of our opinions, was adorned with divine martyrdom when the philosopher

[1] See Introduction, pp. li, lii.   [2] See Introduction, pp. l, li.

Κρήσκεντος (τὸν φερώνυμον δ' οὗτος τῇ Κυνικῇ
προσηγορίᾳ βίον τε καὶ τρόπον ἐζήλου) τὴν ἐπιβουλὴν αὐτῷ καττύσαντος, ἐπειδὴ πλεονάκις ἐν
διαλόγοις ἀκροατῶν παρόντων εὐθύνας αὐτόν,
τὰ νικητήρια τελευτῶν ἧς ἐπρέσβευεν ἀληθείας
διὰ τοῦ μαρτυρίου τοῦ κατ' αὐτὸν ἀνεδήσατο.

Τοῦτο δὲ καὶ αὐτὸς ὁ ταῖς ἀληθείαις φιλο- 2
σοφώτατος ἐν τῇ δεδηλωμένῃ ἀπολογίᾳ σαφῶς
οὕτως, ὥσπερ οὖν καὶ ἔμελλεν ὅσον οὔπω περὶ
αὐτὸν συμβήσεσθαι, προλαβὼν ἀποσημαίνει τού-
Justin, *Apol.*
2, 3
*Chron.
Pasch.* 482,
10-483, 7τοις τοῖς ῥήμασιν· "κἀγὼ οὖν προσδοκῶ ὑπό 3
τινος τῶν ὠνομασμένων ἐπιβουλευθῆναι καὶ ξύλῳ
ἐντιναγῆναι ἢ κἂν ὑπὸ Κρήσκεντος τοῦ ἀφιλο-
σόφου καὶ φιλοκόμπου· οὐ γὰρ φιλόσοφον εἰπεῖν
ἄξιον τὸν ἄνδρα, ὅς γε περὶ ὧν μὴ ἐπίσταται,
δημοσίᾳ καταμαρτυρεῖ ὡς ἀθέων καὶ ἀσεβῶν
Χριστιανῶν ὄντων, πρὸς χάριν καὶ ἡδονὴν τῶν
πολλῶν τῶν πεπλανημένων τοῦτο πράττων. εἴτε 4
γὰρ μὴ ἐντυχὼν τοῖς τοῦ Χριστοῦ διδάγμασιν
κατατρέχει ἡμῶν, παμπόνηρός ἐστι καὶ ἰδιωτῶν
πολὺ χείρων, οἳ φυλάττονται πολλάκις περὶ ὧν
οὐκ ἐπίστανται, διαλέγεσθαι καὶ ψευδομαρτυρεῖν·
καὶ εἰ ἐντυχὼν μὴ συνῆκεν τὸ ἐν αὐτοῖς μεγαλεῖον
ἢ συνεὶς πρὸς τὸ μὴ ὑποπτευθῆναι τοιοῦτος ταῦτα
ποιεῖ, πολὺ μᾶλλον ἀγεννὴς καὶ παμπόνηρος,
ἰδιωτικῆς καὶ ἀλόγου δόξης καὶ φόβου ἐλάττων
ὤν. καὶ γὰρ προθέντα με καὶ ἐρωτήσαντα αὐτὸν 5
ἐρωτήσεις τινὰς τοιαύτας, μαθεῖν καὶ ἐλέγξαι
*Chron.
Pasch.* 482,
10-483, 7ὅτι ἀληθῶς μηδὲν ἐπίσταται, εἰδέναι ὑμᾶς βούλομαι,
καὶ ὅτι ἀληθῆ λέγω, εἰ μὴ ἀνηνέχθησαν ὑμῖν αἱ
κοινωνίαι τῶν λόγων, ἕτοιμος καὶ ἐφ' ὑμῶν

Crescens, who strove in life and behaviour to justify the name of cynic which he bore, instigated the plot against him, for Justin had often defeated him in debate in the presence of hearers, and finally bound on himself the trophies of victory by his martyrdom for the truth of which he was an ambassador.

This he, who was in truth a supreme philosopher, sets forth in advance, in the above-mentioned Apology, just as clearly as in fact it was almost at once to happen to him, using these words: " I too expect to be plotted against by one of those who have been mentioned, and to be stretched on the rack, or even by Crescens, that lover not of wisdom but of boasting, for the man is not worthy to be called 'philosopher' seeing that he publicly testifies about what he does not know, to the effect that the Christians are atheists and impious, and he does this to gain the grace and pleasure of the many who have been deceived. For either he controverts us without attending to the teachings of Christ, and is a complete rascal and far worse than the uneducated, who often avoid discussing and giving false testimony on subjects of which they have no knowledge ; and if he has studied and does not understand the greatness in them, or though he does understand them is base enough to do what he does to avoid suspicion, he is more ignoble and rascally, for he succumbs to ignorant and unreasonable opinion and fear. For I would have you to know that I put forward and asked him certain questions of this kind in order to find out and prove that he really knows nothing ; and to show that I am speaking the truth, in case the information as to the arguments was not brought to you, I am ready to communicate the

κοινωνεῖν τῶν ἐρωτήσεων πάλιν· βασιλικὸν δ'
ἂν καὶ τοῦτο ἔργον εἴη. εἰ δὲ καὶ ἐγνώσθησαν 6
ὑμῖν αἱ ἐρωτήσεις μου καὶ αἱ ἐκείνου ἀποκρίσεις,
φανερὸν ὑμῖν ἐστιν ὅτι οὐδὲν τῶν ἡμετέρων ἐπί-
σταται· ἢ εἰ ἐπίσταται, διὰ τοὺς ἀκούοντας δὲ οὐ
τολμᾷ λέγειν, ὡς πρότερον ἔφην, οὐ φιλόσοφος,
ἀλλὰ φιλόδοξος ἀνὴρ δείκνυται, ὅς γε μηδὲ τὸ
Σωκρατικόν, ἀξιέραστον ὄν, τιμᾷ."

Ταῦτα μὲν οὖν ὁ Ἰουστῖνος· ὅτι δὲ κατὰ τὴν 7
αὐτοῦ πρόρρησιν πρὸς τοῦ Κρήσκεντος συσκευασθεὶς

Tatian, p.
36, 26

ἐτελειώθη, Τατιανός, ἀνὴρ τὸν πρῶτον αὐτοῦ βίον
σοφιστεύσας ἐν τοῖς Ἑλλήνων μαθήμασι καὶ
δόξαν οὐ σμικρὰν ἐν αὐτοῖς ἀπενηνεγμένος πλεῖστά
τε ἐν συγγράμμασιν αὐτοῦ καταλιπὼν μνημεῖα,

Tatian, p.
20, 15-17

ἐν τῷ Πρὸς Ἕλληνας ἱστορεῖ, λέγων ὧδε· "καὶ
ὁ θαυμασιώτατος Ἰουστῖνος ὀρθῶς ἐξεφώνησεν
ἐοικέναι τοὺς προειρημένους λησταῖς." εἶτ' ἐπει- 8
πών τινα περὶ τῶν φιλοσόφων, ἐπιλέγει ταῦτα·

Tatian, p.
21, 1-6

" Κρήσκης γοῦν ὁ ἐννεοττεύσας τῇ μεγάλῃ πόλει
παιδεραστίᾳ μὲν πάντας ὑπερήνεγκεν, φιλαργυρίᾳ
δὲ πάνυ προσεχὴς ἦν· θανάτου δὲ ὁ καταφρονεῖν 9
συμβουλεύων οὕτως αὐτὸς ἐδεδίει τὸν θάνατον,
ὡς καὶ Ἰουστῖνον, καθάπερ μεγάλῳ κακῷ, τῷ
θανάτῳ περιβαλεῖν πραγματεύσασθαι, διότι κηρύτ-
των τὴν ἀλήθειαν λίχνους τοὺς φιλοσόφους καὶ
ἀπατεῶνας συνήλεγχεν." καὶ τὸ μὲν κατὰ Ἰουστῖνον μαρτύριον τοιαύτην εἴληχεν αἰτίαν.

XVII. Ὁ δ' αὐτὸς ἀνὴρ πρὸ τοῦ κατ' αὐτὸν ἀγῶ- 1
νος ἑτέρων πρὸ αὐτοῦ μαρτυρησάντων ἐν τῇ προτέρᾳ
μνημονεύει ἀπολογίᾳ, χρησίμως τῇ ὑποθέσει καὶ

Justin, Apol.
2, 2

ταῦτα ἱστορῶν· γράφει δὲ ὧδε· "γυνή τις συνεβίου 2
ἀνδρὶ ἀκολασταίνοντι, ἀκολασταίνουσα καὶ αὐτὴ

questions again before you, and this would be a task worthy of an Emperor. But if my questions and his answers are known to you, it is plain to you that he knows nothing of our position, or, if he does know, does not dare say so because of the listeners, and, as I said before, is proved to be a man who loves not wisdom but reputation and does not even honour the saying of Socrates, worthy of affection as it is." [1]

So says Justin; and that, according to his own prophecy, he was caught by Crescens and suffered martyrdom, Tatian, a man who in early life was trained in the learning of the Greeks and gained great distinction in it and has left many monuments of himself in writing, narrates as follows in his treatise against the Greeks: " And the wonderful Justin rightly exclaimed that those mentioned are like brigands." Then continuing about the philosophers, he proceeds: " Crescens, who lurked in the great city, surpassed all in unnatural vice and was also wholly devoted to the love of money. He counselled others to despise death but himself was so afraid of it that he intrigued to inflict death on Justin, as though it were a great evil, because Justin by preaching the truth convicted the philosophers as gluttons and impostors." Such was the cause of the martyrdom of Justin.

XVII. The same writer mentions in his first Apology that before his own contest others had been martyrs before him. He narrates this profitably to our subject and he writes thus: " A certain woman lived with a dissipated husband, and at first she too

---

[1] Eusebius forgot to copy the passage quoted by Justin, " A man must not be honoured above the truth " (Plato, *Republic*, x. 595 c).

πρότερον· ἐπειδὴ δὲ τὰ τοῦ Χριστοῦ διδάγματα
ἔγνω, ἐσωφρονίσθη, καὶ τὸν ἄνδρα ὁμοίως σω-
φρονεῖν πείθειν ἐπειρᾶτο, τὰ διδάγματα ἀναφέρουσα
τήν τε μέλλουσαν τοῖς οὐ σωφρόνως καὶ μετὰ
λόγου ὀρθοῦ βιοῦσιν ἔσεσθαι ἐν αἰωνίῳ πυρὶ
κόλασιν ἀπαγγέλλουσα. ὁ δὲ ταῖς αὐταῖς ἀσελ- 3
γείαις ἐπιμένων, ἀλλοτρίαν διὰ τῶν πράξεων
ἐποιεῖτο τὴν γαμετήν· ἀσεβὲς γὰρ ἡγουμένη τὸ
λοιπὸν ἡ γυνὴ συγκατακλίνεσθαι ἀνδρὶ παρὰ τὸν
τῆς φύσεως νόμον καὶ παρὰ τὸ δίκαιον πόρους
ἡδονῆς ἐκ παντὸς πειρωμένῳ ποιεῖσθαι, τῆς
συζυγίας χωρισθῆναι ἐβουλήθη. καὶ ἐπειδὴ ἐξ- 4
εδυσωπεῖτο ὑπὸ τῶν αὐτῆς, ἔτι προσμένειν συμ-
βουλευόντων ὡς εἰς ἐλπίδα μεταβολῆς ἥξοντός
ποτε τοῦ ἀνδρός, βιαζομένη ἑαυτὴν ἐπέμενεν·
ἐπειδὴ δὲ ὁ ταύτης ἀνὴρ εἰς τὴν Ἀλεξάνδρειαν 5
πορευθείς, χαλεπώτερα πράττειν ἀπηγγέλθη, ὅπως
μὴ κοινωνὸς τῶν ἀδικημάτων καὶ ἀσεβημάτων
γένηται μένουσα ἐν τῇ συζυγίᾳ καὶ ὁμοδίαιτος καὶ
ὁμόκοιτος γινομένη, τὸ λεγόμενον παρ' ὑμῖν
ῥεπούδιον δοῦσα ἐχωρίσθη. ὁ δὲ καλὸς κἀγαθὸς 6
ταύτης ἀνήρ, δέον αὐτὸν χαίρειν ὅτι ἃ πάλαι μετὰ
τῶν ὑπηρετῶν καὶ τῶν μισθοφόρων εὐχερῶς
ἔπραττεν μέθαις χαίρουσα καὶ κακίᾳ πάσῃ, τούτων
μὲν τῶν πράξεων πέπαυτο καὶ αὐτὸν τὰ αὐτὰ
παύσασθαι πράττοντα ἐβούλετο, μὴ βουλομένου
ἀπαλλαγείσης, κατηγορίαν πεποίηται, λέγων αὐτὴν
Χριστιανὴν εἶναι. καὶ ἡ μὲν βιβλίδιόν σοι τῷ 7
αὐτοκράτορι ἀνέδωκεν, πρότερον συγχωρηθῆναι
αὐτῇ διοικήσασθαι τὰ ἑαυτῆς ἀξιοῦσα, ἔπειτα
ἀπολογήσασθαι περὶ τοῦ κατηγορήματος μετὰ
τὴν τῶν πραγμάτων αὐτῆς διοίκησιν, καὶ συν-

was dissipated, but when she knew the doctrine of
Christ she reformed, and tried to persuade her
husband to reform likewise, relating the doctrine to
him, and announcing the punishment in eternal fire
which will be the lot of those who do not live soberly
and in accordance with right teaching. But he remained in his dissoluteness, and through his acts
broke up his marriage, for his wife thought it was
wicked to continue consorting with a husband who
tried every kind of pleasure contrary to the law
of nature and to righteousness, and wished to be
separated from wedlock. Owing to the importunity
of her family, who counselled her to stay with him
because there was always a hope that the husband
would change, she constrained herself to stay with
him, but when her husband went to Alexandria, and
she heard that he was behaving worse, in order not
to be a partner of wickedness and impiety by remaining in wedlock and sharing in his board and
bed, she gave him what you call a writ of divorce
and was separated. But though her noble husband
ought to have rejoiced that she, who had formerly
light-heartedly engaged with servants and hirelings
in drunken pleasure and in all vices, had given up
these habits and wished him too to give up following
them, he disliked her conversion and brought an
accusation alleging that she was a Christian. She
filed a petition with you, as Emperor, begging that
she be allowed first to settle her affairs and then to
answer the accusation after the settlement of her

ἐχώρησας τοῦτο· ὁ δὲ ταύτης ποτὲ ἀνὴρ πρὸς 8
ἐκείνην μὲν μὴ δυνάμενος τὰ νῦν ἔτι λέγειν, πρὸς
Πτολεμαῖόν τινα, ὃν Οὐρβίκιος ἐκολάσατο, διδάσκαλον ἐκείνης τῶν Χριστιανῶν μαθημάτων
γενόμενον, ἐτράπετο διὰ τοῦδε τοῦ τρόπου. ἑκα- 9
τόνταρχον εἰς δεσμὰ ἐμβαλόντα τὸν Πτολεμαῖον,
φίλον αὐτῷ ὑπάρχοντα, ἔπεισε λαβέσθαι τοῦ
Πτολεμαίου καὶ ἀνερωτῆσαι εἰ, αὐτὸ τοῦτο μόνον,
Χριστιανός ἐστιν. καὶ τὸν Πτολεμαῖον, φιλαλήθη
ἀλλ' οὐκ ἀπατηλὸν οὐδὲ ψευδολόγον τὴν γνώμην
ὄντα, ὁμολογήσαντα ἑαυτὸν εἶναι Χριστιανόν, ἐν
δεσμοῖς γενέσθαι ὁ ἑκατόνταρχος πεποίηκεν, καὶ
ἐπὶ πολὺν χρόνον ἐν τῷ δεσμωτηρίῳ ἐκολάσατο·
τελευταῖον δὲ ὅτε ἐπὶ Οὐρβίκιον ἤχθη ὁ ἄνθρωπος, 10
ὁμοίως αὐτὸ τοῦτο μόνον ἐξητάσθη, εἰ εἴη Χρι-
στιανός· καὶ πάλιν, τὰ καλὰ ἑαυτῷ συνεπιστάμενος
διὰ τὴν ἀπὸ τοῦ Χριστοῦ διδαχήν, τὸ διδασκαλεῖον
τῆς θείας ἀρετῆς ὡμολόγησεν. ὁ γὰρ ἀρνούμενος 11
ὁτιοῦν ἢ κατεγνωκὼς τοῦ πράγματος ἔξαρνος
γίνεται ἢ ἑαυτὸν ἀνάξιον ἐπιστάμενος καὶ ἀλλό-
τριον τοῦ πράγματος τὴν ὁμολογίαν φεύγει· ὧν
οὐδὲν πρόσεστιν τῷ ἀληθινῷ Χριστιανῷ. καὶ τοῦ 12
Οὐρβίκιου κελεύσαντος αὐτὸν ἀπαχθῆναι, Λούκιός
τις, καὶ αὐτὸς ὢν Χριστιανός, ὁρῶν τὴν ἀλόγως
οὕτως γενομένην κρίσιν, πρὸς τὸν Οὐρβίκιον ἔφη
'τίς ἡ αἰτία τοῦ μήτε μοιχὸν μήτε πόρνον μήτε
ἀνδροφόνον μήτε λωποδύτην μήτε ἅρπαγα μήτε
ἁπλῶς ἀδίκημά τι πράξαντα ἐλεγχόμενον, ὀνόματος

---

[1] The point appears to be that the settlement of the lady's
estate meant an accounting to her by her husband, and probably considerable payment by him to her, so that the situation

affairs. This you granted. But her former husband being now unable to attack her,[1] turned in the following way against a certain Ptolemy, who had been her teacher in Christian doctrines and was punished by Urbicius. He persuaded a centurion who was a friend of his to arrest Ptolemy, and to ask him this one thing, whether he was a Christian. And Ptolemy, being a lover of the truth, and not deceitful nor of false disposition, confessed that he was a Christian. The centurion caused him to be put in prison and tortured him for a long while in the jail. Finally, when the man was brought before Urbicius he was similarly asked only this same question, whether he was a Christian, and again, conscious of the good which came to him because of the teaching of Christ, he confessed the school of divine virtue. For he who denies anything either condemns the fact and rejects it, or knowing that he is himself unworthy and alien from the fact, avoids confession, and neither of these is the case with the real Christian. When Urbicius ordered him to be executed, a certain Lucius, who was himself a Christian, seeing the verdict which was thus given contrary to all reason, said to Urbicius, ' What is the reason for punishing this man who has not been convicted of adultery or fornication or murder or theft or robbery or, in a word, of having done anything

was that if he wished to gratify his grudge against her he would have to pay more than he desired, while if she wished to escape a martyr's crown she must sacrifice some of her property to her husband. Justin's point of view is obvious, but the emperor may have thought that wives who refused to join in their husband's amusements scarcely deserved to be executed yet might well pay for the privilege of having failed to convert their husbands to their own way of thinking.

δὲ Χριστιανοῦ προσωνυμίαν ὁμολογοῦντα, τὸν ἄνθρωπον τοῦτον ἐκολάσω; οὐ πρέποντα Εὐσεβεῖ αὐτοκράτορι οὐδὲ φιλοσόφῳ Καίσαρος παιδὶ οὐδὲ ἱερᾷ συγκλήτῳ κρίνεις, ὦ Οὐρβίκιε.' καὶ ὅς, ι οὐδὲν ἄλλο ἀποκρινάμενος, καὶ πρὸς τὸν Λούκιον ἔφη ' δοκεῖς μοι καὶ σὺ εἶναι τοιοῦτος,' καὶ τοῦ Λουκίου φήσαντος ' μάλιστα,' πάλιν καὶ αὐτὸν ἀπαχθῆναι ἐκέλευσεν· ὁ δὲ χάριν εἰδέναι ὡμολόγεε πονηρῶν γὰρ δεσποτῶν τῶν τοιούτων ἀπηλλάχθαι ἐπεῖπεν καὶ παρὰ ἀγαθὸν πατέρα καὶ βασιλέα τὸν θεὸν πορεύεσθαι. καὶ ἄλλος δὲ τρίτος ἐπελθὼν κολα- σθῆναι προσετιμήθη.'' τούτοις ὁ Ἰουστῖνος εἰκότως καὶ ἀκολούθως ἃς προεμνημονεύσαμεν αὐτοῦ φωνὰς ἐπάγει λέγων '' κἀγὼ οὖν προσδοκῶ ὑπό τινος τῶν ὠνομασμένων ἐπιβουλευθῆναι '' καὶ τὰ λοιπά.

XVIII. Πλεῖστα δὲ οὗτος καταλέλοιπεν ἡμῖν πε- 1 παιδευμένης διανοίας καὶ περὶ τὰ θεῖα ἐσπουδακυίας ὑπομνήματα, πάσης ὠφελείας ἔμπλεα· ἐφ' ἃ τοὺς φιλομαθεῖς ἀναπέμψομεν, τὰ εἰς ἡμετέραν γνῶσιν ἐλθόντα χρησίμως παρασημηνάμενοι. ὁ μέν τίς 2 ἐστιν αὐτῷ λόγος πρὸς Ἀντωνῖνον τὸν Εὐσεβῆ προσαγορευθέντα καὶ τοὺς τούτου παῖδας τήν τε Ῥωμαίων σύγκλητον προσφωνητικὸς ὑπὲρ τῶν καθ' ἡμᾶς δογμάτων, ὁ δὲ δευτέραν περιέχων ὑπὲρ τῆς ἡμετέρας πίστεως ἀπολογίαν, ἣν πε- ποίηται πρὸς τὸν τοῦ δεδηλωμένου αὐτοκράτορος διάδοχόν τε καὶ ὁμώνυμον Ἀντωνῖνον Οὐῆρον, οὗ τὰ κατὰ τοὺς χρόνους ἐπὶ τοῦ παρόντος διέξιμεν· καὶ ἄλλος ὁ πρὸς Ἕλληνας, ἐν ᾧ μακρὸν περὶ 3 πλείστων παρ' ἡμῖν τε καὶ τοῖς Ἑλλήνων φιλοσόφοις ζητουμένων κατατείνας λόγον, περὶ τῆς τῶν δαιμόνων διαλαμβάνει φύσεως· ἃ οὐδὲν ἂν ἐπείγοι

wrong, but merely confesses that he bears the Christian name ? Your judgement, Urbicius, is unworthy of the emperor called Pius, or of Caesar's son, the philosopher, or of the sacred Senate.' And Urbicius made no reply except to say to Lucius, ' You seem to me to be a Christian yourself.' And when Lucius said, ' Certainly,' he ordered him to be executed also. Lucius expressed his gratitude, for he said he was being removed from wicked lords like these and going to God, the good Father and King. A third man, who also came forward, Urbicius commanded to be punished." To this Justin naturally and suitably adds the words which we quoted above, " So I expect myself to suffer a plot from one of those named," etc.

XVIII. Justin has left us treatises of an educated intelligence trained in theology, which are full of helpfulness, and to them we will refer students, indicating what has come usefully to our knowledge. There is a treatise by him, on behalf of our opinions, addressed to Antoninus, surnamed Pius, and his children, and to the Roman Senate another, containing a second Apology for our defence, which he made to the successor and namesake of the above mentioned emperor, Antoninus Verus, whose period we are at present discussing ; and another to the Greeks, in which, after a long and expanded argument about very many things inquired into both by Christians and the philosophers of the Greeks, he discourses on the nature of demons, which there is no urgency to quote at present.

369

τὰ νῦν παρατίθεσθαι. καὶ αὖθις ἕτερον πρὸς 4
Ἕλληνας εἰς ἡμᾶς ἐλήλυθεν αὐτοῦ σύγγραμμα,
ὃ καὶ ἐπέγραψεν Ἔλεγχον, καὶ παρὰ τούτους ἄλλο
περὶ θεοῦ μοναρχίας, ἣν οὐ μόνον ἐκ τῶν παρ᾽ ἡμῖν
γραφῶν, ἀλλὰ καὶ τῶν Ἑλληνικῶν συνίστησιν
βιβλίων· ἐπὶ τούτοις ἐπιγεγραμμένον Ψάλτης, 5
καὶ ἄλλο σχολικὸν Περὶ ψυχῆς, ἐν ᾧ διαφόρους
πεύσεις προτείνας περὶ τοῦ κατὰ τὴν ὑπόθεσιν
προβλήματος, τῶν παρ᾽ Ἕλλησιν φιλοσόφων παρατίθεται τὰς δόξας, αἷς καὶ ἀντιλέξειν ὑπισχνεῖται
τήν τε αὐτὸς αὐτοῦ δόξαν ἐν ἑτέρῳ παραθήσεσθαι
συγγράμματι. καὶ διάλογον δὲ πρὸς Ἰουδαίους 6
συνέταξεν, ὃν ἐπὶ τῆς Ἐφεσίων πόλεως πρὸς
Τρύφωνα τῶν τότε Ἑβραίων ἐπισημότατον πε-
Justin, Dial.
2-8 ποίηται· ἐν ᾧ τίνα τρόπον ἡ θεία χάρις αὐτὸν ἐπὶ
τὸν τῆς πίστεως παρώρμησε λόγον, δηλοῖ ὁποίαν
τε πρότερον περὶ τὰ φιλόσοφα μαθήματα σπουδὴν
εἰσενήνεκται καὶ ὅσην ἐποιήσατο τῆς ἀληθείας
ἐκθυμοτάτην ζήτησιν. ἱστορεῖ δ᾽ ἐν ταὐτῷ περὶ 7
Ἰουδαίων ὡς κατὰ τῆς τοῦ Χριστοῦ διδασκαλίας
ἐπιβουλὴν συσκευασαμένων, αὐτὰ ταῦτα πρὸς
Justin, Dial.
17 τὸν Τρύφωνα ἀποτεινόμενος· "οὐ μόνον δὲ οὐ
μετενοήσατε ἐφ᾽ οἷς ἐπράξατε κακῶς, ἀλλὰ ἄνδρας
ἐκλεκτοὺς ἐκλεξάμενοι τότε ἀπὸ Ἰερουσαλὴμ
ἐξεπέμψατε εἰς πᾶσαν τὴν γῆν, λέγοντες αἵρεσιν
ἄθεον Χριστιανῶν πεφάνθαι καταλέγοντές τε ταῦτα
ἅπερ καθ᾽ ἡμῶν οἱ ἀγνοοῦντες ἡμᾶς πάντες λέγουσιν,
ὥστε οὐ μόνον ἑαυτοῖς ἀδικίας αἴτιοι ὑπάρχετε,
ἀλλὰ καὶ τοῖς ἄλλοις ἅπασιν ἁπλῶς ἀνθρώποις."
Justin, Dial.
82
Justin, Dial.
81 Γράφει δὲ καὶ ὡς ὅτι μέχρι καὶ αὐτοῦ χαρίσματα 8
προφητικὰ διέλαμπεν ἐπὶ τῆς ἐκκλησίας, μέμνηταί
τε τῆς Ἰωάννου Ἀποκαλύψεως, σαφῶς τοῦ

Again a second treatise against the Greeks has reached us, which he entitled *A Confutation*, and besides them another about the Sovereignty of God which he compiled not only from our own scriptures but also from the books of the Greeks. Besides these he wrote the book entitled *Psaltes* and another disputation *On the Soul*, in which he propounds various questions concerning the problem under discussion and adduces the opinion of the Greek philosophers ; these he promises to refute and to give his own opinion in another book. He also composed a dialogue against the Jews, which he held in the city of Ephesus against Trypho, the most distinguished Jew of the day. In this he explains how the grace of God brought him to the word of the faith, and how he had formerly been zealous for philosophic learning and made deep and enthusiastic inquiry into the truth. In the same book he narrates about the Jews how they plotted against the teaching of Christ, and presses the same point against Trypho. " Not only did you not repent of the evil that you did but you chose out picked men at that time and sent them from Jerusalem to the whole world saying that a seditious sect of Christians had arisen, and uttering the calumnies which all those who do not know us make against us, so that you are not only guilty of unrighteousness against yourselves but also against absolutely all other men."

He also writes that even up to his own time prophetic gifts illuminated the church, and quotes the Apocalypse of John, saying clearly that it is the work

371

Justin, *Dial.*
71-73 ἀποστόλου αὐτὴν εἶναι λέγων· καὶ ῥητῶν δέ τινων
προφητικῶν μνημονεύει, διελέγχων τὸν Τρύφωνα
ὡς δὴ περικοψάντων αὐτὰ Ἰουδαίων ἀπὸ τῆς
γραφῆς. πλεῖστα δὲ καὶ ἕτερα παρὰ πολλοῖς
φέρεται ἀδελφοῖς τῶν αὐτοῦ πόνων, οὕτωσὶ δὲ 9
σπουδῆς εἶναι ἄξιοι καὶ τοῖς παλαιοῖς ἐδόκουν οἱ
τἀνδρὸς λόγοι, ὡς τὸν Εἰρηναῖον ἀπομνημονεύειν
αὐτοῦ φωνάς, τοῦτο μὲν ἐν τῷ τετάρτῳ Πρὸς τὰς
Iren. 4, 6, 2 αἱρέσεις αὐτὰ δὴ ταῦτα ἐπιλέγοντα· "καὶ καλῶς
ὁ Ἰουστῖνος ἐν τῷ πρὸς Μαρκίωνα συντάγματί
φησιν ὅτι αὐτῷ τῷ κυρίῳ οὐκ ἂν ἐπείσθην ἄλλον
θεὸν καταγγέλλοντι παρὰ τὸν δημιουργόν," τοῦτο
δὲ ἐν τῷ πέμπτῳ τῆς αὐτῆς ὑποθέσεως διὰ τούτων·
Iren. 5, 26, 2 "καὶ καλῶς ὁ Ἰουστῖνος ἔφη ὅτι πρὸ μὲν τῆς τοῦ
κυρίου παρουσίας οὐδέποτε ἐτόλμησεν ὁ σατανᾶς
βλασφημῆσαι τὸν θεόν, ἅτε μηδέπω εἰδὼς αὐτοῦ
τὴν κατάκρισιν." καὶ ταῦτα δὲ ἀναγκαίως εἰρήσθω 10
εἰς προτροπὴν τοῦ μετὰ σπουδῆς τοὺς φιλομαθεῖς
καὶ τοὺς τούτου περιέπειν λόγους. καὶ τὰ μὲν κατὰ
τόνδε τοιαῦτα ἦν.

XIX. Ἤδη δὲ εἰς ὄγδοον ἐλαυνούσης ἔτος τῆς 1
δηλουμένης ἡγεμονίας, τῆς Ῥωμαίων ἐκκλησίας
τὴν ἐπισκοπὴν Ἀνίκητον ἕνδεκα τοῖς πᾶσιν ἔτεσιν
διελθόντα Σωτὴρ διαδέχεται, ἀλλὰ καὶ τῆς Ἀλεξανδρέων παροικίας Κελαδίωνος τέτταρσιν ἐπὶ δέκα
ἔτεσιν προστάντος, XX. τὴν διαδοχὴν Ἀγριππίνος 1
διαλαμβάνει, καὶ ἐπὶ τῆς Ἀντιοχέων δὲ ἐκκλησίας Θεόφιλος ἕκτος ἀπὸ τῶν ἀποστόλων ἐγνωρίζετο, τετάρτου μὲν τῶν ἐκεῖσε μετὰ Ἥρωνα
καταστάντος Κορνηλίου, μετὰ δὲ αὐτὸν πέμπτῳ
βαθμῷ τὴν ἐπισκοπὴν Ἔρωτος διαδεξαμένου.

XXI. Ἤκμαζον δ' ἐν τούτοις ἐπὶ τῆς ἐκκλησίας 1

of the apostle. And he also quotes some texts from the prophets bringing the charge against Trypho that the Jews had cut them out of the Scripture. There are also many works of his extant among many Christians, and thus the books of this writer seemed even to the ancients worthy of study, for Irenaeus quotes his works, doing so in the fourth book *Against Heresies* in these very words : " And well does Justin say in his treatise against Marcion that he would not have believed the Lord himself had he preached a God other than the Creator." Again, in the fifth book of the same treatise he quotes him as follows : " And well did Justin say that before the coming of the Lord Satan dared not blaspheme God, seeing that he did not yet know his condemnation." These points must serve to encourage students to follow his arguments zealously and such are the facts about him.

XIX. Now when the reign of this emperor was approaching the eighth year[1] Soter succeeded Anicetus in the bishopric of Rome, who had completed eleven years altogether, and when Celadion had presided over the diocese of the Alexandrians for fourteen years, XX. Agrippinus took up the succession, and in the church of the Antiochians, the famous Theophilus was the sixth from the Apostles, the fourth having been Cornelius, who was appointed after Hero, and after Cornelius Eros had succeeded to the bishopric in the fifth place.

XXI. At this time there flourished in the church

[1] A.D. 168.

Ἡγήσιππός τε, ὃν ἴσμεν ἐκ τῶν προτέρων, καὶ
Διονύσιος Κορινθίων ἐπίσκοπος Πινυτός τε ἄλλος
τῶν ἐπὶ Κρήτης ἐπίσκοπος Φίλιππός τε ἐπὶ
τούτοις καὶ Ἀπολινάριος καὶ Μελίτων Μουσανός
τε καὶ Μόδεστος καὶ ἐπὶ πᾶσιν Εἰρηναῖος, ὧν καὶ
εἰς ἡμᾶς τῆς ἀποστολικῆς παραδόσεως ἡ τῆς
ὑγιοῦς πίστεως ἔγγραφος κατῆλθεν ὀρθοδοξία.

XXII. Ὁ μὲν οὖν Ἡγήσιππος ἐν πέντε τοῖς εἰς 1
ἡμᾶς ἐλθοῦσιν ὑπομνήμασιν τῆς ἰδίας γνώμης πληρεστάτην μνήμην καταλέλοιπεν· ἐν οἷς δηλοῖ ὡς πλείστοις ἐπισκόποις συμμίξειεν ἀποδημίαν στειλάμενος
μέχρι Ῥώμης, καὶ ὡς ὅτι τὴν αὐτὴν παρὰ πάντων
παρείληφεν διδασκαλίαν. ἀκοῦσαί γέ τοι πάρεστιν
μετά τινα περὶ τῆς Κλήμεντος πρὸς Κορινθίους
ἐπιστολῆς αὐτῷ εἰρημένα ἐπιλέγοντος ταῦτα· "καὶ 2
ἐπέμενεν ἡ ἐκκλησία ἡ Κορινθίων ἐν τῷ ὀρθῷ
λόγῳ μέχρι Πρίμου ἐπισκοπεύοντος ἐν Κορίνθῳ·
οἷς συνέμιξα πλέων εἰς Ῥώμην καὶ συνδιέτριψα
τοῖς Κορινθίοις ἡμέρας ἱκανάς, ἐν αἷς συνανεπάη-
μεν τῷ ὀρθῷ λόγῳ· γενόμενος δὲ ἐν Ῥώμῃ, 3
διαδοχὴν ἐποιησάμην μέχρις Ἀνικήτου· οὗ διάκονος
ἦν Ἐλεύθερος, καὶ παρὰ Ἀνικήτου διαδέχεται
Σωτήρ, μεθ᾽ ὃν Ἐλεύθερος. ἐν ἑκάστῃ δὲ διαδοχῇ
καὶ ἐν ἑκάστῃ πόλει οὕτως ἔχει ὡς ὁ νόμος κηρύσσει
καὶ οἱ προφῆται καὶ ὁ κύριος."

Ὁ δ᾽ αὐτὸς καὶ τῶν κατ᾽ αὐτὸν αἱρέσεων τὰς 4
ἀρχὰς ὑποτίθεται διὰ τούτων· "καὶ μετὰ τὸ
μαρτυρῆσαι Ἰάκωβον τὸν δίκαιον, ὡς καὶ ὁ κύριος,
ἐπὶ τῷ αὐτῷ λόγῳ, πάλιν ὁ ἐκ θείου αὐτοῦ Συμεὼν
ὁ τοῦ Κλωπᾶ καθίσταται ἐπίσκοπος, ὃν προέθεντο
πάντες, ὄντα ἀνεψιὸν τοῦ κυρίου δεύτερον. διὰ
τοῦτο ἐκάλουν τὴν ἐκκλησίαν παρθένον, οὔπω γὰρ

Hegesippus, whom we know from former narratives, and Dionysius, bishop of the Corinthians, and Pinytus, another bishop of the Cretans, and Philip, and in addition to them Apolinarius and Melito and Musanus and Modestus and, above all, Irenaeus, and their correct opinions on the sound faith of the apostolic tradition have come down to us in writing.

XXII. Hegesippus has left a complete record of his own opinion in five treatises which have come down to us. In them he explains how when travelling as far as Rome he mingled with many bishops and that he found the same doctrine among them all. But it is well to listen to what he said after some remarks about the epistle of Clement to the Corinthians : " And the church of the Corinthians remained in the true doctrine until Primus was bishop of Corinth, and I conversed with them on my voyage to Rome, and spent some days with the Corinthians during which we were refreshed by the true word. When I was in Rome I recovered the list of the succession until Anicetus, whose deacon was Eleutherus ; Soter succeeded Anicetus, and after him came Eleutherus. In each list and in each city things are as the law, the prophets, and the Lord preach."

The same writer also describes the beginning of the heresies of his time as follows : " After James the Just had suffered martyrdom for the same reason as the Lord, Symeon, his cousin, the son of Clopas was appointed bishop, whom they all proposed because he was another cousin of the Lord. For this cause they called the church virgin, for it had not

ἔφθαρτο ἀκοαῖς ματαίαις· ἄρχεται δὲ ὁ Θέβουθις 5
διὰ τὸ μὴ γενέσθαι αὐτὸν ἐπίσκοπον ὑποφθείρειν
ἀπὸ τῶν ἑπτὰ αἱρέσεων, ὧν καὶ αὐτὸς ἦν, ἐν τῷ
λαῷ, ἀφ' ὧν Σίμων, ὅθεν Σιμωνιανοί, καὶ Κλεόβιος,
ὅθεν Κλεοβιηνοί, καὶ Δοσίθεος, ὅθεν Δοσιθιανοί,
καὶ Γορθαῖος, ὅθεν Γοραθηνοί, καὶ Μασβώθεοι.
ἀπὸ τούτων Μενανδριανισταὶ καὶ Μαρκιανισταὶ
καὶ Καρποκρατιανοὶ καὶ Οὐαλεντινιανοὶ καὶ Βασι-
λειδιανοὶ καὶ Σατορνιλιανοὶ ἕκαστος ἰδίως καὶ
ἑτεροίως ἰδίαν δόξαν παρεισηγάγοσαν, ἀπὸ τούτων 6
ψευδόχριστοι, ψευδοπροφῆται, ψευδαπόστολοι, οἵ-
τινες ἐμέρισαν τὴν ἕνωσιν τῆς ἐκκλησίας φθορι-
μαίοις λόγοις κατὰ τοῦ θεοῦ καὶ κατὰ τοῦ Χριστοῦ
αὐτοῦ."

Ἔτι δ' ὁ αὐτὸς καὶ τὰς πάλαι γεγενημένας παρὰ 7
Ἰουδαίοις αἱρέσεις ἱστορεῖ λέγων· "ἦσαν δὲ
γνῶμαι διάφοροι ἐν τῇ περιτομῇ ἐν υἱοῖς Ἰσραηλιτῶν κατὰ τῆς φυλῆς Ἰούδα καὶ τοῦ Χριστοῦ
αὗται· Ἐσσαῖοι Γαλιλαῖοι Ἡμεροβαπτισταὶ Μασβώθεοι Σαμαρεῖται Σαδδουκαῖοι Φαρισαῖοι."

Καὶ ἕτερα δὲ πλεῖστα γράφει, ὧν ἐκ μέρους ἤδη 8
πρότερον ἐμνημονεύσαμεν, οἰκείως τοῖς καιροῖς
τὰς ἱστορίας παραθέμενοι, ἔκ τε τοῦ καθ' Ἑβραίους
εὐαγγελίου καὶ τοῦ Συριακοῦ καὶ ἰδίως ἐκ τῆς
Ἑβραΐδος διαλέκτου τινὰ τίθησιν, ἐμφαίνων ἐξ
Ἑβραίων ἑαυτὸν πεπιστευκέναι, καὶ ἄλλα δὲ ὡς
ἐξ Ἰουδαϊκῆς ἀγράφου παραδόσεως μνημονεύει. οὐ
Iren. 4, 20, 3 μόνος δὲ οὗτος, καὶ Εἰρηναῖος δὲ καὶ ὁ πᾶς τῶν 9
ἀρχαίων χορὸς πανάρετον Σοφίαν τὰς Σολομῶνος
Παροιμίας ἐκάλουν. καὶ περὶ τῶν λεγομένων δὲ

---

¹ "The people" usually means the Jews, but here it

yet been corrupted by vain messages, but Thebouthis, because he had not been made bishop, begins its corruption by the seven heresies, to which he belonged, among the people.[1] Of these were Simon, whence the Simonians, and Cleobius, whence the Cleobians, and Dositheus, whence the Dosithians, and Gorthaeus, whence the Goratheni and the Masbothei. From these come the Menandrianists and the Marcianists and the Carpocratians and the Valentinians and the Basilidians and Saturnilians ; each of these puts forward in its own peculiar way its own opinion, and from them come the false Christs and false prophets and false apostles who destroy the unity of the church by their poisonous doctrine against God and against his Christ.''

The same writer also described the sects which once existed among the Jews as follows : " Now there were various opinions among the circumcision, among the children of Israel, against the tribe of Judah and the Messiah, as follows : Essenes, Galileans, Hemerobaptists, Masbothei, Samaritans, Sadducees, and Pharisees.''

He also wrote much more, from which we have already made some quotations, arranging the narratives chronologically, and he makes extracts from the Gospel according to the Hebrews, and from the Syriac and particularly from the Hebrew language, showing that he had been converted from among the Hebrews, and he mentions points as coming from the unwritten tradition of the Jews. And not only he but also Irenaeus and the whole company of the ancients called the Proverbs the All-virtuous Wisdom. And in dis-

seems to mean Palestinian Christians. But the passage is not clear, and possibly the text is corrupt.

ἀποκρύφων διαλαμβάνων, ἐπὶ τῶν αὐτοῦ χρόνων
πρός τινων αἱρετικῶν ἀναπεπλάσθαι τινὰ τούτων
ἱστορεῖ. ἀλλὰ γὰρ ἐφ' ἕτερον ἤδη μεταβατέον.

XXIII. Καὶ πρῶτόν γε περὶ Διονυσίου φατέον ὅτι 1
τε τῆς ἐν Κορίνθῳ παροικίας τὸν τῆς ἐπισκοπῆς ἐγκεχείριστο θρόνον, καὶ ὡς τῆς ἐνθέου φιλοπονίας
οὐ μόνοις τοῖς ὑπ' αὐτόν, ἀλλ' ἤδη καὶ τοῖς ἐπὶ
τῆς ἀλλοδαπῆς ἀφθόνως ἐκοινώνει, χρησιμώτατον
ἅπασιν ἑαυτὸν καθιστὰς ἐν αἷς ὑπετυποῦτο καθο-
λικαῖς πρὸς τὰς ἐκκλησίας ἐπιστολαῖς· ὧν ἐστιν ἡ
μὲν πρὸς Λακεδαιμονίους ὀρθοδοξίας κατηχητικὴ 2
εἰρήνης τε καὶ ἑνώσεως ὑποθετική, ἡ δὲ πρὸς
Ἀθηναίους διεγερτικὴ πίστεως καὶ τῆς κατὰ τὸ
εὐαγγέλιον πολιτείας, ἧς ὀλιγωρήσαντας ἐλέγχει
ὡς ἂν μικροῦ δεῖν ἀποστάντας τοῦ λόγου ἐξ οὗπερ
τὸν προεστῶτα αὐτῶν Πούπλιον μαρτυρῆσαι κατὰ
τοὺς τότε συνέβη διωγμούς. Κοδράτου δὲ μετὰ 3
τὸν μαρτυρήσαντα Πούπλιον καταστάντος αὐτῶν
ἐπισκόπου μέμνηται, ἐπιμαρτυρῶν ὡς διὰ τῆς
αὐτοῦ σπουδῆς ἐπισυναχθέντων καὶ τῆς πίστεως
Acts 17, 34 ἀναζωπύρησιν εἰληχότων· δηλοῖ δ' ἐπὶ τούτοις ὡς
καὶ Διονύσιος ὁ Ἀρεοπαγίτης ὑπὸ τοῦ ἀποστόλου
Παύλου προτραπεὶς ἐπὶ τὴν πίστιν κατὰ τὰ ἐν
ταῖς Πράξεσιν δεδηλωμένα, πρῶτος τῆς Ἀθήνησι
παροικίας τὴν ἐπισκοπὴν ἐγκεχείριστο. ἄλλη δ' 4
ἐπιστολή τις αὐτοῦ πρὸς Νικομηδέας φέρεται,
ἐν ᾗ τὴν Μαρκίωνος αἵρεσιν πολεμῶν τῷ τῆς
ἀληθείας παρίσταται κανόνι. καὶ τῇ ἐκκλησίᾳ 5
δὲ τῇ παροικούσῃ Γόρτυναν ἅμα ταῖς λοιπαῖς
κατὰ Κρήτην παροικίαις ἐπιστείλας, Φίλιππον
ἐπίσκοπον αὐτῶν ἀποδέχεται ἅτε δὴ ἐπὶ πλείσταις
μαρτυρουμένης ἀνδραγαθίαις τῆς ὑπ' αὐτὸν ἐκ-
378

cussing the so-called Apocrypha, he relates that some of them were fabricated by certain heretics in his own time. But we must now pass on to another writer.

XXIII. Concerning Dionysius it must first be said that he was appointed to the throne of the episcopate of the diocese of Corinth, and that he communicated his divine industry ungrudgingly not only to those under him but also to those at a distance, rendering himself most useful to all in the general epistles which he drew up for the churches.[1] Among them the letter to the Lacedaemonians is an instruction in orthodoxy on the subject of peace and unity, and the letter to the Athenians is a call to faith and to life according to the gospel, and for despising this he rebukes them as all but apostates from the truth since the martyrdom of Publius,[2] their leader, in the persecution of that time. He mentions that Quadratus was appointed their bishop after the martyrdom of Publius and testifies that through his zeal they had been brought together and received a revival of their faith. Moreover, he mentions that Dionysius the Areopagite was converted by the Apostle Paul to the faith, according to the narrative in the Acts, and was the first to be appointed to the bishopric of the diocese of Athens. There is another extant letter of his to the Nicomedians in which he combats the heresy of Marcion and compares it with the rule of the truth. He also wrote to the church sojourning in Gortyna together with the other Cretan dioceses, and welcomes their bishop Philip for the reputation

---

[1] None of his writings are extant.
[2] Nothing more is known of this Publius.

κλησίας, τήν τε τῶν αἱρετικῶν διαστροφὴν ὑπο
μιμνήσκει φυλάττεσθαι. καὶ τῇ ἐκκλησίᾳ δὲ τῇ 6
παροικούσῃ Ἄμαστριν ἅμα ταῖς κατὰ Πόντον
ἐπιστείλας, Βακχυλίδου μὲν καὶ Ἐλπίστου ὡς ἂν
αὐτὸν ἐπὶ τὸ γράψαι προτρεψάντων μέμνηται,
γραφῶν τε θείων ἐξηγήσεις παρατέθειται, ἐπί
σκοπον αὐτῶν ὀνόματι Πάλμαν ὑποσημαίνων·
πολλὰ δὲ περὶ γάμου καὶ ἁγνείας τοῖς αὐτοῖς
παραινεῖ, καὶ τοὺς ἐξ οἵας δ᾽ οὖν ἀποπτώσεως,
εἴτε πλημμελείας εἴτε μὴν αἱρετικῆς πλάνης,
ἐπιστρέφοντας δεξιοῦσθαι προστάττει. ταύταις 7
ἄλλη ἐγκατείλεκται πρὸς Κνωσίους ἐπιστολή, ἐν
ᾗ Πινυτὸν τῆς παροικίας ἐπίσκοπον παρακαλεῖ
Matt. 11, 30 μὴ βαρὺ φορτίον ἐπάναγκες τὸ περὶ ἁγνείας τοῖς
ἀδελφοῖς ἐπιτιθέναι, τῆς δὲ τῶν πολλῶν κατα
στοχάζεσθαι ἀσθενείας· πρὸς ἣν ὁ Πινυτὸς ἀντι 8
γράφων, θαυμάζει μὲν καὶ ἀποδέχεται τὸν Διονύσιον,
1 Cor. 3, 1. 2
Heb. 5, 12-14 ἀντιπαρακαλεῖ δὲ στερροτέρας ἤδη ποτὲ μεταδιδόναι
τροφῆς, τελειοτέροις γράμμασιν εἰς αὖθις τὸν παρ᾽
αὐτῷ λαὸν ὑποθρέψαντα, ὡς μὴ διὰ τέλους τοῖς
γαλακτώδεσιν ἐνδιατρίβοντες λόγοις τῇ νηπιώδει
ἀγωγῇ λάθοιεν καταγηράσαντες· δι᾽ ἧς ἐπιστολῆς
καὶ ἡ τοῦ Πινυτοῦ περὶ τὴν πίστιν ὀρθοδοξία τε
καὶ φροντὶς τῆς τῶν ὑπηκόων ὠφελείας τό τε
λόγιον καὶ ἡ περὶ τὰ θεῖα σύνεσις ὡς δι᾽ ἀκρι
βεστάτης ἀναδείκνυται εἰκόνος.

Ἔτι τοῦ Διονυσίου καὶ πρὸς Ῥωμαίους ἐπι 9
στολὴ φέρεται, ἐπισκόπῳ τῷ τότε Σωτῆρι προσ
φωνοῦσα· ἐξ ἧς οὐδὲν οἷον τὸ καὶ παραθέσθαι
λέξεις δι᾽ ὧν τὸ μέχρι τοῦ καθ᾽ ἡμᾶς διωγμοῦ
φυλαχθὲν Ῥωμαίων ἔθος ἀποδεχόμενος ταῦτα
γράφει· “ ἐξ ἀρχῆς γὰρ ὑμῖν ἔθος ἐστὶν τοῦτο, 10

of the church in his charge for many noble acts, and he enjoins care against heretical error. He also wrote to the church sojourning in Amastris, together with the churches in Pontus, and mentions that Bacchylides and Elpistus had urged him to write ; he adduces interpretations of the divine scriptures, and mentions by name their bishop Palmas. He gave them many exhortations about marriage and chastity, and orders them to receive those who are converted from any backsliding, whether of conduct or heretical error. To this list has been added another epistle to Cnossus, in which he exhorts Pinytos, the bishop of the diocese, not to put on the brethren a heavy compulsory burden concerning chastity and to consider the weaknesses of the many. To this Pinytos replied that he admired and welcomed Dionysius, but exhorted him in turn to provide at some time more solid food, and to nourish the people under him with another more advanced letter, so that they might not be fed continually on milky words, and be caught unaware by old age while still treated as children. In this letter the orthodoxy of Pinytos in the faith, his care for those under him, his learning and theological understanding are shown as in a most accurate image.

There is, moreover, extant a letter of Dionysius to the Romans addressed to Soter who was then bishop, and there is nothing better than to quote the words in which he welcomes the custom of the Romans, which was observed down to the persecution in our own times. " This has been your custom from the be-

πάντας μὲν ἀδελφοὺς ποικίλως εὐεργετεῖν ἐκκλησίαις τε πολλαῖς ταῖς κατὰ πᾶσαν πόλιν ἐφόδια πέμπειν, ὧδε μὲν τὴν τῶν δεομένων πενίαν ἀναψύχοντας, ἐν μετάλλοις δὲ ἀδελφοῖς ὑπάρχουσιν ἐπιχορηγοῦντας δι' ὧν πέμπετε ἀρχῆθεν ἐφοδίων πατροπαράδοτον ἔθος Ῥωμαίων Ῥωμαῖοι φυλάττοντες, ὃ οὐ μόνον διατετήρηκεν ὁ μακάριος ὑμῶν ἐπίσκοπος Σωτήρ, ἀλλὰ καὶ ηὔξηκεν, ἐπιχορηγῶν μὲν τὴν διαπεμπομένην δαψίλειαν τὴν εἰς τοὺς ἁγίους, λόγοις δὲ μακαρίοις τοὺς ἀνιόντας ἀδελφούς, ὡς τέκνα πατὴρ φιλόστοργος, παρακαλῶν.''

Ἐν αὐτῇ δὲ ταύτῃ καὶ τῆς Κλήμεντος πρὸς 11 Κορινθίους μέμνηται ἐπιστολῆς, δηλῶν ἀνέκαθεν ἐξ ἀρχαίου ἔθους ἐπὶ τῆς ἐκκλησίας τὴν ἀνάγνωσιν αὐτῆς ποιεῖσθαι· λέγει γοῦν· ''τὴν σήμερον οὖν κυριακὴν ἁγίαν ἡμέραν διηγάγομεν, ἐν ᾗ ἀνέγνωμεν ὑμῶν τὴν ἐπιστολήν, ἣν ἕξομεν ἀεί ποτε ἀναγινώσκοντες νουθετεῖσθαι, ὡς καὶ τὴν προτέραν ἡμῖν διὰ Κλήμεντος γραφεῖσαν.''

Ἔτι δ' ὁ αὐτὸς καὶ περὶ τῶν ἰδίων ἐπιστολῶν 12 ὡς ῥαδιουργηθεισῶν ταῦτά φησιν· ''ἐπιστολὰς γὰρ Matt. 13, 25 ἀδελφῶν ἀξιωσάντων με γράψαι ἔγραψα. καὶ ταύτας οἱ τοῦ διαβόλου ἀπόστολοι ζιζανίων Rev. 22, 18, γεγέμικαν, ἃ μὲν ἐξαιροῦντες, ἃ δὲ προστιθέντες· 19 οἷς τὸ οὐαὶ κεῖται. οὐ θαυμαστὸν ἄρα εἰ καὶ τῶν κυριακῶν ῥαδιουργῆσαί τινες ἐπιβέβληνται γραφῶν, ὁπότε καὶ ταῖς οὐ τοιαύταις ἐπιβεβουλεύκασιν.''

Καὶ ἄλλη δέ τις παρὰ ταύτας ἐπιστολὴ τοῦ 13 Διονυσίου φέρεται Χρυσοφόρᾳ πιστοτάτῃ ἀδελφῇ

---

[1] The mines were constantly used by the Romans as convict establishments, as work in them was regarded as unfit even for slaves.

ginning, to do good in manifold ways to all Christians, and to send contributions to the many churches in every city, in some places relieving the poverty of the needy, and ministering to the Christians in the mines,[1] by the contribution which you have sent from the beginning, preserving the ancestral custom of the Romans, true Romans as you are. Your blessed bishop Soter has not only carried on this habit but has even increased it, by administering the bounty distributed to the saints and by exhorting with his blessed words the brethren who come to Rome, as a loving father would his children."

In this same letter he also quotes the letter of Clement to the Corinthians, showing that from the beginning it had been the custom to read it in the church. "To-day we observed the holy day of the Lord, and read out your letter, which we shall continue to read from time to time for our admonition, as we do with that which was formerly sent to us through Clement."[2]

The same writer speaks as follows about the falsification of his own letters. "When Christians asked me to write letters I wrote them, and the apostles of the devil have filled them with tares, by leaving out some things and putting in others. But woe awaits them. Therefore it is no wonder that some have gone about to falsify even the scriptures of the Lord when they have plotted against writings so inferior."

Besides these there is extant another letter of Dionysius to Chrysophora, a most faithful Christian,

---

[2] It is to be noticed that Dionysius regards both the letter of Soter and the letter of Clement as coming from the church of Rome of which they are the first and second epistles. There is much to be said for A. von Harnack's view that the letter which we call II. Clement is really the letter of Soter.

ἐπιστείλαντος, ᾗ τὰ κατάλληλα γράφων, τῆς
προσηκούσης καὶ αὐτῇ μετεδίδου λογικῆς τροφῆς.
καὶ τὰ μὲν τοῦ Διονυσίου τοσαῦτα.

XXIV. Τοῦ δὲ Θεοφίλου, ὃν τῆς Ἀντιοχέων 1
ἐκκλησίας ἐπίσκοπον δεδηλώκαμεν, τρία τὰ πρὸς
Αὐτόλυκον στοιχειώδη φέρεται συγγράμματα, καὶ
ἄλλο Πρὸς τὴν αἵρεσιν Ἑρμογένους τὴν ἐπιγραφὴν
ἔχον, ἐν ᾧ ἐκ τῆς Ἀποκαλύψεως Ἰωάννου κέχρηται
μαρτυρίαις· καὶ ἕτερα δέ τινα κατηχητικὰ αὐτοῦ
φέρεται βιβλία. τῶν γε μὴν αἱρετικῶν οὐ χεῖρον

Matt. 13, 25 καὶ τότε ζιζανίων δίκην λυμαινομένων τὸν εἰλικρινῆ
τῆς ἀποστολικῆς διδασκαλίας σπόρον, οἱ παν-
ταχόσε τῶν ἐκκλησιῶν ποιμένες, ὥσπερ τινὰς
θῆρας ἀγρίους τῶν Χριστοῦ προβάτων ἀποσο-
βοῦντες, αὐτοὺς ἀνεῖργον τοτὲ μὲν ταῖς πρὸς τοὺς
ἀδελφοὺς νουθεσίαις καὶ παραινέσεσιν, τοτὲ δὲ
πρὸς αὐτοὺς γυμνότερον ἀποδυόμενοι, ἀγράφοις
τε εἰς πρόσωπον ζητήσεσι καὶ ἀνατροπαῖς, ἤδη
δὲ καὶ δι' ἐγγράφων ὑπομνημάτων τὰς δόξας
αὐτῶν ἀκριβεστάτοις ἐλέγχοις διευθύνοντες. ὅ γέ
τοι Θεόφιλος σὺν τοῖς ἄλλοις κατὰ τούτων στρα-
τευσάμενος δῆλός ἐστιν ἀπό τινος οὐκ ἀγεννῶς
αὐτῷ κατὰ Μαρκίωνος πεπονημένου λόγου, ὃς
καὶ αὐτὸς μεθ' ὧν ἄλλων εἰρήκαμεν εἰς ἔτι νῦν
διασέσωσται. τοῦτον μὲν οὖν ἕβδομος ἀπὸ τῶν
ἀποστόλων τῆς Ἀντιοχέων ἐκκλησίας διαδέχεται
Μαξιμῖνος.

XXV. Φίλιππός γε μήν, ὃν ἐκ τῶν Διονυσίου 1
φωνῶν τῆς ἐν Γορτύνῃ παροικίας ἐπίσκοπον ἔγνωμεν, πάνυ γε σπουδαιότατον πεποίηται καὶ αὐτὸς
κατὰ Μαρκίωνος λόγον, Εἰρηναῖός τε ὡσαύτως καὶ
Μόδεστος, ὃς καὶ διαφερόντως παρὰ τοὺς ἄλλους
384

in which he writes to her, suitably imparting to her the proper spiritual food. Such are the facts about Dionysius.

XXIV. Of Theophilus, whom we have mentioned as bishop of the church of the Antiochians, three elementary treatises are extant, addressed to Autolycus, and another with the title, *Against the Heresy of Hermogenes*, in which he has quoted the Apocalypse of John, and there are also extant some other books of his on instruction. Heretics were even then no less defiling the pure seed of apostolic teaching like tares, and the shepherds of the churches in every place, as though driving off wild beasts from Christ's sheep, excluded them at one time by rebukes and exhortations to the brethren, at another by their more complete exposure, by unwritten and personal inquiry and conversation, and ultimately correcting their opinions by accurate arguments in written treatises. It is clear that Theophilus joined with the others in this campaign against them from a noble treatise which he made against Marcion, which has been preserved until now with the others that we have mentioned. His successor in the church of the Antiochians was Maximinus, seventh from the apostles.

XXV. Philip, whom we know from the words of Dionysius as bishop of the diocese in Gortyna, also made a most excellent treatise against Marcion. Irenaeus, likewise, and Modestus,[1] who excels beyond

---

[1] Nothing more is known of Modestus, though Jerome appears to have been acquainted with his writings (*De vir. ill.* 32).

τὴν τοῦ ἀνδρὸς εἰς ἔκδηλον τοῖς πᾶσιν κατεφώρασε
πλάνην, καὶ ἄλλοι δὲ πλείους, ὧν παρὰ πλείστοις
τῶν ἀδελφῶν εἰς ἔτι νῦν οἱ πόνοι διαφυλάττονται.

XXVI. Ἐπὶ τῶνδε καὶ Μελίτων τῆς ἐν Σάρδεσιν 1
παροικίας ἐπίσκοπος Ἀπολινάριός τε τῆς ἐν
Ἱεραπόλει διαπρεπῶς ἤκμαζον, οἳ καὶ τῷ δηλωθέντι κατὰ τοὺς χρόνους Ῥωμαίων βασιλεῖ λόγους
ὑπὲρ τῆς πίστεως ἰδίως ἑκάτερος ἀπολογίας
προσεφώνησαν.   τούτων εἰς ἡμετέραν γνῶσιν 2
ἀφῖκται τὰ ὑποτεταγμένα· Μελίτωνος, τὰ Περὶ
τοῦ πάσχα δύο καὶ τὸ Περὶ πολιτείας καὶ προφητῶν
καὶ ὁ Περὶ ἐκκλησίας καὶ ὁ Περὶ κυριακῆς λόγος,
ἔτι δὲ ὁ Περὶ πίστεως ἀνθρώπου καὶ ὁ Περὶ
Heb. 5, 14 πλάσεως, καὶ ὁ Περὶ ὑπακοῆς πίστεως [καὶ Περὶ]
αἰσθητηρίων καὶ πρὸς τούτοις ὁ Περὶ ψυχῆς καὶ
σώματος [ἡ γένοισ] καὶ ὁ Περὶ λουτροῦ καὶ Περὶ
ἀληθείας καὶ Περὶ πίστεως καὶ γενέσεως Χριστοῦ
καὶ λόγος αὐτοῦ προφητείας καὶ Περὶ ψυχῆς καὶ
σώματος καὶ ὁ Περὶ φιλοξενίας καὶ ἡ Κλεὶς καὶ
τὰ Περὶ τοῦ διαβόλου καὶ τῆς Ἀποκαλύψεως
Ἰωάννου καὶ ὁ Περὶ ἐνσωμάτου θεοῦ, ἐπὶ πᾶσι
καὶ τὸ Πρὸς Ἀντωνῖνον βιβλίδιον.

Ἐν μὲν οὖν τῷ Περὶ τοῦ πάσχα τὸν χρόνον καθ' 3
ὃν συνέταττεν, ἀρχόμενος σημαίνει ἐν τούτοις·
"ἐπὶ Σερουιλλίου Παύλου ἀνθυπάτου τῆς Ἀσίας,
ᾧ Σάγαρις καιρῷ ἐμαρτύρησεν, ἐγένετο ζήτησις

---

[1] Marcus Aurelius (A.D. 161-180).
[2] This conjecture seems necessary and was made by
Rufinus and Jerome, but the words bracketed in Greek
are omitted in all the Greek manuscripts.
[3] Some Greek manuscripts add " or mind " and others
three words which make no sense. The most probable

the rest in exposing to everyone the man's error, did the same, and there are many others, too, whose works are still preserved among many Christians.

XXVI. In their time, too, Melito, bishop of the diocese of Sardis, and Apolinarius, bishop of Hierapolis, were at the height of their fame, and each addressed apologetic arguments of their own to the emperor [1] of the Romans of that day, who has been already mentioned. The following of their works have come to our knowledge. Of Melito two books *On the Passover*, a treatise *On Christian Life and the Prophets*, *On the Church*, and *On the Lord's Day*; besides these *On the Faith of Man*, and *On Creation*, and *On the Obedience of Faith*, and *On the Senses* [2]; besides these, *On the Soul and Body*,[3] and *On Baptism* and *Truth* and *Faith and Christ's Birth*,[4] and a treatise of his prophecy [5] and *On Soul and Body*, and *On Hospitality*, and the *Key*, and the books *On the Devil* and the *Apocalypse of John*, and *On God Incarnate*; above all, the little book *To Antoninus*.[6]

At the beginning of the book *On the Passover* he indicates the time at which he was composing it as follows : " In the time of Servillius Paulus,[7] proconsul, of Asia, at the time when Sagaris was martyred,

solution is that of M'Giffert who thinks that " or mind " is a gloss upon the word " soul."

[4] These appear to be the chapters of a single book.

[5] Such must be the meaning of the Greek, but a περί may have dropped out by accident. It is found in some MSS., but probably only as an emendation.

[6] *i.e.* Antoninus Verus, usually called Marcus Aurelius.

[7] Servilius Paulus is not known, but Rufinus emended the name to Sergius Paulus, who was consul for the second time in 168, and may have been proconsul of Asia about 164-166. See Waddington, *Fastes des provinces asiatiques*, and McGiffert's note *ad loc.*

πολλὴ ἐν Λαοδικείᾳ περὶ τοῦ πάσχα, ἐμπεσόντος
κατὰ καιρὸν ἐν ἐκείναις ταῖς ἡμέραις, καὶ ἐγράφη
ταῦτα." τούτου δὲ τοῦ λόγου μέμνηται Κλήμης
ὁ Ἀλεξανδρεὺς ἐν ἰδίῳ Περὶ τοῦ πάσχα λόγῳ, ὃν
ὡς ἐξ αἰτίας τῆς τοῦ Μελίτωνος γραφῆς φησιν
ἑαυτὸν συντάξαι. ἐν δὲ τῷ πρὸς τὸν αὐτοκράτορα
βιβλίῳ τοιαῦτά τινα καθ' ἡμῶν ἐπ' αὐτοῦ γεγονέναι
ἱστορεῖ· "τὸ γὰρ οὐδεπώποτε γενόμενον, νῦν
διώκεται τὸ τῶν θεοσεβῶν γένος καινοῖς ἐλαυ-
νόμενον δόγμασιν κατὰ τὴν Ἀσίαν. οἱ γὰρ ἀναι-
δεῖς συκοφάνται καὶ τῶν ἀλλοτρίων ἐρασταὶ τὴν
ἐκ τῶν διαταγμάτων ἔχοντες ἀφορμήν, φανερῶς
λῃστεύουσι, νύκτωρ καὶ μεθ' ἡμέραν διαρπάζοντες
τοὺς μηδὲν ἀδικοῦντας." καὶ μεθ' ἕτερά φησιν·
"καὶ εἰ μὲν σοῦ κελεύσαντος τοῦτο πράττεται,
ἔστω καλῶς γινόμενον· δίκαιος γὰρ βασιλεὺς οὐκ
ἂν ἀδίκως βουλεύσαιτο πώποτε, καὶ ἡμεῖς ἡδέως
φέρομεν τοῦ τοιούτου θανάτου τὸ γέρας· ταύτην
δέ σοι μόνην προσφέρομεν δέησιν ἵνα αὐτὸς
πρότερον ἐπιγνοὺς τοὺς τῆς τοιαύτης φιλονεικίας
ἐργάτας, δικαίως κρίνειας εἰ ἄξιοι θανάτου καὶ
τιμωρίας ἢ σωτηρίας καὶ ἡσυχίας εἰσίν. εἰ δὲ
παρὰ σοῦ μὴ εἴη ἡ βουλὴ αὕτη καὶ τὸ καινὸν τοῦτο
διάταγμα, ὃ μηδὲ κατὰ βαρβάρων πρέπει πολεμίων,
πολὺ μᾶλλον δεόμεθά σου μὴ περιιδεῖν ἡμᾶς ἐν
τοιαύτῃ δημώδει λεηλασίᾳ." τούτοις αὖθις ἐπιφέρει λέγων· "ἡ γὰρ καθ' ἡμᾶς φιλοσοφία πρότερον μὲν ἐν βαρβάροις ἤκμασεν, ἐπανθήσασα δὲ
τοῖς σοῖς ἔθνεσιν κατὰ τὴν Αὐγούστου τοῦ σοῦ
προγόνου μεγάλην ἀρχήν, ἐγενήθη μάλιστα τῇ
σῇ βασιλείᾳ αἴσιον ἀγαθόν. ἔκτοτε γὰρ εἰς μέγα
καὶ λαμπρὸν τὸ Ῥωμαίων ηὐξήθη κράτος· οὗ σὺ

there was a great discussion about the Passover, which fell according to the season in those days, and this was written." Clement of Alexandria quotes this treatise in his own *On the Passover*, which he says that he compiled in consequence of the writing of Melito. And in the book to the emperor he relates that in his time we were treated as follows : " It has never before happened as it is now that the race of the religious should be persecuted and driven about by new decrees throughout Asia. For shameless informers and lovers of other people's property have taken advantage of the decrees, and pillage us openly, harrying night and day those who have done nothing wrong." And after other points he says: " And if this is done as your command, let it be assumed that it is well done, for no righteous king would ever have an unrighteous policy, and we gladly bear the honour of such death. But we submit to you this single request, that you will first take cognizance yourself of the authors of such strife, and judge righteously whether they are worthy of death and punishment, or of acquittal and immunity. But, if it be not from you that there comes this counsel and this new decree (and it would be improper even against barbarian enemies), we beseech you all the more not to neglect us in this brigandage by a mob." He then continues as follows : " Our philosophy first grew up among the barbarians, but its full flower came among your nation in the great reign of your ancestor Augustus, and became an omen of good to your empire, for from that time the power of the Romans became great and splendid. You are now his

διάδοχος εὐκταῖος γέγονάς τε καὶ ἔσῃ μετὰ τοῦ παιδός, φυλάσσων τῆς βασιλείας τὴν σύντροφον καὶ συναρξαμένην Αὐγούστῳ φιλοσοφίαν, ἣν καὶ οἱ πρόγονοί σου πρὸς ταῖς ἄλλαις θρησκείαις ἐτίμησαν, καὶ τοῦτο μέγιστον τεκμήριον τοῦ πρὸς ἀγαθοῦ τὸν καθ' ἡμᾶς λόγον συνακμάσαι τῇ καλῶς ἀρξαμένῃ βασιλείᾳ, ἐκ τοῦ μηδὲν φαῦλον ἀπὸ τῆς Αὐγούστου ἀρχῆς ἀπαντῆσαι, ἀλλὰ τοὐναντίον ἅπαντα λαμπρὰ καὶ ἔνδοξα κατὰ τὰς πάντων εὐχάς. μόνοι πάντων, ἀναπεισθέντες ὑπό τινων βασκάνων ἀνθρώπων, τὸν καθ' ἡμᾶς ἐν διαβολῇ καταστῆσαι λόγον ἠθέλησαν Νέρων καὶ Δομετιανός, ἀφ' ὧν καὶ τὸ τῆς συκοφαντίας ἀλόγῳ συνηθείᾳ περὶ τοὺς τοιούτους ῥυῆναι συμβέβηκεν ψεῦδος· ἀλλὰ τὴν ἐκείνων ἄγνοιαν οἱ σοὶ εὐσεβεῖς πατέρες ἐπηνωρθώσαντο, πολλάκις πολλοῖς ἐπιπλήξαντες ἐγγράφως, ὅσοι περὶ τούτων νεωτερίσαι ἐτόλμησαν· ἐν οἷς ὁ μὲν πάππος σου Ἀδριανὸς πολλοῖς μὲν καὶ ἄλλοις, καὶ Φουνδανῷ δὲ τῷ ἀνθυπάτῳ, ἡγουμένῳ δὲ τῆς Ἀσίας, γράφων φαίνεται, ὁ δὲ πατήρ σου, καὶ σοῦ τὰ σύμπαντα διοικοῦντος αὐτῷ, ταῖς πόλεσι περὶ τοῦ μηδὲν νεωτερίζειν περὶ ἡμῶν ἔγραψεν, ἐν οἷς καὶ πρὸς Λαρισαίους καὶ πρὸς Θεσσαλονικεῖς καὶ Ἀθηναίους καὶ πρὸς πάντας Ἕλληνας. σὲ δὲ καὶ μᾶλλον περὶ τούτων τὴν αὐτὴν ἐκείνοις ἔχοντα γνώμην καὶ πολύ γε φιλανθρωποτέραν καὶ φιλοσοφωτέραν, πεπείσμεθα πάντα πράσσειν ὅσα σου δεόμεθα.''

Ἀλλὰ ταῦτα μὲν ἐν τῷ δηλωθέντι τέθειται λόγῳ· ἐν δὲ ταῖς γραφείσαις αὐτῷ Ἐκλογαῖς ὁ

happy successor, and shall be so along with your son,[1] if you protect the philosophy which grew up with the empire and began with Augustus. Your ancestors nourished it together with the other cults, and the greatest proof that our doctrine flourished for good along with the empire in its noble beginning is the fact that it met no evil in the reign of Augustus, but on the contrary everything splendid and glorious according to the wishes of all men.[2] The only emperors who were ever persuaded by malicious men to slander our teaching were Nero and Domitian, and from them arose the lie, and the unreasonable custom of falsely accusing Christians. But their ignorance was corrected by your pious fathers, who wrote many rebukes to many, whenever any dared to take new measures against Christians. Your grandfather Hadrian shows this in his letters to many, and especially to the proconsul Fundanus, the governor of Asia, and your father, while you were joined with him [3] in the administration of the world, wrote to the cities that no new measures should be taken concerning us. Among these are letters to the Larisians and to the Thessalonians and the Athenians and to all the Greeks. Since you hold the same opinion about them and, indeed, one which is far kinder and more philosophic, we are persuaded of your doing all which we beg of you."

These words are found in the treatise quoted, but in the *Extracts* which he wrote the same writer begins

---

[1] The Emperor and his son are Marcus Aurelius and his son the Emperor Commodus.

[2] The defect in this argument is that Augustus was dead some time before the foundation of the Christian church.

[3] Translating Wilamowitz's emendation συνδιοικοῦντος, which must be right for Melito, even if not for Eusebius.

αὐτὸς κατὰ τὸ προοίμιον ἀρχόμενος τῶν ὁμολογουμένων τῆς παλαιᾶς διαθήκης γραφῶν ποιεῖται
κατάλογον· ὃν καὶ ἀναγκαῖον ἐνταῦθα καταλέξαι,
γράφει δὲ οὕτως· " Μελίτων Ὀνησίμῳ τῷ ἀδελφῷ 1
χαίρειν. ἐπειδὴ πολλάκις ἠξίωσας, σπουδῇ τῇ
πρὸς τὸν λόγον χρώμενος, γενέσθαι σοι ἐκλογὰς
ἔκ τε τοῦ νόμου καὶ τῶν προφητῶν περὶ τοῦ
σωτῆρος καὶ πάσης τῆς πίστεως ἡμῶν, ἔτι δὲ
καὶ μαθεῖν τὴν τῶν παλαιῶν βιβλίων ἐβουλήθης
ἀκρίβειαν πόσα τὸν ἀριθμὸν καὶ ὁποῖα τὴν τάξιν
εἶεν, ἐσπούδασα τὸ τοιοῦτο πρᾶξαι, ἐπιστάμενός
σου τὸ σπουδαῖον περὶ τὴν πίστιν καὶ φιλομαθὲς
περὶ τὸν λόγον ὅτι τε μάλιστα πάντων πόθῳ τῷ
πρὸς τὸν θεὸν ταῦτα προκρίνεις, περὶ τῆς αἰωνίου
σωτηρίας ἀγωνιζόμενος. ἀνελθὼν οὖν εἰς τὴν 1
ἀνατολὴν καὶ ἕως τοῦ τόπου γενόμενος ἔνθα
ἐκηρύχθη καὶ ἐπράχθη, καὶ ἀκριβῶς μαθὼν τὰ
τῆς παλαιᾶς διαθήκης βιβλία, ὑποτάξας ἔπεμψά
σοι· ὧν ἐστι τὰ ὀνόματα· Μωυσέως πέντε, Γένεσις
Ἔξοδος Ἀριθμοὶ Λευιτικὸν Δευτερονόμιον, Ἰησοῦς
Ναυῆ, Κριταί, Ῥούθ, Βασιλειῶν τέσσαρα, Παρα-
λειπομένων δύο, Ψαλμῶν Δαυίδ, Σολομῶνος
Παροιμίαι ἡ καὶ Σοφία, Ἐκκλησιαστής, Ἄισμα
Ἀισμάτων, Ἰώβ, Προφητῶν Ἡσαΐου Ἰερεμίου
τῶν δώδεκα ἐν μονοβίβλῳ Δανιήλ, Ἰεζεκιήλ,
Ἔσδρας· ἐξ ὧν καὶ τὰς ἐκλογὰς ἐποιησάμην, εἰς
ἓξ βιβλία διελών." καὶ τὰ μὲν τοῦ Μελίτωνος
τοσαῦτα.

XXVII. Τοῦ δ' Ἀπολιναρίου πολλῶν παρὰ 1
πολλοῖς σῳζομένων τὰ εἰς ἡμᾶς ἐλθόντα ἐστὶν τάδε·
λόγος ὁ πρὸς τὸν προειρημένον βασιλέα καὶ Πρὸς
Ἕλληνας συγγράμματα πέντε καὶ Περὶ ἀληθείας

in his preface by making a list of the recognized scriptures of the Old Testament, which it is necessary to enumerate here, and he writes as follows : " Melito to Onesimus his brother, greeting. Since you often desired, in your zeal for the true word, to have extracts from the Law and the Prophets concerning the Saviour, and concerning all our faith, and, moreover, since you wished to know the accurate facts about the ancient writings, how many they are in number, and what is their order, I have taken pains to do thus, for I know your zeal for the faith and interest in the word, and that in your struggle for eternal salvation you esteem these things more highly than all else in your love towards God. Accordingly when I came to the east and reached the place where these things were preached and done, and learnt accurately the books of the Old Testament, I set down the facts and sent them to you. These are their names : five books of Moses, Genesis, Exodus, Numbers, Leviticus, Deuteronomy, Joshua the son of Nun, Judges, Ruth, four books of Kingdoms, two books of Chronicles, the Psalms of David, the Proverbs of Solomon and his Wisdom, Ecclesiastes, the Song of Songs, Job, the prophets Isaiah, Jeremiah, the Twelve in a single book, Daniel, Ezekiel, Ezra. From these I have made extracts and compiled them in six books." Such are the facts about Melito.

XXVII. Of the many writings of Apolinarius which have been widely preserved the following have reached us : A treatise to the above mentioned emperor,[1] five books *Against the Greeks*, and books one and two *On the Truth*, one and two *Against the*

---

[1] Marcus Aurelius.

α′ β′ καὶ Πρὸς Ἰουδαίους α′ β′ καὶ ἃ μετὰ ταῦτα
συνέγραψε κατὰ τῆς τῶν Φρυγῶν αἱρέσεως, μετ'
οὐ πολὺν καινοτομηθείσης χρόνον, τότε γε μὴν
ὥσπερ ἐκφύειν ἀρχομένης, ἔτι τοῦ Μοντανοῦ ἅμα
ταῖς αὐτοῦ ψευδοπροφήτισιν ἀρχὰς τῆς παρεκ-
τροπῆς ποιουμένου.

XXVIII. Καὶ Μουσανοῦ δέ, ὃν ἐν τοῖς φθάσασιν [1]
κατελέξαμεν, φέρεταί τις ἐπιστρεπτικώτατος λόγος,
πρός τινας αὐτῷ γραφεὶς ἀδελφοὺς ἀποκλίναντας ἐπὶ
τὴν τῶν λεγομένων Ἐγκρατιτῶν αἵρεσιν, ἄρτι
τότε φύειν ἀρχομένην ξένην τε καὶ φθοριμαίαν
ψευδοδοξίαν εἰσάγουσαν τῷ βίῳ· XXIX. ἧς παρεκ- [1]
τροπῆς ἀρχηγὸν καταστῆναι Τατιανὸν λόγος ἔχει,
οὗ μικρῷ πρόσθεν τὰς περὶ τοῦ θαυμασίου Ἰουστίνου
παρατεθείμεθα λέξεις, μαθητὴν αὐτὸν ἱστοροῦντες
τοῦ μάρτυρος. δηλοῖ δὲ τοῦτο Εἰρηναῖος ἐν τῷ
πρώτῳ τῶν Πρὸς τὰς αἱρέσεις, ὁμοῦ τά τε περὶ
αὐτοῦ καὶ τῆς κατ' αὐτὸν αἱρέσεως οὕτω γράφων·

Iren. 1, 28, 1 " ἀπὸ Σατορνίνου καὶ Μαρκίωνος οἱ καλούμενοι [2]
Ἐγκρατεῖς ἀγαμίαν ἐκήρυξαν, ἀθετοῦντες τὴν
ἀρχαίαν πλάσιν τοῦ θεοῦ καὶ ἠρέμα κατηγοροῦντες
τοῦ ἄρρεν καὶ θῆλυ εἰς γένεσιν ἀνθρώπων πεποιη-
κότος, καὶ τῶν λεγομένων παρ' αὐτοῖς ἐμψύχων
ἀποχὴν εἰσηγήσαντο, ἀχαριστοῦντες τῷ πάντα
πεποιηκότι θεῷ, ἀντιλέγουσί τε τῇ τοῦ πρωτο-
πλάστου σωτηρίᾳ. καὶ τοῦτο νῦν ἐξευρέθη παρ' [3]
αὐτοῖς Τατιανοῦ τινος πρώτως ταύτην εἰσενέγ-
καντος τὴν βλασφημίαν· ὃς Ἰουστίνου ἀκροατὴς
γεγονώς, ἐφ' ὅσον μὲν συνῆν ἐκείνῳ, οὐδὲν ἐξ-
έφηνεν τοιοῦτον, μετὰ δὲ τὴν ἐκείνου μαρτυρίαν

---

[1] See book v. 14-19 (pp. 470-94)
[2] Their name was derived from the Greek ἐγκράτεια,

Jews, and after this the treatises which he wrote against the heresy of the Phrygians, which had begun its innovations not long before and was then, as it were, beginning to sprout, while Montanus with his false prophetesses[1] was making the beginnings of the error.

XXVIII. And of Musanus, whom we have mentioned in a previous passage, there is extant a certain very eloquent discourse which he wrote to some Christians who had fallen away to the heresy of the so-called Encratites,[2] which was at that time just beginning to sprout and to introduce into life its strange and corrupting false doctrine. XXIX. The story goes that Tatian was the author of this error, whose words we quoted a little above concerning the marvellous Justin, and related that he was a disciple of the martyr. Irenaeus states this in his first book, *Against the Heresies*, and in the same place writes thus concerning him and his heresy. "The so-called Encratites proceeding from Saturninus and Marcion preached against marriage, annulling the original creation of God, and tacitly condemning him who made male and female. They also introduced abstention from what they called ' animate ' things in ingratitude to the God who has made all things, and they deny the salvation of the first created man. This innovation was recently made by them when a certain Tatian first introduced this blasphemy. He had been a hearer of Justin but so long as he was with him, he produced nothing of this kind, but after the martyrdom of Justin he left the church, being

---

"continence," and they seem to have preached an ascetic doctrine somewhat resembling that of the later Manichaeans.

ἀποστὰς τῆς ἐκκλησίας, οἰήματι διδασκάλου ἐπ-
αρθεὶς καὶ τυφωθεὶς ὡς διαφέρων τῶν λοιπῶν, ἴδιον
χαρακτῆρα διδασκαλείου συνεστήσατο, αἰῶνάς
τινας ἀοράτους ὁμοίως τοῖς ἀπὸ Οὐαλεντίνου
μυθολογήσας γάμον τε φθορὰν καὶ πορνείαν
παραπλησίως Μαρκίωνι καὶ Σατορνίνῳ ἀναγορεύ-
σας, τῇ δὲ τοῦ Ἀδὰμ σωτηρίᾳ παρ᾽ ἑαυτοῦ τὴν
ἀντιλογίαν ποιησάμενος.'' ταῦτα μὲν ὁ Εἰρηναῖος 4
τότε· σμικρῷ δὲ ὕστερον Σευῆρός τις τοὔνομα
κρατύνας τὴν προδεδηλωμένην αἵρεσιν, αἴτιος τοῖς
ἐξ αὐτῆς ὡρμημένοις τῆς ἀπ᾽ αὐτοῦ παρηγμένης
Σευηριανῶν προσηγορίας γέγονεν. χρῶνται μὲν 5
οὖν οὗτοι νόμῳ καὶ προφήταις καὶ εὐαγγελίοις,
ἰδίως ἑρμηνεύοντες τῶν ἱερῶν τὰ νοήματα γραφῶν·
βλασφημοῦντες δὲ Παῦλον τὸν ἀπόστολον, ἀθετοῦσιν αὐτοῦ τὰς ἐπιστολάς, μηδὲ τὰς Πράξεις
τῶν ἀποστόλων καταδεχόμενοι. ὁ μέντοι γε πρό- 6
τερος αὐτῶν ἀρχηγὸς ὁ Τατιανὸς συνάφειάν τινα
καὶ συναγωγὴν οὐκ οἶδ᾽ ὅπως τῶν εὐαγγελίων
συνθείς, Τὸ διὰ τεσσάρων τοῦτο προσωνόμασεν,
ὃ καὶ παρά τισιν εἰς ἔτι νῦν φέρεται· τοῦ δ᾽ ἀποστόλου φασὶ τολμῆσαί τινας αὐτὸν μεταφράσαι φωνάς,
ὡς ἐπιδιορθούμενον αὐτῶν τὴν τῆς φράσεως
σύνταξιν. καταλέλοιπεν δὲ οὗτος πολύ τι πλῆθος 7
συγγραμμάτων, ὧν μάλιστα παρὰ πολλοῖς μνημονεύεται διαβόητος αὐτοῦ λόγος ὁ Πρὸς Ἕλληνας,
ἐν ᾧ καὶ τῶν ἀνέκαθεν χρόνων μνημονεύσας, τῶν
παρ᾽ Ἕλλησιν εὐδοκίμων ἁπάντων προγενέστερον
Μωυσέα τε καὶ τοὺς Ἑβραίων προφήτας ἀπέ-
φηνεν· ὃς δὴ καὶ δοκεῖ τῶν συγγραμμάτων ἁπάντων
αὐτοῦ κάλλιστός τε καὶ ὠφελιμώτατος ὑπάρχειν.
καὶ τὰ μὲν κατὰ τούσδε τοιαῦτα ἦν.

exalted by the idea of becoming a teacher and puffed up as superior to others. He established his own type of doctrine, telling stories of invisible Aeons, like the followers of Valentinus, and rejecting marriage as corruption and fornication similarly to Marcion and Saturninus. And as his own contribution he denied the salvation of Adam." Irenaeus wrote thus at that time. But a little later a certain man named Severus strengthened the above mentioned heresy, and is the reason why those who have sprung from it obtained the name of Severiani from him. These indeed use the Law and the Prophets and the Gospels, though they interpret the facts of the sacred scriptures in their own way, but they blaspheme the Apostle Paul, and reject his epistles and do not receive the Acts of the Apostles. Their former leader Tatian composed in some way a combination and collection of the gospels, and gave this the name of *The Diatessaron*,[1] and this is still extant in some places. And they say that he ventured to paraphrase some words of the apostle, as though correcting their style. He has left a great number of writings, of which the most famous, quoted by many, is his discourse *Against the Greeks*. In it he deals with primitive history, and shows that Moses and the prophets of the Hebrews preceded all those who are celebrated among the Greeks. This seems to be the best and most helpful of all his writings. Such are the facts of this period.

[1] See Introduction, p. lii.

XXX. Ἐπὶ δὲ τῆς αὐτῆς βασιλείας, πληθυουσῶν 1 τῶν αἱρέσεων ἐπὶ τῆς Μέσης τῶν ποταμῶν, Βαρδη- σάνης, ἱκανώτατός τις ἀνὴρ ἔν τε τῇ Σύρων φωνῇ διαλεκτικώτατος, πρὸς τοὺς κατὰ Μαρκίωνα καί τινας ἑτέρους διαφόρων προϊσταμένους δογμάτων διαλόγους συστησάμενος τῇ οἰκείᾳ παρέδωκεν γλώττῃ τε καὶ γραφῇ μετὰ καὶ πλείστων ἑτέρων αὐτοῦ συγγραμμάτων· οὓς οἱ γνώριμοι (πλεῖστοι δὲ ἦσαν αὐτῷ δυνατῶς τῷ λόγῳ παρισταμένῳ) ἐπὶ τὴν Ἑλλήνων ἀπὸ τῆς Σύρων μεταβεβλήκασι φωνῆς· ἐν οἷς ἐστιν καὶ ὁ πρὸς Ἀντωνῖνον ἱκανώ- 2 τατος αὐτοῦ Περὶ εἱμαρμένης διάλογος ὅσα τε ἄλλα φασὶν αὐτὸν προφάσει τοῦ τότε διωγμοῦ συγγράψαι. ἦν δ' οὗτος πρότερον τῆς κατὰ 3 Οὐαλεντῖνον σχολῆς, καταγνοὺς δὲ ταύτης πλεῖστά τε τῆς κατὰ τοῦτον μυθοποιίας ἀπελέγξας, ἐδόκει μέν πως αὐτὸς ἑαυτῷ ἐπὶ τὴν ὀρθοτέραν γνώμην μετατεθεῖσθαι, οὐ μὴν καὶ παντελῶς γε ἀπερρύψατο τὸν τῆς παλαιᾶς αἱρέσεως ῥύπον.

Ἐν τούτῳ γε μὴν καὶ ὁ τῆς Ῥωμαίων ἐκκλησίας ἐπίσκοπος Σωτὴρ τελευτᾷ.

XXX. In the same reign heresies increased in Mesopotamia, and Bardesanes, a most able man and skilled in Syriac, composed dialogues against the Marcionites and other leaders of various opinions, and he issued them in his own language and script, together with many other of his writings. Those who knew them, and they were many, for he was a powerful arguer, have translated them from Syriac into Greek. Among them is his very powerful dialogue with Antoninus *Concerning Fate*, and they say that he wrote many other works in consequence of the persecution of that time. He had been first a member of the Valentinians, but condemned this school and refuted many of their fables, and himself thought that he had changed to orthodox opinion, but in fact he did not completely clean off the filth of his ancient heresy.

At this time Soter, bishop of Rome, died.

Ε

Τάδε καὶ ἡ πέμπτη περιέχει βίβλος τῆς
Ἐκκλησιαστικῆς ἱστορίας

Ā Ὅσοι καὶ ὅπως κατὰ Οὐῆρον ἐπὶ τῆς Γαλλίας
τὸν ὑπὲρ τῆς εὐσεβείας διεξῆλθον ἀγῶνα.

Β̄ Ὡς οἱ θεοφιλεῖς μάρτυρες τοὺς ἐν τῷ διωγμῷ
διαπεπτωκότας ἐθεράπευον δεξιούμενοι.

Γ̄ Ὁποία τῷ μάρτυρι Ἀττάλῳ δι’ ὀνείρου
γέγονεν ἐπιφάνεια.

Δ̄ Ὅπως οἱ μάρτυρες τὸν Εἰρηναῖον δι’ ἐπιστολῆς παρετίθεντο.

Ε̄ Ὡς Μάρκῳ Αὐρηλίῳ Καίσαρι ταῖς τῶν
ἡμετέρων εὐχαῖς οὐρανόθεν ὁ θεὸς ἐπακούσας
ὗσεν.

Ϛ̄ Τῶν ἐπὶ Ῥώμης ἐπισκοπευσάντων κατάλογος.

Ζ̄ Ὡς καὶ μέχρι τῶν τότε καιρῶν διὰ τῶν
πιστῶν δυνάμεις ἐνηργοῦντο παράδοξοι.

Η̄ Ὅπως ὁ Εἰρηναῖος τῶν θείων μνημονεύει
γραφῶν.

Θ̄ Οἱ κατὰ Κόμοδον ἐπισκοπεύσαντες.

Ī Περὶ Πανταίνου τοῦ φιλοσόφου.

ĪĀ Περὶ Κλήμεντος τοῦ Ἀλεξανδρέως.

ĪΒ̄ Περὶ τῶν ἐν Ἱεροσολύμοις ἐπισκόπων.

ĪΓ̄ Περὶ Ῥόδωνος καὶ ἧς ἐμνημόνευσεν κατὰ
Μαρκίωνα διαφωνίας.

400

CONTENTS OF BOOK V

The contents of the fifth book of the History of the Church are as follows :

I. The number and behaviour of those who in the time of Verus underwent in Gaul the struggle for religion.

II. How the martyrs, beloved of God, gave the hand of fellowship and healing to those who had fallen in the persecution.

III. The vision which appeared in a dream to the martyr Attalus.

IV. How the martyrs commended Irenaeus by a letter.

V. How God sent rain from heaven to Marcus Aurelius Caesar in response to the prayers of the Christians.

VI. The list of those who were bishops in Rome.

VII. How even until those times strange miracles were wrought by the faithful.

VIII. How Irenaeus quotes the divine Scriptures.

IX. Those who were bishops under Commodus.

X. On Pantaenus the philosopher.

XI. On Clement of Alexandria.

XII. On the bishops in Jerusalem.

XIII. On Rhodo and the dissensions which he mentions among the Marcionites.

ΙΔ Περὶ τῶν κατὰ Φρύγας ψευδοπροφητῶν.

ΙΕ Περὶ τοῦ κατὰ Βλάστον ἐπὶ Ῥώμης γενομένου σχίσματος.

ΙϚ Ὅσα περὶ Μοντανοῦ καὶ τῶν μετ᾽ αὐτοῦ
ψευδοπροφητῶν μνημονεύεται.

ΙΖ Περὶ Μιλτιάδου καὶ ὧν συνέταξε λόγων.

ΙΗ Ὅσα καὶ Ἀπολλώνιος τοὺς κατὰ Φρύγας
ἀπήλεγξεν καὶ τίνων ἐμνημόνευσεν.

ΙΘ Σεραπίωνος περὶ τῆς τῶν Φρυγῶν αἱρέσεως.

Κ Ὅσα Εἰρηναῖος τοῖς ἐπὶ Ῥώμης σχισματικοῖς
ἐγγράφως διείλεκται.

ΚΑ Ὅπως ἐπὶ Ῥώμης Ἀπολλώνιος ἐμαρτύρησεν.

ΚΒ Τίνες κατὰ τούτους ἐπίσκοποι ἐγνωρίζοντο.

ΚΓ Περὶ τοῦ τότε κινηθέντος ἀμφὶ τοῦ πάσχα
ζητήματος.

ΚΔ Περὶ τῆς κατὰ τὴν Ἀσίαν διαφωνίας.

ΚΕ Ὅπως τοῖς πᾶσι μία ψῆφος περὶ τοῦ πάσχα
συνεφωνήθη.

ΚϚ Ὅσα τῆς Εἰρηναίου φιλοκαλίας καὶ εἰς ἡμᾶς
κατῆλθεν.

ΚΖ Ὅσα καὶ τῶν λοιπῶν τῶν τηνικάδε συν-
ηκμακότων.

ΚΗ Περὶ τῶν τὴν Ἀρτέμωνος αἵρεσιν ἐξ ἀρχῆς
προβεβλημένων οἷοί τε τὸν τρόπον γεγόνασιν
καὶ ὅπως τὰς ἁγίας γραφὰς διαφθεῖραι
τετολμήκασιν.

ECCLESIASTICAL HISTORY, V. CONTENTS

XIV. On the Montanist [1] false prophets.

XV. About the schism at Rome under Blastus.

XVI. The tradition concerning Montanus and those who were false prophets together with him.

XVII. On Miltiades and the treatises which he composed.

XVIII. How Apollonius also refuted the Montanists and the quotations which he made.

XIX. Of Serapion on Montanism.

XX. The discussions of Irenaeus in writing with the schismatics at Rome.

XXI. How Apollonius was martyred in Rome.

XXII. What bishops were famous in these times.

XXIII. On the paschal controversy which was then active.

XXIV. On the division in Asia.

XXV. How unanimous decision was reached concerning Easter.

XXVI. How much of the eloquent work of Irenaeus has come down to us.

XXVII. How much also of the others who flourished with him at that time.

XXVIII. On those who at the beginning put forward the heresy of Artemon, what manner of men they were, and how they have dared to corrupt the holy Scriptures.

[1] Literally " Among Phrygians " but this is one of the usual names of the Montanists, and passed into Latin as " Catafrygae."

E

Ὁ μὲν οὖν τῆς Ῥωμαίων ἐκκλησίας ἐπίσκοπος **1**
Σωτὴρ ἐπὶ ὄγδοον ἔτος ἡγησάμενος τελευτᾷ τὸν
βίον· τοῦτον δωδέκατος ἀπὸ τῶν ἀποστόλων
Ἐλεύθερος διαδέχεται, ἔτος δ᾽ ἦν ἑπτακαιδέκατον
αὐτοκράτορος Ἀντωνίνου Οὐήρου· ἐν ᾧ κατά τινα
μέρη τῆς γῆς σφοδρότερον ἀναρριπισθέντος τοῦ
καθ᾽ ἡμῶν διωγμοῦ, ἐξ ἐπιθέσεως τῶν κατὰ πόλεις
δήμων μυριάδας μαρτύρων διαπρέψαι στοχασμῷ
λαβεῖν ἔνεστιν ἀπὸ τῶν καθ᾽ ἓν ἔθνος συμβεβηκότων, ἃ καὶ γραφῇ τοῖς μετέπειτα παραδοθῆναι,
ἀλήστου μνήμης ὡς ἀληθῶς ἐπάξια ὄντα, συμβέβηκεν. τῆς μὲν οὖν περὶ τούτων ἐντελεστάτης **2**
ὑφηγήσεως τὸ πᾶν σύγγραμμα τῇ τῶν μαρτύρων
ἡμῖν κατατέτακται συναγωγῇ, οὐχ ἱστορικὴν αὐτὸ
μόνον, ἀλλὰ καὶ διδασκαλικὴν περιέχον διήγησιν·
ὁπόσα γέ τοι τῆς παρούσης ἔχοιτο πραγματείας,
ταῦτ᾽ ἐπὶ τοῦ παρόντος ἀναλεξάμενος παραθήσομαι.
ἄλλοι μὲν οὖν ἱστορικὰς ποιούμενοι διηγήσεις, **3**
πάντως ἂν παρέδωκαν τῇ γραφῇ πολέμων νίκας
καὶ τρόπαια κατ᾽ ἐχθρῶν στρατηγῶν τε ἀριστείας
καὶ ὁπλιτῶν ἀνδραγαθίας, αἵματι καὶ μυρίοις
φόνοις παίδων καὶ πατρίδος καὶ τῆς ἄλλης ἕνεκεν
περιουσίας μιανθέντων· ὁ δέ γε τοῦ κατὰ θεὸν **4**

404

BOOK V

Soter, the bishop of the church of Rome, ended his life in the eighth year of his rule. To him succeeded Eleutherus, the twelfth from the apostles, and it was the seventeenth year of the Emperor Antoninus Verus.[1] In this time the persecution of us in some parts of the world was rekindled more violently by popular violence in the cities, and, to judge from the events in one nation, myriads were distinguished by martyrdom. The story has chanced to be handed down in writing for posterity, and it is truly worthy of unceasing remembrance. Since the whole record of its complete treatment has been embodied in our collection of martyrs,[2] and contains not merely the narrative itself but also an exposition of doctrine, I will at present select and quote merely such points as belong to the present undertaking. Other writers of historical works have confined themselves to the written tradition of victories in wars, of triumphs over enemies, of the exploits of generals and the valour of soldiers, men stained with blood and with countless murders for the sake of children and country and other possessions; but it is wars most peaceful,

---

[1] That is, Marcus Aurelius. His seventeenth year was A.D. 177.

[2] That is, the *Acts of the Martyrs* which Eusebius collected. See Introduction, p. xxiii.

πολιτεύματος διηγηματικὸς ἡμῖν λόγος τοὺς ὑπὲρ
αὐτῆς τῆς κατὰ ψυχὴν εἰρήνης εἰρηνικωτάτους
πολέμους καὶ τοὺς ἐν τούτοις ὑπὲρ ἀληθείας
μᾶλλον ἢ πατρίδος καὶ μᾶλλον ὑπὲρ εὐσεβείας ἢ
τῶν φιλτάτων ἀνδρισαμένους αἰωνίαις ἀναγράψεται
στήλαις, τῶν εὐσεβείας ἀθλητῶν τὰς ἐνστάσεις καὶ
τὰς πολυτλήτους ἀνδρείας τρόπαιά τε τὰ κατὰ
δαιμόνων καὶ νίκας τὰς κατὰ τῶν ἀοράτων ἀντι-
πάλων καὶ τοὺς ἐπὶ πᾶσι τούτοις στεφάνους εἰς
αἰώνιον μνήμην ἀνακηρύττων.

I. Γαλλία μὲν οὖν ἡ χώρα ἦν, καθ' ἣν τὸ τῶν 1
δηλουμένων συνεκροτεῖτο στάδιον, ἧς μητροπόλεις
ἐπίσημοι καὶ παρὰ τὰς ἄλλας τῶν αὐτόθι δια-
φέρουσαι βεβόηνται Λούγδουνος καὶ Βίεννα, δι'
ὧν ἀμφοτέρων τὴν ἅπασαν χώραν πολλῷ τῷ ῥεύματι
περιρρέων ὁ Ῥοδανὸς ποταμὸς διέξεισιν. τὴν 2
οὖν περὶ τῶν μαρτύρων γραφὴν αἱ τῇδε δια-
φανέσταται ἐκκλησίαι ταῖς κατὰ τὴν Ἀσίαν καὶ
Φρυγίαν διαπέμπονται, τὰ παρ' αὐταῖς πραχθέντα
τοῦτον ἀνιστοροῦσαι τὸν τρόπον, παραθήσομαι 3
δὲ τὰς αὐτῶν φωνάς· " οἱ ἐν Βιέννῃ καὶ Λουγδούνῳ
τῆς Γαλλίας παροικοῦντες δοῦλοι Χριστοῦ τοῖς
κατὰ τὴν Ἀσίαν καὶ Φρυγίαν τὴν αὐτὴν τῆς
ἀπολυτρώσεως ἡμῖν πίστιν καὶ ἐλπίδα ἔχουσιν
ἀδελφοῖς· εἰρήνη καὶ χάρις καὶ δόξα ἀπὸ θεοῦ
πατρὸς καὶ Χριστοῦ Ἰησοῦ τοῦ κυρίου ἡμῶν."

Εἶτα τούτοις ἑξῆς ἕτερα προοιμιασάμενοι, τὴν 4
τοῦ λόγου καταρχὴν ποιοῦνται ἐν τούτοις· " τὸ
μὲν οὖν μέγεθος τῆς ἐνθάδε θλίψεως καὶ τὴν
τοσαύτην τῶν ἐθνῶν εἰς τοὺς ἁγίους ὀργὴν καὶ ὅσα
ὑπέμειναν οἱ μακάριοι μάρτυρες, ἐπ' ἀκριβὲς οὔθ'
ἡμεῖς εἰπεῖν ἱκανοὶ οὔτε μὴν γραφῇ περιληφθῆναι

waged for the very peace of the soul, and men who therein have been valiant for truth rather than for country, and for piety rather than for their dear ones, that our record of those who order their lives according to God will inscribe on everlasting monuments: it is the struggles of the athletes of piety and their valour which braved so much, trophies won from demons, and victories against unseen adversaries, and the crowns at the end of all, that it will proclaim for everlasting remembrance.

I. Gaul was the country in which was prepared the stage for these events. Its capital cities, famous and more renowned than the others in the district, were Lyons and Vienne, through both of which passes the river Rhone, flowing in an ample stream through the whole district. The distinguished churches of this country sent the document about the martyrs to the churches in Asia and Phrygia, in this way recording what happened among them, and I will quote their words : " The servants sojourning in Vienne and Lyons in Gaul to the brethren in Asia and Phrygia, who have the same faith and hope of redemption as you. Peace, grace, and glory from God the Father and Jesus Christ, our Lord."

Then after other prefatory remarks they begin their narrative thus : " The greatness of the persecution here, and the terrible rage of the heathen against the saints, and the suffering of the blessed martyrs, are more than we can narrate accurately, nor can they be put down in writing. For with all

407

δυνατόν. παντὶ γὰρ σθένει ἐνέσκηψεν ὁ ἀντικεί- 5
μενος, προοιμιαζόμενος ἤδη τὴν ἀδεῶς μέλλουσαν
ἔσεσθαι παρουσίαν αὐτοῦ, καὶ διὰ πάντων διῆλθεν,
ἐθίζων τοὺς ἑαυτοῦ καὶ προγυμνάζων κατὰ τῶν
δούλων τοῦ θεοῦ, ὥστε μὴ μόνον οἰκιῶν καὶ
βαλανείων καὶ ἀγορᾶς εἴργεσθαι, ἀλλὰ καὶ τὸ
καθόλου φαίνεσθαι ἡμῶν τινα αὐτοῖς ἀπειρῆσθαι
ἐν ὁποίῳ δήποτε τόπῳ. ἀντεστρατήγει δὲ ἡ 6
χάρις τοῦ θεοῦ, καὶ τοὺς μὲν ἀσθενεῖς ἐρρύετο,
1 Tim. 3, 15 ἀντιπαρέτασσε δὲ στύλους ἑδραίους δυναμένους
διὰ τῆς ὑπομονῆς πᾶσαν τὴν ὁρμὴν τοῦ πονηροῦ
Heb. 10, 33 εἰς ἑαυτοὺς ἑλκύσαι· οἳ καὶ ὁμόσε ἐχώρουν, πᾶν
εἶδος ὀνειδισμοῦ καὶ κολάσεως ἀνεχόμενοι· οἳ καὶ
τὰ πολλὰ ὀλίγα ἡγούμενοι ἔσπευδον πρὸς Χριστόν,
Rom. 8, 18 ὄντως ἐπιδεικνύμενοι ὅτι οὐκ ἄξια τὰ παθήματα
τοῦ νῦν καιροῦ πρὸς τὴν μέλλουσαν δόξαν ἀπο-
καλυφθῆναι εἰς ἡμᾶς.

"Καὶ πρῶτον μὲν τὰ ἀπὸ τοῦ ὄχλου πανδημεὶ 7
σωρηδὸν ἐπιφερόμενα γενναίως ὑπέμενον, ἐπιβοήσεις καὶ πληγὰς καὶ συρμοὺς καὶ διαρπαγὰς
καὶ λίθων βολὰς καὶ συγκλείσεις καὶ πάνθ' ὅσα
ἠγριωμένῳ πλήθει ὡς πρὸς ἐχθροὺς καὶ πολεμίους
φιλεῖ γίνεσθαι, καὶ δὴ ἀναχθέντες εἰς τὴν ἀγορὰν 8
ὑπό τε τοῦ χιλιάρχου καὶ τῶν προεστηκότων τῆς
πόλεως ἐξουσιῶν ἐπὶ παντὸς τοῦ πλήθους ἀνακρι-
θέντες καὶ ὁμολογήσαντες, συνεκλείσθησαν εἰς τὴν
εἱρκτὴν ἕως τῆς τοῦ ἡγεμόνος παρουσίας· μετ- 9
έπειτα δὲ ἐπὶ τὸν ἡγεμόνα ἀχθέντων αὐτῶν κἀκείνου
πάσῃ τῇ πρὸς ἡμᾶς ὠμότητι χρωμένου, Οὐέττιος
Ἐπάγαθος, εἷς ἐκ τῶν ἀδελφῶν, πλήρωμα ἀγάπης
τῆς πρὸς τὸν θεὸν καὶ πρὸς τὸν πλησίον κεχωρηκώς,
οὗ καὶ ἐπὶ τοσοῦτον ἠκρίβωτο ἡ πολιτεία, ὡς

his might the adversary attacked us, foreshadowing
his coming which is shortly to be, and tried everything, practising his adherents and training them
against the servants of God, so that we were not
merely excluded from houses and baths and markets,
but we were even forbidden to be seen at all in any
place whatever. But against them the grace of God
did captain us; it rescued the weak, and marshalled
against them steadfast pillars of men able by patience
to draw to themselves all the attack of the enemy.
They came together and endured every kind of abuse
and punishment, they counted many things as few in
their zeal for Christ, and did indeed prove that the
sufferings of this present time are not worthy to be
compared with the glory which shall be revealed
to us.

"First they endured nobly all that was heaped upon
them by the mob, howls and stripes and dragging
about, and rapine and imprisonment and stoning,
and all things which are wont to happen at the
hands of an infuriated populace against its supposed
enemies and foes; then they were dragged into the
market-place by the tribune and by the chief
authorities of the city, were indicted and confessed,
and at last they were shut up until the coming of
the governor. Then they were brought before the
governor, and when he used all his cruelty against
them, then intervened Vettius Epagathus, one of
the brethren, filled with love towards God and
towards his neighbour, the strictness of whose life

Luke 1, 16 καίπερ ὄντα νέον συνεξισοῦσθαι τῇ τοῦ πρεσβυτέρου Ζαχαρίου μαρτυρίᾳ· πεπόρευτο γοῦν ἐν
πάσαις ταῖς ἐντολαῖς καὶ δικαιώμασι τοῦ κυρίου
ἄμεμπτος καὶ πάσῃ τῇ πρὸς τὸν πλησίον λειτουργίᾳ
ἄοκνος, ζῆλον θεοῦ πολὺν ἔχων καὶ ζέων τῷ
πνεύματι· τοιοῦτος δή τις ὤν, τὴν οὕτως καθ' ἡμῶν
ἀλόγως γινομένην κρίσιν οὐκ ἐβάστασεν, ἀλλ'
ὑπερηγανάκτησεν καὶ ἠξίου καὶ αὐτὸς ἀκουσθῆναι
ἀπολογούμενος ὑπὲρ τῶν ἀδελφῶν ὅτι μηδὲν ἄθεον
μηδὲ ἀσεβές ἐστιν ἐν ἡμῖν. τῶν δὲ περὶ τὸ βῆμα 10
καταβοησάντων αὐτοῦ, καὶ γὰρ ἦν ἐπίσημος,
καὶ τοῦ ἡγεμόνος μὴ ἀνασχομένου τῆς οὕτως ὑπ'
αὐτοῦ δικαίας προταθείσης ἀξιώσεως, ἀλλὰ μόνον
τοῦτο πυθομένου εἰ καὶ αὐτὸς εἴη Χριστιανός, τοῦ
δὲ λαμπροτάτῃ φωνῇ ὁμολογήσαντος, ἀνελήφθη καὶ
αὐτὸς εἰς τὸν κλῆρον τῶν μαρτύρων, παράκλητος
Χριστιανῶν χρηματίσας, ἔχων δὲ τὸν παράκλητον
Luke 1, 67 ἐν ἑαυτῷ, τὸ πνεῦμα τοῦ Ζαχαρίου, ὃ διὰ τοῦ
1 John 3, 16 πληρώματος τῆς ἀγάπης ἐνεδείξατο, εὐδοκήσας
1 Thes. 2, 8 ὑπὲρ τῆς τῶν ἀδελφῶν ἀπολογίας καὶ τὴν ἑαυτοῦ
θεῖναι ψυχήν· ἦν γὰρ καὶ ἔστιν γνήσιος Χριστοῦ
Rev. 14, 4 μαθητής, ἀκολουθῶν τῷ ἀρνίῳ ὅπου ἂν ὑπάγῃ.

" Ἐντεῦθεν δὴ διεκρίνοντο οἱ λοιποί, καὶ φανεροὶ 11
καὶ ἕτοιμοι ἐγίνοντο πρωτομάρτυρες, οἳ καὶ μετὰ
πάσης προθυμίας ἀνεπλήρουν τὴν ὁμολογίαν τῆς
μαρτυρίας, ἐφαίνοντο δὲ καὶ οἱ ἀνέτοιμοι καὶ
ἀγύμναστοι καὶ ἔτι ἀσθενεῖς, ἀγῶνος μεγάλου

had gone so far that in spite of his youth his reputation was equal to that of the elder Zacharias.[1] He walked in all the commandments and ordinances of the Lord blameless and was unwearied in all ministrations to his neighbours, having much zeal toward God and being fervent in spirit. His character forbade him to endure the unreasonable judgement given against us, and, overcome with indignation, he asked to be heard himself in defence of the brethren to the effect that there was nothing atheistic or impious among us. He was howled down by those around the judgement-seat, for he was a man of position,[2] and the governor would not tolerate the just requests which he had put forward but merely asked if he were a Christian himself. He then confessed in clear tones and was himself taken into the ranks of the martyrs. He was called the 'Comforter of Christians,' but had the Comforter in himself, the spirit of Zacharias which he had shown by the fullness of his love when he chose to lay down even his own life for the defence of the brethren, for he was and he is [3] a true disciple of Christ, and he follows the Lamb whithersoever he goes.

"The rest were then divided and the first martyrs were obviously ready, and they fulfilled the confession of martyrdom with all readiness, but some others appeared not to be ready, and failed in training and in strength, unable to endure the strain

---

[1] Zacharias the father of John the Baptist, as is shown by the allusion to Luke i. 6 in the following line.

[2] Apparently the meaning is that his social position made the crowd even more indignant at his advocacy of Christians.

[3] It is almost incredible that this " is " was interpreted by Renan and others as showing that Vettius was not actually put to death.

τόνον ἐνεγκεῖν μὴ δυνάμενοι· ὧν καὶ ἐξέτρωσαν
ὡς δέκα τὸν ἀριθμόν· οἳ καὶ μεγάλην λύπην καὶ
πένθος ἀμέτρητον ἐνεποίησαν ἡμῖν καὶ τὴν προθυμίαν τῶν λοιπῶν τῶν μὴ συνειλημμένων ἐνέκοψαν·
οἳ καίπερ πάντα τὰ δεινὰ πάσχοντες, ὅμως συμ-
παρῆσαν τοῖς μάρτυσιν καὶ οὐκ ἀπελείποντο
αὐτῶν, τότε δὲ οἱ πάντες μεγάλως ἐπτοήθημεν 12
διὰ τὸ ἄδηλον τῆς ὁμολογίας, οὐ τὰς ἐπιφερομένας
κολάσεις φοβούμενοι, ἀλλὰ τὸ τέλος ἀφορῶντες
καὶ τὸ ἀποπεσεῖν τινα δεδιότες. συνελαμβάνοντο 13
μέντοι καθ᾽ ἑκάστην ἡμέραν οἱ ἄξιοι τὸν ἐκείνων
ἀναπληροῦντες ἀριθμόν, ὥστε συλλεγῆναι ἐκ τῶν
δύο ἐκκλησιῶν πάντας τοὺς σπουδαίους καὶ δι᾽
ὧν μάλιστα συνεστήκει τὰ ἐνθάδε· συνελαμβάνοντο 14
δὲ καὶ ἐθνικοί τινες οἰκέται τῶν ἡμετέρων, ἐπεὶ
δημοσίᾳ ἐκέλευσεν ὁ ἡγεμὼν ἀναζητεῖσθαι πάντας
ἡμᾶς· οἳ καὶ κατ᾽ ἐνέδραν τοῦ σατανᾶ, φοβηθέντες
τὰς βασάνους ἃς τοὺς ἁγίους ἔβλεπον πάσχοντας,
τῶν στρατιωτῶν ἐπὶ τοῦτο παρορμώντων αὐτούς,
κατεψεύσαντο ἡμῶν Θυέστεια δεῖπνα καὶ Οἰδιπο-
δείους μίξεις καὶ ὅσα μήτε λαλεῖν μήτε νοεῖν θέμις
ἡμῖν, ἀλλὰ μηδὲ πιστεύειν εἴ τι τοιοῦτο πώποτε
παρὰ ἀνθρώποις ἐγένετο. τούτων δὲ φημισθέντων, 15
πάντες ἀπεθηριώθησαν εἰς ἡμᾶς, ὥστε καὶ εἴ τινες
Acts 7, 54 τὸ πρότερον δι᾽ οἰκειότητα ἐμετρίαζον, τότε
μεγάλως ἐχαλέπαινον καὶ διεπρίοντο ἐφ᾽ ἡμῖν·
ἐπληροῦτο δὲ τὸ ὑπὸ τοῦ κυρίου ἡμῶν εἰρημένον
John 16, 2 ὅτι ἐλεύσεται καιρὸς ἐν ᾧ πᾶς ὁ ἀποκτείνας ὑμᾶς
δόξει λατρείαν προσφέρειν τῷ θεῷ. ἐνταῦθα λοιπὸν 16
ὑπεράνω πάσης ἐξηγήσεως ὑπέμενον κολάσεις οἱ
ἅγιοι μάρτυρες, φιλοτιμουμένου τοῦ σατανᾶ καὶ

of a great conflict, and about ten in number failed, as those born out of due time. They caused us great grief and immeasurable mourning, and hindered the zeal of the others who had not been arrested. Yet they, although suffering all the terrors, nevertheless remained with the martyrs and did not desert them. But at that point we were all greatly terrified by uncertainty as to their confession, not fearing the threatened punishment but looking towards the end and afraid lest some one should fall away. Yet day by day those who were worthy went on being arrested, completing their number, so as to collect from the two churches all the zealous and those through whom the life of the locality was kept together. There were also arrested certain heathen slaves of our members, since the governor had publicly commanded that we should all be prosecuted, and these by the snare of Satan, fearing the tortures which they saw the saints suffering, when the soldiers urged them, falsely accused us of Thyestean feasts and Oedipodean intercourse,[1] and things which it is not right for us either to speak of or to think of or even to believe that such things could ever happen among men. When this rumour spread all men turned like beasts against us, so that even if any had formerly been lenient for friendship's sake they then became furious and raged against us, and there was fulfilled that which was spoken by our Lord that 'the time will come when whosoever killeth you will think that he doeth God service.' Then at last the holy martyrs endured sufferings beyond all description, for Satan was striving to wring some

---

[1] According to Greek mythology Thyestes had unconsciously eaten his children and Oedipus had married his mother.

413

δι' ἐκείνων ῥηθῆναί τι τῶν βλασφήμων· ὑπερ- 17
βεβλημένως δὲ ἐνέσκηψεν ἡ ὀργὴ πᾶσα καὶ ὄχλου
καὶ ἡγεμόνος καὶ στρατιωτῶν εἰς Σάγκτον τὸν
διάκονον ἀπὸ Βιέννης καὶ εἰς Μάτουρον, νεο-
φώτιστον μέν, ἀλλὰ γενναῖον ἀγωνιστήν, καὶ εἰς
1 Tim. 3, 15 Ἄτταλον Περγαμηνὸν τῷ γένει, στῦλον καὶ
ἑδραίωμα τῶν ἐνταῦθα ἀεὶ γεγονότα, καὶ εἰς
Βλανδῖναν, δι' ἧς ἐπέδειξεν ὁ Χριστὸς ὅτι τὰ παρὰ
ἀνθρώποις εὐτελῆ καὶ ἀειδῆ καὶ εὐκαταφρόνητα
φαινόμενα μεγάλης καταξιοῦται παρὰ θεῷ δόξης
διὰ τὴν πρὸς αὐτὸν ἀγάπην τὴν ἐν δυνάμει δεικνυ-
μένην καὶ μὴ ἐν εἴδει καυχωμένην. ἡμῶν γὰρ 18
πάντων δεδιότων καὶ τῆς σαρκίνης δεσποίνης
αὐτῆς, ἥτις ἦν καὶ αὐτὴ τῶν μαρτύρων μία ἀγωνί-
στρια, ἀγωνιώσης μὴ οὐδὲ τὴν ὁμολογίαν δυνήσεται
παρρησιάσασθαι διὰ τὸ ἀσθενὲς τοῦ σώματος, ἡ
Βλανδῖνα τοσαύτης ἐπληρώθη δυνάμεως, ὥστε
ἐκλυθῆναι καὶ παρεθῆναι τοὺς κατὰ διαδοχὰς
παντὶ τρόπῳ βασανίζοντας αὐτὴν ἀπὸ ἑωθινῆς
ἕως ἑσπέρας, καὶ αὐτοὺς ὁμολογοῦντας ὅτι νενίκην-
ται μηδὲν ἔχοντες μηκέτι ὃ ποιήσωσιν αὐτῇ, καὶ
θαυμάζειν ἐπὶ τῷ παραμένειν ἔμπνουν αὐτήν,
παντὸς τοῦ σώματος περιερρωγότος καὶ ἠνεῳγ-
μένου, καὶ μαρτυρεῖν ὅτι ἓν εἶδος στρεβλώσεως
ἱκανὸν ἦν πρὸς τὸ ἐξαγαγεῖν τὴν ψυχήν, οὐχ ὅτι
γε τοιαῦτα καὶ τοσαῦτα. ἀλλ' ἡ μακαρία ὡς 19
γενναῖος ἀθλητὴς ἀνενέαζεν ἐν τῇ ὁμολογίᾳ καὶ
ἦν αὐτῆς ἀνάληψις καὶ ἀνάπαυσις καὶ ἀναλγησία
τῶν συμβαινόντων τὸ λέγειν ὅτι 'Χριστιανή εἰμι
καὶ παρ' ἡμῖν οὐδὲν φαῦλον γίνεται.'
"Ὁ δὲ Σάγκτος καὶ αὐτὸς ὑπερβεβλημένως 20
καὶ ὑπὲρ πάντα ἄνθρωπον πάσας τὰς ἐξ ἀνθρώπων

blasphemy even from them, and all the fury of the mob and of the governor and of the soldiers was raised beyond measure against Sanctus, the deacon from Vienne, and against Maturus, who was a novice but a noble contender, and against Attalus. a Pergamene by race, who had always been a pillar and support of the Christians there, and against Blandina, through whom Christ showed that things which are mean and obscure and contemptible among men are vouchsafed great glory with God because of the love towards him shown in power and not boasted of in appearance. For while we were all afraid, and her human mistress, who was herself one of the contenders among the martyrs, was in distress lest she should not be able, through the weakness of her body, to be bold enough even to make confession, Blandina was filled with such power that she was released and rescued from those who took turns in torturing her in every way from morning until evening, and they themselves confessed that they were beaten, for they had nothing left to do to her, and they marvelled that she still remained alive, seeing that her whole body was broken and opened, and they testified that any one of these tortures was sufficient to destroy life, even when they had not been magnified and multiplied. But the blessed woman, like a noble athlete, kept gaining in vigour in her confession, and found comfort and rest and freedom from pain from what was done to her by saying, ' I am a Christian woman and nothing wicked happens among us.'

" Sanctus also himself endured nobly, beyond measure or human power, all the ill-treatment of

αἰκίας γενναίως ὑπομένων, τῶν ἀνόμων ἐλπιζόντων
διὰ τὴν ἐπιμονὴν καὶ τὸ μέγεθος τῶν βασάνων
ἀκούσεσθαί τι παρ' αὐτοῦ τῶν μὴ δεόντων, τοσαύτῃ
ὑποστάσει ἀντιπαρετάξατο αὐτοῖς, ὥστε μήτε τὸ
ἴδιον κατειπεῖν ὄνομα μήτε ἔθνους μήτε πόλεως
ὅθεν ἦν, μήτε εἰ δοῦλος ἢ ἐλεύθερος εἴη· ἀλλὰ πρὸς
πάντα τὰ ἐπερωτώμενα ἀπεκρίνατο τῇ Ῥωμαϊκῇ
φωνῇ 'Χριστιανός εἰμι'· τοῦτο καὶ ἀντὶ ὀνόματος
καὶ ἀντὶ πόλεως καὶ ἀντὶ γένους καὶ ἀντὶ παντὸς
ἐπαλλήλως ὡμολόγει, ἄλλην δὲ φωνὴν οὐκ ἤκουσαν
αὐτοῦ τὰ ἔθνη· ὅθεν δὴ καὶ φιλονεικία μεγάλη τοῦ 21
τε ἡγεμόνος καὶ τῶν βασανιστῶν ἐγένετο πρὸς
αὐτόν, ὥστε ὁπότε μηκέτι μηδὲν εἶχον ὃ ποιήσωσιν
αὐτῷ, τὸ τελευταῖον χαλκᾶς λεπίδας διαπύρους
προσεκόλλων τοῖς τρυφερωτάτοις μέλεσι τοῦ σώματος αὐτοῦ. καὶ ταῦτα μὲν ἐκαίετο, αὐτὸς δὲ 22
παρέμενεν ἀνεπίκαμπτος καὶ ἀνένδοτος, στερρὸς
John 7, 88 πρὸς τὴν ὁμολογίαν, ὑπὸ τῆς οὐρανίου πηγῆς τοῦ
ὕδατος τῆς ζωῆς τοῦ ἐξιόντος ἐκ τῆς νηδύος τοῦ
Χριστοῦ δροσιζόμενος καὶ ἐνδυναμούμενος· τὸ 23
Is. 53, 2. 5 δὲ σωμάτιον μάρτυς ἦν τῶν συμβεβηκότων, ὅλον
τραῦμα καὶ μώλωψ καὶ συνεσπασμένον καὶ ἀπο-
βεβληκὸς τὴν ἀνθρώπειον ἔξωθεν μορφήν, ἐν ᾧ
πάσχων Χριστὸς μεγάλας ἐπετέλει δόξας, καταργῶν
1 Tim. 1. 16 τὸν ἀντικείμενον καὶ εἰς τὴν τῶν λοιπῶν ὑπο-
τύπωσιν ὑποδεικνύων ὅτι μηδὲν φοβερὸν ὅπου
πατρὸς ἀγάπη, μηδὲ ἀλγεινὸν ὅπου Χριστοῦ δόξα.
τῶν γὰρ ἀνόμων μεθ' ἡμέρας πάλιν στρεβλούντων 24
τὸν μάρτυρα καὶ νομιζόντων ὅτι οἰδούντων καὶ
φλεγμαινόντων τῶν σωμάτων, εἰ τὰ αὐτὰ προσ-
ενέγκοιεν κολαστήρια, περιέσοιντο αὐτοῦ, ὁπότε
οὐδὲ τὴν ἀπὸ τῶν χειρῶν ἁφὴν ἠνείχετο, ἢ ὅτι

men, for though the wicked hoped through persistence and the rigour of his tortures to wring from him something wrong, he resisted them with such constancy that he did not even tell his own name, or the race or the city whence he was, nor whether he was slave or free, but to all questions answered in Latin, ' I am a Christian.' This he said for name and city and race and for everything else, and the heathen heard no other sound from him. For this reason the governor and the torturers were very ambitious to subdue him, so that when they had nothing left at all to do to him at last they fastened plates of heated brass to the tenderest parts of his body. His limbs were burning, but he continued himself unbending and unyielding, firm in his confession, refreshed and strengthened by the heavenly spring of the water of life which proceeds forth from the body of Christ. His body was a witness to his treatment ; it was all one wound and bruise, wrenched and torn out of human shape, but Christ suffering in him manifested great glory, overthrowing the adversary and showing for the example of the others how there is nothing fearful where there is the love of the Father nor painful where there is the glory of Christ. For when the wicked after some days again tortured the martyr they thought that they might overcome him now that his body was swollen and inflamed if they applied the same tortures, seeing that he could not even endure to be

ἐναποθανὼν ταῖς βασάνοις φόβον ἐμποιήσειεν τοῖς λοιποῖς, οὐ μόνον οὐδὲν περὶ αὐτὸν τοιοῦτο συνέβη, ἀλλὰ καὶ παρὰ πᾶσαν δόξαν ἀνθρώπων ἀνέκυψεν καὶ ἀνωρθώθη τὸ σωμάτιον ἐν ταῖς μετέπειτα βασάνοις, καὶ τὴν ἰδέαν ἀπέλαβεν τὴν προτέραν καὶ τὴν χρῆσιν τῶν μελῶν, ὥστε μὴ κόλασιν, ἀλλ' ἴασιν διὰ τῆς χάριτος τοῦ Χριστοῦ τὴν δευτέραν στρέβλωσιν αὐτῷ γενέσθαι.

"Καὶ Βιβλίδα δέ, μίαν τῶν ἠρνημένων, ἤδη 25 δοκῶν ὁ διάβολος καταπεπωκέναι, θελήσας δὲ καὶ διὰ βλασφημίας κατακρῖναι, ἦγεν ἐπὶ κόλασιν, ἀναγκάζων εἰπεῖν τὰ ἄθεα περὶ ἡμῶν, ὡς εὔθραυστον ἤδη καὶ ἄνανδρον· ἡ δὲ ἐν τῇ στρεβλώσει ἀνένηψεν 26 καὶ ὡς ἂν εἰπεῖν ἐκ βαθέος ὕπνου ἀνεγρηγόρησεν, ὑπομνησθεῖσα διὰ τῆς προσκαίρου τιμωρίας τὴν αἰώνιον ἐν γεέννῃ κόλασιν, καὶ ἐξ ἐναντίας ἀντεῖπεν τοῖς βλασφήμοις, φήσασα ' πῶς ἂν παιδία φάγοιεν οἱ τοιοῦτοι, οἷς μηδὲ ἀλόγων ζῴων αἷμα φαγεῖν ἐξόν;' καὶ ἀπὸ τοῦδε Χριστιανὴν ἑαυτὴν ὡμολόγει καὶ τῷ κλήρῳ τῶν μαρτύρων προσετέθη.

"Καταργηθέντων δὲ τῶν τυραννικῶν κολα- 27 στηρίων ὑπὸ τοῦ Χριστοῦ διὰ τῆς τῶν μακαρίων ὑπομονῆς, ἑτέρας μηχανὰς ὁ διάβολος ἐπενόει, τὰς κατὰ τὴν εἱρκτὴν ἐν τῷ σκότει καὶ τῷ χαλε- πωτάτῳ χωρίῳ συγκλείσεις καὶ τὰς ἐν τῷ ξύλῳ διατάσεις τῶν ποδῶν, ἐπὶ πέμπτον διατεινομένων τρύπημα, καὶ τὰς λοιπὰς αἰκίας, ὅσας εἰώθασιν ὀργιζόμενοι ὑπουργοὶ καὶ ταῦτα διαβόλου πλήρεις διατιθέναι τοὺς ἐγκλειομένους· ὥστε ἀποπνιγῆναι τοὺς πλείστους ἐν τῇ εἱρκτῇ, ὅσους γε ὁ κύριος οὕτως ἐξελθεῖν ἠθέλησεν, ἐπιδεικνύων τὴν αὐτοῦ δόξαν. οἱ μὲν γὰρ βασανισθέντες πικρῶς ὥστε 28

touched by the hand, or that by dying under torture he would put fear into the rest. Yet not only did nothing of this kind happen, but, beyond all human expectation, he raised himself up and his body was straightened in the subsequent tortures, and he regained his former appearance and the use of his limbs, so that through the grace of Christ the second torturing became not torment but cure.

"Biblis, too, one of those who had denied, did the devil bring to torture (thinking that he had already swallowed her up and wishing to condemn her through blasphemy as well), to force her to say impious things about us, as though she were already broken and weak. But she recovered under torture, and, as it were, woke up out of deep sleep, being reminded through this transitory punishment of the eternal torments in hell, and contradicted the blasphemers, saying, ' How would such men eat children, when they are not allowed to eat the blood even of irrational animals?' And after this she confessed herself a Christian and was added to the ranks of the martyrs.

"But when the tyrant's torments had been brought to naught by Christ through the endurance of the blessed saints, the devil thought of other devices, imprisonment in the jail in darkness and in the most horrible place, and stretching their feet in the stocks, separated to the fifth hole, and the other outrages which angry warders filled with the devil are accustomed to inflict on the prisoners. Thus most of them were strangled in the prison, being all those whom the Lord had chosen thus to depart manifesting his glory. Some were tortured so cruelly

δοκεῖν μηδὲ τῆς πάσης θεραπείας τυχόντας ἔτι
ζῆσαι δύνασθαι, παρέμενον ἐν τῇ εἱρκτῇ, ἔρημοι
μὲν τῆς παρὰ ἀνθρώπων ἐπιμελείας, ἀναρρωννύμενοι
δὲ ὑπὸ κυρίου καὶ ἐνδυναμούμενοι καὶ σώματι καὶ
ψυχῇ καὶ τοὺς λοιποὺς παρορμῶντες καὶ παραμυθού-
μενοι· οἱ δὲ νεαροὶ καὶ ἄρτι συνειλημμένοι, ὧν μὴ
προκατήκιστο τὰ σώματα, τὸ βάρος οὐκ ἔφερον
τῆς συγκλείσεως, ἀλλ' ἔνδον ἐναπέθνησκον.

" Ὁ δὲ μακάριος Ποθεινός, ὁ τὴν διακονίαν τῆς 29
ἐπισκοπῆς ἐν Λουγδούνῳ πεπιστευμένος, ὑπὲρ τὰ
ἐνενήκοντα ἔτη τῆς ἡλικίας γεγονὼς καὶ πάνυ
ἀσθενὴς τῷ σώματι, μόλις μὲν ἐμπνέων διὰ τὴν
προκειμένην σωματικὴν ἀσθένειαν, ὑπὸ δὲ προθυμίας πνεύματος ἀναρρωννύμενος διὰ τὴν ἐγκειμένην τῆς μαρτυρίας ἐπιθυμίαν, καὶ αὐτὸς ἐπὶ τὸ
βῆμα ἐσύρετο, τοῦ μὲν σώματος καὶ ὑπὸ τοῦ
2 Cor. 2, 14 γήρως καὶ ὑπὸ τῆς νόσου λελυμένου, τηρουμένης
δὲ τῆς ψυχῆς ἐν αὐτῷ, ἵνα δι' αὐτῆς Χριστὸς
θριαμβεύσῃ· ὃς ὑπὸ τῶν στρατιωτῶν ἐπὶ τὸ βῆμα 30
κομισθείς, παραπεμπόντων αὐτὸν τῶν πολιτικῶν
ἐξουσιῶν καὶ παντὸς τοῦ πλήθους, ἐπιβοήσεις
παντοίας ποιουμένων ὡς αὐτοῦ ὄντος τοῦ Χριστοῦ,
ἀπεδίδου τὴν καλὴν μαρτυρίαν. ἀνεταζόμενος δὲ 31
ὑπὸ τοῦ ἡγεμόνος τίς εἴη Χριστιανῶν ὁ θεός, ἔφη
'ἐὰν ᾖς ἄξιος, γνώσῃ' ἐντεῦθεν δὲ ἀφειδῶς
ἐσύρετο καὶ ποικίλας ἔπασχε πληγάς, τῶν μὲν
σύνεγγυς χερσὶν καὶ ποσὶν ἐνυβριζόντων παντοίως,
μηδὲ τὴν ἡλικίαν αἰδουμένων αὐτοῦ, τῶν δὲ
μακράν, ὃ μετὰ χεῖρας ἕκαστος εἶχεν, εἰς αὐτὸν
ἀκοντιζόντων, πάντων δὲ ἡγουμένων μεγάλως
πλημμελεῖν καὶ ἀσεβεῖν, εἴ τις ἀπολειφθείη τῆς
εἰς αὐτὸν ἀσελγείας· καὶ γὰρ τοὺς θεοὺς αὐτῶν

that it seemed impossible for them to live even if
they had had every care, yet survived in the prison,
bereft of human attention but strengthened by the
Lord and given power in body and soul, and looking
after and comforting the rest. But the younger
ones, who had lately been arrested, whose bodies
had not become accustomed to it, did not endure the
burden of confinement but died in prison.

"The blessed Pothinus, who had been entrusted
with the ministry of the bishopric at Lyons, was over
ninety years old and very weak physically. He was
scarcely breathing through the physical weakness
which had already come upon him, but was strengthened by zeal of spirit through urgent desire of
martyrdom. He was dragged before the judgement-
seat, and although his body was weakened by old
age and disease, his soul was kept in him in order
that through it Christ might triumph. He was
brought by soldiers to the judgement-seat; the local
authorities accompanied him, and all the populace,
uttering all kinds of howls at him as though he was
Christ himself, but he gave noble testimony. When
asked by the governor, Who was the God of the
Christians, he said, 'If you are worthy, you will
know.' And then he was dragged about without
mercy, and suffered many blows; for those who were
near ill-treated him with feet and hands and in
every way, without respect even for his old age, and
those who were at a distance each threw at him
whatever he had at hand, and all thought that it
would be a great transgression and impiety to omit
any abuse against him. For they thought that in

ᾤοντο οὕτως ἐκδικήσειν. καὶ μόγις ἐμπνέων
ἐρρίφη ἐν τῇ εἰρκτῇ καὶ μετὰ δύο ἡμέρας ἀπέψυξεν.

"Ἐνταῦθα δὴ μεγάλη τις οἰκονομία θεοῦ 3.
ἐγίνετο καὶ ἔλεος ἀμέτρητον ἀνεφαίνετο Ἰησοῦ,
σπανίως μὲν ἐν τῇ ἀδελφότητι γεγονός, μὴ ἀπο-
λειπόμενον δὲ τῆς τέχνης Χριστοῦ. οἱ γὰρ κατὰ 3.
τὴν πρώτην σύλληψιν ἔξαρνοι γενόμενοι συνεκλείοντο καὶ αὐτοὶ καὶ μετεῖχον τῶν δεινῶν· οὐδὲ
γὰρ ἐν τῷ καιρῷ τούτῳ ὄφελός τι αὐτοῖς ἡ ἐξάρνησις
ἐγίνετο, ἀλλ' οἱ μὲν ὁμολογοῦντες ὃ καὶ ἦσαν,
συνεκλείοντο ὡς Χριστιανοί, μηδεμιᾶς ἄλλης αἰτίας
αὐτοῖς ἐπιφερομένης, οὗτοι δὲ λοιπὸν ὡς ἀνδρο-
φόνοι καὶ μιαροὶ κατείχοντο, διπλότερον παρὰ
τοὺς λοιποὺς κολαζόμενοι. ἐκείνους μὲν γὰρ ἐπ- 3.
εκούφιζεν ἡ χαρὰ τῆς μαρτυρίας καὶ ἡ ἐλπὶς τῶν
ἐπηγγελμένων καὶ ἡ πρὸς τὸν Χριστὸν ἀγάπη
καὶ τὸ πνεῦμα τὸ πατρικόν, τούτους δὲ τὸ συνειδὸς
μεγάλως ἐτιμωρεῖτο, ὥστε καὶ παρὰ τοῖς λοιποῖς
ἅπασιν κατὰ τὰς παρόδους διαδήλους τὰς ὄψεις
αὐτῶν εἶναι. οἳ μὲν γὰρ ἱλαροὶ προῄεσαν, δόξης 3.

Ps. 44, 14 καὶ χάριτος πολλῆς ταῖς ὄψεσιν αὐτῶν συγκεκρα-
μένης, ὥστε καὶ τὰ δεσμὰ κόσμον εὐπρεπῆ περι-
κεῖσθαι αὐτοῖς, ὡς νύμφῃ κεκοσμημένῃ ἐν κροσσω-
2 Cor. 2, 15 τοῖς χρυσοῖς πεποικιλμένοις, τὴν εὐωδίαν ὀδωδότες
ἅμα τὴν Χριστοῦ, ὥστε ἐνίους δόξαι καὶ μύρῳ
κοσμικῷ κεχρῖσθαι αὐτούς· οἱ δὲ κατηφεῖς καὶ
ταπεινοὶ καὶ δυσειδεῖς καὶ πάσης ἀσχημοσύνης
ἀνάπλεοι, προσέτι δὲ καὶ ὑπὸ τῶν ἐθνῶν ὀνειδιζό-
μενοι ὡς ἀγεννεῖς καὶ ἄνανδροι, ἀνδροφόνων μὲν
ἐγκλήματα ἔχοντες, ἀπολωλεκότες δὲ τὴν πάντιμον
καὶ ἔνδοξον καὶ ζωοποιὸν προσηγορίαν. ταῦτα
δὴ οἱ λοιποὶ θεωροῦντες ἐστηρίχθησαν, καὶ οἱ

this way they would vindicate their gods. And he was thrown into prison scarcely breathing and after two days yielded up the ghost.

" Then a great dispensation of God was given, and the measureless mercy of Jesus was so manifested, as has rarely happened among the brethren, but is not beyond the skill of Christ. For those who at the first arrest had denied were imprisoned themselves and shared in the terrors, for this time not even their denial was any advantage to them; but those who confessed what they were were imprisoned as Christians, no other accusation being brought against them, the others however were held as murderers and foul persons and punished twice as much as the rest. For the burden of the former was lightened by the joy of martyrdom and the hope of the promises, and by love towards Christ and by the Spirit of the Father; but the latter were greatly punished by their conscience so that they were conspicuous among all the rest by their faces when they were taken out. For the one went forth gladly; glory and great grace were mingled on their faces, so that they wore even their fetters as a becoming ornament, like a bride adorned with golden lace of many patterns, and they were perfumed with the sweet savour of Christ, so that some supposed that they had been anointed with worldly unguents; but the others were depressed and humble and wretched and filled with every kind of unseemliness, and in addition were insulted by the heathen as ignoble and cowardly; they had gained the accusation of murder, but had lost the name which is full of honour and glory and gives life. When the others saw this they were strengthened and those who

423

συλλαμβανόμενοι ἀδιστάκτως ὡμολόγουν, μηδὲ
ἔννοιαν ἔχοντες διαβολικοῦ λογισμοῦ.''

Τούτοις μεταξύ τινα ἐπειπόντες, αὖθις ἐπι- 36
φέρουσιν· ''μετὰ ταῦτα δὴ λοιπὸν εἰς πᾶν εἶδος
διῃρεῖτο τὰ μαρτύρια τῆς ἐξόδου αὐτῶν. ἐκ
διαφόρων γὰρ χρωμάτων καὶ παντοίων ἀνθῶν
ἕνα πλέξαντες στέφανον προσήνεγκαν τῷ πατρί·
ἐχρῆν δ' οὖν τοὺς γενναίους ἀθλητὰς ποικίλον
ὑπομείναντας ἀγῶνα καὶ μεγάλως νικήσαντας
ἀπολαβεῖν τὸν μέγαν τῆς ἀφθαρσίας στέφανον. ὁ 37
μὲν οὖν Μάτουρος καὶ ὁ Σάγκτος καὶ ἡ Βλανδῖνα
καὶ Ἄτταλος ἤγοντο ἐπὶ τὰ θηρία εἰς τὸ δημόσιον
καὶ εἰς κοινὸν τῶν ἐθνῶν τῆς ἀπανθρωπίας θέαμα,
ἐπίτηδες τῆς τῶν θηριομαχίων ἡμέρας διὰ τοὺς
ἡμετέρους διδομένης. καὶ ὁ μὲν Μάτουρος καὶ 38
ὁ Σάγκτος αὖθις διῄεσαν ἐν τῷ ἀμφιθεάτρῳ διὰ
πάσης κολάσεως, ὡς μηδὲν ὅλως προπεπονθότες,
μᾶλλον δ' ὡς διὰ πλειόνων ἤδη κλήρων ἐκβεβια-
κότες τὸν ἀντίπαλον καὶ περὶ τοῦ στεφάνου αὐτοῦ
τὸν ἀγῶνα ἔχοντες, ὑπέφερον πάλιν τὰς διεξόδους
τῶν μαστίγων τὰς ἐκεῖσε εἰθισμένας καὶ τοὺς
ἀπὸ τῶν θηρίων ἑλκηθμοὺς καὶ πάνθ' ὅσα μαινό-
μενος ὁ δῆμος, ἄλλοι ἀλλαχόθεν, ἐπεβόων καὶ
ἐπεκελεύοντο, ἐπὶ πᾶσιν τὴν σιδηρᾶν καθέδραν,
ἐφ' ἧς τηγανιζόμενα τὰ σώματα κνίσης αὐτοὺς
ἐνεφόρει. οἱ δ' οὐδ' οὕτως ἔληγον, ἀλλ' ἔτι καὶ 39
μᾶλλον ἐξεμαίνοντο, βουλόμενοι νικῆσαι τὴν ἐκείνων
ὑπομονήν, καὶ οὐδ' ὡς παρὰ Σάγκτου ἕτερόν τι
εἰσήκουσαν παρ' ἣν ἀπ' ἀρχῆς εἴθιστο λέγειν
τῆς ὁμολογίας φωνήν.

---

[1] Schwartz thinks with much probability that κοινόν is
a gloss. If so, the meaning of the original would be " to the
424

were arrested confessed without hesitation and gave no thought to the arguments of the devil."

After a few more sentences they go on again: "After this the testimony of their death fell into every kind of variety. For they wove various colours and all kinds of flowers into one wreath to offer to the Father, and so it was necessary for the noble athletes to undergo a varied contest, and after great victory to receive the great crown of immortality. Maturus and Sanctus and Blandina and Attalus were led forth to the wild beasts, to the public,[1] and to a common exhibition of the inhumanity of the heathen, for the day of fighting with beasts was specially appointed for the Christians. Maturus and Sanctus passed again through all torture in the amphitheatre as though they had suffered nothing before, but rather as though, having conquered the opponent in many bouts,[2] they were now striving for his crown, once more they ran the gauntlet in the accustomed manner, endured the worrying of the wild beasts, and everything which the maddened public, some in one way, some in another, were howling for and commanding, finally, the iron chair on which the roasting of their own bodies clothed them with its reek. Their persecutors did not stop even here, but went on growing more and more furious, wishing to conquer their endurance, yet gained nothing from Sanctus beyond the sound of the confession which he had been accustomed to make from the beginning.

public exhibition," but it seems just possible that τὸ δημόσιον is used substantively.

[2] Literally, "lots," but the word was used in a technical sense, for the gladiators used to draw lots as to who should fight. See the note of Valesius on this passage, and compare Lucian, *Hermotimus*. The opponent is Satan.

"Οὗτοι μὲν οὖν, δι' ἀγῶνος μεγάλου ἐπὶ πολὺ 40
παραμενούσης αὐτῶν τῆς ψυχῆς, τοὖσχατον ἐτύθησαν, διὰ τῆς ἡμέρας ἐκείνης ἀντὶ πάσης τῆς ἐν
τοῖς μονομαχίοις ποικιλίας αὐτοὶ θέαμα γενόμενοι
τῷ κόσμῳ· ἡ δὲ Βλανδῖνα ἐπὶ ξύλου κρεμασθεῖσα 41
προύκειτο βορὰ τῶν εἰσβαλλομένων θηρίων· ἣ καὶ
διὰ τοῦ βλέπεσθαι σταυροῦ σχήματι κρεμαμένη
διὰ τῆς εὐτόνου προσευχῆς πολλὴν προθυμίαν
τοῖς ἀγωνιζομένοις ἐνεποίει, βλεπόντων αὐτῶν ἐν
τῷ ἀγῶνι καὶ τοῖς ἔξωθεν ὀφθαλμοῖς διὰ τῆς
ἀδελφῆς τὸν ὑπὲρ αὐτῶν ἐσταυρωμένον, ἵνα πείσῃ
τοὺς πιστεύοντας εἰς αὐτὸν ὅτι πᾶς ὁ ὑπὲρ τῆς
Χριστοῦ δόξης παθὼν τὴν κοινωνίαν ἀεὶ ἔχει
μετὰ τοῦ ζῶντος θεοῦ. καὶ μηδενὸς ἁψαμένου 42
τότε τῶν θηρίων αὐτῆς, καθαιρεθεῖσα ἀπὸ τοῦ
ξύλου ἀνελήφθη πάλιν εἰς τὴν εἱρκτήν, εἰς ἄλλον
Is. 27, 1 ἀγῶνα τηρουμένη, ἵνα διὰ πλειόνων γυμνασμάτων
νικήσασα, τῷ μὲν σκολιῷ ὄφει ἀπαραίτητον
ποιήσῃ τὴν καταδίκην, προτρέψηται δὲ τοὺς
ἀδελφούς, ἡ μικρὰ καὶ ἀσθενὴς καὶ εὐκαταφρόνητος
Rom. 13, 14 μέγαν καὶ ἀκαταγώνιστον ἀθλητὴν Χριστὸν ἐνδε-
Gal. 3, 27 δυμένη, διὰ πολλῶν κλήρων ἐκβιάσασα τὸν ἀντικείμενον καὶ δι' ἀγῶνος τὸν τῆς ἀφθαρσίας στεψαμένη
στέφανον.

" Ὁ δὲ Ἄτταλος καὶ αὐτὸς μεγάλως ἐξαιτηθεὶς 43
ὑπὸ τοῦ ὄχλου (καὶ γὰρ ἦν ὀνομαστός), ἕτοιμος
εἰσῆλθεν ἀγωνιστὴς διὰ τὸ εὐσυνείδητον, ἐπειδὴ
γνησίως ἐν τῇ Χριστιανῇ συντάξει γεγυμνασμένος
ἦν καὶ ἀεὶ μάρτυς ἐγεγόνει παρ' ἡμῖν ἀληθείας.
καὶ περιαχθεὶς κύκλῳ τοῦ ἀμφιθεάτρου, πίνακος 44
αὐτὸν προάγοντος ἐν ᾧ ἐγέγραπτο Ῥωμαϊστὶ
'οὗτός ἐστιν Ἄτταλος ὁ Χριστιανός,' καὶ τοῦ

"Thus after a long time, when their life still remained in them through the great contest, they were at last sacrificed, having been made a spectacle to the world throughout that day as a substitute for all the variations of gladiatorial contests; but Blandina was hung on a stake and offered as a prey to the wild beasts that were let in. She seemed to be hanging in the shape of a cross, and by her continuous prayer gave great zeal to the combatants, while they looked on during the contest, and with their outward eyes saw in the form of their sister him who was crucified for them, to persuade those who believe on him that all who suffer for the glory of Christ have for ever fellowship with the living God. Then when none of the beasts would touch her she was taken down from the stake and brought back into the jail, and was thus preserved for another contest, in order that by winning through more trials she might make irrevocable the condemnation of the crooked serpent, and might encourage the brethren; for small and weak and despised as she was, she had put on the great and invincible athlete, Christ; she had overcome the adversary in many contests, and through the struggle had gained the crown of immortality.

"But Attalus was himself loudly called for by the crowd, for he was well known. He went in, a ready combatant, for his conscience was clear, and he had been nobly trained in Christian discipline and had ever been a witness for truth among us. He was led round the amphitheatre and a placard was carried before him on which was written in Latin, 'This is Attalus, the Christian.' The people were very bitter

δήμου σφόδρα σφριγῶντος ἐπ' αὐτῷ, μαθὼν ὁ ἡγεμὼν ὅτι Ῥωμαῖός ἐστιν, ἐκέλευσεν αὐτὸν ἀναληφθῆναι μετὰ καὶ τῶν λοιπῶν τῶν ἐν τῇ εἰρκτῇ ὄντων, περὶ ὧν ἐπέστειλεν τῷ Καίσαρι καὶ περιέμενεν τὴν ἀπόφασιν τὴν ἀπ' ἐκείνου.

2 Peter 1, 8

" Ὁ δὲ διὰ μέσου καιρὸς οὐκ ἀργὸς αὐτοῖς οὐδὲ 45 ἄκαρπος ἐγίνετο, ἀλλὰ διὰ τῆς ὑπομονῆς αὐτῶν τὸ ἀμέτρητον ἔλεος ἀνεφαίνετο Χριστοῦ· διὰ γὰρ τῶν ζώντων ἐζωοποιοῦντο τὰ νεκρά, καὶ μάρτυρες

2 Cor. 2, 7
Col. 3, 13

τοῖς μὴ μάρτυσιν ἐχαρίζοντο, καὶ ἐνεγίνετο πολλὴ χαρὰ τῇ παρθένῳ μητρί, οὓς ὡς νεκροὺς ἐξέτρωσε, τούτους ζῶντας ἀπολαμβανούσῃ. δι' ἐκείνων γὰρ 46 οἱ πλείους τῶν ἠρνημένων ἀνεμετροῦντο καὶ ἀνεκυΐσκοντο καὶ ἀνεζωπυροῦντο καὶ ἐμάνθανον ὁμολογεῖν καὶ ζῶντες ἤδη καὶ τετονωμένοι προσ-

Ezek. 12, 23;
33, 11

ῄεσαν τῷ βήματι, ἐγγλυκαίνοντος τοῦ τὸν μὲν θάνατον τοῦ ἁμαρτωλοῦ μὴ βουλομένου, ἐπὶ δὲ τὴν μετάνοιαν χρηστευομένου θεοῦ, ἵνα καὶ πάλιν ἐπερωτηθῶσιν ὑπὸ τοῦ ἡγεμόνος. ἐπιστείλαντος 47 γὰρ τοῦ Καίσαρος τοὺς μὲν ἀποτυμπανισθῆναι, εἰ δέ τινες ἀρνοῖντο, τούτους ἀπολυθῆναι, τῆς ἐνθάδε πανηγύρεως (ἔστιν δὲ αὕτη πολυάνθρωπος ἐκ πάντων τῶν ἐθνῶν συνερχομένων εἰς αὐτήν) ἀρχομένης συνεστάναι, ἀνῆγεν ἐπὶ τὸ βῆμα θεατρίζων τοὺς μακαρίους καὶ ἐμπομπεύων τοῖς ὄχλοις· δι' ὃ καὶ πάλιν ἀνήταζεν, καὶ ὅσοι μὲν ἐδόκουν πολιτείαν Ῥωμαίων ἐσχηκέναι, τούτων ἀπέτεμνε τὰς κεφαλάς, τοὺς δὲ λοιποὺς ἔπεμπεν εἰς θηρία. ἐδοξάζετο δὲ μεγάλως ὁ Χριστὸς ἐπὶ 48 τοῖς πρότερον ἀρνησαμένοις, τότε παρὰ τὴν τῶν ἐθνῶν ὑπόνοιαν ὁμολογοῦσιν. καὶ γὰρ ἰδίᾳ οὗτοι ἀνητάζοντο ὡς δῆθεν ἀπολυθησόμενοι, καὶ ὁμο-

against him, but when the governor learnt that he was a Roman, he commanded him to be put back with the rest, who were in the jail, about whom he had written to the emperor and was waiting for his reply.

"But the intervening time was not idle or fruitless for them but through their endurance was manifested the immeasurable mercy of Christ, for through the living the dead were being quickened and martyrs gave grace to those who had denied. And there was great joy to the Virgin Mother who had miscarried with them as though dead, and was receiving them back alive. For through them the majority of those who had denied were again brought to birth [1] and again conceived and quickened again, and learned to confess, and now alive and vigorous, made happy by God who wills not the death of the sinner, but is kind towards repentance, went to the judgement-seat, in order that they might again be interrogated by the governor. For Caesar had written that they should be tortured to death, but that if any should recant they should be let go, and at the beginning of the local feast (and this is widely attended by the concourse of all the heathen to it) the governor led them to the judgement-seat, making a show and spectacle of the blessed men to the mob. He accordingly examined them again, beheaded all who appeared to possess Roman citizenship, and sent the rest to the beasts. And Christ was greatly glorified by those who had formerly denied but then confessed contrary to the expectation of the people. For they were examined by themselves with the intention of then letting them

---

[1] The Greek text ἀνεμετροῦντο is meaningless. I have translated Schwartz's ἀνεμαιοῦντο, "brought to birth," though it is not quite satisfactory.

λογοῦντες προσετίθεντο τῷ τῶν μαρτύρων κλήρῳ·
ἔμειναν δὲ ἔξω οἱ μηδὲ ἴχνος πώποτε πίστεως μηδὲ
αἴσθησιν ἐνδύματος νυμφικοῦ μηδὲ ἔννοιαν φόβου
θεοῦ σχόντες, ἀλλὰ καὶ διὰ τῆς ἀναστροφῆς αὐτῶν
βλασφημοῦντες τὴν ὁδόν, τοῦτ' ἐστὶν οἱ υἱοὶ τῆς
ἀπωλείας, οἱ δὲ λοιποὶ πάντες τῇ ἐκκλησίᾳ προσ-
ετέθησαν· ὧν καὶ ἀνεταζομένων, Ἀλέξανδρός τις, 49
Φρὺξ μὲν τὸ γένος, ἰατρὸς δὲ τὴν ἐπιστήμην,
πολλοῖς ἔτεσιν ἐν ταῖς Γαλλίαις διατρίψας καὶ
γνωστὸς σχεδὸν πᾶσιν διὰ τὴν πρὸς θεὸν ἀγάπην
καὶ παρρησίαν τοῦ λόγου (ἦν γὰρ καὶ οὐκ ἄμοιρος
ἀποστολικοῦ χαρίσματος), παρεστὼς τῷ βήματι
καὶ νεύματι προτρέπων αὐτοὺς πρὸς τὴν ὁμολογίαν,
φανερὸς ἦν τοῖς περιεστηκόσιν τὸ βῆμα ὥσπερ
ὠδίνων. ἀγανακτήσαντες δὲ οἱ ὄχλοι ἐπὶ τῷ 50
τοὺς πρότερον ἠρνημένους αὖθις ὁμολογεῖν, κατε-
βόησαν τοῦ Ἀλεξάνδρου ὡς ἐκείνου τοῦτο ποιοῦντος,
καὶ ἐπιστήσαντος τοῦ ἡγεμόνος καὶ ἀνετάσαντος
αὐτὸν τίς εἴη, τοῦ δὲ φήσαντος ὅτι 'Χριστιανός,'
ἐν ὀργῇ γενόμενος κατέκρινεν αὐτὸν πρὸς θηρία.
καὶ τῇ ἐπιούσῃ εἰσῆλθεν μετὰ καὶ τοῦ Ἀττάλου,
καὶ γὰρ καὶ τὸν Ἄτταλον τῷ ὄχλῳ χαριζόμενος
ὁ ἡγεμὼν ἐξέδωκε πάλιν πρὸς θηρία· οἳ καὶ διὰ 51
πάντων διελθόντες τῶν ἐν τῷ ἀμφιθεάτρῳ πρὸς
κόλασιν ἐξηυρημένων ὀργάνων καὶ μέγιστον ὑπο-
μείναντες ἀγῶνα, τοὔσχατον ἐτύθησαν καὶ αὐτοί, τοῦ
μὲν Ἀλεξάνδρου μήτε στενάξαντος μήτε γρύξαντός
τι ὅλως, ἀλλὰ κατὰ καρδίαν ὁμιλοῦντος τῷ θεῷ,
ὁ δὲ Ἄτταλος, ὁπότε ἐπὶ τῆς σιδηρᾶς ἐπετέθη 52
καθέδρας καὶ περιεκαίετο, ἡνίκα ἡ ἀπὸ τοῦ
σώματος κνῖσα ἀνεφέρετο, ἔφη πρὸς τὸ πλῆθος
τῇ Ῥωμαϊκῇ φωνῇ 'ἰδοὺ τοῦτό ἐστιν ἀνθρώπους

Matt. 22, 11-
13
Rom. 2. 24

John 17, 12

Acts 4, 29-31

go, but confessed and were added to the ranks of the martyrs. Those indeed remained without who had never had any vestige of faith, nor perception of the bridal garment, nor idea of the fear of God, but even through their behaviour blasphemed the Way—they are the sons of perdition — but all the rest were added to the church. When they too were being examined a certain Alexander, a Phrygian by race and a physician by profession, who had lived in Gaul for many years and was known to almost every one for his love toward God and boldness of speech (for he was not without a share of the apostolic gift), stood by the judgement-seat and by signs encouraged them to confession, and seemed to those who were standing by as though he were in travail. But the crowd, angry that those who had formerly denied were confessing again, howled at Alexander as though he were responsible for this. The governor summoned him and asked him who he was, and when he said 'a Christian,' he flew into a rage and condemned him to the beasts. And the next day he went into the arena together with Attalus; for to please the mob the governor had given Attalus back to the beasts. They passed through all the instruments of torture which were prepared in the amphitheatre, and endured a great contest. Finally they too were sacrificed. Alexander uttered neither groan nor moan at all, but conversed with God in his heart, and Attalus, when he was put on the iron chair and was being burned and the reek arose from his body, said to the crowd in Latin, 'Lo, this which

ἐσθίειν, ὃ ποιεῖτε ὑμεῖς· ἡμεῖς δὲ οὔτε ἀνθρώπους ἐσθίομεν οὔθ᾽ ἕτερόν τι πονηρὸν πράσσομεν.' ἐπερωτώμενος δὲ τί ὄνομα ἔχει ὁ θεός, ἀπεκρίθη ' ὁ θεὸς ὄνομα οὐκ ἔχει ὡς ἄνθρωπος.'

" Ἐπὶ πᾶσι δὲ τούτοις τῇ ἐσχάτῃ λοιπὸν ἡμέρᾳ 53 τῶν μονομαχιῶν ἡ Βλανδῖνα πάλιν εἰσεκομίζετο μετὰ καὶ Ποντικοῦ, παιδαρίου ὡς πεντεκαίδεκα ἐτῶν, οἳ καὶ καθ᾽ ἡμέραν εἰσήγοντο πρὸς τὸ βλέπειν τὴν τῶν λοιπῶν κόλασιν· καὶ ἠναγκάζοντο ὀμνύναι κατὰ τῶν εἰδώλων αὐτῶν, καὶ διὰ τὸ ἐμμένειν εὐσταθῶς καὶ ἐξουθενεῖν αὐτοὺς ἠγριώθη πρὸς αὐτοὺς τὸ πλῆθος, ὡς μήτε τὴν ἡλικίαν τοῦ παιδὸς οἰκτεῖραι μήτε τὸ γύναιον αἰδεσθῆναι, πρὸς 54 πάντα δὲ τὰ δεινὰ παρέβαλλον αὐτοὺς καὶ διὰ πάσης ἐν κύκλῳ διῆγον κολάσεως, ἐπαλλήλως ἀναγκάζοντες ὀμόσαι, ἀλλὰ μὴ δυνάμενοι τοῦτο πρᾶξαι. ὁ μὲν γὰρ Ποντικὸς ὑπὸ τῆς ἀδελφῆς παρωρμημένος, ὡς καὶ τὰ ἔθνη βλέπειν ὅτι ἐκείνη ἦν προτρεπομένη καὶ στηρίζουσα αὐτόν, πᾶσαν κόλασιν γενναίως ὑπομείνας ἀπέδωκεν τὸ πνεῦμα· ἡ δὲ μακαρία Βλανδῖνα πάντων ἐσχάτη, καθάπερ 55 μήτηρ εὐγενὴς παρορμήσασα τὰ τέκνα καὶ νικηφόρους προπέμψασα πρὸς τὸν βασιλέα, ἀναμετρουμένη καὶ αὐτὴ πάντα τὰ τῶν παίδων ἀγωνίσματα ἔσπευδεν πρὸς αὐτούς, χαίρουσα καὶ ἀγαλλιωμένη ἐπὶ τῇ ἐξόδῳ, ὡς εἰς νυμφικὸν δεῖπνον κεκλημένη, ἀλλὰ μὴ πρὸς θηρία βεβλημένη· καὶ μετὰ τὰς μάστιγας, μετὰ τὰ θηρία, μετὰ τὸ 56 τήγανον, τοὔσχατον εἰς γυργαθὸν βληθεῖσα ταύρῳ παρεβλήθη, καὶ ἱκανῶς ἀναβληθεῖσα πρὸς τοῦ ζῴου μηδὲ αἴσθησιν ἔτι τῶν συμβαινόντων ἔχουσα διὰ τὴν ἐλπίδα καὶ ἐποχὴν τῶν πεπιστευμένων καὶ

you are doing is to eat men, but we neither eat men nor do anything else wicked.' And when he was asked what name God has, he replied, ' God has not a name as a man has.'

" In addition to all this, on the last day of the gladiatorial sports, Blandina was again brought in with Ponticus, a boy of about fifteen years old, and they had been brought in every day to see the torture of the others, and efforts were made to force them to swear by the idols, and the mob was furious against them because they had remained steadfast and disregarded them, so that there was neither pity for the youth of the boy nor respect for the sex of the woman. They exposed them to all the terrors and put them through every torture in turn, trying to make them swear, but not being able to do so. For Ponticus was encouraged by the Christian sister, so that even the heathen saw that she was exhorting and strengthening him, and after nobly enduring every torture he gave up his spirit. But the blessed Blandina, last of all, like a noble mother who had encouraged her children and sent them forth triumphant to the king, having herself endured all the tortures of the children, hastened to them, rejoicing and glad at her departure as though invited to a marriage feast rather than cast to the beasts. And after scourging, after the beasts, after the gridiron, she was at last put in a net and thrown to a bull. She was tossed about a long time by the beast, having no more feeling for what happened to her through her hope and hold on what had been en-

ὁμιλίαν πρὸς Χριστόν, ἐτύθη καὶ αὐτή, καὶ αὐτῶν
ὁμολογούντων τῶν ἐθνῶν ὅτι μηδεπώποτε παρ'
αὐτοῖς γυνὴ τοιαῦτα καὶ τοσαῦτα ἔπαθεν.

" 'Αλλ' οὐδ' οὕτως κόρον ἐλάμβανεν αὐτῶν ἡ 57
μανία καὶ ἡ πρὸς τοὺς ἁγίους ὠμότης. ὑπὸ γὰρ
ἀγρίου θηρὸς ἄγρια καὶ βάρβαρα φῦλα ταραχθέντα
δυσπαύστως εἶχεν, καὶ ἄλλην ἰδίαν ἀρχὴν ἐπὶ τοῖς
σώμασιν ἐλάμβανεν ἡ ὕβρις αὐτῶν· τὸ γὰρ νενικῆ- 58
σθαι αὐτοὺς οὐκ ἐδυσώπει διὰ τὸ μὴ ἔχειν ἀνθρώ-
πινον ἐπιλογισμόν, μᾶλλον δὲ καὶ ἐξέκαιεν αὐτῶν
τὴν ὀργὴν καθάπερ θηρίου, καὶ τοῦ ἡγεμόνος καὶ
τοῦ δήμου τὸ ὅμοιον εἰς ἡμᾶς ἄδικον ἐπιδεικ-
Rev. 22, 11 νυμένων μῖσος, ἵνα ἡ γραφὴ πληρωθῇ ' ὁ ἄνομος
ἀνομησάτω ἔτι, καὶ ὁ δίκαιος δικαιωθήτω ἔτι.'
καὶ γὰρ τοὺς ἐναποπνιγέντας τῇ εἱρκτῇ παρ- 59
έβαλλον κυσίν, ἐπιμελῶς παραφυλάσσοντες νύκτωρ
καὶ μεθ' ἡμέραν μὴ κηδευθῇ τις ὑφ' ἡμῶν· καὶ
τότε δὴ προθέντες τά τε τῶν θηρίων τά τε τοῦ
πυρὸς λείψανα, πῆ μὲν ἐσπαραγμένα, πῆ δὲ
ἠνθρακευμένα, καὶ τῶν λοιπῶν τὰς κεφαλὰς σὺν
τοῖς ἀποτμήμασιν αὐτῶν ὡσαύτως ἀτάφους παρεφύλαττον μετὰ στρατιωτικῆς ἐπιμελείας ἡμέραις
Acts 7, 54 συχναῖς. καὶ οἱ μὲν ἐνεβριμοῦντο καὶ ἔβρυχον 60
τοὺς ὀδόντας ἐπ' αὐτοῖς, ζητοῦντές τινα περισ-
σοτέραν ἐκδίκησιν παρ' αὐτῶν λαβεῖν, οἱ δὲ
ἐνεγέλων καὶ ἐπετώθαζον, μεγαλύνοντες ἅμα τὰ
εἴδωλα αὐτῶν καὶ ἐκείνοις προσάπτοντες τὴν
τούτων τιμωρίαν, οἱ δὲ ἐπιεικέστεροι καὶ κατὰ
ποσὸν συμπαθεῖν δοκοῦντες ὠνείδιζον πολύ, λέγοντες ' ποῦ ὁ θεὸς αὐτῶν καὶ τί αὐτοὺς ὤνησεν
ἡ θρησκεία, ἣν καὶ πρὸ τῆς ἑαυτῶν εἵλαντο ψυχῆς; '
καὶ τὰ μὲν ἀπ' ἐκείνων τοιαύτην εἶχε τὴν ποικιλίαν, 61
434

trusted to her and her converse with Christ. And so she too was sacrificed, and the heathen themselves confessed that never before among them had a woman suffered so much and so long.

" Not even thus was their madness and cruelty to the saints satisfied, for, incited by a wild beast,[1] wild and barbarous tribes could scarcely stop, and their violence began again in a new way on the bodies ; for that they had been conquered[2] did not shame them, because they had no human reason, but it rather inflamed their wrath as of a wild beast, and the governor and the people showed the like unrighteous hatred against us that the Scripture might be fulfilled, ' Let him that is unlawful be unlawful still, and he that is righteous be righteous still.' For those who had been strangled in the jail they threw to the dogs, and watched carefully night and day that none should be cared for by us. Then they threw out the remains left by the beasts and by the fire, torn and charred, and for many days watched with a military guard the heads of the rest, together with their trunks, all unburied. And some raged and gnashed their teeth at the remains, seeking some further vengeance from them, others laughed and jeered, glorifying their idols and ascribing to them the punishment of the Christians, and the gentler, who seemed to have a little sympathy, mocked greatly, saying, ' Where is their god and what good to them was their worship, which they preferred beyond their lives ? ' Their conduct thus

---

[1] That is, by the Devil.
[2] Because they had been unable to break the courage of the martyrs.

τὰ δὲ καθ' ἡμᾶς ἐν μεγάλῳ καθειστήκει πένθει διὰ
τὸ μὴ δύνασθαι τὰ σώματα κρύψαι τῇ γῇ· οὔτε
γὰρ νὺξ συνεβάλλετο ἡμῖν πρὸς τοῦτο οὔτε ἀργύρια
ἔπειθεν οὔτε λιτανεία ἐδυσώπει, παντὶ δὲ τρόπῳ
παρετήρουν, ὡς μέγα τι κερδανοῦντες, εἰ μὴ
τύχοιεν ταφῆς.''

Τούτοις ἑξῆς μεθ' ἕτερά φασιν· '' τὰ οὖν σώματα 62
τῶν μαρτύρων παντοίως παραδειγματισθέντα καὶ
αἰθριασθέντα ἐπὶ ἡμέρας ἕξ, μετέπειτα καέντα
καὶ αἰθαλωθέντα ὑπὸ τῶν ἀνόμων κατεσαρώθη εἰς
τὸν Ῥοδανὸν ποταμὸν πλησίον παραρρέοντα, ὅπως
μηδὲ λείψανον αὐτῶν φαίνηται ἐπὶ τῆς γῆς ἔτι.
καὶ ταῦτ' ἔπραττον ὡς δυνάμενοι νικῆσαι τὸν θεὸν 63
καὶ ἀφελέσθαι αὐτῶν τὴν παλιγγενεσίαν, ἵνα, ὡς
ἔλεγον ἐκεῖνοι, 'μηδὲ ἐλπίδα σχῶσιν ἀναστάσεως,
ἐφ' ᾗ πεποιθότες ξένην τινὰ καὶ καινὴν εἰσάγουσιν
ἡμῖν θρησκείαν καὶ καταφρονοῦσι τῶν δεινῶν,
ἕτοιμοι καὶ μετὰ χαρᾶς ἥκοντες ἐπὶ τὸν θάνατον
νῦν ἴδωμεν εἰ ἀναστήσονται καὶ εἰ δύναται βοηθῆσαι
αὐτοῖς ὁ θεὸς αὐτῶν καὶ ἐξελέσθαι ἐκ τῶν χειρῶν
ἡμῶν.' ''

II. Τοιαῦτα καὶ τὰ κατὰ τὸν δεδηλωμένον αὐτο- 1
κράτορα ταῖς Χριστοῦ συμβέβηκεν ἐκκλησίαις,
ἀφ' ὧν καὶ τὰ ἐν ταῖς λοιπαῖς ἐπαρχίαις ἐνηργημένα
εἰκότι λογισμῷ στοχάζεσθαι πάρεστιν. ἄξιον τούτοις ἐκ τῆς αὐτῆς ἐπισυνάψαι γραφῆς λέξεις
ἑτέρας, δι' ὧν τὸ ἐπιεικὲς καὶ φιλάνθρωπον τῶν
δεδηλωμένων μαρτύρων ἀναγέγραπται τούτοις
αὐτοῖς τοῖς ῥήμασιν· '' οἳ καὶ ἐπὶ τοσοῦτον ζηλωταὶ 2

Phil. 2, 6
καὶ μιμηταὶ Χριστοῦ ἐγένοντο, ὃς ἐν μορφῇ θεοῦ
ὑπάρχων οὐχ ἁρπαγμὸν ἡγήσατο τὸ εἶναι ἴσα θεῷ,
ὥστε ἐν τοιαύτῃ δόξῃ ὑπάρχοντες καὶ οὐχ ἅπαξ

436

varied, but in our circle great grief obtained, because we could not bury the bodies in the earth, for night did not avail us for this, nor did money persuade nor entreaty shame, but in every way they watched, as though they would make some great gain, that the bodies should not obtain burial."

Further on they say: "Thus the bodies of the martyrs, after having been exposed and insulted in every way for six days, and afterwards burned and turned to ashes, were swept by the wicked into the river Rhone which flows near by, that not even a relic of them might still appear upon the earth. And this they did as though they could conquer God and take away their rebirth in order, as they said, ' that they might not even have any hope of resurrection, through trusting in which they have brought in strange and new worship and despised terrors, going readily and with joy to death; now let us see if they will rise again, and if their God be able to help them and to take them out of our hands.' "

II. Such things happened to the churches of Christ under the emperor mentioned, and from them it is possible to form a reasonable conclusion as to what was done in the other provinces. It is worth while to add other statements from the same document, in which the gentleness and the kindness of the martyrs already mentioned have been set down in these very words. " And they carried so far their zeal and imitation of Christ, ' who being in the form of God, thought it not robbery to be equal with God,' that for all their glory, and though they had

οὐδὲ δὶς ἀλλὰ πολλάκις μαρτυρήσαντες καὶ ἐκ
θηρίων αὖθις ἀναληφθέντες καὶ τὰ καυτήρια καὶ
τοὺς μώλωπας καὶ τὰ τραύματα ἔχοντες περι-
κείμενα, οὔτ' αὐτοὶ μάρτυρας ἑαυτοὺς ἀνεκήρυττον
οὔτε μὴν ἡμῖν ἐπέτρεπον τούτῳ τῷ ὀνόματι
προσαγορεύειν αὐτούς, ἀλλ' εἴ ποτέ τις ἡμῶν δι'
ἐπιστολῆς ἢ διὰ λόγου μάρτυρας αὐτοὺς προσεῖπεν,
ἐπέπλησσον πικρῶς. ἡδέως γὰρ παρεχώρουν τὴν **3**

Rev. 3, 14
Rev. 1, 5
Acts 3, 15

τῆς μαρτυρίας προσηγορίαν τῷ Χριστῷ, τῷ πιστῷ
καὶ ἀληθινῷ μάρτυρι καὶ πρωτοτόκῳ τῶν νεκρῶν
καὶ ἀρχηγῷ τῆς ζωῆς τοῦ θεοῦ, καὶ ἐπεμιμνήσκον-
το τῶν ἐξεληλυθότων ἤδη μαρτύρων καὶ ἔλεγον
'ἐκεῖνοι ἤδη μάρτυρες, οὓς ἐν τῇ ὁμολογίᾳ Χριστὸς
ἠξίωσεν ἀναληφθῆναι, ἐπισφραγισάμενος αὐτῶν
διὰ τῆς ἐξόδου τὴν μαρτυρίαν, ἡμεῖς δὲ ὁμόλογοι
μέτριοι καὶ ταπεινοί,' καὶ μετὰ δακρύων παρ-
εκάλουν τοὺς ἀδελφοὺς δεόμενοι ἵνα ἐκτενεῖς εὐχαὶ
γίνωνται πρὸς τὸ τελειωθῆναι αὐτούς. καὶ τὴν **4**
μὲν δύναμιν τῆς μαρτυρίας ἔργῳ ἐπεδείκνυντο,
πολλὴν παρρησίαν ἄγοντες πρὸς τὰ ἔθνη, καὶ τὴν
εὐγένειαν διὰ τῆς ὑπομονῆς καὶ ἀφοβίας καὶ
ἀτρομίας φανερὰν ἐποίουν, τὴν δὲ πρὸς τοὺς
ἀδελφοὺς τῶν μαρτύρων προσηγορίαν παρῃτοῦντο,
ἐμπεπλησμένοι φόβου θεοῦ.''

1 Peter 5, 6

Καὶ αὖθις μετὰ βραχέα φασίν· '' ἐταπείνουν **5**
ἑαυτοὺς ὑπὸ τὴν κραταιὰν χεῖρα, ὑφ' ἧς ἱκανῶς
νῦν εἰσιν ὑψωμένοι. τότε δὲ πᾶσι μὲν ἀπελογοῦντο,
κατηγόρουν δὲ οὐδενός· ἔλυον ἅπαντας, ἐδέσμευον

---

[1] Or "witness." The translation of all this passage is
rendered difficult by the impossibility of translating the
Greek word μαρτύς by the same English word in all passages.
" Martyr " has been adopted so far as possible but the sense
of " witness " is much more present than it is in the English

testified not once or twice but many times, and had
been taken back from the beasts and were covered
with burns and scars and wounds, they neither proclaimed themselves as martyrs, nor allowed us to
address them by this title. But if ever any one of
us called them martyrs either in a letter or in speech
they rebuked him sharply. For they gladly con-
ceded the title of martyrdom to Christ, the faithful
and true martyr [1] and first-born from the dead and
author of the life of God. And they reminded us of
the martyrs who had already passed away, and said
' they are already martyrs, whom Christ vouchsafed
to be taken up at their confession, and sealed their
witness by their departure, but we are lowly and
humble confessors.' [2] And they besought the
brethren with tears, begging that earnest prayers
might be made for their consecration. The power
of martyrdom they actually showed, having great
boldness towards the heathen, and they made plain
their nobleness by endurance and absence of fear or
timidity ; but the title of martyr they refused from
the brethren, for they were filled with the fear of
God."

A little further on they say: "They humbled
themselves under the mighty hand and by it they
have now been greatly exalted. At that time they
made defence for all men, against none did they
bring accusation ; they released all and bound none ;

word, for though it is used in a more or less technical sense,
it does not as yet imply death.

[2] The sense must be as given above, but the Greek word
does not appear to be used in this sense. It is corrected
in later manuscripts to ὁμολογηταί. Schwartz thinks that
it is a primitive error for ὁμολογο[ῦντες ἔτ]ι, and Wendland
suggested ὁμόδουλοι.

δὲ οὐδένα· καὶ ὑπὲρ τῶν τὰ δεινὰ διατιθέντων
ηὔχοντο, καθάπερ Στέφανος ὁ τέλειος μάρτυς
'κύριε, μὴ στήσῃς αὐτοῖς τὴν ἁμαρτίαν ταύτην.'
εἰ δ' ὑπὲρ τῶν λιθαζόντων ἐδέετο, πόσῳ μᾶλλον
ὑπὲρ τῶν ἀδελφῶν.''

Καὶ αὖθίς φασι μεθ' ἕτερα· ''οὗτος γὰρ καὶ 6
μέγιστος αὐτοῖς πρὸς αὐτὸν ὁ πόλεμος ἐγένετο
διὰ τὸ γνήσιον τῆς ἀγάπης, ἵνα ἀποπνιχθεὶς ὁ θὴρ
οὓς πρότερον ᾤετο καταπεπωκέναι, ζῶντας ἐξεμέσῃ.
οὐ γὰρ ἔλαβον καύχημα κατὰ τῶν πεπτωκότων,
ἀλλ' ἐν οἷς ἐπλεόναζον αὐτοί, τοῦτο τοῖς ἐνδεε-
στέροις ἐπήρκουν μητρικὰ σπλάγχνα ἔχοντες, καὶ
πολλὰ περὶ αὐτῶν ἐκχέοντες δάκρυα πρὸς τὸν
πατέρα, ζωὴν ᾐτήσαντο, καὶ ἔδωκεν αὐτοῖς· ἣν 7
καὶ συνεμερίσαντο τοῖς πλησίον, κατὰ πάντα
νικηφόροι πρὸς θεὸν ἀπελθόντες. εἰρήνην ἀγα-
πήσαντες ἀεὶ καὶ εἰρήνην ἡμῖν παρεγγυήσαντες,
μετ' εἰρήνης ἐχώρησαν πρὸς θεόν, μὴ καταλιπόντες
πόνον τῇ μητρὶ μηδὲ στάσιν καὶ πόλεμον τοῖς
ἀδελφοῖς ἀλλὰ χαρὰν καὶ εἰρήνην καὶ ὁμόνοιαν
καὶ ἀγάπην.'' ταῦτα καὶ περὶ τῆς τῶν μακαρίων 8
ἐκείνων πρὸς τοὺς παραπεπτωκότας τῶν ἀδελφῶν
στοργῆς ὠφελίμως προκείσθω τῆς ἀπανθρώπου
καὶ ἀνηλεοῦς ἕνεκα διαθέσεως τῶν μετὰ ταῦτα
ἀφειδῶς τοῖς Χριστοῦ μέλεσιν προσενηνεγμένων.

III. Ἡ δ' αὐτὴ τῶν προειρημένων μαρτύρων 1
γραφὴ καὶ ἄλλην τινὰ μνήμης ἀξίαν ἱστορίαν περιέχει, ἣν καὶ οὐδεὶς ἂν γένοιτο φθόνος μὴ οὐχὶ τῶν

---

[1] The "beast" is the Devil, and those whom he had
swallowed are those who had at first recanted; the hope of
the confessors was to regain backsliders and so rescue them
from the Devil's maw.   [2] That is, the Church.

and they prayed for those who had inflicted torture, even as did Stephen, the perfect martyr, ' Lord, lay not this sin to their charge.' And if he prayed for those who were stoning him, how much more for the brethren ? "

And again after other details, they say : " For their greatest contest, through the genuineness of their love, was this, that the beast[1] should be choked into throwing up alive those whom he had at first thought to have swallowed down. For they did not boast over the fallen, but from their own abundance supplied with a mother's love those that needed, and shedding many tears for them to the Father, they prayed for life, and he gave it to them, and they divided it among their neighbours, and then departed to God, having in all things carried off the victory. They ever loved peace ; peace they commended to us ; and with peace they departed to God ; for their mother[2] they left behind no sorrow, and for the brethren no strife and war, but glory, peace, concord, and love." Let this profitable extract suffice concerning the love of those blessed ones for their brethren who had fallen, for the sake of the inhuman and merciless disposition of those who after these events acted unsparingly to the members of Christ.[3]

III. The same document of the aforementioned martyrs contains also another story worthy of memory, and none could grudge our bringing it to

[3] Eusebius wishes to emphasize the charity of these martyrs towards backsliders in contrast to the hardness of soul of his own contemporaries, notably the Donatists and Novatians.

ἐντευξομένων εἰς γνῶσιν προθεῖναι· ἔχει δὲ οὕτως. Ἀλκιβιάδου γάρ τινος ἐξ αὐτῶν πάνυ αὐχμηρὸν 2 βιοῦντος βίον καὶ μηδενὸς ὅλως τὸ πρότερον μεταλαμβάνοντος, ἀλλ᾽ ἢ ἄρτῳ μόνῳ καὶ ὕδατι χρωμένου πειρωμένου τε καὶ ἐν τῇ εἱρκτῇ οὕτω διάγειν, Ἀττάλῳ μετὰ τὸν πρῶτον ἀγῶνα ὃν ἐν τῷ ἀμφιθεάτρῳ ἤνυσεν, ἀπεκαλύφθη ὅτι μὴ καλῶς ποιοίη ὁ Ἀλκιβιάδης μὴ χρώμενος τοῖς κτίσμασι τοῦ θεοῦ καὶ ἄλλοις τύπον σκανδάλου ὑπολειπόμε- νος. πεισθεὶς δὲ ὁ Ἀλκιβιάδης πάντων ἀνέδην 3 μετελάμβανεν καὶ ηὐχαρίστει τῷ θεῷ· οὐ γὰρ ἀνεπίσκεπτοι χάριτος θεοῦ ἦσαν, ἀλλὰ τὸ πνεῦμα τὸ ἅγιον ἦν σύμβουλον αὐτοῖς. καὶ ταῦτα μὲν ὡδὶ ἐχέτω.

Τῶν δ᾽ ἀμφὶ τὸν Μοντανὸν καὶ Ἀλκιβιάδην καὶ 4 Θεόδοτον περὶ τὴν Φρυγίαν ἄρτι τότε πρῶτον τὴν περὶ τοῦ προφητεύειν ὑπόληψιν παρὰ πολλοῖς ἐκφερομένων (πλεῖσται γὰρ οὖν καὶ ἄλλαι παρα- δοξοποιίαι τοῦ θείου χαρίσματος εἰς ἔτι τότε κατὰ διαφόρους ἐκκλησίας ἐκτελούμεναι πίστιν παρὰ πολλοῖς τοῦ κἀκείνους προφητεύειν παρεῖχον) καὶ δὴ διαφωνίας ὑπαρχούσης περὶ τῶν δεδηλω- μένων, αὖθις οἱ κατὰ τὴν Γαλλίαν ἀδελφοὶ τὴν ἰδίαν κρίσιν καὶ περὶ τούτων εὐλαβῆ καὶ ὀρθο- δοξοτάτην ὑποτάττουσιν, ἐκθέμενοι καὶ τῶν παρ᾽ αὐτοῖς τελειωθέντων μαρτύρων διαφόρους ἐπι- στολάς, ἃς ἐν δεσμοῖς ἔτι ὑπάρχοντες τοῖς ἐπ᾽ Ἀσίας καὶ Φρυγίας ἀδελφοῖς διεχάραξαν, οὐ μὴν ἀλλὰ καὶ Ἐλευθέρῳ τῷ τότε Ῥωμαίων ἐπισκόπῳ, τῆς τῶν ἐκκλησιῶν εἰρήνης ἕνεκα πρεσβεύοντες.

the knowledge of those who are about to study. It runs thus : There was among them a certain Alcibiades, who was living a very austere life, and at first was not partaking of anything at all, but used merely bread and water and was trying to live thus even in the jail. But it was revealed to Attalus after the first contest which he underwent in the amphitheatre that Alcibiades was not doing well in not making use of the creations of God, and offering an example of offence [1] to others. Alcibiades was persuaded and began to partake of everything without restraint and gave thanks to God ; for they were not without help from the grace of God but the Holy Spirit was their counsellor. Let this suffice for this point.

Just at that time the party of Montanus and Alcibiades and Theodotus in Phrygia began first to engender among many their views concerning prophecy (for the many other wonderful works of the grace of God which were still being wrought up to that time in divers churches produced the belief among many that they also were prophets), and when dissension arose about the persons mentioned the brethren in Gaul again formulated their own judgement, pious and most orthodox, concerning them, subjoining various letters from the martyrs who had been consecrated among them, which letters while they were still in prison they had composed for the brethren in Asia and Phrygia, and also for Eleutherus, who was then bishop of the Romans, and so they were ambassadors for the sake of the peace of the churches.

[1] An " example of offence " because it might seem to support the heretical doctrine that matter is evil, as some Gnostics maintained.

IV. Οἱ δ' αὐτοὶ μάρτυρες καὶ τὸν Εἰρηναῖον, πρεσ- 1
βύτερον ἤδη τότ' ὄντα τῆς ἐν Λουγδούνῳ παροικίας,
τῷ δηλωθέντι κατὰ Ῥώμην ἐπισκόπῳ συνίστων,
πλεῖστα τῷ ἀνδρὶ μαρτυροῦντες, ὡς αἱ τούτον
ἔχουσαι τὸν τρόπον δηλοῦσι φωναί· " χαίρειν ἐν 2
θεῷ σε πάλιν εὐχόμεθα καὶ ἀεί, πάτερ Ἐλεύθερε.

Rev. 1, 9

ταῦτά σοι τὰ γράμματα προετρεψάμεθα τὸν
ἀδελφὸν ἡμῶν καὶ κοινωνὸν Εἰρηναῖον διακομίσαι,
καὶ παρακαλοῦμεν ἔχειν σε αὐτὸν ἐν παραθέσει,
ζηλωτὴν ὄντα τῆς διαθήκης Χριστοῦ. εἰ γὰρ
ᾔδειμεν τόπον τινὶ δικαιοσύνην περιποιεῖσθαι, ὡς
πρεσβύτερον ἐκκλησίας, ὅπερ ἐστὶν ἐπ' αὐτῷ, ἐν
πρώτοις ἂν παρεθέμεθα."

Τί δεῖ καταλέγειν τὸν ἐν τῇ δηλωθείσῃ γραφῇ 3
τῶν μαρτύρων κατάλογον, ἰδίᾳ μὲν τῶν ἀποτμήσει
κεφαλῆς τετελειωμένων, ἰδίᾳ δὲ τῶν θηρσὶν εἰς
βορὰν παραβεβλημένων, καὶ αὖθις τῶν ἐπὶ τῆς
εἱρκτῆς κεκοιμημένων, τόν τε ἀριθμὸν τῶν εἰς
ἔτι τότε περιόντων ὁμολογητῶν; ὅτῳ γὰρ φίλον,
καὶ ταῦτα ῥᾴδιον πληρέστατα διαγνῶναι μετὰ
χεῖρας ἀναλαβόντι τὸ σύγγραμμα, ὃ καὶ αὐτὸ τῇ
τῶν μαρτύρων συναγωγῇ πρὸς ἡμῶν, ὡς γοῦν
ἔφην, κατείλεκται. ἀλλὰ τὰ μὲν ἐπ' Ἀντωνίνου
τοιαῦτα.

V. Τούτου δὴ ἀδελφὸν Μάρκον Αὐρήλιον Καίσαρα 1
λόγος ἔχει Γερμανοῖς καὶ Σαρμάταις ἀντιπαρα-
ταττόμενον μάχῃ, δίψει πιεζομένης αὐτοῦ τῆς
στρατιᾶς, ἐν ἀμηχανίᾳ γενέσθαι· τοὺς δ' ἐπὶ τῆς
Μελιτηνῆς οὕτω καλουμένης λεγεῶνος στρατιώτας
διὰ πίστεως ἐξ ἐκείνου καὶ εἰς δεῦρο συνεστώσης
ἐν τῇ πρὸς τοὺς πολεμίους παρατάξει γόνυ θέντας
ἐπὶ γῆν κατὰ τὸ οἰκεῖον ἡμῖν τῶν εὐχῶν ἔθος ἐπὶ

IV. Irenaeus also, who was at that time already a presbyter of the diocese at Lyons, the same martyrs commended to the afore-mentioned bishop of Rome, and gave him much good testimony, as is shown by words to the following effect: " Once more and always, Father Eleutherus, we wish you greeting in God. We have asked our brother and companion, Irenaeus, to bring this letter to you and we beg you to hold him in esteem, for he is zealous for the covenant of Christ. For had we known that rank can confer righteousness on anyone, we should first of all have recommended him as being a presbyter of the church, for that is his position."

What need is there to transcribe the list of the martyrs in the above mentioned document, some consecrated by beheading, some cast out to be eaten by the wild beasts, others who fell asleep in the jail, and the number of the confessors which still survived at that time ? For whoever wishes can easily read the full account by taking the description which has been included in our collection of martyrs,[1] as I said before. Such were the events which happened under Antoninus.

V. It is said that when his brother, Marcus Aurelius Caesar, was engaging in battle with the Germans and Sarmatians, he was in difficulties, because his army was oppressed by thirst ; but the soldiers of the legion which is called after Melitene,[2] knelt on the ground according to our own custom of prayer, in the faith which has sustained them from that time to this in their contests with their enemies, and turned

---

[1] See Introduction, p. xxiii.
[2] Melitene is in eastern Cappadocia.

τὰς πρὸς τὸν θεὸν ἱκεσίας τραπέσθαι, παραδόξου 2
δὲ τοῖς πολεμίοις τοῦ τοιούτου δὴ θεάματος
φανέντος, ἄλλο τι λόγος ἔχει παραδοξότερον ἐπι-
καταλαβεῖν αὐτίκα, σκηπτὸν μὲν εἰς φυγὴν καὶ
ἀπώλειαν συνελαύνοντα τοὺς πολεμίους, ὄμβρον δὲ
ἐπὶ τὴν τῶν τὸ θεῖον παρακεκληκότων στρατιάν,
πᾶσαν αὐτὴν ἐκ τοῦ δίψους μέλλουσαν ὅσον οὔπω
διαφθείρεσθαι ἀνακτώμενον.

Ἡ δ' ἱστορία φέρεται μὲν καὶ παρὰ τοῖς πόρρω 3
τοῦ καθ' ἡμᾶς λόγου συγγραφεῦσιν οἷς μέλον
γέγονεν τῆς κατὰ τοὺς δηλουμένους γραφῆς,
δεδήλωται δὲ καὶ πρὸς τῶν ἡμετέρων. ἀλλὰ τοῖς
μὲν ἔξωθεν ἱστορικοῖς, ἅτε τῆς πίστεως ἀνοικείοις,
τέθειται μὲν τὸ παράδοξον, οὐ μὴν καὶ ταῖς τῶν
ἡμετέρων εὐχαῖς τοῦθ' ὡμολογήθη γεγονέναι· τοῖς
δέ γε ἡμετέροις, ἅτε ἀληθείας φίλοις, ἁπλῷ καὶ
ἀκακοήθει τρόπῳ τὸ πραχθὲν παραδέδοται. τού- 4
των δ' ἂν εἴη καὶ Ἀπολινάριος, ἐξ ἐκείνου φήσας
τὴν δι' εὐχῆς τὸ παράδοξον πεποιηκυῖαν λεγεῶνα
οἰκείαν τῷ γεγονότι πρὸς τοῦ βασιλέως εἰληφέναι
προσηγορίαν, κεραυνοβόλον τῇ Ῥωμαίων ἐπι-
κληθεῖσαν φωνῇ. μάρτυς δὲ τούτων γένοιτ' ἂν 5
ἀξιόχρεως ὁ Τερτυλλιανός, τὴν Ῥωμαϊκὴν τῇ
συγκλήτῳ προσφωνήσας ὑπὲρ τῆς πίστεως ἀπολογίαν, ἧς καὶ πρόσθεν ἐμνημονεύσαμεν, τήν τε
ἱστορίαν βεβαιῶν σὺν ἀποδείξει μείζονι καὶ ἐναρ-
γεστέρᾳ· γράφει δ' οὖν καὶ αὐτός, λέγων Μάρκου 6
τοῦ συνετωτάτου βασιλέως ἐπιστολὰς εἰς ἔτι νῦν
φέρεσθαι ἐν αἷς αὐτὸς μαρτυρεῖ ἐν Γερμανίᾳ

Tertull.
Apol. 5

---

[1] Dio Cassius, lxxi. 8, who ascribes the miracle to the
Egyptian magician, Arnuphis. Capitolinus in the life of
Marcus Aurelius ascribes it to the prayer of the emperor, and

towards supplications to God. Now though this kind of spectacle seemed strange to the enemy, the story goes that another still more marvellous overcame them at once, for lightning drove the enemy to flight and destruction, and a shower falling on the army which had prayed to God, refreshed them all when they were on the point of destruction from thirst

The story is both told among writers who are foreign to our faith who have undertaken to write of the times of the above mentioned emperors,[1] and has also been recorded by Christians. By the heathen writers, inasmuch as they were strangers to the faith, the miracle is related, but it was not confessed that it happened through the prayers of the Christians ; but in our own writers, inasmuch as they are the friends of truth, what happened has been described in a simple and harmless fashion. Among these would be also Apolinarius, who states that after that time the legion which had wrought the miracle through prayer had received a name from the emperor appropriate to what had happened, and was called in Latin the "Thundering Legion."[2] Tertullian is also a worthy witness of these things, who in addressing in Latin an apology for our faith to the Senate, which we have quoted already, confirmed the story with more and clearer proof. In his writing he says that letters of Marcus, the most prudent emperor, were still extant, in which he testifies himself that when his army was on the point

the emperor himself on his coins represents Jupiter as hurling thunderbolts against the Germans.

[2] But from Dio Cassius and from inscriptions, it would appear that the legion had certainly this name in the time of Nero, and probably in that of Augustus.

ὕδατος ἀπορίᾳ μέλλοντα αὐτοῦ τὸν στρατὸν
διαφθείρεσθαι ταῖς τῶν Χριστιανῶν εὐχαῖς σε-
σῶσθαι, τοῦτον δέ φησιν καὶ θάνατον ἀπειλῆσαι
τοῖς κατηγορεῖν ἡμῶν ἐπιχειροῦσιν· οἷς ὁ δηλωθεὶς
ἀνὴρ καὶ ταῦτα προσεπιλέγει· "ποταποὶ οὖν οἱ 7
νόμοι οὗτοι, οὓς καθ' ἡμῶν μόνων ἕπονται ἀσεβεῖς
ἄδικοι ὠμοί; οὓς οὔτε Οὐεσπασιανὸς ἐφύλαξεν,
καίτοι γε Ἰουδαίους νικήσας, οὓς Τραϊανὸς ἐκ
μέρους ἐξουθένησεν, κωλύων ἐκζητεῖσθαι Χριστιανούς, οὓς οὔτε Ἀδριανός, καίτοι γε πάντα τὰ
περίεργα πολυπραγμονῶν, οὔτε ὁ Εὐσεβὴς ἐπι-
κληθεὶς ἐπεκύρωσεν." ἀλλὰ ταῦτα μὲν ὅπῃ τις
ἐθέλοι, τιθέσθω· μετίωμεν δ' ἡμεῖς ἐπὶ τὴν τῶν
ἑξῆς ἀκολουθίαν.

Ποθεινοῦ δὴ ἐφ' ὅλοις τῆς ζωῆς ἔτεσιν ἐνενήκοντα 8
σὺν τοῖς ἐπὶ Γαλλίας μαρτυρήσασιν τελειωθέντος,
Εἰρηναῖος τῆς κατὰ Λούγδουνον ἧς ὁ Ποθεινὸς
ἡγεῖτο παροικίας τὴν ἐπισκοπὴν διαδέχεται· Πολυκάρπου δὲ τοῦτον ἀκουστὴν γενέσθαι κατὰ τὴν
νέαν ἐμανθάνομεν ἡλικίαν. οὗτος τῶν ἐπὶ Ῥώμης 9
τὴν διαδοχὴν ἐπισκόπων ἐν τρίτῃ συντάξει τῶν
πρὸς τὰς αἱρέσεις παραθέμενος, εἰς Ἐλεύθερον,
οὗ τὰ κατὰ τοὺς χρόνους ἡμῖν ἐξετάζεται, ὡς ἂν
δὴ κατ' αὐτὸν σπουδαζομένης αὐτῷ τῆς γραφῆς,
Iren. 3, 3. 3   τὸν κατάλογον ἵστησι, γράφων ὧδε· VI. "θεμελιώ- 1
σαντες οὖν καὶ οἰκοδομήσαντες οἱ μακάριοι ἀπό-
στολοι τὴν ἐκκλησίαν, Λίνῳ τὴν τῆς ἐπισκοπῆς
λειτουργίαν ἐνεχείρισαν· τούτου τοῦ Λίνου Παῦλος
2 Tim. 4, 21   ἐν ταῖς πρὸς Τιμόθεον ἐπιστολαῖς μέμνηται.
διαδέχεται δ' αὐτὸν Ἀνέγκλητος, μετὰ τοῦτον δὲ 2
τρίτῳ τόπῳ ἀπὸ τῶν ἀποστόλων τὴν ἐπισκοπὴν
κληροῦται Κλήμης, ὁ καὶ ἑορακὼς τοὺς μακαρίους

of destruction in Germany from lack of water it had been saved by the prayers of the Christians, and Tertullian says that the emperor also threatened death to those who attempted to accuse us. The author goes on as follows : " What kind of laws are these which wicked, unrighteous, and cruel men use against us alone ? Vespasian did not observe them although he conquered the Jews. Trajan partially allowed them, but forbade Christians to be sought out. Neither Hadrian, though busy in all curious matters, nor Pius, as he is called, ratified them." But let these things be as anyone will, we must pass on to the train of further events.

When Pothinus was consecrated with the martyrs in Gaul at the age of full ninety years, Irenaeus received the episcopacy of the diocese in Lyons,[1] of which Pothinus had been the head, and we have been told that he had been a listener to Polycarp in his early youth. In his third book against the heresies he gives the succession of the bishops in Rome as far as Eleutherus, the events of whose days are now being discussed by us, as though his book had been composed at that time, and he gives the list, writing as follows. VI. " Therefore when the blessed apostles had found and built the church they gave the ministry of the episcopate to Linus. Paul mentioned this Linus in his epistle to Timothy. Anencletus succeeded him, and after him Clement obtained the episcopate in the third place from the apostles He had seen the blessed apostles and

[1] That is, in A.D. 177. *Cf.* v. 1. 1, p. 407.

ἀποστόλους καὶ συμβεβληκὼς αὐτοῖς καὶ ἔτι
ἔναυλον τὸ κήρυγμα τῶν ἀποστόλων καὶ τὴν
παράδοσιν πρὸ ὀφθαλμῶν ἔχων, οὐ μόνος· ἔτι
γὰρ πολλοὶ ὑπελείποντο τότε ὑπὸ τῶν ἀποστόλων
δεδιδαγμένοι. ἐπὶ τούτου οὖν τοῦ Κλήμεντος 3
στάσεως οὐκ ὀλίγης τοῖς ἐν Κορίνθῳ γενομένης
ἀδελφοῖς, ἐπέστειλεν ἡ ἐν Ῥώμῃ ἐκκλησία ἱκανω-
τάτην γραφὴν τοῖς Κορινθίοις, εἰς εἰρήνην συμ-
βιβάζουσα αὐτοὺς καὶ ἀνανεοῦσα τὴν πίστιν αὐτῶν
καὶ ἣν νεωστὶ ἀπὸ τῶν ἀποστόλων παράδοσιν
εἰλήφει."

Iren. 3, 3, 3 Καὶ μετὰ βραχέα φησίν· "τὸν δὲ Κλήμεντα 4
τοῦτον διαδέχεται Εὐάρεστος καὶ τὸν Εὐάρεστον
Ἀλέξανδρος, εἶθ᾽ οὕτως ἕκτος ἀπὸ τῶν ἀποστόλων
καθίσταται Ξύστος, μετὰ δὲ τοῦτον Τελεσφόρος,
ὃς καὶ ἐνδόξως ἐμαρτύρησεν· ἔπειτα Ὑγῖνος, εἶτα
Πίος, μεθ᾽ ὃν Ἀνίκητος. διαδεξαμένου τὸν Ἀνίκητον Σωτῆρος, νῦν δωδεκάτῳ τόπῳ τὸν τῆς ἐπισκοπῆς ἀπὸ τῶν ἀποστόλων κατέχει κλῆρον
Ἐλεύθερος. τῇ αὐτῇ τάξει καὶ τῇ αὐτῇ διδαχῇ 5
ἥ τε ἀπὸ τῶν ἀποστόλων ἐν τῇ ἐκκλησίᾳ παράδοσις καὶ τὸ τῆς ἀληθείας κήρυγμα κατήντηκεν
εἰς ἡμᾶς."

VII. Ταῦτα ὁ Εἰρηναῖος ἀκολούθως ταῖς προ- 1
διεξοδευθείσαις ἡμῖν ὑπογράψας ἱστορίαις ἐν οἷς
ἐπέγραψεν, πέντε οὖσι τὸν ἀριθμόν, Ἐλέγχου καὶ
1 Tim. 6, 20 ἀνατροπῆς τῆς ψευδωνύμου γνώσεως, ἐν δευτέρῳ
τῆς αὐτῆς ὑποθέσεως, ὅτι δὴ καὶ εἰς αὐτὸν ὑποδείγματα τῆς θείας καὶ παραδόξου δυνάμεως ἐν ἐκκλησίαις τισὶν ὑπολέλειπτο, διὰ τούτων ἐπισημαίνεται,

---

[1] The letter in question is generally called "the First
Epistle of Clement," but the true title is "the Epistle of the
450

conversed with them and the teaching of the apostles still rang in his ears, their tradition was held before his eyes. Nor was he alone in this, for there were still many surviving at that time who had been taught by the apostles. When in the time of this Clement no little dissension arose among the Christians at Corinth, the church in Rome sent a most powerful letter to the Corinthians urging them to peace and renewing their faith and the tradition which they had recently received from the apostles.[1] "

And after a little he says : " Evarestus succeeded to this Clement and Alexander to Evarestus, and then Xystus was appointed as the sixth from the apostles, and after him Telesphorus, who also was martyred gloriously ; then Hyginus, then Pius, after him Anicetus. Soter succeeded Anicetus, and now, in the twelfth place from the apostles, Eleutherus holds the lot of the episcopate. The tradition from the apostles in the church and the preaching of the truth have reached us in the same order and the same teaching." [2]

VII. These things Irenaeus recounts, according to the extracts which we have made already, in the books, five in number, to which he gave the title of *Refutation and Overthrow of Knowledge falsely so-called*, and in the second book of this work he proves in the following words that manifestations of the divine and marvellous power had remained in some

Church in Rome to the Church in Corinth " Probably the subject of εἰλήφει in the last sentence is the church in Corinth supplied from the general sense of the preceding paragraph, as it clearly refers to Corinth and not to Rome.

[2] It is probable that " teaching " is a mistake in the text of Eusebius for διαδοχή, " succession," which is implied by the Latin version of Irenaeus.

Iren. 2, 31, 2 λέγων· "τοσοῦτον δὲ ἀποδέουσιν τοῦ νεκρὸν 2 ἐγεῖραι, καθὼς ὁ κύριος ἤγειρεν καὶ οἱ ἀπόστολοι διὰ προσευχῆς καὶ ἐν τῇ ἀδελφότητι πολλάκις διὰ τὸ ἀναγκαῖον καὶ τῆς κατὰ τόπον ἐκκλησίας πάσης αἰτησαμένης μετὰ νηστείας καὶ λιτανείας πολλῆς ἐπέστρεψεν τὸ πνεῦμα τοῦ τετελευτηκότος καὶ ἐχαρίσθη ὁ ἄνθρωπος ταῖς εὐχαῖς τῶν ἁγίων."

Iren. 2, 32, 4 καὶ αὖθίς φησιν μεθ' ἕτερα· "εἰ δὲ καὶ τὸν κύριον 3 φαντασιωδῶς τὰ τοιαῦτα πεποιηκέναι φήσουσιν, ἐπὶ τὰ προφητικὰ ἀνάγοντες αὐτούς, ἐξ αὐτῶν ἐπιδείξομεν πάντα οὕτως περὶ αὐτοῦ καὶ προειρῆσθαι καὶ γεγονέναι βεβαίως καὶ αὐτὸν μόνον εἶναι τὸν υἱὸν τοῦ θεοῦ· δι' ὃ καὶ ἐν τῷ ἐκείνου ὀνόματι οἱ ἀληθῶς αὐτοῦ μαθηταί, παρ' αὐτοῦ λαβόντες τὴν χάριν ἐπιτελοῦσιν ἐπ' εὐεργεσίᾳ τῇ τῶν λοιπῶν ἀνθρώπων, καθὼς εἷς ἕκαστος τὴν δωρεὰν εἴληφεν παρ' αὐτοῦ. οἱ μὲν γὰρ δαίμονας 4 ἐλαύνουσιν βεβαίως καὶ ἀληθῶς, ὥστε πολλάκις καὶ πιστεύειν ἐκείνους αὐτοὺς τοὺς καθαρισθέντας ἀπὸ τῶν πονηρῶν πνευμάτων καὶ εἶναι ἐν τῇ ἐκκλησίᾳ, οἱ δὲ καὶ πρόγνωσιν ἔχουσιν τῶν μελλόντων καὶ ὀπτασίας καὶ ῥήσεις προφητικάς, ἄλλοι δὲ τοὺς κάμνοντας διὰ τῆς τῶν χειρῶν ἐπιθέσεως ἰῶνται καὶ ὑγιεῖς ἀποκαθιστᾶσιν, ἤδη δέ, καθὼς ἔφαμεν, καὶ νεκροὶ ἠγέρθησαν καὶ παρέμειναν σὺν ἡμῖν ἔτεσιν ἱκανοῖς, καί, τί γάρ; οὐκ 5 ἔστιν ἀριθμὸν εἰπεῖν τῶν χαρισμάτων ὧν κατὰ παντὸς τοῦ κόσμου ἡ ἐκκλησία παρὰ θεοῦ λαβοῦσα ἐν τῷ ὀνόματι Ἰησοῦ Χριστοῦ τοῦ σταυρωθέντος ἐπὶ Ποντίου Πιλάτου ἑκάστης ἡμέρας ἐπ' εὐεργεσίᾳ

---

[1] Eusebius seems to slip in making his extract from Irenaeus, and by omitting the end of the sentence leaves " so

452

churches even as far as his time : " But they fall so far [1] short of raising the dead, as did the Lord and his apostles through prayer (and often among the brethren, because of necessity and at the request of the whole church in the neighbourhood, with fasting and much supplication, the spirit of him who had died returned, and the man was given to the prayers of the saints)." And again he says after other things : " But if they say that the Lord has done all these things merely in appearance we will take them back to the prophetic writings, and show from them that all these things had been foretold concerning him, and that they certainly happened, and that he alone is the Son of God ; for which cause also his true disciples having received grace from him use it in his name for the benefit of the rest of men, even as each has received the gift from him. For some drive out demons with certainty and truth, so that often those who have themselves been cleansed from the evil spirits believe and are in the church, and some have foreknowledge of things to be, and visions and prophetic speech, and others cure the sick by the laying on of hands and make them whole, and even as we have said, the dead have been raised and remained with us for many years. And why should I say more ? It is not possible to tell the number of the gifts which the church throughout the whole world, having received them from God in the name of Jesus Christ, who was crucified under Pontius Pilate, uses each day for the

far " hanging in the air. In the original the sentence runs : " They fall so far short of raising the dead, as did the Lord etc. . . ., that they do not even believe that it can be done." The " they " referred to are the Simonians and Carpocratians —two early heresies.

τῇ τῶν ἐθνῶν ἐπιτελεῖ, μήτε ἐξαπατῶσά τινας

Matt. 10, 8 μήτε ἐξαργυριζομένη· ὡς γὰρ δωρεὰν εἴληφεν παρὰ
θεοῦ, δωρεὰν καὶ διακονεῖ." καὶ ἐν ἑτέρῳ δὲ τόπῳ

Iren. 5, 6, 1 ὁ αὐτὸς γράφει· "καθὼς καὶ πολλῶν ἀκούομεν
ἀδελφῶν ἐν τῇ ἐκκλησίᾳ προφητικὰ χαρίσματα
ἐχόντων καὶ παντοδαπαῖς λαλούντων διὰ τοῦ πνεύματος γλώσσαις καὶ τὰ κρύφια τῶν ἀνθρώπων
εἰς φανερὸν ἀγόντων ἐπὶ τῷ συμφέροντι καὶ τὰ
μυστήρια τοῦ θεοῦ ἐκδιηγουμένων." ταῦτα καὶ
περὶ τοῦ διαφορὰς χαρισμάτων μέχρι καὶ τῶν
δηλουμένων χρόνων παρὰ τοῖς ἀξίοις διαμεῖναι.

VIII. Ἐπεὶ δὲ ἀρχόμενοι τῆς πραγματείας ὑπό-
σχεσιν πεποιήμεθα παραθήσεσθαι κατὰ καιρὸν εἰπόν-
τες τὰς τῶν ἀρχαίων ἐκκλησιαστικῶν πρεσβυτέρων
τε καὶ συγγραφέων φωνὰς ἐν αἷς τὰς περὶ τῶν
ἐνδιαθήκων γραφῶν εἰς αὐτοὺς κατελθούσας παραδόσεις γραφῇ παραδεδώκασιν, τούτων δὲ καὶ ὁ
Εἰρηναῖος ἦν, φέρε, καὶ τὰς αὐτοῦ παραθώμεθα
λέξεις, καὶ πρώτας γε τὰς περὶ τῶν ἱερῶν εὐ-

Iren. 3, 1, 1 αγγελίων, οὕτως ἐχούσας· "ὁ μὲν δὴ Ματθαῖος ἐν
τοῖς Ἑβραίοις τῇ ἰδίᾳ αὐτῶν διαλέκτῳ καὶ γραφὴν
ἐξήνεγκεν εὐαγγελίου, τοῦ Πέτρου καὶ τοῦ Παύλου
ἐν Ῥώμῃ εὐαγγελιζομένων καὶ θεμελιούντων τὴν
ἐκκλησίαν· μετὰ δὲ τὴν τούτων ἔξοδον Μάρκος,
ὁ μαθητὴς καὶ ἑρμηνευτὴς Πέτρου, καὶ αὐτὸς τὰ
ὑπὸ Πέτρου κηρυσσόμενα ἐγγράφως ἡμῖν παρα-
δέδωκεν· καὶ Λουκᾶς δέ, ὁ ἀκόλουθος Παύλου, τὸ
ὑπ' ἐκείνου κηρυσσόμενον εὐαγγέλιον ἐν βίβλῳ κατ-
έθετο. ἔπειτα Ἰωάννης, ὁ μαθητὴς τοῦ κυρίου,

John 13, 25. ὁ καὶ ἐπὶ τὸ στῆθος αὐτοῦ ἀναπεσών, καὶ αὐτὸς
21, 20 ἐξέδωκεν τὸ εὐαγγέλιον, ἐν Ἐφέσῳ τῆς Ἀσίας
διατρίβων."

benefit of the heathen, deceiving none and making profit from none. For as it received freely from God, it ministers also freely." And in another place the same author writes : "Just as also we hear many brethren in the church who have gifts of prophecy, and who speak through the Spirit with all manner of tongues, and who bring the hidden things of men into clearness for the common good and expound the mysteries of God." So much on the point that variety of gifts remained among the worthy up till the time spoken of.

VIII. At the beginning of this work we made a promise to quote from time to time the sayings of the presbyters and writers of the church of the first period, in which they have delivered the traditions which came down to them about the canonical Scriptures. Now Irenaeus was one of these, so let us quote his words, and in the first place those which refer to the sacred Gospels, as follows : " Now Matthew published among the Hebrews a written gospel [1] also in their own tongue, while Peter and Paul were preaching in Rome and founding the church. But after their death Mark also, the disciple and interpreter of Peter, himself handed down to us in writing the things which were preached by Peter, and Luke also, who was a follower of Paul, put down in a book the gospel which was preached by him. Then John, the disciple of the Lord, who had even rested on his breast, himself also gave forth the gospel, while he was living at Ephesus in Asia."

---

[1] The point of the καὶ γραφήν is that it was a written as well as a spoken gospel.

Ταῦτα μὲν οὖν ἐν τρίτῳ τῆς εἰρημένης ὑποθέσεως 5
τῷ προδηλωθέντι εἴρηται, ἐν δὲ τῷ πέμπτῳ περὶ

Rev. 13, 18 τῆς Ἰωάννου Ἀποκαλύψεως καὶ τῆς ψήφου τῆς
τοῦ ἀντιχρίστου προσηγορίας οὕτως διαλαμβάνει·

Iren. 5, 30, 1 "τούτων δὲ οὕτως ἐχόντων καὶ ἐν πᾶσι δὲ τοῖς
σπουδαίοις καὶ ἀρχαίοις ἀντιγράφοις τοῦ ἀριθμοῦ
τούτου κειμένου καὶ μαρτυρούντων αὐτῶν ἐκείνων
τῶν κατ' ὄψιν τὸν Ἰωάννην ἑορακότων καὶ τοῦ
λόγου διδάσκοντος ἡμᾶς ὅτι ὁ ἀριθμὸς τοῦ ὀνόματος τοῦ θηρίου κατὰ τὴν Ἑλλήνων ψῆφον διὰ
τῶν ἐν αὐτῷ γραμμάτων ἐμφαίνεται." καὶ ὑπο- 6

Iren. 5, 30, 3 καταβὰς περὶ τοῦ αὐτοῦ φάσκει· "ἡμεῖς οὖν οὐκ
ἀποκινδυνεύομεν περὶ τοῦ ὀνόματος τοῦ ἀντιχρίστου ἀποφαινόμενοι βεβαιωτικῶς. εἰ γὰρ ἔδει
ἀναφανδὸν ⟨ἐν⟩ τῷ νῦν καιρῷ κηρύττεσθαι τοὔνομα αὐτοῦ, δι' ἐκείνου ἂν ἐρρέθη τοῦ καὶ τὴν
ἀποκάλυψιν ἑορακότος· οὐδὲ γὰρ πρὸ πολλοῦ
χρόνου ἑωράθη, ἀλλὰ σχεδὸν ἐπὶ τῆς ἡμετέρας
γενεᾶς, πρὸς τῷ τέλει τῆς Δομετιανοῦ ἀρχῆς."

Iren. 3, 16, 5. Ταῦτα καὶ περὶ τῆς Ἀποκαλύψεως ἱστόρηται 7
8
[1 John 2, 18- τῷ δεδηλωμένῳ· μέμνηται δὲ καὶ τῆς Ἰωάννου
22. 4, 1-3. 5,
1] πρώτης ἐπιστολῆς, μαρτυρίας ἐξ αὐτῆς πλείστας
Iren. 4, 9, 2.
5, 7, 2. 4, 16, εἰσφέρων, ὁμοίως δὲ καὶ τῆς Πέτρου προτέρας.
5
[1 Peter 1, 8. οὐ μόνον δὲ οἶδεν, ἀλλὰ καὶ ἀποδέχεται τὴν τοῦ
2, 16]
Iren. 4, 20, 2 Ποιμένος γραφήν, λέγων· "καλῶς οὖν ἡ γραφὴ
[Herm.
mand. 1] ἡ λέγουσα πρῶτον πάντων πίστευσον ὅτι εἷς
ἐστιν ὁ θεὸς ὁ τὰ πάντα κτίσας καὶ καταρτίσας"
καὶ τὰ ἑξῆς. καὶ ῥητοῖς δέ τισιν ἐκ τῆς Σολομῶνος 8

Iren. 4, 88. 3 Σοφίας κέχρηται, μόνον οὐχὶ φάσκων· "ὅρασις
456

These things were said by the writer referred to in the third book of his treatise which has been quoted before, and in the fifth book he discourses thus about the Apocalypse of John and the number of the name of the Antichrist.[1] " Now since this is so, and since this number is found in all the good and ancient copies, and since those who have seen John face to face testify, and reason teaches us that the number of the name of the beast appears according to the numeration of the Greeks by the letters in it . . ." And going on later he says concerning the same point, " We therefore will not take the risk of making any positive statement concerning the name of the Antichrist. For if it had been necessary for his name to have been announced clearly at the present time, it would have been spoken by him who also saw the Revelation ; for it was not even seen a long time ago, but almost in our own generation towards the end of the reign of Domitian."

The author quoted says this about the Apocalypse, and he also mentions the first Epistle of John, making many quotations from it, and likewise the first Epistle of Peter. And he not only knew but also received [2] the writing of the Shepherd, saying, " Well did the Scripture say ' first of all believe that God is one who created and fitted together all things,' and so on." He also made some quotations all but verbally from the Wisdom of Solomon, " And

---

[1] According to Rev. xiii. 18 the Number of the Beast is 666. The point is that in ancient times the letters of the alphabet were used as numbers ; thus the writer means that if the letters in the name of the Beast be taken as numbers they will when added up amount to 666. The difficulty is that with a little ingenuity this can be proved to be true of almost any unpopular person.   [2] *i.e.* as Scripture.

EUSEBIUS

Wisd. 6, 20 δὲ θεοῦ περιποιητικὴ ἀφθαρσίας, ἀφθαρσία δὲ
Iren. 4, 27, 1.
2, 28, 1. 30, 1.
31, 1. 32, 1 ἐγγὺς εἶναι ποιεῖ θεοῦ." καὶ ἀπομνημονευμάτων
δέ ἀποστολικοῦ τινος πρεσβυτέρου, οὗ τοὔνομα
σιωπῇ παρέδωκεν, μνημονεύει ἐξηγήσεις τε αὐτοῦ
Iren. 4, 6, 2.
5, 26, 2. 28, 4 θείων γραφῶν παρατέθειται. ἔτι καὶ Ἰουστίνου 9
τοῦ μάρτυρος καὶ Ἰγνατίου μνήμην πεποίηται,
μαρτυρίαις αὖθις καὶ ἀπὸ τῶν τούτοις γραφέντων
Iren. 1, 27. 4 κεχρημένος, ἐπήγγελται δ' αὐτὸς ἐκ τῶν Μαρκίωνος
συγγραμμάτων ἀντιλέξειν αὐτῷ ἐν ἰδίῳ σπου-
δάσματι.

Καὶ περὶ τῆς κατὰ τοὺς ἑβδομήκοντα ἑρμηνείας 10
τῶν θεοπνεύστων γραφῶν ἄκουε οἷα κατὰ λέξιν
Iren. 3, 21, 1 γράφει· "ὁ θεὸς οὖν ἄνθρωπος ἐγένετο καὶ αὐτὸς
κύριος ἔσωσεν ἡμᾶς, δοὺς τὸ τῆς παρθένου σημεῖον,
ἀλλ' οὐχ ὡς ἔνιοί φασιν τῶν νῦν τολμώντων
Is. 7, 14 μεθερμηνεύειν τὴν γραφήν, 'ἰδοὺ ἡ νεᾶνις ἐν
γαστρὶ ἕξει καὶ τέξεται υἱόν'· ὡς Θεοδοτίων
ἡρμήνευσεν ὁ Ἐφέσιος καὶ Ἀκύλας ὁ Ποντικός,
ἀμφότεροι Ἰουδαῖοι προσήλυτοι, οἷς κατακολουθήσαντες οἱ Ἐβιωναῖοι ἐξ Ἰωσὴφ αὐτὸν γε-
γενῆσθαι φάσκουσιν." τούτοις ἐπιφέρει μετὰ 11
Iren. 3, 21, 2 βραχέα λέγων· "πρὸ τοῦ γὰρ Ῥωμαίους κρατῦναι
τὴν ἀρχὴν αὐτῶν, ἔτι τῶν Μακεδόνων τὴν Ἀσίαν
κατεχόντων, Πτολεμαῖος ὁ Λάγου φιλοτιμούμενος
τὴν ὑπ' αὐτοῦ κατεσκευασμένην βιβλιοθήκην ἐν
Ἀλεξανδρείᾳ κοσμῆσαι τοῖς πάντων ἀνθρώπων
συγγράμμασιν ὅσα γε σπουδαῖα ὑπῆρχεν, ᾐτήσατο
παρὰ τῶν Ἱεροσολυμιτῶν εἰς τὴν Ἑλληνικὴν
διάλεκτον σχεῖν αὐτῶν μεταβεβλημένας τὰς γραφάς.
οἱ δέ, ὑπήκουον γὰρ ἔτι τοῖς Μακεδόσιν τότε, τοὺς 12
παρ' αὐτοῖς ἐμπειροτάτους τῶν γραφῶν καὶ
ἀμφοτέρων τῶν διαλέκτων, ἑβδομήκοντα πρεσβυ-

the vision of God produces incorruptibility and incorruptibility brings us near to God." He also
quotes treatises of a certain apostolic presbyter
whose name he passes by in silence and gives his
interpretation of divine Scripture. Moreover, he has
made mention of Justin Martyr and Ignatius, making
frequent quotations from their writings, and he
promised to give in a special work a refutation of
Marcion from his own writings.

Hear also, word for word, what he writes about the
interpretation of the inspired Scriptures according to
the Septuagint. " So God became man and the
Lord himself saved us, giving us the sign of the
virgin, but not as some say, who at the present time
venture to translate the Scriptures, ' behold a young
woman shall conceive and bear a son,' as Theodotion
the Ephesian translated it and Aquila from Pontus,
both of them Jewish proselytes, whom the Ebionites
follow and aver that he was begotten by Joseph."
After a little he goes on thus : " For before the
Romans established their government, while the
Macedonians still possessed Asia, Ptolemy, the son
of Lagus,[1] being very anxious to adorn the library,
which he had founded in Alexandria, with all the
best extant writings of all men, asked from the
inhabitants of Jerusalem to have their Scriptures
translated into Greek. They, for they were at that
time still subject to the Macedonians, sent to Ptolemy
seventy elders, the most experienced they had

[1] Usually called Ptolemy Soter ; he reigned from 323 to
285 B.C.

τέρους, ἔπεμψαν Πτολεμαίῳ, ποιήσαντος τοῦ θεοῦ
ὅπερ ἠβούλετο. ὁ δὲ ἰδίᾳ πεῖραν αὐτῶν λαβεῖν 13
θελήσας εὐλαβηθείς τε μή τι ἄρα συνθέμενοι
ἀποκρύψωσι τὴν ἐν ταῖς γραφαῖς διὰ τῆς ἑρμηνείας
ἀλήθειαν, χωρίσας αὐτοὺς ἀπ' ἀλλήλων ἐκέλευσε
τοὺς πάντας τὴν αὐτὴν ἑρμηνείαν γράφειν, καὶ
τοῦτ' ἐπὶ πάντων τῶν βιβλίων ἐποίησεν. συνελ- 14
θόντων δὲ αὐτῶν ἐπὶ τὸ αὐτὸ παρὰ τῷ Πτολεμαίῳ
καὶ συναντιβαλόντων ἑκάστου τὴν ἑαυτοῦ ἑρμηνείαν,
ὁ μὲν θεὸς ἐδοξάσθη, αἱ δὲ γραφαὶ ὄντως θεῖαι
ἐγνώσθησαν, τῶν πάντων τὰ αὐτὰ ταῖς αὐταῖς
λέξεσιν καὶ τοῖς αὐτοῖς ὀνόμασιν ἀναγορευσάντων
ἀπ' ἀρχῆς μέχρι τέλους, ὥστε καὶ τὰ παρόντα
ἔθνη γνῶναι ὅτι κατ' ἐπίπνοιαν τοῦ θεοῦ εἰσιν
ἑρμηνευμέναι αἱ γραφαί. καὶ οὐδέν γε θαυμαστὸν 15
τὸν θεὸν τοῦτο ἐνηργηκέναι, ὅς γε καὶ ἐν τῇ
ἐπὶ Ναβουχοδονόσορ αἰχμαλωσίᾳ τοῦ λαοῦ δια-
φθαρεισῶν τῶν γραφῶν καὶ μετὰ ἑβδομήκοντα ἔτη
τῶν Ἰουδαίων ἀνελθόντων εἰς τὴν χώραν αὐτῶν,
ἔπειτα ἐν τοῖς χρόνοις Ἀρταξέρξου τοῦ Περσῶν
1 Ezra 9, 38-   βασιλέως ἐνέπνευσεν Ἔσδρᾳ τῷ ἱερεῖ ἐκ τῆς
41   φυλῆς Λευὶ τοὺς τῶν προγεγονότων προφητῶν
πάντας ἀνατάξασθαι λόγους καὶ ἀποκαταστῆσαι
τῷ λαῷ τὴν διὰ Μωϋσέως νομοθεσίαν.'' τοσαῦτα
ὁ Εἰρηναῖος.

IX. Ἐννέα δὲ καὶ δέκα ἔτεσιν τῇ βασιλείᾳ δι- 1
αρκέσαντος Ἀντωνίνου, Κόμοδος τὴν ἡγεμονίαν
παραλαμβάνει· οὗ κατὰ τὸ πρῶτον ἔτος τῶν κατ'
Ἀλεξάνδρειαν ἐκκλησιῶν Ἰουλιανὸς ἐγχειρίζεται
τὴν ἐπισκοπήν, ἐπὶ δυοκαίδεκα ἔτεσιν Ἀγριππίνου
τὴν λειτουργίαν ἀποπλήσαντος.

in the Scriptures and in both languages, and God thus wrought what he willed. But Ptolemy, wishing to make trial of them in his own way, and being afraid lest they should have made some agreement to conceal by their translation the truth in the Scriptures, separated them from one another and commanded them all to write the same translation. And this he did in the case of all the books. But when they came together to Ptolemy, and compared each his own translation, God was glorified and the Scriptures were recognized as truly divine, for they all rendered the same things in the same words and the same names, from beginning to end, so that even the heathen who were present knew that the Scriptures had been translated by the inspiration of God. And it is no marvel that God did this, for when the Scriptures had been destroyed in the captivity of the people in the days of Nebuchadnezzar, and the Jews had gone back to their country after seventy years, then in the times of Artaxerxes, the king of the Persians, he inspired Ezra, the priest of the tribe of Levi, to restore all the sayings of the prophets who had gone before, and to restore to the people the law given by Moses." [1] So much says Irenaeus.

IX. When Antoninus had held the empire for nineteen years, Commodus [2] received the sovereignty, and in his first year Julian was appointed to the episcopate of the churches in Alexandria when Agrippinus had completed his ministry after twelve years.

---

[1] The source of this tradition seems to be the *Letter of Aristeas*, which purports to be the work of a Persian noble in the time of Ptolemy Philadelphus (285-247 B.C.). See E. Schürer, *GJV*. vol. ii. [2] In A.D. 180.

X. Ἡγεῖτο δὲ τηνικαῦτα τῆς τῶν πιστῶν αὐτόθι 1
διατριβῆς ἀνὴρ κατὰ παιδείαν ἐπιδοξότατος, ὄνομα
αὐτῷ Πάνταινος, ἐξ ἀρχαίου ἔθους διδασκαλείου
τῶν ἱερῶν λόγων παρ' αὐτοῖς συνεστῶτος· ὃ καὶ εἰς
ἡμᾶς παρατείνεται καὶ πρὸς τῶν ἐν λόγῳ καὶ τῇ
περὶ τὰ θεῖα σπουδῇ δυνατῶν συγκροτεῖσθαι
παρειλήφαμεν, ἐν δὲ τοῖς μάλιστα κατ' ἐκεῖνο
καιροῦ διαλάμψαι λόγος ἔχει τὸν δεδηλωμένον,
οἷα καὶ ἀπὸ φιλοσόφου ἀγωγῆς τῶν καλουμένων
Στωϊκῶν ὡρμημένον. τοσαύτην δ' οὖν φασι 2
αὐτὸν ἐκθυμοτάτῃ διαθέσει προθυμίαν περὶ τὸν
θεῖον λόγον ἐνδείξασθαι, ὡς καὶ κήρυκα τοῦ κατὰ
Χριστὸν εὐαγγελίου τοῖς ἐπ' ἀνατολῆς ἔθνεσιν
ἀναδειχθῆναι, μέχρι καὶ τῆς Ἰνδῶν στειλάμενον
γῆς. ἦσαν γάρ, ἦσαν εἰς ἔτι τότε πλείους εὐαγγελισταὶ τοῦ λόγου, ἔνθεον ζῆλον ἀποστολικοῦ
μιμήματος συνεισφέρειν ἐπ' αὐξήσει καὶ οἰκοδομῇ
τοῦ θείου λόγου προμηθούμενοι· ὧν εἷς γενόμενος
καὶ ὁ Πάνταινος, καὶ εἰς Ἰνδοὺς ἐλθεῖν λέγεται, 3
ἔνθα λόγος εὑρεῖν αὐτὸν προφθάσαν τὴν αὐτοῦ παρουσίαν τὸ κατὰ Ματθαῖον εὐαγγέλιον παρά τισιν
αὐτόθι τὸν Χριστὸν ἐπεγνωκόσιν, οἷς Βαρθολομαῖον
τῶν ἀποστόλων ἕνα κηρῦξαι αὐτοῖς τε Ἑβραίων
γράμμασι τὴν τοῦ Ματθαίου καταλεῖψαι γραφήν,
ἣν καὶ σῴζεσθαι εἰς τὸν δηλούμενον χρόνον. ὅ 4
γε μὴν Πάνταινος ἐπὶ πολλοῖς κατορθώμασι τοῦ
κατ' Ἀλεξάνδρειαν τελευτῶν ἡγεῖται διδασκαλείου,
ζώσῃ φωνῇ καὶ διὰ συγγραμμάτων τοὺς τῶν
θείων δογμάτων θησαυροὺς ὑπομνηματιζόμενος.

XI. Κατὰ τοῦτον ταῖς θείαις γραφαῖς συν- 1
ασκούμενος ἐπ' Ἀλεξανδρείας ἐγνωρίζετο Κλήμης,
ὁμώνυμος τῷ πάλαι τῆς Ῥωμαίων ἐκκλησίας

X. At that time a man very famous for his learning named Pantaenus had charge of the life of the faithful in Alexandria, for from ancient custom a school of sacred learning existed among them. This school has lasted on to our time, and we have heard that it is managed by men powerful in their learning and zeal for divine things, but tradition says that at that time Pantaenus was especially eminent, and that he had been influenced by the philosophic system of those called Stoics. They say that he showed such zeal in his warm disposition for the divine word that he was appointed as a herald for the gospel of Christ to the heathen in the East, and was sent as far as India. For indeed there were until then many evangelists of the word who had forethought to use inspired zeal on the apostolic model for the increase and the building up of the divine word. One of these was Pantaenus, and it is said that he went to the Indians, and the tradition is that he found there that among some of those there who had known Christ the Gospel according to Matthew had preceded his coming ; for Bartholomew, one of the apostles, had preached to them and had left them the writing of Matthew in Hebrew letters, which was preserved until the time mentioned. Pantaenus, after many achievements, was at the head of the school in Alexandria until his death, and orally and in writing expounded the treasures of the divine doctrine.

XI. In his time Clement, the namesake of the pupil of the apostles who had once ruled the church of Rome, was famous in Alexandria for his study

ἡγησαμένῳ φοιτητῇ τῶν ἀποστόλων· ὃς δὴ καὶ 2
ὀνομαστὶ ἐν αἷς συνέταξεν Ὑποτυπώσεσιν ὡς ἂν
διδασκάλου τοῦ Πανταίνου μέμνηται, τοῦτόν τε
αὐτὸν καὶ τῶν Στρωματέων ἐν πρώτῳ συγγράμματι αἰνίττεσθαί μοι δοκεῖ, ὅτε τοὺς ἐμφανεστέρους
ἧς κατείληφεν ἀποστολικῆς διαδοχῆς ἐπισημηνάμενος ταῦτά φησιν· " ἤδη δὲ οὐ γραφῇ εἰς ἐπίδειξιν 3
τετεχνασμένη ἥδε ἡ πραγματεία, ἀλλά μοι ὑπομνήματα εἰς γῆρας θησαυρίζεται, λήθης φάρμακον,
εἴδωλον ἀτεχνῶς καὶ σκιαγραφία τῶν ἐναργῶν καὶ
ἐμψύχων ἐκείνων ὧν κατηξιώθην ἐπακοῦσαι λόγων
τε καὶ ἀνδρῶν μακαρίων καὶ τῷ ὄντι ἀξιολόγων.
τούτων ὁ μὲν ἐπὶ τῆς Ἑλλάδος, ὁ Ἰωνικός, ὁ δὲ 4
ἐπὶ τῆς μεγάλης Ἑλλάδος, τῆς Κοίλης ἅτερος
αὐτῶν Συρίας ἦν, ὁ δὲ ἀπ' Αἰγύπτου, ἄλλοι δὲ
ἀνὰ τὴν ἀνατολήν, καὶ ταύτης ὁ μέν τις τῶν
Ἀσσυρίων, ὁ δὲ ἐν τῇ Παλαιστίνῃ Ἑβραῖος
ἀνέκαθεν· ὑστάτῳ δὲ περιτυχών, δυνάμει δὲ ἄρα
πρῶτος ἦν, ἀνεπαυσάμην, ἐν Αἰγύπτῳ θηράσας
λεληθότα. ἀλλ' οἱ μὲν τὴν ἀληθῆ τῆς μακαρίας 5
σῴζοντες διδασκαλίας παράδοσιν εὐθὺς ἀπὸ Πέτρου
καὶ Ἰακώβου Ἰωάννου τε καὶ Παύλου τῶν ἁγίων
ἀποστόλων παῖς παρὰ πατρὸς ἐκδεξάμενος (ὀλίγοι
δὲ οἱ πατράσιν ὅμοιοι), ἧκον δὴ σὺν θεῷ καὶ εἰς
ἡμᾶς, τὰ προγονικὰ ἐκεῖνα καὶ ἀποστολικὰ κατα-
θησόμενοι σπέρματα."

XII. Ἐπὶ τούτων τῆς ἐν Ἱεροσολύμοις ἐκκλη- 1
σίας ἐπίσκοπος ὁ παρὰ πολλοῖς εἰς ἔτι νῦν βεβοημένος Νάρκισσος ἐγνωρίζετο, πεντεκαιδεκάτην
ἄγων διαδοχὴν ἀπὸ τῆς τῶν Ἰουδαίων κατὰ
Ἁδριανὸν πολιορκίας, ἐξ οὗ δὴ πρῶτον τὴν
αὐτόθι ἐκκλησίαν ἐξ ἐθνῶν συστῆναι μετὰ τοὺς

Clem. Strom.
1, 11

of the Holy Scriptures with Pantaenus. In the
Hypotyposes which he composed he mentioned
Pantaenus by name as his teacher, and he seems to
me to allude to him in the first book of the *Stromateis*,[1]
when he speaks thus in reference to the more distinguished members of the apostolic succession which
he had received. "This work is not a writing composed for show, but notes stored up for my old age,
a remedy against forgetfulness, an image without
art, and a sketch of those clear and vital words which
I was privileged to hear, and of blessed and truly
notable men. Of these one, the Ionian, was in
Greece, another in South Italy, a third in Coele-
Syria,[2] another from Egypt, and there were others
in the East, one of them an Assyrian, another in
Palestine of Hebrew origin. But when I had met
the last, and in power he was indeed the first, I
hunted him out from his concealment in Egypt and
found rest. But these men preserved the true tradition of the blessed teaching directly from Peter and
James and John and Paul, the holy apostles, son receiving it from father (but there were few like their
fathers), and by the blessing of God they came down
to us to deposit those ancestral and apostolic seeds."

XII. In their time there flourished Narcissus,
bishop of the church at Jerusalem, who is still widely
famous. He held the succession in the fifteenth
place after the siege of the Jews under Hadrian,
and we have stated already that from that time the
church in that city was composed of Gentiles, in

[1] See Introduction, p. xlv.
[2] That is, the district of the Lebanon.

ἐκ περιτομῆς καθηγήσασθαί τε αὐτῶν πρῶτον
ἐξ ἐθνῶν ἐπίσκοπον Μάρκον ἐδηλώσαμεν· μεθ' ὃν 2
ἐπισκοπεῦσαι Κασσιανὸν αἱ τῶν αὐτόθι διαδοχαὶ
περιέχουσιν, καὶ μετὰ τοῦτον Πούπλιον, εἶτα
Μάξιμον, καὶ ἐπὶ τούτοις Ἰουλιανόν, ἔπειτα Γάϊον,
μεθ' ὃν Σύμμαχον, καὶ Γάϊον ἕτερον, καὶ πάλιν
ἄλλον Ἰουλιανόν, Καπίτωνά τε πρὸς τούτοις καὶ
Οὐάλεντα καὶ Δολιχιανόν, καὶ ἐπὶ πᾶσι τὸν
Νάρκισσον, τριακοστὸν ἀπὸ τῶν ἀποστόλων κατὰ
τὴν τῶν ἑξῆς διαδοχὴν γεγενημένον.

XIII. Ἐν τούτῳ καὶ Ῥόδων, γένος τῶν ἀπὸ 1
Ἀσίας, μαθητευθεὶς ἐπὶ Ῥώμης, ὡς αὐτὸς ἱστορεῖ,
Τατιανῷ, ὃν ἐκ τῶν πρόσθεν ἔγνωμεν, διάφορα
συντάξας βιβλία, μετὰ τῶν λοιπῶν καὶ πρὸς τὴν
Μαρκίωνος παρατέτακται αἵρεσιν· ἣν καὶ εἰς
διαφόρους γνώμας κατ' αὐτὸν διαστᾶσαν ἱστορεῖ,
τοὺς τὴν διάστασιν ἐμπεποιηκότας ἀναγράφων
ἐπ' ἀκριβές τε τὰς παρ' ἑκάστῳ τούτων ἐπινενοη-
μένας διελέγχων ψευδολογίας. ἄκουε δ' οὖν καὶ
αὐτοῦ ταῦτα γράφοντος· "διὰ τοῦτο καὶ παρ' 2
ἑαυτοῖς ἀσύμφωνοι γεγόνασιν, ἀσυστάτου γνώμης
ἀντιποιούμενοι. ἀπὸ γὰρ τῆς τούτων ἀγέλης
Ἀπελλῆς μέν, ὁ τὴν πολιτείαν σεμνυνόμενος καὶ
τὸ γῆρας, μίαν ἀρχὴν ὁμολογεῖ, τὰς δὲ προφητείας
ἐξ ἀντικειμένου λέγει πνεύματος, πειθόμενος ἀπο-
φθέγμασι παρθένου δαιμονώσης, ὄνομα Φιλουμένης·
ἕτεροι δέ, καθὼς καὶ αὐτὸς ὁ ναύτης [Μαρκίων], 3
δύο ἀρχὰς εἰσηγοῦνται· ἀφ' ὧν εἰσιν Ποτῖτός τε
καὶ Βασιλικός. καὶ οὗτοι μὲν κατακολουθήσαντες 4
τῷ Ποντικῷ λύκῳ καὶ μὴ εὑρίσκοντες τὴν διαίρεσιν

succession to the Jewish Christians, and that the first of the Gentile bishops was Marcus. After him the local successions record that Cassian was bishop, and after him Publius, then Maximus, in addition to them Julian, then Gaius, after him Symmachus and Gaius the second, and then another Julian, and Capito, and in addition to them Valens and Dolichianus, and after them all Narcissus, the thirtieth from the apostles according to the regular succession.[1]

XIII. At this time too Rhodo, of Asiatic race, was, as he narrates himself, the pupil at Rome of Tatian, whom we have mentioned above, and composed various books, among others especially one directed against the heresy of Marcion. He says that it was divided in his time into various opinions, and, describing accurately those who had caused the divergence, he refutes the false teaching devised by each of them. Listen then to him when he writes thus : " Therefore they have ceased to agree among themselves, maintaining inconsistent opinions. One of their herd is Apelles, who is reverenced for his life and old age. He admits that there is one Principle,[2] but says that the prophecies are of an opposing spirit, and he was persuaded by the utterances of a possessed maiden named Philoumene. But others, such as the captain himself (Marcion), introduced two Principles. To them belong Potitus and Basilicus. These followed the wolf of Pontus,[3] not perceiving

---

[1] This only gives thirteen names from Marcus to Narcissus, but Eusebius says that Narcissus is the fifteenth. Comparison with the *Chronicon* shows that after Capito the names of Maximus the second and Antoninus should be inserted.

[2] Or " Source of being," " Beginning," or almost " God."

[3] That is, Marcion, who is said to have been the son of a bishop in Pontus.

τῶν πραγμάτων, ὡς οὐδ' ἐκεῖνος, ἐπὶ τὴν εὐχέρειαν
ἐτράποντο καὶ δύο ἀρχὰς ἀπεφήναντο ψιλῶς καὶ
ἀναποδείκτως· ἄλλοι δὲ πάλιν ἀπ' αὐτῶν ἐπὶ τὸ
χεῖρον ἐξοκείλαντες, οὐ μόνον δύο, ἀλλὰ καὶ τρεῖς
ὑποτίθενται φύσεις· ὧν ἐστιν ἀρχηγὸς καὶ προ-
στάτης Συνέρως, καθὼς οἱ τὸ διδασκαλεῖον αὐτοῦ
προβαλλόμενοι λέγουσιν.''

Γράφει δὲ ὁ αὐτὸς ὡς καὶ εἰς λόγους ἐληλύθει 5
τῷ 'Απελλῇ, φάσκων οὕτως· ''ὁ γὰρ γέρων
'Απελλῆς συμμίξας ἡμῖν, πολλὰ μὲν κακῶς λέγων
ἠλέγχθη· ὅθεν καὶ ἔφασκεν μὴ δεῖν ὅλως ἐξετάζειν
τὸν λόγον, ἀλλ' ἕκαστον, ὡς πεπίστευκεν, δια-
μένειν· σωθήσεσθαι γὰρ τοὺς ἐπὶ τὸν ἐσταυρωμένον
ἠλπικότας ἀπεφαίνετο, μόνον ἐὰν ἐν ἔργοις ἀγαθοῖς
εὑρίσκωνται· τὸ δὲ πάντων ἀσαφέστατον ἐδογμάτι-
ζετο αὐτῷ πρᾶγμα, καθὼς προειρήκαμεν, τὸ περὶ
θεοῦ. ἔλεγεν μὲν γὰρ μίαν ἀρχὴν καθὼς καὶ ὁ
ἡμέτερος λόγος.'' εἶτα προθεὶς αὐτοῦ πᾶσαν τὴν 6
δόξαν, ἐπιφέρει φάσκων· ''λέγοντος δὲ πρὸς
αὐτόν ' πόθεν ἡ ἀπόδειξις αὕτη σοι, ἢ πῶς δύνασαι
λέγειν μίαν ἀρχήν; φράσον ἡμῖν ' ἔφη τὰς μὲν
προφητείας ἑαυτὰς ἐλέγχειν διὰ τὸ μηδὲν ὅλως
ἀληθὲς εἰρηκέναι· ἀσύμφωνοι γὰρ ὑπάρχουσι καὶ
ψευδεῖς καὶ ἑαυταῖς ἀντικείμεναι. τὸ δὲ πῶς ἐστιν
μία ἀρχή, μὴ γινώσκειν ἔλεγεν, οὕτως δὲ κινεῖσθαι
μόνον. εἶτ' ἐπομοσαμένου μου τἀληθὲς εἰπεῖν, 7
ὤμνυεν ἀληθεύων λέγειν μὴ ἐπίστασθαι πῶς εἷς
ἐστιν ἀγένητος θεός, τοῦτο δὲ πιστεύειν. ἐγὼ δὲ
γελάσας κατέγνων αὐτοῦ, διότι διδάσκαλος εἶναι
λέγων, οὐκ ᾔδει τὸ διδασκόμενον ὑπ' αὐτοῦ
κρατύνειν.''

Ἐν τῷ αὐτῷ δὲ συγγράμματι Καλλιστίωνι 8

the division of things, any more than he, and turning to a simple solution, announced two principles, baldly and without proof. Others again, passing into worse error, supposed that there are not only two but even three Natures. Of them the chief and leader is Syneros, as those state who represent his school."

The same writer (Rhodo) says that he conversed with Apelles, and states it thus: "For the old man Apelles when he consorted with us, was proved to make many false statements. Hence also he used to say that it is not necessary to investigate the argument fully, but that each should remain in his own belief, for he asserted that those who placed their hope on the Crucified would be saved, if they persisted in good works. But as we have said before, the most obscure part of all the doctrines which he put forward were about God. For he kept on saying that there is only one Principle just as our doctrine states." Then after expounding all his opinions he goes on as follows: "And when I said to him, 'Where is this proof of yours, or how can you say that there is one Principle? Tell us,' he said that the prophecies refute themselves by not having spoken the truth at all, for they are inconsistent and false and contradict themselves, but as to how there is one Principle he said that he did not know it, but merely inclined to that view. Then when I adjured him to speak the truth he swore that he was speaking the truth, when he said that he did not know how the unbegotten God is one but that he believed it. But I laughed at him and condemned him, because though he called himself a teacher he did not know how to establish what he taught."

In the same work, speaking to Kallistio, the same

προσφωνῶν ὁ αὐτὸς μεμαθητεῦσθαι ἐπὶ Ῥώμης
Τατιανῷ ἑαυτὸν ὁμολογεῖ· φησὶν δὲ καὶ ἐσπουδάσθαι
τῷ Τατιανῷ Προβλημάτων βιβλίον· δι' ὧν τὸ
ἀσαφὲς καὶ ἐπικεκρυμμένον τῶν θείων γραφῶν
παραστήσειν ὑποσχομένου τοῦ Τατιανοῦ, αὐτὸς ὁ
Ῥόδων ἐν ἰδίῳ συγγράμματι τὰς τῶν ἐκείνου
προβλημάτων ἐπιλύσεις ἐκθήσεσθαι ἐπαγγέλλεται.
φέρεται δὲ τοῦ αὐτοῦ καὶ εἰς τὴν ἑξαήμερον
ὑπόμνημα. ὅ γέ τοι Ἀπελλῆς οὗτος μυρία κατὰ 9
τοῦ Μωυσέως ἠσέβησεν νόμου, διὰ πλειόνων
συγγραμμάτων τοὺς θείους βλασφημήσας λόγους
εἰς ἔλεγχόν τε, ὥς γε δὴ ἐδόκει, καὶ ἀνατροπὴν
αὐτῶν οὐ μικρὰν πεποιημένος σπουδήν. ταῦτα
μὲν οὖν περὶ τούτων·

XIV. Μισόκαλός γε μὴν ἐς τὰ μάλιστα καὶ 1
φιλοπόνηρος ὢν ὁ τῆς ἐκκλησίας τοῦ θεοῦ πολέμιος,
μηδένα τε μηδαμῶς τῆς κατὰ τῶν ἀνθρώπων
ἀπολιπὼν ἐπιβουλῆς τρόπον, αἱρέσεις ξένας αὖθις
ἐπιφύεσθαι κατὰ τῆς ἐκκλησίας ἐνήργει· ὧν οἱ
μὲν ἰοβόλων δίκην ἑρπετῶν ἐπὶ τῆς Ἀσίας καὶ
Φρυγίας εἷρπον, τὸν μὲν δὴ παράκλητον Μοντανόν,
τὰς δ' ἐξ αὐτοῦ γυναῖκας, Πρίσκιλλαν καὶ Μαξί-
μιλλαν, ὡς ἂν τοῦ Μοντανοῦ προφήτιδας γεγονυίας,
αὐχοῦντες· XV. οἱ δ' ἐπὶ Ῥώμης ἤκμαζον, ὧν 1
ἡγεῖτο Φλωρῖνος, πρεσβυτερίου τῆς ἐκκλησίας
ἀποπεσών, Βλάστος τε σὺν τούτῳ, παραπλησίῳ
πτώματι κατεσχημένος· οἳ καὶ πλείους τῆς ἐκκλησίας περιέλκοντες ἐπὶ τὸ σφῶν ὑπῆγον βούλημα,
θάτερος ἰδίως περὶ τὴν ἀλήθειαν νεωτερίζειν πειρώ-
μενος.

XVI. Πρὸς μὲν οὖν τὴν λεγομένην κατὰ Φρύγας 1
αἵρεσιν ὅπλον ἰσχυρὸν καὶ ἀκαταγώνιστον ἐπὶ τῆς

writer states that he had been himself a disciple of Tatian at Rome, and he says that Tatian had prepared a book on Problems, in which he undertook to set out what was unclear and hidden in the divine Scriptures, and Rhodo himself in his own work announces that he will set out the answers to Tatian's Problems. There is also extant a treatise of Rhodo on the Hexaëmeron.[1] Apelles, however, uttered countless impieties against the law of Moses, and in many treatises blasphemed the divine words with no little zeal, as it seemed, for their refutation and overthrow, as he at least thought. So much then concerning these.

XIV. The enemy of the church of God, who hates good and loves deeply all that is wicked, left untried no kind of plot against men and again strove to raise up strange heresies against the church. Of these some like poisonous reptiles crawled over Asia and Phrygia, and boasted that Montanus was the Paraclete and that the women of his sect, Priscilla and Maximilla, were the prophetesses of Montanus. XV. Others flourished in Rome of which Florinus was the leader. He had been turned out of the presbytery of the church and with him was Blastus who had suffered a similar fall. These drew away more of the church and brought them to their own opinion, each trying to introduce innovations about the truth in his own way.

XVI. Against the so-called Cataphrygian[2] heresy the power which champions the truth raised up a powerful and invincible weapon at Hierapolis in

---

[1] That is, the Narrative of Creation in six days.

[2] *i.e.* Montanist.

Ἱεραπόλεως τὸν Ἀπολινάριον, οὗ καὶ πρόσθεν
μνήμην ὁ λόγος πεποίητο, ἄλλους τε σὺν αὐτῷ
πλείους τῶν τηνικάδε λογίων ἀνδρῶν ἡ τῆς ἀληθείας
ὑπέρμαχος ἀνίστη δύναμις, ἐξ ὧν καὶ ἡμῖν ἱστορίας
πλείστη τις ὑπόθεσις καταλέλειπται. ἀρχόμενος **2**
γοῦν τῆς κατ᾽ αὐτῶν γραφῆς, τῶν εἰρημένων δή
τις πρῶτον ἐπισημαίνεται ὡς καὶ ἀγράφοις τοῖς
κατ᾽ αὐτῶν ἐπεξέλθοι ἐλέγχοις· προοιμιάζεται
γοῦν τοῦτον τὸν τρόπον· " ἐκ πλείστου ὅσου καὶ **3**
ἱκανωτάτου χρόνου, ἀγαπητὲ Ἀουίρκιε Μάρκελλε,
ἐπιταχθεὶς ὑπὸ σοῦ συγγράψαι τινὰ λόγον εἰς τὴν
τῶν κατὰ Μιλτιάδην λεγομένων αἵρεσιν, ἐφεκτικώ-
τερόν πως μέχρι νῦν διεκείμην, οὐκ ἀπορίᾳ τοῦ
δύνασθαι ἐλέγχειν μὲν τὸ ψεῦδος, μαρτυρεῖν δὲ τῇ
ἀληθείᾳ, δεδιὼς δὲ καὶ ἐξευλαβούμενος μή πη
Rev. 22, 18.
19 δόξω τισὶν ἐπισυγγράφειν ἢ ἐπιδιατάσσεσθαι τῷ
τῆς τοῦ εὐαγγελίου καινῆς διαθήκης λόγῳ, ᾧ
μήτε προσθεῖναι μήτε ἀφελεῖν δυνατὸν τῷ κατὰ
τὸ εὐαγγέλιον αὐτὸ πολιτεύεσθαι προῃρημένῳ.
προσφάτως δὲ γενόμενος ἐν Ἀγκύρᾳ τῆς Γαλατίας **4**
καὶ καταλαβὼν τὴν κατὰ τόπον ἐκκλησίαν ὑπὸ
τῆς νέας ταύτης, οὐχ, ὡς αὐτοί φασιν, προφητείας,
πολὺ δὲ μᾶλλον, ὡς δειχθήσεται, ψευδοπροφητείας
διατεθρυλημένην, καθ᾽ ὅσον δυνατόν, τοῦ κυρίου
παρασχόντος, περὶ αὐτῶν τε τούτων καὶ τῶν
προτεινομένων ὑπ᾽ αὐτῶν ἕκαστά τε διελέχθημεν
ἡμέραις πλείοσιν ἐν τῇ ἐκκλησίᾳ, ὡς τὴν μὲν
ἐκκλησίαν ἀγαλλιαθῆναι καὶ πρὸς τὴν ἀλήθειαν
ἐπιρρωσθῆναι, τοὺς δ᾽ ἐξ ἐναντίας πρὸς τὸ παρὸν
ἀποκρουσθῆναι καὶ τοὺς ἀντιθέτους λυπηθῆναι.
ἀξιούντων οὖν τῶν κατὰ τόπον πρεσβυτέρων ὅπως **5**
τῶν λεχθέντων κατὰ τῶν ἀντιδιατιθεμένων τῷ τῆς
472

Apolinarius, who has already been mentioned in this work, and with him many others of the learned men of that time, from whom abundant material for history has been left to us. One of these at the beginning of his treatise against the Montanists indicates that he had also taken part in oral controversy against them. He writes a preface in this way : " For a long and protracted time, my dear Abercius Marcellus, I have been urged by you to compose a treatise against the sect of those called after Miltiades,[1] but until now I was somewhat reluctant, not from any lack of ability to refute the lie and testify to the truth, but from timidity and scruples lest I might seem to some to be adding to the writings or injunctions of the word of the new covenant of the gospel, to which no one who has chosen to live according to the gospel itself can add and from which he cannot take away. But when I had just come to Ancyra in Galatia and perceived that the church in that place was torn in two by this new movement which is not, as they call it, prophecy but much rather, as will be shown, false prophecy, I disputed concerning these people themselves and their propositions so far as I could, with the Lord's help, for many days continuously [2] in the church. Thus the church rejoiced and was strengthened in the truth, but our opponents were crushed for the moment and our adversaries were distressed. Therefore the presbyters of the place asked me to leave some note of what had been said against the opponents of the

---

[1] See Introduction, p. lv. Miltiades was apparently a leader of the Montanists.
[2] This translates Schwartz's emendation of ἐκτενέστατα instead of the impossible ἕκαστά τε.

ἀληθείας λόγῳ ὑπόμνημά τι καταλείπωμεν, παρόντος καὶ τοῦ συμπρεσβυτέρου ἡμῶν Ζωτικοῦ τοῦ
'Οτρηνοῦ, τοῦτο μὲν οὐκ ἐπράξαμεν, ἐπηγγειλάμεθα
δέ, ἐνθάδε γράψαντες, τοῦ κυρίου διδόντος, διὰ
σπουδῆς πέμψειν αὐτοῖς.''

Ταῦτα καὶ ἑξῆς τούτοις ἕτερα κατ' ἀρχὰς εἰπὼν 6
τοῦ λόγου, τὸν αἴτιον τῆς δηλουμένης αἱρέσεως
προϊὼν τοῦτον ἀνιστορεῖ τὸν τρόπον· ''ἡ τοίνυν
ἔνστασις αὐτῶν καὶ πρόσφατος τοῦ ἀποσχίσματος
αἵρεσις πρὸς τὴν ἐκκλησίαν τὴν αἰτίαν ἔσχε
τοιαύτην. κώμη τις εἶναι λέγεται ἐν τῇ κατὰ τὴν 7
Φρυγίαν Μυσίᾳ, καλουμένη 'Αρδαβαῦ τοὔνομα·
ἔνθα φασί τινα τῶν νεοπίστων πρώτως, Μοντανὸν
τοὔνομα, κατὰ Γρᾶτον 'Ασίας ἀνθύπατον, ἐν ἐπι-
θυμίᾳ ψυχῆς ἀμέτρῳ φιλοπρωτείας δόντα πάροδον
εἰς ἑαυτὸν τῷ ἀντικειμένῳ πνευματοφορηθῆναί
τε καὶ αἰφνιδίως ἐν κατοχῇ τινι καὶ παρεκστάσει
γενόμενον ἐνθουσιᾶν ἄρξασθαί τε λαλεῖν καὶ
ξενοφωνεῖν, παρὰ τὸ κατὰ παράδοσιν καὶ κατὰ
διαδοχὴν ἄνωθεν τῆς ἐκκλησίας ἔθος δῆθεν προ-
φητεύοντα. τῶν δὲ κατ' ἐκεῖνο καιροῦ ἐν τῇ τῶν 8
νόθων ἐκφωνημάτων ἀκροάσει γενομένων οἱ μὲν
ὡς ἐπὶ ἐνεργουμένῳ καὶ δαιμονῶντι καὶ ἐν πλάνης
πνεύματι ὑπάρχοντι καὶ τοὺς ὄχλους ταράττοντι
ἀχθόμενοι, ἐπετίμων καὶ λαλεῖν ἐκώλυον, με-
Matt. 7, 15 μνημένοι τῆς τοῦ κυρίου διαστολῆς τε καὶ ἀπειλῆς
πρὸς τὸ φυλάττεσθαι τὴν τῶν ψευδοπροφητῶν
ἐγρηγορότως παρουσίαν· οἱ δὲ ὡς ἁγίῳ πνεύματι
καὶ προφητικῷ χαρίσματι ἐπαιρόμενοι καὶ οὐχ
ἥκιστα χαυνούμενοι καὶ τῆς διαστολῆς τοῦ κυρίου
ἐπιλανθανόμενοι, τὸ βλαψίφρον καὶ ὑποκοριστικὸν
καὶ λαοπλάνον πνεῦμα προυκαλοῦντο, θελγόμενοι
474

word of the truth, when Zoticus of Otrous, our fellow presbyter, was also present. Though we did not do so, we promised to write from home if the Lord permitted, and to send it to them speedily."

Continuing with other similar remarks at the beginning of his treatise, he proceeds to narrate as follows the cause of the heresy referred to :—" Their opposition and their recent heretical schism from the church had the following origin. In Phrygian Mysia there is said to be a village called Ardabav. There they say that a recent convert called Montanus, when Gratus was proconsul of Asia, in the unbounded lust of his soul for leadership gave access to himself to the adversary, became obsessed, and suddenly fell into frenzy and convulsions. He began to be ecstatic and to speak and to talk strangely, prophesying contrary to the custom which belongs to the tradition and succession of the church from the beginning. Of those who at that time heard these bastard utterances some were vexed, thinking that he was possessed by a devil and by a spirit of error, and was disturbing the populace ; they rebuked him, and forbade him to speak, remembering the distinction made by the Lord, and his warning to keep watchful guard against the coming of the false prophets ; but others, as though elevated by a holy spirit and a prophetic gift, and not a little conceited, forgot the Lord's distinction, and encouraged the mind-injuring and seducing and people-misleading

καὶ πλανώμενοι ὑπ' αὐτοῦ, εἰς τὸ μηκέτι κωλύεσθαι
σιωπᾶν. τέχνῃ δέ τινι, μᾶλλον δὲ τοιαύτῃ μεθόδῳ 9
κακοτεχνίας ὁ διάβολος τὴν κατὰ τῶν παρηκόων
ἀπώλειαν μηχανησάμενος καὶ παρ' ἀξίαν ὑπ'
αὐτῶν τιμώμενος ὑπεξήγειρέν τε καὶ προσεξέκαυσεν
αὐτῶν τὴν ἀποκεκοιμημένην ἀπὸ τῆς κατ' ἀλήθειαν
πίστεως διάνοιαν, ὡς καὶ ἑτέρας τινὰς δύο γυναῖκας
ἐπεγεῖραι καὶ τοῦ νόθου πνεύματος πληρῶσαι, ὡς
καὶ λαλεῖν ἐκφρόνως καὶ ἀκαίρως καὶ ἀλλοτριο-
τρόπως, ὁμοίως τῷ προειρημένῳ. καὶ τοὺς μὲν
χαίροντας καὶ χαυνουμένους ἐπ' αὐτῷ μακαρίζοντος
τοῦ πνεύματος καὶ διὰ τοῦ μεγέθους τῶν ἐπαγ-
γελμάτων ἐκφυσιοῦντος, ἔσθ' ὅπῃ δὲ καὶ κατα-
κρίνοντος στοχαστικῶς καὶ ἀξιοπίστως αὐτοὺς
ἄντικρυς, ἵνα καὶ ἐλεγκτικὸν εἶναι δοκῇ (ὀλίγοι
δ' ἦσαν οὗτοι τῶν Φρυγῶν ἐξηπατημένοι), τὴν δὲ
καθόλου καὶ πᾶσαν τὴν ὑπὸ τὸν οὐρανὸν ἐκκλησίαν
βλασφημεῖν διδάσκοντος τοῦ ἀπηυθαδισμένου πνεύματος, ὅτι μήτε τιμὴν μήτε πάροδον εἰς αὐτὴν τὸ 10
ψευδοπροφητικὸν ἐλάμβανε πνεῦμα, τῶν γὰρ κατὰ
τὴν Ἀσίαν πιστῶν πολλάκις καὶ πολλαχῇ τῆς
Ἀσίας εἰς τοῦτο συνελθόντων καὶ τοὺς προσφάτους
λόγους ἐξετασάντων καὶ βεβήλους ἀποφηνάντων
καὶ ἀποδοκιμασάντων τὴν αἵρεσιν, οὕτω δὴ τῆς
τε ἐκκλησίας ἐξεώσθησαν καὶ τῆς κοινωνίας
εἴρχθησαν."

Ταῦτα ἐν πρώτοις ἱστορήσας καὶ δι' ὅλου τοῦ 11
συγγράμματος τὸν ἔλεγχον τῆς κατ' αὐτοὺς
πλάνης ἐπαγαγών, ἐν τῷ δευτέρῳ περὶ τῆς τελευτῆς

---

[1] The meaning is plain, though it is not quite clear whether
the subject of the infinitives (κωλύεσθαι σιωπᾶν) is Montanus or
the " seducing spirit," but there is a word too much in the

spirit, being cheated and deceived by it so that he could not be kept silent.[1] But by some art, or rather by such an evil scheme of artifice, the devil wrought destruction for the disobedient, and receiving unworthy honours from them stimulated and inflamed their understanding which was already dead to the true faith; so that he raised up two more women and filled them with the bastard spirit so that they spoke madly and improperly and strangely, like Montanus. The spirit[2] gave blessings to those who rejoiced and were proud in him, and puffed them up by the greatness of its promises. Yet sometimes it flatly condemned them completely, wisely, and faithfully, that it might seem to be critical, though but few of the Phrygians were deceived. But when the arrogant spirit taught to blaspheme the whole Catholic church throughout the world, because the spirit of false prophecy received from it neither honour nor entrance, for the Christians of Asia after assembling for this purpose many times and in many parts of the province, tested the recent utterances, pronounced them profane, and rejected the heresy, —then at last the Montanists were driven out of the church and excommunicated."

He tells this story at the beginning, and throughout the book continues the refutation of the error, but in the second book he speaks as follows about the

Greek and either κωλύεσθαι or σιωπᾶν must be an interpolation.

[2] That is to say, the false spirit speaking through Montanus. It is important to notice that Abercius fully believed in the supernatural gift of Montanus but ascribed it to the Devil instead of to the Holy Spirit. It was the difficulty of distinguishing except on subjective grounds between these two sources of inspiration which led to so much trouble.

τῶν προδεδηλωμένων ταῦτά φησιν· "ἐπειδὴ τοίνυν 12
καὶ προφητοφόντας ἡμᾶς ἀπεκάλουν, ὅτι μὴ τοὺς
ἀμετροφώνους αὐτῶν προφήτας ἐδεξάμεθα (τού-

John 14, 26 τους γὰρ εἶναί φασιν οὕσπερ ἐπηγγείλατο τῷ λαῷ
πέμψειν ὁ κύριος), ἀποκρινάσθωσαν ἡμῖν πρὸς
θεοῦ· ἔστιν τις, ὦ βέλτιστοι, τούτων τῶν ἀπὸ
Μοντανοῦ καὶ τῶν γυναικῶν λαλεῖν ἀρξαμένων

Matt. 23, 34 ὅστις ὑπὸ Ἰουδαίων ἐδιώχθη ἢ ὑπὸ παρανόμων
ἀπεκτάνθη; οὐδείς. οὐδέ γέ τις αὐτῶν κρατηθεὶς
ὑπὲρ τοῦ ὀνόματος ἀνεσταυρώθη; οὐ γὰρ οὖν.
οὐδὲ μὴν οὐδὲ ἐν συναγωγαῖς Ἰουδαίων τῶν
γυναικῶν τις ἐμαστιγώθη ποτὲ ἢ ἐλιθοβολήθη;
οὐδαμόσε οὐδαμῶς, ἄλλῳ δὲ θανάτῳ τελευτῆσαι 13
λέγονται Μοντανός τε καὶ Μαξίμιλλα. τούτους
γὰρ ὑπὸ πνεύματος βλαψίφρονος ἑκατέρους ὑπο-
κινήσαντος λόγος ἀναρτῆσαι ἑαυτοὺς οὐχ ὁμοῦ,
κατὰ δὲ τὸν τῆς ἑκάστου τελευτῆς καιρὸν φήμη
πολλὴ καὶ οὕτω δὲ τελευτῆσαι καὶ τὸν βίον κατα-
στρέψαι Ἰούδα προδότου δίκην, καθάπερ καὶ τὸν 14
θαυμαστὸν ἐκεῖνον τὸν πρῶτον τῆς κατ᾽ αὐτοὺς
λεγομένης προφητείας οἷον ἐπίτροπόν τινα Θεόδοτον πολὺς αἱρεῖ λόγος ὡς αἱρόμενόν ποτε καὶ
ἀναλαμβανόμενον εἰς οὐρανοὺς παρεκστῆναί τε
καὶ καταπιστεῦσαι ἑαυτὸν τῷ τῆς ἀπάτης πνεύματι
καὶ δισκευθέντα κακῶς τελευτῆσαι· φασὶ γοῦν
τοῦτο οὕτως γεγονέναι. ἀλλὰ μὴ ἄνευ τοῦ ἰδεῖν 15
ἡμᾶς ἐπίστασθαί τι τῶν τοιούτων νομίζωμεν, ὦ
μακάριε· ἴσως μὲν γὰρ οὕτως, ἴσως δὲ οὐχ οὕτως
τετελευτήκασιν Μοντανός τε καὶ Θεόδοτος καὶ ἡ
προειρημένη γυνή."

Αὖθις δ᾽ ἐν τῷ αὐτῷ φησιν λόγῳ τοὺς τότε 16
ἱεροὺς ἐπισκόπους πεπειρᾶσθαι μὲν τὸ ἐν τῇ

end of the persons referred to : " Since then they called us murderers of the prophets because we did not receive their chattering prophets (for they say that these ·are those whom the Lord promised to send to the people), let them answer us before God. Is there anyone, good people, of those whose talking began with Montanus and the women, who was persecuted by Jews or killed by the wicked ? Not one. Or was there any one of them who was taken and crucified for the name ? No, there was not. Or was any one of the women ever scourged in the synagogues of the Jews or stoned ? Never anywhere. It was a different death that Montanus and Maximilla are said to have died ; for the story goes that each of them was inspired by a mind-destroying spirit to commit suicide, though not together, and there was much gossip at the time of the death of each. But thus it was that they died, and destroyed their lives like the traitor Judas. So also general report says that a certain Theodotus, that remarkable man, the first steward as it were of their alleged prophecy, was sometimes taken up and raised to Heaven, when he fell into a trance and trusted himself to the spirit of deceit, but was hurled down and died miserably. They say, at least, that this happened thus. But not having seen them ourselves we do not claim to have any knowledge of such things, my friend, for perhaps Montanus and Theodotus and the above mentioned woman died in this way, but perhaps they did not."

Again in the same book he says that the sacred bishops of that time tried to refute the spirit that

Μαξιμίλλῃ πνεῦμα διελέγξαι, κεκωλῦσθαι δὲ πρὸς
ἑτέρων, συνεργούντων δηλαδὴ τῷ πνεύματι· γράφει 17
δὲ οὕτως· " καὶ μὴ λεγέτω ἐν τῷ αὐτῷ λόγῳ
τῷ κατὰ Ἀστέριον Ὀρβανὸν τὸ διὰ Μαξιμίλλης
πνεῦμα ' διώκομαι ὡς λύκος ἐκ προβάτων· οὐκ
εἰμὶ λύκος· ῥῆμά εἰμι καὶ πνεῦμα καὶ δύναμις,'
ἀλλὰ τὴν ἐν τῷ πνεύματι δύναμιν ἐναργῶς δειξάτω
καὶ ἐλεγξάτω καὶ ἐξομολογεῖσθαι διὰ τοῦ πνεύματος καταναγκασάτω τοὺς τότε παρόντας εἰς τὸ
δοκιμάσαι καὶ διαλεχθῆναι τῷ πνεύματι λαλοῦντι,
ἄνδρας δοκίμους καὶ ἐπισκόπους, Ζωτικὸν ἀπὸ
Κουμάνης κώμης καὶ Ἰουλιανὸν ἀπὸ Ἀπαμείας,
ὧν οἱ περὶ Θεμίσωνα τὰ στόματα φιμώσαντες
οὐκ εἴασαν τὸ ψευδὲς καὶ λαοπλάνον πνεῦμα ὑπ'
αὐτῶν ἐλεγχθῆναι."

Ἐν ταὐτῷ δὲ πάλιν ἕτερα μεταξὺ πρὸς ἔλεγχον 18
τῶν τῆς Μαξιμίλλης ψευδοπροφητειῶν εἰπών,
ὁμοῦ τόν τε χρόνον καθ' ὃν ταῦτ' ἔγραφεν, σημαίνει
καὶ τῶν προρρήσεων αὐτῆς μέμνηται δι' ὧν
πολέμους ἔσεσθαι καὶ ἀκαταστασίας προεμαν-
τεύσατο, ὧν καὶ τὴν ψευδολογίαν εὐθύνει, ὧδε
λέγων· " καὶ πῶς οὐ καταφανὲς ἤδη γέγονεν καὶ 19
τοῦτο τὸ ψεῦδος; πλείω γὰρ ἢ τρισκαίδεκα ἔτη
εἰς ταύτην τὴν ἡμέραν ἐξ οὗ τετελεύτηκεν ἡ γυνή,
καὶ οὔτε μερικὸς οὔτε καθολικὸς κόσμῳ γέγονεν
πόλεμος, ἀλλὰ καὶ Χριστιανοῖς μᾶλλον εἰρήνη
διάμονος ἐξ ἐλέου θεοῦ."

Καὶ ταῦτα δ' ἐκ τοῦ δευτέρου συγγράμματος. 20
καὶ ἀπὸ τοῦ τρίτου δὲ σμικρὰς παραθήσομαι

---

[1] Or possibly, Urbanus. Nothing is known about him,
but Valesius thinks that the words " according to Asterius
Orbanus " are a misplaced marginal note giving the name

was in Maximilla, but were prevented by others who plainly co-operated with the spirit, and he writes thus : " And let not the spirit which speaks through Maximilla say, in the same work according to Asterius Orbanus,[1] ' I am driven away like a wolf from the sheep. I am not a wolf, I am word and spirit and power.' But let him show clearly and prove the power in the spirit, and let him through the spirit force to recognize him those who were then present for the purpose of testing and conversing with the spirit as it spoke,—eminent men and bishops, Zoticus from the village Cumane, and Julian from Apamea, whose mouths the party of Themiso muzzled, and did not allow the false spirit which deceived the people to be refuted by them."

In the same book, again, after other refutations of the false prophecies of Maximilla, in a single passage he both indicates the time at which he wrote this, and quotes her predictions, in which she foretold future wars and revolutions, and he corrects the falsehood of them as follows : " Has it not been made obvious already that this is another lie ? For it is more than thirteen years to-day since the woman died, and there has been in the world neither local nor universal war, but rather by the mercy of God continuing peace even for Christians." [2]

This is from his second book. And from the third I will also quote a few words in which he speaks as

of the writer of this treatise. The phrase certainly is awkward, but it seems equally possible that the text is right and that Asterius was the name of a Montanist writer.

[2] This probably means the period before the wars of Septimus Severus. There seem to have been no important wars in the reign of Commodus, and though there were some persecutions there were less than in the earlier reigns.

481

EUSEBIUS

λέξεις, δι᾽ ὧν πρὸς τοὺς αὐχοῦντας ὡς ἄρα πλείους
καὶ αὐτῶν μεμαρτυρηκότες εἶεν, ταῦτά φησιν·
" ὅταν τοίνυν ἐν πᾶσι τοῖς εἰρημένοις ἐλεγχθέντες
ἀπορήσωσιν, ἐπὶ τοὺς μάρτυρας καταφεύγειν πει-
ρῶνται, λέγοντες πολλοὺς ἔχειν μάρτυρας καὶ
τοῦτ᾽ εἶναι τεκμήριον πιστὸν τῆς δυνάμεως τοῦ
παρ᾽ αὐτοῖς λεγομένου προφητικοῦ πνεύματος.
τὸ δ᾽ ἐστὶν ἄρα, ὡς ἔοικεν, παντὸς μᾶλλον οὐκ
ἀληθές. καὶ γὰρ τῶν ἄλλων αἱρέσεών τινες 21
πλείστους ὅσους ἔχουσι μάρτυρας, καὶ οὐ παρὰ
τοῦτο δήπου συγκαταθησόμεθα, οὐδὲ ἀλήθειαν
ἔχειν αὐτοὺς ὁμολογήσομεν. καὶ πρῶτοί γε οἱ
ἀπὸ τῆς Μαρκίωνος αἱρέσεως Μαρκιανισταὶ καλούμενοι πλείστους ὅσους ἔχειν Χριστοῦ μάρτυρας
λέγουσιν, ἀλλὰ τόν γε Χριστὸν αὐτὸν κατ᾽ ἀλήθειαν
οὐχ ὁμολογοῦσιν."

Καὶ μετὰ βραχέα τούτοις ἐπιφέρει λέγων· " ὅθεν 22
τοι καὶ ἐπειδὰν οἱ ἐπὶ τὸ τῆς κατ᾽ ἀλήθειαν πίστεως
μαρτύριον κληθέντες ἀπὸ τῆς ἐκκλησίας τύχωσι
μετά τινων τῶν ἀπὸ τῆς τῶν Φρυγῶν αἱρέσεως
λεγομένων μαρτύρων, διαφέρονταί τε πρὸς αὐτοὺς
καὶ μὴ κοινωνήσαντες αὐτοῖς τελειοῦνται διὰ τὸ
μὴ βούλεσθαι συγκαταθέσθαι τῷ διὰ Μοντανοῦ
καὶ τῶν γυναικῶν πνεύματι. καὶ ὅτι τοῦτ᾽ ἀληθές,
καὶ ἐπὶ τῶν ἡμετέρων χρόνων ἐν Ἀπαμείᾳ τῇ πρὸς
Μαιάνδρῳ τυγχάνει γεγενημένον ἐν τοῖς περὶ
Γάϊον καὶ Ἀλέξανδρον ἀπὸ Εὐμενείας μαρτυρήσασι
πρόδηλον."

XVII. Ἐν τούτῳ δὲ τῷ συγγράμματι καὶ 1
Μιλτιάδου συγγραφέως μέμνηται, ὡς λόγον τινὰ
καὶ αὐτοῦ κατὰ τῆς προειρημένης αἱρέσεως γε-
γραφότος· παραθέμενος γοῦν αὐτῶν λέξεις τινάς,
482

follows against those who boasted that they had had more martyrs. "So when they have been refuted in the whole discussion and have nothing to reply, they try to take refuge in martyrs, saying that they have many martyrs and that this is a trustworthy proof of the power of the alleged prophetic spirit among them. But this appears to be actually further from the truth than anything. For some of the other heresies have innumerable martyrs, but I do not suppose that we shall accept them for that reason, nor admit that they have the truth. In the first place, indeed, the so-called Marcianists of the heresy of Marcion say that they have innumerable martyrs to Christ but nevertheless Christ himself they do not confess according to truth."

And after a little he goes on as follows : " Wherefore whenever members of the church who have been called to martyrdom for the true faith meet any of the so-called martyrs of the Montanist heresy, they separate from them and die without communicating with them, because they refuse to agree with the spirit in Montanus and the women. And that this is true, and that it happened in our time in Apamea on the Meander, is shown by the case of those who were martyred with Gaius and Alexander of Eumeneia."

XVII. And in this work he also quotes Miltiades as a writer who had also himself written a treatise against the heresy mentioned. After quoting some

ἐπιφέρει λέγων· "ταῦτα εὑρὼν ἔν τινι συγγράμματι αὐτῶν ἐνισταμένων τῷ Ἀλκιβιάδου τοῦ ἀδελφοῦ συγγράμματι, ἐν ᾧ ἀποδείκνυσιν περὶ τοῦ μὴ δεῖν προφήτην ἐν ἐκστάσει λαλεῖν, ἐπετεμόμην." ὑπο- **2** καταβὰς δ᾽ ἐν ταὐτῷ τοὺς κατὰ τὴν καινὴν διαθήκην προπεφητευκότας καταλέγει, ἐν οἷς καταριθμεῖ Ἀμμίαν τινὰ καὶ Κοδρᾶτον, λέγων οὕτως· "ἀλλ᾽ ὅ γε ψευδοπροφήτης ἐν παρεκστάσει, ᾧ ἕπεται ἄδεια καὶ ἀφοβία, ἀρχομένου μὲν ἐξ ἑκουσίου ἀμαθίας, καταστρέφοντος δὲ εἰς ἀκούσιον μανίαν ψυχῆς, ὡς προείρηται. τοῦτον δὲ τὸν τρόπον οὔτε **3** τινὰ τῶν κατὰ τὴν παλαιὰν οὔτε τῶν κατὰ τὴν καινὴν πνευματοφορηθέντα προφήτην δεῖξαι δυνή-

Acts 11, 28.
21, 10. 15, 32
21, 9 σονται, οὔτε Ἄγαβον οὔτε Ἰούδαν οὔτε Σίλαν οὔτε τὰς Φιλίππου θυγατέρας, οὔτε τὴν ἐν Φιλαδελφίᾳ Ἀμμίαν οὔτε Κοδρᾶτον, οὔτε εἰ δή τινας ἄλλους μηδὲν αὐτοῖς προσήκοντας καυχήσονται." καὶ αὖθις δὲ μετὰ βραχέα ταῦτά φησιν· "εἰ γὰρ **4** μετὰ Κοδρᾶτον καὶ τὴν ἐν Φιλαδελφίᾳ Ἀμμίαν, ὥς φασιν, αἱ περὶ Μοντανὸν διεδέξαντο γυναῖκες τὸ προφητικὸν χάρισμα, τοὺς ἀπὸ Μοντανοῦ καὶ τῶν γυναικῶν τίνες παρ᾽ αὐτοῖς διεδέξαντο,

Eph. 4, 11 ff.
1 Cor. 1, 7 δειξάτωσαν· δεῖν γὰρ εἶναι τὸ προφητικὸν χάρισμα ἐν πάσῃ τῇ ἐκκλησίᾳ μέχρι τῆς τελείας παρουσίας ὁ ἀπόστολος ἀξιοῖ. ἀλλ᾽ οὐκ ἂν ἔχοιεν δεῖξαι τεσσαρεσκαιδέκατον ἤδη που τοῦτο ἔτος ἀπὸ τῆς Μαξιμίλλης τελευτῆς."

Οὗτος μὲν δὴ τοσαῦτα· ὅ γέ τοι πρὸς αὐτοῦ **5** δεδηλωμένος Μιλτιάδης καὶ ἄλλας ἡμῖν τῆς ἰδίας περὶ τὰ θεῖα λόγια σπουδῆς μνήμας καταλέλοιπεν

---

¹ Schwartz and almost all editors except McGiffert emend this to Miltiades. This emendation certainly seems

of their sayings he continues as follows : " I have given this abstract of what I found in a work of theirs when they were attacking the work of Alcibiades [1] the Christian in which he shows that a prophet need not to speak in ecstasy." And he goes on in the same work to give a catalogue of those who have been prophets of the New Testament, and among them he numbers a certain Ammia and Quadratus and says thus : " But the false prophet speaks in ecstasy, after which follow ease and freedom from fear ; he begins with voluntary ignorance, but turns to involuntary madness of soul, as has been said before. But they cannot show that any prophet, either of those in the Old Testament or of those in the New, was inspired in this way ; they can boast neither of Agabus, nor of Judas, nor of Silas, nor of the daughters of Philip, nor of Ammia in Philadelphia, nor of Quadratus, nor of any others who do not belong to them." And again after a little he goes on, " For if the Montanist women succeeded to Quadratus and Ammia in Philadelphia in the prophetic gift, let them show who among them succeeded the followers of Montanus and the women, for the apostle grants that the prophetic gift shall be in all the church until the final coming, but this they could not show, seeing that this is already the fourteenth year from the death of Maximilla."

He, therefore, so writes. But the Miltiades mentioned by him has also left us other monuments of his own zeal for the oracles of God in the treatises which

to be correct so far as historical fact is concerned, but the evidence of the mss. seems equally to prove that the mistake is due to Eusebius himself, and as such ought to appear in the text. See Introduction, p. lv., and *cf.* McGiffert's note *ad loc.*

ἔν τε οἷς πρὸς Ἕλληνας συνέταξε λόγοις καὶ τοῖς
πρὸς Ἰουδαίους, ἑκατέρᾳ ἰδίως ὑποθέσει ἐν δυσὶν
ὑπαντήσας συγγράμμασιν, ἔτι δὲ καὶ πρὸς τοὺς
κοσμικοὺς ἄρχοντας ὑπὲρ ἧς μετῄει φιλοσοφίας
πεποίηται ἀπολογίαν.

XVIII. Τῆς δὲ κατὰ Φρύγας καλουμένης αἱρέ- 1
σεως καὶ Ἀπολλώνιος, ἐκκλησιαστικὸς συγγραφεύς,
ἀκμαζούσης εἰς ἔτι τότε κατὰ τὴν Φρυγίαν ἔλεγχον
ἐνστησάμενος, ἴδιον κατ' αὐτῶν πεποίηται σύγγραμμα, τὰς μὲν φερομένας αὐτῶν προφητείας
ψευδεῖς οὔσας κατὰ λέξιν εὐθύνων, τὸν δὲ βίον τῶν
τῆς αἱρέσεως ἀρχηγῶν ὁποῖός τις γέγονεν, διελέγ-
χων· αὐτοῖς δὲ ῥήμασιν περὶ τοῦ Μοντανοῦ ταῦτα
λέγοντος ἄκουε· "ἀλλὰ τίς ἐστιν οὗτος ὁ πρόσ- 2
φατος διδάσκαλος, τὰ ἔργα αὐτοῦ καὶ ἡ διδασκαλία
δείκνυσιν. οὗτός ἐστιν ὁ διδάξας λύσεις γάμων,
ὁ νηστείας νομοθετήσας, ὁ Πέπουζαν καὶ Τύμιον
Ἱερουσαλὴμ ὀνομάσας (πόλεις δ' εἰσὶν αὗται
μικραὶ τῆς Φρυγίας), τοὺς πανταχόθεν ἐκεῖ συν-
αγαγεῖν ἐθέλων, ὃ πράκτηρας χρημάτων καταστήσας,
ὁ ἐπ' ὀνόματι προσφορῶν τὴν δωροληψίαν ἐπιτεχνώμενος, ὁ σαλάρια χορηγῶν τοῖς κηρύσσουσιν
αὐτοῦ τὸν λόγον, ἵνα διὰ τῆς γαστριμαργίας ἡ
διδασκαλία τοῦ λόγου κρατύνηται."

Καὶ ταῦτα μὲν περὶ τοῦ Μοντανοῦ· καὶ περὶ τῶν 3
προφητίδων δὲ αὐτοῦ ὑποκαταβὰς οὕτω γράφει·
"δείκνυμεν οὖν αὐτὰς πρώτας τὰς προφήτιδας
ταύτας, ἀφ' οὗ τοῦ πνεύματος ἐπληρώθησαν, τοὺς
ἄνδρας καταλιπούσας. πῶς οὖν ἐψεύδοντο Πρίσκιλλαν παρθένον ἀποκαλοῦντες; εἶτ' ἐπιφέρει 4
λέγων· "δοκεῖ σοι πᾶσα γραφὴ κωλύειν προφήτην
λαμβάνειν δῶρα καὶ χρήματα; ὅταν οὖν ἴδω τὴν

he composed against the Gentiles and against the Jews, treating each subject separately in two treatises, and besides this he wrote an Apology to the secular rulers on behalf of the philosophy which he held.

XVIII. Apollonius also, a writer of the church when the so-called Montanist heresy was still flourishing in Phrygia, composed a refutation and published it as a separate work against them, proving word by word that their alleged prophecies are false and showing the true character of the life of the leaders of the heresy. Listen to the actual words which he uses about Montanus. " But the deeds and the teachings of this recent teacher show his character. It is he who taught the annulment of marriage, who enacted fasts, who gave the name of Jerusalem to Pepuza and Tymion, which are little towns in Phrygia, and wished to hold assemblies there from everywhere, who appointed collectors of money, who organized the receiving of gifts under the name of offerings, who provided salaries for those who preached his doctrine in order that its teaching might prevail through gluttony."

So he says about Montanus. And a little further on he writes thus about the prophetesses. " Thus we prove that these first prophetesses themselves deserted their husbands from the moment that they were filled with the spirit. What a lie it is then for them to call Priscilla a virgin." Then he goes on saying : " Does not all Scripture seem to you to forbid a prophet from receiving gifts and money ? There-

προφῆτιν εἰληφυῖαν καὶ χρυσὸν καὶ ἄργυρον καὶ
πολυτελεῖς ἐσθῆτας, πῶς αὐτὴν μὴ παραιτήσωμαι.''

Αὖθις δ' ὑποκαταβὰς περί τινος τῶν κατ' 5
αὐτοὺς ὁμολογητῶν ταῦτά φησιν· '' ἔτι δὲ καὶ
Θεμίσων, ὁ τὴν ἀξιόπιστον πλεονεξίαν ἠμφι-
εσμένος, ὁ μὴ βαστάσας τῆς ὁμολογίας τὸ σημεῖον,
ἀλλὰ πλήθει χρημάτων ἀποθέμενος τὰ δεσμά, δέον
ἐπὶ τούτῳ ταπεινοφρονεῖν, ὡς μάρτυς καυχώμενος,
ἐτόλμησεν, μιμούμενος τὸν ἀπόστολον, καθολικήν
τινα συνταξάμενος ἐπιστολήν, κατηχεῖν μὲν τοὺς
ἄμεινον αὐτοῦ πεπιστευκότας, συναγωνίζεσθαι δὲ
τοῖς τῆς κενοφωνίας λόγοις, βλασφημῆσαι δὲ
εἰς τὸν κύριον καὶ τοὺς ἀποστόλους καὶ τὴν ἁγίαν
ἐκκλησίαν.'' καὶ περὶ ἑτέρου δὲ αὖθις τῶν κατ' 6
αὐτοὺς τετιμημένων ὡς δὴ μαρτύρων οὕτω γράφει·
'' ἵνα δὲ μὴ περὶ πλειόνων λέγωμεν, ἡ προφῆτις
ἡμῖν εἰπάτω τὰ κατὰ Ἀλέξανδρον, τὸν λέγοντα
ἑαυτὸν μάρτυρα, ᾧ συνεστιᾶται, ᾧ προσκυνοῦσιν
καὶ αὐτῷ πολλοί· οὗ τὰς λῃστείας καὶ τὰ ἄλλα
τολμήματα ἐφ' οἷς κεκόλασται, οὐχ ἡμᾶς δεῖ
λέγειν, ἀλλὰ ὁ ὀπισθόδομος ἔχει. τίς οὖν τίνι
χαρίζεται τὰ ἁμαρτήματα; πότερον ὁ προφήτης 7
τὰς λῃστείας τῷ μάρτυρι ἢ ὁ μάρτυς τῷ προφήτῃ
τὰς πλεονεξίας; εἰρηκότος γὰρ τοῦ κυρίου μὴ
Matt. 10, 9. 10 κτήσησθε χρυσὸν μήτε ἄργυρον μηδὲ δύο χιτῶνας,
οὗτοι πᾶν τοὐναντίον πεπλημμελήκασιν περὶ τὰς
τούτων τῶν ἀπηγορευμένων κτήσεις. δείξομεν
γὰρ τοὺς λεγομένους παρ' αὐτοῖς προφήτας καὶ

---

[1] This is the text of all mss. except one which reads " the
prophet." Probably this is a correction, but the context
shows that it is right and that the reference is to Themiso.
Apparently Themiso and Alexander lived together.

fore when I see that the prophetess has received gold
and silver and expensive clothes, how should I refrain
from blaming her ? "

Then further on he says this about one of their
confessors : " Moreover, Themiso too, who was garbed
with specious covetousness, who did not endure the
sign of confession but exchanged prison for wealth
when he ought to have been humble-minded on this
account, and boasted that he was a martyr, dared,
in imitation of the apostle, to compose an epistle
general, to instruct those whose faith was better
than his, and to contend with empty sounding words
and to blaspheme against the Lord and the apostles
and the holy church." And again he writes thus
about another of those who were honoured among
them as martyrs : " But in order that we may not
speak about more of them, let the prophetess [1] tell
us the story of Alexander, who calls himself a
martyr, with whom she joins in revels, to whom many
pay reverence. We need not tell of his robberies
and the other crimes for which he has been punished,
but the record-house [2] has them. Which then for-
gives the other's sins ? Does the prophet absolve
the martyr of robbery or the martyr forgive the
prophet for avarice ? For the Lord said, ' Provide
neither gold nor silver nor two coats '; but these,
doing wholly otherwise, have transgressed by the
acquisition of these forbidden things. For we will
show that their so-called prophets and martyrs make

---

[1] ὀπισθόδομος, literally " back room." It originally referred to a back room in the temple of Athena on the
Acropolis at Athens which was used as the treasury, and it
was afterwards extended to any room used for this or similar
public purposes.

μάρτυρας μὴ μόνον παρὰ πλουσίων, ἀλλὰ καὶ
παρὰ πτωχῶν καὶ ὀρφανῶν καὶ χηρῶν κερματιζο-
μένους. καὶ εἰ πεποίθησιν ἔχουσιν, στήτωσαν ἐν 8
τούτῳ καὶ διορισάσθωσαν ἐπὶ τούτοις, ἵνα ἐὰν
ἐλεγχθῶσιν, κἂν τοῦ λοιποῦ παύσωνται πλημ-
μελοῦντες. δεῖ γὰρ τοὺς καρποὺς δοκιμάζεσθαι
Matt. 12, 33 τοῦ προφήτου· ἀπὸ γὰρ τοῦ καρποῦ τὸ ξύλον 9
γινώσκεται. ἵνα δὲ τοῖς βουλομένοις τὰ κατὰ
Ἀλέξανδρον ᾖ γνώριμα, κέκριται ὑπὸ Αἰμιλίου
Φροντίνου ἀνθυπάτου ἐν Ἐφέσῳ, οὐ διὰ τὸ
ὄνομα, ἀλλὰ δι᾿ ἃς ἐτόλμησεν λῃστείας, ὧν ἤδη
παραβάτης· εἶτ᾿ ἐπιψευσάμενος τῷ ὀνόματι τοῦ
κυρίου, ἀπολέλυται, πλανήσας τοὺς ἐκεῖ πι-
στούς, καὶ ἡ ἰδία παροικία αὐτόν, ὅθεν ἦν,
οὐκ ἐδέξατο διὰ τὸ εἶναι αὐτὸν λῃστήν, καὶ
οἱ θέλοντες μαθεῖν τὰ κατ᾿ αὐτὸν ἔχουσιν τὸ
τῆς Ἀσίας δημόσιον ἀρχεῖον· ὃν ὁ προφήτης
συνόντα πολλοῖς ἔτεσιν ἀγνοεῖ. τοῦτον ἐλέγ- 10
χοντες ἡμεῖς, δι᾿ αὐτοῦ καὶ τὴν ὑπόστασιν ἐξ-
ελέγχομεν τοῦ προφήτου. τὸ ὅμοιον ἐπὶ πολλῶν
δυνάμεθα ἀποδεῖξαι, καὶ εἰ θαρροῦσιν, ὑπομεινά-
τωσαν τὸν ἔλεγχον."

Πάλιν τε αὖ ἐν ἑτέρῳ τόπῳ τοῦ συγγράμματος 11
περὶ ὧν αὐχοῦσι προφητῶν ἐπιλέγει ταῦτα· " ἐὰν
ἀρνῶνται δῶρα τοὺς προφήτας αὐτῶν εἰληφέναι,
τοῦθ᾿ ὁμολογησάτωσαν ὅτι ἐὰν ἐλεγχθῶσιν εἰλη-
φότες, οὐκ εἰσὶ προφῆται, καὶ μυρίας ἀποδείξεις
τούτων παραστήσομεν. ἀναγκαῖον δέ ἐστιν πάντας
καρποὺς δοκιμάζεσθαι προφήτου. προφήτης, εἰπέ
μοι, βάπτεται; προφήτης στιβίζεται; προφήτης
φιλοκοσμεῖ; προφήτης τάβλαις καὶ κύβοις παίζει;
προφήτης δανείζει; ταῦτα ὁμολογησάτωσαν πό-

gain not only from the rich but from the poor and from orphans and widows. And if they have the courage let them stop at this point and discuss these matters in order that if they are convicted they may at least cease transgressing for the future. For it is necessary to test the fruits of the prophet, for from the fruits the tree is known. But, that the story of Alexander may be known to those who wish, he was convicted by Aemilius Pompinus, proconsul in Ephesus, not for being a Christian but for his daring robberies, and he was an old offender. Then, by falsely claiming the name of the Lord he was released, having deceived the Christians there, and his own diocese from which he came would not receive him because he was a robber, and those who wish to learn his story have the public records of Asia at their disposition.[1] The prophet is ignorant about him though he lived with him for many years, but we have exposed him, and through him expose also the nature of the prophet. We can show the same in many instances, and, if they dare, let them stand the test."

And again in another part of the book he says this about their boasted prophets : " If they deny that their prophets have taken gifts let them admit this, that if they have been convicted, they are not true prophets, and we will give countless proofs of this. But it is necessary to test all the fruits of a prophet. Tell me, does a prophet dye his hair ? Does he pencil his eyelids ? Does he love ornaments ? Does he gamble and dice ? Does he lend money ? Let them state

---

[1] The story is an interesting parallel to Lucian's account of Peregrinus.

τερον ἔξεστιν ἢ μή, ἐγὼ δ᾽ ὅτι γέγονεν παρ᾽
αὐτοῖς, δείξω.''

Ὁ δ᾽ αὐτὸς οὗτος Ἀπολλώνιος κατὰ τὸ αὐτὸ 12
σύγγραμμα ἱστορεῖ ὡς ἄρα τεσσαρακοστὸν ἐτύγ-
χανεν ἔτος ἐπὶ τὴν τοῦ συγγράμματος αὐτοῦ
γραφὴν ἐξ οὗ τῇ προσποιήτῳ αὐτοῦ προφητείᾳ
ὁ Μοντανὸς ἐπικεχείρηκεν, καὶ πάλιν φησὶν ὡς
ἄρα Ζωτικός, οὗ καὶ ὁ πρότερος συγγραφεὺς ἐ- 13
μνημόνευσεν, ἐν Πεπούζοις προφητεύειν δὴ προσ-
ποιουμένης τῆς Μαξιμίλλης ἐπιστὰς διελέγξαι τὸ
ἐνεργοῦν ἐν αὐτῇ πνεῦμα πεπείραται, ἐκωλύθη γε
μὴν πρὸς τῶν τὰ ἐκείνης φρονούντων. καὶ Θρασέα
δέ τινος τῶν τότε μαρτύρων μνημονεύει. ἔτι δὲ 14
ὡς ἐκ παραδόσεως τὸν σωτῆρά φησιν προστετα-
χέναι τοῖς αὐτοῦ ἀποστόλοις ἐπὶ δώδεκα ἔτεσιν
μὴ χωρισθῆναι τῆς Ἱερουσαλήμ, κέχρηται δὲ
καὶ μαρτυρίαις ἀπὸ τῆς Ἰωάννου Ἀποκαλύψεως,
καὶ νεκρὸν δὲ δυνάμει θείᾳ πρὸς αὐτοῦ Ἰωάννου
ἐν τῇ Ἐφέσῳ ἐγηγέρθαι ἱστορεῖ, καὶ ἄλλα τινά
φησιν, δι᾽ ὧν ἱκανῶς τῆς προειρημένης αἱρέσεως
πληρέστατα διηύθυνεν τὴν πλάνην. ταῦτα καὶ
ὁ Ἀπολλώνιος.

XIX. Τῶν δὲ Ἀπολιναρίου κατὰ τῆς δηλωθείσης 1
αἱρέσεως μνήμην πεποίηται Σεραπίων, ὃν ἐπὶ τῶν
δηλουμένων χρόνων μετὰ Μαξιμῖνον ἐπίσκοπον
τῆς Ἀντιοχέων ἐκκλησίας γενέσθαι κατέχει λόγος·
μέμνηται δ᾽ αὐτοῦ ἐν ἰδίᾳ ἐπιστολῇ τῇ πρὸς
Καρικὸν καὶ Πόντιον, ἐν ᾗ διευθύνων καὶ αὐτὸς
τὴν αὐτὴν αἵρεσιν, ἐπιλέγει ταῦτα· "ὅπως δὲ 2
καὶ τοῦτο εἰδῆτε ὅτι τῆς ψευδοῦς ταύτης τάξεως
τῆς ἐπικαλουμένης νέας προφητείας ἐβδέλυκται ἡ
ἐνέργεια παρὰ πάσῃ τῇ ἐν κόσμῳ ἀδελφότητι,

whether these things are right or not, and I will show that they have been done among them."

This same Apollonius in the same book says that it was forty years from the time when Montanus plotted his fictitious prophecy, to the time when he wrote his book. And again he says that Zoticus, whom the former writer mentioned, when Maximilla pretended to prophesy in Pepuza had tried in opposition to confute the spirit which worked in her, but was prevented by those who agreed with her. He also mentions a certain Thraseas [1] as one of the martyrs of that time. Moreover, he says, as though from tradition, that the Saviour ordered his apostles not to leave Jerusalem for twelve years. He also makes quotations from the Apocalypse of John and tells how by divine power a dead man was raised by John himself at Ephesus. And he says other things by which he demonstrated powerfully and completely the error of the heresy under discussion. So far says Apollonius.

XIX. Tradition says that Serapion was bishop of Antioch after Maximinus at the time referred to, and he has mentioned the works of Apolinarius against the heresy described. He mentions him in his own letter to Caricus and Pontius, in which he also himself refutes the same heresy, and continues thus : " And in order that you may know this, that the working of the so-called new prophecy of this false order is abominated in the whole of Christendom

---

[1] *Cf. H.E.* v. 24.

πέπομφα ὑμῖν καὶ Κλαυδίου Ἀπολιναρίου, τοῦ μακαριωτάτου γενομένου ἐν Ἱεραπόλει τῆς Ἀσίας ἐπισκόπου, γράμματα." ἐν ταύτῃ δὲ τῇ τοῦ 3 Σεραπίωνος ἐπιστολῇ καὶ ὑποσημειώσεις φέρονται διαφόρων ἐπισκόπων, ὧν ὁ μέν τις ὧδέ πως ὑποσεσημείωται· " Αὐρήλιος Κυρίνιος μάρτυς ἐρρῶσθαι ὑμᾶς εὔχομαι," ὁ δέ τις τοῦτον τὸν τρόπον· "Αἴλιος Πούπλιος Ἰούλιος ἀπὸ Δεβελτοῦ κολωνίας τῆς Θρᾴκης ἐπίσκοπος· ζῇ ὁ θεὸς ὁ ἐν τοῖς οὐρανοῖς, ὅτι Σωτᾶς ὁ μακάριος ὁ ἐν Ἀγχιάλῳ ἠθέλησε τὸν δαίμονα τὸν Πρισκίλλης ἐκβαλεῖν, καὶ οἱ ὑποκριταὶ οὐκ ἀφῆκαν." καὶ ἄλλων δὲ πλειόνων τὸν ἀριθμὸν 4 ἐπισκόπων συμψήφων τούτοις ἐν τοῖς δηλωθεῖσιν γράμμασιν αὐτόγραφοι φέρονται σημειώσεις. καὶ τὰ μὲν κατὰ τούτους ἦν τοιαῦτα.

XX. Ἐξ ἐναντίας δὲ τῶν ἐπὶ Ῥώμης τὸν ὑγιῆ 1 τῆς ἐκκλησίας θεσμὸν παραχαραττόντων, Εἰρηναῖος διαφόρους ἐπιστολὰς συντάττει, τὴν μὲν ἐπιγράψας Πρὸς Βλάστον περὶ σχίσματος, τὴν δὲ Πρὸς Φλωρῖνον περὶ μοναρχίας ἢ περὶ τοῦ μὴ εἶναι τὸν θεὸν ποιητὴν κακῶν. ταύτης γάρ τοι τῆς γνώμης οὗτος ἐδόκει προασπίζειν· δι' ὃν αὖθις ὑποσυρόμενον τῇ κατὰ Οὐαλεντῖνον πλάνῃ καὶ τὸ Περὶ ὀγδοάδος συντάττεται τῷ Εἰρηναίῳ σπούδασμα, ἐν ᾧ καὶ ἐπισημαίνεται τὴν πρώτην τῶν ἀποστόλων κατειληφέναι ἑαυτὸν διαδοχήν· ἔνθα πρὸς τῷ τοῦ συγ- 2 γράμματος τέλει χαριεστάτην αὐτοῦ σημείωσιν εὑρόντες, ἀναγκαίως καὶ ταύτην τῇδε καταλέξομεν τῇ γραφῇ, τοῦτον ἔχουσαν τὸν τρόπον· " ὁρκίζω σε τὸν μεταγραψόμενον τὸ βιβλίον τοῦτο κατὰ τοῦ κυρίου ἡμῶν Ἰησοῦ Χριστοῦ καὶ κατὰ τῆς ἐνδόξου παρουσίας αὐτοῦ, ἧς ἔρχεται κρῖναι ζῶντας καὶ

throughout the world, I have sent you the writings
of Claudius Apolinarius, the bishop of Hierapolis in
Asia, of blessed memory." And in this letter of
Serapion there are preserved the signatures of various
bishops, of whom one signed himself " I, Aurelius
Cyrenaeus, a martyr, pray for your welfare." Another as follows : " I, Aelius Publius Julius, bishop
of Debeltum, a colony of Thrace. As God lives in
the heavens the blessed Sotas in Anchialus wished
to drive the devil out of Priscilla and the hypocrites
would not let him." The autograph signatures of
many other bishops who agreed with them are also
preserved in the above mentioned writing. So far
concerning them.

XX. In opposition to those in Rome who were
discarding the sound ordinance of the church,
Irenaeus composed various letters. He addressed
one to Blastus *On Schism*, another to Florinus, *On
the Sole Sovereignty* [1] or *That God is not the Author of
Evil*, for Florinus seemed to be defending this
opinion. For his sake too, when he was attracted
by the Valentinian error, a work was composed by
Irenaeus *On the Ogdoad*,[2] in which he also indicates
that he had himself received the first succession of
the apostles, and in it, at the end of the work, we
find a most acceptable notice from him which we
are obliged to give in this book and it runs as follows :
" I adjure thee, who shalt copy out this book, by
our Lord Jesus Christ, by his glorious advent when
he comes to judge the living and the dead, that thou

---

[1] The μοναρχία became the technical term for the assertion
of the Unity of the Godhead, without—as it was thought
—due regard to the reality of the Persons of the Trinity,
though " Person " (or ὑπόστασις) was not yet used in this
sense.　　　　[2] Some Gnostics regarded God as eightfold.

νεκρούς, ἵνα ἀντιβάλῃς ὃ μετεγράψω, καὶ κατ-
ορθώσῃς αὐτὸ πρὸς τὸ ἀντίγραφον τοῦτο ὅθεν
μετεγράψω, ἐπιμελῶς· καὶ τὸν ὅρκον τοῦτον ὁμοίως
μεταγράψεις καὶ θήσεις ἐν τῷ ἀντιγράφῳ." καὶ 3
ταῦτα δὲ ὠφελίμως ὑπ' ἐκείνου λελέχθω πρὸς
ἡμῶν τε ἱστορείσθω, ὡς ἂν ἔχοιμεν ἄριστον
σπουδαιοτάτης ἐπιμελείας τοὺς ἀρχαίους ἐκείνους
καὶ ὄντως ἱεροὺς ἄνδρας ὑπόδειγμα.

Ἐν ᾗ γε μὴν προειρήκαμεν πρὸς τὸν Φλωρῖνον 4
ὁ Εἰρηναῖος ἐπιστολῇ αὖθις τῆς ἅμα Πολυκάρπῳ
συνουσίας αὐτοῦ μνημονεύει, λέγων· "ταῦτα τὰ
δόγματα, Φλωρῖνε, ἵνα πεφεισμένως εἴπω, οὐκ
ἔστιν ὑγιοῦς γνώμης· ταῦτα τὰ δόγματα ἀσύμφωνά
ἐστιν τῇ ἐκκλησίᾳ εἰς τὴν μεγίστην ἀσέβειαν περι-
βάλλοντα τοὺς πειθομένους αὐτοῖς· ταῦτα τὰ
δόγματα οὐδὲ οἱ ἔξω τῆς ἐκκλησίας αἱρετικοὶ
ἐτόλμησαν ἀποφήνασθαί ποτε· ταῦτα τὰ δόγματα
οἱ πρὸ ἡμῶν πρεσβύτεροι, οἱ καὶ τοῖς ἀποστόλοις
συμφοιτήσαντες, οὐ παρέδωκάν σοι. εἶδον γάρ 5
σε, παῖς ἔτι ὤν, ἐν τῇ κάτω Ἀσίᾳ παρὰ Πολυκάρπῳ, λαμπρῶς πράσσοντα ἐν τῇ βασιλικῇ αὐλῇ
καὶ πειρώμενον εὐδοκιμεῖν παρ' αὐτῷ. μᾶλλον
γὰρ τὰ τότε διαμνημονεύω τῶν ἔναγχος γινομένων
(αἱ γὰρ ἐκ παίδων μαθήσεις συναύξουσαι τῇ ψυχῇ, 6
ἑνοῦνται αὐτῇ), ὥστε με δύνασθαι εἰπεῖν καὶ τὸν
τόπον ἐν ᾧ καθεζόμενος διελέγετο ὁ μακάριος
Πολύκαρπος, καὶ τὰς προόδους αὐτοῦ καὶ τὰς
εἰσόδους καὶ τὸν χαρακτῆρα τοῦ βίου καὶ τὴν τοῦ
σώματος ἰδέαν καὶ τὰς διαλέξεις ἃς ἐποιεῖτο πρὸς
τὸ πλῆθος, καὶ τὴν μετὰ Ἰωάννου συναναστροφὴν
ὡς ἀπήγγελλεν καὶ τὴν μετὰ τῶν λοιπῶν τῶν
ἑορακότων τὸν κύριον, καὶ ὡς ἀπεμνημόνευεν τοὺς

compare what thou shalt transcribe and correct it with this copy whence thou art transcribing, with all care, and thou shalt likewise transcribe this oath and put it in the copy." May his words be spoken to our profit and be narrated in order that we may keep those primitive and truly sacred men as the best example of the most zealous care.

In the letter to Florinus, which we have spoken of above, Irenaeus again mentions his intercourse with Polycarp, and says : " These opinions, O Florinus, that I may speak sparingly, do not belong to sound doctrine. These opinions are inconsistent with the church, and bring those who believe in them into the greatest impiety. These opinions not even the heretics outside the church ever dared to proclaim. These opinions those who were presbyters before us, they who accompanied the apostles, did not hand on to you. For while I was still a boy I knew you in lower Asia in Polycarp's house when you were a man of rank in the royal hall and endeavouring to stand well with him. I remember the events of those days more clearly than those which happened recently, for what we learn as children grows up with the soul and is united to it, so that I can speak even of the place in which the blessed Polycarp sat and disputed, how he came in and went out, the character of his life, the appearance of his body, the discourses which he made to the people, how he reported his intercourse with John and with the others who had seen the Lord, how he remembered their words, and what

497

λόγους αὐτῶν, καὶ περὶ τοῦ κυρίου τίνα ἦν ἃ παρ'
ἐκείνων ἀκηκόει, καὶ περὶ τῶν δυνάμεων αὐτοῦ,
καὶ περὶ τῆς διδασκαλίας, ὡς παρὰ τῶν αὐτοπτῶν
τῆς ζωῆς τοῦ λόγου παρειληφὼς ὁ Πολύκαρπος
ἀπήγγελλεν πάντα σύμφωνα ταῖς γραφαῖς. ταῦτα 7
καὶ τότε διὰ τὸ ἔλεος τοῦ θεοῦ τὸ ἐπ' ἐμοὶ γεγονὸς
σπουδαίως ἤκουον, ὑπομνηματιζόμενος αὐτὰ οὐκ
ἐν χάρτῃ, ἀλλ' ἐν τῇ ἐμῇ καρδίᾳ· καὶ ἀεὶ διὰ τὴν
χάριν τοῦ θεοῦ γνησίως αὐτὰ ἀναμαρυκῶμαι, καὶ
δύναμαι διαμαρτύρασθαι ἔμπροσθεν τοῦ θεοῦ ὅτι εἴ
τι τοιοῦτον ἀκηκόει ἐκεῖνος ὁ μακάριος καὶ ἀποστολικὸς πρεσβύτερος, ἀνακράξας ἂν καὶ ἐμφράξας
τὰ ὦτα αὐτοῦ καὶ κατὰ τὸ σύνηθες αὐτῷ εἰπών
' ὦ καλὲ θεέ, εἰς οἵους με καιροὺς τετήρηκας, ἵνα
τούτων ἀνέχωμαι,' πεφεύγει ἂν καὶ τὸν τόπον ἐν
ᾧ καθεζόμενος ἢ ἑστὼς τῶν τοιούτων ἀκηκόει
λόγων. καὶ ἐκ τῶν ἐπιστολῶν δὲ αὐτοῦ ὧν 8
ἐπέστειλεν ἤτοι ταῖς γειτνιώσαις ἐκκλησίαις, ἐπι-
στηρίζων αὐτάς, ἢ τῶν ἀδελφῶν τισί, νουθετῶν
αὐτοὺς καὶ προτρεπόμενος, δύναται φανερωθῆναι.''
ταῦτα ὁ Εἰρηναῖος.

XXI. Κατὰ δὲ τὸν αὐτὸν τῆς Κομόδου βασιλείας 1
χρόνον μεταβέβλητο μὲν ἐπὶ τὸ πρᾶον τὰ καθ'
ἡμᾶς, εἰρήνης σὺν θείᾳ χάριτι τὰς καθ' ὅλης τῆς
οἰκουμένης διαλαβούσης ἐκκλησίας· ὅτε καὶ ὁ
σωτήριος λόγος ἐκ παντὸς γένους ἀνθρώπων πᾶσαν
ὑπήγετο ψυχὴν ἐπὶ τὴν εὐσεβῆ τοῦ τῶν ὅλων θεοῦ
θρησκείαν, ὡς ἤδη καὶ τῶν ἐπὶ Ῥώμης εὖ μάλα
πλούτῳ καὶ γένει διαφανῶν πλείους ἐπὶ τὴν σφῶν
ὁμόσε χωρεῖν πανοικεί τε καὶ παγγενεῖ σωτηρίαν.
οὐκ ἦν δὲ ἄρα τοῦτο τῷ μισοκάλῳ δαίμονι βασκάνῳ 2
ὄντι τὴν φύσιν οἰστόν, ἀπεδύετο δ' οὖν εἰς αὖθις,

were the things concerning the Lord which he had heard from them, and about their miracles, and about their teaching, and how Polycarp had received them from the eyewitnesses of the word of life, and reported all things in agreement with the Scriptures. I listened eagerly even then to these things through the mercy of God which was given me, and made notes of them, not on paper but in my heart, and ever by the grace of God do I truly ruminate on them, and I can bear witness before God that if that blessed and apostolic presbyter had heard anything of this kind he would have cried out, and shut his ears, and said according to his custom, ' O good God, to what time hast thou preserved me that I should endure this ? ' He would have fled even from the place in which he was seated or standing when he heard such words. And from his letters which he sent either to the neighbouring churches, strengthening them, or to some of the brethren, exhorting and warning them, this can be made plain." So says Irenaeus.

XXI. And at the same time in the reign of Commodus our treatment was changed to a milder one, and by the grace of God peace came on the churches throughout the whole world. The word of salvation began to lead every soul of every race of men to the pious worship of the God of the universe, so that now many of those who at Rome were famous for wealth and family turned to their own salvation with all their house and with all their kin. This was unendurable to the demon who hates good, envious as he is by nature, and he again stripped for conflict,

ποικίλας τὰς καθ' ἡμῶν μηχανὰς ἐπιτεχνώμενος. ἐπὶ γοῦν τῆς Ῥωμαίων πόλεως Ἀπολλώνιον, ἄνδρα τῶν τότε πιστῶν ἐπὶ παιδείᾳ καὶ φιλοσοφίᾳ βεβοημένον, ἐπὶ δικαστήριον ἄγει, ἔνα γέ τινα τῶν εἰς ταῦτ' ἐπιτηδείων αὐτῷ διακόνων ἐπὶ κατηγορίᾳ τἀνδρὸς ἐγείρας. ἀλλ' ὁ μὲν δείλαιος παρὰ καιρὸν 3 τὴν δίκην εἰσελθών, ὅτι μὴ ζῆν ἐξὸν ἦν κατὰ βασιλικὸν ὅρον τοὺς τῶν τοιῶνδε μηνυτάς, αὐτίκα κατάγνυται τὰ σκέλη, Περεννίου δικαστοῦ τοιαύτην κατ' αὐτοῦ ψῆφον ἀπενέγκαντος· ὁ δέ γε θεο- 4 φιλέστατος μάρτυς, πολλὰ λιπαρῶς ἱκετεύσαντος τοῦ δικαστοῦ καὶ λόγον αὐτὸν ἐπὶ τῆς συγκλήτου βουλῆς αἰτήσαντος, λογιωτάτην ὑπὲρ ἧς ἐμαρτύρει πίστεως ἐπὶ πάντων παρασχὼν ἀπολογίαν, κεφαλικῇ κολάσει ὡς ἂν ἀπὸ δόγματος συγκλήτου τελειοῦται, μηδ' ἄλλως ἀφεῖσθαι τοὺς ἅπαξ εἰς δικαστήριον παριόντας καὶ μηδαμῶς τῆς προθέσεως μεταβαλλομένους ἀρχαίου παρ' αὐτοῖς

Acta Martyr.
sel. ed. Geb-
hardt, p. vi

νόμου κεκρατηκότος. τούτου μὲν οὖν τὰς ἐπὶ τοῦ 5 δικαστοῦ φωνὰς καὶ τὰς ἀποκρίσεις ἃς πρὸς πεῦσιν πεποίητο τοῦ Περεννίου, πᾶσάν τε τὴν πρὸς τὴν σύγκλητον ἀπολογίαν, ὅτῳ διαγνῶναι φίλον, ἐκ τῆς τῶν ἀρχαίων μαρτύρων συναχθείσης ἡμῖν ἀναγραφῆς εἴσεται.

XXII. Δεκάτῳ γε μὴν τῆς Κομόδου βασιλείας 1 ἔτει δέκα πρὸς τρισὶν ἔτεσιν τὴν ἐπισκοπὴν λελειτουργηκότα Ἐλεύθερον διαδέχεται Βίκτωρ· ἐν ᾧ καὶ Ἰουλιανοῦ δέκατον ἔτος ἀποπλήσαντος, τῶν κατ' Ἀλεξάνδρειαν παροικιῶν τὴν λειτουργίαν ἐγχειρίζεται Δημήτριος· καθ' οὓς καὶ τῆς Ἀντιοχέων ἐκκλησίας ὄγδοος ἀπὸ τῶν ἀποστόλων ὁ πρόσθεν ἤδη δεδηλωμένος ἔτι τότε Σεραπίων

and prepared various devices against us. In the city of the Romans he brought before the court Apollonius, a man famous among the Christians of that time for his education and philosophy, and raised up to accuse him one of his servants who was suitable for this. But the coward entered the case at a bad time, for according to imperial decree informers on such points were not allowed to live; so they broke his legs at once, for the judge Perennius decreed this sentence against him. But the martyr, beloved of God, when the judge earnestly begged and prayed him to defend himself before the senate, made before everyone a most learned defence of the faith for which he was a martyr, and was consecrated by beheading as if by decree of the senate; for an ancient law obtained among them that there should be no other issue for the case of those who once appeared before the court and did not change their opinion. The words of Apollonius before the judge and the answers which he made to the interrogation of Perennius, and all the defence which he made to the senate, can be read by anyone who wishes in the compilation which we have made of the ancient martyrs.[1]

XXII. In the tenth year of the reign of Commodus [2] Victor succeeded Eleutherus who had served in the episcopate thirteen years. In the same year Julian had completed his tenth year, and Demetrius was appointed to the administration of the Alexandrian dioceses, and at the same time the famous Serapion, whom we mentioned before, was bishop of the church

---

[1] See Introduction, p. xxiii. The facts as to Apollonius are obscure; but the servant was probably executed in accordance with the law against slaves who betrayed their masters.

[2] That is, in A.D. 189.

ἐπίσκοπος ἐγνωρίζετο. Καισαρείας δὲ τῆς Παλαιστίνων ἡγεῖτο Θεόφιλος, καὶ Νάρκισσος δὲ ὁμοίως,
οὗ καὶ πρόσθεν ὁ λόγος μνήμην ἐποιήσατο, τῆς
ἐν Ἱεροσολύμοις ἐκκλησίας ἔτι τότε τὴν λειτουργίαν
εἶχεν, Κορίνθου δὲ τῆς καθ᾽ Ἑλλάδα κατὰ τοὺς
αὐτοὺς ἐπίσκοπος ἦν Βάκχυλλος καὶ τῆς ἐν Ἐφέσῳ
παροικίας Πολυκράτης. καὶ ἄλλοι δ᾽, ὥς γε εἰκός,
ἐπὶ τούτοις μυρίοι κατὰ τούσδε διέπρεπον· ὧν γε
μὴν ἔγγραφος ἡ τῆς πίστεως εἰς ἡμᾶς κατῆλθεν
ὀρθοδοξία, τούτους εἰκότως ὀνομαστὶ κατελέξαμεν.

XXIII. Ζητήσεως δῆτα κατὰ τούσδε οὐ σμικρᾶς 1
ἀνακινηθείσης, ὅτι δὴ τῆς Ἀσίας ἁπάσης αἱ
παροικίαι ὡς ἐκ παραδόσεως ἀρχαιοτέρας σελήνης
τὴν τεσσαρεσκαιδεκάτην ᾤοντο δεῖν ἐπὶ τῆς τοῦ
σωτηρίου πάσχα ἑορτῆς παραφυλάττειν, ἐν ᾗ
θύειν τὸ πρόβατον Ἰουδαίοις προηγόρευτο, ὡς
δέον ἐκ παντὸς κατὰ ταύτην, ὁποίᾳ δ᾽ ἂν ἡμέρᾳ
τῆς ἑβδομάδος περιτυγχάνοι, τὰς τῶν ἀσιτιῶν
ἐπιλύσεις ποιεῖσθαι, οὐκ ἔθους ὄντος τοῦτον
ἐπιτελεῖν τὸν τρόπον ταῖς ἀνὰ τὴν λοιπὴν ἅπασαν
οἰκουμένην ἐκκλησίαις, ἐξ ἀποστολικῆς παραδόσεως
τὸ καὶ εἰς δεῦρο κρατῆσαν ἔθος φυλαττούσαις, ὡς
μηδ᾽ ἑτέρᾳ προσήκειν παρὰ τὴν τῆς ἀναστάσεως
τοῦ σωτῆρος ἡμῶν ἡμέρᾳ τὰς νηστείας ἐπιλύεσθαι,
σύνοδοι δὴ καὶ συγκροτήσεις ἐπισκόπων ἐπὶ 2
ταὐτὸν ἐγίνοντο, πάντες τε μιᾷ γνώμῃ δι᾽ ἐπιστολῶν
ἐκκλησιαστικὸν δόγμα τοῖς πανταχόσε διετυποῦντο
ὡς ἂν μηδ᾽ ἐν ἄλλῃ ποτὲ τῆς κυριακῆς ἡμέρᾳ τὸ
τῆς ἐκ νεκρῶν ἀναστάσεως ἐπιτελοῖτο τοῦ κυρίου
μυστήριον, καὶ ὅπως ἐν ταύτῃ μόνῃ τῶν κατὰ τὸ

of Antioch and the eighth from the apostles. Theophilus ruled Caesarea in Palestine, and Narcissus, whom our work has mentioned before, was still holding the administration of the church at Jerusalem, and at the same time Bacchyllus was bishop of Corinth in Greece and Polycrates of the diocese of Ephesus. There were also, of course, countless other famous men at this time, but we have naturally given the names of those the orthodoxy of whose faith has been preserved to us in writing.

XXIII. At that time no small controversy arose because all the dioceses of Asia thought it right, as though by more ancient tradition, to observe for the feast of the Saviour's passover the fourteenth day of the moon, on which the Jews had been commanded to kill the lamb. Thus it was necessary to finish the fast on that day, whatever day of the week it might be.[1] Yet it was not the custom to celebrate in this manner in the churches throughout the rest of the world, for from apostolic tradition they kept the custom which still exists that it is not right to finish the fast on any day save that of the resurrection of our Saviour. Many meetings and conferences with bishops were held on this point, and all unanimously formulated in their letters the doctrine of the church for those in every country that the mystery of the Lord's resurrection from the dead could be celebrated on no day save Sunday,[2] and

---

[1] That is, instead of Good Friday as the anniversary of the Lord's death the Asiatic Christians observed the Jewish feast on the fourteenth day after the new moon with which the month Nisan began. Hence they are often called Quartodecimans.

[2] And therefore the celebration of the crucifixion must come on a Friday.

πάσχα νηστειῶν φυλαττοίμεθα τὰς ἐπιλύσεις. φέρεται δ᾽ εἰς ἔτι νῦν τῶν κατὰ Παλαιστίνην 3 τηνικάδε συγκεκροτημένων γραφή, ὧν προυτέτακτο Θεόφιλος τῆς ἐν Καισαρείᾳ παροικίας ἐπίσκοπος καὶ Νάρκισσος τῆς ἐν Ἱεροσολύμοις, καὶ τῶν ἐπὶ Ῥώμης δ᾽ ὁμοίως ἄλλη περὶ τοῦ αὐτοῦ ζητήματος, ἐπίσκοπον Βίκτορα δηλοῦσα, τῶν τε κατὰ Πόντον ἐπισκόπων, ὧν Πάλμας ὡς ἀρχαιότατος προυτέτακτο, καὶ τῶν κατὰ Γαλλίαν δὲ 4 παροικιῶν, ἃς Εἰρηναῖος ἐπεσκόπει, ἔτι τε τῶν κατὰ τὴν Ὀσροηνὴν καὶ τὰς ἐκεῖσε πόλεις, καὶ ἰδίως Βακχύλλου τῆς Κορινθίων ἐκκλησίας ἐπισκόπου, καὶ πλείστων ὅσων ἄλλων, οἳ μίαν καὶ τὴν αὐτὴν δόξαν τε καὶ κρίσιν ἐξενηνεγμένοι, τὴν αὐτὴν τέθεινται ψῆφον.

XXIV. Καὶ τούτων μὲν ἦν ὅρος εἷς, ὁ δεδηλω- 1 μένος· τῶν δὲ ἐπὶ τῆς Ἀσίας ἐπισκόπων τὸ πάλαι πρότερον αὐτοῖς παραδοθὲν διαφυλάττειν ἔθος χρῆναι διισχυριζομένων ἡγεῖτο Πολυκράτης· ὃς καὶ αὐτὸς ἐν ᾗ πρὸς Βίκτορα καὶ τὴν Ῥωμαίων ἐκκλησίαν διετυπώσατο γραφῇ τὴν εἰς αὐτὸν ἐλθοῦσαν παράδοσιν ἐκτίθεται διὰ τούτων· "ἡμεῖς 2 οὖν ἀραδιούργητον ἄγομεν τὴν ἡμέραν, μήτε προστιθέντες μήτε ἀφαιρούμενοι. καὶ γὰρ κατὰ τὴν Ἀσίαν μεγάλα στοιχεῖα κεκοίμηται· ἅτινα ἀναστήσεται τῇ ἡμέρᾳ τῆς παρουσίας τοῦ κυρίου, ἐν ᾗ ἔρχεται μετὰ δόξης ἐξ οὐρανῶν καὶ ἀναζητήσει πάντας τοὺς ἁγίους, Φίλιππον τῶν δώδεκα ἀποστόλων, ὃς κεκοίμηται ἐν Ἱεραπόλει καὶ δύο θυγατέρες αὐτοῦ γεγηρακυῖαι παρθένοι καὶ ἡ ἑτέρα αὐτοῦ θυγάτηρ ἐν ἁγίῳ πνεύματι πολιτευσαμένη ἐν Ἐφέσῳ ἀναπαύεται· ἔτι δὲ καὶ 3

that on that day alone we should celebrate the end of the paschal fast. There is still extant a writing of those who were convened in Palestine, over whom presided Theophilus, bishop of the diocese of Caesarea, and Narcissus, bishop of Jerusalem; and there is similarly another from those in Rome on the same controversy, which gives Victor as bishop; and there is one of the bishops of Pontus over whom Palmas presided as the oldest; and of the dioceses of Gaul, of which Irenaeus was bishop; and yet others of those in Osrhoene and the cities there; and particularly of Bacchyllus, the bishop of the church of Corinth; and of very many more who expressed one and the same opinion and judgement, and gave the same vote.

XXIV. These issued the single definition which was given above; but the bishops in Asia were led by Polycrates in persisting that it was necessary to keep the custom which had been handed down to them of old. Polycrates himself in a document which he addressed to Victor and to the church of Rome, expounds the tradition which had come to him as follows. " Therefore we keep the day undeviatingly, neither adding nor taking away, for in Asia great luminaries [1] sleep, and they will rise on the day of the coming of the Lord, when he shall come with glory from heaven and seek out [2] all the saints. Such were Philip of the twelve apostles, and two of his daughters who grew old as virgins, who sleep in Hierapolis, and another daughter of his, who lived in the Holy Spirit, rests at Ephesus. Moreover,

---

[1] στοιχεῖα in late Greek often means the planets.
[2] Some mss. (AB) read ἀναστήσει, " raise up," and this may be the right reading.

Ex. 28, 32 ff.
36, 38 ff.

Ἰωάννης ὁ ἐπὶ τὸ στῆθος τοῦ κυρίου ἀναπεσών,
ὃς ἐγενήθη ἱερεὺς τὸ πέταλον πεφορεκὼς καὶ
μάρτυς καὶ διδάσκαλος· οὗτος ἐν Ἐφέσῳ κε- 4
κοίμηται, ἔτι δὲ καὶ Πολύκαρπος ἐν Σμύρνῃ, καὶ
ἐπίσκοπος καὶ μάρτυς· καὶ Θρασέας καὶ ἐπίσκοπος
καὶ μάρτυς ἀπὸ Εὐμενείας, ὃς ἐν Σμύρνῃ κεκοί- 5
μηται. τί δὲ δεῖ λέγειν Σάγαριν ἐπίσκοπον καὶ
μάρτυρα, ὃς ἐν Λαοδικείᾳ κεκοίμηται, ἔτι δὲ καὶ
Παπίριον τὸν μακάριον καὶ Μελίτωνα τὸν εὐνοῦχον,
τὸν ἐν ἁγίῳ πνεύματι πάντα πολιτευσάμενον, ὃς
κεῖται ἐν Σάρδεσιν περιμένων τὴν ἀπὸ τῶν οὐρανῶν
ἐπισκοπὴν ἐν ᾗ ἐκ νεκρῶν ἀναστήσεται; οὗτοι 6
πάντες ἐτήρησαν τὴν ἡμέραν τῆς τεσσαρεσκαι-
δεκάτης τοῦ πάσχα κατὰ τὸ εὐαγγέλιον, μηδὲν
παρεκβαίνοντες, ἀλλὰ κατὰ τὸν κανόνα τῆς πίστεως
ἀκολουθοῦντες· ἔτι δὲ κἀγὼ ὁ μικρότερος πάντων
ὑμῶν Πολυκράτης, κατὰ παράδοσιν τῶν συγγενῶν
μου, οἷς καὶ παρηκολούθησά τισιν αὐτῶν. ἑπτὰ
μὲν ἦσαν συγγενεῖς μου ἐπίσκοποι, ἐγὼ δὲ ὄγδοος·
καὶ πάντοτε τὴν ἡμέραν ἤγαγον οἱ συγγενεῖς μου
ὅταν ὁ λαὸς ἤρνυεν τὴν ζύμην. ἐγὼ οὖν, ἀδελφοί, 7
ἑξήκοντα πέντε ἔτη ἔχων ἐν κυρίῳ καὶ συμ-
Philipp. 1, 28 βεβληκὼς τοῖς ἀπὸ τῆς οἰκουμένης ἀδελφοῖς καὶ
πᾶσαν ἁγίαν γραφὴν διεληλυθώς, οὐ πτύρομαι ἐπὶ
τοῖς καταπλησσομένοις· οἱ γὰρ ἐμοῦ μείζονες εἰρή-
Acts 5, 29 κασι ʼ πειθαρχεῖν δεῖ θεῷ μᾶλλον ἢ ἀνθρώποις.ʼ ʼ̓

Τούτοις ἐπιφέρει περὶ τῶν γράφοντι συμπαρόντων 8
αὐτῷ καὶ ὁμοδοξούντων ἐπισκόπων ταῦτα λέγων
" ἐδυνάμην δὲ τῶν ἐπισκόπων τῶν συμπαρόντων
μνημονεῦσαι, οὓς ὑμεῖς ἠξιώσατε μετακληθῆναι
ὑπʼ ἐμοῦ καὶ μετεκαλεσάμην· ὧν τὰ ὀνόματα ἐὰν
γράφω, πολλὰ πλήθη εἰσίν· οἱ δὲ εἰδότες τὸν

there is also John, who lay on the Lord's breast,
who was a priest wearing the breastplate, and a
martyr, and teacher. He sleeps at Ephesus. And
there is also Polycarp at Smyrna, both bishop and
martyr, and Thraseas, both bishop and martyr,
from Eumenaea, who sleeps in Smyrna. And why
should I speak of Sagaris, bishop and martyr, who
sleeps at Laodicaea, and Papirius, too, the blessed,
and Melito the eunuch, who lived entirely in the
Holy Spirit, who lies in Sardis, waiting for the
visitation from heaven when he will rise from the
dead ? All these kept the fourteenth day of the
passover according to the gospel, never swerving,
but following according to the rule of the faith.
And I also, Polycrates, the least of you all, live
according to the tradition of my kinsmen, and some
of them have I followed. For seven of my family
were bishops and I am the eighth, and my kinsmen
ever kept the day when the people put away the
leaven. Therefore, brethren, I who have lived sixty-
five years in the Lord and conversed with brethren
from every country, and have studied all holy
Scripture, am not afraid of threats, for they have
said who were greater than I, ' It is better to obey
God rather than men.' "

He continues about the bishops who when he wrote
were with him and shared his opinion, and says
thus : " And I could mention the bishops who are
present whom you required me to summon, and I
did so. If I should write their names they would
be many multitudes ; and they knowing my feeble

μικρόν μου ἄνθρωπον συνηυδόκησαν τῇ ἐπιστολῇ, εἰδότες ὅτι εἰκῇ πολιὰς οὐκ ἤνεγκα, ἀλλ᾽ ἐν Χριστῷ Ἰησοῦ πάντοτε πεπολίτευμαι.''

Ἐπὶ τούτοις ὁ μὲν τῆς Ῥωμαίων προεστὼς 9 Βίκτωρ ἀθρόως τῆς Ἀσίας πάσης ἅμα ταῖς ὁμόροις ἐκκλησίαις ·τὰς παροικίας ἀποτέμνειν, ὡς ἂν ἑτεροδοξούσας, ·ῆς κοινῆς ἑνώσεως πειρᾶται, καὶ στηλιτεύει γε διὰ γραμμάτων ἀκοινωνήτους πάντας ἄρδην τοὺς ἐκεῖσε ἀνακηρύττων ἀδελφούς· ἀλλ᾽ οὐ πᾶσί γε τοῖς ἐπισκόποις ταῦτ᾽ ἠρέσκετο. 10 ἀντιπαρακελεύονται δῆτα αὐτῷ τὰ τῆς εἰρήνης καὶ τῆς πρὸς τοὺς πλησίον ἑνώσεώς τε καὶ ἀγάπης φρονεῖν, φέρονται δὲ καὶ αἱ τούτων φωναὶ πλη- κτικώτερον καθαπτομένων τοῦ Βίκτορος· ἐν οἷς 11 καὶ ὁ Εἰρηναῖος ἐκ προσώπου ὧν ἡγεῖτο κατὰ τὴν Γαλλίαν ἀδελφῶν ἐπιστείλας, παρίσταται μὲν τῷ δεῖν ἐν μόνῃ τῇ τῆς κυριακῆς ἡμέρᾳ τὸ τῆς τοῦ κυρίου ἀναστάσεως ἐπιτελεῖσθαι μυστήριον, τῷ γε μὴν Βίκτορι προσηκόντως, ὡς μὴ ἀποκόπτοι ὅλας ἐκκλησίας θεοῦ ἀρχαίου ἔθους παράδοσιν ἐπιτηρούσας, πλεῖστα ἕτερα παραινεῖ, καὶ αὐτοῖς δὲ ῥήμασιν τάδε ἐπιλέγων· '' οὐδὲ γὰρ μόνον περὶ 12 τῆς ἡμέρας ἐστὶν ἡ ἀμφισβήτησις, ἀλλὰ καὶ περὶ τοῦ εἴδους αὐτοῦ τῆς νηστείας. οἱ μὲν γὰρ οἴονται μίαν ἡμέραν δεῖν αὐτοὺς νηστεύειν, οἱ δὲ δύο, οἱ δὲ καὶ πλείονας· οἱ δὲ τεσσαράκοντα ὥρας ἡμερινάς τε καὶ νυκτερινὰς συμμετροῦσιν τὴν ἡμέραν αὐτῶν. καὶ τοιαύτη μὲν ποικιλία τῶν ἐπιτηρούντων οὐ 13 νῦν ἐφ᾽ ἡμῶν γεγονυῖα, ἀλλὰ καὶ πολὺ πρότερον

---

[1] It appears to have been some time before the Church adopted the Lenten fast of forty days. Oddly enough, according to the historian Socrates (*Hist. Eccl.* v. 22) the

humanity, agreed with the letter, knowing that not in vain is my head grey, but that I have ever lived in Christ Jesus."

Upon this Victor, who presided at Rome, immediately tried to cut off from the common unity the dioceses of all Asia, together with the adjacent churches, on the ground of heterodoxy, and he indited letters announcing that all the Christians there were absolutely excommunicated. But by no means all were pleased by this, so they issued counter-requests to him to consider the cause of peace and unity and love towards his neighbours. Their words are extant, sharply rebuking Victor. Among them too Irenaeus, writing in the name of the Christians whose leader he was in Gaul, though he recommends that the mystery of the Lord's resurrection be observed only on the Lord's day, yet nevertheless exhorts Victor suitably and at length not to excommunicate whole churches of God for following a tradition of ancient custom, and continues as follows : " For the controversy is not only about the day, but also about the actual character of the fast ; for some think that they ought to fast one day, others two, others even more, some count their day as forty hours, day and night.[1] And such variation of observance did not begin in our own time,[2] but much earlier, in the days of our predecessors who,

Greek name for Lent ($\tau\epsilon\sigma\sigma\alpha\rho\alpha\kappa\sigma\sigma\tau\dot{\eta}$=fortieth) is older than the custom of fasting forty days. Forty hours was the traditional interval between the death and resurrection of Jesus. The present limits of Lent appear to have been fixed in the seventh century. See Smith's *Dictionary of Christian Antiquities*, s.v. *Lent*.

[2] The construction of the Greek is harsh : $\gamma\epsilon\gamma\sigma\nu\nu\hat{\iota}\alpha$ seems a mistake for $\gamma\acute{\epsilon}\gamma\sigma\nu\epsilon$.

ἐπὶ τῶν πρὸ ἡμῶν, τῶν παρὰ τὸ ἀκριβές, ὡς εἰκός,
κρατούντων τὴν καθ᾽ ἁπλότητα καὶ ἰδιωτισμὸν
συνήθειαν εἰς τὸ μετέπειτα πεποιηκότων, καὶ οὐδὲν
ἔλαττον πάντες οὗτοι εἰρήνευσάν τε καὶ εἰρηνεύομεν
πρὸς ἀλλήλους, καὶ ἡ διαφωνία τῆς νηστείας τὴν
ὁμόνοιαν τῆς πίστεως συνίστησιν.''

Τούτοις καὶ ἱστορίαν προστίθησιν, ἣν οἰκείως 14
παραθήσομαι, τοῦτον ἔχουσαν τὸν τρόπον· '' ἐν
οἷς καὶ οἱ πρὸ Σωτῆρος πρεσβύτεροι, οἱ προ-
στάντες τῆς ἐκκλησίας ἧς σὺ νῦν ἀφηγῇ, Ἀνίκητον
λέγομεν καὶ Πίον Ὑγῖνόν τε καὶ Τελεσφόρον καὶ
Ξύστον, οὔτε αὐτοὶ ἐτήρησαν οὔτε τοῖς μετ᾽ αὐτῶν
ἐπέτρεπον, καὶ οὐδὲν ἔλαττον αὐτοὶ μὴ τηροῦντες
εἰρήνευον τοῖς ἀπὸ τῶν παροικιῶν ἐν αἷς ἐτηρεῖτο,
ἐρχομένοις πρὸς αὐτούς· καίτοι μᾶλλον ἐναντίον
ἦν τὸ τηρεῖν τοῖς μὴ τηροῦσιν. καὶ οὐδέποτε 15
διὰ τὸ εἶδος τοῦτο ἀπεβλήθησάν τινες, ἀλλ᾽ αὐτοὶ
μὴ τηροῦντες οἱ πρὸ σοῦ πρεσβύτεροι τοῖς ἀπὸ
τῶν παροικιῶν τηροῦσιν ἔπεμπον εὐχαριστίαν, καὶ 16
τοῦ μακαρίου Πολυκάρπου ἐπιδημήσαντος τῇ
Ῥώμῃ ἐπὶ Ἀνικήτου καὶ περὶ ἄλλων τινῶν μικρὰ
σχόντες πρὸς ἀλλήλους, εὐθὺς εἰρήνευσαν, περὶ
τούτου τοῦ κεφαλαίου μὴ φιλεριστήσαντες εἰς
ἑαυτούς. οὔτε γὰρ ὁ Ἀνίκητος τὸν Πολύκαρπον
πεῖσαι ἐδύνατο μὴ τηρεῖν, ἅτε μετὰ Ἰωάννου τοῦ
μαθητοῦ τοῦ κυρίου ἡμῶν καὶ τῶν λοιπῶν ἀποστόλων οἷς συνδιέτριψεν, ἀεὶ τετηρηκότα, οὔτε
μὴν ὁ Πολύκαρπος τὸν Ἀνίκητον ἔπεισεν τηρεῖν,

---

[1] That is, the Quartodeciman practice; see note on p.
503.

[2] The meaning appears to be that the previous generation of Romans had not made an issue out of the Quartodeciman practice, even when Asiatics visiting Rome

it would appear, disregarding strictness maintained
a practice which is simple and yet allows for
personal preference, establishing it for the future,
and none the less all these lived in peace, and we
also live in peace with one another and the disagree-
ment in the fast confirms our agreement in the
faith."

He adds to this a narrative which I may suitably
quote, running as follows : " Among these too were
the presbyters before Soter, who presided over the
church of which you are now the leader, I mean
Anicetus and Pius and Telesphorus and Xystus.
They did not themselves observe it,[1] nor did they
enjoin it on those who followed them, and though they
did not keep it they were none the less at peace
with those from the dioceses in which it was observed
when they came to them, although to observe it was
more objectionable to those who did not do so.[2] And
no one was ever rejected for this reason, but the presbyters before you who did not observe it sent the
Eucharist to those from other dioceses who did ; and
when the blessed Polycarp was staying in Rome in
the time of Anicetus, though they disagreed a little
about some other things as well, they immediately
made peace, having no wish for strife between them
on this matter. For neither was Anicetus able to
persuade Polycarp not to observe it, inasmuch as he
had always done so in company with John the disciple of our Lord and the other apostles with whom
he had associated ; nor did Polycarp persuade
Anicetus to observe it, for he said that he ought to

observed it. The difficulty can be seen best if it be
remembered that the Quartodeciman practice would sometimes mean that Asiatics treated as Easter day what the
Romans regarded as Good Friday.

λέγοντα τὴν συνήθειαν τῶν πρὸ αὐτοῦ πρεσβυτέρων ὀφείλειν κατέχειν. καὶ τούτων οὕτως ἐχόντων, 17
ἐκοινώνησαν ἑαυτοῖς, καὶ ἐν τῇ ἐκκλησίᾳ παρ-
εχώρησεν ὁ Ἀνίκητος τὴν εὐχαριστίαν τῷ Πολυκάρπῳ, κατ' ἐντροπὴν δηλονότι, καὶ μετ' εἰρήνης
ἀπ' ἀλλήλων ἀπηλλάγησαν, πάσης τῆς ἐκκλησίας
εἰρήνην ἐχόντων, καὶ τῶν τηρούντων καὶ τῶν μὴ
τηρούντων."

Καὶ ὁ μὲν Εἰρηναῖος φερώνυμός τις ὢν τῇ 18
προσηγορίᾳ αὐτῷ τε τῷ τρόπῳ εἰρηνοποιός,
τοιαῦτα ὑπὲρ τῆς τῶν ἐκκλησιῶν εἰρήνης παρεκάλει
τε καὶ ἐπρέσβευεν, ὁ δ' αὐτὸς οὐ μόνῳ τῷ Βίκτορι,
καὶ διαφόροις δὲ πλείστοις ἄρχουσιν ἐκκλησιῶν
τὰ κατάλληλα δι' ἐπιστολῶν περὶ τοῦ κεκινη-
μένου ζητήματος ὡμίλει.

XXV. Οἵ γε μὴν ἐπὶ Παλαιστίνης, οὓς ἀρτίως 1
διεληλύθαμεν, ὅ τε Νάρκισσος καὶ Θεόφιλος, καὶ
σὺν αὐτοῖς Κάσσιος τῆς κατὰ Τύρον ἐκκλησίας
ἐπίσκοπος καὶ Κλᾶρος τῆς ἐν Πτολεμαΐδι οἵ τε
μετὰ τούτων συνεληλυθότες, περὶ τῆς κατελθούσης
εἰς αὐτοὺς ἐκ διαδοχῆς τῶν ἀποστόλων περὶ τοῦ
πάσχα παραδόσεως πλεῖστα διειληφότες, κατὰ
τὸ τέλος τῆς γραφῆς αὐτοῖς ῥήμασιν ἐπιλέγουσιν
ταῦτα· "τῆς δ' ἐπιστολῆς ἡμῶν πειράθητε κατὰ
πᾶσαν παροικίαν ἀντίγραφα διαπέμψασθαι, ὅπως
μὴ ἔνοχοι ὦμεν τοῖς ῥᾳδίως πλανῶσιν ἑαυτῶν τὰς
ψυχάς. δηλοῦμεν δὲ ὑμῖν ὅτι τῇ αὐτῇ ἡμέρᾳ
καὶ ἐν Ἀλεξανδρείᾳ ἄγουσιν ἧπερ καὶ ἡμεῖς·
παρ' ἡμῶν γὰρ τὰ γράμματα κομίζεται αὐτοῖς
καὶ ἡμῖν παρ' αὐτῶν, ὥστε συμφώνως καὶ ὁμοῦ
ἄγειν ἡμᾶς τὴν ἁγίαν ἡμέραν."

XXVI. Ἀλλὰ γὰρ πρὸς τοῖς ἀποδοθεῖσιν Εἰρη- 1

keep the custom of those who were presbyters before him. And under these circumstances they communicated with each other, and in the church Anicetus yielded the celebration of the Eucharist to Polycarp, obviously out of respect, and they parted from each other in peace, for the peace of the whole church was kept both by those who observed and by those who did not."

And Irenaeus, who deserved his name, making an eirenicon in this way, gave exhortations of this kind for the peace of the church and served as its ambassador, for in letters he discussed the various views on the issue which had been raised, not only with Victor but also with many other rulers of churches.

XXV. The Palestinians whom we have recently mentioned, that is to say Narcissus and Theophilus, and with them Cassius, the bishop of the church in Tyre, and Clarus, the bishop of the church in Ptolemais, and those who assembled with them, treated at length the tradition concerning the passover which had come down to them from the succession of the apostles, and at the end of their writing they add as follows : " Try to send copies of our letter to every diocese that we may not be guilty towards those who easily deceive their own souls. And we make it plain to you that in Alexandria also they celebrate the same day as do we, for letters have been exchanged between them and us, so that we observe the holy day together and in agreement."

XXVI In addition to the published treatises

ναίου συγγράμμασιν καὶ ταῖς ἐπιστολαῖς φέρεταί
τις αὐτοῦ πρὸς Ἕλληνας λόγος συντομώτατος
καὶ τὰ μάλιστα ἀναγκαιότατος, Περὶ ἐπιστήμης
ἐπιγεγραμμένος, καὶ ἄλλος, ὃν ἀνατέθεικεν ἀδελφῷ
Μαρκιανῷ τοὔνομα εἰς ἐπίδειξιν τοῦ ἀποστολικοῦ
κηρύγματος, καὶ βιβλίον τι διαλέξεων διαφόρων,
ἐν ᾧ τῆς πρὸς Ἑβραίους ἐπιστολῆς καὶ τῆς
λεγομένης Σολομῶνος Σοφίας μνημονεύει, ῥητά
τινα ἐξ αὐτῶν παραθέμενος. καὶ τὰ μὲν εἰς
ἡμετέραν ἐλθόντα γνῶσιν τῶν Εἰρηναίου τοσαῦτα.

Κομόδου δὲ τὴν ἀρχὴν ἐπὶ δέκα καὶ τρισὶν
ἔτεσιν καταλύσαντος, αὐτοκράτωρ Σευῆρος οὐδ'
ὅλοις μησὶν ἓξ μετὰ τὴν Κομόδου τελευτὴν Περτί-
νακος διαγενομένου κρατεῖ. XXVII. πλεῖστα μὲν 1
οὖν παρὰ πολλοῖς εἰς ἔτι νῦν τῶν τότε σῴζεται
παλαιῶν καὶ ἐκκλησιαστικῶν ἀνδρῶν ἐναρέτου
σπουδῆς ὑπομνήματα· ὧν γε μὴν αὐτοὶ διέγνωμεν,
εἴη ἂν τὰ Ἡρακλείτου εἰς τὸν ἀπόστολον, καὶ τὰ
Μαξίμου περὶ τοῦ πολυθρυλήτου παρὰ τοῖς αἱρε-
σιώταις ζητήματος τοῦ πόθεν ἡ κακία, καὶ περὶ
τοῦ γενητὴν ὑπάρχειν τὴν ὕλην, τά τε Κανδίδου
εἰς τὴν ἑξαήμερον, καὶ Ἀπίωνος εἰς τὴν αὐτὴν
ὑπόθεσιν, ὁμοίως Σέξτου περὶ ἀναστάσεως, καὶ
ἄλλη τις ὑπόθεσις Ἀραβιανοῦ, καὶ μυρίων ἄλλων,
ὧν διὰ τὸ μηδεμίαν ἔχειν ἀφορμὴν οὐχ οἷόν τε
οὔτε τοὺς χρόνους παραδοῦναι γραφῇ οὔθ' ἱστορίας
μνήμην ὑποσημήνασθαι. καὶ ἄλλων δὲ πλείστων,
ὧν οὐδὲ τὰς προσηγορίας καταλέγειν ἡμῖν δυνατόν,
ἦλθον εἰς ἡμᾶς λόγοι, ὀρθοδόξων μὲν καὶ ἐκκλη-

---

[1] Commodus was killed on December 31, A.D. 192.
Pertinax succeeded him, but was killed by the Praetorian
guard on March 28, 193. The Praetorians sold the empire

and to the letters of Irenaeus, there is extant a concise and extremely convincing treatise of his against the Greeks, entitled *Concerning Knowledge,* and another which he has dedicated to a Christian named Marcian on the *Demonstration of the Apostolic Preaching,* and a little book of various discourses in which he mentions the Epistle to the Hebrews and the so-called Wisdom of Solomon, quoting certain passages from them. Such is the extent of our knowledge of the works of Irenaeus.

When Commodus had finished his reign after thirteen years Severus became emperor not quite six months after the death of Commodus, Pertinax coming in the interval.[1] XXVII. Many works of the virtuous zeal of the ancient members of the church of that time have still been widely preserved until now, and we have read them ourselves. Such are the writings of Heraclitus on the Epistles,[2] and the writings of Maximus on the problem of the source of evil, so much traversed by the heretics, and on whether matter has an origin, the works of Candidus on the Hexaëmeron,[3] and of Apion on the same subject, also of Sextus on the Resurrection, and another treatise of Arabianus, and countless others of which we are unable from lack of evidence to give the date or any accounts of their history. And there are many others also which have reached us, but we cannot even give their names, yet they are orthodox

---

to Didius Iulianus, but the Pannonian legions acclaimed Severus, who marched on Rome. The Senate then turned against Didius Iulianus who was beheaded after a reign of only sixty-six days.

[2] Literally " on the apostle," which in ecclesiastical Greek regularly means the Epistles of Paul, not the Acts of the Apostles.   [3] That is, the Six days of creation.

σιαστικῶν, ὥς γε δὴ ἡ ἑκάστου παραδείκνυσιν τῆς θείας γραφῆς ἑρμηνεία, ἀδήλων δ' ὅμως ἡμῖν, ὅτι μὴ τὴν προσηγορίαν ἐπάγεται τῶν συγγραψαμένων.

XXVIII. Τούτων ἔν τινος σπουδάσματι κατὰ 1 τῆς Ἀρτέμωνος αἱρέσεως πεπονημένῳ, ἣν αὖθις ὁ ἐκ Σαμοσάτων Παῦλος καθ' ἡμᾶς ἀνανεώσασθαι πεπείραται, φέρεταί τις διήγησις ταῖς ἐξεταζομέναις ἡμῖν προσήκουσα ἱστορίαις. τὴν γάρ τοι 2 δεδηλωμένην αἵρεσιν ψιλὸν ἄνθρωπον γενέσθαι τὸν σωτῆρα φάσκουσαν οὐ πρὸ πολλοῦ τε νεωτερισθεῖσαν διευθύνων, ἐπειδὴ σεμνύνειν αὐτὴν ὡς ἂν ἀρχαίαν οἱ ταύτης ἤθελον εἰσηγηταί, πολλὰ καὶ ἄλλα εἰς ἔλεγχον αὐτῶν τῆς βλασφήμου ψευδηγορίας παραθεὶς ὁ λόγος ταῦτα κατὰ λέξιν ἱστορεῖ· "φασὶν γὰρ τοὺς μὲν προτέρους ἅπαντας 3 καὶ αὐτοὺς τοὺς ἀποστόλους παρειληφέναι τε καὶ δεδιδαχέναι ταῦτα ἃ νῦν οὗτοι λέγουσιν, καὶ τετηρῆσθαι τὴν ἀλήθειαν τοῦ κηρύγματος μέχρι τῶν Βίκτορος χρόνων, ὃς ἦν τρισκαιδέκατος ἀπὸ Πέτρου ἐν Ῥώμῃ ἐπίσκοπος· ἀπὸ δὲ τοῦ διαδόχου αὐτοῦ Ζεφυρίνου παρακεχαράχθαι τὴν ἀλήθειαν. ἦν δ' ἂν τυχὸν πιθανὸν τὸ λεγόμενον, εἰ μὴ πρῶ- 4 τον μὲν ἀντέπιπτον αὐτοῖς αἱ θεῖαι γραφαί· καὶ ἀδελφῶν δέ τινων ἔστιν γράμματα, πρεσβύτερα τῶν Βίκτορος χρόνων, ἃ ἐκεῖνοι καὶ πρὸς τὰ ἔθνη ὑπὲρ τῆς ἀληθείας καὶ πρὸς τὰς τότε αἱρέσεις ἔγραψαν, λέγω δὲ Ἰουστίνου καὶ Μιλτιάδου καὶ Τατιανοῦ καὶ Κλήμεντος καὶ ἑτέρων πλειόνων, ἐν οἷς ἅπασιν θεολογεῖται ὁ Χριστός. τὰ γὰρ 5 Εἰρηναίου τε καὶ Μελίτωνος καὶ τῶν λοιπῶν τίς ἀγνοεῖ βιβλία, θεὸν καὶ ἄνθρωπον καταγγέλλοντα

and Christian, as their interpretation of the divine
Scripture demonstrates, but the writers are unknown
to us because their names are not given in their
writings.

XXVIII. In a treatise worked out by one of these
against the heresy of Artemon, which Paul of
Samosata has tried to renew in our time, there is
extant an account which bears on the history which
we are examining. For he criticizes the above-
mentioned heresy (which claims that the Saviour
was a mere man) as a recent innovation, because
those who introduced it wished to make it respectable
as being ancient. Among many other points adduced
in refutation of their blasphemous falsehood, the
treatise relates this: "For they say that all who
went before and the apostles themselves received
and taught what they now say, and that the truth
of the teaching was preserved until the times of
Victor, who was the thirteenth bishop in Rome after
Peter, but that the truth had been corrupted from
the time of his successor, Zephyrinus. What they
said might perhaps be plausible if in the first place
the divine Scriptures were not opposed to them, and
there are also writings of certain Christians, older
than the time of Victor, which they wrote to the
Gentiles on behalf of the truth and against the
heresies of their own time. I mean the works of
Justin and Miltiades and Tatian and Clement and
many others in all of which Christ is treated as God.
For who is ignorant of the books of Irenaeus and
Melito and the others who announced Christ as God

517

τὸν Χριστόν, ψαλμοὶ δὲ ὅσοι καὶ ᾠδαὶ ἀδελφῶν 6
ἀπ᾽ ἀρχῆς ὑπὸ πιστῶν γραφεῖσαι τὸν λόγον τοῦ
θεοῦ τὸν Χριστὸν ὑμνοῦσιν θεολογοῦντες; πῶς
οὖν ἐκ τοσούτων ἐτῶν καταγγελλομένου τοῦ
ἐκκλησιαστικοῦ φρονήματος, ἐνδέχεται τοὺς μέχρι
Βίκτορος οὕτως ὡς οὗτοι λέγουσιν κεκηρυχέναι;
πῶς δὲ οὐκ αἰδοῦνται ταῦτα Βίκτορος κατα-
ψεύδεσθαι, ἀκριβῶς εἰδότες ὅτι Βίκτωρ Θεόδοτον
τὸν σκυτέα, τὸν ἀρχηγὸν καὶ πατέρα ταύτης τῆς
ἀρνησιθέου ἀποστασίας, ἀπεκήρυξεν τῆς κοινωνίας,
πρῶτον εἰπόντα ψιλὸν ἄνθρωπον τὸν Χριστόν; εἰ
γὰρ Βίκτωρ κατ᾽ αὐτοὺς οὕτως ἐφρόνει ὡς ἡ
τούτων διδάσκει βλασφημία, πῶς ἂν ἀπέβαλεν
Θεόδοτον τὸν τῆς αἱρέσεως ταύτης εὑρετήν;"

Καὶ τὰ μὲν κατὰ τὸν Βίκτορα τοσαῦτα· τούτου 7
δὲ ἔτεσιν δέκα προστάντος τῆς λειτουργίας
διάδοχος καθίσταται Ζεφυρῖνος ἀμφὶ τὸ ἔνατον
τῆς Σευήρου βασιλείας ἔτος. προστίθησιν δὲ ὁ
τὸ προειρημένον συντάξας περὶ τοῦ κατάρξαντος
τῆς δηλωθείσης αἱρέσεως βιβλίον καὶ ἄλλην κατὰ
Ζεφυρῖνον γενομένην πρᾶξιν, ὧδέ πως αὐτοῖς
ῥήμασι γράφων· "ὑπομνήσω γοῦν πολλοὺς τῶν 8
Matt. 11, 23 ἀδελφῶν πρᾶγμα ἐφ᾽ ἡμῶν γενόμενον, ὃ νομίζω
ὅτι εἰ ἐν Σοδόμοις ἐγεγόνει, τυχὸν ἂν κἀκείνους
ἐνουθέτησεν. Νατάλιος ἦν τις ὁμολογητής, οὐ
πάλαι, ἀλλ᾽ ἐπὶ τῶν ἡμετέρων γενόμενος καιρῶν.
οὗτος ἠπατήθη ποτὲ ὑπὸ Ἀσκληπιοδότου καὶ 9
ἑτέρου Θεοδότου τινὸς τραπεζίτου· ἦσαν δὲ οὗτοι
ἄμφω Θεοδότου τοῦ σκυτέως μαθηταὶ τοῦ πρώτου
ἐπὶ ταύτῃ τῇ φρονήσει, μᾶλλον δὲ ἀφροσύνῃ,
ἀφορισθέντος τῆς κοινωνίας ὑπὸ Βίκτορος, ὡς

and man ? And all the Psalms and hymns which were written by faithful Christians from the beginning sing of the Christ as the Logos of God and treat him as God. How then is it possible that after the mind of the church had been announced for so many years that the generation before Victor can have preached as these say ? Why are they not ashamed of so calumniating Victor when they know quite well that Victor excommunicated Theodotus the cobbler, the founder and father of this insurrection which denies God, when he first said that Christ was a mere man ? For if Victor was so minded towards them as their blasphemy teaches, how could he have thrown out Theodotus who invented this heresy ? "

Such were the events of the time of Victor. When he had held his office ten years, Zephyrinus was appointed his successor in the ninth year of the reign of Severus.[1] And the author of the book mentioned about the founder of the above-mentioned heresy adds another incident which happened in the time of Zephyrinus and writes as follows : " I will at least remind many of the brethren of an event which happened in our time which I think would have probably been a warning to the men of Sodom had it happened in their city. There was a certain confessor, Natalius, not long ago but in our own time. He was deceived by Asclepiodotus and by a second Theodotus, a banker. These were both disciples of Theodotus the cobbler, who was first excommunicated by Victor, who, as I said, was then bishop, for this way

[1] That is, A.D. 201. But reckoning backwards from the time of Callistus who seems to have become bishop of Rome in 217, when Zephyrinus had been bishop for eighteen years (cf. Eusebius, *Hist. Eccl.* vi. 21), it would seem that this date is somewhat too late.

ἔφην, τοῦ τότε ἐπισκόπου. ἀνεπείσθη δὲ ὁ Νατά- 10
λιος ὑπ' αὐτῶν ἐπὶ σαλαρίῳ ἐπίσκοπος κληθῆναι
ταύτης τῆς αἱρέσεως, ὥστε λαμβάνειν παρ' αὐτῶν
μηνιαῖα δηνάρια ρν΄. γενόμενος οὖν σὺν αὐτοῖς, 11
δι' ὁραμάτων πολλάκις ἐνουθετεῖτο ὑπὸ τοῦ
κυρίου· ὁ γὰρ εὔσπλαγχνος θεὸς καὶ κύριος ἡμῶν
Ἰησοῦς Χριστὸς οὐκ ἐβούλετο ἔξω ἐκκλησίας
γενόμενον ἀπολέσθαι μάρτυρα τῶν ἰδίων παθῶν.
ἐπεὶ δὲ ῥᾳθυμότερον τοῖς ὁράμασιν προσεῖχεν, 12
δελεαζόμενος τῇ τε παρ' αὐτοῖς πρωτοκαθεδρίᾳ
καὶ τῇ πλείστους ἀπολλυούσῃ αἰσχροκερδίᾳ, τελευταῖον ὑπὸ ἁγίων ἀγγέλων ἐμαστιγώθη δι' ὅλης
τῆς νυκτὸς οὐ μικρῶς αἰκισθείς, ὥστε ἕωθεν
ἀναστῆναι καὶ ἐνδυσάμενον σάκκον καὶ σποδὸν
καταπασάμενον μετὰ πολλῆς σπουδῆς καὶ δακρύων
προσπεσεῖν Ζεφυρίνῳ τῷ ἐπισκόπῳ, κυλιόμενον
ὑπὸ τοὺς πόδας οὐ μόνον τῶν ἐν κλήρῳ, ἀλλὰ καὶ
τῶν λαϊκῶν, συγχέαι τε τοῖς δάκρυσιν τὴν εὔσπλαγ-
χνον ἐκκλησίαν τοῦ ἐλεήμονος Χριστοῦ πολλῇ τε
τῇ δεήσει χρησάμενον δείξαντά τε τοὺς μώλωπας
ὧν εἰλήφει πληγῶν μόλις κοινωνηθῆναι.''

Τούτοις ἐπισυνάψωμεν καὶ ἄλλας περὶ τῶν 13
αὐτῶν τοῦ αὐτοῦ συγγραφέως φωνάς, τοῦτον
ἐχούσας τὸν τρόπον· ''γραφὰς μὲν θείας ἀφόβως
ῥεραδιουργήκασιν, πίστεώς τε ἀρχαίας κανόνα
ἠθετήκασιν, Χριστὸν δὲ ἠγνοήκασιν, οὐ τί αἱ
θεῖαι λέγουσιν γραφαί, ζητοῦντες, ἀλλ' ὁποῖον
σχῆμα συλλογισμοῦ εἰς τὴν τῆς ἀθεότητος σύστασιν
εὑρεθῇ, φιλοπόνως ἀσκοῦντες. κἂν αὐτοῖς προ-
τείνῃ τις ῥητὸν γραφῆς θεϊκῆς, ἐξετάζουσιν πό-

of thinking, or rather of not thinking. Natalius was persuaded by them to be called bishop of this heresy with a salary, so that he was paid a hundred and fifty denarii a month by them.[1] When he was with them he was often warned by the Lord in visions, for our merciful God and Lord, Jesus Christ, did not wish that there should go out of the church and perish one who had been a witness of his own sufferings.[2] But when he paid indifferent attention to the visions, for he was entrapped by his leading rank among them and by that covetousness which ruins so many, he was at last scourged all night long by holy angels, and suffered not a little, so that in the morning he got up, put on sackcloth, and covered himself with ashes, and went with much haste, and fell down with tears before Zephyrinus the bishop, rolling at the feet not only of the clergy but also of the laity, and moved with his tears the compassionate church of the merciful Christ. But for all his prayers and the exhibition of the weals of the stripes he had received, he was scarcely admitted into communion."

We would add to this some other words of the same author on the same persons, which run as follows : " They have not feared to corrupt divine Scriptures, they have nullified the rule of ancient faith, they have not known Christ, they do not inquire what the divine Scriptures say, but industriously consider what syllogistic figure may be found for the support of their atheism. If anyone adduced to them a text of divine Scripture they

[1] That is, rather more than £5. This is the first clear instance of the payment of bishops, but compare chapter 18. 2.

[2] This does not mean more than " had been a confessor " —a witness in court to the " sufferings of Christ."

τερον συνημμένον ἢ διεζευγμένον δύναται ποιῆσαι
σχῆμα συλλογισμοῦ· καταλιπόντες δὲ τὰς ἁγίας 14
τοῦ θεοῦ γραφάς, γεωμετρίαν ἐπιτηδεύουσιν, ὡς
ἂν ἐκ τῆς γῆς ὄντες καὶ ἐκ τῆς γῆς λαλοῦντες καὶ
τὸν ἄνωθεν ἐρχόμενον ἀγνοοῦντες. Εὐκλείδης γοῦν
παρά τισιν αὐτῶν φιλοπόνως γεωμετρεῖται, Ἀριστο-
τέλης δὲ καὶ Θεόφραστος θαυμάζονται· Γαληνὸς
γὰρ ἴσως ὑπό τινων καὶ προσκυνεῖται. οἱ δὲ ταῖς 15
τῶν ἀπίστων τέχναις εἰς τὴν τῆς αἱρέσεως αὐτῶν
γνώμην ἀποχρώμενοι καὶ τῇ τῶν ἀθέων πανουργίᾳ
τὴν ἁπλῆν τῶν θείων γραφῶν πίστιν καπηλεύοντες,
ὅτι μηδὲ ἐγγὺς πίστεως ὑπάρχουσιν, τί δεῖ καὶ
λέγειν; διὰ τοῦτο ταῖς θείαις γραφαῖς **ἀφόβως**
ἐπέβαλον τὰς χεῖρας, λέγοντες αὐτὰς διωρθωκέναι.
καὶ ὅτι τοῦτο μὴ καταψευδόμενος αὐτῶν λέγω, 16
ὁ βουλόμενος δύναται μαθεῖν. εἰ γάρ τις θελήσει
συγκομίσας αὐτῶν ἑκάστου τὰ ἀντίγραφα ἐξετάζειν πρὸς ἄλληλα, κατὰ πολὺ ἂν εὕροι δια-
φωνοῦντα. ἀσύμφωνα γοῦν ἔσται τὰ Ἀσκλη- 17
πιάδου τοῖς Θεοδότου, πολλῶν δὲ ἔστιν εὐπορῆ-
σαι διὰ τὸ φιλοτίμως ἐκγεγράφθαι τοὺς μαθητὰς
αὐτῶν τὰ ὑφ' ἑκάστου αὐτῶν, ὡς αὐτοὶ καλοῦσιν,
κατωρθωμένα, τοῦτ' ἐστὶν ἠφανισμένα· πάλιν δὲ
τούτοις τὰ Ἑρμοφίλου οὐ συνᾴδει. τὰ γὰρ
Ἀπολλωνιάδου οὐδὲ αὐτὰ ἑαυτοῖς ἐστιν σύμφωνα·
ἔνεστιν γὰρ συγκρῖναι τὰ πρότερον ὑπ' αὐτῶν
κατασκευασθέντα τοῖς ὕστερον πάλιν ἐπιδιαστρα-

---

[1] Lit. "earth-measurement." Note the play on the words.

[2] Apparently the meaning of the passage is that these persons tried to introduce Greek learning generally into

inquire whether it can be put in the form of a conjunctive or a disjunctive syllogism. They abandon the holy Scripture of God and study geometry,[1] for they are of the earth and they speak of the earth and him who comes from above they do not know. Some of them, forsooth, study the geometry of Euclid and admire Aristotle and Theophrastus. Galen perhaps is even worshipped by some of them.[2] When they make a bad use of the arts of unbelievers for the opinions of their heresy, and adulterate the simple faith of the divine scriptures by the cunning of the godless, what need is there to say that they are not even near the faith ? For this cause they did not fear to lay hands on the divine scriptures, saying that they had corrected them. And that I do not calumniate them in saying this any who wish can learn, for if any be willing to collect and compare with each other the texts of each of them, he would find them in great discord, for the copies [3] of Asclepiades do not agree with those of Theodotus, and it is possible to obtain many of them because their disciples have diligently written out copies corrected, as they say, but really corrupted by each of them. Again the copies of Hermophilus do not agree with these, the copies of Apolloniades are not even consistent with themselves, for the copies prepared by them at first can be compared with those which later on underwent a second corruption, and they

the interpretation of Scripture. Though little noted at the time or since, their rejection by the Church is perhaps one of the turning-points of history.

[3] That is, the copies of Scripture used by Asclepiades. Apparently these Roman heretics added textual criticism to the sin of using Aristotle's logic, and were unable to resist the temptations of conjectural emendation.

φεῖσιν καὶ εὑρεῖν κατὰ πολὺ ἀπᾴδοντα. ὅσης δὲ 18
τόλμης ἐστὶ τοῦτο τὸ ἁμάρτημα, εἰκὸς μηδὲ
ἐκείνους ἀγνοεῖν. ἢ γὰρ οὐ πιστεύουσιν ἁγίῳ
πνεύματι λελέχθαι τὰς θείας γραφάς, καί εἰσιν
ἄπιστοι· ἢ ἑαυτοὺς ἡγοῦνται σοφωτέρους τοῦ
ἁγίου πνεύματος ὑπάρχειν, καὶ τί ἕτερον ἢ δαι-
μονῶσιν; οὐδὲ γὰρ ἀρνήσασθαι δύνανται ἑαυτῶν
εἶναι τὸ τόλμημα, ὁπόταν καὶ τῇ αὐτῶν χειρὶ ᾖ
γεγραμμένα, καὶ παρ' ὧν κατηχήθησαν, μὴ
τοιαύτας παρέλαβον τὰς γραφάς, καὶ δεῖξαι
ἀντίγραφα ὅθεν αὐτὰ μετεγράψαντο, μὴ ἔχωσιν.
ἔνιοι δ' αὐτῶν οὐδὲ παραχαράσσειν ἠξίωσαν 19
αὐτάς, ἀλλ' ἁπλῶς ἀρνησάμενοι τόν τε νόμον καὶ
τοὺς προφήτας, ἀνόμου καὶ ἀθέου διδασκαλίας
προφάσει χάριτος εἰς ἔσχατον ἀπωλείας ὄλεθρον
κατωλίσθησαν.''

Καὶ ταῦτα μὲν τοῦτον ἱστορήσθω τὸν τρόπον.

will be found to disagree greatly. The impudence of this sin can scarcely be unknown even to them, for either they do not believe that the divine scriptures were spoken by the Holy Spirit, and if so they are unbelievers, or they think that they are wiser than the Holy Spirit, and what are they but demoniacs? For they cannot even deny that this crime is theirs, seeing that the copies were written in their own hand, and they did not receive the scriptures in this condition from their teachers, nor can they show originals from which they made their copies. Some of them have not thought it necessary even to emend the text, but simply deny the Law and the Prophets, and thus on the pretence [1] of their wicked and godless teaching have fallen to the lowest destruction of perdition." And let this suffice for these things.

[1] χάριτος seems to be a primitive error, for though it is found in all the mss. it is impossible to give it any reasonable sense. Possibly a word has fallen out which would give the meaning " they have fallen from grace, etc."

Printed in Great Britain by R. & R. CLARK, LIMITED, *Edinburgh*

THE LOEB CLASSICAL LIBRARY

VOLUMES ALREADY PUBLISHED

LATIN AUTHORS

AMMIANUS MARCELLINUS. J. C. Rolfe. 3 Vols.

APULEIUS : THE GOLDEN ASS (METAMORPHOSES). W. Adlington (1566). Revised by S. Gaselee.

ST. AUGUSTINE: CITY OF GOD. 7 Vols. Vol. I. G. E. McCracken. Vol. II. W. M. Green. Vol. III. D. Wiesen. Vol. IV. P. Levine. Vol. V. E. M. Sanford and W. M. Green. Vol. VI. W. C. Greene. Vol. VII. W. M. Green.

ST. AUGUSTINE, CONFESSIONS OF. W. Watts (1631). 2 Vols.

ST. AUGUSTINE : SELECT LETTERS. J. H. Baxter.

AUSONIUS. H. G. Evelyn White. 2 Vols.

BEDE. J. E. King. 2 Vols.

BOETHIUS : TRACTS AND DE CONSOLATIONE PHILOSOPHIAE. Rev. H. F. Stewart and E. K. Rand. Revised by S. J. Tester.

CAESAR : ALEXANDRIAN, AFRICAN AND SPANISH WARS. A. G. Way.

CAESAR : CIVIL WARS. A. G. Peskett.

CAESAR : GALLIC WAR. H. J. Edwards.

CATO AND VARRO : DE RE RUSTICA. H. B. Ash and W. D. Hooper.

CATULLUS. F. W. Cornish ; TIBULLUS. J. B. Postgate ; and PERVIGILIUM VENERIS. J. W. Mackail.

CELSUS : DE MEDICINA. W. G. Spencer. 3 Vols.

CICERO : BRUTUS AND ORATOR. G. L. Hendrickson and H. M. Hubbell.

CICERO : DE FINIBUS. H. Rackham.

CICERO : DE INVENTIONE, etc. H. M. Hubbell.

CICERO : DE NATURA DEORUM AND ACADEMICA. H. Rackham.

CICERO : DE OFFICIIS. Walter Miller.

CICERO: DE ORATORE, etc. 2 Vols. Vol. I: DE ORATORE, Books I and II. E. W. Sutton and H. Rackham. Vol. II: DE ORATORE, Book III ; DE FATO ; PARADOXA STOICORUM ; DE PARTITIONE ORATORIA. H. Rackham.

CICERO : DE REPUBLICA, DE LEGIBUS. Clinton W. Keyes.

THE LOEB CLASSICAL LIBRARY

CICERO: DE SENECTUTE, DE AMICITIA, DE DIVINATIONE.
W. A. Falconer.

CICERO: IN CATILINAM, PRO MURENA, PRO SULLA, PRO
FLACCO. New version by C. Macdonald.

CICERO: LETTERS TO ATTICUS. E. O. Winstedt. 3 Vols.

CICERO: LETTERS TO HIS FRIENDS. W. Glynn Williams,
M. Cary, M. Henderson. 4 Vols.

CICERO: PHILIPPICS. W. C. A. Ker.

CICERO: PRO ARCHIA, POST REDITUM, DE DOMO, DE HA-
RUSPICUM RESPONSIS, PRO PLANCIO. N. H. Watts.

CICERO: PRO CAECINA, PRO LEGE MANILIA, PRO CLUENTIO,
PRO RABIRIO. H. Grose Hodge.

CICERO: PRO CAELIO, DE PROVINCIIS CONSULARIBUS, PRO
BALBO. R. Gardner.

CICERO: PRO MILONE, IN PISONEM, PRO SCAURO, PRO
FONTEIO, PRO RABIRIO POSTUMO, PRO MARCELLO, PRO
LIGARIO, PRO REGE DEIOTARO. N. H. Watts.

CICERO: PRO QUINCTIO, PRO ROSCIO AMERINO, PRO ROSCIO
COMOEDO, CONTRA RULLUM. J. H. Freese.

CICERO: PRO SESTIO, IN VATINIUM. R. Gardner.

[CICERO]: RHETORICA AD HERENNIUM. H. Caplan.

CICERO: TUSCULAN DISPUTATIONS. J. E. King.

CICERO: VERRINE ORATIONS. L. H. G. Greenwood. 2 Vols.

CLAUDIAN. M. Platnauer. 2 Vols.

COLUMELLA: DE RE RUSTICA, DE ARBORIBUS. H. B. Ash,
E. S. Forster, E. Heffner. 3 Vols.

CURTIUS, Q.: HISTORY OF ALEXANDER. J. C. Rolfe. 2 Vols.

FLORUS. E. S. Forster; and CORNELIUS NEPOS. J. C. Rolfe.

FRONTINUS: STRATAGEMS AND AQUEDUCTS. C. E. Bennett
and M. B. McElwain.

FRONTO: CORRESPONDENCE. C. R. Haines. 2 Vols.

GELLIUS. J. C. Rolfe. 3 Vols.

HORACE: ODES AND EPODES. C. E. Bennett.

HORACE: SATIRES, EPISTLES, ARS POETICA. H. R. Fairclough.

JEROME: SELECT LETTERS. F. A. Wright.

JUVENAL AND PERSIUS. G. G. Ramsay.

LIVY. B. O. Foster, F. G. Moore, Evan T. Sage, A. C.
Schlesinger and R. M. Geer (General Index). 14 Vols.

LUCAN. J. D. Duff.

LUCRETIUS. W. H. D. Rouse. Revised by M. F. Smith.

MANILIUS. G. P. Goold.

MARTIAL. W. C. A. Ker. 2 Vols. Revised by E. H.
Warmington.

MINOR LATIN POETS: from PUBLILIUS SYRUS to RUTILIUS
NAMATIANUS, including GRATTIUS, CALPURNIUS SICULUS,

THE LOEB CLASSICAL LIBRARY

NEMESIANUS, AVIANUS, with "Aetna," "Phoenix" and other poems. J. Wight Duff and Arnold M. Duff.

OVID: THE ART OF LOVE AND OTHER POEMS. J. H. Mozley. Revised by G. P. Goold.

OVID: FASTI. Sir James G. Frazer.   [by G. P. Goold.

OVID: HEROIDES AND AMORES. Grant Showerman. Revised

OVID: METAMORPHOSES. F. J. Miller. 2 Vols. Vol. I revised by G. P. Goold.

OVID: TRISTIA AND EX PONTO. A. L. Wheeler.

PETRONIUS. M. Heseltine; SENECA: APOCOLOCYNTOSIS. W. H. D. Rouse. Revised by E. H. Warmington.

PHAEDRUS AND BABRIUS (Greek). B. E. Perry.

PLAUTUS. Paul Nixon. 5 Vols.

PLINY: LETTERS, PANEGYRICUS. B. Radice. 2 Vols.

PLINY: NATURAL HISTORY. 10 Vols. Vols. I-V. H. Rackham. Vols. VI-VIII. W. H. S. Jones. Vol. IX. H. Rackham. Vol. X. D. E. Eichholz.

PROPERTIUS. H. E. Butler.

PRUDENTIUS. H. J. Thomson. 2 Vols.

QUINTILIAN. H. E. Butler. 4 Vols.

REMAINS OF OLD LATIN. E. H. Warmington. 4 Vols. Vol. I (Ennius and Caecilius). Vol. II (Livius, Naevius, Pacuvius, Accius). Vol. III (Lucilius, Laws of the XII Tables). Vol. IV (Archaic Inscriptions).

SALLUST. J. C. Rolfe.

SCRIPTORES HISTORIAE AUGUSTAE. D. Magie. 3 Vols.

SENECA: APOCOLOCYNTOSIS. Cf. PETRONIUS.

SENECA: EPISTULAE MORALES. R. M. Gummere. 3 Vols.

SENECA: MORAL ESSAYS. J. W. Basore. 3 Vols.

SENECA: NATURALES QUAESTIONES. T. H. Corcoran. 2 Vols.

SENECA: TRAGEDIES. F. J. Miller. 2 Vols.

SENECA THE ELDER. M. Winterbottom. 2 Vols.

SIDONIUS: POEMS AND LETTERS. W. B. Anderson. 2 Vols.

SILIUS ITALICUS. J. D. Duff. 2 Vols.

STATIUS. J. H. Mozley. 2 Vols.

SUETONIUS. J. C. Rolfe. 2 Vols.

TACITUS: AGRICOLA AND GERMANIA. M. Hutton; DIALOGUS. Sir Wm. Peterson. Revised by R. M. Ogilvie, E. H. Warmington, M. Winterbottom.

TACITUS: HISTORIES AND ANNALS. C. H. Moore and J. Jackson. 4 Vols.

TERENCE. John Sargeaunt. 2 Vols.

TERTULLIAN: APOLOGIA AND DE SPECTACULIS. T. R. Glover; MINUCIUS FELIX. G. H. Rendall.

VALERIUS FLACCUS. J. H. Mozley.

VARRO : DE LINGUA LATINA. R. G. Kent. 2 Vols.
VELLEIUS PATERCULUS AND RES GESTAE DIVI AUGUSTI.
F. W. Shipley.
VIRGIL. H. R. Fairclough. 2 Vols.
VITRUVIUS : DE ARCHITECTURA. F. Granger. 2 Vols.

GREEK AUTHORS

ACHILLES TATIUS. S. Gaselee.
AELIAN : ON THE NATURE OF ANIMALS. A. F. Scholfield.
3 Vols.
AENEAS TACTICUS, ASCLEPIODOTUS AND ONASANDER. The
Illinois Greek Club.
AESCHINES. C. D. Adams.
AESCHYLUS. H. Weir Smyth. 2 Vols.
ALCIPHRON, AELIAN AND PHILOSTRATUS : LETTERS. A. R.
Benner and F. H. Fobes.
APOLLODORUS. Sir James G. Frazer. 2 Vols.
APOLLONIUS RHODIUS. R. C. Seaton.
THE APOSTOLIC FATHERS. Kirsopp Lake. 2 Vols.
APPIAN : ROMAN HISTORY. Horace White. 4 Vols.
ARATUS. Cf. CALLIMACHUS : HYMNS AND EPIGRAMS.
ARISTIDES. C. A. Behr. 4 Vols. Vol. I.
ARISTOPHANES. Benjamin Bickley Rogers. 3 Vols. Verse
trans.
ARISTOTLE : ART OF RHETORIC. J. H. Freese.
ARISTOTLE : ATHENIAN CONSTITUTION, EUDEMIAN ETHICS.
VIRTUES AND VICES. H. Rackham.
ARISTOTLE : THE CATEGORIES. ON INTERPRETATION. H. P.
Cooke ; PRIOR ANALYTICS. H. Tredennick.
ARISTOTLE : GENERATION OF ANIMALS. A. L. Peck.
ARISTOTLE : HISTORIA ANIMALIUM. A. L. Peck. 3 Vols.
Vols. I and II.
ARISTOTLE : METAPHYSICS. H. Tredennick. 2 Vols.
ARISTOTLE : METEOROLOGICA. H. D. P. Lee.
ARISTOTLE : MINOR WORKS. W. S. Hett. " On Colours,"
" On Things Heard," " Physiognomics," " On Plants,"
" On Marvellous Things Heard," " Mechanical Prob-
lems," " On Invisible Lines," " Situations and Names of
Winds," " On Melissus, Xenophanes, and Gorgias."
ARISTOTLE : NICOMACHEAN ETHICS. H. Rackham.
ARISTOTLE : OECONOMICA AND MAGNA MORALIA. G. C.
Armstrong. (With METAPHYSICS, Vol. II.)
ARISTOTLE : ON THE HEAVENS. W. K. C. Guthrie.

THE LOEB CLASSICAL LIBRARY

ARISTOTLE: ON THE SOUL, PARVA NATURALIA, ON BREATH.
W. S. Hett.

ARISTOTLE: PARTS OF ANIMALS. A. L. Peck: MOVEMENT
AND PROGRESSION OF ANIMALS. E. S. Forster.

ARISTOTLE: PHYSICS. Rev. P. Wicksteed and F. M. Corn-
ford. 2 Vols.

ARISTOTLE: POETICS; LONGINUS ON THE SUBLIME. W. Ham-
ilton Fyfe; DEMETRIUS ON STYLE. W. Rhys Roberts.

ARISTOTLE: POLITICS. H. Rackham.

ARISTOTLE: POSTERIOR ANALYTICS. H. Tredennick; TOPICS.
E. S. Forster.

ARISTOTLE: PROBLEMS. W. S. Hett. 2 Vols.

ARISTOTLE: RHETORICA AD ALEXANDRUM. H. Rackham.
(With PROBLEMS, Vol. II.)

ARISTOTLE: SOPHISTICAL REFUTATIONS. COMING-TO-BE AND
PASSING-AWAY. E. S. Forster; ON THE COSMOS. D. J.
Furley.

ARRIAN: HISTORY OF ALEXANDER AND INDICA. 2 Vols.
Vol. I. P. Brunt. Vol. II. Rev. E. Iliffe Robson.

ATHENAEUS: DEIPNOSOPHISTAE. C. B. Gulick. 7 Vols.

BABRIUS AND PHAEDRUS (Latin). B. E. Perry.

ST. BASIL: LETTERS. R. J. Deferrari. 4 Vols.

CALLIMACHUS: FRAGMENTS. C. A. Trypanis; MUSAEUS:
HERO AND LEANDER. T. Gelzer and C. Whitman.

CALLIMACHUS: HYMNS AND EPIGRAMS, AND LYCOPHRON.
A. W. Mair; ARATUS. G. R. Mair.

CLEMENT OF ALEXANDRIA. Rev. G. W. Butterworth.

COLLUTHUS. Cf. OPPIAN.

DAPHNIS AND CHLOE. Cf. LONGUS.

DEMOSTHENES I: OLYNTHIACS, PHILIPPICS AND MINOR
ORATIONS: I-XVII AND XX. J. H. Vince.

DEMOSTHENES II: DE CORONA AND DE FALSA LEGATIONE.
C. A. and J. H. Vince.

DEMOSTHENES III: MEIDIAS, ANDROTION, ARISTOCRATES,
TIMOCRATES, ARISTOGEITON. J. H. Vince.

DEMOSTHENES IV-VI: PRIVATE ORATIONS AND IN NEAERAM.
A. T. Murray.

DEMOSTHENES VII: FUNERAL SPEECH, EROTIC ESSAY, EX-
ORDIA AND LETTERS. N. W. and N. J. DeWitt.

DIO CASSIUS: ROMAN HISTORY. E. Cary. 9 Vols.

DIO CHRYSOSTOM. 5 Vols. Vols. I and II. J. W. Cohoon.
Vol. III. J. W. Cohoon and H. Lamar Crosby. Vols. IV
and V. H. Lamar Crosby.

DIODORUS SICULUS. 12 Vols. Vols. I-VI. C. H. Oldfather.
Vol. VII. C. L. Sherman. Vol. VIII. C. B. Welles. Vols.

IX and X. Russel M. Geer. Vols. XI and XII. F. R. Walton. General Index. Russel M. Geer.

DIOGENES LAERTIUS. R. D. Hicks. 2 Vols. New Introduction by H. S. Long.

DIONYSIUS OF HALICARNASSUS : CRITICAL ESSAYS. S. Usher. 2 Vols.

DIONYSIUS OF HALICARNASSUS : ROMAN ANTIQUITIES. Spelman's translation revised by E. Cary. 7 Vols.

EPICTETUS. W. A. Oldfather. 2 Vols.

EURIPIDES. A. S. Way. 4 Vols. Verse trans.

EUSEBIUS : ECCLESIASTICAL HISTORY. Kirsopp Lake and J. E. L. Oulton. 2 Vols.

GALEN : ON THE NATURAL FACULTIES. A. J. Brock.

THE GREEK ANTHOLOGY. W. R. Paton. 5 Vols.

THE GREEK BUCOLIC POETS (THEOCRITUS, BION, MOSCHUS). J. M. Edmonds.

GREEK ELEGY AND IAMBUS WITH THE ANACREONTEA. J. M. Edmonds. 2 Vols.

GREEK MATHEMATICAL WORKS. Ivor Thomas. 2 Vols.

HERODES. Cf. THEOPHRASTUS : CHARACTERS.

HERODIAN. C. R. Whittaker. 2 Vols.

HERODOTUS. A. D. Godley. 4 Vols.

HESIOD AND THE HOMERIC HYMNS. H. G. Evelyn White.

HIPPOCRATES AND THE FRAGMENTS OF HERACLEITUS. W. H. S. Jones and E. T. Withington. 4 Vols.

HOMER : ILIAD. A. T. Murray. 2 Vols.

HOMER : ODYSSEY. A. T. Murray. 2 Vols.

ISAEUS. E. S. Forster.

ISOCRATES. George Norlin and LaRue Van Hook. 3 Vols.

[ST. JOHN DAMASCENE]: BARLAAM AND IOASAPH. Rev. G. R. Woodward, Harold Mattingly and D. M. Lang.

JOSEPHUS. 9 Vols. Vols. I-IV. H. St. J. Thackeray. Vol. V. H. St. J. Thackeray and Ralph Marcus. Vols. VI and VII. Ralph Marcus. Vol. VIII. Ralph Marcus and Allen Wikgren. Vol. IX. L. H. Feldman.

JULIAN. Wilmer Cave Wright. 3 Vols.

LIBANIUS : SELECTED WORKS. A. F. Norman. 3 Vols. Vols. I and II.

LONGUS : DAPHNIS AND CHLOE. Thornley's translation revised by J. M. Edmonds ; and PARTHENIUS. S. Gaselee.

LUCIAN. 8 Vols. Vols. I-V. A. M. Harmon. Vol. VI. K. Kilburn. Vols. VII and VIII. M. D. Macleod.

LYCOPHRON. Cf. CALLIMACHUS : HYMNS AND EPIGRAMS.

LYRA GRAECA. J. M. Edmonds. 3 Vols.

LYSIAS. W. R. M. Lamb.

THE LOEB CLASSICAL LIBRARY

MANETHO. W. G. Waddell; PTOLEMY: TETRABIBLOS. F. E. Robbins.

MARCUS AURELIUS. C. R. Haines.

MENANDER I. New edition by W. G. Arnott.

MINOR ATTIC ORATORS. 2 Vols. K. J. Maidment and J. O. Burtt.

MUSAEUS: HERO AND LEANDER. *Cf.* CALLIMACHUS: FRAGMENTS.

NONNOS: DIONYSIACA. W. H. D. Rouse. 3 Vols.

OPPIAN, COLLUTHUS, TRYPHIODORUS. A. W. Mair.

PAPYRI. NON-LITERARY SELECTIONS. A. S. Hunt and C. C. Edgar. 2 Vols. LITERARY SELECTIONS (Poetry). D. L. Page.

PARTHENIUS. *Cf.* LONGUS.

PAUSANIAS: DESCRIPTION OF GREECE. W. H. S. Jones. 4 Vols. and Companion Vol. arranged by R. E. Wycherley.

PHILO. 10 Vols. Vols. I-V. F. H. Colson and Rev. G. H. Whitaker. Vols. VI-X. F. H. Colson. General Index. Rev. J. W. Earp.

Two Supplementary Vols. Translation only from an Armenian Text. Ralph Marcus.

PHILOSTRATUS: THE LIFE OF APOLLONIUS OF TYANA. F. C. Conybeare. 2 Vols.

PHILOSTRATUS: IMAGINES; CALLISTRATUS: DESCRIPTIONS. A. Fairbanks.

PHILOSTRATUS AND EUNAPIUS: LIVES OF THE SOPHISTS. Wilmer Cave Wright.

PINDAR. Sir J. E. Sandys.

PLATO: CHARMIDES, ALCIBIADES, HIPPARCHUS, THE LOVERS, THEAGES, MINOS AND EPINOMIS. W. R. M. Lamb.

PLATO: CRATYLUS, PARMENIDES, GREATER HIPPIAS, LESSER HIPPIAS. H. N. Fowler.

PLATO: EUTHYPHRO, APOLOGY, CRITO, PHAEDO, PHAEDRUS. H. N. Fowler.

PLATO: LACHES, PROTAGORAS, MENO, EUTHYDEMUS. W. R. M. Lamb.

PLATO: LAWS. Rev. R. G. Bury. 2 Vols.

PLATO: LYSIS, SYMPOSIUM, GORGIAS. W. R. M. Lamb.

PLATO: REPUBLIC. Paul Shorey. 2 Vols.

PLATO: STATESMAN, PHILEBUS. H. N. Fowler; ION. W. R. M. Lamb.

PLATO: THEAETETUS AND SOPHIST. H. N. Fowler.

PLATO: TIMAEUS, CRITIAS, CLITOPHO, MENEXENUS, EPISTULAE. Rev. R. G. Bury.

PLOTINUS. A. H. Armstrong. 6 Vols. Vols. I-III.

THE LOEB CLASSICAL LIBRARY

PLUTARCH : MORALIA. 16 Vols. Vols. I-V. F. C. Babbitt.
Vol. VI. W. C. Helmbold. Vol. VII. P. H. De Lacy and
B. Einarson. Vol. VIII. P. A. Clement, H. B. Hoffleit.
Vol. IX. E. L. Minar, Jr., F. H. Sandbach, W. C.
Helmbold. Vol. X. H. N. Fowler. Vol. XI. L. Pearson,
F. H. Sandbach. Vol. XII. H. Cherniss, W. C. Helmbold.
Vol. XIII, Parts 1 and 2. H. Cherniss. Vol. XIV. P. H.
De Lacy and B. Einarson. Vol. XV. F. H. Sandbach.
PLUTARCH : THE PARALLEL LIVES. B. Perrin. 11 Vols.
POLYBIUS. W. R. Paton. 6 Vols.
PROCOPIUS : HISTORY OF THE WARS. H. B. Dewing. 7 Vols.
PTOLEMY : TETRABIBLOS. *Cf.* MANETHO.
QUINTUS SMYRNAEUS. A. S. Way. Verse trans.
SEXTUS EMPIRICUS. Rev. R. G. Bury. 4 Vols.
SOPHOCLES. F. Storr. 2 Vols. Verse trans.
STRABO : GEOGRAPHY. Horace L. Jones. 8 Vols.
THEOPHRASTUS : CHARACTERS. J. M. Edmonds ; HERODES,
etc. A. D. Knox.
THEOPHRASTUS : DE CAUSIS PLANTARUM. G. K. K. Link and
B. Einarson. 3 Vols. Vol. I.
THEOPHRASTUS : ENQUIRY INTO PLANTS. Sir Arthur Hort.
2 Vols.
THUCYDIDES. C. F. Smith. 4 Vols.
TRYPHIODORUS. *Cf.* OPPIAN.
XENOPHON : ANABASIS. C. L. Brownson.
XENOPHON : CYROPAEDIA. Walter Miller. 2 Vols.
XENOPHON : HELLENICA. C. L. Brownson.
XENOPHON : MEMORABILIA AND OECONOMICUS. E. C. Mar-
chant ; SYMPOSIUM AND APOLOGY. O. J. Todd.
XENOPHON : SCRIPTA MINORA. E. C. Marchant and G. W.
Bowersock.

DESCRIPTIVE PROSPECTUS ON APPLICATION

CAMBRIDGE, MASS.	LONDON
HARVARD UNIV. PRESS	WILLIAM HEINEMANN LTD